CW01558866

CONFLICTED LIFE

WILLIAM JERDAN, 1782–1869

For Theo

CONFLICTED LIFE

WILLIAM JERDAN, 1782–1869

LONDON EDITOR, AUTHOR AND CRITIC

SUSAN MATOFF

sussex
ACADEMIC
PRESS
Brighton • Portland • Toronto

2 4 6 8 10 9 7 5 3 1

First published in 2011 by
SUSSEX ACADEMIC PRESS
PO Box 139
Eastbourne BN24 9BP

and in the United States of America by
SUSSEX ACADEMIC PRESS
920 NE 58th Ave   Suite 300
Portland, Oregon 97213-3786

and in Canada by
SUSSEX ACADEMIC PRESS (CANADA)
90 Arnold Avenue, Thornhill, Ontario L4J 1B5

British Library Cataloguing in Publication Data
A CIP catalogue record for this book is available from the British Library.

Library of Congress Cataloging-in-Publication Data
Matoff, Susan.
Conflicted life : William Jerdan, 1782–1869, London editor, author and critic / Susan Matoff.
p. cm.
Includes bibliographical references and index.
ISBN 978-1-84519-417-8 (h/b : alk. paper)
   1. Jerdan, William, 1782–1869. 2. Authors, English—19th century—Biography. 3. Journalism—Great Britain—History—19th century. 4. Criticism —Great Britain. I. Title.
PR4825.J25Z78 2010
828'.7'09—dc22
[B]

2010016824

Papers used by Sussex Academic Press are natural, renewable and recyclable products from well-managed forests and certified in accordance with the rules of the Forest Stewardship Council.

Typeset and designed by Sussex Academic Press, Brighton & Eastbourne.
Printed by TJ International, Padstow, Cornwall.
This book is printed on acid-free paper.

Contents

Contents

❦ List of Illustrations ❦

Cover illustrations: William Jerdan aged 33, 1815; artist, G. H. Harlow; engraver, H. Robinson. Scanned from author's copy of Jerdan's *Autobiography*, Vol. I; author's photographs of Jerdan Place, Fulham, London, named in Jerdan's honour by the Metropolitan Board of Works in 1876.

Illustrations are placed after page 276.

Exeter 'Change in the Strand. G. Cooke, c. 1830. Collage, City of London Archives.

7   Ella Stuart, Melbourne, Australia. Courtesy of Michael Gorman private collection.
Emily Ella Stuart, Port-of-Spain, Trinidad. Courtesy of Michael Gorman private collection.

8   Charles Stuart Jerdan. Courtesy of Michael Gorman private collection.
John Jerdan, 1892. Courtesy of Gail Wallis and Bonnie Sayles.

❧ Preface ❧

This biography is a chronological reconstruction of William Jerdan's life, tracing his early battles to avoid the study of law through his rise in journalism which eventually led to editorship of the *Literary Gazette*, the first British weekly review of literature and the arts. His position as Editor gave him extraordinary access to those in power in Britain during the post-Napoleonic and early Victorian times, which Jerdan called "a stirring and wonderful period". He was a friend, acquaintance or associate of almost every person of note during this era and he owned a grand mansion where he lavishly entertained a social circle including Prime Minister George Canning. Sadly however, from 1850 until his death in 1869, William Jerdan struggled to keep afloat financially, writing fiction, polemical articles and verse. He also wrote a long series of articles for the *Leisure Hour* magazine, based upon the vast amount of knowledge he had amassed about important and well-known men. The income was still scarcely enough to provide for his large family, and his life ended in poverty.

Jerdan was a man whose livelihood lay in writing, from his early journalism to his late caustic observations on contemporary society. In between he wrote scores of critical reviews for his *Literary Gazette*, few of which can be definitely attributed to him, as no records or office books appear to have survived. Jerdan was personally responsible for over seventeen hundred issues of the *Literary Gazette* and although this period undoubtedly represented his most important and influential time, it was nevertheless only a part of the whole picture of Jerdan's life. Over three hundred letters from him have been found in various archives, of which a mere handful make any reference to his private life, complicated domestic arrangements or innermost thoughts. However, some of these matters have been deduced through other documentation, mainly statutory records.

William Jerdan is an enigma – a writer who left few written clues as to his personal life – no diaries or journals, and almost no private letters. He did, however, leave an autobiography. He was a secretive man who concealed much of his personal and professional life from those nearest to him. Today he has become a somewhat forgotten figure, featuring only peripherally in the recorded lives of others. In his day however, he was a vital facilitator and promoter of aspirants to literature and many other cultural endeavours.

Jerdan's conflicted character produced a far more complex man than his "riches to rags" story might suggest. His exceptional social skills and affability led inexorably to an excessive appetite for women, drink and "tuft-hunting". In parallel with his professional vicissitudes this biography examines what is known of his three families which numbered about twenty-three children (three with his young protégée, the famous poet Letitia Landon, better known as L.E.L.). Jerdan's generosity, kindness and charitable activities were legendary, but his trusting nature led to foolhardy and disastrous financial decisions.

His *Autobiography* in four volumes was written in 1852–53 when he was seventy years of age, but he still had another seventeen years of an emotional tumultuous life ahead. This present narrative has drawn largely on the *Autobiography* especially for his early years. However, as he was averse to recording dates, either in his memoir or in many of his letters, there were difficulties in reconstructing some aspects of his life.

In his *Autobiography* Jerdan claimed to have tried to be truthful, but *"was not artist enough to paint a complete picture"*. In his view, *"the great end of biography is to convey a complete and accurate idea of the individual who forms its subject in its inner, and in his external life; especially as that it is shaped and coloured by the society and circumstances in which he is placed."* This book expands on Jerdan's own memoir, filling in some considerable gaps of events that he either forgot or chose not to mention. It paints a more "complete picture" of a complex and one-time highly influential figure in English periodical literature and journalism of the late Georgian and early Victorian eras.

Acknowledgments

My first acknowledgment and deep appreciation is to Cynthia Lawford and Julie Watt, whose joyous company has so enhanced this Jerdan journey.

Michael Gorman of Kurashiki, Japan, direct descendant of William Jerdan and Letitia Landon, and Bonnie Sayles of Georgia, USA, direct descendant of William Jerdan and Mary Maxwell, have been unstinting in their encouragement and in sharing family information and images with me.

To Cary Fagan, who opened windows to other worlds, I owe an eternal debt.

I wish to thank Francis J. Sypher and Patrick Leary for their friendly advice, and my sons Simon Curran and Andrew Curran for their unfailing interest in this project.

Thanks are due to the Royal Literary Fund, and Lady Willoughby de Eresby for permission to quote from their archives. All documents from Hertfordshire Archives and Local Studies are by courtesy of Knebworth House – www.knebworthhouse. com.

Finally but crucially, the loving and immutable support of my husband, Theo Matoff, without whom this book would never have been finished.

❧ A Note on Money ❧

During Jerdan's lifetime British currency was in pounds, shillings and pence.

One pound (£1) = 20 shillings, 240 pennies.

One shilling (1s) = 12 pennies (12d).

Payments were frequently made in guineas. One guinea was £1 1s.

Money mentioned in this book is within the period 1810–1870, during which time the country experienced severe fluctuations in its currency. Comparing monetary values then and now is a virtually impossible task, depending on which data are used. However, based on estimates by the Office of National Statistics in the U.K. it has been suggested that as a quick rule of thumb, prices today are about eighty times those of the nineteenth century. Wages have risen just over three times faster than prices, resulting in a suggested factor of two hundred and fifty times a nineteenth-century wage.[1] These factors will of course differ considerably between individuals such as, for example, a labourer who, in 1827 earned £31 a year and a lawyer on £522 a year,[2] but will serve as an average equivalent overall.

In 1828, a peak earning year for Jerdan, his salary for editing the *Literary Gazette* was £10.10s (ten guineas) per issue, amounting to £546 a year, plus his one-third share of its profits which, in the same year, amounted to £1444, so his total income for 1828 was almost £2000. Using the average factor of 250 above, this is the equivalent of £500,000 today.

As a contemporary indication of Jerdan's financial status, the popular "Mrs Rundell's New System of Domestic Economy" published a few years earlier, indicates that an establishment of ten, including house servants, coachman and footman, and the upkeep of a carriage and pair, could be run to a high standard on £1000 a year, or £250,000 at today's value, half of Jerdan's income for the year mentioned.

At this midpoint of his career, therefore, William Jerdan was highly paid, and a man in exceedingly comfortable circumstances. However, his inability to manage his finances, and misfortune with his investments resulted in his eventual penury.

Part I

The Early Years, 1782–1817

Of all species of authorship, faithful and satisfactory biography is the most difficult. The impossibility of being perfectly certain of facts is the first stumbling block; the risk of drawing right conclusions from those you are fortunate enough to obtain is the next; and the delicacy required for steering by the lamp of truth, without flattery or offence, consummates the obstacles to authentic personal history.

WILLIAM JERDAN
Autobiography
Vol. IV, p. 303

1

From the River Tweed to the River Thames

The huge crowd was silent, the only sound the muffled beat of crepe-covered drums. The young surgeon's clerk, William Jerdan, stood on the deck of the guardship *Gladiator* in Portsmouth Harbour. He was watching the *Victory*, flag at half-mast, bring home the embalmed remains of Horatio, Lord Nelson from the Battle of Trafalgar. The date was 2 December 1805, a day the nation would remember. An historic day too, for the man Jerdan loathed. As Nelson's body sailed into harbour, Napoleon Buonaparte was decimating the armies of Russia and Austria on the battlefield of Austerlitz.

Jerdan was a surgeon's clerk in name only; his uncle Stuart, the ship's surgeon, had despaired of helping his young nephew to recover from a recurrent debilitating illness unless he was able to supervise him closely. He realised that this was possible only if William enrolled into the Royal Navy. Jerdan's time was spent reading, and he occasionally risked a flogging for not dousing his light when ordered. As so often in his youth he was spoilt, being given a cabin and cot by a Captain of Marines who lived ashore, and he was invited to eat with the officers in the gunners' mess. He often remarked, during later life, that he was spoilt from childhood by indulgence, and felt very strongly that this had created fatal flaws in his character.

William Jerdan was born on 16 April 1782 into a family who were large fish in the small pond of Kelso, a Borders town at the junction of the Rivers Tweed and Teviot. The Jerdans were amongst the gentry, one of the families of whom the local physician, Dr Douglas, noted, "The higher class of inhabitants in this parish are courteous in their manners, liberal in their sentiments, and benevolent in their dispositions."[1] John Jerdan, William's father, came from a long line of respectable landowners who had tenanted property around Kelso for over three hundred years. As a young man John Jerdan had wished to improve his prospects by being appointed as purser to an East Indiaman. Whether by accident or design he failed to arrive in London in time to join his ship. Too embarrassed to return home he stayed in London for a while, and in 1760–61 made a 'volunteer voyage' to India, an expedition rarely undertaken by a private gentleman at that time, and one that had unforeseen and tragic consequences for his sons.

When John Jerdan returned home he did not deploy his apparently considerable talents, being content merely to own his few fields, which brought in only a small revenue. He spent much of his time reading, acquiring factual knowledge. He was a portly man, easy-going, hospitable and a little indolent. Despite his modest income he married and produced a large family. His wife was Agnes Stuart, who claimed descent from an Abbot of Melrose and an illegitimate son of a "certain King James".[2] William Jerdan himself was doubtful about the truth of the royal element of his maternal ancestry, as most respectable families in Scotland claimed some sort of similar lineage.[3] Jerdan's mother, Agnes Stuart, was born in 1746, daughter of John Stuart, who held the first appointment as surgeon to the Kelso Dispensary from 1777–89. The family lived in a large stone house called Paradise, in Kelso; the house still stands, now called Halidon. Possibly Agnes felt that in marrying into the Jerdan family she needed to create a more distinguished ancestry for herself, and so the myth of Melrose was born.

The marriage of Agnes Stuart and John Jerdan produced four daughters, followed by four sons, of whom William was the third. The sisters hardly feature in Jerdan's reminiscences, although he did compose a poem to his sister Mary. His brothers played a more important part in his life. The eldest, John Stuart, was born in 1778, followed at two-year intervals by Gilbert, William himself, and George.

William Jerdan's childhood was idyllic, spent amidst glorious countryside. For Jerdan this was "one of the sweetest rural localities upon the face of the earth"[4] and implanted in him a love of beauty in nature. The scene he recalled so nostalgically when he came to write his *Autobiography* at the age of seventy-four is little changed in the first decade of the twenty-first century; the tiny island, 'Ana', is just as he knew it, a home to wild birds, with Fleurs (now Floors) Castle, home of the Duke of Roxburgh, presiding over the landscape from a short distance.

The house where William was born was called "Lang Linkie", and described as a mansion two centuries old.[5] The family soon moved out, and the building became used as a place for town meetings, dancing schools and warehouses; it then became a distillery, and the small road leading to the site is still named "Distillery Lane". The Jerdans' new home was situated opposite the "Ana", and boasted a fine walled garden. Both "Lang Linkie" and the Jerdans' cottage have vanished, the chalk cliffs to which they clung being eroded over time. However, there is still a wall above the river bank showing infilled windows where they once stood, above the Cobby, a broad strip of grass between the riverside and the gable wall of "Lang Linkie". The Cobby was the venue for many of the Jerdan children's games. Favourites were Set-a-foot, Cock's Odin, Boys and Girls, and Willie Wassle. Even at the age of eighty-five Jerdan remembered these games clearly.[6] Both sexes and all classes could play together with impunity, a situation Jerdan looked back on fondly in his old age, sorry for the children of his present-day, who were much more strictly bound by rules of propriety and prudery. He recalled the teams of boys, one representing the Scots, the other the English, the former taunting the latter to "set-a-foot" on their territory, using heaps of discarded clothing to mark the border. Monkey battles of small boys on the shoulders of bigger boys usually resulted in torn jackets, and bruised shins. Bathing in the river was another favourite past-time, and one which caused Jerdan repercussions when he jumped into the cold water before properly recovering from smallpox. This debilitated him, and he suffered throughout his life from recurrent bouts of severe illnesses.

William's father John Jerdan was appointed by the Duke of Roxburgh, holder of the feudal Barony, to the office of the Baron's Bailiff, known as the Baron Baillie of Kelso. In effect this made John Jerdan the governor of the town, assisted by fifteen stent-masters.[7] A duty of the Baron Baillie was to act as the Duke's representative in the weekly court, administering justice as necessary. As an act of kindness, he was 'assisted' in this duty by the local harmless idiot Willy Hawick who, Jerdan maintained, was the original for Walter Scott's fictional creation Goose Gibby.[8] Walter Scott's frequent summer visits to his relation, Captain Scott of Rosebank in Kelso, led to his acquaintance with the Jerdan family. He was to become a useful connection in William Jerdan's later life. Scott and Willy Hawick were both frequent visitors to the Jerdan household, even after Willy smashed two large and valuable Chinese mandarins John Jerdan had brought home, because he was sure they nodded and made faces at him! Scott, recalling with gratitude that it was John Jerdan who was the first to encourage his love of poetry, eventually asked William to watch over his own son Charles when he came to London. Thus John Jerdan, a man who was too indolent to make a mark for himself, was highly influential in nurturing the greatest novelist of the period, and his own son, who was to become an important influence on contemporary literature.

William Jerdan spent a great deal of time with his father who not only took him, aged three, to see the great Lunardi's balloon flight,[9] but actually fired the starting pistol himself. This was the first cross-border hot-air balloon flight, from Kelso graveyard to Doddington Moor, the initiator of the many spectacles which William enjoyed all his life. When he was five years old, his father called him from play to introduce him to the poet Robert Burns, with whom he had been walking. By the time he was seven, the Revolution was raging in France, but as a child this had no impact on him. Far more important to him was the day in 1795 when the whole family turned out to wave farewell to his beloved older brother John, just seventeen, as he set off on his pony from Ednam, happy to be going to India as a soldier. John Stuart Jerdan's cadetcy had been arranged through his father's friendship with the influential Mr Kerr, an eminent Scottish solicitor and Governor of Bombay, whom he had met on his own trip to the East some thirty years earlier.

Ednam was a village two miles from Kelso,[10] and John's pony came from the wealthy farm of his mother's brother John Stuart, "downright but gentlemanly, frank and hospitable, and inhabiting a land of Goshen".[11] This uncle was to be of great assistance in William's early life. Ednam had another strong association for William. It was the birthplace of the famous poet James Thomson, the author of *Seasons*, a poem in four parts, 'Winter' being inspired by the Borders countryside. William Jerdan wrote a sketch of the poet, a few copies of which were privately printed. He was deeply influenced by Thomson: in his old age he mused about Thomson's life, recognizing that "at the distance of nearly a century, research into the private circumstances of an individual career could hope but for small reward in the shape of prominent discoveries".[12] He noted particularly how much Thomson was influenced by his mother, a circumstance that Jerdan could wholly identify and sympathize with.

While he admired his mother as "one of the best of wives that ever fell to the lot of man",[13] Jerdan idolized his father, recognizing that "in his limited provincial sphere [he] stood almost alone for a genuine and cultivated taste in literature".[14] He encouraged William into an ardent and life-long interest in Scottish Ballads and Border lore, taking him to meet with old weavers, cobblers, and others whose snatches of song and legend he remembered all his life. In pursuance of this interest, the thirteen year old William visited the "gipsy haunts of Yetholm and the legendary den of the Worm of Wormielaw".[15] Whilst he was away, in the autumn of 1796, his father died suddenly.

In his *Autobiography* Jerdan said that a few months after his father's death, his mother also died. In fact, Agnes lived on until 1820. The "mother" he mentioned was likely to have been a relation of his real mother's, a Mrs Walker, wife of the Supervisor of Excise, who had "adopted" him from an early age. Jerdan did not explain why he was adopted by the Walkers, neither did he mention whether any of his brothers or sisters were similarly brought up by other than their parents. In any event, his adoptive parents spoilt and cossetted him, were over-generous with spending money, and allowed him considerable freedom. He believed that this caused him to grow up "petulant and self-willed; and it is only extraordinary that the process did not also render me vicious and selfish".[16] He believed that he was saved by inheriting his father's easy-going disposition. Jerdan never took responsibility for trying to improve his flawed character, always blaming the way he was "spoilt" so often, by so many, in his early years.

The town of Kelso where young William grew up was a prosperous and lively place with a population of 3557.[17] It had expanded greatly in the previous fifty years, largely because many small farmers and labourers came into the town to find other ways to make a living. Leather by-products were a staple industry of the town; William Jerdan's grandfather John had been a skinner and tanner, and like others in his trade dried animal skins in the churchyard, a practice deplored by the local physician Dr Douglas, on moral as well as hygiene grounds. This churchyard was overlooked by Rosebank, the home of Sir Walter Scott's uncle and aunt.

Kelso had benefited from a public library since 1750, housing a valuable collection of books, the stock being regularly updated. Perhaps its most famous volume was the copy of Percy's *Reliques* that first inspired Sir Walter Scott. Kelso also boasted a coffee house supplied with the London, Edinburgh and local papers, so that the Jerdans, with other literate residents of the town, had access to current news, opinions and literature. William Jerdan's father and brother were directly and deeply involved in the public press from the very beginning of the nineteenth century,[18] an example which William Jerdan was eventually to follow for most of his long life.

As would be natural in such an educated and literate town, Kelso supported several schools, the main ones being the English parochial school, and an upper Latin school. At a very young age William Jerdan was outstanding at arithmetic, often invited to perform calculations to earn treats of gingerbread and sweets. (Unfortunately for his peace of mind in adult life, this talent vanished as soon as he learnt to read.) He attended the parochial English school with around 130 pupils who were expected to tip the master, the boy who gave the largest tip being made school captain, an open and frank acknowledgement of favour purchased. The school was attended by all classes of boys, from sons of the gentry to sons of the farm servant. No distinction was made for religious differences, either – only the schooling itself was important. Reading, writing, arithmetic and grammar, broadened into "moral precept and unsectarian advice"[19] as the boys grew older. All his life Jerdan believed this was an ideal educational model, free from attempts to subvert the student to any particular creed or opinion.

Leaving the English school Jerdan moved to Kelso's upper Latin school. His master Mr Taylor left shortly afterwards to establish his own academy in Musselburgh, which William's elder brother John attended until his education was completed. William, however, stayed in the Latin school for six years under the able tuition of Mr Dymock. Jerdan learnt Latin by drudgery and Greek "by love of its soft and sonorous structure".[20] Dymock later moved to Glasgow and edited many educational and classical works which Jerdan was to review in the *Literary Gazette*, the publication he edited and wrote for over a period of thirty-four years.

Jerdan's literary interests, fostered by his father, became more defined and encouraged by a fortunate circumstance – another instance where he saw himself as being "spoilt". As he was ready to leave Mr Dymock's school, Dr Rutherford who had run a boarding school in Uxbridge retired and settled in Maxwellheugh, just across the river, assisting the Minister of the Established Kirk. He brought with him a young man who had been one of his boarders, entrusted to his care by a family in India. As a result of his achievements at school where he had won many prizes, William Jerdan was chosen to be this young man's fellow-student. The time spent with Dr Rutherford cultivated Jerdan's mind beyond mere learning. For about a year he found himself in an environment of "great intelligence and refinement of manners"[21] which offered him opportunities in a life and society he had never before known. In his spare time he "scribbled" in the offices of James Hume, a Writer (as solicitors in Scotland were called), to prepare himself for the career in law that he was supposed to follow. Hume's amusing jumble of Latin and English was especially enjoyed by Jerdan, who was fascinated by language, and so prepared him for the constant puns and word-play for which he was to become well-known.

In 1800 Jerdan met the three Pollock brothers, with whom he formed life-long friendships, from which he derived much happiness and benefit. The three boys – David, William and Frederick – were sons of David Pollock, originally from Berwick-on-Tweed, saddler to His Majesty King George III. Through distant relationships by marriage, the Pollock boys became guests in the Jerdan household for about ten days, long enough to forge ties with the three younger Jerdans of the same age as themselves, Gilbert, William and George. The provincial Jerdans were in awe of their sophisticated, London-educated friends. The eighteen-year old William thought he knew less of life than a ten-year old brought up in the capital. His particular attachment was to Frederick Pollock, a year his junior, but benefitting from an education at St Paul's School in London. For the first time Jerdan felt himself weighed in the balance, and discomfited, but between the two young men there nevertheless was established a mutual regard and strong friendship. This brief encounter made Jerdan restless with the idea of studying law in Edinburgh; he was filled with longing to try his luck in London. He believed that he was ready to launch himself into the world.

Jerdan's whim was yet again indulged, and on his nineteenth birthday, 16 April 1801, he left home and sailed from Berwick to London in a smack. Nine days later he landed at Wapping, was met by his uncle, Mr Stuart, Surgeon, RN, and introduced to the West Indian Merchant House of Messrs Samuel, Samuel and Charles Turner, which employed him as a clerk at fifty pounds a year. He was a poor clerk, bad at figures and at copying, and expected to be dismissed. Instead, again he was spoilt and petted, even when caught in office hours writing verses, as he had done since the age of twelve. Paradoxically, his penchant for writing was his entrée to a grand social circle at the home of his employer Charles Turner, where he was invited to mingle with people of rank and station. His uncle Stuart supplied him liberally with funds, so Jerdan did not take the idea of work too seriously; he was much more interested in pranks and fun, such as breaking eggs into a cask of fine madeira, thereby ruining it, an act greeted by laughter rather than dismay or punishment. Charles Turner's son was one of Jerdan's closest companions at this time, and their friendship was renewed years later on a steamship from Liverpool to Dublin. This was a British Association visit[22] and Turner represented the ship's owners. After an excellent dinner, toasts were made, and in proposing Jerdan's health, Turner regaled the company with a ludicrous account of Jerdan's youthful inability to add up, or to copy ledgers neatly, while praising his achievements in the world of literature.[23]

The Pollock brothers featured largely in these early days in London. Jerdan was welcomed hospitably to their home, and treated almost as another son. When David Pollock was called to the Bar of the Middle Temple, his chambers at Elm Court were a favourite haunt of Jerdan's; David Pollock eventually became Chief Justice of Bombay. William Pollock, also a lawyer, died prematurely in 1817 and his brother Frederick, Jerdan's special friend, studied law at Cambridge, later becoming Lord Chief Baron in Her Majesty's Court of Exchequer. A younger Pollock brother, John, became a highly-placed civic official, and yet another, George, covered himself in glory at the Khyber Pass. The family eventually boasted three knighthoods and attained the highest ranks of the legal and military professions, examples of character and self-discipline which might have exerted a very positive effect upon a young man from a Borders town who was more focussed than Jerdan, and not as keen on pursuits of pleasure.

The Pollocks were not Jerdan's only acquaintances to make good in the world: the foreman of their saddlers' shop, Peter Laurie, was destined to become Lord Mayor of London, as was a fellow-clerk of Jerdan's, John Pirie. Jerdan proudly attended both inauguration dinners at the Guildhall. All these models of hard work and involvement must have impressed him, but he was not induced to follow their example.

Jerdan was always a sociable man, and one of his pleasures at this time was a small society formed to read and discuss papers on various subjects. The three Pollock brothers and other rising young men were also members, as was Thomas Wilde, later Lord Truro, Lord High Chancellor of England. Looking back on this period of his life, Jerdan recognized that he himself had equally good prospects as those of his friends, and was acknowledged by them as clever. Although he did eventually exert a considerable influence, his career did not attain the dizzy heights achieved by his young friends. True to his generous character he rejoiced at their success; he acknowledged this was earned by their unflagging hard work and dedication to their chosen path, a will to succeed and certainty in their own ability. He, on the other hand, forsook a profession, the law, and soon found himself "leaning for life on the fragile crutch of literature for my support".[24] But this clear understanding came with hindsight and by no means concerned the young Jerdan as he gleefully enjoyed life in London with his friends and associates. They were a lively, often rowdy group, but not violent or vicious. They indulged in harmless frolics, one of which was quoting passages of Homer in Greek to a bemused constable who took their witness statements after they had seen a man beating a drunken woman in the street.[25]

At one of many jovial dinners, talk turned to the subject of secret ciphers, of which the company had little knowledge.[26] Jerdan brashly asserted that it could not be difficult to invent one, and that he could easily design a secret unbreakable code. Thomas Wilde instantly offered him a wager, the forfeit being to provide the company with a dinner. On consulting the 'Cyclopaedia' Jerdan was horrified to discover that many schemes had already been devised and broken, and retired to bed discontent with his own pretensions. However, in the morning he found that his subconscious had been at work, and he arose with a system complete in his head. He confided this to a barrister friend, who immediately grasped the importance to the Government of such a scheme and urged Jerdan not to waste such treasure on a trivial bet. Wilde agreed to this proposal. True to form, Jerdan wove his castle in the air, anticipating a huge reward for his scheme. He and Wilde obtained letters of introduction and gained an audience with the private secretary to Lord Sidmouth, Mr Serjeant, who politely received their precious secret cipher and told them to return the following week for a fuller meeting. When they did so, Serjeant had forgotten the whole affair and being reminded, recalled that he had the papers safely in his drawer. More meetings followed but, due to illness, Jerdan was forced to leave the matter in Wilde's hands and heard nothing more.

There was a sequel to this incident: several years later, around 1813, he was momentarily alone in the office of Rolleston, Under-Secretary to the Foreign Office in Downing Street; seating himself at Rolleston's desk he saw papers covered in hieroglyphics and figures he recognized as his own cipher. Returning to the office, Rolleston laughed and told Jerdan he could publish the content of the papers if he could decipher them. Not having the key to hand, Jerdan could not do this, but explained to Rolleston that he was the inventor of the cipher, describing to him the system employed. Rolleston admitted this cipher was widely used in the Foreign Office for all matters of secrecy. Unfairly, Jerdan received no acknowledgement, much less reward, for his cipher. However, always happy to be of use to his friends, he claimed a key role in being the instrument (through his cipher) by which Thomas Wilde entered into the hallowed halls of government, later rising to the eminence of Lord Chancellor. This gave Jerdan particular pleasure as Wilde came from a modest family, his father being only a junior partner in a small law firm. Wilde had not attended University and furthermore suffered from a stammer which he conquered by sheer will. Even as a young man Jerdan basked in his association with men of public distinction, a characteristic that became more noticeable as he progressed through his life.

Restless without regular employment and wanting to escape the heat of the London summer of 1801, Jerdan undertook a walk from London to Edinburgh.[27] Leaving London on a Monday, he arrived at Newcastle on Saturday, passing and being passed by an acquaintance making the same journey by carriage and led horse. He claimed to walk at a rate of 40–50 miles a day, starting before breakfast, stopping for only a light snack at midday, then tackling the longest stretch with the incentive of a good dinner and comfortable bed at a convenient inn, to prepare him for the following day's exertions. From Newcastle he proceeded to Edinburgh via Durham and Alnwick. He talked to everyone he met along the way, making a special point of chatting with labourers and working people. By this means he amassed a store of information, both trivial and profound. He continued to employ this practice to great effect on his subsequent travels. In later life he regretted that the advent of rail travel made such pleasurable encounters unlikely.

In the Spring of 1802 Jerdan and David Pollock spent a few days with their friend Burchell, in Amersham. On their way home Jerdan became seriously ill with "brain fever" and was quickly put under the care of his uncle Stuart, the naval surgeon, at his house in Lower Sloane Street. The air here was cleaner, the environment more rural, than in the City where Jerdan had been lodging close to his place of work. He was dangerously ill for a long time, subject to vivid hallucinations. A distinguished physician, Dr Harness, President of the Sick and Hurt Board, attended him and, Jerdan believed, saved his life. When he was able to travel his long-suffering and generous uncle took him back to Kelso and delivered him to his mother. Having subsidised Jerdan's sojourn in London, his uncle must have been sorely disappointed to bring home an emaciated invalid rather than a successful prodigy, but this was not the last time he would come to Jerdan's aid. Wishing for death, Jerdan instead gradually recovered his health and took up his pen again, writing a ten-stanza poem entitled "The Nosegay: To my sister Mary on seeing her gathering wild flowers". Parts of this verse were surprisingly cynical for a twenty-year-old who had been as generously nurtured as Jerdan:

> Nay! Hid beneath Love's warmest smile,
> Lurk falsehood, perfidy, and guile,
>> The female heart t'ensnare;
> And, under friendship's guise,
> Too oft, alas! Foul treachery lies,
>> Deceit and selfish care.

He tried to leave Mary with a more cheerful world view:

> Yet suffer not scowling mistrust
> To make thee to the world unjust,
>> And think the whole one blot:
> For some there are – alas! How few!
> With souls to every virtue true –
>> Heav'n cast with theirs thy lot!

He published this poem ten years later in his journal *The Satirist* and even fifty years after it was written he thought it worth repeating in his *Autobiography*.[28] But he was not yet on the path of literature. Despite his earlier false start, it was once again decided that Jerdan should go to Edinburgh to study law.

By 1803 he was placed with Cornelius Elliott, Writer to the Signet, (a solicitor who was also a member of the august body, The Society of Writers to the Signet), an aged relation whom Jerdan had not previously met. Yet again Jerdan experienced kindness and indulgence. The year he had spent in London set him apart from the other young men, and made him Mr Elliott's favourite. He found lodgings in Thistle Street in the heart of the recently-built New Town, and just around the corner from Queen Street where Cornelius Elliott lived at No. 95, next door to Lord Moira, Commander in Chief of the forces in Scotland. Jerdan fell foul of Lord Moira on several occasions. The most serious incident, and perhaps the most silly of Jerdan's misdemeanours. was when he stumbled home in his red jacket from a night out with the Volunteers, and bribed the sentry guards outside Moira's house to present arms to him. Unluckily this charade was seen by Lord Moira, who had the soldiers imprisoned, and told Jerdan to wait until he was promoted before such honours were due to him. Much mortified next day, Jerdan made frantic petitions to Moira until the soldiers were released. Jerdan's penalty was that henceforth Moira greeted him as "Marshal Jourdan", a reminder not to get above his station.

Jerdan's daily "studies" mainly consisted of an hour copying deeds, or taking dictation from Mr Elliot, after which they went out to breakfast. Jerdan still heartily disliked the law, eschewing his prescribed classes, but attending instead lectures on medicine and chemistry, which he much preferred. His social life however, made up for the daily drudgery. Elliott's circle included his beautiful daughters and their bevy of female friends, and the entertainments on offer differed vastly from those he had experienced in London. There was a streak of eccentricity in Edinburgh which appealed to Jerdan. Once he was almost shot as a result of a silly quarrel with a fiery West Indian student, participating in a duel in which, seeing his opponent's bullet hit the ground, Jerdan did not fire a shot in return. His days were filled with rounds of billiards, luncheons, dinners, drinking and oyster fêtes. Without the benign and balanced influence of his London friends, Jerdan was unable to resist so much temptation and lived to regret the time he later considered wasted.

However, not all of his time was spent on entirely frivolous pursuits: he was initiated into the Ancient Lodge of the Canongate Kilwinning No. 2,[29] which ironically made the much put-upon Lord Moira his Brother in Freemasonry. He also served in the 1st (Gentleman's) Regiment of Edinburgh Volunteers. The system of Volunteers had a considerable effect at a dangerous time in Britain's war, as evidenced by a false invasion alarm caused by the accidental lighting of beacons which brought out between twenty and twenty-five thousand armed men from the region between the Tweed and the Forth alone. This caused Jerdan to reflect that when arms are entrusted to the disaffected, men respond to such confidence with loyalty and patriotism. (The authors of the Bill of Rights amendments to the American Constitution only twelve years earlier may have had this same belief when they decreed that all men could bear arms.) Thousands of Volunteers served in the field, most of whom were killed. Although Jerdan did not see active service, he took part in training manouevres at Craigmillar Castle, a prototype for the storming of Badajoz and San Sebastian. At Craigmillar, however, the only casualty was a careless hare.

Literature continued to be a constant tug as Jerdan continued to scribble poems at the same time as indulging in revelries, half-heartedly pursuing law studies and his various other interests. He was in the right place for an aspiring author. For the last two decades of the eighteenth century Scotland's most profitable trade was book-selling, leading to a boom in the printing industry, of which Scott and Ballantyne were a vital part. Prior to the advent of trains the proximity of Berwick-on-Tweed facilitated transport of books by sea, and books printed in Scotland were sold in London bookshops run by Scotsmen. Periodicals were an influential part of this huge expansion in print, the most notable at this early period being the Liberal *Edinburgh Review* and the *Critical Review.* These publications commented on new books, and quoted extensively from them, a template Jerdan was to emulate in his own *Literary Gazette* some years in the future. The circle whom Jerdan met at Elliott's house, to which he had been admitted for his literary proclivities, would certainly have subscribed to at least one of these journals, broadening their horizons from the merely provincial to the wider world. The huge success of the novels of Sir Walter Scott gave an enormous boost to the industry of literature, rendering inconceivable the disaster that finally befell him, Ballantyne and Constable which was still some years away.[30]

The good life became altogether too much of a good thing: Jerdan's always delicate health declined, partly as a result of too much high living, and partly caused by the shock of hearing that his West Indian duelling partner, with whom he had remained on the friendliest terms, had committed suicide. Hoping to cheer Jerdan up, Cornelius Elliott played a joke on him, sending him to obtain a signature from a lady client in the town, warning Jerdan not to be overcome by her extraordinary beauty. The lady turned out to be an ancient crone with a beard. Having extracted from Jerdan the reason for his badly-disguised amusement, she luckily turned out to have a sense of humour as well. This escapade did not achieve the desired effect of improving Jerdan's health. Too much partying had given way to a frantic attempt to make up for months of lost study time, and he was reading avidly, putting a strain on his fragile constitution. He was so ill he was thought to be dying of consumption, and had given himself up for dead.

Salvation came in the form of a client of Elliott's, whose legal action required minute inspection of parish registers throughout Peebleshire and Tweeddale. Correctly discerning that this task would greatly benefit Jerdan's health, Elliott sent him off on horseback, and for several weeks he combed the hills, visiting every Manse, enjoying the priests' simple way of life, and their hospitality, amid the wild countryside. His health restored, he made a final break with any pretence of studying law, and three years after he had been forced by illness to leave London, returned there with no fixed plan, but with a vague notion about pursuing a literary life. In his own words, "Like a child I could only see the gilt edges and gay binding of the book, and little apprehended the toil of the text, the labour of the brain, and all the troubles and ills that were concealed within!"[31]

At the end of January 1805 Jerdan spent several days on board an East Indiaman, a splendid ship called the *Earl of Abergavenney*, berthed at Northfleet in Kent.[32] The following week the ship left on its fifth voyage, with a diverse cargo funded from a huge investment by the entire family of the poet William Wordsworth. The plan was that the proceeds of the voyage would enable the poet to concentrate wholly on his poetry. In the Solent the weather deteriorated so badly that a pilot was employed to guide the ship safely out to sea; instead, he grounded her so severely on a notorious reef that, despite the valiant efforts of the crew to pump her out she sank, drowning almost everyone on board, including Commander John Wordsworth, brother of the poet. According to an eye-witness the Commander made no effort to save himself, but went down with his ship. Having met the officers and men so recently, Jerdan felt this dreadful accident most keenly.

Jerdan's inability to keep his own accounts or to budget within his income, coupled with the profligate high-living habits developed in Edinburgh had not been of much concern to him in that city. In London however, his financial difficulties multiplied and he was in debt. Although these debts were settled for him, more than likely by his patient uncle, Jerdan was – finally – overcome by mortification and shame. He had been flattered since childhood as to his talents, his cleverness, his wit, but here he was in London with no work and little prospect of finding his place in the world. He again succumbed to illness, this time of a severely depressive nature. Once more, his uncle Stuart stepped in to rescue him.

At this time Stuart was the surgeon aboard the gunship *Gladiator* in Portsmouth Harbour, and enrolling Jerdan as "Able-Seaman Samuel Moses" took him aboard to take care of him and restore him to health. Jerdan served from 1 October 1805 to 28 February 1806 when he was honourably discharged, receiving the sum of £5 3s 1d.[33] (He claimed that he later returned this sum to Disraeli to clear his conscience for not having in fact *earned* these wages.) Having no naval duties to attend to, he read voraciously. John Price, Lieutenant to the Dockyard, befriended him, taking him for cruises between Portsmouth and Ryde, thus restoring his mental and physical well-being. These five months considerably matured Jerdan. He discovered that he enjoyed soaking up knowledge and became sharply observant of people and events. This proved to be excellent training for his literary endeavours, as both journalist and editor. He watched the return of the *Victory*, bearing Nelson's body, and heard many tales from the seamen who came ashore from the *Téméraire*, the *Mars*, the *Tonant* and other battle-worn ships returning from Trafalgar. He saw scenes of horror and human misery, finding two bodies on the shore washed up from a recent wreck, and was uncomfortably aware of the proximity of a convict ship moored near to the *Gladiator*. The disgusting spectacle of a man flogged through the fleet stayed in his mind; the wretched criminal was taken on a specially-fitted boat alongside every ship and lacerated a prescribed number of times at each vessel, with the crews forced to watch. Although removed to hospital the man soon died. Jerdan reported that this experience made him a fervent supporter of reform in the matter of corporal punishment in both navy and army, and he rejoiced when the change in law ensured that such scenes were never to recur.[34]

He still managed to find ways to enjoy his enforced naval "service". Lieutenant John Price introduced him to pleasant society in Gosport; he was allowed to visit the local Haslar Hospital to further his interests in medicine and surgical science and, most excitingly for Jerdan, had his first poem published in "the Portsmouth paper".[35] The subject was Wilberforce, who was annually raising Motions in the House of Commons to abolish slavery, a campaign that bore fruit in 1807. Seeing his work in print thrilled Jerdan; he carried the newspaper cutting in his pocket checking it frequently, and was convinced that all who saw him knew him to be the poet. (He kept the precious paper safe and, twenty years later, when he was purchasing Wilberforce's house in Brompton, he was able to show the great man the poem written in his honour.)

The excitement of being a published poet confirmed Jerdan in his literary ambitions, a path down which his uncle Stuart refused to fund him further. His old friend, Lieutenant John Price, stepped into the breach and provided the money that enabled the young adventurer to again try his luck in London, not in the hated law studies as previously, but in the uncertain and fickle world of letters.[36]

~2~

Embarking on Journalism

When Jerdan arrived back in London early in 1806 the country was in a dangerous state. The severe economic distress caused by the French wars and bad harvests had resulted in food riots in 1801–2; the price of wheat and other foods was at an all-time high. The Peace of Amiens, which failed after a year, had given Napoleon time to enlarge his Empire in Europe. Britain therefore had to redirect attention from the people's clamour for reform to the patriotic imperative to crush Napoleon. The task fell to William Pitt the Younger who, in May 1804, had resumed the office of Prime Minister. During his Ministry Spain declared war on Britain, leading to the Battle of Trafalgar in October 1805. The nation's victory over the Spanish was tempered only by its mourning for the loss of Lord Nelson.

Thus 1806 and the ensuing years were a turbulent time for the whole country and life in the capital was no exception. Spurred on by events and by his earlier publishing success Jerdan wrote a long verse, *The British Eclogue for the Year 1805*, which was printed in a forty-eight page pamphlet by T. Wilson in 1806. As a pseudonym, the author used an anagram of his name, W. J. André. The pamphlet also included two minor works of Jerdan's, *The Lord Mayor's Day* and *A Tale for the Benefit of the Ugly*. The *Eclogue* filled thirty pages with 870 lines in couplets. Near the beginning of his verse he reflected on the uncertain state of the country:

> The social compact, once, without alloy,
> A source of safety, truth and love and joy,
> Transform'd by baleful passions now appears
> A scene of rapine, treachery and tears: –
> From such a man of folly, vice and pride
> Satire disgusted, turns with scorn aside
> Even Misanthropy with tearful eye
> Deplores the aggregate of misery –

He attacked the government as being "exalted far above the storms" as they "never feel the unpropitious hour/ Of chilling penury's resistless power". The government had little use for soldiers who had suffered so much and fought for thirty years for King and Country, but would now only "clog the state machine." Such men had a chance of preferment only if they had a wife or sister with "handsome legs or pretty face", to bestow upon some Lordling:

> Let his sweet partner some soft moment find,
> Her noble gull to dalliance inclined;
> Then beg (when he's in such an am'rous mood)
> He'd give her *kinsman* some appointment good.
> 'Tis but to ask, he surely will eftsoons,
> Strut forth a gaudy Captain of Dragoons,
> Or else, perhaps, a Counsellor of State
> Or, may-be, a Physician to the Fleet,
> Or, likely, a Comptroller of Finance,
> Or even an Ambassador to France.
> But has he talents? Do not ask such stuff –
> *She* has, – and certes, that is quite enough.

Injustice, corruption, unfair treatment of Catholics, and unseemly behaviour of the clergy were among the ills scourged by Jerdan's satiric pen; he made personal attacks too, using asterisks instead of names, but his references would surely have been clear to his contemporary readers. In his *Autobiography* Jerdan mourned that he had not kept a copy of his *Eclogue;*[1] he had been proud of it, and it is indeed an unusually highly political and critical work for Jerdan to have produced at the very outset of his career.

Satire could be a defence against what Jerdan perceived as injustice, as in his *Eclogue*. It had seemed inadequate to address an incident in which he unwittingly became involved when he visited David Pollock in Elm Court Chambers. Jerdan found a pocket-book belonging to a letter-carrier who was thus was exposed as having been stealing money from letters. Jerdan was appalled at the prospect of having any part in a capital prosecution and pleaded illness. Served with a subpoena he was forced to appear in court where the letter-carrier, a German called Nicolai was tried, sentenced and later executed. Whilst the lawyers adjourned to enjoy a merry evening, Jerdan deplored their apparent levity, and could not get the misfortunes of the poor man out of his mind.

Despite such a distressing incident, Jerdan plainly relished his carefree bachelor life, but his status, if not his habits, were about to change. He made scant reference to this important life event in his *Autobiography*. Rather oddly, in Volume I he noted that "In enumerating misfortunes, I will close this chapter with the publication of banns, and the commission of matrimony".[2] This was Jerdan's sole reference to his wife Frances in the four volumes of his

Autobiography, a circumstance rendered more noticeable as he dedicated one of these volumes, and devoted several chapters to the poetess L.E.L.

William Jerdan's wife was Frances Eggar; he did not reveal how or when they met, or where they married, and these facts are, so far, unknown.[3] Frances was christened on 2 March 1781 in the church of Elstead, Surrey. Her parents John and Mary (née Knight) already had three children, and after Frances's birth they moved to Bentley, just across the county boundary in Hampshire. Here four more children were born, of all whom were duly christened. The Eggars were part of a large family, farming in nearby Binsted as well as Bentley, and were renowned for their hops. The family name is memorialised today by Eggar's Field, and Eggar's School. It could be expected that from such a respectable background, Frances would have been married in the local church surrounded by her family, or in nearby Winchester, but no such record exists in any parish church in Surrey, Hampshire or Sussex.[4] The absence of a marriage record might suggest that the family disapproved of her bridegroom, a young Scotsman with a history of failed starts behind him, so that the couple were forced to marry elsewhere. Jerdan's reference to the "publication of banns" implies that a formal church ceremony took place. The mention of banns also indicates that the traditional Scottish practice of hand-fasting was not used, which might otherwise explain why no record has been discovered. It is just possible that Jerdan's reference to banns covered up an omission of any official marriage, but this seems unlikely, given the status in their local societies of both families.

At the end of 1806, probably about the time of his marriage, Jerdan found his first employment. It could be that he needed work in order to afford to marry Frances, or that having found employment already, he was in a position to contemplate matrimony. In any event, he began work on a new newspaper. Its prototype was the successful *Morning Advertiser*, which had prospered under the guidance of publicans. The new paper was conceived by a group of hotel keepers and landlords of major inns and taverns in the West End of London, a class above that of their model. Such a society was well suited to Jerdan's appreciation of *bonhomie*, and he recalled that the planning and consultation meetings were held in the hotels of the proprietors where the participants were generously entertained. The atmosphere was one of confidence in the paper's success and a determination to create a reputable and impartial organ of news.[5]

The new paper appeared on 19 January 1807 on the birthday of Queen Charlotte, and was named for her, the *Aurora*. The first issue was a splendidly elegant affair printed on white silk, but is now not easy to read; subsequent issues appeared on good quality paper with clear typography.[6] The *Aurora's* first Editorial claimed that there was "a peculiar difficulty in starting a paper in such a political turmoil". Its declared object was to establish a free press in the Metropolis, unassailable by venality or corruption, politically unbiased, impartial, independent, morally upright so as not to offend "the Fair" (possibly an attempt to obtain a wider readership by reassuring women that the paper could safely be read by them without danger of shock or horror). Reporters, claimed the Editorial, would not make speeches for Members of the Legislature, "but shall inform the People what their Representatives did say, not what they ought to have said". This was to be Jerdan's job. The paper would aim to always uphold the British Constitution and the Law, and to "assert and defend equally against the levelling hand of Republicanism and the encroachments of Court, or Ministerial influence." This was not the high-Tory line of Jerdan's family, and especially not of that arch-conservative his brother George, with his ultra-reactionary policy dominating the *Kelso Mail*. For Jerdan however, it was a useful introduction to journalism. The *Aurora* largely comprised political reporting, and also carried news of ships' movements, and columns on fine art, exhibitions at the Royal Academy, and police business.

Jerdan was twenty-five, keen to make a name for himself, full of enthusiasm and impatience. His colleagues were older, set in their ways, and mainly concerned, it seemed to Jerdan, with finding ways to avoid doing any actual work. As a raw recruit, Jerdan had as yet little experience of reporting parliamentary debates, but his superiors, rather than undertake the job themselves, threw him in at the deep end to report on the Chancellor's budget speech. His work somehow managed to pass muster, but the Editor was not as demanding in his duties as his impressive mission-statement had implied. Jerdan recalled that he tended to write his editorial leaders after midnight, in fits and starts, a line or two at a time, in between smoking his pipe, drinking his porter and dozing. By three a.m. he had usually produced an acceptable column.

At first Jerdan found his new occupation absorbing and exciting, and he enjoyed the challenge of understanding the issues and questions raised in the House. He was very conscious of the journalist's responsibility to his readers to present the truth as best he could. After a while however, he found the routine dull and irksome with only occasional highlights in the parliamentary business. To relieve his boredom he started to frequent clubs and taverns on his way between the House and the printing office.[7] In this habit he claimed to be merely emulating the practice of his fellow-journalists, but nevertheless always had to deliver his report in time for the morning paper. The young Charles Knight, about to start work as an apprentice reporter, was taken to a coffee house near the House of Commons to meet other reporters. He recalled, "I especially remember [Jerdan] as looking upon the laughing side of human affairs, and never unmindful of the enjoyment of the passing hour, even amidst the monotonous performance of his duty in the reporter's function."[8] After long acquaintance with Jerdan, Knight's first impressions were unchanged: "Age could not wither, nor custom stale, the infinite sociality of William Jerdan, as I knew him in the years when the third and fourth Georges had passed away."[9]

Although Jerdan was reporting before the electric telegraph made communication amazingly speedy, technology was beginning to make itself felt in the streets. As a demonstration, Pall Mall was now lit by a few gas lights, and the advent of coal-gas for domestic use was only a few years in the future. Parliamentary reporters had not yet been given the convenience of a Press gallery to which reporters could come and go at will, so that newspapers could arrange for their staff to cover the day's business in shifts. In Jerdan's day the Reporters' Bench was at the back of the Strangers' Gallery. To reach it, the reporter thrust his way through the crowd and then through a doorway about two feet wide. A journalist who suffered the same difficulties as Jerdan described how "There were, perhaps, a hundred seats under him, benches filled with 'strangers' and in this back bench it was very difficult to hear. When he sought egress he had a hard fight with the intervening legs and arms to reach his own door; often jaded, heated and laden with anxiety, he had absolutely to push his way in and out – struggling to make room for his successor who was pushing his way in."[10] Jerdan found that the back row of the gallery was the prized position, so that the journalist's frantically writing arm would not be jogged by the knees of anyone seated behind him.[11]

In an area set apart outside the Members' Dining room, excellent meals could be purchased for three shillings and sixpence. Once, when this place was full, Jerdan was permitted access to the Members' Dining Room, and found himself a place at a table shared by the Marquis of Wellesley, the Duke of Wellington and Mr Canning (later Prime Minister).[12] George Canning was to become Jerdan's "idolised friend" and godfather to one of his sons.

At the *Aurora* the dozy pipe-smoking Editor soon retired, and only months after the paper was launched Jerdan was appointed to succeed him. Things proceeded satisfactorily enough for a time but cracks soon appeared. Jerdan found the proprietors intelligent and sensible but they were neither literary men nor journalists. They even differed from each other in their politics and two or three of them wrote leaders upholding opposing views. Jerdan had neither the authority nor experience enough to take a firm hold. He recalled that readers became confused by the paper's vacillations and within a short time the *Aurora's* sun had set and it was no more.

Throughout this period Jerdan worked steadily at various jobs, needing a sufficient income to provide for his young family. His first son John Stuart was born in February 1807, and daughter Frances-Agnes in September 1809.[13] They were christened together in October 1810, a delay which suggests that church attendance was not a significant part of William and Frances Jerdan's domestic routine, and may also reflect the question of whether an official marriage had taken place. They had started wedded life in furnished rooms in Craven Street, Strand and then in Curzon Street, Mayfair. As Jerdan's income improved they moved to Cromwell Cottage, Old Brompton, a large unfurnished old house, near to Gloucester Lodge, home of George Canning. They settled here for several years, Jerdan happy to be in the neighbourhood of many "noticeable" people. Throughout his *Autobiography*, written in 1852–3, he name-dropped continually, as if to increase his own importance by association with the famous. This was a central trait of Jerdan's character, and one which often guided his actions.

His main employment (although not long-lived) commenced in the Spring of 1808, when he joined the *Pilot*, an evening newspaper which had been launched in January 1807. The proprietors were all educated gentlemen and Jerdan flourished in their company, finding this a very different and much more congenial environment than the *Aurora*. The *Pilot* had links with the Horse Guards, from whom it derived prime information; additionally, the officers shared some excellent dinner parties with the newspaper's officials, a bonus welcomed by Jerdan.

Newspapers at this time had the sword of Damocles hanging over them, wielded by the Attorney-General Sir Vicary Gibbs (called by Queen Caroline, Jerdan says, "Vinegar Gibbs"[14]). Gibbs had the power of issuing *ex-officio* 'informations' against writers, printers, booksellers and publishers whom he considered offensive or dangerous to the government. In exchange for not proceeding to trial he exacted their promise to desist from publishing such material again. Gibbs was a man feared by the press but he was not their only concern – the price of paper rose, and could not be absorbed by putting up the cost of the newspaper, as the Stamp Office confined a 10 percent discount on duty payable only to newspapers costing less than sixpence.[15] Mr Huskisson MP proposed to offer some relief to newspapers and a Bill to this effect was passed by Pitt and the House in 1809.

Issues of the *Pilot* ran to four pages, each of four columns; the paper dealt almost entirely with politics and war, news from Portugal and Spain, and listed London shipping and passengers. It carried a small section on actions in the law courts, and extracts of official reports such as the Committee on Public Expenditure. None of these features gave Jerdan much opportunity to flex his journalistic muscle, but he had several more irons in the fire.

At the same time as his parliamentary reporting for the *Pilot*, for nearly eight years Jerdan also had a lucrative sideline in editing a provincial newspaper, the *Sheffield Mercury*, and at other times papers in Birmingham, Staffordshire and Ireland (although he was never paid for the latter), all without leaving London.[16] He found this a satisfactory occupation which worked well, as political news emanated from the capital and had in any event to be sent out to the provinces, while local sub-editors provided local news. Jerdan remarked that this system was "to the sound edification of their readers, and the entire relief of their proprietors, who had nothing to do but eat their puddings and hold their tongues".[17] His exact contributions to these newspapers are untraceable as no names were appended to articles.

Jerdan also helped to translate Madame de Staël's *Corinne* with which he was pleased. Coincidentally, this novel was to have a great influence on his protégée Letitia Landon's poem *The Improvisatrice* several years later. Jerdan was, however, dissatisfied with a novel he wrote in collaboration with a Michael Nugent, based on material furnished by an unnamed captain, and entitled *New Canterbury Tales*.[18] This is a bawdy exchange between a Major-General without prospect of a regiment, and a retired general. They journey together to Canterbury and meet two other characters. Their talk is full of puns and sarcasm; one character jeers at another 'Your Scotch brogue unfitted you for any character beyond a mute in Mahomet',[19] a jibe that Jerdan may well have heard addressed to himself. The work was published by Henry Colburn, an aggressive publisher who played a crucial role in Jerdan's subsequent life.

Jerdan published many essays in both prose and verse, most anonymously, but occasionally using the name 'Teutha', an ancient name of the River Tweed.[20] Under his earlier pseudonym as the author of the *British Eclogue*, W.J. André also published a poem on the occasion of George III's Jubilee, admitting later that he had lost his copy.[21] Jerdan prefaced his 590 lines of fairly pedestrian verse with a breathlessly apologetic explanation and excuse for its poor quality, claiming that as the country had decided only in September to celebrate the King's Jubilee, he had not had time to polish his work. The verse is replete with footnotes, in one of which he took the golden opportunity of mentioning his favourite theme: patronage for literature. The note declared that the King alone had been the sole patron of genius and science for the preceding fifty years, no Minister having been appointed to patronize literature. The stanza in which he drove this point home gives a flavour of the entire tribute:

> No Minister in Britain's isle
> Of late has risen, alas the while!
> To rescue genius from neglect,
> Unshielded merits to protect,
> To dissipate poor Talent's gloom,
> Or bid the buds of Poesy bloom –
> 'Tis his alone – 'tis GEORGE'S praise,
> Neglected genius to praise,
> To Merit's modest plea t'attend,
> And lowly Talent to befriend –
> In him alone does Britain find
> Mecenas and Augustus joined.

There is no doubt that Jerdan had a genuine deep regard and affection for his King, and would have preferred time to perfect this celebratory tribute to do his Monarch justice. This tribute was not intended to be ironic. Jerdan's regard for George III was genuine, confirmed by his later strenuous efforts to ensure that a statue was erected in his memory.

Having completed his short time with the *Pilot,* although he still continued to edit the provincial papers, Jerdan wrote regularly for the *Morning Post.* This, like most newspapers of the day, was mainly concerned with political matters and also included news from overseas, law reports and extracts from the *London Gazette.* He considered that his most effective contributions were leaders on the hot topic of the day: the conduct of the Duke of York and his mistress, Mary Ann Clarke.[22] This scandal took up a considerable amount of parliamentary time, and it was Jerdan's task to report on the debates. Jerdan's leaders in the *Morning Post* staunchly supported the Royalist cause, "denouncing the conspiracy against him and exposing the misdeeds of his enemies".[23] This partisan approach proved disastrous to the *Morning Post,* and within two weeks the circulation was dropping by hundreds every day. This galling fact did not reflect the enormous effort Jerdan was putting into his articles. He attended the House every night, making notes on the entire debate, after which he went to the offices of the *Morning Post* in the Strand, to prepare the next day's column. From there, often at 3 a.m., he virtually sleep-walked three miles home to Brompton, to partake of a pint of mulled madeira, a bit of dry toast, and four hours' sleep, until the whole circus started again next day.

William Jerdan was not a man to miss a chance to meet a member of "the Fair", so when Mary Ann Clarke invited him to her house in the King's Road, he accepted eagerly. Her purpose was to cajole him into softening his acerbic leaders which cast her as the villain of the scandal. He was conscious of, and enjoyed, her obvious feminine wiles and seductive skills, to the extent that he did indeed moderate his tone about her.

Benefitting from his intensive experience in reporting parliamentary debates, Jerdan subsequently covered three sessions of Parliament for the daily *British Press or Morning Literary Advertiser.* He also contributed to a monthly publication called *The Satirist, or Monthly Meteor* which was soon to become an important part of his life.

Somehow, in between all his frantic journalistic activity, and family demands, Jerdan still found time for a social life, and even some trips. In the summer of 1809 he managed a holiday of almost a month, including a visit to the mess of the 95th Rifle Regiment at Hythe, in Kent, where he admired the soldiers' devotion to their military duties, and their equal devotion to dinners and balls. He became well acquainted with many of the officers and men, marching with them to their embarkation at Deal, where he stayed on board the *Superb* and *Seraphis,* at the invitation of a surgeon colleague of his uncle Stuart. A sight never to be forgotten was the departure of over three hundred vessels sailing down the Channel. Most of the men with whom he had made friends in the soldiers' mess were lost either in the ill-fated Walcheren expedition,[24] or later, in the Peninsular Campaigns.

On a lighter note, in 1810 Jerdan attended the "stately and brilliant" proceedings which installed Lord Grenville (one of the controversial "Ministry of all the Talents" and later Prime Minister) as Chancellor of Oxford University. He grumbled, though, at having to pay five guineas a week for a "3-pair back room", suggesting, with his tongue in his cheek, that the expense "may, perhaps, account for my education not being finished as it might have been!"[25] In the autumn of that year he returned to his beloved Tweedside for a short visit, and the following year spent almost ten days at Harlow Bush near Cambridge enjoying shooting, one of his favourite sports. Although all his professional life was to be spent in London, his heart was always in the country, and he escaped at every possible opportunity to shoot, hunt, fish, or merely to bask in the peace of a rural setting.

Jerdan earned extra income by attending series of committee meetings discussing the Regent's Canal, producing a précis of half a sheet after each meeting. For this he earned a total of one hundred and fifty pounds, a surprisingly considerable sum for a simple task.[26]

One of Jerdan's more endearing traits was his wish to help people in distress; this characteristic evinced itself quite early in his London life when a friend and Brompton neighbour, 23 year old George Hammon, found himself in deep trouble. He had defrauded his employers, the banking house of Birch & Co. He could have escaped to France but was caught, and sentenced to death. He wrote to Jerdan from Tothill-fields prison, begging for help. Appalled, Jerdan wrote to government authorities asking for mercy for his friend, raising a petition, and using his position as parliamentary reporter to plead for leniency. Although by no means condoning Hammon's actions, Jerdan felt, at the prospect of Hammon's execution, that "there were palliatives in the case which might make stern Virtue pause, and Justice hesitate".[27] Visiting Hammon in his cell, he found himself locked in, an experience which so upset him that he fainted, and suffered nervous attacks for several weeks afterwards. He took Hammon's wife to plead before the Recorder of London, the infamous "Black Jack" who, as a condition of offering to help, propositioned the distraught wife. Through Jerdan's efforts, and with assistance from Canning, Hammon's death sentence was commuted to transportation for life. Jerdan arranged for him to be employed with a wine merchant in Bordeaux, but caught sight of him many years later on an incognito and risky visit to England. He was later seen as a dapper waiter in a hotel between Calais and Paris, while his blameless wife retired to the north of England. This exploit to help someone in distress was one of the more dramatic of Jerdan's interventions. As time went on and he acquired influence in certain circles, he was frequently instrumental in arranging financial and other assistance when it was most desperately needed.

A mood of desperation and depression was the norm in the England of 1810: Napoleon was at the height of his power; the Industrial Revolution was causing social and economic upheaval; King George III was increasingly incapacitated, and in 1811 the Prince Regent was installed. This was an uneasy year, when the Regent's political allegiances changed dramatically as he betrayed those who had supported him. The poet Anna Barbauld marked the year with her poem entitled *Eighteen Hundred and Eleven*, giving a gloomy view of the present and future prospects for the country; John and Leigh Hunt labelled it "a strange and perplexing year".[28] The following year Napoleon marched on Moscow and the United States Congress declared war on Great Britain.

Britain was about to face a unique situation. Following Lord Grenville's Whig Ministry, the Duke of Portland had assembled a coalition of Tories in 1807. However, Portland was old and ill, and Spencer Perceval was effectively the chief minister. In 1809 he was formally appointed Prime Minister, to the displeasure of most senior statesmen who absented themselves from his government. However, the economic health of the country was gradually benefitting from the improvements Perceval's government was making. The Prime Minister had held office for two years and 221 days[29] when, on 11 May 1812, he was assassinated, the only British Prime Minister to have died in this manner.

At the fatal moment Jerdan was within inches of Spencer Perceval. He had arrived at the House of Commons at 5 p.m. for his usual stint of attending and reporting debates, at the same moment as the Prime Minister walked through the lobby on his way to the Chamber to attend an inquiry into the recent Luddite riots. Jerdan greeted him, and was saluted in return. As Jerdan held open the door for Perceval to pass into the Chamber, Jerdan heard nothing, but saw

a small curling wreath of smoke rise above his head, as if the breath of a cigar; I saw him reel back against the ledge on the inside of the door; I heard him exclaim, 'Oh God!' or 'Oh my God!' and nothing more . . . I saw him totter forward, not half way, and drop dead between the four pillars which stood there in the centre of the space, with a slight trace of blood issuing from his lips.[30]

In the ensuing alarm and confusion several men rushed forward to carry Perceval's body into a side room. Hearing a clerk call out "That is the murderer!" Jerdan seized the assassin by the collar, a feat not too heroic, as by this time Bellingham was sitting quietly on a bench, offering no resistance. The discharged pistol was beside him, and another, loaded and primed, removed from his pocket. An opera glass, papers and other articles were also found on his person. A surgeon pronounced Perceval dead, the shot having entered his heart in a slanting direction as Bellingham was a tall man, and Perceval of short stature. To Jerdan, at such close quarters, it was clear that Bellingham was in a state of considerable agitation:

His countenance wore the hue of the grave, blue and cadaverous; huge drops of sweat ran down from his forehead, like rain on the window-pane in a heavy storm, and coursing his pallid cheeks, fell upon his person where their moisture was distinctly visible; and from the bottom of his chest to his gorge, rose and receded, with almost every breath, a spasmodic action, as if a body, as large or larger than a billiard-ball, were choking him. The miserable wretch repeatedly struck his chest with the palm of his hand to abate this sensation, but it refused to be repressed.[31]

Jerdan himself was close to fainting, and long remembered the kindness of a friend who found some water to revive him. Jerdan took charge of the pair of pistols until the trial, taking the opportunity of tracing them onto a piece of paper to show their size and strength. He also retained, and kept for many years, Bellingham's opera-glass in a red case, used by the assassin in several visits to the House of Commons to survey the assembly. Bellingham was escorted to the bar of the House, with Jerdan still holding him firmly by the collar. He was then taken before magistrates, and remanded to Newgate until his trial three days later.

Reflecting upon the legal procedures of the Grand Jury many years later, Jerdan expressed his concerns about what he called "the evils of the system". He identified particularly the perversion of facts that could so easily arise when witnesses are kept together in one room prior to the hearing, so that they may compare notes and potentially change their stories to fit another's recollection. He believed that the Scottish system of law, as of education, was superior, as this situation could not occur there. In Scotland, a case conducted by the public prosecutor contributed "admirably to the pure and satisfactory administration of justice, between the country and the accused".[32] Jerdan was subpoenaed to appear at Bellingham's trial on 15 May, but was not examined. The outcome of the proceedings was a foregone conclusion: Bellingham was found with the pistol that killed Perceval in his possession, and had admitted his guilt. However, the transcript throws light upon his reason for the killing which was not directed against Perceval the individual, but Perceval as the representative of a government against whom Bellingham harboured a deep and abiding resentment.[33] In instructing the jury, the judge burst into tears when speaking of Spencer Perceval, and the reverence in which he was held. The jury was out for fourteen minutes, returning a verdict of guilty. Bellingham was hanged on 18 May, a week after his violent and desperate act. Jerdan ensured that his own connection with the case lived on in his subsequent writings.

Jerdan never claimed to have played a pivotal role in the arrest of Bellingham, admitting that "there is little to boast of in having seized an unresisting man", but was at pains to make it clear that there were those who let it be known they had faced with courage the danger of a loaded pistol, although in truth there had never been the slightest possibility of the second pistol being fired. In 1830

Jerdan wrote the entries for individuals portrayed in Fisher's *National Portrait Gallery*. In his entry on Spencer Perceval, Jerdan published a facsimile of the manuscript petition he and Mr Dowling had removed from Bellingham's jacket at the time of his arrest, identified by the initials JH, those of Mr Hume, to whom the papers had been passed for the trial. In this article Jerdan also provided a detailed sketch of the lobby of the House of Commons, showing the numbered positions of himself, Perceval and Bellingham at the moment the shot was fired, as well as those of various other witnesses. Jerdan also published the outline he had made of Bellingham's pistol, as part of his article. Of the eleven pages of text that comprised his article on Perceval, Jerdan devoted four pages to the minutiae of the murder, an indulgence for which he could be excused as he was, first and foremost a journalist, and was at exactly the right place and time when the most heinous political crime in British history took place – a scoop indeed![34]

The experience was so important to him, that he relived the incident again almost fifty years later, giving it considerable coverage in his *Autobiography*. His part may not have been as crucial as he implied: he was not called upon as a witness, despite his close proximity to the victim, neither was his name mentioned by any of the several witnesses called upon at the trial. Nevertheless, it would have been an unnerving experience. News of the murder travelled fast, causing alarm and uneasiness. The assassination changed the political leadership of the country. Within days the Earl of Liverpool had been appointed as Prime Minister, and retained this position until 1827.

For Jerdan, life went on as usual. He attended and wrote up reports of debates in the House, and met all his other journalistic commitments. He continued to contribute to *The Satirist or Monthly Meteor* with pleasure but only rarely, over a period of several years. This journal had been launched in October 1807 by George Manners, and to Jerdan it came to represent "a very essential section of my literary career".[35] Its tone was a relief from the turgid reports of parliament with which he had been so involved. He commented that "its talent and virulence very speedily attracted general notice, warm partisanship, and bitter hate". Against the economic depression and political uncertainty in the difficult days of 1812, some sections of the press wielded a potent weapon: satire. In the visual arts, Rowlandson and Cruikshank were among the foremost political cartoonists and their work sometimes found a place in *The Satirist*. Each issue included a political cartoon on a fold-out sheet, and few were safe. One such caricature appeared which included Lord Grenville, the long-suffering Lord Moira of Jerdan's Edinburgh days, Sheridan, John Kemble, and many other public literary, political and dramatic figures, all with the figure of the Satirist looming over them, brandishing his whip. The Whig government, the "Ministry of all the Talents" came in for especial virulence. *The Satirist* was more than a solely political journal; it was a magazine with various features, and Jerdan particularly relished, and contributed enthusiastically to one entitled "Comparative

Criticism" in which contradictory reviews of plays, and new publications, from other periodicals were placed in juxtaposition to each other, highlighting how ridiculous it was to place any reliance upon such opinions.

In January 1808 Jerdan had provided *The Satirist* with an introduction to his political drama *Vox et Praeterea Nihil, or Parliamentary Debates in Rhyme*,[36] a comic ridicule against Opposition leaders and adherents. The 'drama' itself followed in the February issue. Wrapped in the conceit of a letter to "Mr Satirist", Jerdan introduced his subject, explaining: "Anxious to rescue from disgrace and obloquy a certain body of political worthies, *self-* named ALL THE TALENTS, I long ago exerted all my *talents* to discover a method of doing justice to their *virtuous patriotism*; but so much had been written and said upon their arrogance in power, their meanness while falling, and their rancour since that lamentable event, that I began to dispair [sic] of success." After twenty false starts, he continued, he lit upon the notion of presenting his characters in the process of deliberating upon their future actions in the format of a "tragic-comic-melo-drame in rhyme". Jerdan clearly enjoyed choosing the names of his *dramatis personae*, including the easily identifiable Mr Grin-vile, Mr Chance-seller and Mr Wind-I-am. Readers were advised that four acts of the play were concerned with the usual "lamenting, regretting, groaning, reviling, quarrelling, bragging and cursing" of the various characters, but in the fifth act the author must make a happy ending. In this drama, the final act was a discussion about creating the means to harass their successors in office, noting with heavy irony that:

> the old palaver about the freedom of the people, reform of parliament, liberty of the press etc. etc. won't go down now, since they have been tried and found wanting. At last, however, they agree that nothing can render them more *hateful, despicable and ridiculous* than they are already and determine to rail against ministers for . . . speaking in a haughty tone to America, for vexing and thwarting the designs of Buonaparte etc. etc. and above all, for not *promising any thing* while they perform a great deal, which *my* heroes conclude is not done from any love to the country, but solely with the design, Mr Satirist, of satirising them!!!

Complaining that both Drury Lane and Covent Garden had rejected his drama, Jerdan begged "Mr Satirist" to show the world how clever he was by publishing his work, not in its original dramatic form, but in monthly instalments of rhyming debates. He did not need to notice the present ministry of course, as "they never say or do anything worth preserving" and could not compare with the virtues of a C_nn_ng or a P__l, and various other almost-named Tories. He declared to the "great Satirist" "what a grand thing it will be to consecrate *all the effusions of All the Talents;* not in the slovenly way of a daily paper – not choaked with the numerous weeds which spring up so luxuriantly with every little flower of rhetoric, vanity and patriotism – not buried beneath the dross of extraneous matter . . . " and so on and on, and with a final ironic flourish, signs himself "Brevis Curtis". The actual "drama" appearing in the February issue consisted of a few maudlin drunken exchanges between his main characters; it was the minor roles of Mistresses Fitz and Bucks (called Mrs and Miss Prompter) who were given the thrust of the scene:

Miss P.	Nay, dearest Mother, prithee cease to sorrow,
	Tho' wrong today, all may be right tomorrow:
	Pray take some ratafia to quell these shocks,
	The *Talents* yet may overthrow the *Blocks*.
Mrs P.	Ah! By the virgin! That will never be,
	They've bragged and blundered on to that degree,
	The people's eyes are opened to their shame,
	And all the world, save France, detest their name.
	How could these lips so foolishly persuade
	Prompter to lend such cursed fools his aid.

Jerdan concluded his address to "Mr Satirist" by remarking that the public had been greatly deprived by the refusal of the theatres to produce his drama – ironic to the end.

Given its nature, *The Satirist* was a journal which was constantly in trouble with the law, monthly battling law-suits, writs for libel and assaults on its proprietor.[37] Despite these unfavourable conditions, when George Manners wished to dispose of his interest in the paper Jerdan purchased the copyright from him, together with the house at 267 Strand in which it was published. The house purchase proved to be an albatross around Jerdan's neck. He took over editorship of *The Satirist* on 1 July 1812 and eliminated from its tone the vituperative rancour that had made it so popular and notorious. He was not sanctimonious about this, however, stating his aims clearly, if rather lengthily. Recognising that satire was a potent instrument, he announced that he intended to use it impartially, to correct crimes "that flaunt in the broad face of day", but not to gratify envy, disseminate slander, or poison the confidence of social intercourse.[38] He dropped "Comparative Criticism" but introduced a new feature called "The Moon", offering lighter literature such as anecdotes and epigrams. Jerdan intended to greatly expand articles on politics, theatre, and critical reviews. He continued to include a cartoon at the beginning of every issue, with an "Explanation of the Caricature". One, dated 1 August 1812, depicted *The Satirist* under new management: Jerdan driving a coach and four, symbolizing the magazine, trampling on a woman, Vice, who has dropped her sword. The image contained witches, thunderbolts and sunrays, with a crest of the letters SNS

(Satirist New Series), a laurel wreath, a snake and crossed pens.[39] For a few months, his new approach was successful.

In his second volume, January–June 1813, Jerdan printed *The Satirist*'s first advertisement, announcing that advertising would henceforth be a regular feature.[40] It was apparently unsuccessful, as no more appeared.[41] The third volume of *The Satirist* commenced in July 1813 and Jerdan deemed it a success. The tone of his editorial leader in the issue for September of that year was entirely serious and political, and concerned the Congress for Peace at Prague. Napoleon was in trouble on all sides; he had left his army retreating from Moscow, Prussia had declared war on France, and Napoleon had allowed Metternich to attempt to mediate peace. Napoleon had just lost Spain as a result of Wellington's victory at Vitoria. Even from such a disadvantaged position, Napoleon declined the terms offered to him under the Congress of Prague. Jerdan was cynical – or perhaps realistic – about the Congress, calling it

> the solemn trickery in which every sovereign of Europe engages, well-knowing that it will lead to nothing – the breathing-time armistice . . . the most hostile meeting for pacific purposes that Form and Folly ever exhibited to an astonished world . . . is it not a shame . . . that credulous mankind should yet, . . . be so marvellously stupid as to be blinded by the flimsy pretexts. Alas! When will age bring wisdom to this same world of ours . . . But perhaps, in *after* ages, when all our other labours are forgotten, and the bright pages of this work are buried in the dust of oblivious antiquity so deeply, that not even black-letter zeal will venture to assail the mouldering heap; in those days when the fingers which form these letters, and the stump with which they are written, shall be alike insensible; it may be remembered, that, at least, one miserable scribbler could tell his country to expect nothing but war from the pantomime at Prague.[42]

He was right. Napoleon's rejection of the Congress for Peace offer resulted in Austria joining Russia, Prussia, Britain and Spain in the war on France and the fighting continued.

A fourth volume of *The Satirist* followed but Jerdan rapidly became disenchanted with it, partly because Napoleon's defeat in 1814 left a large void, where previously space given to attacks on him had been increasing.[43] His publisher, Williams, had been persuaded by the Duke of York's old adversary, Mary Ann Clarke, to produce a libellous pamphlet against Fitzgerald, the Chancellor of the Irish Exchequer. Jerdan wrote to Fitzgerald to apologise for his publisher's part, and then went to visit Mrs Clarke who had been arrested, finding her as self-satisfied and cheerful as ever. She was sentenced to nine months in the Marshalsea Prison, from where she sent out cards proclaiming "Mrs M. A. Clarke At Home every Evening till farther notice". At this time Jerdan started an association with the *Sun* newspaper and could not devote sufficient attention to *The Satirist*. Its circulation dropped, because the paper did not titillate the public as the original version had, and Jerdan ceased publication. He attempted to revive it under another name, *The Tripod or New Satirist*, but this paper lasted only a very short time; as he said "it had soon hardly a leg to stand upon, and so was kicked over",[44] ceasing in August 1814.[45]

The property in the Strand that Jerdan acquired from George Manners in the purchase of *The Satirist* proved to be a drain rather than a benefit to his resources. Not only did the paper fail, but so did his feeble attempts to be a land-lord. At the time of purchase Jerdan was assured the tenants were respectable – but he was not ruthless enough to force them to pay rent, and was led a merry dance. The mantua-maker and her young assistants, tenants of the first floor, laughed in his face when he called for the rent; his threats against another tenant, an agent for a wealthy Welsh mine, resulted in the man sending him the door-key to the Strand house in a letter for which, to add insult to injury, Jerdan had to pay the postage. He received nothing at all for his property, which he continued to own for five years. He still owned it when he commenced work on the *Literary Gazette* in 1817 when it became the publishing offices of Pinnock and Maunder. Thus the property-owning venture was a disaster for Jerdan. Even when he eventually managed to dispose of it, he received bills on the Newbury bank for the price, but this bank was robbed, and payment was stopped. Jerdan had to wait a further twelve years before the purchasers finally paid him the debt due.

Fortunately for him, Jerdan was now firmly launched upon the path of jour-nalism: he had written up parliamentary debates for the *Aurora*, the *Pilot*, and the *Morning Post;* he had tried his hand at writing for, and editing *The Satirist* and *Tripod* and published several poems. With this wealth of experience (but little to show in the way of financial benefit) he was ready for his next step, into the *Sun*.

3

Editor of the *Sun*

In 1812 when Jerdan started to work on the *Sun*, the paper's fortunes were in decline. It had been an organ of Pitt politics and had been earlier been convicted of a libel on a Lord St Vincent, resulting in Mr Herriot, the *Sun's* editor, being imprisoned for six months, while the printer and Scripps the publisher were each imprisoned for one month, and John Taylor the drama critic given a fine of one hundred marks. Such draconian measures to punish newspapers were not uncommon.

On 10 May 1813 Jerdan was appointed editor of the *Sun*. The paper's proprietors were George Herriot who owned five shares, and Robert Clarke who owned three shares, both former editors of the paper, and John Taylor, in whose ability the other two proprietors had lost confidence. It was for this reason that Jerdan had been brought in. He and Taylor owned one share each. In addition to his one-tenth share in the *Sun*, Jerdan was to receive a weekly salary of between five and six hundred pounds a year, and was assured of the 'entire control' of the paper. This seemed clear enough, and Jerdan was satisfied with the arrangement, although financially he was not as well paid as he had been when combining a range of journalistic activities. He saw himself as the saviour of the *Sun* and so was willing to take a reduction in his income.

Shortly after he joined the *Sun* he published a declaration of his principles, from which he later claimed he had never swerved, believing them to be the "true elements of the true Press". He stated that the British nation should be informed of "the truth, the whole truth and nothing but the truth", even though he acknowledged that mistakes can happen. News that created excitement (and, implicitly, sales) which next day proved a fallacy, was inconsistent with his principles, as was the practice of promoting "the sordid purposes of gambling and stock-jobbing". The *Sun*, he insisted, would never be prostituted by doing such things. The public should be given bad news undiluted, because after twenty years of upheaval they had learnt to overcome unpleasant tidings; they should also be given good news, but this should not be exaggerated. Having set out his stall, Jerdan embarked upon the task of editing the *Sun*.

His first leader appeared on the anniversary of Perceval's death. The political debate on the position of Roman Catholics, to whom Perceval had been antagonistic, had continued. Jerdan took the Protestant, opposition side, claiming that he "wrote so well that the *Sun* was publicly stigmatised and burnt by the Romish party in Dublin".[1]

This was the period of Jerdan's most active and ferocious political writing. The fervent Toryism he shared with his father and brother George found another outlet in almost daily attacks on the Whig opposition, through his editorial and leader writings in the *Sun*, against the Whig paper, the *Morning Chronicle*. The *Chronicle*'s editor was James Perry, in later years a friend of Jerdan's with whom he shared "the pleasant field of literature", after Jerdan had come to view Perry as merely the tool of the party.[2] (Interestingly, he did not make any comment about his own position vis-à-vis the Tory party.) In 1813, however, Wellington was engaged in the Peninsular Wars. Jerdan was incensed at the opposition's evident admiration for Napoleon's powers when the *Morning Chronicle* opined in July, as Wellington triumphantly entered Madrid, that Buonaparte was merely delaying his war in Spain until a more convenient opportunity. It was an exciting time, watching the progression of Napoleon's downfall in a succession of events of unparalleled consequence. On most nights the evening papers published up to four or even five editions, as they attempted to keep up with the speed of extraordinary news arriving from all fronts on the continent. Jerdan was proud to uphold traditional Tory values, losing no opportunity to promulgate them in the *Sun*, as well as attacking the opposition views in the *Morning Chronicle*. He published a nine-stanza verse entitled "A Brace of Opposition Similes", likening the all-the-talents crew to curs tied to a cart, impotent to perform real service.[3]

Six weeks after Jerdan's installation as editor, he and his fellow shareholder John Taylor joined forces in contravention of their contractual obligation. This was a clause prohibiting them to bail a third party on pain of forfeiture of their shares. However, they agreed to do just that, giving bail for a stricken journalist, Mr Proby, Lord's reporter for the *Morning Chronicle* and, according to Jerdan, a 'great oddity' in his day.[4] This small infraction would normally have bound the two rebels closely together, but this did not last.

Jerdan's tasks as editor were undoubtedly demanding, but he was a likeable man who gathered a circle of associates to encourage and stimulate him. His friends assembled in the office in the afternoons, to give and receive news and information. Mr Proby, the 'oddity' from the *Morning Chronicle*, was a frequent visitor, surprising given the fierce rivalry between the two newspapers. Francis (later Sir Francis) Freeling, the actor John Kemble and Robert Clarke, shareholder in the *Sun*, were other regular callers.

The *Sun* was an evening newspaper, so the mornings were full of frantic activity. Once the paper had gone to press, around two o'clock in the afternoon, Jerdan had another two or three hours of lighter work in preparation for the following day. Before the advent of rail and telegraph, much important news reached London in the afternoons. Laws prohibited the importation of news-papers from the continent, but they were sometimes smuggled in for sale. A single paper could fetch up to one hundred guineas if it was recent, especially if it carried news of Buonaparte's German campaigns. Occasionally it happened that news thus obtained and printed in the papers was the first time the govern-ment heard of it. Jerdan mentioned at least two letters from Downing Street which revealed this situation. He became a habitué of the corridors of power, familiar with ministers and officials in various departments. He was to be found on his knees in the Foreign Office, crawling over maps spread on the floor, whilst he and the Under-Secretary struggled to find the unfamiliar place-names where Buonaparte's army was marching.

Jerdan was glad to see the end of 1813, penning a 'vale' :

> Eighteen hundred and thirteen, I bid you adieu,
> In the dark to eternity jog;
> Before you took leave you had got out of view,
> And now you are lost in a fog.

His new year started well, with a visit to Drury Lane to see the famous actor Kean in 'Shylock' (sic). Jerdan became a great fan of Kean and followed his theatrical career with interest, seeing in his Richard III and Othello perfect vehi-cles for his physique and talent but he did not think that Kean was so successful in the roles of Romeo, Hamlet or Lear. January also brought the great Frost Fair on the Thames, when sheep were roasted on the ice – or rather 'scorched' as Jerdan grumpily remarked. This was a time when every available printing press was ready to satisfy the huge demand by authors of all abilities – or none. Continuing the sheep theme, Jerdan remarked that many would-be authors were thereby 'fleeced'. The icy grip on the country lasted until mid-March, bringing snow and fog. Mail could not be delivered and the price of bread and coal soared. On the plus side, there were sideshows and merry-go-rounds on the Thames to amuse the populace.

In this period Jerdan started to educate himself about art, a passion which lasted throughout his life. His entrée to this world was through the British Institution, where fine art was exhibited and offered for sale.[5] He became espe-cially interested in British art. The press of the time gave only scant attention to the subject, but Jerdan later claimed to be responsible for bringing public attention to the Arts throughout the ensuing thirty-six years of his journalis-tic career. Moreover, he believed he had enough influence "to guide the judgment and influence the taste of the country".[6] The *Sun*, a highly political paper, was not to be the vehicle for this guidance; the journal where Jerdan was to play a significant role in forming taste in both art and literature was still three years away, but it was whilst editor of the *Sun* that his deep interest in art was formed.

William Jerdan was widening not only his professional circle, becoming acquainted with writers of all genres, politicians, booksellers and merchants, but also found opportunity to make new friends outside of the *Sun* and its interests. At home, Cromwell Cottage was becoming crowded: on 2 March 1814 a daughter was born, named Mary Felicity Dawn.[7] In his *Autobiography*, Jerdan made virtually no reference to his domestic life, and what little is known has to be pieced together from inference and from scattered mentions in surviving correspondence. At this stage of his life it appears that Jerdan was happy in his work, fulfilled in his family life, and sufficiently free to indulge in his many social and personal interests and activities. He needed these distractions to alleviate the gruelling mornings spent in preparing the paper for its daily appearance, and trying to keep abreast of wars on multiple fronts.

At the beginning of 1814 important events were taking place: British forces attacked Washington DC, burning the White House and the Capitol; the first steam-driven war ship was developed by the British navy, and the Corn Laws were passed.[8] Finally, and crucially – or so it seemed – Napoleon had been vanquished and exiled to Elba, a cause of great relief and rejoicing by the Allies. Curiosity about his place of exile encouraged Jerdan to translate a French account of a recent visit to that island by Arsenne Thiebaut de Berneaud. *Voyage to the Isle of Elba* was published as a single octavo volume by Longman & Co. in June 1814. Jerdan dedicated his translated book to Charles Long (later 1st Baron Farnborough), a close friend of Pitt, in esteem and admiration for his untiring support of Pitt's principles through his work as a legislator and holder of various government offices. (Long had also dissuaded Jerdan from publishing criticism of the judicial system at the time of Perceval's murder, and in retrospect, Jerdan was grateful for his advice.)

Jerdan's objective was to translate Thiebaut's French as closely as possible, to give his readers "a perfect idea of the manner in which Members of the French Institute and men of science in that country, direct their inquiries". Thiebaut's own Introduction ran to fifteen pages. Jerdan acknowledged that were the author "less a scholar, he would be more entertaining", but facts were so interwoven with learning, Jerdan could not separate them. He merely moved the chapter on Geology from second to fourth place, as being of less interest to the general reader. The book was dry in content, consisting of chapters on a General View of the Isle of Elba, Population, Natural History, Agriculture, Industry, Political History, Geology and Topography. It does not appear to have been a success and was not reprinted. Jerdan commented that it did not add much to his resources. He sent a copy as a gift to Walter Scott, whose letter of thanks recalled with pleasure the kindness he received at Kelso from Jerdan's father, although he thought that Jerdan himself had probably been too young to remember him from those days.[9]

Napoleon's exile immediately made a voyage to France possible. The country had been closed to English visitors since the breakdown of the Peace of Amiens in 1802. Even before the signing of the Cessation of Hostilities, Jerdan saw it as his duty, as editor of a political paper, to lose no time in leaving London to investigate the newly-opened country across the Channel. He left Robert Clarke, his co-proprietor, in charge of the *Sun*.

Although William Jerdan had, by 1814, contributed a great deal of political comment and leaders to the *Sun* and various other newspapers, these were unsigned, and thus his authorship of specific pieces can seldom be indisputably verified. Jerdan's largest body of *attributable* journalistic writing was a series entitled "Journal of a Trip to Paris", thirty-one articles signed 'Viator', written between April and September 1814, and published in the *Sun*.[10] In his *Autobiography*, published in 1852, he identified these articles as his own. These reports therefore afford the earliest substantial opportunity to note his journalistic style and capabilities; most of his later writing for periodicals was also unsigned, but here, in the *Sun*, Jerdan was free to choose his topics, his politics (which, like the *Sun*, were strongly Tory), and safe in the certainty that whatever he sent back to London would be published within a few days. An "in-joke" which only he and a very few others would appreciate, was in the text of one Journal entry, where he addressed himself to "Mr Editor", saying "I must be allowed occasionally to riot on trifles, drop and resume subjects *ad libitum*, and, in short, write just as chance and whim determine."[11] Clarke, as Acting Editor, was hardly likely to overrule or alter the contributions of his permanent editor who saw himself as a pioneer of travel journalism, an early *Rough Guide* or *Lonely Planet*, forging into newly accessible territory to tempt and guide future travellers. Jerdan's stated aim in the first entry of the "Journal of a Trip to Paris" was to add "the minute touches which generally escape the common picture-drawers for the public". All the newspapers covered politics, but 'Viator' would give his public colour, sounds, sights and personal observations of the state of the country not seen for many years since the advent of Napoleon. Discipline and structure were never Jerdan's strong points, although the way in which his lively journalistic observations of Paris tumbled out, mixing national character and politics with trivia, and tourist guide with art criticism, make them immediate, and real, giving a strong flavour of post-revolutionary Paris.

Jerdan sailed from Dover on 19 April 1814 on the first regular Packet, the *Lady Francis*, his friend Francis Freeling having obtained his passage.[12] Even before leaving Dover, Jerdan witnessed an event which so moved him, he mentioned it not only in his "Journal", but repeated it thirty-eight years later in his *Autobiography*. A beautiful girl, about twenty years of age, had just arrived from France. She flung herself upon "the free land of Albion", weeping tears of joy at the end of eleven years' captivity in a foreign land. Jerdan insisted he did not want to create a 'sentimental journey', like Sterne; however, he *was* a sentimentalist, so could not resist this emotional image of freedom from the bonds of the hated Corsican tyrant.

The energy and enthusiasm with which Jerdan embarked on his adventure was immediately apparent. With his 'tour guide' hat on, he urged travellers, especially ladies, not to be seduced into accepting passage on the numerous opportunistic boats taking advantage of the crowds wishing to get to France quickly, but only to trust to regular Packets for their safety and convenience. He vividly described the chaotic, absurd disembarkation at Calais, whereby men and luggage were decanted from the *Lady Francis* into a six-oared boat, and were set upon by hundreds of men, women and children spilling from the shore into the sea, trying to grab hold of some piece of luggage and carry it to dry land. The passengers too were seized upon and bodily carried ashore. Jerdan reported that a "sturdy fisherwoman with a long paddle in her hand took violent possession of my person, which she disposed of as the Indian females do their children"[13] and so he came ashore to start the great adventure. Thoroughly soaked from the rain above and the sea below, travellers and baggage were reunited at the Customs House and then continued on their way.

Jerdan's "Journal" entries described the arduous journey from Calais to Paris, a total of thirty-six hours on the road. His observations ranged "from politics to agriculture and from serious matters to trifles". He had a knack for the quick sketch, an evocative word-picture, such as the postillion he acquired at one post, dressed in pre-Revolutionary costume: "The large cocked hat, the powdered and ponderous queue, the ragged dress, and beyond all, the enormous jack-boots into which this veritable Frenchman inserted his pony limbs."[14] The poverty, misery and beggary along the way affected Jerdan deeply, as did the almost total absence of young men. Horses, cattle and sheep were gone too, requisitioned or eaten. Very old men, women and children worked the fields, pulling ploughs and harrows. He constantly passed or came upon companies of soldiers, such as Prussian Hussars in Boulogne, contrasting with the wretched condition of French conscripts. These conscripts, some only fifteen or sixteen years old, were sick, wounded and broken "by a complication of distress, these most miserable of human beings consigned, in the very flower of youth, to premature old age, and an early grave".

Such heavy matters were leavened by some humorous observations – Jerdan was seldom down-hearted for long, and he wanted to entertain as well as to instruct. He delighted in describing the antics of postillions, who took every opportunity to show off to their English *milords*, by skilful whip-cracking, singing and general good-nature. These were the only young men met with upon the journey who were not soldiers.

Transport was an important topic on which he expended several column inches, explaining the differences between French and English systems. He zealously gave details of each post between Calais and Paris and the charges for each post and horse, so that those who planned a similar trip would be able to calculate their financial needs. The currency exchange rate was not favourable, losing about two to three hundred pounds for every thousand pounds brought from England.[15]

English visitors were warmly welcomed by all kinds of French peasants with whom Jerdan spoke, seeking them out in their huts and houses. The English were seen as the source of regeneration and trade, and it was Jerdan's opinion that it was the very struggle for superiority between England and France over six hundred years which "exalted these nations, respectively, in the consideration of each other . . . with 400,000 victorious Russians, Austrians and Prussians over-spreading their country . . . the French think more highly of the power of Great Britain . . . than they consider the rest of the world together".[16] He believed this confidence would prove to be of mutual advantage.

Throughout these "Journals" his despair at the pitiful scenes on all sides was clearly evident. He was surprised, however, that whilst the French spoke of Buonaparte with disgust, he discerned "a coolness in their hate which I cannot reconcile with that temper and character of a people which I could admire".[17] From a longer perspective, it may not in fact have been coolness, rather a lack of energy caused by the privations suffered by the population over so many years, in the cause of the bloody revolution.

Jerdan's highly charged emotions threatened to overwhelm his journalistic style as he contemplated events that resulted in collaborators being rewarded with the land and possessions of murdered noblemen. He tried to be even-handed, to understand the plight of some who had no choice but to serve Buonaparte, but was unforgiving of those men he named who "waded through blood and infamy to these favours from an infamous Master . . . scoundrels, whose atrocities are unparalleled in history".[18] Epithets such as "demon", "butcher" "Corsican Tamerlane" abounded; his heartfelt loathing for the man who had so decimated an entire country and culture could not be contained.

He felt sympathy for the ignominy of the people. The military were quartered everywhere, each village and hut housing a one-time enemy. Jerdan expressed the hope that such close quarters would alleviate any feelings of hostility, create a mutual understanding, and pave the way for future harmony in Europe. This seems a naïve idea for a political journalist. After a long and weary war, to have a soldier of the occupying force living under one's roof must have been salt in the wound, and a situation highly unlikely to generate the harmony that Jerdan expected.

Jerdan's route into Paris took him from St Denis through Montmartre, so recently the scene of Buonaparte's final defeat. So recent, indeed, that dead horses still lay unburied and, in Jerdan's colourful words:

In other respects, however, all was as if no such battle had ever been fought.

The fields, so lately stained with human blood, and disfigured with the mutilated corpses of the slain, were green with cultivation – over the road formed by the transport of artillery, the plough and the roller were drawn in tranquillity – where the bugle and the trumpet so recently sounded the dreadful charge; where the noisy drum drowned the groans of the dying, and confounded in rude clamour all the agonies of battle; where carnage revelled, and the smoke, and fire, and thunder of war was terrible; even there, within so short a space, rural quiet and pastoral simplicity reigned with an undisturbed sovereignty. The song of the labourer in the field had entirely succeeded to the strife of the warrior; the lovely herbage did not seem as if its roots had been moistened with human gore. The celebrated heights of Montmartre on the left, crowned with windmills in full activity, looked gay and animated. So wonderful and mutable are the affairs of men![19]

Entering Paris affected Jerdan deeply. He mused upon Arabian Tales, mythical meetings of Princes, gatherings of Warriors, and reflected that the real-life equivalents of all these heroes, and more, were crowded within the walls of Paris; figments of his rich imagination, fuelled by his wide literary knowledge, were about to become reality.

Jerdan believed that Buonaparte's most heinous crime, amongst a litany of atrocities, was his plan for the defence of Paris. Flimsy wooden barriers which could not have withstood a single assault had been erected; if Marshal Marmont, whose corps was defending the city, had attempted to repel the Allies at this vulnerable point, this would have "produced a catastrophe so horrid, that nature shrinks at the bare apprehension of it".[20] As it was, Marmont's men stood their ground, fighting from every height for thirty miles, taking countless Allied lives. Only when Montmartre and Belleville, on the doorstep of Paris, were stormed, and Paris lay at the feet of the 200,000 Allied troops who surrounded the capital, was a Capitulation proposed and agreed. The corps of Marmont, Duke of Ragusa, had defected, making continued resistance impossible. This defection gave rise to a new French verb, *raguser*, to betray.[21] Looking back at these events which had happened only a few weeks earlier on 31 March when it was clear that the Allies had triumphed, Jerdan said the French, "a gay and giddy people", did not seem to care. One emperor was much the same as another.[22]

Jerdan's overall impression of Paris was of a "miserable, ill-built, irregular, dirty, and disgusting place",[23] hardly a ringing endorsement to his readers, as potential travellers and tourists. Its only splendour was in its palaces, "and even there the toe of meanness does so tread upon the heel of magnificence, that it galls its kibe".[24] He explained the problem of finding one's way around the streets of Paris, exacerbated by the many name changes, which the locals knew, but the tourist did not. There were ancient names, revolutionary names, then imperial names, and currently, changes back to Bourbon nomenclature. He mentioned what he called "the greatest ornament" of Paris, the circle around the city of wide Boulevarts (sic) planted on each side with trees. However, other streets were narrow, with central gutters awash, and no pavements for pedestrians who took their chances between passing carriages.

Aware of his self-appointed task as 'pioneer' and tour guide, Jerdan realised that accommodation was what the traveller required. He was at pains to explain clearly the various types of lodging available and their prices. He was unusually practical too, advising those who preferred private lodgings to hotels "that they ought to be provided by some friend or agent before you arrive in Paris; otherwise you are apt to be annoyed in searching for them, and *more imposed upon in your bargain*".[25] He reassured the timid that lodging houses were licensed by the Police and their proprietors were therefore unlikely to cheat, for fear of having the license rescinded. Jerdan himself finally negotiated a room in a hotel in the Rue Vivienne, not far from the Louvre, later moving to the Hôtel du Rome.

Shoals of would-be servants offered themselves for hire, but picking the honest and faithful one was the challenge. Jerdan was sympathetic up to a point; he knew that periods of work and enforced idleness create need, and addiction to bad habits. Illustrating the problem, he admitted how he was duped by one such servant, to whom he gave an important package to post to London, with six francs for postage; three days later the package was found at the British Ambassador's office, whence the man had taken it, pocketing the six francs. Thenceforth he managed with just the hotel's servant.

Jerdan offered his readers some notion of prices of staple foods. Whilst he showed that most provisions were cheaper in France, coffee, tea and sugar cost more than in England. He found the tea undrinkable, one brew being made from dried birch leaves. The cheapness of wine was a delight to him, table Burgundy being less than a shilling, and the best Claret and Champagne only two to four shillings a bottle. This, he said, was the "fair side of the picture". However, if an Englishman chose to live in France, he "must consent to the surrender of almost all the *domestic comforts of life*".[26] On this point Jerdan became severely moralistic, maintaining that the French were strangers to cleanliness and delicacy; filth and grandeur mixed indiscriminately; they were an unsociable people who, as a legacy of a terrible revolution, had lax principles and were morally subverted. He seemed genuinely shocked at this moral turpitude: "the obvious absence of every idea of honour in the high, and of honesty in the low".[27] His implication was that such behaviour was unknown in England. This critical and rather negative view of the French was balanced by his oft-repeated claim that the French people he met throughout his trip were unfailingly polite, willing to assist the traveller, and always helpful.

An entire "Journal" entry was devoted to one of the best restaurants in Paris, Beauvilliers. Jerdan described its Bill of Fare and Wine List, the layout of the restaurant, the *modus operandi* of the staff, and the discernible national manners or lack of them, of customers from Austria, Prussia and Russia as well as the French and English. In his *Autobiography* in 1852 he still remembered Beauvillier's fondly, saying there was no longer a restaurant in Paris to match it.[28]

One event was so momentous that it is curious Jerdan did not mention it in his "Journal of a Trip to Paris". It must have made a deep impression upon him, as he recounted it vividly in his *Autobiography*. On 4 May Louis XVIII entered Paris. This magnificent occasion was celebrated with a parade on the banks of the Seine by the elite of the Allied Forces and the colourful presence of Russian, Prussian and Austrian uniforms. The Duke of Wellington had come from Toulouse, and paraded in plain clothes to avoid attention, but the news soon spread, and Jerdan tells us "They hurra'd and shouted as if they were demented, and a French conqueror of Great Britain had suddenly descended upon them. 'Vive Vellington! Vive Vellington!' resounded from ten thousand throats." [29] The *Sun* readers would surely have been gratified to know how their hero was fêted in Paris, and Jerdan may have known that the event would be widely covered in the news columns of his paper. People of many nations were in the crowd, and the rejoicing completely overshadowed even the jubilation caused by Buonaparte's exit from Fontainbleau to his exile on Elba only two weeks earlier. Workmen were frantically busy replacing the Imperial crowns, Ns and Bees wherever they were found, and the air was thick with jokes punning on the initials. White flags flew, and it seemed to Jerdan that only white doves were allowed in the skies. The day ended with a grand ball given by Sir Charles Stewart, the British Ambassador, to which Jerdan was admitted with a ticket given to him by Lord Burghersh, later Earl of Westmoreland.

One of the promised "trivial" episodes which Jerdan found worth recounting, was the early morning, unannounced visit of a group of five "*Dames des Halles*", alias *Poissardes* (fishwives). Naked and sleepy, he was no match for these gaudily dressed women armed with flowers, who sandwiched him into his bed, noisily demanding 5 francs of the English *milord*. He used to feel contempt, he said, for those warriors beaten by the Amazons, but now he understood their situation better!

His personal interest in the arts coincided with the journalistic necessity to report on the major institutions and buildings of the newly liberated city. Eager to see whatever Paris had to offer, he hurried to the Louvre, the most important public building. He found the experience overwhelming; examining the sublime collection of art on display, he was "agitated with delight and rapture and astonishment".[30] Running from one marvel to another, he found himself "dissatisfied with that narrowness of intellectual power" which impeded fixing every piece upon his memory. From this first visit he selected only the Apollo Belvedere which he venerated "as if a divinity were before you". He could not tear himself away from the Louvre until closing time. In his later life Jerdan exhibited this same deep love and respect for works of art, perhaps too often calling them works of 'genius', but nevertheless, responding to and respecting serious artistic endeavours. His use of the word 'genius' was applied to those of talent and potential and in his time was generally used more freely than the more rarefied connotation recognized today.

Jerdan later visited another great institution, the Hotel des Invalides or, as he called it, the Chelsea Hospital of France. Being an Englishman he was warmly welcomed and, as before, commented that to be an Englishman was

> a passport to civility and attention everywhere. I wish I could reflect on the politeness shewn to Foreigners, *because they are foreigners*, in England, with the same complacency, but in this respect the French are far our superiors.[31]

He inspected the Hospital's church, now devoid of its religious decorations and of military trophies, which had now been returned to their rightful owners. The Common Hall was decorated with pictures of French victories, and he "enjoyed a secret national pride in observing that not one of them was over the English". In his view, this Hospital should be on every tourist's list, unlike the Ecole Militaire which was disappointing and dilapidated.

He reported that the huge ground of the Champ de Mars, where the "Corsican Tyrant" had displayed his military power to subjugate his people, now offered a very different scene: encampments of soldiers, some with their families or with women of the town, horses, camp fires and tents, dancing, drinking and story-telling, the whole forming a spectacle he felt his "humble pen" could not adequately describe. He took a gleeful pleasure in noticing that the Fountain of the Invalides, ornamented with the Lion of Venice appropriated by Buonaparte and decorated with glorifying inscriptions to the usurper, slaked the thirst of a Cossack's horse drinking from its basin. His piece ended, "What a comment!"[32]

Jerdan also visited the Cossack encampment on the banks of the Seine, describing it as a "great gipsy party". So that his readers at home could picture this scene, he likened its picturesque wildness to a scene by Dr Loutherberg.[33] He admired the Cossacks' strength and courage, but not their table manners:

> They were at dinner, standing around a pot upon the channel, and with spoons conveyed its contents to their mouths, by insinuating the spoon most adroitly through more hair than any "hill horse Dobbin" has upon his tail. When they arrived at a lump of meat, it was torn to pieces with great dispatch, and with the ceremony of a cannibal.[34]

Another Cossack habit was to "water" the gardens of houses where they were billeted, not, as the owners thought, out of gratitude for a roof over their heads, but knowing that valuables were often buried in anticipation of their approach; the water immediately sank where the ground had been recently dug, but remained longer on the surface where it had not, instantly indicating to the Cossacks where a search was likely to reveal hidden treasures.[35]

Jerdan seemed bemused by the Parisian lifestyle – rising at five or six, the Court was in session by seven, and by nine the Tuileries were crowded with Civil and Military Officers attending to their various functions. By noon, all business was concluded, and while women continued to shop all afternoon, the men idled, gambled and went to the theatre. He feared this "strange kind of gossiping, lounging life" would be "the source of immorality, licentiousness and disorder", but hoped it was a temporary reaction to the recent terrors the country had passed through.

As an example of this gossiping life, Jerdan described how in public gardens such as the Luxembourg and the Tuileries, dozens of stalls were filled with newspapers and journals. These were for sale or, for one sou lent, to readers to regale passers-by with the news. At this low price, he noted, "the very poorest of the people are enabled to become great politicians at the cheapest rate". Seeing the press as "the most potent moral engine that exists"[36] Jerdan deplored the censorship which had not yet been lifted from the French press, contrary to the idea of liberty, the founding principle of the new order. On the firm ground of his own experience, Jerdan noted that "the news of the day at Paris is infinitely more various and uncertain than in London".[37] London papers reported on news great and small, whereas the Paris press, having been so long under repressive constraints, which he hoped would soon be lifted, barely published more than official news, for fear of offence and punishment.

Jerdan was horrified at the lack of observance of the Sabbath. Christian devotion ended with the Revolution. The shops were open, and there was no rest, but for him the most shocking were the occupations of Sunday evening: theatres crowded with inferior ranks, dancing houses full of music and riotous behaviour, scenes of revelry he calls a "Saturnalia". Such non-observance could only result in even more moral turpitude. The disappearance of religion from France was evident in the deconsecration of the Church of Saint Genevieve, and its renaming as the Pantheon, designed to be the resting-place of great men who oppressed their fellow creatures and defied Heaven.[38] He challenged the inscription that these were '*grands hommes*' deserving of the admiration of posterity.

Jerdan the Moralist is again evident in a diatribe against the venal French habit of gaming, seeing it as a "general laxity of principle and depravity of morals".[39] He visited all classes of gaming-house, from those of Princes to the lowest public rooms, and even pavement games, to ascertain their levels of pollution. He likened some to Hogarth's 'Rakes Progress', and in the interests of journalism, studied the subject closely enough to describe in detail the methods of gambling at Faro and Hazard, solely of course for the edification of his readers.

The loyalty of large numbers of French people to the House of Bourbon was an eye-opener to Jerdan, who understood the huge risks taken in keeping images and reminders of the monarchy throughout the tyrannical rule of Buonaparte. They had risked death, in the belief that the monarchy would ultimately be returned to power. Some objects were immense oil paintings, often including portraits of men who subsequently collaborated with Buonaparte; Jerdan remarked how their presence in the pictures was simply ignored, the owners being interested only in what a man is, not what he was. In Versailles, Jerdan admired a pair of portraits of the late King and Queen and wished to purchase them. His offer was refused, but he was shown the vast hiding place behind the kitchen where these paintings and numerous other objects had lain hidden for years. The touching faith of the French in the restoration of the Bourbons made Jerdan ever more angry about the despotic rule of Buonaparte. He was at his most lucid in raging against this hated tyrant, and the way in which he had deliberately kept all France plunged into ignorance and barbarity, in order to exert his sovereignty:

> Thus, though I have for years entertained a determined hatred to the system of the Usurper, and had conceived a pretty strong picture of his iniquitous misrule, the variety, the extent, the perfection of his infamy was not to be imagined; and only now, when I have it before me in a tangible shape, can I form any idea of the audacity and turpitude of this Corsican Demon. You will scarcely credit me when I tell you, that there is not only no classical instruction among the rising generation of France, but they are actually as dark and uninformed as the Vandals of ancient ages[40]

He apparently believed that such ignorance of the classics, of history, and of Greek and Latin poets would have dire consequences for the French who, he maintained, had been in a state of delusion.

After having been in Paris for several weeks, Jerdan set off in July on a tour of towns to the east of the city, including Laon, Reims, and Troyes, so recently the theatre of war. He gathered eyewitness information from all types of inhabitants and shopkeepers, and the local Prefectures made their records available to him. He discovered, and reported in his "Journal", that the people's bitterness was directed not against the Allies, but against their own countrymen. Buildings were torn apart for firewood, and in Soissons the destruction of over thirty churches and abbeys begun in the Revolution, was completed by the French soldiery. The enemy was still at Laon, twenty miles away, when French soldiers, anticipating their arrival, razed the town to the ground. Many of the people had no option but to live in the underground vaults of the destroyed churches. The

Prefects assessed losses at Soissons alone at four million francs. Such military action against their own compatriots clearly shocked and upset Jerdan, but as a journalist he had a duty to report on what he found.

Somehow Jerdan found time to wine and dine with huge enjoyment, at his favourite restaurant Beauvilliers. On one especially memorable evening he met Davidoff, the formidable leader of the Black Cossacks, and another famous general, with both of whom he exchanged compliments and toasts. With a surfeit of wine loosening his tongue, he let it be known that he was editor of a major English newspaper, and thus could speak for England. This news swiftly circulated throughout the restaurant. Suddenly, a seedy-looking personage arrived. Noting the deference paid to him, Jerdan enquired as to his identity. This man was none other than the fabled Marshal Blucher who, even at this date before the Battle of Waterloo, England regarded as a hero for his fight against Napoleon. Jerdan had learnt during his time in Paris, that Blucher was an inveterate but unlucky gambler, and thus France was revenged upon him! Blucher hated everything French to such a degree that when King Louis wished to give him a medal, Blucher refused as he had so many there was nowhere to hang a new one, and it would have to go on his back. "Well," he was told, "put it there and I'll be bound it will be where no enemy will ever hit it!" Jerdan remarked that Blucher had an eye for good art, and had earmarked many fine paintings in the Louvre to be removed and sent away to Berlin, Potsdam etc. It was only with great difficulty that he was persuaded to relinquish his hold on some of these works. Blucher's hatred of the French extended to his refusal to listen to the language, but Jerdan did not know this. On sending over his compliments to the Marshal, Jerdan was astounded to see the old man rise, and come across to his table to talk to him. Jerdan addressed him in French, which Blucher ignored. Jerdan then spoke to him in English, which was translated into German for Blucher. The two men must have enjoyed each other's company, for next morning they breakfasted together. This meeting was a memorable high point for Jerdan, but not so memorable apparently for Blucher. When Jerdan met him again in London a few months later, Blucher, tired out by the constant adulation of the English crowds, had forgotten their earlier Parisian encounter.

Jerdan's stay in Paris was by no means all taken up with serious political reporting. One evening, having dined too late to attend the theatre, he visited a couple of dwarfs instead. He described this meeting in great detail, clearly enamoured with their height and appearance, and evidently admiring the lady's talent for pianoforte and her fluency in four languages. Another time he went to a freak show of an abnormally "Fat Child", and from this spectacle to another, showing paintings depicting Naples and Amsterdam, and Prevost's panorama of Boulogne. These encounters were entirely in keeping with his life-long interest in and attraction to all kinds of the unusual, and to all types of show, which later in London included other dwarfs and the freaks so popular at the time.

The Theatre Français came in for his criticism: its ticket purchase system was crowded and dangerous, the mere act of paying for your ticket being to risk a dislocated shoulder or other injury. Once inside, the Theatre was disgraceful, mean and filthy. Jerdan's article knowledgeably discussed the performance by the famous tragedian Talma. He likened the production to one which might have been seen half a century earlier in England, before the advent of Garrick's intro-duction of 'Nature'; he thought the French drama unnatural and the language not expressive of the passions it declaims. Not to denigrate the tragedic abilities of Talma, Jerdan likened him to "a race-horse in a broad wheeled wagon-team" unable to show the true nature of the tragedy.[41] The topic of dramatic language seems to have bothered Jerdan, who returned to it in a later "Journal" entry, explaining that :

It is not alone the everlasting jingle of the rhyme, which in French tragedy impresses the English ear with the idea of burlesque, but the mode of laying the emphasis in delivering this heroic poetry, adds to the grating effect. The words are pronounced in an entirely different manner from common life. All the emphases are not only thrown upon the ends of words, but also upon the termination of verses, and thus the drawl of monotony is most disagreeably and unnaturally perfected.[42]

Furthermore, he noted, "the universal French shrug . . . is very ill-suited to our ideas of dignity in Tragedy."

On his final Sunday in Paris, Jerdan attended the King's Chapel in the Tuileries, and was impressed with the surroundings and the service. In the evening he went to the Olympic Circus, watching horses perform and two stags jump through fire, an act he thought singular for such a timid animal. His grand Finale to the "Journal of a Trip to Paris" was a visit to the Bibliothèque du Roi, the last two words having just been imposed over the ubiquitous "Imperiale". Jerdan's own words are eloquent of his admiration and envy:

Indeed, it is impossible for an Englishman to visit or speak of the Institutions for the promotion of Literature in France, without experi-encing a secret pang of mortification, and of regrets, that, with all its wealth, magnificence, and power, *there is nothing like them in his own country*. The facility of access afforded to strangers, the magnitude and value of the collections, the excellence of their arrangement and keeping, the unreservedness with which their choicest stores are unlocked to the researches of students of all nations, as well as to natives, are, in truth, worthy of our imitation. In France, these opportunities are valuable: in England where the light of science is so generally diffused over the mass of the people, they would be beyond all value![43]

It seems appropriate that this considerable body of Jerdan's journalism should end with a prospectus for the promotion of Literature in England; perhaps it was this one experience, beyond all the myriad other memories he took home from his trip to Paris, which became the engine of the enormous time and effort he expended throughout his life to further the cause of Literature.

4

Turbulent Times

Eventually the time came for Jerdan to leave Paris, with all its charms and difficulties, and return to London. He was fortunate in finding a congenial travelling companion in Douglas Kinnaird, a member of the Drury Lane Management Committee, but was told a story that astonished and upset him: Jerdan had published some mildly critical remarks on some lines of Byron's (concerning a Mrs Charlemont, his lady's attendant), which had offended the poet. Byron, using Kinnaird as his messenger, had demanded satisfaction by challenging Jerdan to a duel. Kinnaird soon told Byron that his quarry was nowhere to be found as newspaper men were notoriously difficult to pin down, and were often drunk. He suggested to Lord Byron that it was "beneath his dignity to call out a paltry scribbler" who might accidentally kill him. His ploy worked and Byron acceded to his advice, thus ensuring that the world was deprived of neither Jerdan nor Byron. Jerdan was conscious that he owed his life to Kinnaird for his kindly intercession, for Byron was renowned as a certain shot.[1]

Safely back in London in the summer of 1814, Jerdan resumed his editorial duties on the *Sun*. He could not resist creating his own private celebratory verse, producing a ballad entitled *Everywhere Happy* [2] to be sung to the old Scots tune of 'Maggy Lauder'. A single verse will suffice to give the general idea of his gloating over Napoleon's downfall:

> At Paris, then, I took my way,
> No scoundrel e'er went further,
> And revell'd nobly night and day,
> In rapine, blood and murther;
> For when the Jacobins began
> Their Revolution Free tricks,
> They found I was their very man,
> And Ubicumque Felix! [chorus]

At this time he also wrote *Serpentine Sea Song*,[3] with the refrain "We've caught the [fellow] at last" (the word used, he thought, was not suitable for ladies to hear). This was again a celebratory song about the transportation of the "Corsican Felon" to Elba. He never believed these works to be of immense literary value, but thought them interesting enough to include in his *Autobiography*, as they were "smart enough for immediate purpose and display cleverness and talent well fitted for the small ready change of temporary currency".[4] Jerdan ingenuously assured his readers that he could judge his own works as fairly as if they had been written by somebody else. He certainly enjoyed playing with words; puns and anagrams were his favourites, and he celebrated Napoleon's exile with:

ANAGRAM: BONAPARTE IN ELBA
In *Elba* is placed (an appropriate station!)
Napoleon, *once ABLE – once feared by each nation;*
Now stript of his empire, his legions dispersed,
His real situation is ABLE reversed.

Although the country still suffered from the costs of the long war, London was full of continental visitors; luxuries which had been forbidden for so long were now being imported. Art treasures, hidden from Napoleon's armies, found their way on to the English market, and for the first time in more than twenty years peace reigned. London hurled itself into pleasure: fêtes and entertainments abounded. A particularly popular event was the great Peace Jubilee, with bridges and pagodas in St James's Park,[5] and a model fleet on the Serpentine, causing Jerdan to remark, slightly cynically perhaps, that "all rulers who take the trouble to devise amusements for the populace know what they are about, and how to smother disaffection, and create loyal attachment. The effect of a genuine holiday upon a working population is not to be calculated, and politicians would do well to study the problem."[6]

Whilst the country, for the time being putting aside economic despondency, resounded with rejoicings at the cessation of war, all was not well within the Royal household. As an ardent Monarchist as well as a political journalist, the situation would have been of great concern to Jerdan. In 1811 King George III's sufferings from porphyria had necessitated the appointment of his son, George Prince of Wales, as Regent, a role he fulfilled until he became King on George III's death in 1820. On the positive side the Regency saw the arts, literature and architecture blossom as never before. On the negative side, the Prince of Wales was widely despised for his marital and domestic problems and financial profligacy. In exchange for the King paying off his enormous debts, George had been forced into marriage in 1795 with Princess Caroline of Brunswick, even though, to his father's disgust and rage, he was already (illegally) married to the Catholic Maria Fitzherbert. Princess Caroline was famously repulsive to her husband, but they had an only child, Princess Charlotte, who became the prize in a tug of war between her parents. Caroline was effectively banished to Blackheath in South London. She was heard to remark bitterly, "Je suis la fille d'un Hero; la femme d'un Zero."[7]

As a consequence of this unsatisfactory childhood, Charlotte grew up rebellious and reckless and was virtually imprisoned in Cranbourne Lodge in Windsor Great Park for eighteen months, to prevent unsuitable liaisons. Byron and Shelley both wrote poetry praising her and attacking the Prince Regent for his behaviour towards her. At the same time as her daughter was under virtual house arrest in Windsor, Princess Caroline had her own severe problems. An investigation had been launched into whether a four-year old child, who formed part of her entourage, was the offspring of the Princess and one of her footmen. She turned for comfort and advice to George Canning,[8] (see illustration no. 4,) and it was at this point that the story of the royal difficulties touched upon the life of William Jerdan.

Canning was a career politician and a man of principle and sympathy, with a love of literature; these aspects of his character endeared him to William Jerdan, who grew to idolize him. He admired Canning's "profundity and firmness", his "simplicity and playfulness", his sweet tone of voice and courteous manner.[9] Lest this sound like too much hagiography, Jerdan also related that Canning expressed contempt and disgust when confronted by anything base.

At the time of Princess Caroline's distress in 1814, Canning was appointed as Ambassador to Lisbon, where he was to stay until the autumn of the following year. Before he left for Lisbon, the Princess sometimes visited him at Gloucester Lodge, his home in Brompton, a few minutes from Jerdan's Cromwell Cottage. Jerdan was in the habit of dropping in to see Canning, often on a Sunday after church. In good weather they strolled in the garden for a couple of hours, and if wet, sat talking in the library. Jerdan appreciated and relished being so warmly welcomed into Canning's home and circle, which included poets, painters, philosophers, and wits as well as the inevitable statesmen.

One Sunday afternoon as he approached Canning's house for their regular meeting, Jerdan saw Princess Caroline's coach at the door. As he hesitated to intrude, the Princess, highly flushed, came out of the house, escorted by Canning who seemed emotional. She entered her coach and drove off. Canning motioned Jerdan to go inside, where he entered the room and stood with his arm on the mantelpiece. Canning came in, in an excited and agitated state, and theatrically exclaimed: "Take care, sir, what you do! Your arm is bathing in the tears of a Princess!"[10] Caroline had indeed been weeping on the very spot, having just then accepted the advice of Canning and Lord Gower that she should leave England. She left on 9 August 1814 for her native Brunswick, and did not return until 1820, three years after the death of her twenty-one year old daughter Charlotte, in childbirth.[11] Canning and Gower's advice that Caroline leave England was partly for sound political reasons, to create more tranquillity in the country, but also to remove a source of royal scandal which was a perpetual harassment to the ailing King George and a thorn in the side of the Prince Regent. This was not to be the end of Canning's advice and sympathy towards Princess Caroline, a loyalty which would cost him dearly.

Once the Princess had left England, Canning began to make preparations for his departure to Lisbon, and Jerdan found the atmosphere at Gloucester Lodge more cheerful. He affectionately recalled a particular quirk of Canning's: on meeting a mere acquaintance, he offered only one or perhaps two fingers when shaking hands, and Jerdan had been pleased to graduate to receiving three fingers. After the episode of the Princess's tears, however, Canning shook hands with the delighted Jerdan using his whole hand, a sign of esteem given by Canning to very few.

Jerdan gained obvious benefits from such proximity to a senior politician: as a political journalist, he was at the very centre of things. Canning, apart from enjoying Jerdan's good company, was pleased to have an opportunity to learn from him what people thought about political matters, knowing that in his daily work the journalist met with intelligent men in many fields, such as literature, agriculture, mercantile and professional. On one occasion Jerdan recalled that he went too far in his outspokenness, and Canning mentioned this to another MP who took him to task over it. Jerdan defended himself on the grounds that he believed Canning would prefer truth rather than concealment, and he was forgiven his trespasses.

Jerdan's interest in Canning's appointment to Lisbon was personal as well as professional. Canning had agreed that he should look in on Gloucester Lodge and its gardens in his absence, and report on any problems to Canning's 'man of business' for action. Canning also asked Jerdan and his friend Francis Freeling to send butter and mutton to Portugal for his family. Jerdan enjoyed the correspondence he received from Canning, especially those personal notes from such an exalted person familiarly addressing him as "My dear Sir" and ending "Yours most sincerely". (Political or business letters were more formally just "Sir" and "Yours respectfully".) Canning received sets of the *Sun* by every packet, in fact two sets, and asked Jerdan to cancel one, sent from the Foreign Office.

Canning's appointment as Ambassador to Lisbon and his tenure there was the subject of much animosity in the House of Commons and therefore was reported in the Press. Jerdan, of course, ensured that the *Sun* supported Canning in the opposition war being waged against him. In the absence of his idol, Jerdan was in constant touch with William Huskisson, MP.[12] Huskisson corresponded with Jerdan concerning Canning's financial difficulties in maintaining a fitting Representation of the Court in Lisbon on an inadequate allowance, and also about incorrect rumours of Canning's early return to Britain. These matters and others were for Jerdan's private ear only, and not for publication. The *Sun* merely announced that Canning was remaining in Portugal in his personal, not state, capacity, and firmly refuted rumours spread by the Whig *Morning Chronicle*, Jerdan's old nemesis.

In the autumn of 1814 there existed fifteen daily papers in Britain, of which eight were published in the morning and seven in the evening. Jerdan classified these as Ministerial or pro-government, Opposition or Neutral. This latter group he dismissed as being not truly independent, but leaning merely a little more or a little less to one side or the other. His own paper, the *Sun*, was indeed a Tory organ, but in an article on 21 October 1814 he was insistent that he and it were never mere tools of the Party. Politicians, he said, had no influence on what went into his paper and no influence on what was omitted. The same held true in reverse: the paper would not attempt to influence politicians to uphold any particular action or opinion. Jerdan strongly maintained that the connections between politics and the Press were natural but never corrupt. This was his published manifesto.

However, he had other interests besides the politicians: he was always keen to make everyday lives better, and claimed to be "one of the boldest and earliest, if not the very earliest, champion for cheap bread, cheap food, and cheap clothing for the poorer classes, and the downfall of war prices, which enriched only one class, the agricultural, including landlords and tenants!" [13] For Jerdan, his newspaper was a powerful tool in achieving his laudable aims. Throughout that autumn his pieces in the *Sun* reflected his campaign to improve the lot of the working classes. He called persuasively for lower food prices, fairer prices for imported goods, wages that would enable British manufacturers to compete with continental rivals, and a properly regulated property tax.

Whilst promulgating these economic theories, Jerdan did not lose sight of his first love. Now that the war was over – or so it was believed – he was finally able to turn his attention, coupled with his journalistic experience, to the literary leanings nurtured by his schoolteacher Dr Rutherford. He printed a verse called "The March to Moscow", accepting it from a Mr Sayer, an official in the Tower. The author was many years later revealed as the Poet Laureate, Robert Southey. Jerdan reprinted this 'jeu d'esprit' in Volume I of his *Autobiography* in 1852, and referred to Southey's trick again in an article in 1866. To celebrate the peace, Jerdan launched a new feature in the *Sun*, a Review of new Works. This, he said, was the first of its kind in a newspaper, and from the small beginning grew, over the years, press influence upon the literature of the nation – a grandiose claim that Jerdan made more than once, and its truth has not been challenged by subsequent historians of the press. "When I look around me at this date," mused Jerdan forty years later, "I cannot but feel a sensible gratification on witnessing this little plant become the parent of a vast tree that overspreads the land and possesses a universal influence upon the interests of literature." [14] The newspapers of the time paid scant attention to any of the arts, merely listing exhibitions, seldom mentioning books. The arts were the province of the monthly, or quarterly, reviews of which there were several competing for circulation and sales.

This was an optimistic and productive time for Jerdan. But then, to use a meteorological metaphor, storm clouds erupted, threatening to obscure the *Sun*. The clouds were in the shape of Jerdan's colleague and co-proprietor of the *Sun*, John Taylor.

Taylor was a 'character', known by London society, especially the worlds of theatre and literature; he was a favourite of actors, knew how to flatter them, and enjoyed their company above all others. Jerdan saw this as a failure of intellect, and thought that Taylor lived in a make-believe world of theatre, not in the real world. His facility for puns attracted Jerdan, who displayed a similar ability and appreciation for word-play. As the creator of "Monsieur Tonson", Taylor was known as a prolific versifier, who turned out rhymes on the instant, a collection of which was published by John Murray in 1812. Jerdan esteemed this talent of Taylor's, and as both men were famous for their good company, they should, by all outward signs, have been good friends. Indeed, at the outset of Jerdan's editorship of the *Sun* they were friends and compatible working colleagues.

Taylor was of unusual appearance, having a 'death's head' skull, weak shoulders, and a thin torso, but muscular legs, fetchingly displayed in knee breeches and silk stockings. The humorist George Colman nicknamed him 'Merrydeath', declaring that "Taylor's body would do for any legs, and his legs for any body!"[15] His father, or possibly grandfather, was the Chevalier Taylor, famous in his time (but quickly forgotten) as an 'Opthalmiator', or quack oculist. In 1761 he produced a book described by Jerdan as 'one of the most amusing and ludicrous books in the English language'. This colourful character was welcomed into the Courts of Europe where he was believed to exercise amazing healing powers, to such an extent that a grateful and rich widow of ninety years of age, whose sight he had apparently restored, proposed marriage to him. Jerdan included extracts from the Chevalier's book in his own *Autobiography*, as a token of his admiration.

Not long after Jerdan joined the paper, the majority shareholders Herriot and Clarke, apparently overlooking their dissatisfaction with John Taylor, sold Taylor their shares, thereby making him a nine-tenths owner of the *Sun*. Jerdan believed that Clarke was tired of arguments with his co-proprietor and sold out to him rather than being continually at loggerheads. Unfortunately, this transfer of shares had an immediate and deleterious effect upon Jerdan.

The *Sun's* circulation had improved noticeably since Jerdan became editor, but when Taylor acquired nine-tenths of the shares in the paper, he tried to annul Jerdan's contract and assume control over the paper's content, the very area of Jerdan's complete control according to his agreement. This was a red rag to a bull, and in retelling the escalating controversy Jerdan was aware how childish it sounded, but at the time it was a very real threat to his autonomy. The struggle was not only about who was boss, who had the say-so of what was published, but in Jerdan's eyes it became a struggle about issues of morality. Taylor would try to insert articles or opinions that were contrary to Jerdan's notions of public propriety. In his professional life at least, Jerdan saw himself as a highly moral man, admitting that although he had his "fallings-off", he "never consented to the promulgation of an opinion or sentiment in the press under my direction that could deprave the moral obligations of society, or sully the purity of innocence".[16] This was a retrospective view of his literary career, written at the age of seventy; how much more fiery was his reaction at age thirty-one, when Taylor tried to hi-jack improper material into the *Sun*. Jerdan reacted furiously, inveighing against Taylor's interference into his realm of editorial control. His opponent's mind was disturbed. Taylor, living in his theatrical, fantasy world, behaved as if on stage, acting out his passions in a violent manner. Jerdan noted that "At the wildest time of our differences he would cast himself down upon his knees, clasp his hands, gnash his teeth, and imprecate curses on my head for five minutes together, till some one humanely lifted him up and led him away to privacy."[17]

Jerdan found that his misfortunes did not come singly. In the midst of his battles with Taylor, he suffered a crushing financial blow. He had developed a close friendship with Peter Begbie, whose daughters Anna and Helen wrote poetry for the *Sun*, and later for the *Literary Gazette*. Jerdan enjoyed twice-weekly visits to the Begbie home, where he met Mr Whitehead, principal of the long-established and respectable bankers, Whitehead, Howard and Haddock. Jerdan lodged his hard-won savings with the bank, but on 17 November 1814 it was forced to wind up its business and stopped all payments. It took Jerdan two years to recover from this disaster, which he cited as one of the myriad misfortunes that can befall literary men. (It would be a misfortune for anyone, but when he wrote his memoirs Jerdan was focussed on dissuading young people from a literary life.) These two years of poverty shook Jerdan's sense of security for ever; once on the slopes of financial struggle, he found himself preyed upon by those who in all ages take advantage of such victims. His friend David Pollock later observed that "Jerdan has always been kept back for the want of those few hundred pounds".[18] It was a bad way to end a year that had started with such promise.

In March 1815 another, more far-reaching disaster occurred. Napoleon escaped from Elba and landed in France. On the day the news broke in London, Jerdan was leaving his office in the Strand early, at five o'clock. The *Sun* had been reduced to only two or three editions a day as, with the advent of peace, there was not enough news to fill the five or six editions of the previous year. As he stepped out of his door, he saw a thin pale youth whom he knew slightly, shouting, laughing and rejoicing that "Our old friend Bonny's got loose again, hurra! old Bonny for ever!" Jerdan put his unpatriotic enthusiasm down to the effects of drink, but the youth was not the only one who thought well of Buonaparte. There had been some in Britain who supported his ambition for Empire, such as Hazlitt who published a *Life of Napoleon Buonaparte* in 1830. His escape revitalised the newspapers: at last there was news again. On 18 June, at the Battle of Waterloo, Napoleon was finally defeated by the combined armies of Wellington and Blucher and again exiled, this time to St. Helena.

Whilst this renewed and longer-lasting peace once again allowed Jerdan to develop his ground-breaking reviews of art and literature in the *Sun*, his problems with Taylor had not gone away. Taylor became obsessed with what he saw as Jerdan's villainy and oppression. He wrote about it to ministers, harangued his friends, and publicised his grievances. According to Jerdan his actions "ruined the paper". Whilst Jerdan recognized his partner's talents and ability, he also knew that some vital part was missing in Taylor's understanding of the world.[19] In the presence of Robert Clarke, who tried to mediate between the warring proprietors, Jerdan offered to relinquish his control of political writing in the *Sun* if Taylor would name the major European capital cities. This he was quite unable to do. Thus Jerdan was forced to edit his paper alongside a majority shareholder who appeared to be unstable, unpredictable and psychologically unbalanced. They fought their battle in public, in the paper: Jerdan refused to print paragraphs Taylor wrote if he considered them indecorous; Taylor became mad with rage over Jerdan's tyranny. They may eventually have somehow resolved their differences in the interests of the *Sun*, but as their fire raged on, someone came forward to throw more fuel upon it.

This someone was Acheson, a founder of the Pitt Club, whose private views on the treaty of America were at odds with those of the government. He wrote a long letter to Jerdan, endeavouring to persuade him to publish his views; these, of course, went against Jerdan's own opinions as a fervent Tory supporter. Acheson's motivation was not political but mercantile: his interest was in promoting the import and export of Canadian timber in which he had invested. Jerdan absolutely refused to go against the government, so Acheson's next target was to lobby Taylor. By working on his already violent resentment of Jerdan, Acheson contrived to link Taylor to him, leading Taylor to "years of delusion into pecuniary distress".[20] Taylor's obsession had deprived him of whatever judgment he had, and although he lived to deeply regret his alliance with Acheson, even apologising to Jerdan years later, for his behaviour, the damage to the *Sun* was severe. In September 1815 Jerdan published a notice to the effect that all communications to the *Sun* must be addressed solely to him, and for a month all was calm. In October, against Jerdan's remonstrances, Taylor inserted a notice which appeared several times, demanding that his "friends" write only to him with their contributions, with all general letters to be addressed to the editor. The staff were confused, not knowing whose instructions to obey, and were witness to daily scenes of unedifying squabbling between the two proprietors. The climax came in a form that to the combatants was a lethal weapon: poetry.

Taylor published a sonnet to Byron; Jerdan thought it was not only bad poetry, but far worse, bad taste, as it referred to Byron's well-known marital difficulties. Rashly, Jerdan responded the following day with a doggerel parody on this sonnet, signed "W. J. Extempore, Poet Laureate". Infuriated, Taylor advised readers of the *Sun* that the perpetrator of this attack on Byron was by William Jerdan and that it had been inserted in Taylor's absence.

These doggerel verses were not the only examples to appear in the *Sun*. Both Jerdan and Taylor indulged their tastes for punning and word-play, sometimes on harmless neutral topics. Jerdan however, used his abilities in this area to fight his political fights. He especially loathed an opposition MP named Whitbread, who had been an ardent Buonapartist, and had earned a reputation for pestering Ministers in the House of Commons with constant questions. In the paper of 25 April Jerdan published a 'squib' against him, which included a verse parodying Whitbread's constant questioning. The next verse ended:

> But the cream of the jest is the fellow, odd rot it,
> Can never make use of a fact when he's got it.

Much as he detested his quarry, on hearing of Whitbread's death Jerdan was in the middle of writing an appreciative obituary of his adversary's "indefatigable diligence, perseverance and constancy" when he was told that Whitbread had committed suicide, news which "stopped my pen".

Jerdan's passions ran high, but he did not bear grudges; he was by nature an optimist who inherited his father's relaxed attitude, a Panglossian view that in life all is for the best in the best of all possible worlds. He did his best to forward the interests of his friends, such as William Todd, printer and proprietor of the *Sheffield Mercury* for which, earlier in his career, Jerdan had written leaders for six or seven years. Through Francis Freeling, Jerdan was instrumental in Todd's appointment as Postmaster of Sheffield. Freeling was also instrumental, at Jerdan's behest, in obtaining permission for the artist William Pyne to have access to the royal apartments in Windsor, to make drawings for his book on royal palaces. This negotiation was delicate in the extreme, because of the King's illness and unpredictable behaviour.[21]

Jerdan's Scottish heritage was of utmost importance to him, so he had been happy to accept an invitation in June 1815 to exhort the Scottish community in London to subscribe to the erection of a monument over the grave of Scotland's national poet, Robert Burns, in Dumfries. His appeal was well-received and followed up in May 1816 by a dinner and meeting at the Freemasons' Tavern. Jerdan worked hard to arrange this event, and was cheered to find that the name of Burns was a "rallying-point for Scotchmen at home or abroad". The Earl of Aberdeen took the Chair, and the thirty supporters, not all of whom could attend the dinner, included Peter Laurie, Jerdan's old acquaintance from Kelso days and later Lord Mayor of London, the Royal Academician David Wilkie, the writer Thomas Campbell, Cosmo Orme who was to become Jerdan's publisher at Longman's, and various Lords, Admirals and Generals. The Scotsmen knew how to enjoy themselves whilst raising funds for their cause. The Chairman made a moving speech acknowledging that Burns had not received recognition in his lifetime and had died in obscurity, so their monument was an attempt to make amends. There were innumerable toasts, giving rise to innumerable responses; Campbell had written an Ode for the occasion and subsequently printed and distributed with two other works, one by 'an English lady', the other by Jerdan – an "After Battle Sang" in Scots dialect, lauding the Scotsmen who had fought with Wellington. A band played, and the mandatory Scottish piper paraded in full costume with a melody Jerdan admitted as "only ravishing, at such close quarters, to Scottish ears." Robert Burns's son was present at the Dinner, enabling Jerdan to make another of his helpful and kindly intercessions, by introducing him to a fellow guest, Charles Grant. Grant assisted young Burns to a cadetcy in India, from which he eventually returned to Britain as a respected and prosperous officer.

Jerdan's contribution to the evening's proceedings were in his capacity as Hon. Secretary, when he read out the list of subscriptions, amounting to three hundred and fifty pounds. Peter Laurie proposed Jerdan's health, flattering him as "the individual who had originated this Commemoration, and whose exertions, for the last two years, to accomplish this interesting object, had been as great and unremitting as they had ultimately proved successful".[22] Jerdan naturally responded to the toast, and was well satisfied with the entire event. He appreciated a subscription from James Perry, editor of the abhorred *Morning Chronicle*, who gallantly disregarded "the hostility of rival editors". His secretarial work continued after the Dinner, chasing those who "forgot" their promises, and sorting out the finances. David Wilkie sent ticket money for himself and his friends to Jerdan, with a letter suggesting that future festivals take place to benefit Burns's family; as Jerdan had done such a good job, he should organise them. Long after, Jerdan was "almost ashamed to confess I never made an effort" to comply with Wilkie's suggestion.[23] Thomas Hunt, the architect of Burns's monument never received any payment for his work, but Peter Turnerelli received two hundred and twenty pounds in part payment for his sculpture. The Burns Monument was completed in September 1817.

His ongoing tensions with Taylor apart, Jerdan was happy and engaged with his work. Family news was encouraging: his brother, John Stuart Jerdan, whom he had last seen aged seventeen, setting off from Ednam, had been promoted to Major and commanded a battalion in the expedition to Kutch, in western India. His name was mentioned in despatches, although misspelled 'Jardine'. John wrote to William that he was pleased to have seen his younger brother's name also "honourably mentioned" in a magazine. Jerdan was understandably delighted that his fame had spread so far and had impressed his successful older brother. On the home front, William and Frances Jerdan's family of three children was joined by the addition, on 30 June 1816, of William Freeling Jerdan.[24] He was the first (but not the last) of Jerdan's children to be named to honour a distinguished friend. (Francis Freeling was at this time Secretary of the General Post Office.)[25]

Some time in 1815, when Jerdan was thirty-three years old, he sat for his portrait to the painter George Henry Harlow, a young artist whose talent and facility astonished him. One day Harlow kept him waiting for his sitting and rushing in, asked Jerdan to wait while he made a memorandum of a Rubens landscape he had just seen at the British Institution. Within a very short time he had produced a painting in an impressive feat of memory that Jerdan said compared minutely with the original when he had a chance to see the two together. Five years later Harlow toured Italy, and was lavished with honours in all the great cities, but on returning to London fell ill and died in February 1819, aged thirty-two. The portrait he painted of William Jerdan, engraved by Robinson, adorns the first volume of Jerdan's *Autobiography*, and shows a good-looking young man with unruly dark hair, large dark eyes looking directly at the viewer, straight nose and full lips, wearing a fashionable stock and leaning with a clenched left fist on some papers. The gaze is challenging, and slightly humorous, a young man who has started upon his life's work, and is ready for anything. (See cover illustration.)

During 1815 Jerdan translated Jouy's *L'Hermite de la Chaussée d'Antin*. His work was dedicated to Canning and appeared in three volumes under the title of *The Paris Spectator*, published by Longman, Hurst, Rees, Orme, and Brown. Jerdan had seen the original version whilst in Paris, and thought the English public might welcome his selection. Longman's advertisement in *The Times* of 21 September read:

> This lively and entertaining view of the State of Society in Paris, at the most eventful period of its annals, obtained great celebrity in that city, and has been unanimously accorded a high rank among the periodical productions of French literature. The amusements, annoyances, pleasures and discomforts of a Paris fashionable life are sketched with a humorous and witty hand: nor has there ever issued from the press of that country a more animated and close imitation of our own exquisite Spectator.

Sales were not spectacular and the book was re-advertized three months later. Jerdan sent a copy to Sir Walter Scott in 1815, as a token of his "esteem and admiration". Begun as a recreation, he said, it had become "a serious toil, and I am ashamed to see how many blunders have escaped me, how much the style ought to have been polished, and in short how incautiously I have exposed myself to the critical lash . . . I must abide the consequence with all my imperfections on my head."[26] Jouy himself made some critical and some amusing comments on Jerdan's translation, and translated his next book himself. *The Paris Spectator* was favourably received, but not reprinted, and brought Jerdan scant financial reward.

The end of the year saw the death of Jerdan's beloved friend Peter Begbie, who succumbed to consumption leaving a widow, several children and no money. Begbie's friends, including Jerdan and Freeling, were of great practical help in finding employment for the sons. Was Jerdan disingenuous, or merely vain, when he chose to print in his *Autobiography* Mrs Begbie's letters of gratitude for his help? He made the point, in case his readers should miss it, "that in this, as in many an other instance, my character, from youth to age, was genial, kindly of heart, and rejoicing in the privilege of doing good when in my power".[27] His own excuse, or reason, for this pat on his own back was that as his memoirs openly admitted his failures, he was therefore at liberty to also disclose his good deeds.

A few days after Begbie's miserable death Jerdan took the fast-deteriorating battle with Taylor into his own hands. His spirits were at a low ebb, the *Sun* was fading. As Taylor became even more demented, Jerdan's reaction was often anger, and he admitted that he provoked Taylor, sometimes without real cause. To taunt his adversary, who had accused Jerdan of a false alias when he signed his Jubilee poem of 1809 'Teutha', Jerdan inserted doggerel couplets into the *Sun* using the same pseudonym. Another provocation was his refusal to publish a particular poem of Taylor's, although it was no worse than much that was being published. (As a belated gesture to make some amends Jerdan included the verse in his *Autobiography*, but too late, of course, to appease its author.) Jerdan was aware that the *Sun*'s standards had dropped, and in desperation to stop the rapid slide into oblivion, he applied for an injunction in Chancery to prevent Taylor's interference with his running of the newspaper; to refrain from inserting any article without Jerdan's consent; and not to give any instructions to the staff or printers of the paper, on the penalty of forfeiting five thousand pounds.

Predictably, Taylor responded with another outburst of rage. Worn out and weary, Jerdan wrote him a letter in February 1816, in which he clearly set out his case.[28] He was no longer prepared to submit to Taylor's daily interference and distraction in his running of the paper, and had decided that the only course was to have nothing to do with him. Such a drastic step had been brought about by Taylor's persecution and ill-usage. He could not understand how Taylor could expect his insults and enmity to be returned by courtesy and friendship. Should Taylor attempt to reverse the injunction placed upon him, the *Sun* would close in a fortnight; it would close if Taylor published one line injurious to Jerdan, and if Jerdan was to be ruined, then so would Taylor, who had invested about four-teen hundred pounds in the paper.

Taylor's insults and accusations continued and Jerdan was forced to law again, aware that some stigma always adheres to a man slandered, even if the accusations are proved groundless. He was advised that no action could be taken against the slanders, as Taylor had not imputed any felonious act to him. He could sue for libel, but even then Taylor's abusive letters might be construed as just within the law. The problem lay in that although Taylor called him "a thief", Jerdan had no control over any monies to do with the *Sun*. He was its editor, and his control was solely over its content. Taylor could therefore not be shown to accuse him of any financial felony. This bruising experience soured Jerdan's opinion of the law, and he warned literary men to steer clear of it, as the law would punish them, the police ridicule them, and justice balk them. They would suffer in purse, person and hopes.[29] It is easy to understand his jaundiced view.

In an attempt to find a way to carry on working with Taylor for the good of the *Sun*, Jerdan asked his lawyer to demand that Taylor write him a reference, stating that he knew of nothing that could militate against Jerdan's reputation as an honest man, or his honour as a gentleman. Jerdan was sinking under the weight of legal expenses, and hoped this would end the sorry quarrel without further ado. His salary was due and he did not wish to incur further expense to secure it. He was amazed to discover that Taylor was talking about either selling his share in the *Sun*, or purchasing all of it, that is, Jerdan's one-tenth share. Furthermore, Jerdan was appalled to hear that Taylor denied there had ever been a partnership deed between the two protagonists. His lawyer advised him that this plea would fail, and the only question would be the amount of damages granted. By October nothing had been resolved, and Jerdan's lawyer consulted Frederick Pollock for his learned advice. Pollock recommended that Jerdan settle for only moderate damages to enable the working relationship, such as it was, to proceed. He urged that Jerdan should not consider indicting Taylor for perjury as that would prevent any continuation of the paper. He suggested appointing a mutual friend as arbitrator, but Taylor refused the mediation of the original proprietors of the paper, Herriot and Clarke, and also turned down others in the publishing business.

These damaging and unsettling skirmishes were only a microcosm of what was happening in the country, as it struggled to return to peace. Riots and revolutionary meetings had been occurring since 1811, of which the best known were the Luddites. Demonstrations were becoming more common as the economic depression deepened. The price of wheat rose again, income tax was abolished as the wars were over, but the Stamp Act of 1815 had increased newspaper tax to four pence a copy, making the retail price of six pence or seven pence beyond the reach of many. Every advertisement incurred a duty of three shillings and six pence, so that these imposts added to the cost of papers, reporters, printing etc. left very little profit for publishers. The collective name for the whole raft of problems was "The Condition of England Question".

The parlous "Condition of England" had encouraged another Scotsman, John Trotter, to a new venture, one which Jerdan strongly supported even in the midst of his contretemps with Taylor. Trotter had been an army contractor who became rich during the Napoleonic Wars, and finding himself with a huge ware-house in Soho Square and no further need to store army equipment, turned it into a Bazaar, then a venture unique in Europe, and the first time the term 'Bazaar' had been used in Britain.[30] This was not merely a mercantile operation, but had been conceived to provide an opportunity for the wives and daughters of army officers to sell their handiwork. Stalls could be hired for threepence per foot, and the Bazaar was entirely enclosed, affording security to the stall-holders, who had to be vetted before admission. Jerdan interceded for an acquaintance, Mrs Sell, for a position there, and even she had to be closely vetted by the Trotters. Trotter asked Jerdan to write an explanatory notice about the Bazaar so that the public could understand its nature and objects. This notice, in the form of a letter, was inserted into the *New Monthly Magazine*.[31] Jerdan's seven-page article on the Bazaar noted that its purpose was partly to relieve the current state of wretched-ness. "Alas Sir! The miseries of mankind are too certain, too universal, too obvious, to admit of doubts either as to their reality, their extent or their afflic-tiveness ... there is no class free from its share in the common lot of humanity." The Bazaar was not a charity, he explained, but designed "to encourage FEMALE AND DOMESTIC INDUSTRY". His long article clarified how this was to be done, noting particularly the difficulties of providing for daughters in large families. Setting them up in the Bazaar would make them prudent and industrious. The Bazaar was also to function as a Gallery to encourage arts. The moral value of the Bazaar was incalculable, both for those selling and for purchasers, with the Bazaar acting as a union to ensure fair prices for goods sold by respectable women in a safe environment. Jerdan's article was shortly after-wards enlarged into a pamphlet sold in the Bazaar for a few pence.[32]

A year later Trotter presented Jerdan with a substantial cheque, the proceeds of the pamphlet's sale. Jerdan was persuaded to accept the money only when Trotter produced his "Big Book" (Jerdan called it his conjuring-book) in which meticulous accounts were kept, and also minute details on every aspect of Trotter's business transactions, from the great to the insignificant, proving the extent of the pamphlet's sales. So precise was Trotter that the government relied upon his records for recovering stores left behind in foreign parts by the army. Jerdan greatly admired such accurate record-keeping, but was utterly unable to emulate it in his own affairs – his early facility with numbers had vanished when he learnt to read, and he did not have a methodical bone in his body;[33] he did not keep good records, nor even copies of his own published works, an odd over-sight, until one recognizes the pace at which he had to work, and the vast amounts of paper crossing his desk every day, all demanding review or reply, writing with his scratchy pen by candlelight, far into the night.

Jerdan was also in awe of Trotter's domestic felicity and his inventiveness. Trotter's eldest daughter, Stuart, was a help to her father in one of his inventions, a universal language. Jerdan was always intrigued by such ciphers, and was mindful of the one he had invented that the government failed to acknowledge. Trotter's system was based on pasigraphs, which work by using characters to represent ideas not words, perhaps similar to Chinese where the written sign is understood in all parts of the country, but spoken language differs from one area to another. Jerdan tested this out by giving young Stuart a passage in a language she did not know, and she was able to transpose this to prove her understanding of it. To Jerdan's eternal regret the system was never written down. Stuart died shortly afterwards, and Jerdan was moved to write a verse to comfort her bereaved parents.

John Trotter and his two brothers, like the Pollocks, had come to London and made a great success, one becoming a partner in Coutts Bank, and the other an advisor to Lord Melville. They were yet more examples of achievement that Jerdan highlighted with admiration, and apparently without envy. He and John Trotter remained close friends for many years. Trotter sent him a gift of a small milking cow to Brompton, sympathetic to the needs of Jerdan's growing family. He took Jerdan in his own carriage to the coronation of George IV, a privilege Jerdan recognized that "few literary gentleman could hope to emulate". He and Trotter were to co-operate on one or two other projects in the years to come.

One of the most famous confrontations during this period of the "Condition of England Question" was the Spa Fields riot, in December 1816, which led directly to severe consequences for publishers, editors and writers. A meeting had been called in November for the purpose of raising a petition to the Prince Regent from the people of London asking for poor relief and parliamentary reform in the shape of universal suffrage (males only), annual general elections and a secret ballot. The organizers were prevented from delivering the petition leading to the Spa Fields Riot which at last brought home to the government the realization that discontent had been brewing for years, and that a revolution in England was entirely possible. This belief was reinforced when the Prince Regent's carriage was mobbed and its windows broken after the State opening of parliament. This led to the "Gag Acts" being quickly passed, suspending Habeas Corpus and banning seditious meetings; the government also attempted to arraign printers and writers responsible for blasphemous material, but this move failed as juries refused to risk the freedom of the press. The *Sun*, in the person of a writer called Mr Mulock,[34] treated the Spa Fields Riot with the lash of satire. His humour and wit were not unworthy of Dean Swift, according to Jerdan, who reprinted some of these stinging attacks in his memoirs. Canning, who had returned from Portugal in June, made a special request for copies of these articles, which would have amused him in those tumultuous days.

In the new year 1817, Jerdan's own tumultuous time with Taylor was finally to reach its climax. At the beginning of February Taylor wrote a letter to Jerdan, full of complaints and accusations, but here and there with a ring of credibility, such as that Jerdan came late to the office, and turned it into a coffee-room and a gossiping mart – presumably one at which Taylor was not welcome.[35] Taylor claimed that he and Herriot had not taken their salaries for two years, enabling Jerdan to take out £800 which he owed to the paper. Jerdan was also accused of taking £131 5s for French papers he never bought, and £116 for legal expenses involved in a breach of covenant whereby he hired writers without Taylor's consent. These dull figures belie Taylor's frantic tone, question after question tumbling cross the page: "Is it not your absolute tyranny over my property a continued provocation to me? Is your conduct to be reconciled to any principle of justice, any feeling of shame?" and so on. Jerdan had apologized to Taylor's wife for his reactions to her husband's provocations, and Taylor hit back with "I most heartily pity your poor wife, for her afflictions must be heightened by the consideration that you bring all that she suffers on *yourself* by your conduct towards me." This may have been a spiteful, retaliatory remark that Frances Jerdan's "afflictions" were in having to live with Jerdan, or merely that she had several children to take care of whilst he was so distracted by his work.

Taylor's next letter, a few days later, threw more missiles Jerdan's way. He disbelieved Jerdan's friendship with Canning, and argued that he would advise Francis Freeling (to whom Jerdan had presented the bound copy of Bellingham's manuscript which he had taken from the assassin at the time of Perceval's murder), to surrender it to the widow or the law. Jerdan, who had received a note of gratitude from Freeling, said his friend would merely laugh at Taylor's advice. In evident frustration and desperation, Taylor asked point blank what Jerdan would take to sever his connection with the *Sun* which, he said, Jerdan had "nearly ruined". He worked himself into a frenzy, saying "You have often accused me of attempting to undermine your character _____ *your* character !!!" his emphasis and punctuation encapsulating all his contempt for his one-time friend and colleague.

Taylor went to see landscape painter Joseph Farington, well connected to many influential people. In his diary Farington recorded that:

> Taylor I met. Taylor sd. that Jordain (sic.) had offered to give up His share and situation as Editor, if a settlement of £200 per annum for Life were assured to Him. Taylor thought he might be induced to do it if £1000 shd be offered Him, and as He himself had no money, if His friend wd raise that sum they shd have interest for their money and the principal gradually liquidated. He sd He stood so well with Men in high official

situations, and with eminent Literary Characters that could He get possession of the Editorship He cd soon raise the character of the Sun.[36]

Taylor came to dinner two days later, when Sir Thomas Lawrence was also a guest. He explained the present situation concerning shares in the newspaper, but Farington took an objective view:

> I remarked to Him that he had purchased 8 of the 9 shares He possessed of the paper after he had full knowledge of Jerdain's (sic) character. – He granted it; but sd He cd not suppose that Jerdain wd continue to act towards Him as He had done when He became Proprietor of all the Shares but one which Jerdain held. Nothing followed from this conversation; nothing was said about purchasing the Editorship from Jerdain for £1000.

In his diary Farington noted that when Jerdan had been made Editor of the *Sun*, Herriot held seven shares, Clarke had two and Taylor one share.

> One of Heriott's shares was then made over to Jerdain and by this deed Taylor was to have apartments at the Sun office and £200 per annum. Heriott at that time valued his seven shares at £3000; but their value was lessened after Jerdain became Editor and I understood from Taylor that He purchased six shares from Heriott and two from Clarke for about £700. He spoke of Heriott with much dissatisfaction and also of Freeling of the Post Office who, he said, had aided Jerdan's interest with the Government. The Deed secured to Jerdain the Editorship of the *Sun* for 900 years.

The dispute rumbled on. Jerdan told his lawyers he would accept one thousand pounds in salary, which was between five and six hundred pounds in arrears, and profits as his due as proprietor of the paper, together with a well-secured annuity of two hundred pounds for life. Taylor countered with an offer of twenty shillings annuity as long as the *Sun* was published. The impasse was eventually resolved: Jerdan settled for eight hundred pounds for his four years' work which, at five hundred and forty-six pounds a year should have brought him nearly two thousand two hundred pounds. This substantial loss was the outcome of Jerdan's appeal to Chancery, where it was deemed by the Master that his co-partnership deed entitled him to a salary of ten guineas weekly. In allowing the arrears to accumulate rather than drawing his salary regularly (how did he live, meanwhile?), the law decided he was not entitled to a verdict. Despite representations from Fladgate who drew up the deed, and Robert Clarke a party to it, giving evidence that this had not been their intention, the judge decreed that the case was so hard he would not give judgment in it. Jerdan knew that even had the decision gone in his favour, the *Sun* could not have paid him out, but the victory of principle would have been his.

Jerdan's ever-loyal friend Francis Freeling made funds available to him so that he could keep his head above water for some time. Freeling also tried to salvage Jerdan's share in the *Sun*, but Taylor's abusive letters to all and sundry continued and Jerdan was nervous that some impressions would stick. In the Spring of 1817 he gladly sold his one-tenth share for three hundred pounds, and the dissolution of partnership was announced in the *Gazette* of 3 May.[37] Taylor placed a notice in the *Sun* saying that it was now entirely under his control. A second notice announced that Taylor had become a member of the Pitt Club, "as a pledge for his upholding the principles of the paper founded under the auspices of the illustrious Pitt", evidence to Jerdan that the abhorred Acheson still had Taylor in his grasp.[38]

Thus Jerdan was once again free from commitments, and without income. With his wife and children to support, he needed urgently to find his next employment. He could not know that the exhausting fight with Taylor, and the loss of the *Sun* was to lead him into a position offering power, influence, riches and ultimately penury that he was to experience for the next thirty-four exciting and challenging years.

Part II

The *Literary Gazettte* –
The First Decade,
1817–1827

5

The *Literary Gazette* – An Ideal Occupation

Whilst he looked around for another position Jerdan did not neglect his pleasures. He was a keen theatre-goer, but sometimes wondered if an "ill-natured fairy" had whispered at his birth, "William, have a taste".[1] In his old age he reflected that even more than in art, bad dramatic performances disgusted him to the same extent as immoral actions. That he could claim this when looking back at his life, it is clear that he plainly believed his private life would remain just that – private – but history and biographers seldom respect such hopes. Paradoxically, given the way he led his life in the years to come, Jerdan was a strongly moral man who somehow overlooked his own lapses. In pursuit of pleasures to his 'taste', Jerdan took the front seat in the stage-box one evening, to see John Kemble's gripping performance as Coriolanus. Next day Kemble told Jerdan that he had spotted him in the box, and played the part just for him alone. Jerdan greatly admired the famous trage-dian's comic talents in his private life, recounting how Kemble hid at the close of a dinner party at Freeling's Hampstead house, whilst he and the other guests departed. It was subsequently reported to him that Kemble reappeared with a bottle of claret from Freeling's cellar, saying it was "too good for those fellows" and that he and his host could drink it in peace.[2] Jerdan observed that Kemble was very fond of a bottle or more of wine – a predilection that Jerdan himself was well-known to indulge.

On 23 June 1817 Kemble gave his emotional farewell performance to a crowded theatre, on an excessively hot evening; a few days later the Freemasons' Tavern (where the Burns Dinner had been held) saw a convivial dinner in his honour attended by many noblemen, and "nearly all the eminent poets, artists and literary men of the metropolis" including Jerdan. The gathering was enter-tained by one of Campbell's Odes, and addressed by Talma, the acclaimed French tragedian, whose dramatic delivery Jerdan had strongly criticised in Paris.[3] Jerdan met Talma more personally at a dinner given by Dr Croly, where the actor spoke of his admiration for Kemble, but thought another major actor, Kean, deficient in intellect and dignity. He demonstrated their differences by declaiming speeches in their individual styles, a performance Jerdan thought original and entertaining.

In the hiatus between employments, Jerdan wrote two books, both parodies of the genre of fiction/travel writing currently popular as France became more familiar to travellers from Britain. His three-volume work, each volume of about two hundred and forty pages, entitled *Six Weeks in Paris, or, a Cure for the Gallomania, by a late Visitant*, was published in September 1817 by J. Johnston of Cheapside and Macredie & Co. of Edinburgh. It purports to be written by an English nobleman, and has been characterised as "a cautionary roman-à-clef . . . arguing that the weak-minded and unwary could easily be drawn into a vortex of vice, tolerated by French moral passivity, yet fatal to English ingenuousness . . . Jerdan's novel imitates travel description so well that one suspects it is based on an actual journey . . . "[4] – which of course it was. Advertizements for the book echo some of the intentions claimed in Jerdan's *Sun* "Journal of a Trip to Paris" three years earlier: to educate, warn and advise. Taken from the Preface to the book, and used in advertizements for it, "his Lordship" announces that for the good of his countrymen, emigrating in shoals "to encounter French hatred, deceit, rapacity" the work "is intended as an antidote to the poison of other Publications, teeming with gross exaggerations, fictitious characters and anecdotes, and notoriously false fabrications". The book is written as a dialogue between two main characters and other occasional participants, who discuss food, religion, the streets, theatre, and all aspects of French life. The tone of the writing is arch and humorous, sometimes biting and sarcastic. The third volume is a love story which is almost a novel in itself. The work was reprinted in 1818, the first time that a work of Jerdan's enjoyed sufficient popularity to merit a reprint, and more important, the first work of his own imagination, not merely a translation or reporting.

He followed this with "*Six Weeks at Long's by a late Resident*", also in three volumes each of about two hundred and twenty pages, written with Michael Nugent, from material furnished by a military officer who paid them for their literary assistance.[5] Long's was a hotel in London's fashionable Bond Street, and Jerdan opened the book with a description of the street, filled with carriages taking occupants to their secret assignations. The style of the book is similar to that of *Six Weeks in Paris* and of the *New Canterbury Tales*, also written with Michael Nugent, being a conversation between two or three main characters, notable for irony and wit, including portraits of contemporary literary figures such as Lord Leander (Byron) and also pillorying Beau Brummell. The book falls into the genre of 'portrait novels' in Regency satirical fiction, but

> these Portraits fail to stress how their satiric attack pertains to issues of general or public interest . . . [they] have an inconsistency of purpose at

their core. On the one hand they profess corrective intent . . . At the end of *Six Weeks at Long's*, its authors indicate that they consider attacks on particular real people a service to the public: 'When we see them inveigling others into their snares; rendering the weak, wicked; the wealthy, poor; and the innocent flagitious; we should feel ourselves in some measure parties to their atrocity, if we did not endeavour to unmask them.' [III, 220–221][6]

This was the selling point of the novel: an advertisement in the *New Monthly Magazine* of 1 April 1817 claimed that:

Works of fiction, we apprehend, are seldom more likely to be really beneficial than when they actually exhibit the portraits of existing characters and scenes with which the world is acquainted. These may perhaps be highly coloured, and rendered in some respects ridiculous through such a vehicle, yet if, in the narrative, the basis of truth be observed, and the prominent features of the actors are faithfully delineated, the cause of virtue will gain by a caricatured castigation of irregularities and persons which the laws cannot reach.

Six Weeks at Long's reached a third edition, but Jerdan was not proud of it, saying that it was "a personal satire of an order never tolerated by me as a critic."[7] His excuse, or reason, was simple: poverty. This book was reviewed in the 5th issue of the *Literary Gazette* as "a caustic portraiture of 'noble profligates and honourable dupes'", a timely connection with Jerdan's next, and most important career move.

The aggressive and successful publisher Henry Colburn had produced the first issue of the weekly *Literary Gazette* on 25 January 1817, principally as a way of promoting or "puffing" the books he published, but also to take advantage of the rising literacy and interest in reading amongst the middle classes. It was in a lighter vein and more readable than its forerunners, the ponderous quarterly and monthly reviews. The first nine issues of the *Literary Gazette* were each of sixteen pages printed in two columns, at a price of one shilling; on the tenth issue Colburn changed its format to three columns per page, at which it remained for many years. The journal was printed by A. J. Valpy and published by Colburn from 159 Strand, just down the road from number 267, Jerdan's own building acquired as part of his purchase of *The Satirist*. Looking back at this venture from a perspective of forty years, Jerdan believed that the country was indebted to Colburn not only for all subsequent imitators of the new journal, but for the introduction of hitherto new and undiscussed topics into the periodical press. The *Literary Gazette* became a leading and innovative periodical, and aimed to cover:

Original Correspondence, foreign and domestic; Critical Analyses of New Publications; Varieties on all subjects connected with Polite Literature, such as Discoveries and Improvements, Philosophical Researches, Scientific Inventions, Sketches of Society, Proceedings of Public Bodies; Biographical Memoirs of distinguished persons; Original Letters and Anecdotes of remarkable personages; Essays and Critiques on the Fine Arts; and Miscellaneous Articles on the Drama, Music, and Literary Intelligence: so as to form at the end of the year, a clear and instructive picture of the moral and literary improvement of the times, and a complete, and authentic Chronological Literary Record for general reference.[8]

This was a highly ambitious plan, especially for a weekly publication. Hitherto, publications which covered only a part of Colburn's grand scheme had been published as monthly, or even quarterly, reviews and were aimed at a different, more "up" market and were overtly political. One of the most famous was the *Quarterly Review*, begun in 1809 by John Murray, the notable London publisher and a man of strong political and religious opinions. He wished to challenge the popularity of the *Edinburgh Review*, a literary journal whose views were opposed to his own. Walter Scott and George Canning were active supporters of the *Quarterly Review*, and the publication was edited by William Gifford, a protégé and close associate of Canning. The *Quarterly Review* played a formative role in the criticism of Romantic writers. It was positive about Wordsworth and Scott but vilified the works of Leigh Hunt, Hazlitt, Shelley and Keats. However, the *Quarterly Review* was a political journal first and foremost, an influential supporter of the Tory party. Depending on which side of the political divide one stood upon, it was considered to be an agent of dark forces, or the disseminator of inside governmental information. For Canning, it was a medium by which he could influence the press. As this last consideration was to become a hot topic between Canning and Jerdan, Canning's participation in the *Quarterly Review* is significant. Furthermore, when Jerdan consulted Canning for his advice on taking the editor's position for the *Literary Gazette*, Canning counselled him to take the job, but "Avoid politics and polemics". Jerdan heeded this advice throughout his entire career, and when in any doubt, asked himself "What would Mr Canning's opinion be?"

In the Spring of 1817 William Blackwood, who was John Murray's agent in Edinburgh, started the *Edinburgh Magazine*, shortly changed to *Blackwood's Edinburgh Magazine,* a monthly publication, of a lighter tone than the *Quarterly*. *Maga* as Blackwood nicknamed it when he took over the editorship from the seventh issue, was published in London as well as Edinburgh, and appealed to a similar readership to that of the *Literary Gazette*. *Blackwood's* was joined by John Gibson Lockhart, aged twenty-three (later to be Sir Walter Scott's son-in-law) and John Wilson, aged thirty-two. They attacked the "Cockney School" of Poetry, criticising the works of Keats, Hazlitt and Leigh Hunt as disreputable and political. Hiding behind the pen-name 'Z', Lockhart, whom Blackwood had told to "sharpen his pen", launched himself at the "Cockneys", deriding their low birth, their habits, ideologies and free versification, accusing them of "extreme moral depravity" in sarcastic and biting language. These articles continued for several months, echoed by Gifford, editor of the *Quarterly* who had a grudge against Hunt for mocking him in his "The Feast of the Poets". Hunt, however, took these vicious attacks as "motivated by political more than literary animus".[9] Jerdan's instinct was to agree that the work of the so-called "Cockneys" could not compare with classical, romantic poetry, even with that of Byron, although some of the latter's work was to cause a storm in the *Literary Gazette*. *Maga* became well-known from 1822 for 'Noctes Ambrosianae', written by John Wilson under the pen-name Christopher North. The 'Noctes' were imaginary discussions about literary and topical subjects, and as time went on, Jerdan became one of those mentioned. The biggest difference between *Blackwood's* and the *Literary Gazette* was that the former published original fiction, often serialised, whereas the *Literary Gazette* was a paper of review and notices. *Blackwood's* has been evaluated as one of the three most important of the nineteenth-century magazines, the others being the *New Monthly Magazine* and the *London Magazine*"[10]

The *New Monthly* was, like the *Literary Gazette,* published by Henry Colburn who, together with Frederic Shoberl, started it in early 1814. It was a liberal, anti-Napoleonic journal, with much the same list of departments as Colburn announced for the *Literary Gazette*, with the addition of political reports and digests. Future editors of the *New Monthly* were such luminaries as Thomas Campbell, Bulwer Lytton, Theodore Hook and Harrison Ainsworth. As with the *Literary Gazette*, Colburn saw his publication as historic. The first issue declared that the *New Monthly Magazine* was to be a "complete record and chronicle of the times". The *London Magazine* was published between 1820 and 1829, so was not a contender when Jerdan took up his pen to write for the *Literary Gazette* for the first time.

Jerdan's first contribution to the *Literary Gazette,* a critique on *Zuma* by Madame de Genlis,[11] appeared in its twenty-fifth issue, on 12 July 1817. The following week he became editor of the journal, a position he held for thirty-four years. With the change of editor came a change of ownership of the *Literary Gazette*. Jerdan acquired a one-third interest, but whether he paid for this, possibly out of the money he received from the *Sun,* or whether Colburn gave him the shares as an incentive, is not known. Jerdan's income from the *Literary Gazette* depended on its profits, and at this time in his career there is no evidence that he was drawing any salary; the shrewd Colburn would have seen the exchange of one-third of the shares as a good investment to keep his new editor on board, loyal and hard-working. Colburn himself held one-third, and the final third was held by Pinnock and Maunder, publishers of the *Literary Gazette* who presumably paid Colburn for their share, reimbursing him for his investment in the new paper.

Under Jerdan's editorship the offices of the *Literary Gazette* were moved to the building he owned at 267 Strand, opposite St Clement Danes church. Jerdan grew to dislike the monotonous chime of the bells, which made him feel dull and melancholy. At one end of the Strand was Waterloo Bridge which had just been opened in June 1817. The architect Rennie had modelled the bridge on the one he had built in 1800–1803 in Jerdan's home town of Kelso, a visual link between his London working life and his old home. As a consequence of moving the *Literary Gazette* into the building which had caused him so much aggravation and financial loss, Jerdan sold the building to Pinnock and Maunder. The men were brothers-in-law, but of very different temperament. Maunder was reliable and steady, but Pinnock was volatile and restless, perpetually dissatisfied. His flawed personality was to have an adverse effect on Jerdan and the *Literary Gazette*.

However, at the outset, the new job was a godsend to Jerdan. He did not feel himself to be a natural writer, "the dignity and stilts of authorship never suited me. If I tried to write grand or fine I was sure to fail".[12] However, he admitted to an ability to write clearly and intelligibly, a talent crucial for the vast amount of comment and review that he undertook over the ensuing decades. He was fortunate in the timing of his new venture: Scott's Waverley novels had appeared by 1817, whetting the middle classes' appetite for literature, and Byron had raised popular interest in poetry; the arts were burgeoning in the absence of war, the world had opened up to travellers who wrote copiously of their adventures, theatre was overflowing with talented actors and many productions, shows and exhibitions were all the rage. The reading public was expanding rapidly, and with the rise of literacy came demand for ever-more and cheap books. The newly literate needed guidance as to taste and quality, and Jerdan's *Literary Gazette* was ideally placed to cater for their needs. Technology developed to facilitate and speed printing, as lithography became used more widely, an invention of which the *Literary Gazette* was among the first to take advantage. Thus everything conspired to promote the aims of the *Literary Gazette* in a rich and fulfilling way. For the affable Jerdan, it was a perfect vehicle, giving him an entrée into many different societies and groups, who were keen to nurture his interest in order to further their own. It was a busy world, and Jerdan was happy to be among those "stirring".

The importance of the *Literary Gazette* and the vital part Jerdan was to play as its editor, were recalled years later by Samuel Carter Hall, an acquaintance but no friend of Jerdan's, whose opinion is therefore more valuable:

It would be difficult now to comprehend the immense power exercised by the *Literary Gazette* . . . between 1820 and 1840. A laudatory review there was almost certain to sell an edition of a book, and an author's fame was established when he had obtained the praise of the journal. People do not, perhaps, think more for themselves now than they did then; but the hands that bestowed the laurels were at that time few . . . for a quarter of a century there was but one who was accepted as an 'authority'. The *Gazette* stood alone as the arbiter of fate, literary and artistic.[13]

Over the period Jerdan edited the *Literary Gazette* it contained, exclusive of advertisements, "roughly 25,000 words per issue, a million and a quarter per year, totalling over 42 million words – the vast majority written by Jerdan himself".[14] A massive task lay ahead, one that Jerdan surely relished.

Among his first tasks was to assemble a core group of contributors, including "laborious Lloyd" (Hannibal Evans Lloyd) of the Foreign Post Office, who collected and translated foreign intelligence, and had probably edited the first few numbers of the *Literary Gazette* before Jerdan took over. There was also Thomasina Ross, daughter of a *Times* reporter, a translator who had assisted Lloyd.[15] More well-known and prolific contributors were the Rev. Dr. Croly, the artist Richard Dagley, both of whom became lifelong friends to Jerdan, and others whose names were famous in their day. Jerdan valued these assistants, but at the beginning, he undertook the bulk of the work himself:

> In my capacity I was omnivorous – at all in the ring – and produced hebdomadally [*weekly*], Reviews, Criticisms of the Arts and Drama, *jeux d'esprit* in prose and in verse; and in truth, played every part, as Bottom, the weaver, wished to do; and it might be only from the good luck of having, in reality, several able coadjutors (though I announced publicly I had them), that the paper did not sink under my manning, in addition to my pilotage.[16]

One scholar has interpreted Jerdan's statement to mean that he wrote the bulk of the *Literary Gazette* himself, being too penurious to pay others, and that this remained the case throughout his editorship.[17] An opposing view, taken by a later scholar, suggests that Jerdan meant that he was involved in the writing of some of many parts of the *Gazette*; that there is evidence to corroborate the interpretation that he employed many contributors.[18] He claimed, in a response to an attack by Hazlitt in the *Edinburgh Review*, that a dozen different writers had contributed to the last number of the *Gazette*.[19] Almost no evidence is available concerning rates paid to *Literary Gazette* contributors, largely because of Jerdan's self-confessed carelessness in keeping records, and because one of his later partners, Longman & Co., saw to the business side of the journal. Only a comment from Gerald Griffin referring to "a liberal remuneration – a guinea a page", and indications that Pyne received three to four pounds for each 'Wine and Walnuts' sketch (averaging less than three pages), give any clear idea of early *Literary Gazette* payments.

Under his new editorship, circulation of the *Literary Gazette* seemed to be turning "Up, and but for a few incidental or accidental crosses, would have been Up-per".[20] There is the ubiquitous Jerdan "but" again: such "crosses" were the integral and repeating pattern of Jerdan's life: his poor health (and his unwillingness) had impeded his legal studies, *The Satirist* readers had not welcomed his changes to a more morally respectable journal, and Taylor had blighted his partnership in the *Sun*.

At the start of his connection with the *Literary Gazette*, however, all was hopeful. The publisher, Henry Colburn, already had a reputation as an aggressive promoter of his books; he was an entrepreneur through and through, seemingly more interested in the bottom line of accounts than in the promotion of literature. Colburn's origins were mysterious, rumours suggesting that he was the illegitimate son of the Duke of York, or of Lord Lansdowne.[21] He began his life in the book trade whilst still a youth, and by 1808 was at the British and Foreign Library in Conduit Street, London, publishing books under his own name. He soon became sole proprietor. Within weeks of starting the *Literary Gazette* in 1817 Colburn employed William Jerdan as editor, but his mercantile interests remained foremost, a fact which Jerdan overlooked at his peril. Colburn's relentless promotion of his books and Jerdan's desire for a journal of objective literary review were a potent recipe for a clash. Indeed the subject of "puffery" or in-house advertising, became one that, within a few years, created strife for the participants (and a minor industry for subsequent literary researchers).

Hopeless as he was at record-keeping, Jerdan related that he had found a notebook stating that "income from the *Literary Gazette* in its early days (in a January, but not stating which year, a typical Jerdan omission), was in the order of £5, £3, £2 and £4 3s 6d, totalling £14 3s 6d".[22] Succeeding months were "worse for balances". Things were quickly to improve.

Through a friend he had acquired a manuscript of Captain Tuckey's *Voyage to the Congo*, later published as a book by John Murray in 1818. This account appeared weekly in the *Literary Gazette* from its thirtieth issue (16 August 1817) and proved unexpectedly popular. This surprising upward turn of events bore out Jerdan's principle of journalistic prosperity: "Sleeping will not do", one must be ever alert to opportunity. According to him, sales of the journal rose by over five hundred, equal to about one thousand pounds a year, and improved Jerdan's expectations of a share in profits.[23] However, trouble came in the shape of Sir John Barrow, Secretary of the Admiralty, who told him Tuckey's had been a government expedition and details had been published which should not have been made public. Barrow blamed a particular officer, but Jerdan protested that his informant, whose identity he did not know at that time, should not be castigated. He and Barrow quarrelled, and although Jerdan was soon able to prove that the accused officer was innocent, the culprit being some lowly clerk, relations were cool for a while. Moreover, the *Literary Gazette* publication of Tuckey's manuscript anticipated Murray's book publication by some months, causing the famous publisher to resent Jerdan's pre-emption.

During his first few months in charge, Jerdan widened his circle of contributors to the *Literary Gazette*, to include the poet George Crabbe (admired by Byron), writers Miss Mitford and Thomas Gaspey, artists John Preston Neale and Henry Howard RA, and the architect William Wilkins (who, to Jerdan's disgust, was later to design the National Gallery). Jerdan was especially proud of the *Literary Gazette*'s coverage of Fine Arts, so dear to him, and hitherto neglected by the majority of the press. He cultivated acquaintance with the "leading men of the period", and his own social standing rose as a consequence. Success breeds success, and he later claimed that "the present highly improved system of our periodical literature may, in great measure, be traced and attributed to the pioneering of so humble an individual as myself".[24] That he did indeed play a major role is evident, but it would have been more dignified, perhaps, to let others blow his trumpet for him.

By the summer of 1817 the Jerdan family had moved house again, this time to Rose Cottage, Old Brompton. He quickly found himself giving evidence at the Old Bailey, following the arrest by a watchman of an eighteen-year old man, for stealing three live tame geese from his coach house, and seven eggs value sixpence from his hen house. The culprit was found guilty, and transported for seven years.[25] Whilst his "quiet and pretty residence" was being made ready, the family had temporarily stayed in Little Chelsea, neighbours to the Princess of Condé, daughter of the murdered King of France, Louis XVI. Jerdan called upon her several times, mostly on local matters, and noted her thick-soled boots and dress no better than a milkmaid's. (Some years later, Jerdan was riding in a carriage with the President of France, Louis Napoleon, and pointed out to him the modest house where his kinswoman had lived. This greatly moved the President, who referred to it on many subsequent meetings with Jerdan.)

However, at the time Jerdan was not hobnobbing with Presidents. His own finances were in a parlous state. During his turbulent time at the *Sun* he had incurred debts, and these, coupled with the failure of Whitehead's Bank where he had entrusted his savings, conspired to throw him "behind-hand with the world". The money he received from the *Sun* was not sufficient to clear his debts and pay his current expenses, and it was to be three years before the *Literary Gazette* became profitable enough to provide even the most basic subsistence. To add insult to injury, he received a bill for eighty-eight pounds from his lawyers for the *Sun* litigation. He brooded that he was so encumbered by debts, he would have been wiser to appear in the <u>London</u> *Gazette* (which listed bankruptcies) rather than the *Literary Gazette*, a sombre joke which was to prove prophetic. From this period on, interest on his debts accumulated and he paid "thirty or forty shillings for every pound[26] and got plentifully belied and abused by my unsatiated plunderers".[27] In an effort to improve his resources he applied for some kind of government employment, but was turned down.

Somehow he kept his ironical sense of humour. In the *Literary Gazette* of August 1817 he published a letter he had written addressed to "My dearest Friend", i.e. himself. "Why am I writing this?" he asked his correspondent, "when I could so easily speak to you in person." He answered that he didn't begrudge the postage, and believed a formal communication would get his attention: taking on the challenge of the *Literary Gazette* requires

> the strength of Hercules, united to the talents of the admirable Crichton, and the calculating powers of the American boy, would not suffice for the execution of such a task. I am afraid you have over-rated your capabili-ties . . . Mr Editor! I am afraid you have not well considered either your difficulties or your dangers . . . You review new books forsooth; every censure makes an author and his partisans your foes. You criticise the drama; . . . You will be pilloried in a farce, caricatured by Matthews and transfixed by as many thousand shafts of ridicule as the wit of modern dramatic writers can supply. You also criticise the arts: artists are even more irritable . . . If your literary intelligence is not a string of puffs, publishers will abominate as much as authors abhor you . . .

His "letter" went on to tell the tale of a dog so beset by a swarm of bees that despite the writer's success in freeing him, the pain was so great that the dog died – he left it to himself to connect the analogy of this tale to his own life. It is evident that from the outset of his editorship of the *Literary Gazette*, Jerdan was sensitive to the dangerous waters he swam in. Not only would writers and artists resent a bad review, but publishers whose books he did not actively promote would despise him. Censuring society would deprive him of a welcome everywhere. It is a wonder that he had the courage to proceed at all.

At the height of popularity of the 'Gothic novel', the *Literary Gazette* reviewed Thomas Love Peacock's *Nightmare Abbey*, which satirized the vogue. Peacock's barbs were directed at Byron and Coleridge, in the guise of his two main characters, the first of whom Jerdan strongly disapproved because of his perceived immorality. However, he seemed to have missed Peacock's point, reviewing the novel as "executed with greater license than nature and with more humour than wit", puzzling over the novel as not fitting into the known genres of "romances, novels, tales, nor treatises, but a mixture of all these combined." Jerdan has been accused of being "hostile to satire",[28] an accusation perhaps based on his failed attempt to rid *The Satirist* when he bought the paper, of its more scurrilous aspect, but a view which ignores his satirical verse of *Vox et Praterea Nihil* and the *British Eclogue* of a few years earlier. Jerdan was to pen several more pieces of satirical work over the years, although never with the aim of cruelty that satire often implies. The *Literary Gazette* ignored Jane Austen's *Northanger Abbey* published in the same year, which, with hindsight, was an error of judgment on Jerdan's part.

Reviews in the *Literary Gazette* were not signed, and it is only by recognizing his style of writing that Jerdan's own contributions can be identified. No marked up office copy has been found, an omission in keeping with Jerdan's own often repeated complaint that he was not a record-keeper. Some contributors can be identified by letters that have been found, but in the first three years of Jerdan's editorship it is likely that the majority of literary reviews came from his own pen. And even if they were by someone else, he had to authorize them. Anonymity was deliberate, and Jerdan endeavoured to give the *Literary Gazette* its own identity, rather than as a vehicle for individual writers. He made this clear:

> Some confusion having arisen in consequence of Gentlemen who contribute to the various departments of this journal, as well as others being addressed as the organs of communication, or as responsible for its contents, we beg leave to refer to our Imprint for the proper mode of communication, and to say, that it is uncandid and erroneous to fix upon Individuals as the Writers of Articles, in a publication which boasts a little Republic of Literature.[29]

An exception to his rule was his chief art critic, William Paulet Carey, who was already on the staff of the *Gazette*. A later art critic, revealed by his obituary in the paper of January 1842 was Walter Henry Watts, who had served for over twenty years. Occasionally Jerdan wrote an original piece, and identified one of these in his *Autobiography*, although in the *Literary Gazette* it was signed an unlikely "F. Munchausen Pinto". This piece was a long and amusing story about being thrown from a carriage, concussed, and dreaming of a visit to the Enneabionians, an unknown race in the interior of New Holland, a race where the people had ten lips and nine lives. A diagram was included showing how, as each life was lost, another lip opened. This story is reminiscent of Swift's *Gulliver's Travels* and is, similarly, a political satire in the style of travel writing so popular at the time. Jerdan also satirized the pomposity of anthropologists and other scholars: the traveller told an Enneabionian philosopher of the English phrase used when someone is sad, that he is "down in the mouth", which provoked a two-volume treatise proving that Great Britain was an Enneabionian colony. Politics too are shown as pointless: once actions are taken, politicians are neglected – literature is the only comfort. The moral of the story was that "the poor wretch with only one life is just as happy as the Enneabionian with nine".[30]

Jerdan also indulged in a sci-fi fantasy, with a story wherein the narrator met a mermaid who could see into the future. Unfortunately the narrator was shot whilst she was divulging her experiences to him, and on recovering, he wrote down all that he could remember about 1820, only three years ahead. The world had turned topsy-turvy and no aspect of political or cultural life escaped Jerdan's ascerbic pen. He even wrote, jokingly, of a tunnel from Dover to Calais, and a canal to carry the Nile avoiding cataracts. These were not the only prophetic ideas in this piece: he also suggested that "The greatest improvement in politics seems to be the system of legislating entirely through the medium of newspapers", an idea he obviously thought silly, but is still to this day a topic of debate.

Jerdan's inversions and criticisms of the social and political mores of his times appear in stories such as these last two examples, more than likely as a safer, less confrontational way to bring them to his readers' attention than straightforward journalism. His light and superficially humorous tone takes the sting out of his barbs, and would thus not be overtly offensive to his powerful and influential friends such as Canning. A more cogent reason for cloaking satire and criticism in humour was what has been called "the most decisive single event in shaping the reading of the romantic period".[31] In the 1790s, at the age of nineteen, Robert Southey had written a political verse drama, 'Wat Tyler'. In 1817 a publisher, Sharwood, without asking Southey's permission, printed and sold copies of his manuscript. In the interim Southey had become Poet Laureate, and had changed his views. He believed that his republican work, which (like Jerdan's stories) "ridiculed royal extravagance, oppressive taxes, aggressive wards and cynical churchmen, would encourage unrest and revolution" and the publisher could be prosecuted for sedition. Southey asked for an injunction against the publishing of this work, and damages for breach of copyright, of which he believed he was the owner. His case fell apart because the Lord Chancellor said it was the text itself which was not lawful, and that Southey would need to bring a case for seditious libel against the printer or publisher. This created a vacuum into which pirate publishers jumped, selling 60,000 cheap copies, and the text remained in print for decades. Jerdan would be extremely wary of publishing anything, least of all his own work, against which a charge of sedition could be brought.

The first year of the *Literary Gazette* came to an end on an optimistic note: circulation had risen, largely thanks to the serialization of Tuckey's *Voyage to the Congo*, the number and quality of Jerdan's contributors had widened and the *Literary Gazette* was being read and spoken of by "the superior classes of the educated and intelligent who were addicted to literature".[32] Jerdan reported that its first year receipts were £109 and the paper sold almost one thousand stamped, and two hundred and fifty unstamped copies.[33] It was a solid foundation from which Jerdan could move forward to shape the *Literary Gazette* into an influential guide to contemporary literature and culture.

As his journal rose in popularity, Jerdan became ever more deluged with submissions of prose and verse from would-be contributors, requesting that their work should be favourably 'noticed' in the pages of the *Literary Gazette*. Such importunings, he claimed, did not influence his decisions whether to review or to ignore a work, whether to praise or criticize it. The literary worth of the work was the sole deciding factor. If he could not praise, then censure was to be mild; defects pointed out "in a friendly manner", and severity never exercised, unless "the publication gave great offence, by its immoral and dangerous tendencies".[34] Although at the time literary reviews were believed to be highly influential on opinions and sales, this may not quite be the case; it has been observed that many books were published long before reviews appeared, selling well despite this. Byron's *Childe Harold* was an example. This observer noted that there was "no correlation between reviews, reputations and sales, or between contemporary and later reputation".[35]

The *Literary Gazette* stayed faithful to the promotion of fine arts and literature and was the means of introducing to the public many whose names became famous in their time. Jerdan consulted friends for their advice, and some offered to assist on a voluntary basis for the time being. Jerdan himself was very keen on poetry, a preference inculcated in his late eighteenth-century education, and one that he failed to see was not shared by the public as the century proceeded into the decades of the 1830s and 1840s. At the outset, the *Literary Gazette* was "the wet nurse to bards".[36] An issue in November 1817 was the first publication where Bryan Waller Procter's work appeared, (better known under his penname of Barry Cornwall). The *Literary Gazette* also featured several female poets. Some were already well-known, such as Mrs Rolls, Barbara Hofland and Felicia Hemans. The four daughters of Jerdan's old lamented friend Begbie also wrote for the *Literary Gazette*, as did the sisters of the Rev. Dr Croly, himself a long-time aide to Jerdan and husband to one of Begbie's daughters. The poets helped to establish the reputation of the paper in those early days when, as Jerdan wryly observed, "poetry was not a drug but a public pleasure!"[37] It was indeed a poetical era, boasting Campbell, Scott, Byron, Shelley, Southey, Wordsworth, Coleridge and, their equal in Jerdan's eyes, but forgotten today, George Croly. The *Literary Gazette* of 1818 carried several of what Jerdan called "fine compositions" by Croly, including 'Paris in 1815'. Jerdan usually supported Sir Walter Scott's work; he was a Tory and a Scotsman and a phenomenally successful novelist. However, in a February issue of the *Literary Gazette* Jerdan oddly observed, "we do not like Sir Walter's gratuitous servility, we like Lord Byron's preposterous liberalism little better". Thinking back to this period of the *Literary Gazette*, Jerdan acknowledged that many of the minor poets were forgotten forty years later, but that "The greater and smaller wheels are all necessary to the wonderful machine."[38]

Poetry was therefore a vital component of the *Literary Gazette* but there were other circumstances which also raised the journal's reputation. When the Archdukes of Austria visited the printing press of the *Literary Gazette*'s typographer, Bensley, Jerdan was asked to act as translator. He modestly said his French was indifferent and he hardly knew the technical names of the press in English, but their Imperial Highnesses were impressed and ordered that the *Literary Gazette* be delivered to them regularly, an act which increased its fame and circulation in Germany. The Archdukes wrote about their tour of England, and this was translated for the *Literary Gazette* by the indefatigable Lloyd of the Foreign Post Office together with Miss Ross. Publication of the Archdukes' Remarks boosted the reputation of the *Literary Gazette*, causing Jerdan to muse "On such accidents do many of the important events of literary success, and even of life, often take their hue."[39]

A feature which boosted the circulation of the *Literary Gazette* was the commencement of a series called "The Hermit in London", a spin-off from Jerdan's translation of *A Hermit in Paris* a few years earlier. The author was a Captain Macdonough, who was retired on half pay, and penned over twenty essays in this series of "smart and graphic sketches of society". Colburn initiated the feature, begun in Issue No. 77 on 11 July 1818, as one "written by a person of distinguished rank and title". Jerdan was more impressed that the author was keenly observant, and drew "original pictures from life . . . without trenching upon private matters or personalities".[40] Colburn had also arranged with Stendhal to supply Paris correspondence to the *Literary Gazette* and this arrangement remained in place until Jerdan appeared to end it in March 1822. In the interim he had severely edited Stendhal's letters when he considered them too long or too political. The Frenchman continued to write for the *New Monthly Magazine* after Jerdan had dispensed with his services.[41]

There was always a certain amount of mutual back-scratching with other journals. Jerdan welcomed an opportunity to receive Blackwood's *Maga*. He told a correspondent from the rival house,

> I was much pleased with the one or two numbers which I purchased at Murray's, and would have completed the set, but you can well form an idea of the heavy expense I am at for periodicals, taking as I do most of the French, German and Italian works of literary interest and a great number of the daily, weekly, monthly and quarterly productions of our own prolific island. I have the *Edinburgh Magazine* (Constable's) sent regularly and without charge from Longman's; and have quoted both that and *Blackwood's* in the *Literary Gazette*. Of course, any notice of the L.G. in the *Magazine* would be advantageous, and I trust it is seldom altogether

destitute of interesting matter for quotation. I make it an invariable rule to give honour where honour is due, and never fail to mention the source of any extract I take. This is, in my opinion, the only candid and honourable way of availing ourselves of the fruits of contemporary labour.[42]

This glimpse of the sheer volume of material that Jerdan had to scan each and every week, to ensure that his journal was never behind the competition, and preferably well in advance of it, shows that his reading list was formidable. His letter also declared that the circulation of the *Literary Gazette* rose every week, and that in the previous six months sales had risen by six hundred copies.

In return for citing the source of his quotations from *Blackwood's* and other publications, Jerdan sent Blackwood a copy of Barry Cornwall's poems in May 1819, gently suggesting a notice by being "not injudicious enough to endeavour, did I wish, to warp your judgment … I greatly admire my friend's poetical genius … ".[43] A couple of weeks later he thanked Blackwood for his "attentions" to Barry Cornwall, and warned him that a letter from Paris which *Blackwood's* had printed was not original, but a translation, and gave him the source. Jerdan's sense of honour on professional matters was strong; here he was being helpful, not spiteful, in pointing out an error to his rival editor and friend.

His promotion of Bryan Waller Procter (Barry Cornwall) was one of several examples of Jerdan nurturing a young talent. In his own *Literary Recollections* Procter made no mention of his debt to Jerdan or the *Literary Gazette* despite the fact that Jerdan had discovered him and at least once a month for three years, published some of his work, either poetry or short prose pieces.[44] In May Jerdan took the opportunity, when reviewing Procter's 'Dramatic Scenes and other Poems', to set out his own views on the current state of poetry, and what he considered should be its aims. His statement defended romantic values in opposition to neo-classical, and displayed the schism between his late-eighteenth century upbringing and the modern taste for change in the aftermath of years of war. As Editor of the *Literary Gazette* Jerdan was exceptionally well placed to deliver his opinion to a wide reading public. His opinion was relevant both to his journal and as an explanation of what was to follow in his private life. His language was, as usual, prolix and flowery, but the content is of vital interest in understanding the nature of the man himself, a man who was in an almost unrivalled position to influence large numbers of readers:

The greatest literary revolution, which has turned the taste of England from foreign imitation to her original treasures, is now familiar to our readers. Whatever might have been the cause, whether the passion for novelty, the long exclusion of Continental intercourse, or the vigour of the public mind, first exhibited by the struggle of war, and then exalted by the glories of unexampled victory, the effect has been produced with a fulness and a power that seem to place us beyond the possibility of a relapse. It is forbidden for a writer henceforth to establish a distinguished character upon the minor ingenuity of his weapons; no epigrammatic and pointed turns of wit, no keen and satiric employment of phrase, will be suffered to enter into the lists where the high prize of fame is to be won. A nobler and more lofty stature must be exhibited in that combat; and with all the artificial habilliments of the day flung aside, the prize must be toiled for by the vigour of naked heroic nature. The simplicity of this revived taste is at once a pledge of its truth and of its permanence. Imagination is the Sun of Poetry, all substitutions for that perpetual and sublime splendour must disturb or dim the true colours of nature; from the passing cloud to the total eclipse, there is a gradual loss of beauty in the sphere of vision; and when the full darkness comes at last, no earthly fabricated fire can supply the security, the expansion, and the glory of the great centre of the system. All the authorship of England has felt this change shooting down through its parts; the hasty writing of our public journals displays a general vigour, that twenty years ago would have been considered as the privilege only of the highest names. But the change has been still more obvious in the hallowed garden of poetry; the richness of the oil had slept, but was not dead; and the moment it had ceased to be cut into serpentines and trodden into dust by the capricious and tasteless of the world, its old luxuriousness rose up, and the first flower from above showed us what blooms and beauty might yet expand for our delight and wisdom. Fashion was the guide of the last age, Nature is the guide of the present and our progress must be from grandeur to grandeur; a keener sense of passion, a purer simplicity, a more comprehensive vision of nature, a more majestic, solemn and sacred love of all things lovely, will be wrought upon us in that upward flight, and, like the translated Prophet, the spirit be made sublime its ascent to receive the palm of immortality.[45]

This was high-flown language indeed to set out his vision of the return of the kind of poetry he was brought up on, the kind he did not want to see change. In his own verse, which he sometimes included in his journal, taking advantage of his position, he was not quite so ambitious, although he maintained that being a writer himself, he was better able to judge the efforts of others. One of his verses was uncharacteristically serious. "Night Dreams – Life Dreams!"[46] spoke of the submerging of love, of poverty making life hell, of death and disease and the failure of friends to succour the needy. The poem was composed of Spenserians, with "the personifications of Disease and Poverty looking back to eighteenth century models, though the poem eschews allegory for more natu-ralistic effects".[47] Such dark thoughts did not often surface in Jerdan's writing, which was more likely to be a parody on a Greek verse, or a joke about pimples. He wrote "Night Dreams" at a time when he himself felt insecure and his resources insufficient for his needs, despite the upward trend of his journal.

Insecurity was hardly surprising in this year of the Peterloo Massacre, when armed troops stormed a protest meeting in Manchester killing eleven people and injuring four hundred. Protests were inevitable – the government had clamped down on press freedoms, increased censorship and had not furthered the cause of Catholic emancipation or parliamentary reform. Demonstrations in London followed in September. Jerdan's personal insecurity was much closer to home, in the behaviour of the volatile Pinnock, under whose roof, with Maunder, the *Literary Gazette* was produced. The brothers-in-law were co-partners in the *Literary Gazette* with Colburn and Jerdan. They had a highly successful and lucrative business publishing catechisms and short histories for children, and their provincial contacts were beneficial to the circulation of the *Literary Gazette*. But Pinnock wanted more than this, and dived headfirst into business ventures he knew nothing about. One such, where he thought he could make a fortune, was to corner the market in veneers, and the manufacture of pianofortes. He thought he could create a monopoly and thereby name his own price to all other musical-instrument makers who needed his material. This venture, and other schemes he tried, all failed. These distractions, and Pinnock's lack of attention to the accounts of the *Literary Gazette* were a recipe for disaster. Jerdan's income became more precarious than usual, and by the end of 1819, although circulation had increased considerably, sales were only fifty pounds more than the previous year's one hundred and nine pounds. The cost of newspapers and magazines was well above what the working man could afford, and the reading classes, that is the upper and more substantial middle classes, numbered about one and a half million; this was Jerdan's target market so he still had far to go.

To supplement his income Jerdan found time to write leaders for the *North Staffordshire Potteries Gazette*, and essays for the *Chelmsford Chronicle*. He also saw two books through the press for John Murray, who paid him seventy-five pounds for Fitzclarence's *Journey from India to England*. Fitzclarence, later Lord Munster, remained Jerdan's lifelong friend. Colonel Hippesley's *Voyage to the Orinoko* earned him fifty pounds and Jerdan also negotiated the copyright to Hippesley for one hundred pounds, receiving a "handsome bronze inkstand" from the author as a token of gratitude.[48] (Jerdan identified himself as the author of an article "Origin of the Pindaries" in the *Quarterly Review* of January 1818, perhaps another income-raising attempt; he was aided in this venture by material from Sir John Malcolm.)[49] All this extra work was necessary to keep the wolf from the door, and, as Jerdan said, to stop Rose Cottage becoming Bleak House. His efforts were not enough to prevent him having to sell his horse, and after only a year or so, in May 1819, move from Rose Cottage to 7 Upper Queens

Buildings, facing the Brompton Road.[50] Queens Buildings was home mainly to tradesmen and craftsmen,[51] and the move must have been a blow to the ambitious and social-climbing editor.

Jerdan and Frances' fifth child had arrived on 2 August 1818 and, a year later was christened George Canning Jerdan, together with his sister Mary aged five, and brother William Freeling, aged three.[52] That such an eminent person as Canning agreed to be godfather and give his name to Jerdan's son is surely evidence that he held Jerdan in high regard. Canning even went himself to St Mary Abbots Church, Kensington, to ensure that the child's baptismal name was properly registered in the record book. The minister officiating at this multiple christening was Jerdan's close friend and poetical colleague, the Rev. George Croly.

As well as trying to meet the demands of his family and keep up with all the work entailed in running a weekly journal, Jerdan embarked upon an activity close to his heart: the succour of the needy author. The Literary Fund had been established by the Rev. David Williams in 1790.[53] Williams had initially hoped for it to be a Royal Society of Authors, to include a college for the sons of authors, with a library and archive. This proved too ambitious a plan, and he abandoned these extensions, concentrating instead on the Literary Fund itself.[54] In addition to being one of its first subscribers the Prince Regent had, in 1806, given the Fund a house in Soho to use as offices. Its purpose was to relieve authors in distress; the list of distinguished writers who benefited from it is impressive, and includes Coleridge and Chateaubriand. Several were beneficiaries as a direct result of Jerdan's intercession, which often kept the writer out of debtor's prison. The Fund also helped widows and orphans of writers whose death left their families destitute. In 1842 the Fund was allowed to add 'Royal' to its title. Jerdan was introduced to the Literary Fund by James Christie, and was already involved in its work in 1818, when he decided that the President of the day, the Duke of Somerset, was too slow and lethargic to be effective. Jerdan wrote about the Fund, to stir things up and get it operational again. He found a powerful ally in Sir Benjamin Hobhouse, a Whig MP and social reformer. Within a year £1157 had been raised, of which £820 went to the relief of unfortunate authors.

By the time Jerdan began his involvement with the Literary Fund it had become an established charity with over four hundred subscribers, including peers and baronets. London's most eminent publishers, Longman, Cadell and Murray, also supported it. However, few notable writers were subscribers and Southey was the first of several to attack the Literary Fund on the grounds that it "distributed a pittance which was almost useless and did so with 'despicable ostentation of patronage'".[55] Walter Scott declined to subscribe, explaining that he preferred to give money directly to those in need rather than to a general fund. Such personal assistance was practised by other leading authors. The case of Coleridge highlights the point:"When the Literary Fund gave Coleridge £30 in February 1816 out of their income of about £2000 per annum and stocks worth nearly £17,000, Byron sent him £100 'being at a time when I could not command £150 in the world'."[56] Fortunately for the myriad of impoverished writers who were not known to such exalted beings, and could not expect help from such quarters, but were in dire want of any funding they could get, Jerdan took a different view and gave much energy to his work on behalf of the Literary Fund, recalling that it was "an object of my zealous and ceaseless exertion".[57]

The Literary Fund held fund-raising events, and most importantly an annual dinner designed to raise public awareness of the Fund and to attract new subscribers. To Christie's displeasure, the poet Fitzgerald traditionally gave a recital of his verse at almost every Anniversary Dinner. His theme was frequently the wrongs and sufferings of the literary classes and Jerdan thought one example worth repeating for posterity, even though the poet was so often ridiculed:

> But of all wants with which mankind is curst,
> The accomplished Scholar's are, by far, the worst;
> For generous pride compels him to control
> And hide the worm that gnaws his very soul.
> Though Fortune in her gifts to him is blind,
> Nature bestows nobility of mind,
> That makes him rather endless ills endure,
> Than seek from meanness a degraded cure!
> Yet from his unrequited labours flow
> Half we enjoy, and almost all we know.[58]

These sentiments, and the Literary Fund Anniversary Dinners were of great importance to Jerdan whose sympathy, pity and practical assistance to struggling writers was one of his most enduring and endearing characteristics.

Despite, or perhaps because of, his strict Tory upbringing and beliefs, Jerdan always tried to reform where he saw injustice. His reforming zeal led him to write often in favour of an Equitable Trade Society "for the adjustment of disputed accounts, the prevention of law suits and the benefit of commercial and trading interests".[59] This plan, too, fell on deaf ears. Another of his projects, he claimed, was to campaign for the establishment of free drawing and design schools throughout the kingdom, to encourage fine art. Although this did not happen at the time, Jerdan lived long enough to see some moves towards such schools in his old age. He also worked fervently – he said he was the first to make a public outcry – against cruelty to animals. This too, he saw come to take a positive form in later years.

In the interests of reporting for the *Literary Gazette* and also for his own insatiable curiosity, Jerdan began to attend the many scientific and learned institutions then being established. Publication of their proceedings in his journal was, he felt, his contribution to "remove the bushel from over the candle, so that its light might be diffused over the land."[60]

In the Spring of 1818 an event occurred which meant much to Jerdan: an acquaintance, Sir John Leicester, opened to the public his Gallery of Native Artists in Hill Street, Berkeley Square, in London. He was the first great patron of British Art, an avid collector, with the intention of establishing a National Gallery of British Art. Admission was free to all, an innovation in England where hitherto staff at country houses with art collections were given gratuities for showing visitors around. The *Literary Gazette* took up this topic, when it printed a letter headed 'Admission of the lower orders to Public Exhibitions'.[61] In this letter a (probably fictional) Frenchman urged for free access to art on certain days, reassuring nervous owners of paintings that the populace would be flattered and behave themselves accordingly. Jerdan, as a devoted admirer of art, was delighted with the new Gallery and expressed his appreciation in glowing terms. Sir John assumed Jerdan's eloquence was equal to his knowledge of the subject, and on that basis, welcomed Jerdan into his circle of friends. This, recalled Jerdan, was "one of the most gratifying sources of pleasure and friendship which gave happiness to many days of my chequered life".[62] Many of these days were to be spent at Sir John's estate, Tabley House in Knutsford, Cheshire. Jerdan happened to be visiting on the very day that Sir John received a letter from the Prince Regent raising him to the peerage, and he discussed the choice of title with his visitor. The peer chose de Tabley, but Jerdan suggested Warren, or Fitz-Warenne, on a heraldic basis, and was pleased when de Tabley's heir added this name to his own on his father's death. He noted that a wit suggested "de Tableaux" as more appropriate for a patron of the arts.

Jerdan relished his visits to Tabley House over a number of years. It was to him an earthly paradise, an escape for one so much a slave to the pen. He indulged in the country pursuits of hunting, shooting and fishing, and greatly admired his host's skill with a shotgun. On one of Jerdan's visits, another guest who was also a keen fisherman, was the great painter, J.M.W. Turner,[63] to whom Lord de Tabley had been a generous patron, purchasing nine major works. The peer was an enthusiastic amateur painter himself and had left an unfinished landscape on his easel. Whilst the assembled company stood around discussing the painting, Jerdan stuck a bit of blue paper on to show where he thought it would be improved by a spot of brightness, and unasked, Turner took up a brush and marked a few improvements. Turner then returned to London, and at breakfast the next day de Tabley was furious to receive a bill from him for "Instructions in Painting". Jerdan tried to persuade him to ignore it, but de Tabley paid up, as Turner must have known he would. Jerdan called this a "deplorable instance of Turner's eccentricity" but "as a sort of balance to the human infirmity of the Drawing Master account", also related that Turner invited Thomas Hunt, an authority on Tudor architecture, to accompany him on a continental trip, paying all Hunt's expenses. Tabley House still has Turner's painting depicting the lake in the grounds where he and Jerdan fished, and the grooves cut into the floor by the artist's easel may still be seen.

Returning from one of his visits to Tabley House, Jerdan went to call on Wordsworth at Rydal Mount. The impression stayed in his mind for many years: "I was not unexpected, nor denied the favour of a first home-picture. On walking up the beautiful greensward, on a fine summer afternoon, towards the house, I at once saw the poet seated, almost in attitude, at an open window which descended to the ground, and with a handsome folio poised upon his crossed knee, which he seemed to be reading. Had those been the days of photographs, the position would have been invaluable."[64]

Jerdan's visual memory remained acute, even as an old man; he recalled in some detail many of the shows and art he had seen in his youth. Amongst his favourites were Mr Bullock's displays at the Egyptian Hall in Piccadilly, most particularly Napoleon's carriage, just as he had abandoned it in his flight from Waterloo, complete with its coachman, a great coup for Bullock and one which attracted a total of 220,000 visitors during its seven months on display.[65] Jerdan saved a letter from Bullock exulting over his acquisition, gloating that it had given him "the opportunity of accomplishing in a few months what he [Napoleon] could never succeed in doing; for in that short period I over-ran England, Ireland and Scotland, levying a willing contribution on upwards of 800,000 of his Majesty's subjects; for old and young, rich and poor, clergy and laity, all ages, sexes, and conditions, flocked to pay their poll-tax and gratify their curiosity by an examination of the spoils of the dead lion". Bullock's return on his £2,500 investment was £35,000. Jerdan plainly admired Bullock's entrepreneurship in taking the moribund collection of natural history objects previously displayed at the Leverian Museum, and transforming them, with Bullock's own collection, into a fascinating and educational exhibit, the first English museum to use the device of 'habitat groups' to display specimens as nearly as possible in their natural surroundings. Jerdan recalled this museum minutely in his mini-biography on Bullock more than forty years later. He also recalled how Bullock brought him a pony from Shetland, which Jerdan had to transport across London in a hackney coach, with its head sticking out of the window, transforming its owner into a showman.[66]

It was Jerdan's lot in his life as the *Literary Gazette*'s editor, to be bombarded with requests to print everything he was offered, and he was frequently expected to improve some amateur's attempt at an Ode, or review, or an opinion on any matter. He became inured to the sycophantic language used to entreat his publishing of anything and everything sent to him, and made fun of the flowery terms used by these supplicants who "rejoiced" over a poem, sent with "highest pleasure", "great delight", "astonishment and rapture" and so on. His immediate attention to each offering was demanded, and his mealtimes and scant rest were often broken in upon by such importuners. He, like other editors then and since, could not always do as demanded, and Jerdan felt at the mercy of the wrath of disappointed writers, overlooked painters and poorly reviewed actors. Irritably, he noted that:

> most public characters have such capacious stomachs for applause, that there is no risk of surfeiting them with panegyric; but, on the contrary, much danger of being thought churls and niggardly starvlings for not giving enough, Reviews must be puffs – criticisms must observe no blem- ishes – biographies must make men angels![67]

Jerdan was definitely no angel; he was sorely tried by poets who resented their immortal words being "polished", especially poetesses who entreated him "with downcast eyes and heaving bosom" to print their verses. He was "martyred between the writer and the writing". Actors who opined that their provincial tour was at least as important as the march of a general's victorious army were another thorn in his side. He needed to be a diplomat and counsellor and, above all, focussed on his task of keeping the *Literary Gazette* both interesting and influ- ential. One poet in particular went against the tide of those vying to be included in the *Literary Gazette*. Jerdan approached Wordsworth, on the eve of one of his overseas travels, to write a Diary for the journal; he offered the poet "a consid- erable sum", but was refused on the grounds of "an idleness of disposition".[68]

There were compensations for all these petty annoyances. One was the satis- faction of Jerdan's fervent interest in, and access to, all the variety of shows that London had to offer. These were not stage shows as we would recognize the term today, (although he was also a devotee of the theatre), but what he called 'novelties', recalling decades later that: "for some twenty-five years there was not a known show or curiosity, from the charge of a halfpenny to a guinea, that I did not see . . . giants, dwarfs, mermaids, Albinos, Hottentot Venuses, animals with more heads or legs than 'they ought to', and all other curiosities and monstrosities were 'my affections'."[69] His passionate curiosity about all such popular shows became evident through reviews in the *Literary Gazette*, most if not all, apparently written by the editor himself.

Another compensation for Jerdan's 'martyrdom' was that editorship allowed him access to important people whose acquaintance, and occasional friendship, he valued highly. He kept his friends for many years, often for a lifetime, and such attachments could have been not only for mutual benefit, but for mutual liking and esteem. Colonel Fitzclarence, Earl Munster, whose book Jerdan super- vised through the press, changed from a dilettante to an ardent scholar and writer; he visited Jerdan at home, where his good humour was enjoyed by everyone. Jerdan also called on him at home in Belgravia, to discuss literature and drawing, and where he was able to admire Lord Munster's obvious affection for his family. Jerdan recounted that he was present when Fitzclarence, just after he had been made Earl, met the Earl of Mulgrave, recently raised to Marquis of Normanby. After much "Milording" between them, and with the lubrication of champagne, they agreed to drop their titles, calling each other simply George and Henry. Years later, Munster was accused in an anonymous letter Lord Mulgrave showed to Jerdan, of intriguing with the Duke of Wellington, and of being a "Gorse Hopper". Jerdan and Mulgrave finally realized that Munster's accuser was calling him a "Gossiper" – just the kind of word joke that Jerdan relished.

Jerdan loved parties, and recalled one particular gathering where the company played "Games and Forfeits". He was made to kneel and bury his head in the lap of Lady Caroline Lamb (infamous as having been Byron's mistress), there to answer any questions the other guests proposed. He was asked "What would you do if an injured ghost approached to assault you, for wrongs done in the flesh?" Before he could answer, he was indeed assaulted, with a knock to his head. On taking off his blindfold, he looked up into the face of William Lamb, Lady Caroline's husband, come to collect his wife from the party. Jerdan felt uncomfortable at being the butt of a silly joke, but decided not to call Lamb out for a duel. This was fortunate, for Lamb later became Lord Melbourne, beloved adviser to the young Queen Victoria and future Premier and powerful ruler of the empire. Melbourne and Jerdan became more closely acquainted over the years, but even the ambitious Jerdan did not claim that they became real friends. He tried unsuccessfully to interest the Premier in doing something for literary men, and occasionally published Melbourne's own poems in the *Literary Gazette*. A few years later Jerdan used his access to Melbourne to plead for aid for the widows of the brothers Lander, intrepid explorers of Africa who, in 1830, discovered the course of the River Niger, and one of whom died in 1834; Jerdan helped to procure pensions for them, one of which was still being paid, through him, until at least 1852. On Melbourne's death, in 1848, Jerdan was consulted about his life by Melbourne's friend, Sir Henry Bulwer, an acknowledgement that he was considered to have known the Premier well enough to have something to say about this powerful and esteemed statesman.

Now that he was established at the *Literary Gazette*, Jerdan often found himself in exalted company, not always as a result of any flattery on his part. Horace Twiss, a Tory MP famous for his unconventionally flippant speeches, produced a novel in 1819 called *Carib Chief*. The *Literary Gazette* was mildly critical of this work. A few years later Twiss attained political eminence, which provoked jealousy in some literary men, who ridiculed his wit and lampooned him for his foibles. Despite the paper's indifferent review, Twiss invited Jerdan to dine in his "dark little dining room in Serle Street," Lincolns Inn, with other guests including Lord Eldon, Lord Castlereagh and other Cabinet Ministers. Jerdan and Twiss remained close friends for thirty years, until Twiss's death in 1849, unaffected by the *Literary Gazette*'s misgivings about his literary production.

The *Literary Gazette* gave a warmer reception to Washington Irving's *Sketch Book*. William Pyne sent a copy to Jerdan at Hastings, where he was enjoying a brief respite, accompanying the book with an amusing letter which Jerdan called facetious, correcting Jerdan's assumption that the man who had purchased it in New York "wet from the press" was the author, a pardonable mistake as Irving used the pseudonym Geoffrey Crayon.[70] Jerdan corrected his error in the following issue of the *Literary Gazette*. The *Sketch Book* was a huge success in Britain, and Jerdan received a gratifying note of thanks from Irving: "The author of the *Sketch Book* cannot but feel highly flattered that his Essays should be deemed worthy of insertion in so elegant and polite a miscellany as the *Literary Gazette* . . . he begs leave to add his conviction that he could not have a better introduction to fashionable notice than the favourable countenance of the *Literary Gazette*." Although oblivious to Irving's implicit complaint that the *Literary Gazette* had given too long an extract from his book, Jerdan noted that this was one of the "most grateful incidents of my literary life"; he modestly did not take full credit for the book's success, acknowledging that: "No doubt, without my aid, the beautiful American canoe would soon have been safely launched on the British waters; but as it was, I had the pleasure and honour to launch it at once, fill the sails, and send it on its prosperous voyage."[71] Jerdan entertained Irving in his home, together with Edward and Henry Bulwer, Thomas Moore and others of great literary renown; Irving's retiring character and the editor's hectic life precluded their developing a close friendship, but it was a source of pride to Jerdan that they held each other in high esteem. When a parody of Scott's 'Lay of the Last Minstrel' called 'The Lay of the Scottish Fiddle' was incorrectly advertised in the newspapers as being the work of Washington Irving, Jerdan was asked to set the matter right by an announcement in the *Literary Gazette*.[72]

Irving's discreet hint that the *Literary Gazette*'s extracts from his book were too long, and thus could inhibit sales of his book, became a familiar complaint from authors. Jerdan took no notice, and several years later was still doing the same thing. He enraged Thomas Moore in 1827 by printing the climax of his book *The Epicurean*, whilst praising it generously, thus obviating the need for readers to buy it.

The space Jerdan allocated to book reviews has been calculated from an average of about 1500 words in 1818, representing about 135 works, to 3800 in 1826, representing 425 reviews and notices. Reviews remained within 10 percent of this for the rest of Jerdan's tenure.[73] These averages encompass a review of 12,000 words in 1826, (which was extended in following issues), and any review of Scott which was double the average. Within these figures the quantity of extracted text from the work reviewed rose from about 43% in 1818 to 65% in 1826 and over 80% in 1847. This steep rise in 1847 may have reflected Jerdan's disenchantment with his paper which was by then in rapid decline. The practice of including lengthy extracts was not due to laziness; it was in accord with Jerdan's plan at the outset of his editorship, when he announced his intention to quote at length, a practice which had been common in eighteenth-century magazines and newspapers. On one hand, this filled many columns without the need to pay a reviewer to write long articles, and saved time in getting reviews out before or at publication date of the work discussed. On the other hand, the *Literary Gazette*, aimed as it was at the middle classes and young readers of Scott and the miscellanies, could be read to the family in the evenings, keeping them sufficiently abreast of the content of new books without the necessity of purchasing them. Publishers were in a cleft stick, needing the *Literary Gazette* to review their books, but unhappy if the extracts satisfied readers to the extent they did not purchase the book.

On Saturday 26 June 1819 Bensley's printing house caught fire. That week's *Literary Gazette* had fortunately already been distributed to the publisher and newsmen, but Jerdan lost most of his back stock, records and manuscripts. It was necessary to reprint the lost stock at considerable expense. The *Gazette's* first printer, Messrs Valpy, helped out, a kindly gesture as they had been usurped by Pinnock and Maunder's connection with Bensley. A new printer was shortly engaged, Mr Pople of Chancery Lane, who thereafter printed the *Literary Gazette* for some years.

Pinnock and Maunder's business had now declined to such an extent that they could no longer act as publishers of the *Literary Gazette*. In November their names vanished from the journal and Jerdan, with Colburn, made temporary arrangements for new offices at 268 Strand, and a new publisher. In January 1820 Jerdan appointed William Armiger Scripps of 362 Strand, who had been the publisher of the *Sun* in Jerdan's days there as a journalist; he remained the publisher for over a quarter of a century.

All these changes and difficulties created great strain on Jerdan. Colburn had not made a return on his investment in the first three years of the *Literary Gazette*, and Jerdan said that despite the hard work he had put into the journal, his remuneration was that of a porter and he needed to improve his income. At his wit's end, he wrote to Colburn resigning his editorship. He was in a strong position, having received an offer from the British and Foreign Library in June to edit a new Review. There was a supporting fund of ten thousand pounds and the certainty of a good salary for the Editor. Surprisingly, for one so impecunious, Jerdan turned this generous offer down, being "more inclined to stick to my first love, especially as I was courting a bit of change by way of variety . . . ".[74] This decision was typical of Jerdan, to put an emotional reason above the practical necessity of a certain income.

Jerdan was persuaded by Colburn that when the *Literary Gazette* became profitable, he would reap the benefit; despite trying to pin Colburn down to a definite arrangement, he proved elusive, driving Jerdan to consult Cosmo Orme of the house of Longman, a man with whom he had created a friendly relationship. On a later note from Orme asking Jerdan to confirm the date of their first meeting, Jerdan annotated, "July 1819, present Mr Longman, Mr Rees, Mr Orme."[75] Jerdan was at this time prepared to buy both Colburn's share and Maunder's share, so that he would become sole owner of the *Literary Gazette*. Where he would find the money he did not say. Longmans advised the frustrated Jerdan to tell Colburn that he had sold Maunder's share to Longmans, which would greatly benefit the publication and they would thereafter take care of the management of the sale, and the accounts, aspects of the business which Jerdan called "worldly affairs" and which he found irksome. He asked the advice of his long-time friend Francis Freeling about this new arrangement and was reassured to be told that Freeling had found the Longmans fair and liberal people. He trusted Freeling's judgment not only because he was an old friend, but was also a senior executive in the Post Office and a man involved in literature.[76]

Jerdan was thus able to conclude the arrangement that Longmans suggested, paying Pinnock and Maunder "a handsome douceur for what I had given them gratuitously a year before, to substitute Messrs. Longman in their place as third proprietors . . . the *Literary Gazette* was firmly established in a tripartite partnership, more solid and improvable than had ever as yet been contemplated".[77] The new partner was announced in the *Literary Gazette* of 18 December 1819, and a more settled era began for the now soundly established journal. A legal document dated 1 January 1820 agreed that the three parties – Colburn, Jerdan and Longman & Co. – would continue publication of the *(London) Literary Gazette*.[78]

Spurred on by his acquisition of a share in its future, under Jerdan's editorship and grinding hard work the *Literary Gazette* flourished, fulfilling its stated objectives of reviewing literary works of all genres, and 'noticing' the arts and sciences. Jerdan was satisfied with his achievement.

Whilst his professional life blossomed, he received news of a personal tragedy. On 14 June 1820 his mother Agnes Stuart had died, at the age of 71.[79] She had been staying at 'Paradise' in Kelso, the house which seems to have been her parental home. Jerdan made the briefest of mentions of this event in his *Autobiography* where, thirty years later, he erroneously recalled that she had died in July. "The death was sudden, as my father's had been – a few insensate hours, and the vital flame was extinct. I was deeply affected, but such feelings are not for public obtrusion."[80] Fortunately for him, life was very full. Early in 1820 Jerdan moved his family to "a small cottage" at 1 Michael's Grove, Brompton. Michael's Grove, where Egerton Terrace now stands, was very near to their previous home in Queens Buildings. Horwood's Map of 1799 depicts this property as a terraced house with a long narrow garden, running along-side the ends of gardens in Michael's Place, whose houses fronted Brompton Road.

One day, in the Spring of 1820, Jerdan stood gazing thoughtfully out of the window of his home. His glance fell upon a plump teenager in the garden across the lane. She bowled her hoop with one hand whilst in the other she held a book in which she was engrossed. He knew who she was, because she occasionally played with his own children. William Jerdan could not then have imagined that this young woman would have an enormous impact on his professional and personal life.

6

Love and Literature

The family across the lane was named Landon: the parents were John and Catherine, née Bishop, with three children, Letitia Elizabeth, born in August 1802, Whittington Henry, two years younger and Elizabeth, born in 1812. John Landon's father had been a country rector, but John himself was a midshipman before joining, and eventually becoming a partner in, the army agency Adair & Co. in Pall Mall.

The family lived at 25 Hans Place, Chelsea, where their first two children were born. When Letitia was five she went to school at 22 Hans Place, an establishment run by a Miss Rowden, whose other pupils had included Mary Mitford and Lady Caroline Lamb, the latter taking her own child to the school in due course. Letitia was here for only two years, learning excellent French and nourishing her love of poetry, before the family moved to a large country house, Trevor Park, in East Barnet, where John Landon's brother had just taken the lease. Here, the little girl enjoyed great freedom, roaming in the woods and park of the estate. She was taught by her cousin, Elizabeth, and showed a voracious appetite for reading, feeding her imagination with Scott, *Robinson Crusoe*, Cook's *Voyages* and a *Life of Petrarch*, which gave her a lifelong affection for Italy, although she never travelled there. She had an excellent memory for everything she read, and also evinced a great talent and facility for writing, mostly poetry. She took affectionate care of her young brother Whittington, who showed far less ability, and was a much weaker character. John Landon's experiments in model farming on nearby Coventry Farm were severely affected by the end of the Napoleonic wars, which led to a depression in agriculture, and his interest in the army supply agency also suffered due to the drop in demand. The family returned to London in 1815, living first in Fulham, then moving to Old Brompton in 1816, adjacent to the Jerdans' home. Jerdan referred to the Landon's house as a "mansion" with "a fair garden and paddock", free from the noise of London. A nineteenth-century illustration of the house shows a four bay Georgian brick building, three storeys high, flanked by one storey high wings and a single storey extension in front of the main block. It had nine bedrooms, a "handsome drawing room", and outbuildings which included a double coach house.[1] Landon paid sixty pounds rent for the house, and fifteen pounds for the land, whilst the rent for Jerdan's cottage was forty-five pounds, indicating the difference in the size of their establishments.[2]

Brompton, at this time, was a pretty place, far enough from town to be country, but near enough to be accessible for daily engagements. Haymaking still went on there, honeysuckle and roses flourished; the area drew artists and writers who appreciated the quiet, and the clean air after the noise and pollution of London. Jerdan enjoyed being surrounded by creative people, especially as his daily business was conducted in the rush and grime of the town.

Letitia and Whittington Landon played with the Jerdan children whose ages ranged from thirteen to two years old, the two youngest not yet born. Letitia would have known their mother, Jerdan's wife Frances, when she visited their house to play. Her own parents grew more unhappy as their financial troubles multiplied, and Letitia became used to "the idea of living with secrets".[3] Crucially, she was likely to have seen them put on a "face" or a mask to hide their troubles from the outside world. The habit of hiding secrets behind a misleading exterior was to become a necessary part of her own character and her work.

All through her childhood Letitia Landon wrote poetry for her own amusement, and continued to read hugely. When her father's business ventures failed, the family were in financial difficulties. It was very likely that this was the moment when Letitia's mother and her cousin Elizabeth, who lived with them, conceived the idea of approaching their near neighbour, the well-known editor, William Jerdan. It was an obvious idea – the *Literary Gazette* was famously influential and respected; no shame could attach to their daughter's work being included in such a periodical. In any case, such contributions were generally anonymous, and the family needed income.

Jerdan himself romanticized these early days with Letitia; nothing, as far as is known, survives from this period of their relationship, save the poems themselves. All that exists are Jerdan's own memories, committed to paper many years later, when much water had flowed under their respective bridges. His two accounts differ slightly from each other, as often happens with old memories. Friends of Letitia's also recalled her youth, from a perspective of many years, their recollections fulfilling their own agendas of romanticising the poet.

The occasion when Jerdan first described seeing Letitia from his window was in a Memoir attached to a second edition of her novel *Romance and Reality* in 1848, some thirty years after the event, and is surely coloured by time in his "recognition" of the nascent poet:

When the writer first noticed her from his adjacent residence she appeared to be a girl of some fourteen or fifteen years of age, slightly proportioned, yet with an exuberance of form. In manners she was simplicity itself, and from her previously retired life, and not having associated with children of her own age, strangely combined the infantile with the intellectual. With her book in one hand, reading as well as she could by snatches, she might be seen trundling her hoop, during the hours for exercise, round and round the lawn, and it would have been difficult to suppose that she was doing aught else than combining lesson with play in a curious fashion. But the soul of Poetry was already there; and her first essays in song came with the hoop.

For a man then nearing forty, married, and with a growing family of his own, Jerdan took a close, and maybe not too disinterested, interest in his neighbour's "exuberance of form", a neighbour who was not fourteen or fifteen but nearer to seventeen. As much as her physical attributes, what he found attractive was the combination of the physical with the intellectual, the child within the adult, and having observed Letitia so closely, may have been more than otherwise willing to give her poetry his serious attention.

Revisiting this first glimpse of Letitia Landon five years later, for his *Autobiography*, he reported that

> My first recollection of the future poetess is that of a plump girl, grown enough to be almost mistaken for a woman, bowling a hoop round the walks, with the hoop-stick in one hand and a book in the other, reading as she ran, and as well as she could manage both exercise and instruction at the same time. The exercise was prescribed and insisted upon: the book was her own irrepressible choice.

Jerdan recalled that the first approach came from Mrs Landon, telling him that her daughter was "addicted to poetical composition".[4] She asked him, as a favour, to give his opinion on some of her daughter's efforts. Jerdan doubted that the poems were indeed those of the young hoop-bowler and playmate of his children. He thought instead that they were productions of her cousin Elizabeth, modestly hiding her identity. Elizabeth's two letters indicate that although she herself was not acquainted with the Jerdan family, she knew that at least there was some connection, probably through the young people, and could thus ask for his opinion as to whether "any taste or genius is expressed, or, on the contrary, if he should only call it a waste of time from which no benefit can arise".[5] Jerdan replied immediately, acknowledging some merit, which Elizabeth knew would encourage Letitia to strive for improvement. He considered that her juvenile works were "crude and inaccurate, as might be anticipated, in style, but containing ideas so original and extraordinary, that I found it impossible to believe they emanated from the apparent romp, and singular contradiction of the hoop and volume."[6] Letitia was aware – maybe not at the time, but certainly later – that he had questioned her authorship, telling Samuel Carter Hall that "He would not believe that they were written by the child whom he saw playing with his own children."[7] To try and ascertain without further doubts whether the verses were indeed written by Letitia and not by her cousin Elizabeth as he half suspected, Jerdan set her a test. Driving from London to Brompton one day, they passed St Georges Hospital. He challenged Letitia to produce some verse upon the subject. Immediately after dinner she showed him "a most touching poem of seventy-four lines" thus convincing him finally that her talent and facility were genuine.[8]

That the plan to get Letitia's work published was a family affair is confirmed by a letter (undated) to Jerdan from Mrs Landon, informing him that a friend "wishes much to see a trifle of Letitia's in the Gazette of next or following Saturday. The kindness her family have experienced from Mr and Mrs Jerdan will not be obliterated from the mind of Mrs Landon, it will give her much pleasure to hear they are all well."[9] Whether this was the "trifle" she desired, or another, Letitia's first published poem, "Rome", appeared in the *Literary Gazette* on 11 March 1820. It comprised seven four-line stanzas, and was signed with the single initial "L". Jerdan admitted "crudities" but thought "there was a redeeming quality in some of the epithets and expressions, and the sentiment of the whole an evidence of thought which broods upon its subject".[10] He felt vindicated by her next offering, "The Michelmas Daisy" also published in March, admiring its "touching simplicity" which was more in tune with the trend of the day and the popularity of the 'Lake' poets. Three more poems followed during the course of the year, one in August named "Fragment", that Jerdan called "the germ of the future L.E.L.",[11] the other two in October, all signed only with "L".[12]

Landon's social world was narrow as her parents financial burdens deepened and she went little into "society". She made up for this by creating her own inner worlds, fuelled by the extensive reading she had indulged in all her life. Her head was full of heroines, sacrificing themselves for love. She concocted long narrative poems, convinced of her talent; she had little interest in the commonplace, thinking herself extraordinary.

Jerdan had his own worries in the period of 1819–20. Debts and the needs of his growing family, (his sixth child, Elizabeth Hall Dare[13] was born in September 1820),[14] forced his attention to the circulation of the *Literary Gazette*. Books and poetry overwhelmed him, authors clamoured for reviews and notices, and he had to organize, if not write, all the other information the *Gazette* needed, such as filled the Fine Arts columns, and proceedings of the various societies. Jerdan's own love of poetry was inculcated by his eighteenth-century education; fortunately for him, and for Letitia Landon, the first quarter of the nineteenth century still enjoyed poetry of all kinds, and would-be poets were two-a-penny.

Jerdan acknowledged this in an essay, "Poetry" in the *Literary Gazette* of 3 February 1821:

> This is the age of versification: we know not how many volumes of first, of juvenile, of humble, of unknown, of indifferent, and of qualified essays in poetry, load our table. Unfortunately for those essayists who possess talents which, perhaps, only require development, this is also the age in which many distinguished bards flourish . . . Not to be among the foremost is now to be nothing; there is hardly a medium space between fame and oblivion.

The *Literary Gazette* was itself the 'foremost' of the literary periodicals, the best vehicle for Landon's verses. Even at such an early stage of seeing Landon's poetry, Jerdan recognized that she was out of the ordinary, and that it would be well worth his time to foster her talents for the benefit of the *Literary Gazette*. Fortunate as this was for the young poet, it was also a stroke of luck for Jerdan. "If Letitia really was the poet, and thus a 'child poet', she would be the marvel of his lifetime and, as his protégée, this 'divine' creature had the potential to become his most enduring triumph, her poetry lasting long after his magazines were no longer read."[15] Accordingly, from this time Letitia Landon was more than an occasional contributor. She became Jerdan's pupil, a situation that her family would have encouraged: an experienced editor who could offer the budding poet advice, and a paid outlet for her work, he was a family man who knew her as his children's friend, and she the poet whose parents were acquainted as neighbours with both her tutor and his wife. He recalled this time as idyllic:

> It is the very essence of the being I have so faintly portrayed, not to see things in their actual state, but to imagine, create, exaggerate, and form them into idealities; and then to view them in the light which vivid fancy alone has made them appear. Thus it befel with my tuition of L.E.L. Her poetic emotions and aspirations were intense, usurping in fact almost every other function of the brain; and the assistance I could give her in the ardent pursuit produced an influence not readily to be conceived under other circumstances or a less imaginative nature. The result was a grateful and devoted attachment; all phases of which demonstrate and illumine the origin of her productions. Critics and biographers may guess, and speculate and expatiate for ever; but without this master-key they will make nothing of their reveries.[16]

In such a hothouse atmosphere, flushed with pleasure at the interest the older man took in her writing, it is small wonder that Letitia Landon fell in love with

William Jerdan. The "grateful and devoted attachment" of which he spoke so many years later indeed provides the "master-key" to unlocking the real meaning of the vast quantity of work that Landon produced and is, with a single exception, the only clear and truthful admission made by either Jerdan or Landon about their relationship. But that was still ahead; at this time, Landon had published her first three verses in the *Literary Gazette,* and was about to write her first book, under the watchful protection of her mentor.

In August 1820, as she turned eighteen, Landon began to write a long narrative poem. Taking the first attempt with her, she left Brompton for a four months' visit, probably staying with her paternal grandfather at Tedstone Court in Tedstone Delamere, and seeing other relatives who lived in the area. Dissatisfied, she threw the first draft into the fire, finding it difficult to maintain her confidence without Jerdan's constant encouragement and presence. Reworking her ideas, she tremulously sent him the first of the poem's two Cantos, "too well aware of my many defects . . . your judgement will be most unmurmuringly and implicitly relied on".[17] Jerdan's reply was positive and greatly encouraging. This poem was the first of dozens Landon wrote to Jerdan, her first love. Supported by evidence from Landon's letters to her cousin Elizabeth, it has been clearly shown that he was the subject she addressed:

> the speaker seeks to convey to the beloved how he has pleased her, how she longs to please him further. After she tells the Spirit of the Harp, "I love thee, passionately love!" and "thou enchanting power, my love is thine", she sighs, "But there is a dearer bliss . . .
> ah! canst thou,
> From whom it came, paint the deep joy, or tell
> What the young minstrel feels, when first the song
> Has been rewarded by the thrilling praise
> Of one too partial, but whose lightest word
> Can bid the heart beat quick with happiness –
>
> . . . .
> It is my thought of pride, my cherish'd prize,
> To breathe one song not quite unworthy thee.[18]

It would have taken a strong-minded man to ignore such a blatant declaration from a young and innocent protégée. Jerdan's life was already full; there was a new baby in the house and now he was faced with Landon's open adoration, a heady situation he could not ignore. In telling Jerdan so directly of her feelings for him, she ran the risk of exposing herself to her readers, but she was promoted and perceived as such a child-like ingénue that no such situation crossed anyone's mind. Further verses were sent to him under cover of a letter from her mother, who asked for his opinion and tellingly mentioned, "I believe you are aware of her reasons for wishing to publish". Letitia was worried that she was very young to be rushed into producing a book, but the family needed the money she might make. However, another letter from Catherine Landon of 27 November assured Jerdan that "Without your sanction she feels herself without a hope of success and has no resolution to go on. She has upon her list more than sufficient to defray the expenses of publication – I do not mean by subscription." If Catherine Landon had actually read her daughter's outpouring of love, it is surprising that she would have countenanced sending it on to Jerdan, despite the pressing need for income. More probable is that she did not read it, having never been supportive of, or interested in, Letitia's poetry and story-telling through all the years of her childhood. She informed Jerdan that the famous actress Mrs Siddons, who was a family friend of the Landons, was "shortly going to Oxford, and as we have connections there, is taking it up very warmly".[19] Although in the end no help was forthcoming from Mrs Siddons, the book was dedicated to her, under the initials "L.E.L.". Letitia Landon's grandmother Mrs Bishop, who had independent means, largely paid for the publication of the new book. Jerdan never discovered the source of Mrs Bishop's wealth, "having a confused idea that she was the natural daughter of an aristocratic family", but the mutual affection between her and Letitia endeared her to him.

The Fate of Adelaide, a narrative poem, with additional shorter poems to expand the collection, was published in August 1821, as its author became nineteen. Jerdan seems to have been instrumental in finding the publisher, John Warren of Old Bond Street. Although Landon did not refer specifically to this book when she wrote to her friend Katherine Thomson in 1826, it is likely to be the one she meant, as her subsequent works were eagerly awaited. She told her friend, defending her relationship with Jerdan from the rumours that were then rife:

> I have not had a friend in the world but himself to manage anything of business, whether literary or pecuniary. Your own literary pursuits must have taught you how little, in them, a young woman can do without assistance. Place yourself in my situation. Could you have hunted London for a publisher, endured all the alternate hot and cold water thrown on your exertions; bargained for what sum they might be pleased to give; and after all, canvassed, examined, nay quarrelled over accounts the most intricate in the world . . .[20]

Landon's dreamed-of knight in shining armour had ridden to her rescue, guiding her through the perilous world. Or so it must have seemed to the young and utterly inexperienced Landon. Sadly for the success of her first book, the publisher went bankrupt in the same year, denying her any profit she was due.

A few periodicals reviewed *The Fate of Adelaide* quite favourably and the book, at 7s 6d, sold quite well. Jerdan did what he could to promote the book by reviewing it in the *Literary Gazette* of 4 August. His review failed to mention his own close association with the writer, even to the point of preparing the work for publication. Neither did he mention that the Miss Landon, author of the book, was that same poet who had appeared already in the *Literary Gazette* under the signature "L". Unusually for Jerdan where his friends were concerned, his review did not excessively praise the work. He mentioned her "exuberance of fancy, inequality of diction", but does praise some "touches . . . of genius". As reviewer he opined that "she has the feeling and genius of poesy in her mind, and if she cultivates its mechanical requisites, represses words, cherishes deep thinking and ponders on selection and polish . . . " she would greatly improve. In other words, she needed more tutorial sessions with him. These continued, engendering in Jerdan an emotion he could not combat. Watching over her, he idolized her, as she adored him.

> From day to day, and hour to hour, it was mine to facilitate her studies, to shape her objects, to regulate her taste, to direct her genius, and cultivate the divine organisation of her being. For the divine part was in Her! . . . impossible for me by any description to convey an accurate idea of the dual individuality of L.E.L. In exoteric society she was like others; but in her inmost abstract and visioned moods (and these prevailed) she was the Poet, seen and glorified in her immortal writings.[21]

The "dual individuality" which Jerdan referred to was a characteristic of Landon remarked upon by her later biographers; her ability to switch instantly from the melancholy in which her poems were often born to the gay and witty socialite her world demanded, the "mask" that she had learnt from her parents being used to protect her inner self.

Easy to imagine then, the editor harassed at work, inundated with six children at home, finding solace and gratification in teaching the brilliant and adoring young woman – a situation of mutual idolization, each fulfilling an unmet need in the other. The fact that he suspected her contributions to his magazine would attract attention and increase circulation was his bonus. Her's was the older man's attention and interest in her work and herself, after years of indifference from her own family.

Variously described by her "friends" in their memoirs, all agreed that she was no conventional beauty. Katherine Thomson recalled that she was at this time

> a comely girl with a blooming complexion, small, with very beautiful deep gray eyes, with dark eyelashes: her hair, never very thick, was of a deep brown, and fine as silk: her forehead and eyebrows were perfect; the

one white and clear, the other arched and well-defined. She was inclined rather to be fat; too healthy looking; and then her other features were defective — her nose was *retroussé*. Her mouth, however, without being particularly good, was expressive, and proportioned to her small and delicate face. Her hands and feet were perfect; and in time her figure, which had a girlish redundance of form in it, became slighter and ended by being neat and easy, if not strictly graceful. She had a charming voice . . . [22]

Laman Blanchard, her earliest biographer, described how

Her easy carriage and careless movements would seem to imply an insensibility to the feminine passion for dress; yet she had a proper sense of it, and never disdained the foreign aid of ornament, always provided it was simple, quiet and becoming. . . Her face, though not regular in 'every feature', became beautiful by expression; every flash of thought, every change of colour of feeling, lightened over it as she spoke, when she spoke earnestly . . . her mouth was not less marked by character, and besides the glorious faculty of uttering the pearls and diamonds of fancy and wit, knew how to express scorn, or anger, or pride, as well as it knew how to smile winningly, or to pour forth those short, quick, ringing laughs which, not excepting even her *bon-mots* and aphorisms, were the most delightful things that issued from it. [23]

A later sketch of Landon by her close friend Anna Maria Hall concurred with the dark hair, *retroussé* nose, and unremarkable mouth, mentioned the "peculiar beauty" of her ears, and concluded that "She would have been of perfect symmetry but that her shoulders were rather 'high'. Her movements, when not excited by animated conversation, were graceful and ladylike, but when excited they became sudden and almost abrupt." [24] The several portraits of Landon, mainly by Maclise, are unhelpful in picturing her; they do not resemble each other, and although Mrs Hall believed that Pickersgill's engraving was the closest likeness, Landon's image somehow escapes us, behind that mask she wore in public.

The year of Landon's first published book of poems was a year when much was happening in the world of poetry. Keats published 'Lamia', 'Isabella', and 'The Eve of St Agnes', with other poems including the now famous 'Ode on a Grecian Urn' and 'To a Nightingale'. Shelley's 'Ode to a Skylark', 'The Cenci' and 'Prometheus Unbound' appeared, as did Wordsworth's 'The River Duddon, a Series of Sonnets'. Poetry was still an immensely popular form of literature, and Landon's debut, nurtured so carefully by Jerdan, assured her a place amongst the best of her contemporaries.

Jerdan's treatment of the 'Lake Poets', Wordsworth, Coleridge and Southey, and of Keats, Shelley and others has been fully discussed elsewhere.[25] Although his politics were largely in accord with the former group, it has been alleged that he failed to understand, and disliked, the differing mysticisms of Coleridge and Wordsworth. Even forty years later he had not grasped the importance of Wordsworth:

> there is a strange incongruous mixture of the namby-pamby with the delightful, the ludicrous with the pathetic, and the affected with the natural in Wordsworth — that his poet eye never reached the sublime, or rolled in frenzy, but was chastened into a pervading sobriety of vision, which nevertheless included a magic sphere, sweetly adorned with grace, wisdom and purity.[26]

However, at the time he hailed Southey (whose ten-volume edition of Collected Works was published by Jerdan's *Literary Gazette* partner Longmans), as one for whose works "we have always felt the warmest admiration". He, or at least the *Literary Gazette*, never commented on any specific detail of Southey's poetry, as he did with L.E.L.'s works. In short, "The editor had no mind for subtlety. It is clear that poetry of grandeur was, for Jerdan, poetry in the tradition of Milton . . . In his reviews of Coleridge and Wordsworth especially are two of his outstanding weaknesses: his antipathy towards mysticism and his circumscribed concept of the proper diction and subject matter of poetry."[27] In this personal preference Jerdan clung to his eighteenth-century education, even though in his professional life he was keenly aware that literature was evolving at speed. Within two years of taking charge of the *Literary Gazette* he spoke of his paper as a principal organ of the "great literary revolution",[28] but for him the changes he welcomed veered toward the sentimental and gothic, embodied by the poetry of L.E.L. and Charles Swain.

He was unlikely to wholeheartedly welcome Keats, a friend of Leigh Hunt's and one of the derided "Cockney School". Nevertheless, the *Literary Gazette* gave *Lamia* its first public notice, with merely a non-committal sentence as introduction, but it carried in full *Ode to a Nightingale*, *To Autumn* and *Lines on the Mermaid Tavern*. Jerdan (or Landon) may have had little or nothing to say on these now famous poems, but a biographer of Keats observed that the quotations were probably of more value than a set review in the *Gazette*, "at least if it were written by the editor, William Jerdan, who was said by his fellow-journalists to acquire knowledge of books sent in by cutting the leaves and smelling the paper knife!"[29] This unnecessarily unkind assessment of Jerdan's reviewing abilities is obviously partisan, and equally obviously inaccurate. Many reviews were certainly of a general nature and relied heavily on lengthy extracts, but others showed an understanding of content and substance which demonstrated that the work had been looked at more closely, if not by Jerdan himself then by one of his reviewers.

Jerdan made an unprecedented, personal attack on Shelley upon publication of a new edition of *Queen Mab* in 1821, a unique instance of mentioning any writer's personal affairs, even including Byron's much-publicized immoralities. Jerdan expressed his revulsion in a lengthy four-page review in highly coloured language which he attempted to justify in a footnote to his article:

We are aware, that ordinary criticism has little or nothing to do with the personal conduct of authors; but when the most horrible doctrines are promulgated with appalling force, it is the duty of every man to expose, in every way, the abominations to which they irresistibly drive their odious professors. We declare against receiving our social impulses from a destroyer of every social virtue; our moral creed, from an incestuous wretch; or our religion from an atheist who denied God and reviled the purest institutes of human philosophy and divine ordination, did such a demon exist.[30]

Jerdan's diatribe indicated the *Gazette's* disgust at the gossip surrounding the half-sister of Shelley's wife, who had been living with Mary and Shelley in Switzerland in 1814. Jerdan's outraged sense of morality appeared to have seen no irony in his condemnation of Shelley's behaviour and his own nascent adulterous affair with Landon. He was more upset by Shelley's atheism, calling him an "incarnate driveller . . . miserable worm!", copying the verse containing Alastor's statement "There is no God", solely as a reason to call for censorship to "prohibit the sale of this pernicious book".[31] Instead of merely ignoring an earlier work by Shelley, the *Literary Gazette* reluctantly reviewed *The Cenci*: "We have much doubted whether we ought to notice it; but as watchmen place a light over the common sewer which has been opened in a way dangerous to passengers, so have we concluded it to be our duty to set up a beacon on this noisome and noxious publication".[32] This was not enough to satisfy the outraged reviewer who pronounced the work "a dish of carrion" and "the production of a fiend", but nevertheless quoted extracts from it, for the disapprobation of readers. Three years later, when Shelley was safely dead, Jerdan reviewed his *Posthumous Poems* more kindly, observing that "There is peace, and there is pardon, there is tenderness in the grave. That which in life is denominated crime, is by death almost softened into error, and Pity goes hand in hand with Reprobation."[33]

Whilst Jerdan denounced Shelley's personal immorality, he was busily engaged upon his own close relationship with Landon and with producing the *Literary Gazette*. When not nursing his new protégée, and running the journal, he had many other interests. One of the more important and far-reaching activities he became involved in was the founding of the Royal Society of Literature. Zealous and energetic as he was (and indeed claimed himself to be in all that he undertook)[34] he threw himself into this new project with enthusiasm. King George III had died in January 1820, succeeded by George IV. The new King began divorce proceedings against Queen Caroline whom Canning had tried so hard to comfort before she went into exile, and whom Jerdan had seen leaving Canning's house in tears. She had returned to England to claim her rights as Queen, again supported by Canning and Lord Brougham, and was garnering public sympathy. In July the King wished her to be tried in Parliament under a "Bill of Pains and Penalties", accusing her of licentious behaviour and proposing to dissolve the marriage. Popular outcry forced the abandonment of this trial, but Caroline lost much popular support by her attempt to force an entrance into the Coronation, in July 1821, when she was locked out of Westminster Abbey. Parliament granted her an annuity, but she died a month later, freeing George IV of a burden and embarrassment.

In November 1820, whilst all this was proceeding, the new King had other, more positive plans, including an idea which he asked Dr Burgess, Bishop of St David's, to put into action. (Jerdan thought that the King must have been happy to have a positive and optimistic project to work on, as an antidote to the previous long period of riots and political threats.) The Bishop in turn approached James Christie, a colleague of Jerdan's in the Literary Fund. Christie assured Jerdan that not only the King, but Ministers and Churchmen supported the idea of an institution along the lines of the French Academy, so that Literature would take its place with such established Royal Societies as those for science, fine arts and antiquities. Christie also believed that the new society would, as a side-effect, benefit the work of the Literary Fund by raising the profile of literature generally. Flatteringly, Christie wrote to Jerdan that his opinion was influential and asked him to speak favourably about the project. Of course Jerdan was happy to be invited in on the foundation of such an enterprise, one close to his own interests and especially as it was to be so well-funded by the King, who had agreed to donate one thousand pounds a year, and a hundred guineas annually for two medals for distinguished literary merit. Jerdan thought that the King was at heart a beneficent and generous soul, whose early "sensuous indulgences" had been caused by his pampered upbringing.[35] (Jerdan, it will be remembered, was always an ardent supporter of the King when, as the Duke of York, he had become embroiled in the Mary Ann Clarke affair.)

Accordingly, the *Literary Gazettes* of December 1820, reinforced by a front page feature on 6 January 1821, published the first announcements of the plan for a Royal Society of Literature, (mentioning objections to some inadequacies of the plan, although insisting "But to its spirit, none"), together with an outline of the prospectus submitted to the King, and Jerdan's own comments supporting its aims: "for the encouragement of *indigent* merit and the promotion of *general* literature", with the King as patron, and Dr Burgess at its head. Naturally this declaration was met with instant hostility by opposition papers. The *Morning Chronicle* denounced it as an "'extra-loyal' invention for the benefit of persons in 'high places' to meet", and suggested that a rival establishment be set up. This was never followed through and was summarily dismissed from Jerdan's mind. The *Literary Gazette* article was, unsurprisingly, praised by the head of the Society, the Bishop of St David's, who was delighted that Jerdan "has kept the subject alive ... put it on its right footing ... excited very widely those higher feelings in its favour ... capable of becoming a great instrument of national good".[36] Arranging to meet with Jerdan to promote the Society, the Bishop underlined the two main aims: to reward literary merit, and to excite literary talent. Jerdan himself objected to the phrase "for the encouragement of indigent merit" and proudly reported in the *Literary Gazette* of 17 February that it had subsequently been removed.

Several committee meetings had taken place before Jerdan was invited to join, on 12 April 1821. Many were called, but the work fell upon only half-a-dozen individuals. They judged the best poem on Dartmoor, for a prize of fifty guineas, which was won by Felicia Hemans. The main work of the committee, though, was to prepare the prospectus for publication, a frustrating and onerous task that Jerdan likened to Penelope's web, with "no end to our Odyssey". What was agreed at one meeting was changed at the next, the members attending only sporadically, so that the composition of the gathering was never the same. Nitpicking over specific words resulted in letters flying back and forth, but in May 1821 the committee met again at Hatchards in Piccadilly, believing that agreement had finally been reached. At the last moment it became clear that a spanner had been thrown into the works by Sir Walter Scott, (knighted in this year), who had made known to the Secretary of the Home Department, Lord Sidmouth, that he considered such institutions as the nascent Royal Society of Literature to be injurious rather than beneficial to the interests they espoused.[37] Sidmouth had passed this letter to the King, and then advised Burgess that the plan should not now proceed.

Horrified at the waste of time and effort he had so far invested, Jerdan went to see Burgess, urging him that to abandon a project that the King had personally entrusted to him would be disrespectful, and that the counter-order from Sidmouth should not be credited without recourse to the King himself. Using his "old-boy network", Jerdan wrote to Prince Hoare, an active committee member who was just then with the King at Brighton. Hoare brought the subject to the King's attention, to discover that the monarch knew Scott well, and realized that where the writer did not lead he was not inclined to cooperate, much less to follow. To everyone's relief, word got back that the King expected Dr Burgess to continue with his initiative. If Jerdan's account of the near-strangulation of the budding RSL is accurate, he could justly claim to have saved the institution by his mediation.

Having surmounted that hurdle, Jerdan continued actively to recruit high-ranking men of his acquaintance to take an interest in the RSL. To his dismay, Sir Francis Freeling, his long-time friend, declined. More mortifying, he received a note from George Canning, who had seen the plan in the *Literary Gazette*. His reasons for refusing to become involved were, he said, "partly general, partly personal".

> 1st, I am really of opinion, with Dr Johnson, that the multitudinous personage, called the *Public*, is, after all, the best patron of literature and learned men.
> 2[nd,] A much older authority, Horace, has described the general character of poets (in which other authors may perhaps be comprehended) in a way which would make it unadvisable for any individual who is already in hot water *enough*, as a politician, to prepare another warm bath for himself, as arbiter of literary pretensions and literary rivalries.
> It is obviously much easier to avoid belonging to the institution, than, belonging to it, to decline to execute its functions; and therefore I should very much wish to avoid it[38]

Jerdan had more success with the Duke of Rutland, the Earl of Munster, Lord Willoughby de Eresby, Lord Chief Baron Pollock and others. He also introduced two future presidents to the Society. His fellow council members were Bishops, Lords, a Marquis, Knights of the Realm, several Reverends and other respected, if less exalted figures – just the kind of company which his ambition relished. By the end of the year the RSL was in a good condition. Jerdan had his hands full acting as the President's deputy manager, correcting proofs of the Prospectus and involved in preparing and announcing the topics on which prizes were to be awarded in the coming year. When the list was finally published it was the season when the gentry left town, so that the committee dwindled to two, or often to only one. Jerdan remarked that he felt "like the one soldier from India, who represented Hamilton's regiment at the review".[39] The *Literary Gazette* continued to report on the activities of the RSL, as it did with the other Royal Societies, but this one was always closest to Jerdan's heart. In May he was a Steward at the seventh anniversary of the Artists Benevolent Institution, founded for relief to distressed artists, proving that his concern was not restricted to literary strugglers.

Although Jerdan was grateful to George IV for his philanthropic contributions to the cause of literature, it was George III, on the throne when Jerdan was born and reigning for sixty years, whom he wished to commemorate. His efforts were a long-drawn out story, but they began with a flourish in an advertisement in the *Literary Gazette* of 10 February 1821, where Jerdan's name appeared on the Sub-Committee. This was followed by a large sketch in the issue of 24

February 1821, of a cartoon by Wyatt for a public monument to honour the late King. Four prancing horses pulled an elaborate carriage on which stood the King, as Caesar, wearing a laurel wreath, wrapped in a flowing cloak, carrying a sceptre. Two angels complete with wings danced attendance, one blowing a trumpet, the other holding aloft a wreath. At the horses' feet were cannonballs and strange creatures. Jerdan's accompanying text described more fully the details on the car, which depicted Fame, Victory, Commerce, Arts, Agriculture and Religion. It was intended to carve the names of subscribers on the pedestal of the monument. Jerdan gave five guineas, and the Duke of York one hundred and five pounds.[40] The Duke of York had approved the design as did many of the "illustrious in rank and talent". This was to be a huge monument, befitting the great reign of the King. It was quite unusual for the *Literary Gazette* to include visual images, so the large space devoted to this ambitious drawing would have made a big impression on its readers.

It was another year before the *Literary Gazette* again referred to the monument. On 16 March 1822, a detailed progress report was provided, reminding readers of the prominent men involved in the project. All was proceeding well, until a plan was put forward to hold a public dinner on 4 June, the date of the late King's birthday, for the purpose of raising funds and promoting awareness of the monument. "Strong and active opposition" was aroused, and it was argued that Wyatt's design should not be accepted without a national competition, allowing all artists who wished to submit their ideas. HRH The Duke of York decreed that the anniversary day be merely observed by a dinner, but not used to further the grand project. It was to be attended by the usual great and good but, observed Jerdan, "Thus far the plan was patronized, was carried on, and was paralysed". Subscriptions had reached only five thousand pounds. The objections raised were discussed in the *Literary Gazette*. The writer pointed out that Wyatt's proposal could be executed as planned, and did not preclude the government or anyone else from creating a competition for a second memorial. The King, it was suggested "who had a monument in the hearts of ten millions of his subjects, is deserving of more than one tribute from the Arts, which he encouraged". This was a matter set to run and run.

There were numerous day-to-day problems in compiling the *Literary Gazette* so that it was ahead of the competition in reviewing new books. Timing was crucial, early copies were requested from the publishers, and because the *Gazette* was the most popular literary periodical in London, Jerdan was able to call the tune. With the best will in the world, outside factors intervened, as Scott's publisher was all too aware, when he wrote to Jerdan from Edinburgh on 5 January 1821, enclosing a copy of 'Kenilworth':

when I send it however I cannot but express some doubts about the date of publication – we ship on 9th inst. from Leith and if wind and weather were favourable the bulk might be in London by the following Saturday or Monday, 13th or 15th, but this is uncertain – and I state it thus candidly to you – were the book to get up so as to be out on the Monday, your announcement might appear on the Saturday preceding, that is the 13th, but if any ice in the River or contrary winds come in the way of this, the Announcement of the 13th would play the devil . . . "[41]

Such considerations would have made it almost impossible to time announcements of newly published books to be not too far ahead, and certainly not behind, those of the competition. In the event, Jerdan played it safe and the review appeared on 20 January. Making such judgments was merely one of Jerdan's every day decisions. Clearly, the impact of a review in the *Literary Gazette* was all-important to the success of the book and publishers would court Jerdan's co-operation in timing his reviews very precisely.

Contributors often became friends; Bryan Procter (the poet, Barry Cornwall) who, apologizing that he had no poetry to send, enclosed a hare instead: "You, in your wagging way will say that it has fewer feet". He asked after the "little folks and Mrs. J."[42] and another time suggested that Jerdan bring his daughter Mary to visit.[43] He embroiled Jerdan in his contretemps with the Rev. George Croly, who was offended that the actor Macready had given priority to a work of Procter's despite having been given the opportunity to see Croly's play first. Procter told Jerdan, "I have been endeavouring to serve him in several quarters – <u>Do not mention this</u> (of course) to him or anyone."[44] It was impossible for Jerdan to be detached from the hurly-burly of a wide variety of literary activities undertaken by his vast network of acquaintances, but as Editor he had to remain as objective as possible.

He could not always please everyone. The *Literary Gazette* was quick to denounce what it saw as 'humbug', both in painting and in 'shows'. It poured scorn upon a painting exhibited in Pall Mall by an Italian artist, at the sight of which the *Gazette* reviewer raged: "A miserable, indecent and offensive daub, as a work of art not superior to the pictures which one sees for a half-penny by looking through the magnifying glass of a peep-show, is placed in a darkened room, and by the paltry trick of lighting it from below, made to look like a bad transparency."[45] A later exhibition was attacked by the journal as "a waste of canvas . . . naked forms rendered odious and indecent by bad painting: such constitute the merits of this shameful and shamefully bepuffed Exhibition. We know of no visitors for whom it is fit, except the Agents of the Society for the Suppression of Vice; and we have only to add, that a more indelicate, nasty, impudent, trumpery show, was never offered to a British public."[46]

On the other side of the coin, a very displeased painter, T. C. Hofland, wrote to Jerdan in January 1821 complaining that although the *Literary Gazette* had previously spoken favourably of his works, "I cannot but feel some surprise and

I may add mortification, to find my name totally omitted from your account of the private view of the British Institution, particularly as I exhibit five pictures . . . "[47] The account had probably not been written by Jerdan himself, but as with everything appearing in the *Literary Gazette*, the buck stopped with him, and Hofland should perhaps have been glad to be spared the vehemence of some art reviews in the *Gazette*.

Others took criticism with good-natured humour, which must have cheered up Jerdan's day: a Mr Porden, possibly the distinguished architect, thanked Jerdan for criticism of his poem,

> and would gladly remove the objectionable verb if he were able, for he has so little of the irritability of a Poet that he would alter every word if (as in the present case) there were a good reason for it; being of opinion that in poetry no word or expression should be retained if a better can be found. But after some endeavours he has found himself too stupid to alter the lines in question, and he would rather print the verses as they are, or even forgo the printing altogether, than destroy the picturesque of the passage . . . [48]

Between January and June 1819 Colburn's *New Monthly Magazine* was edited by the twenty-two year old Alaric Watts. On relinquishing this post, Watts began a long and friendly relationship with Jerdan. He contributed both prose and verse regularly to the *Literary Gazette* for about three years between 1819 and 1821, and in Jerdan's absence acted as his 'lieutenant'. The fifteen years difference in their ages did not affect the warmth of their friendship, and even when their opinions differed, this did not change their fundamental respect and liking for each other. Jerdan regretted that, like himself, Watts "did not find literature the path to fortune", but he admired Watts's taste, intelligence and application to work. He was honourable and kind-hearted, said Jerdan, and often sought the advice of his senior, refusing work which might adversely affect Jerdan's own interests.[49] They had a common inaptitude for business matters. Watts, reported his son, "had, I think, much the same dislike to accounts that Dr Johnson admitted himself to entertain of 'clean linen', perhaps for something of the same reason, their cold, unaccommodating character . . . an 'account' . . . is justly to be regarded with apprehension by persons not skilled in the manufacture and use of such engines".[50]

Watts was clearly fond of Jerdan's family; writing to him on literary matters around 1823, he urged Jerdan to take his sons to an exhibition of mechanical models, saying that he had a smaller model by the same artist, which could explain the geography and geology of Montblanc to the Jerdan boys.[51] He also suggested they would enjoy the Automata Chess Player. It was in this same letter that Watts commented momentously, "I don't believe there are two <u>original</u>

thoughts in the whole of 'Don Juan'. It turns out upon close investigation to be a piece merely of elegant mosaic work though put together with a very delicate finger."

In his Memoir of his father, Watts's son commented that these criticisms of Byron would have attracted little attention but for the revulsion that was currently gripping the public upon publication of 'Don Juan.'[52] Until then, the reading public had largely sided with Byron in his marital difficulties, but 'Don Juan' presented a very different and repulsive side to Byron's character, causing readers to feel betrayed, as if they had been fooled in their judgment. Watts had been a great admirer of the poet, and had almost completed a work of scholarship in which he dealt with each of Byron's poems analytically, comparing each with passages in the works of other writers. When Watts showed him this work, Jerdan immediately saw that as it stood it would raise little interest, being too dry. However, with his journalistic experience, he quickly realized that directing attention to the similarities of Byron's poem to other people's work as noted by Watts, would certainly interest the public.

He accordingly advised my father to disembowel his production, and, casting his criticisms to the winds, or reserving them for future use, to concentrate the 'Imitations and Coincidences' into a series of papers for the *Literary Gazette*.[53] Watts insisted that his name as author be appended to the series, believing "that anonymous attacks are cowardly.[54]

This series of articles in the *Literary Gazette* accusing Byron of plagiarism was the means by which Watts came prominently to the public's attention. The articles were electrifying and were taken up by French literary journals, creating what Jerdan termed "A considerable sensation [which] led to much controversy at the time . . . a furious contest".[55]

Watts observed that the monthly periodicals waited to see the *Literary Gazette*'s opinion of new works before making their own pronouncement, especially in the case of Byron's alleged plagiarism. Watts received a complimentary letter from Southey, who praised the plagiarism papers. This was not disinterested as Southey and Byron were shortly to lock horns over the epithet 'Satanic School' applied by Southey and Moore to both Byron and Shelley, believing that their works were marked by a "Satanic spirit of pride and audacious impiety". Byron himself could hardly complain, as he had made a critical charge against Lord Strangford for stealing a single line from Moore; his own borrowings, as shown by Watts, were numerous. Such literary controversies were doubtless encouraged by Jerdan, as a means of increasing sales and readership of the *Literary Gazette*.

As fair and just as he always claimed to be, a few years later Jerdan printed a rebuttal to Watts's charges of Byron's plagiarism by Egerton Brydges.[56] Brydges's argument was that lines and language one has read lodge in the subsconscious mind, and when they rise to the surface cannot be told apart from one's original thoughts. Although giving space to a review of this book by Brydges, the *Literary Gazette* reviewer protested "This is any thing but convincing, for if true, there really is no such thing as plagiarism."

Amongst the deluge of correspondence, contributions and books for review which landed on Jerdan's desk, he especially enjoyed receiving a

> large folio sheet, covered closely all over with manuscript, and supplying me with rich and sparkling matter, to adorn and enliven, at least, two or three successive numbers of the "Miscellaneous Sheet". There was always a perfect shower of varieties; poetry, feeling or burlesque; classic paraphrases, anecdotes, illustrations of famous authors (displaying a vast acquaintance with, and fine appreciation, of, them).[57]

These welcome contributions came from "Mr Crossman" of Cork, in Ireland. The clever, volatile man hiding behind the pseudonym was discovered to be William Maginn, whom Jerdan was to know and befriend until Maginn's early death. Twelve years younger than Jerdan, he had taken a degree in classics at Trinity College Dublin and then assisted his schoolmaster father for a few years. Unlike Jerdan, Maginn completed his studies and in 1819 achieved his doctorate. Drawn to writing, he sent contributions to *Blackwoods* and to the *Literary Gazette*. "At that time, (1819) when Maginn commenced writing for it, the *Literary Gazette* ... conducted as it was with judgment and fairness, obtained extended circulation and considerable influence. In Ireland, more particularly, it supplied a great want, and was no where more esteemed than in Cork. Its great merit was that it kept its readers well acquainted with what was done, doing and intended in the literary world."[58] With his order for a subscription to the *Literary Gazette*, Maginn requested Jerdan to send him information about Swedish literature and books, as he wished to study that language. By the age of twenty-five Maginn spoke and wrote in German, French, Spanish, Portuguese and modern Greek, and could translate Hebrew, Sanscrit and Syrian.[59]

Having had the true name of "Mr Crossman" divulged to him by a mutual acquaintance, Jerdan thought that "the dénouement of the mysterious veiling is a memorable key to the real character of the writer who was, to the end, diffident and unassuming as one unconscious of his extraordinary endowments".[60] Maginn's own reason for the pseudonym was that his pieces were trivial, rushed off as they were between his obligations to school-teaching and the law, and did not deserve a "grave-looking" signature.

In the summer of 1821 Maginn made a short visit to London, to establish a personal connection with Jerdan and other literary figures. He arranged for his correspondence to be delivered to Jerdan, who brought it personally to him at the Angel Hotel, St Clements. Jerdan, always happiest in the company of the large group of Scottish and Irish writers who formed his circle, gave a party for Maginn at Michael's Grove, to introduce him to literary London. Letitia Landon was also invited to this party, perhaps natural in that she was a new contributor to the *Literary Gazette*, but a questionable judgment given the strength of feelings that were boiling away beneath the surface.

When the nineteen-year old poetess entered Jerdan's house to meet William Maginn, then twenty-eight, he was ready to be smitten, and was duly smote. She would have been delighted with his wide knowledge and linguistic skills, enough to ignore the stammer that overtook him "when under the excitement of wine or society". Her charm and wit entranced him and it was rumoured that he proposed marriage to her within a very short time. Landon's friends, Jerdan assuredly amongst them, thought it too soon for her to marry, especially as Maginn had no fortune and little prospects. Maginn returned to Ireland, where he married two years later. He gave up school-teaching and turned to literature for his living.

During this summer visit, Jerdan also introduced Maginn to John Wilson Croker, Secretary to the Admiralty and contributor to the *Quarterly Review*, to John Murray the publisher and to Theodore Hook of *John Bull*.[61] Maginn was thus quite indebted to Jerdan, both for printing his pieces in the *Literary Gazette*, and for his valuable literary introductions. From the evidence of a letter he wrote to William Blackwood, Jerdan's attention and hospitality was carelessly dismissed:

Jeradin (sic) of the L. Gaz. is an ass – but an honest fellow. We impose on him most horribly, he has published things which he would faint if he knew their import. I very often give him a lift, chiefly in the way of poems and parodies and such small beer . . . if you wish, I shall make use of him for you, and that in a way which he wd not have the slightest suspicion.[62]

Such sentiments do not show Maginn in a good light, and compare painfully with the glowing words that Jerdan used about his friend in later years, when the unfolding story between the two men involving Letitia Landon gave him good reason to speak otherwise:

Maginn, the precocious, the prolific, the humorous, the eccentric, the erratic, the versatile, the learned, the wonderfully endowed, the Irish . . . Romancist, parodist, politician, satirist, linguist, poet, critic, scholar – preeminent in all and in the last all but universal – the efflux of his genius was inexhaustible; . . . He jested and he mystified, and he laughed. He played with pebble-stones and nuggets of gold; pelting with the one, and hitting hard with the other . . . In any galaxy he was, indeed, a star of the first magnitude and greatest brilliancy.[63]

On 22 September 1821 the *Literary Gazette* printed the first of Landon's poems to appear for eleven months, an absence during which she had produced the *Fate of Adelaide*, received a marriage proposal, and fallen more in love with Jerdan. The September poems are the first signed as "L.E.L.", a change which "signals that the poet felt ready to be set apart; she felt certain she was good enough to begin establishing a poetic identity by letting readers know the poems were coming from a single source".[64]

The following week's *Gazette* carried an enthusiastic poem in response, by an anonymous writer signing himself A.H.R. For Jerdan, who clearly chose to print this tribute to L.E.L., the reader's admiration convinced him that when her verses were read by others, their not-so-hidden messages of love for him could be interpreted as generic and not specific. By the time he penned his "Memoir of L.E.L." in 1848, fashions had changed, and L.E.L.'s poetry had lost much of its following. Moreover, other memoirs had claimed that she had written her poetry from imagination and not through any genuine feelings, in essence that the social "mask" she wore was the real person, that there was no melancholy Poet behind it. These false reminiscences were more than Jerdan could bear. He wrote: "On the contrary, we think it impossible that such could have been the case with any mind that ever existed." He quoted A.H.R.'s tribute in full, daring only to comment "This seems to us to be no less faithfully descriptive than rationally and metaphysically just, but we must leave speculation to those who will peruse the poetry and draw their own conclusions." In suggesting this, he was not only defending L.E.L.'s genius, but encouraging readers to look again at her work, to keep her name alive because of her poetry, not for the reasons of scandal and titillation which were then ubiquitous.

Encouraged by A.H.R.'s response, and doubtless those of other enthusiasts, Jerdan moved L.E.L.'s next poems in November out of the insignificant "By Correspondents" feature into "Original Poetry". These, in the issue of 10 November, were the "Six Songs of Love, Constancy, Romance, Inconstancy, Truth and Marriage". They seemed traditional enough to appeal to readers who could identify with any, or all, of the situations she had tackled. Perhaps thinking back to Jerdan's party for Maginn, and covering herself for spending too long with her would-be suitor, "Constancy" declared,

> 'Tis love that gilds the mirthful hour
> That lights the smile for me,
> Those smiles would instant lose their power
> Did they not glance on thee!

In "Truth" she mused on two lovers on a deserted isle, realising pragmatically, "And then I thought how very soon/ How very tired we should be." Much of the lure and excitement of her passion for Jerdan was nurtured because of its secrecy, illegitimacy and danger; she was young, but she understood that enforced togetherness would be the death knell of love. She may also have made a virtue out of necessity – the impossibility of a marriage with Jerdan. In this series of verses she may have been toying with him; teasing and satirical, the 'Matrimonial Creed' with which she ended suggested that marriage is for money, not for love:

> He must be rich whom I could love,
> His fortune clear must be,
> Whether in land or in the funds,
> 'Tis all the same to me

This tone is a unique one in Landon's work. "Landon would never again so brazenly betray romantic ideals as she does at the end of these six songs, not in all of her writing over the next seventeen years."[65]

Jerdan marked the end of 1821 by inserting one of his own verses, signed 'Teutha'.[66] Perhaps in a nod to Keats he called it *Adonais*, but subtitled it, "Elegy to my Hat which I took from my Study and hung up in the Lobby last week, when very ill". It ran to seven verses, of which the first is more than enough for a flavour:

> Well! To your peg of brass, old friend.
> It soon may be, unless things mend,
> Worth twice the head you cover;
> These spasms a short time longer dealt,
> I'll feel no more than you have – Felt,
> And be, like you, all over.

Jerdan's love of puns quite often over-rode his judgment and sense of rhythm, but this was meant as a holiday issue of the *Gazette*, not to be taken seriously.

7

Out in Front – Problem Poetics

Keats and Napoleon had both died in 1821, events noted but probably not grieved over by Jerdan. However, 1822 started very sadly for him. He received news of the death of his beloved elder brother John Stuart who had distinguished himself in Kutch, at a cost to his health. Then a Colonel in the 5th Bombay Regiment, he was invalided and on his way home from India when his ship stopped at the Cape of Good Hope. He succumbed to illness and died on 8 January, aged 54. Jerdan allowed himself the indulgence of writing proudly about his brother in his *Autobiography*, sketching his military achievements, noting tributes paid to him as "a gallant officer and a most estimable man".[1] In addition to describing his courage and admirable qualities as an officer, Jerdan dwelt lovingly on his personal tie with his older brother and, in doing so, revealed himself to be well aware of his own faults and frailties:

> His letters to me were of infinite interest, and gave the most vivid accounts of Indian warfare and the manners of the people that ever I read; and yet a stronger proof of his superior intellect was afforded in those parts of his correspondence which were of a private nature. His fraternal advice to me, founded on an exact appreciation of my character, and those foibles or weak points which he thought were calculated to affect my progress in life, showed wonderful discernment, and could hardly be explained with reference to the distance between us and the few opportunities he had of studying that which he certainly understood so well. I used to be surprised by his acumen; and it might have been better for me had I been as sensibly instructed by his wisdom as I was impressed by his fraternal earnestness and astute talent.

The personal loss of such a man was severe indeed, but Jerdan may have been slightly soothed by a letter from George Canning, the postscript of which offered condolences for his bereavement.

The main part of Canning's letter, however, declined Jerdan's invitation to preside over the Literary Fund Anniversary Dinner in the Spring. Embarrassed,

Canning asked to be excused on this occasion, having refused innumerable similar requests, as "it destroys the roundess of my assertion that I do not frequent such meetings".[2] Castlereagh had recently committed suicide, and Canning succeeded him as Foreign Secretary and Tory Leader in the Commons, high offices which made him even more cautious than was his nature. In March Jerdan was elected to the General Committee of the Literary Fund, and continued to enjoy the Anniversary Dinners for many years. As well as being jolly social occasions, they were vital to keep the Fund growing. At this time Croly reported that in the preceding seven years the Literary Fund had aided 239 cases, dispensing the sum of £2294.

Mourning his beloved brother, Jerdan had other things to cheer him at this time. The publication of Landon's *Poetic Sketches* at the beginning of the year marked the appearance of her poetry in almost every issue of the *Literary Gazette* for that year. Eventually there was a series of six *Poetic Sketches*, comprising twenty-eight poems in all, appearing irregularly until 1825. Many of the poems described paintings and contemporary engravings, others came from Landon's imagination. The overall impression was one of repressed emotions, the cruelty of absent lovers, and hopeless passion – the antithesis to what was really happening in her life, another example of the "mask" she hid behind.

In the absence of new evidence coming to light, it can safely be assumed that all of Landon's poetic output at this time was written with Jerdan in mind, and addressed to him directly.[3] Knowing this, the *Poetic Sketches* take on an even more wild and daring aspect: "Call to mind/The arms, the sighs you leave behind." "Breathe not other sighs, love," suggest a sexual closeness to a lover, a closeness that to her readers was unthinkable for an unmarried young woman. If they could have had any clue or suspicion as to the truth, then both Landon and Jerdan were taking considerable risks. Her poetry was also targetting a wider audience than Jerdan: "The erotic hold that Landon may have had on Jerdan was translated into a more culturally acceptable reading in her general public."[4]

For the *Literary Gazette* the *Poetic Sketches* were invaluable, becoming L.E.L.'s 'trademark'. On the publication in the *Gazette* of 9 February of a eulogy "To L.E.L., on his or her Poetic Sketches in the Literary Gazette" by the Quaker poet, Bernard Barton, Jerdan appended a footnote: "We have pleasure in saying that the sweet poems under this signature are by a lady, yet in her teens! The admiration with which they have been so generally read, could not delight their fair author more than it has those who in the *Literary Gazette* cherished her infant genius. – Ed." Thus the mystery of the gender of L.E.L. was revealed. Claiming she was in "her teens" was clever of Jerdan, who knew perfectly well that within six months she would be twenty, but "teens" made her sound even younger, adding to her charm and interest. Even her new signature was a stroke of genius: "The three letters very speedily became a signature of magical interest and curiosity ... Not only was the whole tribe of initialists throughout the land eclipsed, but the initials became *a name* . . . "[5] Her works were eagerly awaited. Bulwer Lytton (see illustration no. 4) described the scene when he was an undergraduate at Cambridge:

> There was always, in the Reading Room of the Union, a rush every Saturday afternoon for "The Literary Gazette", and an impatient anxiety to hasten at once to the corner of the sheet which contained the three magical letters of "L.E.L." And all of us praised the verse, and all of us guessed at the author. We soon learned it was a female, and our admiration was doubled, and our conjectures tripled. Was she young? Was she pretty? And – for there were some embryo fortune-hunters among us – was she rich?[6]

Landon was writing prolifically, and Jerdan made room in the *Literary Gazette* for much of her output. The heat of their joint literary enterprise translated into a consummation of the sexual attraction engendered by the close association. At some point in 1822 their affair started in earnest. In his "Memoir of L.E.L.", Jerdan highlighted 1822 as the year when

> L.E.L. was as full of song as the nightingale in May; and excited a very general enthusiasm by the Sapphic warmth, the mournful emotion, and the imaginative invention, the profound thought and the poetic charm with which she invested every strain.

It was clearly a year imprinted on his memory, for the extraordinary situation in which he found himself – lover of a protégée whose poems were the toast of the town, part owner and editor of a respected and profitable journal, and established family man. Life was indeed good.

The speed with which Landon produced poems was astonishing. Her friend Sarah Sheppard remarked on her

> graceful quickness in every movement; so accordant with that rapidity of thought which is the especial attribute of genius . . . Everything seemed accomplished by her without effort. Her thoughts appeared to spring up spontaneously on any proposed subject; so that her literary tasks were completed with a facility and quickness.[7]

Jerdan already knew that she composed quickly – he had seen it for himself in her poem on St George's Hospital. He knew that because of the speed of her composition errors and flaws were inevitable, but he allowed these to pass into print unchanged, except for punctuation, which was never Landon's strong point. Maybe he felt that sometimes she should take a little longer, and more care, but that would have gone against her very nature, the nature of impulse, wildness and passionate emotions, of love and melancholy, which produced the rising success of the magazine, and the excitement of his own secret liaison with her.

Jerdan's attention to Letitia Landon had to be diverted to other aspects of his responsibilities as editor. At this time a literary quarrel erupted. Byron's *English Bards and Scotch Reviewers* called Southey a "Ballad-monger" and rhymed his name with "quaint and mouthey", ridiculing his works.[8] Southey published a paean to George III in 1821 entitled *The Vision of Judgment*, in the Preface to which he criticized Byron's verse, attacked Shelley's poetry and Mary Shelley's novel, *Frankenstein*. The *Literary Gazette* reviewed Southey's work harshly, doubly surprising as Southey was a Tory and Poet Laureate, and that the *Vision* was published by Jerdan's partners, the Longmans." ... we have no words to describe the mixture of pity and contempt and disapprobation with which the perusal of this piece has filled us", complained the *Literary Gazette*.[9] Jerdan's devastating review was to come back to haunt him later, when Southey took up the cudgels for Charles Lamb against the *Literary Gazette*.

A year after the publication of *The Vision of Judgment* Byron attacked Southey in a poem of his own, using almost the same title, publishing it in the first issue of Leigh Hunt's journal, the *Liberal*. This attack served to titillate public interest and this issue of the *Liberal* made the author a profit of £377.16s, of which he personally pocketed £291.15s.[10] Byron and Hunt were vilified by all who hated the "Cockney School". In a four-page article in the *Literary Gazette*, entitled "Southey and Byron!", the writer, almost certainly Jerdan, remarked that Southey's offence was "a common and venial crime when compared with the enormous guilt of his opponent, who links himself in the closest bonds with that abhorrence of humanity, the avowed Atheist, and devotes his brilliant talents, with fiend-like energy, to subvert all that is valuable in social life or blessed in future hope".[11] Towards the end of the year, in an article celebrating the winding up of Hunt's short-lived *Liberal*, the *Literary Gazette* noted that Byron had contributed "impiety, vulgarity, inhumanity ... Mr Shelley a burlesque upon Goethe; and Mr Leigh Hunt conceit, trumpery, ignorance and wretched verses. The union of wickedness, folly and imbecility is perfect".[12] There is an irony in the *Literary Gazette*'s support of this disparagement of Byron's style, as within the following year or two, L.E.L. became known as "the female Byron".

Byron's name was to bedevil Jerdan in numerous ways. This attack was the second time Jerdan had crossed swords with him (almost literally), the first being the occasion when he had made what Byron considered disrespectful remarks on his lines on Mrs Charlemont, "Born in the garret, in the kitchen bred" in *A Sketch from Private Life*, and had told Jerdan's travelling companion from Paris, Douglas Kinnaird, to challenge Jerdan to a duel, which never occurred. However, Jerdan never attacked Byron in a personal way; his quarrel was with the immorality he perceived in Byron's work. This was in accordance with the view he promulgated later: "In legitimate criticism the main and proper business of the reviewer is with the writings before him; and unless the writer dogmatically parades himself, or inculcates dangerous doctrines, there is not a syllable out of the work, either about him or his history which are within the sphere of justifiable remark."[13]

If, as the saying goes, imitation is the sincerest form of flattery, Jerdan must have been in a rosy haze of self-congratulation in the early days of the *Literary Gazette*'s success. It has been argued that as the *Literary Gazette* was the first periodical of its kind, any that followed had only the *Gazette* as their model, that it had begun "a new species", an achievement that can be credited in large part to Jerdan's efforts.[14]

Imitations abounded: The *Literary Journal* in 1818, which lasted a year and collapsed; the *Literary Chronicle*, which closely followed the content of the *Literary Gazette* had better success, commencing in May 1819, producing 471 issues until it merged with the *Athenaeum* in 1828; and the *Somerset House Gazette* based on the Literary Gazette, but focussed primarily on painting. This last short-lived publication was edited by W. H. Pyne, well known to *Literary Gazette* readers for his essay series 'Wine & Walnuts'. There were others too, that came and went, having little impact on the success of the *Literary Gazette*. In his *Autobiography* Jerdan recalled some of these attempts at imitation quite charitably, saying that "the majority were conducted with commendable talent and in a gentlemanly spirit of competition towards their model, notwithstanding that its pre-occupancy of the public kept them in the background".[15] The *Literary Gazette* was well known in America as early as 1821, when a similarly named journal appeared in Philadelphia, announcing that it would "be conducted very nearly upon the plan of the *London Literary Gazette*, an excellent journal which is deservedly popular." Unlike its model, it lasted for only fifty-two issues.[16]

Two periodicals stood out from the plethora of imitators. The first was Charles Westmacott's *The Gazette of Fashion, Magazine of the Fine Arts, and Belles Lettres,* published from February 1822 until January 1823. The second, eventually to have a defining role in the decline of the *Literary Gazette* and thus on Jerdan's life, was the *Athenaeum*, this latter magazine commencing only in 1828.

Looking back, Jerdan dismissed *The Gazette of Fashion* saying merely that it was "nearly occupied with attacks on me and the *Literary Gazette* and did not last long".[17] The long passage of time between the appearance of Westmacott's vicious journal and Jerdan's reminiscence had mellowed his memory. In fact, *The Gazette of Fashion* flagrantly and continually attacked Jerdan and his magazine. In the fourth issue, on 23 February 1822, appeared a twelve-verse song to be sung to a well-known air. The title was *The Tears of Longman's (alias the Literary) Gazette*. The refrain "When this Gazette was new" purported to extol the hope of high standards offered at the outset of the *Literary Gazette* and mourn the bitter disappointment that Westmacott suggested resulted from its actual performance. The first verse set the scene:

> When this Gazette was new,
> (Tho' that's not many a year,)
> We had, (tho' strange 'tis true)
> A prospect of good cheer.
> But now our wit decays,
> The public proves a shrew,
> And is wiser now-a-days,
> Than when this Gazette was new.

Referring to the well-known practice of Longmans to have weekly meetings, Westmacott did not resist the opportunity to make fun of this, too:

> Then J....n every week
> With L....n went to dine ...

and

> J....n seeks his source,
> And L....n looks quite blue ....

Westmacott brought into his verse the *Literary Gazette*'s well-known attack on Byron, and put into Longman's mouth the words: "Whate'er books you attack/Pass eulogies on our's."

In this, and more specific ways, he held up to ridicule the *Literary Gazette*'s so-called puffing of its partners' books, about which there is more to say as the *Gazette* proceeded. Westmacott's vituperation was unmistakable, subtlety was not his way:

> But now in vain we puff,
> The public wind the trick,
> And all cry out 'Enough,
> Much more will make us sick.'
> We sound the Pirate's praise,
> But ah! It will not do:–
> How diff'rent were the days,
> When this Gazette was new!

The very public feud grew worse. In issue No.10, in April 1822, *The Gazette of Fashion* printed a "Reply to the Duffing Coterie Longman's Duffing Gazette and the Mohawk Magazine". Eschewing his name, which indicates that Jerdan was well-enough known for readers to identify him, Westmacott wrote:"Callous as we thought him, our 'rack of satire' has extracted a groan from the chief of Literary Duffers. He pleads to our charge . . . we believe that there are more than one person attached to Longman's Duffing Gazette, who not only have an 'itching palm', but reason for hire, like the rhetoricians of Athens, on two sides of political and literary questions, at one and the same time." The accusation of bribery is plain enough. In response to the *Literary Gazette*'s attribution of imitation, *The Gazette of Fashion* responded: "First this Mohawk asserts that *The Gazette of Fashion* is an imitation of the Literary Gazette . . . God forbid that we should imitate any thing so maudlin and so vile, so brutally stupid and so impotently dull! We beg our readers to bear in mind that the Gazette of Fashion, from the commencement, has admitted nothing but original papers. It has not been filled like the Duffing Gazette, with thirteen pages of extracts, repeatedly dished up, and three pages of advertisements, principally relative to the book-making manufacture of the proprietors." There was some truth in Westmacott's accusation about the content of the *Literary Gazette*, but the fact remains that the original journal lived on long after the *Gazette of Fashion* had disappeared.

Westmacott continued to make his spurious claims a few months later, boasting that his sales had risen rapidly, with back numbers being reprinted. He claimed too, to have "exposed crippled and palsied the Duffing System". He called on his readers to sing triumphantly that he had bested the opposition: "That the Duffing Gazette should have the meanness to refuse our advertise-ments, was to be expected from its grovelling littleness." This was something of an own goal for Westmacott, who had advertised his *Gazette* in the pages of the journal he vilified and seemed surprised when Jerdan rejected further adver-tising. In his May issue Westmacott attacked various types of literary men, and could not resist a gibe at a (rather glaring) error made in that week's *Literary Gazette* which, published on Saturday, critiqued an actress's performance not delivered until the following Monday. In June 1822 Westmacott disposed of his interest in the *Gazette of Fashion*,[18] and for a while Jerdan and his journal were left to carry on in peace, reaping the benefits of Landon's labours in growing circulation.

The rising circulation caused pressure on space allotted to advertising; Jerdan allowed only advertisements directly connected with literature and the arts, but especially when Parliament was sitting, he had more demand than his space provided. Accordingly, he announced an occasional increase from one to three columns over his normal allotment, but pointed out that at other times the usual two pages were not filled, so the average would stay much the same. He assured his readers that they would not lose by this policy amendment as the type had been changed, and the current number "contains as nearly as possible <u>one third</u> more matter than a Number of the year 1819 . . . without detriment to the beauty of the sheet or the clearness and facility with which it may be perused!"[19]

As Jerdan was not known for his financial acuity, it may have been Longmans who suggested this increase in advertising revenue, as they were keeping the accounting records of the *Literary Gazette*. It made sense to take advantage of the increased circulation of the journal, largely created by L.E.L.'s poetry. A few months later Jerdan noted that a reader had suggested placing advertisements on a separate sheet so as not to encroach upon the magazine proper. The Stamp Act prohibited this, however, but the alteration in type, he claimed, gave the reader one-fourth more matter than it had originally.[20] The onerous Stamp Act was not finally abolished until 1855.

Vital to the success and increased circulation of the *Literary Gazette,* its star poet Letitia Landon was often beset by illness, by spasms, and, a theme recurring in her writing, thoughts of suicide. Her strong emotions, flowing into poetry, were a new and exciting experience for readers of the *Literary Gazette*, sensing a power of expression hitherto unknown from the pen of a very young woman. Paradoxically, although sharing the very essence of herself with the unknown thousands of her fans, Landon cherished her privacy, needing time to be alone, to write and to think, and several of her poems describe this need. Perhaps fortunately for the secrecy of her affair with Jerdan, Landon had no confidantes, and indeed, her friends were frustrated by her apparent self-containment.

If the readers of the *Gazette* had known what has now been revealed, that Landon and Jerdan had become lovers, they would have reacted very differently to the poem that appeared on 4 May. Jerdan recognized it as a key work; it is the one he referred to in his reminiscence of L.E.L. at this time as "excited . . . by the Sapphic warmth". The first poem in the second series *of Poetic Sketches*, L.E.L.'s *Sappho* looks back to a tradition of works upon this subject as far back as Ovid. Landon, however, changed the story in a crucial – and with hindsight, obvious – way, introducing an older man as Sappho's first love, "and attributes the magnetism of Phaon, her second and fatal love, to his resemblance to this unnamed man who, as Sappho's former tutor, occupied a role identical to that of Jerdan vis-à-vis Landon in 1822".[21] Jerdan could not but understand that 'Sappho' was meant for him:

> one had called forth
> The music of her soul: he loved her too,
> But not as she did – she was unto him
> As a young bird, whose early flight he trained,
> Whose first wild songs were sweet, for he had taught
> Those songs – but she looked up to him with all
> Youth's deep and passionate idolatry:
> Love was her heart's sole universe – he was
> To her, Hope, Genius, Energy, the God
> Her inmost spirit worshipped . . . .

He was moved by her image of herself as a young bird, using it twice in later life, once in a letter after L.E.L.'s death, attributing to her the words "we love the bird we taught to sing", a line he repeated as an epigram in his *Autobiography*. No poem of L.E.L.'s has this precise line, but the image of the singing bird being trained by its teacher, harks directly back to *Sappho*. Landon's poetic references to young girls tutored by older men, implied in the *Fate of Adelaide* and explicit in *Sappho*, must have flattered Jerdan, giving him further encouragement, if any were needed, to pursue the affair. From his point of view *he* was the wellspring of inspiration from which her poems emanated so prolifically, a view that Landon herself justified by the many oblique references made to him in her works.

Popular and successful as she was becoming for her regular appearances in the *Literary Gazette*, Landon was experiencing difficulties at home. Her mother thought her conduct with Jerdan was unbecoming and improper. Following bitter arguments, as reported by Katherine Thomson to Bulwer Lytton, "Mrs Landon to this day looks upon Mr Jerdan as the source of her separation from her daughter. As a mother myself, how could I blame her interference?"[22] Both Catherine Landon and the poet's close friend of later years, Katherine Thomson, believed Landon to be utterly virtuous, never suspecting any sexual connection with Jerdan. Just to be accused of improper behaviour with him was, Landon implied, highly offensive to her dignity, and it was for this reason that she left home. The rift with her mother lasted almost up to the time of Landon's death, when one visit and one letter were all that is known to have passed between them. Cousin Elizabeth, the tutor of her younger years, remained living with Landon's mother until the latter's death in 1856, both of them suffering considerable poverty. Elizabeth died four years later. Leaving her father was painful to Landon, and several of the poems appearing in the *Literary Gazette* during the summer of 1822 confirm this.

Landon moved to her grandmother Mrs Bishop's establishment in Sloane Street. This made life easier for her, allowing more freedom of movement, and also the opportunity to establish herself as an independent woman in society. Letitia Bishop had a private income, sufficient to support her granddaughter for a while, until Landon's writing started to earn her a living. It is entirely possible that she was well aware of Landon's affair with Jerdan, especially if she read the poem appearing in the *Literary Gazette* of 18 May 1822, entitled *Rosalie*: "We met in secret: mystery is to love/Like perfume to the flower; the maiden's blush/Looks loveliest when her cheek is pale with fear." Living with her grandmother gave Landon a context of respectability, although quitting her parental home was likely to have raised some eyebrows. Life was more fun now; she adored her grandmother, made frivolous caps for her to wear, and was allowed to have friends to visit. Jerdan was often among the visitors, stopping in most days for only a few minutes, longer on Sundays when he could review her manuscripts. Such personal attention was not the norm for a frantically busy editor, in demand from authors, politicians, publishers and printers. However, she was the star to whom the success of the *Literary Gazette* was hitched, so his frequent visits could, if necessary, be justified.

Now that she was not under her mother's disapproving gaze, Landon was able to go into society more; her companion and escort was frequently Jerdan. He had an endless supply of free tickets and invitations to shows of all kinds – freak shows, panoramas, animal displays, museums, exhibitions, theatres and concerts – everything that London had to offer was his to enjoy. Everyone courted the *Literary Gazette* editor, with an eye to a 'notice' in the magazine which would attract more visitors to their entertainments. In his self-appointed role as tutor, Jerdan was happy to take Landon to exhibitions of paintings, an art form he especially enjoyed, and one which was a direct inspiration for her poetry. Even before this period in her life, Landon had taken pictures and engravings as her subjects, and now she was seeing them at first hand, enhanced by the company of her great love. These outings were an important part of their lives for several years, and were uppermost in Jerdan's mind when he came to write about L.E.L. in his *Autobiography*:

> The world was only opening and unknown to her, and she might – even holding her child-like gratitude in view – both feel and say, "For almost every pleasure I can remember I am indebted to one friend. I love poetry; who taught me to love it but he? I love praise; to whom do I owe so much of it as to him? I love paintings; I have rarely seen them but with him. I love the theatre, and there I have seldom gone but with him. I love the acquisition of ideas; he has conducted me to their attainment. Thus his image has become associated with my enjoyments and the public admiration already accorded to my efforts, and he must be all I picture of kindness, talents, and excellence.[23]

These were not, of course, Landon's own words, but were put into her mouth by Jerdan, perhaps not for self-aggrandizement, but as a way of reassuring himself of the happy times they had shared, although when writing his book he was in a period of deep unhappiness.

Landon accompanied Jerdan not only to exhibitions of paintings, but also to the various 'shows' of the time. Charlatans showed mermaids cobbled together from disparate animals and fish, to deceive the viewer, and a merman was displayed, denounced by the *Literary Gazette* as "a fish tail, an ape body, the head formed of the wolf-fish, the skull of an ape and the fur of a fox".[24] It was the age of the "-ramas"(meaning 'sight'); the Cosmorama was a peep-show where magnifying lenses enlarged small panoramic landscapes. When it moved to Regent Street, the *Gazette* noted disapprovingly that it became "a more agreeable lounge than ever for the various ranks which may be comprised by titles of Idlers, Lovers, Young Folks, Amusement-Seekers, Ice-eaters etc. etc.".[25] The Naturorama was called a "trashy exhibition . . . you are allowed to look through glasses at miserable *models* of places, persons and landscapes, while two or three nasty people sit eating onions and oranges in a corner of the room."[26] The Diorama also came in for criticism from the *Gazette*, complaining about the lack of realism in the images shown. "For example, in this picture, when the waves rise and fall, why are the vessels stationary?"[27] The Diorama was built in four months at a cost of ten thousand pounds, the precursor of yet more "ramas", such as the British Diorama, the Octorama and Padorama, causing the *Literary Gazette* to comment, "the family of Ramas is already large, but it will soon increase to an extent which no verbal Malthus will be able either to limit or to predict, if its members are to be distinguished, like the streets of Washington, by numerical prefixes".[28]

Exeter 'Change in the Strand had staged a major exhibit of waxworks since 1812. This building, just opposite Jerdan's office, displayed "The London Grand Cabinet of Figures".[29] By 1825 waxworks were being used in pseudo-science, to the utter disgust of the *Literary Gazette*: "Under the pretence of imparting anatomical knowledge, this filthy French figure . . . is exhibited . . . as remotely from anatomical precision or utility as any of the sixpenny wooden dolls which you may buy at Bartholomew Fair . . . The thing is a silly imposture, and as indecent as it is wretched."[30]

One of the more bizarre shows was engineered by William Bullock at the Egyptian Hall. As part of a doomed venture to domesticate reindeer in England to provide venison and furs, Bullock imported a Lapland family to "drive a sledge around the Egyptian Hall against a suitably painted background, with sledges, snowshoes and domestic utensils scattered around the room".[31] Bullock took one hundred pounds a day in the first six weeks, but in January the *Literary Gazette* reported that the family were dejected and dilapidated. In March the journal noted that 58,000 visitors had come to see the Laplanders. Jerdan accompanied the exiles to the Haymarket Theatre and remembered "their ecstasies whilst the orchestra were tuning their instruments, only equalled by their disappointment and dislike when they came to play a tune. Lap (sic) ears preferred discord to harmony, beyond all comparison".[32] Much later, perhaps rather ashamed of the misery inflicted on this family, Jerdan recorded that they were returned to their native land "wiser, richer, and happier than any Lapps had been since their earliest migration".[33]

One of the consequences of becoming more involved with the entertainments on offer was that Landon began to write up some of the reviews, perhaps even those just quoted, thus taking some work off Jerdan's hands. It was also at this time that she took over reviewing some of the books that were sent to the *Literary Gazette*. As reviews were unsigned, it is not known definitely who wrote which review, but it would seem that Landon's pile included "publications in general literature, principally in the provinces of poetry, fiction, and romance". Her help was invaluable to Jerdan, and continued for a "number of years", according to Jerdan himself, "for she delighted in the work to the extent of craving for the employment, reading everything voraciously, forming opinions, and adding to her stores of knowledge, writing skilfully, and often beautifully upon her favourite subjects, and, in short, doing little less for the *Gazette* than I did myself".[34] It has been noted that "As the *Gazette* was one of the most influential journals of the time and had a notable influence on the sale of the books reviewed in its pages, Landon wielded a significant amount of power in this role, contributing to a decline of a number of literary reputations."[35] Landon may certainly have written sharp reviews to works she did not think of merit, but the final say was Jerdan's, who would not have published a poor review of something he thought did not deserve it. Kindness was his trademark, and he would have had to be convinced of Landon's reasons – she did not have quite the power attributed to her. It appears doubtful that she was adequately and properly paid for the work she undertook; maybe she did it for love, as a way of legitimately being closer to Jerdan on a daily basis, in a joint venture that was open and aboveboard. In a tally of Landon's earnings, Jerdan gave two hundred pounds as the total she made over ten to twelve years for all her contributions to periodicals and annuals, a niggardly amount for her huge output. Few accounting records exist from this period of Longmans publishing house, which handled all pay for the *Literary Gazette*'s writers between 1820–1841.[36] Jerdan's pay in 1820 for editing every three issues of the *Gazette* was twenty-one pounds, that is seven pounds per issue, or three hundred and sixty-four pounds a year.[37] There was clearly no recognized pay scale for contributors. It may have been that Jerdan was allowed a total rate per issue to pay his writers, and had to juggle the fees to spread the total as thinly as possible; in this regard Landon would have been low down in his priorities as she was happy for the work, had a roof over her head at her grandmother's, and for the moment did not have to rely on her earnings for a livelihood. He probably also weighed in the balance all the benefits she derived from his company in the way of outings and society events, and considered this a part-payment for her work.

Poems about paintings were a common theme for Landon, so in the summer when Jerdan introduced her to his close friend the artist Richard Dagley, who also wrote occasionally for the *Literary Gazette*,[38] she wrote three poems entitled *Sketches from designs by Mr Dagley*, published in August. It is the third of these, *The Cup of Circe* that may mark the start of her actual, as opposed to imaginary, affair with Jerdan. The lines were blatantly seductive:

> And by his side a girl, whose blue eyes, bent
> On the seducer, looked too innocent

> For passion's madness; – but lover's soul was there –
> And for young Love what will not women dare!

The metaphor of the "Circean cup" was in currency at the time – Jerdan used the phrase himself: "The Circean cup was gently replenished"[39] and it was well known that he was an enthusiastic drinker. Moreover, the "seducer" in L.E.L.'s poem was "a white-haired man", hanging on the brim of her wine cup. But who was really the seducer, and who the seduced? In the affair of Jerdan and Landon, it seemed an unanswerable question.

In the same issue of the *Literary Gazette* appeared *Isadore*, a story by L.E.L., of a nineteen-year old girl falling for a man for whom "the day of romance was over; a man above thirty cannot enter into the wild visions of an enthusiastic girl". Landon was a few days from her twentieth birthday, Jerdan had turned forty in April. Placed in the "Sketches of Society" column the story was more serious than was usual in that feature. Landon killed off her heroine who had been rejected, unable to get closer to her beloved than watching him with his "elegant equipage" and his "delicate wife". This is the first expression in Landon's work showing "that her tragic thrust is aimed at the shallow heart of London society".[40] Feeling herself to be somewhat outside of society, Landon had reason to think herself special. Her poems were like none written by a woman before, they were a song of love to her illicit lover, she was living a double life, hiding behind her mask. Jerdan, on the other hand, was a working journalist and editor, who would be vilified by his readers should the truth be discovered. He subscribed whole-heartedly to the myth of L.E.L.'s specialness, keeping up this belief thirty years later when he came to confront the subject of L.E.L. in his *Autobiography*:

> Of the gifted being. I cannot write in a language addressed to common minds or submitted to mere worldly rules. I must appeal to the feeling and the imaginative; for such was L.E.L. She cannot be understood by an ordinary estimate nor measured by an ordinary standard;[41]

Identifying herself with the 'outsider' in a society which she had only recently entered, Landon was strongly influenced by De Staël and Byron. She admired Keats and Shelley, and in this was again 'outside' the bounds prescribed for virtuous young ladies, who were forbidden to read these poets. The *Literary Gazette* was particularly vocal on the matter of morality, and Jerdan insisted that he published nothing that could not be read by young ladies, nothing that could upset their moral code. Jerdan did not want anything to do with Shelley and his subservience to love, and in reviewing *Queen Mab* Jerdan distanced his magazine, advising "A disciple following his tenets would not hesitate to debauch, or after debauching, to abandon any woman."[42] At first glance this would seem to be extremely hypocritical of Jerdan. He may not have "debauched" Landon in the sense that she was an unwilling partner, but he had definitely taken her virginity, compromised her position in society, and her immediate chances of making a suitable marriage. At second glance it has been suggested that both Landon and Jerdan saw social conventions as not applying to *them*, that they should join forces in combatting conformity.[43] This vision of themselves as apart from the common people also found voice in a poem Landon contributed to the *Literary Gazette* in September, in which the man who adores a princess is pitied and mocked by the common people: "They little knew what pride love ever had/In self-devotedness."

By September 1822 Landon's poetry became altogether darker, the first time she had her heroine poison or kill her lover, and penned one of many poems in which the heroine commits suicide. Reading such a poem would have disturbed Jerdan deeply, but his loyalty to her did not waver and in fact got in the way of his literary judgment when, in October, he put L.E.L. on the same pedestal as the long-established famous poet Felicia Hemans; he put the two of them above a pair of unnamed women poets aspiring to the readers' approbation, complaining that he had difficulty finding material good enough to fill his sheet, (other, of course than his protégée's, was what he didn't say). Comparing L.E.L. directly with Hemans in this way threw into vivid contrast her sexually-inspired warmth against the other's more commonplace verse.[44] Her success in the *Literary Gazette* had the effect of encouraging other periodicals to take women poets more seriously, opening more widely for them doors that had previously remained reluctantly ajar.

It was quite an achievement for Landon to produce poetry about pictures in a magazine which did not print the illustrations from which the poems derived, and she wrote another which appeared in the *Literary Gazette* of 16 November. This assuredly related directly to her affair with Jerdan, although the visual image was one popular at the time: *Lines Written under a Picture of a Girl Burning a Love Letter*, something Landon must have routinely done with Jerdan's personal notes, which would have been too dangerous to keep. As far as is known, none have survived. In her poem, the woman fears that love will be destroyed by secrecy.

In the meantime, however, Jerdan and the *Literary Gazette* were still the focus of the appalling Westmacott, who, earlier in the year, had jeered at him with *Tears of Longman*. As the attacks had subsided for a few months, Jerdan would have hoped that was the end of it. The truce was not to last long, however. In November the front page of the *Gazette of Fashion* carried a highly personal, abusive attack which may have been written by Westmacott himself although he was no longer the owner of the paper, or by someone whom he highly influenced. In a reverse kind of way, this attack throws a light on the regard in which Jerdan was held by the publishing community:

It may be deemed a little presumptuous to enter the lists against so formidable an antagonist as the Literary Gazette, more especially when we are aware that, however stupid and obstinate the editor of that puffing journal may be, he had an advantage on his side which no other literary quack in town can boast. Himself the leader of all the piratical and manufacturing authors in the kingdom, he has only, like the captain of a banditti, to sound his horn, and the whole host will attend his summons, and present a group of demi-devils, ready and willing to write and do any thing in defence of a reviewer who has sacrificed his character at the shrine of hack scribblers of every denomination.

The article went on to acknowledge the *Literary Gazette*'s right to praise works without merit, as the public could make up their own mind about the works concerned; it took issue however, when the *Gazette* defamed and injured an individual to gratify its prejudices, an act vulgar and contemptible, and to correct which the *Gazette of Fashion* leapt to the injured party's defence. All this hyperbole was an irony after it had criticized Jerdan himself so publicly and violently. Their complaint, it turned out, was a review of the actor Kean's performance, and quoted some of the *Literary Gazette*'s lines, which were indeed pretty brutal. The *Gazette of Fashion* deduced that, as had happened before, the reviewer had not actually attended the performance, and ended with the slashing comment that "It is rather fortunate for Mr Kean that the *Literary Gazette* is not consulted for theatricals, or looked up to for a candid opinion upon any subject."

The *Literary Gazette* and *Blackwoods* supplied different markets, but there was often cross-fertilization as Jerdan and Blackwood sent each other books to 'notice', the question of who was first to review being always a matter of pride. His tie with Henry Colburn was, from the beginning, a trial to Jerdan. Colburn was a publicist for the books he produced, and expected the *Literary Gazette* to rave about each of them, whatever the reviewer's true opinion. Jerdan insisted on independence, but in the event rarely gave a Colburn book a negative review. These concerns were a constant irritant, shown up in a letter he wrote to Blackwood in March 1823. "I hope you feel that the Literary Gazette is under no trammels as to the notice of your publication. I assure you the suspicion of that fact was utterly without foundation, as I would not endure a silk thread over my Editorship for any advantage it would bring."[45] If Blackwood wanted early reviews, he must send early copies. Furthermore, Jerdan had had to borrow a volume from Croly in order to review it, and demanded of Blackwood, "you should now send me a copy as *droit* and not put me to the expence of a purchase to replace what was besoiled at the Printers so as to be unfit for a Gent's library". To avert any offence Blackwood might take, Jerdan wound up his letter telling him that "Ebony's lucubrations are mighty favourites with me in general, and I take your little flaps occasionally with the best of good humour." Jerdan was often the butt of what he called 'flaps' here, and 'flings' in a later letter.

Whilst the competition was real, there was still a cameraderie between the two Scottish editors, unfortunately not reflected in Jerdan's relationship with his own partner. Colburn was the constant thorn in Jerdan's side, the latter often finding himself between writers and the publisher. Barry Cornwall wrote in March, "I don't see any Advertisement of my book. Colburn is determined to do as little as possible for it . . . It is just like you to take the vexation so good-naturedly – that little Colburn – but I won't rail at him now."[46] The *Literary Gazette* had gained great influence in the few years since Jerdan became Editor. Alaric Watts, who had worked for Jerdan for the past three years, advised William Blackwood in 1821:

> It is without exception the best advertising medium for books there is. . . . I would hint that it is worth your while to be upon civil terms with Jerdan, as he has it in his power to render essential service to your publications. A review in the *Gazette* is of use as an advertising medium . . . [47]

Certainly Colburn used the *Gazette* as an advertising tool for his publications, in a manner which caused Jerdan much trouble as time went on.

As an antidote to the petty squabbles and rivalries that were his every-day fare, Jerdan continued his close involvement with the committees and council of the Royal Society of Literature. Finally, in June 1823, following endless meetings, amendments, quarrels and tussels, a document setting out the Constitution and Regulations of the RSL was presented to the King. The whole enterprise was clearly important to Jerdan, as over thirty years later his memoir went into considerable detail concerning the specific aims, their realization, and the donations, legacies and annuities gifted to the Society. However, he didn't take it all too seriously, seeing the humour in an altercation which ensued over the name by which members could be designated, in line with the other Royal Societies. One or two of these Societies objected to the use of 'Fellow' for the RSL, and the Royal Academy argued against M for Member, as was their own designation. The ludicrous situation was eventually resolved by the adoption of a four-letter title, rather than the three used by the other institutions, and "MRSL" was agreed.

A sociable and always amiable man, Jerdan enjoyed larger-than-life people, and one for whom he had some affection and esteem was Rudolph Ackermann, a German bibliophile, pioneer of lithography, and publisher of fine colour engravings, notably "The Microcosm of London", published monthly between 1808–10. A large, heavy man, eighteen years Jerdan's senior, Ackermann was "sagacious and energetic, good-natured and liberal, simple and far-sighted".[48] His vast knowledge and odd manners impressed Jerdan, as did his heavily-accented language, of which Jerdan made gentle fun. Jerdan dined with Ackermann often when he lived at 101 Strand, then moving to Camberwell, and thence to Ivy Cottage in Fulham Road. Surely at one of these bibulous dinners, Jerdan told Ackermann how he had watched from the deck of the *Gladiator* as Nelson's body was brought home on HMS *Victory*, and in return Ackermann recounted that he had designed Nelson's funeral carriage and the emblems on the Admiral's coffin. Ackermann held "blue parties" where literary ladies outnumbered the gentlemen. Jerdan said that these artistic and literary *conversazioni*, which served to introduce artists to patrons, were the first in London and were subsequently enthusiastically imitated. Being of a charitable bent himself, Jerdan praised Ackermann's tireless efforts to raise money for the relief of widows and orphans in Germany, raising more than forty thousand pounds.[49]

Ackermann was of a generous nature, but when the *Literary Gazette* reviewed a publication of his somewhat critically, he was offended. He told Jerdan he had delivered some 'muzzle' (Moselle) to Grove House (Jerdan's home from 1825), on his way home to Fulham, and thought the review was a poor return, a "shlapp in the mouth".[50] Jerdan asserted that even had he known at the time, the gift would have had no influence on the tone of his review. He was prepared, and indeed happy, to receive gifts and benefits in kind, but recoiled at the notion of accepting "the gross shape of money", seeing this as a form of prostitution. Here, he parted company from a rival editor Leigh Hunt, who "would 'as lief have taken poison' as accepted a free [theatre] ticket".[51] Hunt pioneered independent theatre reviewing at a time when a notice was in effect an advertisement, in other words, a "puff".

Jerdan had been approached by publishers Rodwell and Martin to edit an annual, then unknown in England, following a successful German model, with many engravings. Finding that the cost could not be less than one thousand pounds, the idea was abandoned. Here, Jerdan missed a golden opportunity to be the editor of the very first annual, a position which could have made a great difference to his fortunes. However, Ackermann saw the possibilities of such a plan and in 1822 had published the first annual, the *Forget-Me-Not*, spawning a genre which had many imitators and which, for a short time, were immensely popular and profitable, despite the high costs. Not all annuals met the high standards of Ackermann's *Forget-Me-Not*. Jerdan snarled that some of the imitators were filled "by the names of celebrated authors who sold at a high price their names and sweepings of their studies for the advertising baits of A, B, or C, their contribution being public disappointments, and nearly all the rest of the starved book being unpaid mediocrity".[52] Jerdan contributed to several of these annuals himself as time went on, but was not then in a position to take such an elitist view.

Landon's risky habit of addressing her poems to Jerdan continued. In the first three months of 1823 inventors T. and H. Thomson advertised their set of twelve sealing wafers in the back of the *Literary Gazette*. In the same issues, Landon wrote her series *Medallion Wafers*, an early example of product placement. The seals were of classical subjects, and maybe for this reason Jerdan also 'noticed' them in his Fine Arts column. L.E.L.'s poems on the seals adopted the conceit that they were used for love letters, musing that "Here's many a youth with radiant brow/Darkened by raven curls like thine". A "youth" Jerdan was not, but he did possess a fine head of "raven curls". Another in her series harked back to the Circean cup, the wine that her lover was so attached to:

> She held the cup; and he the while
> Sat gazing on her playful smile,
> As all the wine he wished to sip
> Was one kiss from her rosebud lip.[53]

Her poetry upheld the idea of love as the sole happiness a woman could achieve, and deprived of it she could only be miserable, even suicidal. This was one of her masks: in her real life, Landon knew better than this. She was one of very few women who, if she needed to, could support herself by her writing, especially if she were properly paid for it. This must have given her a measure of satisfaction and independence. Love was a bonus. Jerdan kept her close, reviewing and writing for the *Literary Gazette*, escorting her around town to exhibitions and theatres, and visiting her when he could. All this did not compensate for an undivided, whole-hearted love such as most young women wanted and needed. Whether Landon felt guilt and sorrow over stealing so much of Jerdan away from his wife and family cannot be known. Nothing in her writing suggests remorse, even though as a child she had known Frances Jerdan, playing around her home with the Jerdan children. No letters have been discovered that give any inkling of Landon's thoughts on the matter, and in none of the contemporary biographies is there a murmur of her affair with Jerdan, other than to decry the calumny brought down on Landon's head as time went on. In the absence, therefore, of any evidence to the contrary, it could be assumed that Landon was so immersed in her feelings for Jerdan, there was no room to allow thoughts of his other life and commitments.

No writing of Jerdan's hints at any untoward relationship with L.E.L. save with the hindsight of knowledge of their affair, the part of his *Autobiography* discussing her, and his Memoir of her, are full of the emotion of an old man looking back on a past, lost love. However, at the time, he was not too careful when he treated her, in the *Literary Gazette*, as someone apart from the other contributors. As a footnote to a poem praising L.E.L., in the magazine of 29 January 1823, Jerdan let slip that he regarded L.E.L. and himself as editor of the *Gazette*, as one entity. He says that publishing this tribute to the poet "is something like self-praise by the *Literary Gazette*, but the many tributes we receive to the genius addressed in these lines will escape censure, when we acknowledge them as due to a young and female minstrel, and expressive of feelings very generally excited by her beautiful productions". He did not eulogize like this about his other contributors, mostly male, so this departure from his norm risked attracting too much attention. On the other hand, he had financial as well as personal interest in boosting L.E.L.'s public profile to keep his readers avid for more from her pen.

Early in 1823 Landon prepared a volume for publication the following year, under the title *The Improvisatrice*. Later she told Alaric Watts, "I wrote the *Improvisatrice* in less than five weeks and during that time I often was two or three days without touching it. I never saw the MS till in proof-sheets a year afterwards, and I made no additions, only verbal alterations."[54] At the same time she produced *Leander and Hero*, appearing in the *Literary Gazette* on 22 February, once again blatantly exposing the affair with Jerdan:

> And then their love was secret, – oh it is
> Most exquisite to have a fount of bliss
> Sacred to us alone . . .
> Love's wings are all too delicate to bear
> The open gaze, the common sun and air.

Or, she again implied, the understanding of the "common people". This was risky in the extreme, trumpeting the affair under the collective nose of the readers in a style never before seen in women's poetry. It was risky too on Jerdan's part, to publish it, flaunting his perpetual claim that nothing in the *Literary Gazette* was unsuitable for the eyes of well brought up young ladies. It looked like a game of 'Dare', chancing that L.E.L.'s devoted audience were so besotted with her by now that they looked no further than the surface of her emotional poetry. It was a private game, too. "We must never forget that love poems for the *Gazette* functioned as a part of Landon and Jerdan's affair; that she held up to him images of miserable women left alone who yet kept on loving, while, whatever else he did, Jerdan kept returning to her."[55]

In early April Landon became pregnant, unable to confide in anyone except Jerdan. As the year rolled on however, her changing shape did not go unnoticed. The situation was ripe for mockery. Although Jerdan's nemesis, Westmacott, had moved on from the *Gazette of Fashion*, he had not finished with taunting Jerdan. The editor was not his only target; Westmacott appears in the *Oxford Dictionary of National Biography* described as "journalist and blackmailer", allegedly extorting money from those who wished their names to be either omitted from his paper, or to clear their name from his allegations. He had been well paid by the King's supporters to vilify Queen Caroline, during the 1820s, which did not prevent him from turning his bile on the King later.

It was perhaps rather spiteful and foolish of Jerdan to give space for a notice of Westmacott's slim book, *Points of Misery* published in 1823. This collection of "chiefly original" work by Westmacott was under ten headings of Miseries, such as Authorcraft, Travelling in a Coach, Matrimony etc. The *Literary Gazette* review on 15 November jibed "It is a point of misery beyond any here adduced, to be obliged to read such sad and silly trash as these". Selecting a few (very minor) grammatical errors, the notice opined: "the letter-press [text] is altogether so contemptible as to be below notice . . . " Cruikshank's accompanying etchings were praised, sympathising that he had "such poor materials to labour on". The review concluded that "The handsome paper and printing of the work form a contrast to its slang subjects and low composition." Such a negative and cutting notice was tantamount to lighting the blue touchpaper to Westmacott's fiery temper. He published *Cockney Critics* with a dedication to William Jerdan as Editor of Longman & Co's *Literary Gazette*. Taunting, he opened with a quotation from Dryden:

> To hear an open Slander is a curse,
> But not to find an Answer is a worse.

His dedication declared that the satire which followed had two motives, to draw attention to Jerdan's name, and "to display both your name and character in its true light", hoping that the old-fashioned style of dedication would obtain for Jerdan "that *notoriety* to which your peculiar qualifications have so eminently *entitled* you". He accused Jerdan of having too high an opinion of himself as a censor and judge of literature. He was "a slaughterman of reputation, and you can flay poor authors with as much facility and something less of feeling than a carcase butcher does the bleating lamb." (Contrary to his intention, Westmacott thus confirmed to posterity the extent of Jerdan's importance and influence in the literary world.) Westmacott's diatribe was peppered with angry epithets: he belaboured Jerdan's "Billingsgate style", mentioned his "ravings on the Fine Arts", called him a "nameless thing" and "a hired oracle of an anti-literary faction". He fomented the row over Byron, citing the editor of the *Examiner* who noted Jerdan's dismissal of *Heaven and Earth*, and reluctance to pay a shilling for three Cantos of *Don Juan*. Westmacott compared this with the eight pence price of the *Literary Gazette*, "sixteen pages of little else than a mass of unconnected extracts from about a dozen books". The accusation of Jerdan's taking bribes which he had expressed earlier in *The Gazette of Fashion* surfaced again here, as did his anecdote about the review of an actress who had not yet given her performance.

Hatred and bile pour out of this so-called "Dedication". Jerdan's writings, he said, were "impregnated with sulphurous spirit"; he was obnoxiously sarcastic to those who "have not paid tribute to the Mohawk chieftain of the Cockney literati". For himself, said Westmacott, he was not to be bullied by such a reviewer, jeering that the "trifle" of his which received a poor review in the *Literary Gazette* was received and sold well elsewhere, thus proving "the best reply to your slanders and is a sure criterion of your critical abilities". Jerdan often remarked, throughout his *Autobiography*, that a critic cannot but offend those whose work they either find fault with, or fail to review at all. Westmacott's revenge is an overwhelming example of a writer so offended, and it was over such a "trifle" that he instantly sat down to write his "Dedication" and attack on his enemy. He stated unequivocally that he had long been an enemy of Jerdan's and had "eagerly sought an opportunity of exposing you, upon public principle alone", but his footnote to this sentence was more to the point: in case his readers missed the earlier attack on Jerdan, Westmacott explained that *The Gazette of Fashion*, when he was its proprietor, "exposed" the tricks of "*honest* William Jerdan and his associates", but he had then been subjected to steps taken by the "coterie" to silence him. The Reverend Croly allegedly threatened legal proceedings, though Jerdan himself, taunted Westmacott, "dare not" open his mouth at the time. Instead, Jerdan is accused of "pining in secret over his misery for two years" and had finally found an opportunity for revenge "by pouring out his exuberance of bile in a personal attack upon the author of *Points of Misery*". Had Jerdan in truth been har-bouring such a grudge against Westmacott, he would have come up with a rather stronger notice of his rival's negligible book. Furthermore, Westmacott's vicious attack was very personal, accusing him of "cowardice natural to your character" and of being an assassin, like a tiger springing upon defenceless prey. For him to point the finger at Jerdan's "revenge" is a blatant case of the pot calling the kettle black. In fact, Jerdan's review concerned Westmacott's *work*, not the man himself, and was hardly severe enough to be the fruit of two years' resentment, as Westmacott suggested.

Moving on from the personal, Westmacott set out his "general charges" against Jerdan: that, being the "hired servant of certain booksellers" (identifying Longman & Co., Colburn and Jerdan as owners of the *Literary Gazette*), he must "protect their interests and puff up their publications". Forestalling any response from Jerdan, he rejected any claim that Jerdan had only a share in the work, and was "uncontrolled", on the basis that the major owners were "two great publishers" and, as a junior partner, Jerdan could not act in opposition, by giving impartial or critical reviews of Colburn and Longman's books. Indeed if he were to do so his partners would withdraw, with adverse effects upon the *Literary Gazette* and its Editor. (Westmacott's prognosis turned out to be correct, but this was far in the future.) Not only was Jerdan guilty of 'puffing' his partners' publi-cations, raged Westmacott, but also of denigrating those of their rivals which were in competition against them., charging that this was "a shameful and degrading practice . . . it is a bold union of hypocrisy, malice and ignorance, and a weekly libel upon genius and common sense". Concluding this Dedication,

Westmacott declared it an honour to oppose such a man as Jerdan, "whose censure is the highest possible praise – and whose scurrilous abuse is the best passport to *good* society", and he challenged Jerdan, "Cease, viper! You bite against a file."

Westmacott then launched into the body of his work, a series of verses. The first, an Introduction to the Satirist, did not refer to his target by name, but his meaning was unmistakable:

> The foe of genius, learning's pest,
> A pick-fault, scurvy hack at best,
> Who spreads pollution o'er each page,
> And lives detested by the age.

And then

> Be mine the honour to expose
> The worst of all poor authors' foes,
> The BLOW FLY critic, senseless fool,
> The DEALER'S HACK, and willing tool,
> Who drudges on through slime and gall,
> And lives, to die abhorr'd of all.

Raising a head of steam in his next section, entitled The Blow Fly, Westmacott indulged in a torrential thesaurus of terms such as murky, filthy, vile, heartless, base, pest, curse, fungus, noxious, foul, slimy and so on:

> 'Tis he, the BLOW FLY, critic hack,
> Assassin like behind your back,
> Who'll use the poignard pen;
> You'll trace him by his slimy track
> From ★★★★★★★★★ to the Row and back,
> Where kindred tigers den.

Turning his furious spotlight away from Jerdan, Westmacott went on to denounce "Cockney Critics" in verse and "Cockney Criticism" in prose, railing yet again on his old topics of puffing reviews, partner publishers promoting their books and suppressing independents. "The Coterie" in rhyming couplets harped on a similar theme, followed by "Address of the Cockney Chief to the Coterie", replete with footnotes to strengthen his case against these detested men, especially mentioning Blackwoods and "a fraudful Scottish band". He also hit directly at William Gifford, editor of the *Quarterly Review,*

> Who doth usurp a sov'reign dominion
> O'er me, and all the sooty saucy *host*
> That under L★★gm★★'s banners are enroll'd
> To puff their publications in Gazette . . .

Westmacott's loathing for Jerdan went so deep as to imagine his enemy's death:

> Here rage and envy chok'd his breath,
> His tongue was speechless, pale as death
> His visage: Anon – his giant frame
> Convulsive heaved, with grief and shame;
> His eye-balls, starting, glar'd around,
> He fell, unpitied, on the ground.
> Hysteric laughter filled the room,
> The critic's requiem to the tomb.

Even after killing Jerdan off, Westmacott turned his venom on to George Canning who, he said, rose in status "by the wit of his tongue". However,

> Tho' now he vents his spleen at a second-hand stall,
> And prints with his neighbour at Blunderhead Hall
> At least, 'mong the wags, 'tis currently said
> 'Canning's silver is visible through Jerdan's lead'.
> A sweet reciprocity, tho' much on one side,'
> And that is not George's – these intimates guide.
> Will fathers the Minister's jokes with a grace,
> George gratefully gives to Will's offspring a place;
> And 'tis said, but I know not how far it is true,
> Will, himself, has a something worth having in view."

The author's footnotes to this passage confirm Blunderhead Hall as "Jerdan's villa at Brompton", and "Will's offspring", as "A son of Jerdan's is, I hear, in the Office of the Secretary for Foreign Affairs – One good turn deserves another."

Recalling the vituperation to which he was subjected, Jerdan admitted thirty years later that he had kept a copy of *Cockney Critics*, which still annoyed him then as it had done on publication. Not a man to avoid unpleasantness, he printed Westmacott's scurrilous Dedication and some other quotes from the work for the benefit of contemporary readers, to illustrate the level of opprobrium he had faced. However, he went on to recall "that the *Gazette* and its Editor, so serviceably reviled, reaped every beneficial consequence which was naturally to be expected – the former advancing rapidly in circulation, and the latter being (it might be unduly) more highly appreciated in social and literary life".[56]

In Jerdan's *Autobiography* he loudly rejected accusations that the *Literary Gazette* was a mere tool of the publisher owners. There is no reason to disbelieve him, as by that time he had no connection with the journal and nothing to lose by telling a different story. However, "Nothing could be more untrue than this libel" he claimed. "From first to last I never admitted a whisper of control."[57] In support of this, he quoted a letter from Cosmo Orme, partner in Longman & Co., referring to an unfavourable review of a Colburn book in the *Literary Gazette*. "Our co-partner may be sore; but the lady deserves all she got; and these independent articles do us a world of good", wrote Orme. On another occasion a particular review offended Mr Longman, who told Jerdan that if he could not be positive, he should refrain from any review at all. Jerdan, believing that his journal should report fairly on current literary works, refused to follow this practice, but even so it was widely believed that he followed Longman's precepts. It was of little comfort to him at the time that "I had frequent proofs in my possession where the very parties who spread the report were absolutely prostituting their own service venally to publishers."[58]

Jerdan's journalistic experience had taught him to be on the look-out for scoops for the *Literary Gazette*. He had already made good contacts among the men who had sailed with Captain Parry on his expedition to the Arctic on the *Hecla* and the *Griper*, publishing their accounts in his paper. Talking of Alexander Fisher's *Journal of the Hecla*, Jerdan "procured the publication and saw [it] through the press"; although he does not mention any payment for this, it was another occasion on which he acted as agent for an author. When the expedition returned from their second journey in October 1823, Jerdan took advantage of his friendships and was permitted aboard the ships at Woolwich, on a Wednesday morning, coming up with them to Deptford, where they moored. Amid all the bustle, he managed to acquire much information and arrived home late and tired that night. By working fast and furiously, he was able to give a good account of the expedition in the Saturday's *Gazette*, with a sequel the following week. His strenuous exertions earned an increase of seven hundred copies, so that at the end of 1823 the print run of the *Literary Gazette* was four thousand.[59]

Reliable circulation figures for the *Literary Gazette* are hard to come by, and those given by Jerdan in his *Autobiography* should be treated with caution, as he tried to remember events from a distance of two decades. In comparing figures from Longmans and from Jerdan discrepancies arise, so the following figures should be taken as a guide rather than as a precise statement of fact. In his *Autobiography* Jerdan mentions first year sales of 1250 copies, being 1000 stamped and 250 unstamped. This must be a weekly figure, as in the *Literary Gazette* of 16 June 1821, stamp purchases for 1817 were given as 53,600, an average of a little over a thousand a week. Stamp purchases for 1818 were given as 31,700 and for 1819 as 49,000. By 1820 there were 50,037 stamped copies. Jerdan claimed that unstamped sales were double those for stamped copies, which would mean a printing of 150,000 copies during 1820, an average of 2885 a week. This calculation is largely supported by Longmans' ledgers for January 1820 which show 2000 stamped and about 300 unstamped copies, plus a trade in parts and volumes.[60] Just as Tuckey's *Voyage to the Congo* had increased sales by 500 in 1817, here, discussing his feature on Fisher's *Journal*, Jerdan claimed an increase of 700 copies, raising the *Gazette's* print run to 4000 at the end of 1823. It therefore seems probable that by comparing the 1820 average of 2885 a week with the pre-Fisher's *Journal* figure of 3300 a week, the circulation of the *Literary Gazette* had been boosted by 400 copies a week, which coincides with the increased amount of L.E.L.'s poetry that it contained.[61]

Exhausted by his labours, and by the constant attacks he had suffered, Jerdan inserted a half-joking note in the *Literary Gazette* of 27 December 1823:

> The want of an Editor for the Literary Gazette is immediately anticipated, the present incumbent being nearly smothered to death under reams of heavy poetry accumulated from weekly loads. Candidates may send in their estimates of their own talents (if they admit of measurement); the wages are liberal, but no fees are allowed to be taken for advice, though it is daily asked under every possible shape of circumstances.

Four days later, Jerdan and L.E.L.'s daughter was born.[62]

8

Social Climbing

On 4 April 1824 Jerdan and Landon had their baby daughter christened Ella Stuart, at St. James, Paddington.[1] They gave their names as William and Laetitia Stuart, living in Paddington, with Jerdan's occupation as 'Gentleman'. It was common practice to use a mother's maiden name in cases of illegitimacy, and although this was usually the maternal mother's name, in this case Jerdan clearly had no objection to appropriating that of his own mother. In Scotland it was normal practice for a child to be given the mother's surname in addition to the father's, and although this had not happened in William Jerdan's own case, he would have seen no anomaly in using his mother's Stuart name. At about the same time that Ella was christened, Frances, Jerdan's wife, became pregnant with her last child.

Still heavily involved in meetings and the affairs of the Royal Society of Literature, Jerdan used the *Literary Gazette* to promote and support its objectives. In issue 374 of 20 March 1824 a report of an important meeting was published. This contained an error, describing the appointment of the Royal Associates as proceeding from a *carte blanche* given to the Council by the Sovereign. Jerdan swiftly received an anxious letter from the Society's President, the Bishop of St David's, who was concerned that the King could interpret this as a betrayal of the confidence he had placed in the Bishop. The *carte blanche* had been a personal matter between them and did not apply to the Council; the King had expressed his will, referred to in the report, "that no party or political feelings should be permitted to have the slightest influence in the proceedings of the society".[2] Accordingly, the next issue of the *Literary Gazette* included a correction. One of the first ten Royal Associates, who each received an honorarium of a hundred guineas annually from the King, was Coleridge. The honorary members represented both political parties and, keen to show there was no political or religious bias in the composition of the members, Jerdan recalled how he and Bishop Burgess nominated a certain M. Wiseman, "little foreseeing that he would become a Cardinal and the greatest Roman Catholic authority in England. It is almost enough to stir my venerated old friend in his tomb".[3]

The rapid rise of interest in gift albums had created a large market for writing

which suited this medium, periodicals were started and failed, finances everywhere were becoming a source of concern. Quarrels were inevitable in the fairly
small circle that made up London's literary world. No wonder then, that in such
a hothouse atmosphere, even the most sensible people found fault and picked
arguments over minor matters.

In 1824 Alaric Watts, who had been a regular contributor in the first years
of the *Literary Gazette* and especially renowned for his articles on Byron's plagiarism, founded *The Literary Souvenir*, an annual to compete, amongst many others,
with Ackermann's pioneering *Forget-Me-Not*. Jerdan, always willing to assist a
fellow literary man, gave Alaric Watts permission to use his name in seeking
contributors of some standing for the new annual and sent in an offering of his
own. Watts's gratitude did not prevent him airing grievances against Jerdan's
close friend and contributor the Rev. George Croly, and asking Jerdan's assistance in resolving the matters. They are yet more instances of the petty squabbles
which arose from competitiveness. Belligerently Watts announced "Mr Croly
has been acting a very paltry punt by me and I mean to tell him a piece of my
mind before he is many hours older."[4]

T. K. Hervey, editor of *Friendship's Offering* (and thus a rival to Watts's
Literary Souvenir), had been told by Croly that the poor review of his book of
poems *Australia* in the *Literary Gazette*, was at the instigation of Watts. Watts
had not seen the review but required Jerdan to "oblige me by giving me your
authority to say that I have never attempted to influence you by one word to
the prejudice of the young man. What motive could I have had – Nobody
thinks envy of Mr Hervey's genius!!!" The review, in July, merely said that "it
was not calculated to make a dazzling impression, but there is, nevertheless, a
vein of beauty in his versification which demands our notice and praise. His
chief fault is want of compression . . . a youthful poet of considerable promise.
He has much to unlearn . . . " Watts's other grouse also concerned Croly; he
wanted to "trace the affair home to Mr Croly. He wrote I am told a most bitter and invidious character of me" which was not printed as Croly was afraid
of reprisal. "We stand at bay. Let him look out", warned Watts. This may have
been a story Watts told to his son, who recalled much later that "Jerdan was a
man of genuine bonhomie, and an able and judicious critic. In his hands the
Literary Gazette was conducted in an independent and liberal spirit, unless, perhaps, occasionally, when politics, religious or otherwise, intervened. There was
a powerful clerical pen affected to its service in these days much concerned
with the interests of 'The Throne and the Altar' and very severe in consequence, occasionally, upon 'radicals' and 'atheists'."[5]

Another altercation was averted by the mediation of Owen Rees, a partner
in Longman & Co. Jerdan had reviewed the work of Dr Campbell, allegedly
insinuating that he had included forged letters. Rees insisted that Jerdan had
complete editorial control and, moreover, had supported a request of

Campbell's to the Literary Fund, a matter about which he had been most discreet.[6]

Watts, (whom Lockhart nicknamed 'Attila') was an influential journalist who supported the Tory party before and after his association with Jerdan and the *Literary Gazette*. His new venture, the annual *Literary Souvenir*, provided Landon with another outlet for her poetry. Authors such as Watts and Bernard Barton (who had written the first tribute to L.E.L. in the *Gazette*), ignored the overt tones of sexuality in Landon's poetry, preferring to uphold the virtuous, virginal character that was L.E.L.'s public face, first promoted by Jerdan, as the "young girl yet in her teens".

In the same year Landon's new book of poems *The Improvisatrice* was published. In a letter she sent to Samuel Carter Hall she recalled:

> It was refused by every publisher in London. Mr Murray said peers only should write poetry; Colburn declared poetry was quite out of his way; and for months it remained unpublished. In the meantime the fugitive poems with my signature L.E.L. had attracted much attention in the *Literary Gazette*, and Messrs Hurst and Robinson agreed to publish it.[7]

Jerdan had been instrumental in making the arrangements. The previous November he had sent Hurst and Robinson the manuscript of *The Improvisatrice* together with a press release, directing that the book should be published in March or April, and expecting that "the Annunciation will appear on all your own lists of channels; perhaps in the New Waverley Novels, which is very desirable; say in a slip at the beginning or end".[8] Although he was clearly acting here as Landon's agent, he wanted her to have the final word on the proofs. "The printing should proceed as fastly slow as possible: for though I will correct the press and do every thing in my power for the work, I should wish every page to be revised by the sweet writer whose intelligence will probably be beneficially exercised on the printed copy." He strongly recommended that Richard Dagley design the cover, and also a frontispiece. Confirming his status as a middle-man, Jerdan went on, "I have written to Miss L. to say I have concluded the arrangement with your House, that I shall, as soon as agreeable to you, have the pleasure of enclosing her a draft for thirty guineas, and that the profits are to be divided." Hurst and Robinson paid her three hundred pounds for *The Improvisatrice* and offered to double that for her next work. It seems odd that Longman and Colburn, both partners in the *Literary Gazette* and therefore benefiting from her popularity, refused her book, but perhaps they were not willing to take a chance after the poor sales of *The Fate of Adelaide*.

Once the book was published the press called L.E.L. "the female Byron, the English Sappho, and, after the notoriously independent eponymous heroine of Madame de Staël's novel, the English Corinne".[9] Even the *Literary Chronicle* which had been so cruelly derisive of Jerdan and of Landon's poetry gave *The Improvisatrice* a favourable review, whilst maintaining their contention that she had published too often for one so young.

The *Literary Gazette* reviewed the new offering in the issue of 3 July 1824 (see illustration no. 2). Jerdan overplayed his hand, as usual when mentioning L.E.L.'s productions:

> we can adduce no instance, ancient or modern, of similar talent and excellence ... simplicity, gracefulness, fancy and pathos, seem to gush forth in spontaneous and sweet union, whatever may be the theme ... her poems possess one rare and almost peculiar quality – their style is purely English. In the whole volume before us we do not meet with one ambitious word, one extraneous idition or one affected phrase ... it seems as if by some magic touch mean and household things were changed into the rarest and most brilliant ornaments ...

She would be immortal, he thought. Jerdan's personal taste ran to the sentimental, especially in poetry, and he could generally be relied upon to welcome such contributions to the *Literary Gazette*. However, his unfeigned and excessive admiration for *The Improvisatrice* was not universally mirrored.

He was accused by the *Literary Magnet* of puffing and partiality, of which he was in fact guilty in the case of Landon. The *Literary Magnet* (which would be owned by Alaric Watts between 1825–1828), devoted more than three pages to its review of *The Improvisatrice*, with minimal extracts. The thrust of their article was not so much to praise or to condemn the work itself, but to take issue with the Editor of the *Literary Gazette* for his unqualified encomiums. The *Magnet* called the *Gazette* "A literary journal of talent and celebrity" but protested that "when we see an instance of open bare-faced puffing and undisguised partiality, we cannot too strongly condemn, or too openly expose it". The *Magnet's* reviewer thought L.E.L.'s vast output to be of the same tone, love-sick, melancholic, sadly monotonous, and challenged the *Gazette's* view that the supporting poems in this book "totally differ from each other in sentiment and subject". "The chief fault which pervades the poetry of L.E.L." opined the *Magnet*, "is its unbroken sameness." Quoting a few lines from the *Death Song of Sappho*, he admitted it was "pretty" but could not accept the *Gazette's* opinion that "we are acquainted with nothing more beautiful in our language". This was not the first puff that L.E.L. had received from the Editor of the *Literary Gazette*, noted the *Magnet*, because as she supplied so much to that journal, "the wily Editor is not unmindful of himself". Outraged, the *Magnet* asked, "was the grave Editor of the *Literary Gazette* in his right senses when he sent the following passages to be printed?" referring to Jerdan's assertion of the poet's assured immortality. While the *Magnet* praised L.E.L.'s "high poetical feeling", it regretted that she had "fallen into interested hands, by which her talents are prematurely thrust upon the world, and rated so far beyond their merits". If *The Improvisatrice* had been published anonymously, it wondered, would it have been so lauded by the Editor of the *Literary Gazette*. As a final sword in Jerdan's side, the *Magnet* remarked sententiously, "we shall always remember that there is an unerring standard by which merit may be judged, independently of self-interest, favour or affection" – sentiments which Jerdan himself purported to espouse.

The Westminster Review grudgingly granted the poetry some limited merit, but attacked the book on the grounds that L.E.L. related too much of her poetry to "love". In the poem, they said, there was "very much that is mere verbage, and pages filled with puny and sickly thoughts clothed in glittering language that draws the eye off from their real character and value".[10] In July, Jerdan asked Blackwood quite baldly for a *quid pro quo*: "I am always happy when it is in my power to promote your interests – will you do me a friendly turn by forwarding the success of my favourite Protégée, L.E.L. *The Improvisatrice* where you can."[11] Blackwood complied with Jerdan's request and in the issue of August 1824 a review appeared, written by Maginn. The review was full of personal allusions, even giving Landon's address at her grandmother's house and directions for finding it. In the same issue, the "Noctes Ambrosianae" swung into action:

> "Odoherty (pen-name of Maginn) Literary Gazettes! What a rumpus all that fry have been keeping up about Miss Landon's poetry – the Improvisatrice, I mean.
> North. Why, I always thought you had been one of her greatest admirers, Odoherty. Was it not you that told me she was so very handsome? – A perfect beauty, I think you said.
> Odoherty. And I said truly. She is one of the sweetest little girls in the world and her book is one of the sweetest little books in the world; but Jerdan's extravagant trumpetting has quite sickened everybody; and our friend Alaric has been doing rather too much in the same fashion. This sort of stuff plays the devil with any book. Sappho! And Corinna, forsooth! Proper humbug!"[12]

Whilst Jerdan wanted publicity for Landon's book, he must have found Maginn's comments dangerously personal, and worried that Landon might succumb to such blatant flattery. Samuel Carter Hall, who had known Maginn in Cork back in 1820, commented that "Maginn came to London in 1823–4 with as large a 'stock-in-trade' of knowledge as was ever brought by one man from Ireland to England; yet it was profitless and almost fruitless".[13] Later in life, said Hall the disapproving teetotaller, Maginn frequently got drunk "like a tap house sot". Jerdan had taken Maginn whole-heartedly into his world, and in apologizing for a lack of contribution to the *Literary Gazette*, Maginn told him,

You must think me either dead or very careless. In fact I am neither. But my brain is dry of the affairs I used to write for you, and must get a new supply of moisture before I begin again ... Give my compliments to Mrs J. and my love to your fine boys and girls, or I should say girls and boys out of etiquette and politeness. And remember me to Miss Landon, thanking her in my name for all the pretty L.E.L.'s of her composition I have read since I had the pleasure of seeing her.[14]

Maginn's apparent charm hid a vicious streak of satire which he used to savage effect over the next few years.

Calamity struck the Landon family with the death, in November 1824, of Landon's father, aged sixty-eight. Her brother Whittington was still at University in Oxford, her invalid sister, her mother and cousin Elizabeth were left virtually penniless. Landon became the sole support of her family. Many of L.E.L.'s poems from this time reflect her grief at this bereavement. Despite this, and as ever alert to public tastes, Landon was aware of a shift away from poetry to fiction. She began to add short stories to her repertoire whilst continuing to write poetry.

There was an uneasy tension between the public's devotion to Landon's flowery, emotional, romantic poetry, and their interest in the freak shows of the period, to which Jerdan himself admitted an attraction. The 'ramas', waxworks and pseudo-scientific shows had been popular, and the display of unfortunate humans for amusement was not seen then as distasteful and degrading. The famous 'Hottentot Venus' had come to London in 1810, succeeded in 1822 by Tono Maria, 'The Venus of South America', who was displayed in Bond Street. She bore one hundred scars, one for each act of adultery. She was allowed 104 by her tribe, and would be killed on the 105th.[15] The *Literary Gazette* sought a lesson from this unsavoury display, that Englishmen would hereafter "pay the homage due to the loveliest works of creation, enhanced in value by so wonderful a contrast".[16] Another freak show was the 'Sicilian Fairy' Caroline Cratchami, who was nineteen-and-a-half inches tall, with feet three inches long. In its series, 'The Sights of London', the *Literary Gazette* was ecstatic. The reviewer, who may well have been Jerdan, fell abjectly in love with this tiny creature: "I shall visit her again and again, for she is to me the wonder of wonders. I took her up, caressed, and saluted her; and it was most laughable to see her resent the latter freedom, wiping her cheek, and expressing her dislike of the rough chin."[17] A month later he was back again, describing her appearance and behaviour. A month after that came the stark notice: "Our poor little dwarf is dead. She had been unwell for a few days; and expired on her way home, after enduring the fatigue of receiving above 200 visitors on Thursday last." The 'Fairy' may have been Irish, not Sicilian at all, thought the *Gazette*, but if so such a ruse was unnecessary, "the wonder of so minute a form sustaining the functions of life was sufficiently astonishing".[18] Crachami's skeleton is still to be seen at the Royal College of Surgeons' Hunterian Museum.

The 'Sicilian Fairy' was treated well in comparison to the 'Living Skeleton', who was put on display in Pall Mall in 1825. His skeleton too is supposed to be in the Hunterian collection, but has "unaccountably disappeared".[19] The same source points out that although the display was supposedly of scientific interest, even *The Lancet* called it a disgusting attempt to make a profit out of human suffering and degradation. The *Literary Gazette* furiously attacked the exhibition, railing that the owners of the poor creature made nearly two hundred pounds a week from displaying him, but had agreed to give him more rest time between shows. "Thus he is only required to expose his poor naked frame, in moist or dry, hot or cold, at one, two, three, four, five and six o'clock – to crawl and shuffle round the stage – to have his squalid trunk griped, and his clammy extremities squeezed by hundreds – the beatings of his miserable heart counted, and all his dying symptoms of bone, physiognomy, and distortion commented upon in his hearing, and in terms perfectly clear to his understanding." Angrily, the *Gazette* suggested such displays should be confined to hospitals, as a tourist attraction such as Bethlem once was, perhaps displaying two contrasting patients, one suffering from dropsy, the other from consumption. Despite his evident distaste for such 'shows' and sympathy for the plight of the poor exhibits, Jerdan would visit all of them, both for his own curiosity and more ostensibly, so that they could be written up in the *Literary Gazette,* where he could, and did, attack such barbaric cruelty.

Another, more respectable type of 'show', the exhibition of paintings, was given a boost when, in 1824, the National Gallery opened in Pall Mall with only 38 pictures. It quickly expanded, moving to Angerstein's house also in Pall Mall and, finally, to its new building in Trafalgar Square in 1838.

Whilst visiting all the wide variety of 'shows' on offer, Jerdan's main task was his journal, and encouraging talent wherever he found it. A twenty-year old Irishman, Gerald Griffin, had moved to London in 1823, and was a neighbour of Jerdan's, just as L.E.L. had been. Jerdan recalled that with Griffin he had enjoyed "a literary intercourse rather than a personal intimacy, though of the most agreeable nature".[20] For Griffin however, the acquaintance was more significant. In November 1824 he wrote to his brother:

Since my last I have visited Mr Jerdan several times. The last time he wished me to dine with him, which I happened not to be able to do, and was very sorry for it, for his acquaintance is to me a matter of great impor-tance, not only from the engine he wields – and a formidable one it is, being the most widely circulated journal in Europe – but also because he is acquainted with all the principal literary characters of the day, and a very pleasant kind of man ... There is a young writer here, Miss Landon, the author of "The Improvisatrice", a poem which has made some noise lately, who has been brought out by Jerdan and to be sure he does praise her . . . Jerdan has asked me to meet Alaric Watts at his house, when the latter comes to town"[21]

The following year he told his parents, "I set about writing for those weekly publications, all of which except the *Literary Gazette*, cheated me abominally."

Whatever his other faults, Jerdan tried to be a genuine friend to aspiring authors and to treat them fairly. In contrast, one wonders whether he was somewhat troubled by his unfairness to his family. In the same year that his and Landon's daughter was christened and fostered somewhere, his wife Frances gave birth on 10 December 1824 to Georgiana Leicester King, her last child. Six months later, on 19 July, Georgiana and her sister Elizabeth Hall Dare were christened together.[22]

By 1825 Jerdan had arrived at a time which would prove to be the best period of his life, successful professionally, personally over-endowed with a complex relationship, and now, the accolade of a bust of himself made by the sculptor Peter Turnerelli, was exhibited at the Royal Academy. To have such a bust on display would have made Jerdan immensely proud. The current whereabouts of this sculpture is unknown, and no image of it has so far been discovered.

In February 1825 Jerdan became a member of the Society of Antiquaries, on the recommendation of four sponsors that he was "a Gentleman deeply conversant in English History and Antiquities".[23] In March he paid his admission fee, and gave his Bond for annual payments. Thus in April he was elected a Fellow of the Society, and for a while was involved in its proceedings. In January 1827 his close friend Crofton Croker, author of the recently published *Fairy Legends of Ireland*, also became an F.S.A. and in his turn introduced as Visitors other literary men such as Maginn and Ainsworth. Crofton Croker was active in the Society, giving several papers. At a literary breakfast at Samuel Rogers's recalled many years later, Jerdan and Croker arrived arm-in-arm. They

> presented a striking contrast: the fairy chronicler being little of stature – some four-foot nothing – and Jerdan standing over six feet in his stockings. Little Croker had a shining bald head, a round dumpling, good-humoured face; and Jerdan a physiognomy of hard, Scotch character, that looked as if it had been washed in vinegar and rubbed dry with a nutmeg grater . . . The faces of these gentlemen were by no means indices of their respective dispositions, for it is well known that Croker is by no means indulgent to others; whereas Jerdan is a merciful critic, a kind-hearted man, and a fosterer of struggling men of genius[24]

Predictably, Samuel Carter Hall who disliked Jerdan, also did not have a good word to say for Croker, commenting: "I knew Crofton Croker during many years of his life: he was a small man – small in mind as well as in body; doing many little things, but none of them well."[25] Hall's wife, Anna Maria Hall, also wrote about Irish folk tales, and perhaps Hall's criticism of Croker reflected his loyalty to his wife as much as his literary evaluation of his fellow countryman. Known for his puritanical lifestyle, and never for his *bonhomie*, Hall also pronounced for no apparent reason, "I did not like Hazlitt; nobody did."[26]

Jerdan joined the Horticultural Society, acting as Steward at two of its festivals, and he also promoted the Artists' Fund, noting that there was no benevolent institution in London "to which I did not contribute with pen and purse".[27] One favourite amongst the many clubs and societies of which Jerdan was a member, was the Melodists Club, formed at the house of William Mudford, editor of the *Courier*. The company on that evening included Gaspey, Kitchiner and others of Jerdan's friends, together with the famous singers Braham and Sinclair; the after-dinner conversation turned into a dispute between the singers concerning their vocal range and where falsetto began. Song followed song, and this delightful entertainment was the foundation of the Melodists Club.[28] Their declared object was to encourage the composition of ballads and melodies, with performances both vocal and instrumental. It was a strictly run arrangement, with dinners at the Freemasons Tavern seven times a month in the season, that is between the end of November and the end of June. An annual concert was arranged for which each member received three ladies' and two gentlemen's tickets, and the public were admitted on payment of ten shillings and six pence.[29] There were rules concerning the copyright of the original compositions contributed to the Club. Their convivial meetings became famous for the variety of musical entertainments. From the outset Mudford was elected President, and Jerdan became Vice-President. He valued his association with the Melodists highly and was proud to have been a founder member. The *Age* made fun of an overcrowded Melodists' dinner a while later: "Will Jerdan stuck bolt upright in the chair, as stiff as John Murray, or the Mansion House kitchen poker. By-the-bye, we must stop a moment to enquire how it is that the learned pundit of the *Literary Gazette* contrives to cram himself into so many of these important offices, not that we are jealous of him, or seek to 'push him from his chair' . . . a merry, talkative, three bottle, hard headed gentleman like our friend Jerdan, is no doubt a great acquisition."[30] The *Age* was adept at damning with faint praise.

Literary Gazette matters filled up a large part of Jerdan's time, both in collecting material from his various contributors, and in reviewing major books himself. As a reviewer, Jerdan always erred on the side of kindness. There were exceptions, and he was only human – he could also make the odd mistake. Once instance of this, occurring in July 1825, showed the high regard in which he was held by a well-respected and important literary person, James Ballantyne, erst-while editor of the *Kelso Mail*, then Walter Scott's publisher in Edinburgh. Jerdan had reviewed Scott's *The Crusaders*, and in the last sentence had apparently made the error which upset Ballantyne:

> Any opinion you give as a literary man must of course be free from animadversion: but when you, an authority of great weight, personal as well as literary, tell your readers [that Scott had not written, only corrected *The Betrothed*] had anybody else fallen into, and published this utter error; but from many causes and especially from the uniform sense and caution which characterize your work, it does vex me as having come from you.[31]

Jerdan made a note on this letter, "My mistake about *The Betrothed*. I think Scott never quite forgave it." Scott and Ballantyne, having ridden a huge wave of popularity, were now riding for a catastrophic fall, caught up with so many others in the Panic of 1826. Whilst the financial world was in the state of turmoil which led to a crisis at the end of the year, Jerdan was able to concentrate on his own work. Still apparently in a good mood, 'Teutha' published a poem in the *Literary Gazette* of 25 June, following one of L.E.L.'s. His was entitled *The Inconstant: A Song*:

> Ah! Mary smile not at my woes,
> Nor mock my just upbraiding;
> When you to Henry gave that rose
> Your love to me was fading.
>
> I sacred held the oaths you swore,
> Then wherefore can you wonder
> When Mary Henry's favours wore
> Our ties were torn asunder.
>
> There's but one love – one way of love –
> Whole, changeless: and confiding:
> Let but a doubt th' enchantment move,
> And where's the spell abiding?

Setting aside such sentimental nonsense the following week, 'Teutha' was in punning mode with *The Anniversary – Epigram*:

> Keeping Tom's wedding day, his friends
> Boozed till their brains were addled;
> They frank his *bridal day!* Tom sighed,
> "That same day I was *saddled!*"

Landon would not have known which of these offerings to take as a clue to his frame of mind.

On 16 July 1825 Jerdan's sense of humour temporarily deserted him. In his "To Correspondents" column, he placed an irritable notice castigating a reader, Mr Clerc Smith, for sending an unpaid letter advising that "Agnes Somebody intended to publish a volume of poems. If the same judgment is displayed in that production as in sending such a communication by post, unpaid, we may expect little good of it." The following week he again inserted a notice concerning the unpaid letter, acknowledging that this was "poor rubbish to occupy any part of our Paper". Furious at these attacks, Clerc Smith went to the unprecedented length of taking out a large advertisement in the *Times* of 5 August. He announced himself as "Bookseller and Publisher of St. James's Street", and denied that he had ever written to the *Literary Gazette*, and had so advised the Editor, Mr Jerdan. Appalled that a third notice appeared in the *Gazette* of 30 July, Clerc Smith's advertisement described how he had gone to Jerdan's residence on a Saturday evening, "when, not finding him at home, he left a note pointing out the necessity for an immediate explanation. As Mr Jerdan had neither the good sense nor good manners to return him any answer", Smith had had no choice but to take out the advertisement to appeal against "a wanton and wholly unprovoked attack on the part of the above-named Editor, calculated as it was probably intended, to do material injury in many respects to Mr Smith's character and originating in some unworthy motive which he is wholly at a loss to explain".

In the *Literary Gazette* of 6 August, Jerdan ungraciously caved in, claiming that "someone has been playing tricks with Mr T. Clerc Smith and pestering us with letters in his name, which he denies having written . . . [and] has in consequence fulminated an advertisement in the Times Newspaper, against an individual by name, whom he improperly assumes to be the Editor of the *Literary Gazette* . . . Any complaint he might have, he ought to have addressed to 'The Editor', instead of visiting, as he relates, a private dwelling, and during the absence of its master, leaving an open letter which was calculated to alarm females. The Editor pledges his word that he did not even know who or what Mr Smith was and that he would be very sorry to do him the slightest injury." This was a real tempest in a teapot, arising out of a petty remark of Jerdan's, made on a bad day. His disavowal of being the *Literary Gazette*'s Editor was surely disingenuous, as his position was well known in the literary world in which both he and Clerc Smith, as literature-involved men, travelled. The whole affair seems to have been a practical joke on both of them, which could easily have ended up in a libel court.

While he was himself at the peak of his professional life, Jerdan never forgot that other literary men and women strove for a daily pittance, or sometimes for no pittance at all. One of the most successful features in the *Literary Gazette*'s early days was 'The Hermit in London', written by Felix Macdonough. Of the many desperate cases whom Jerdan helped to get grants from the Literary Fund, Macdonough's was one case which haunted him, especially because of the "extra humiliation of those who try to keep up respectability despite penury".[32] He had been on excellent social terms with the author for several years until Macdonough fell upon very hard times, and was imprisoned in the King's Bench. His application to the Literary Fund in April 1825 admitted that he had been "nursed in the lap of fortune the major part of my life passed in elegant life and in largely, indeed ruinously, assisting others".[33] He wrote to Jerdan, requesting support for his application and asking for "some literary work to do", signing his plea "Author of The Hermit in London" as if Jerdan would not otherwise recognize his friend. Even Henry Colburn was sympathetic, recommending that Macdonough be helped as "Whatever his actions have been, his writings have always upheld good morals." Macdonough had to write several more times to the Literary Fund pleading for grants, receiving ten pounds each time. He died in 1836.

In contrast to Macdonough's sad story, Landon was at the height of her popularity in 1825, when she published *The Troubadour and Other Poems*, inscribed to Jerdan, "This work so much indebted to his kind surveillance". As they had promised, Hurst and Robinson paid her six hundred pounds for it. This was more than they had suggested at the outset of negotiations, and the increase was due to Jerdan's intervention acting as her agent. They had offered her five hundred guineas, (£525), but Jerdan pointed out to Robinson that if the printing of three thousand sold out within six months, which he was sure it would, the firm would gross £1125 at 7s 6d per copy. After production costs of around £350, Hurst Robinson would make a profit of £775. In addition, profits on *The Improvisatrice* were estimated at £250, plus income from further editions. Landon needed the money immediately, Jerdan told Robinson, and asked him to add one hundred guineas to the five already offered ... "or say you do not like this and give her in addition to the 500 guineas offered, 20 guineas for every 500 edition after the 3000 are sold. I really hope and expect you will at once do one of these two things, for I have no doubt whatever but that these volumes will put the thousands in your pocket."[34] For a man who constantly claimed to have no ability for arithmetic, this was a surprisingly compelling letter and resulted in Landon's earning an extra seventy-five pounds for *The Troubadour*, which went into three editions.

This volume was reviewed at length in the *Westminster Review*, the writer finding the influence of L.E.L. "pernicious" by creating dangerous stereotypes of men and women, that she encouraged her young female readers to "weigh one man's merit against those of another, to keep her judgement in suspense, till she learn their comparative excellencies," and of promoting a negative male-warrior stereotype. (Was Landon privately thinking back to her marriage proposal from Maginn, when she weighed him against Jerdan and found him wanting?) This reviewer took her at face-value. It has since been noted that "Though adroit at analysing and criticising some of the formal flaws in L.E.L.'s work, this critic has no sense of the biting irony with which Landon consistently undermines the image of these 'heroes' . . . whenever one of her female characters becomes involved with one of these 'heroic' men, she is emotionally and psychologically destroyed and usually ends up dead."[35]

The *Literary Gazette*'s first review of *The Troubadour* appeared on 16 July 1825, most probably written by Jerdan himself, claiming that it was based on an incomplete volume, as the publication was not quite ready for the printers, (thus highlighting that the *Gazette* had the earliest mention of the book). Explaining that at this time he would abstain from reviewing the main poem, which consisted of about four thousand lines, it was nevertheless "calculated not only to confirm, but to augment and extend the fame of the fair writer". Despite saying he was not reviewing the eponymous poem, the reviewer, mused on the soul of poetry, the creative mind, and metaphysics, and told his readers, "*The Troubadour* is concluded by a finale, in which the personal sentiments of the author are distinctly expressed. Here she leaves fiction and fancy; and after a charming description of the effect which the success of her first work, and the praise it procured for her had upon her heart and spirits so as to lead her to begin a new attempt, she addresses herself to the contrast afforded by its close, when she lost a fond and affectionate father. We never perused anything more honourable to the head and heart of a poet than this natural and pathetic apostrophe." The insertion of this very personal detail about the poet's private life was highly unusual in *Literary Gazette* reviews, and underlines how, at least on this occasion, his intimacy with Landon influenced Jerdan's judgment of her work.

The remainder of this first review was then restricted to discussing the smaller poems only, with the usual extracts, from which Jerdan concluded, in language as emotive as that of the poet herself: "there are so many examples (all of the finest character in their respective kinds) of the deepest natural feeling – of heroic description – of moral tenderness sweetly turned almost in epigram – of poetic romance – of elegant and playful fancy – of elevated pathos – and of lowly interest; it will, we think, be a matter of wonder that it is a youthful female whose pen thus touches so great a variety of themes and adorns every theme it touches."

The *Literary Gazette* issue of 30 July carried another review of *The Troubadour*, with well over four columns of extracts. Tempted though he was to expand into a third week of review, Jerdan noted that he was not "inclined (eminently entitled as we think it is to such distinction) to transgress our usual habits, by carrying our review of a single poetical volume into a third Number". He recovered his objectivity enough to comment, almost in passing, in his conclusion, "We could see some light blemishes too . . . certain irregularities in the versification and some carelessness in repeating rhymes – but we have been too entirely delighted with the copious originality of thought and the ever gushing bursts of true poet-ical genius, to put one objection on record." A second edition of *The Troubadour* appeared on 31 August. The *Literary Gazette* greeted it rather more cautiously than the earlier reviews, though ranking it above *The Improvisatrice*. The *Examiner* cautioned Mr Jerdane (sic) to "be more discriminative and less magnificent in future, especially when a work has benefited from your own 'surveillance'".[36]

Under the *Literary Gazette* section 'Literary and Learned' on 1 October 1825, Jerdan gave a long quotation from the *Revue Encyclopedique*, considering L.E.L.'s *Improvisatrice* and *The Troubadour*. It was of course a review after his own heart, full of phrases such as "Love is the domain of the softer sex . . . the heart of a woman is an inexhaustible source of feelings and passion." Jerdan could only have been delighted that Landon was finding fame on the Continent as well as at home, thus reassuring him that his judgment as to her writing was sound, and not solely coloured by their personal relationship. The same issue that carried this review also had a long poem of Landon's entitled *Stanzas*, one of which was:

> Oh, tell me I shall not forget
> The lesson he has taught me
> Albeit I may not feel so much
> The woe that lesson wrought me.

The poem later said:

> I saw thee change, yet would not see;
> Knew all, yet what I would not know;
> My foolish heart seemed as it feared,
> To own thee false, would make thee so.

It is tempting to read into Landon's lines a shift in her relationship with Jerdan. Perhaps his eye had roved elsewhere, but if so, it was temporary, and they remained close as lovers and as colleagues.

Her poems continued to delight *Literary Gazette* readers, and almost any of them can be interpreted as relating directly to her affair with Jerdan. With their daughter Ella Stuart sequestered somewhere, and possibly unable to visit her often if at all, Landon's poetic mood was occasionally dark. In the *Literary Gazette* of 12 March she asks "Is this your Creed of Love? It is enough/To make one loathe the very name of love." She sounded jealous as if she had seen Jerdan's eye light on another:

> What must a woman feel,
> Whose very soul is given
> To that wild love – whose world must be

> Her all of Hell or Heaven?
> Then to meet the careless smile,
> Look on the altered eye,
> See it on others dwell, and pass
> Herself regardless by.

Another March verse was called *Love's Reproaches* and in April, she published *My heart is wholly changed*. Maybe annoyed by all this moaning and woe, in the issue of 9 April, Jerdan may have been making fun of her, as on the same page as two of her *Songs*, he printed a verse of his own called *Sickness*, and signed with his pseudonym, 'Teutha'.

The notion that Landon's poetry was written entirely with Jerdan in mind has been challenged by an alternative suggestion that she may have been fixated on an earlier unknown love, which had withered on the vine.[37] This idea is supported by a quotation from Landon's friend Emma Roberts noting: "an almost extraordinary want of susceptibility" in Landon's later attachments. This theory is possible certainly, but the evidence of the poetry itself points to her infatuation with Jerdan; perhaps the lack of "susceptibility" was a defensive expression of a (necessarily) selfish character trait exacerbated by watching difficulties in her parents' marriage.

Landon's portrait had been painted by Pickersgill and was exhibited at the Royal Academy. The *Literary Gazette* of 28 May 1825 took special notice of it:

> We have no intention to disguise our knowledge or our admiration of the talents of L.E.L., the author of 'The Improvisatrice' and of numerous poems which have adorned and enriched the numbers of the Literary Gazette; or the excellence of which has been fully recognized by the world of letters, as well as by the public at large. Of the portrait, and its merit as a work of art, we may fairly and truly say, that it is among the happier efforts of the truly able artist's pencil, both in its picturesque arrangement, and its character and expression – where we may venture to quote of the subject, as well as in compliment to his talents, that
> > "There's inspiration in that look, and the rapt eye,
> > Beams with the powers of mental exstacy."

Jerdan was letting himself get carried away with his very partial account of this one portrait, so betraying a most personal interest in its subject (see illustration no. 4).[38]

In recognition of the truth of his statement about Landon's appeal to "the public at large," by the end of 1825 Jerdan had expanded the 'Original Poetry' section of the *Literary Gazette*, sometimes to five or six full columns, mostly filled with the outpourings of L.E.L. In the year-end Index he noted for the first time,

"The poetry of L.E.L. can be found in pages ... ", thus acknowledging that many readers often bought his magazine largely because of her poetry. Another woman poet's first appearance in print was in the *Literary Gazette* of 19 November 1825. Elizabeth Barrett (later Browning), signing her verse E.B.B., contributed *The Rose and the Zephyr*, a feather in Jerdan's cap that he could not have been aware of at the time, and maybe not even later, as he did not mention this debut in his *Autobiography*.

Following the birth of the daughter she could not acknowledge or care for, and the death of her beloved father, Landon had another sadness to contend with. Her sickly little sister Elizabeth died at the age of thirteen, apparently from consumption. These weighty matters, although doubtless felt deeply by Landon, were hidden behind her social mask. Through Jerdan's contacts and, as her popularity grew, on her own account, she was invited to literary salons, welcome and fêted everywhere. Her wit and gaiety were remarked upon. However, even the adoring and sentimental Jerdan noted that "In mixed society she was brilliant and witty, and perhaps it would have been safer and better for herself if she had not also been, with a strong sense of the ridiculous, also sarcastic. This turn, in fact, provoked some to become her enemies, whilst those who knew her were perfectly aware that the character of the satirist was only assumed, and that there was not one grain of ill-will or spitefulness in her disposition. It was, however, a fault, and she paid dearly for it."[39] Another friend of Landon's commented that "the very unguardedness of her innocence served to arm even the feeblest malice with powerful stings; the openness of her nature, and the frankness of her manners, furnished the silly or the ill-natured with abundant materials for gossip. She was always careless as a child of set forms and rules for conduct".[40] When recalling her so fondly for his *Autobiography*, Jerdan put her in yet another, softer, light:

I found in L.E.L. a creature of another sphere, though with fascination which could render her most lovable in our every-day world. The exquisite simplicity of childhood, the fine form of womanhood, the sweetest of dispositions, the utmost charm of unaffected manners, and above all, an impassioned ideal and poetical temperament which absorbed her existence and held all else comparatively as nothing.[41]

There are other glimpses of Landon at this time showing her as playful and affectionate to her grandmother with whom she was still living in Sloane Street. "L.E.L. was a social being and young as she then was – little more than twenty-three – had the gift, so perfect in France, so rare in England, of receiving well. Nothing could be more lively than these little social meetings, and nothing more unexceptionable."[42] The author, Katherine Thomson, was the wife of Landon's physician, Anthony Todd Thomson. She wrote *Queens of Society* with her son

John Cockburn Thomson in 1860, (under the pen names of Grace and Philip Wharton), and included a chapter on Landon. It must be noted that Katherine Thomson's account of L.E.L. in that book is somewhat of a hagiography, and has some factual errors, unsurprising given the lapse of time between the events and her memoir. She remembered her friend as several years younger than her actual age when her early works were published. Her affection for L.E.L. and her eagerness to insist on her friend's adherence to the social mores demanded of a single woman, make her memories unreliable as a source of factual information. Her account is, however, a valuable documentation of how L.E.L. would have been regarded by her readership in general and certainly the female readers. They enjoyed the frisson and titillation of the passionate poetry, whilst believing strongly in the purity and innocence of the author. Landon's other friend and early biographer was Anna Maria Hall, wife of Samuel Carter Hall, both writers. Samuel, at various times, was editor of *New Monthly Magazine, The Amulet* and, in the later part of his life, *The Art Journal*. The memoirs of both these women became the source of much that was known about Landon although they both had their own agendas to ensure that the Landon of their memories remained innocent and pure. Mrs Hall claimed to have seen Landon almost every day and certainly every week for the next thirteen years, a claim which, with that of her other close friend the Doctor's wife, leaves one to wonder how the plain fact of L.E.L.'s next two pregnancies escaped notice. If they were aware of them, both of these close friends were at pains to ignore the facts and to champion Landon's innocence and vilify her victimization in their memoirs of her.

The author William Howitt observed that one had the feeling Landon was playing an assumed part, and that "she seemed to say things for the sake of astonishing you with the very contrast. You felt not only no confidence in the truth of what she was asserting, but a strong assurance that it was said merely for the sake of saying what her hearers would least expect her to say."[43] Howitt had clearly noticed Landon's habit of hiding behind a mask. His wife wrote about Landon in a letter of 28 October 1824, referring to her as "a ward of Jerdan's", that "She is . . . a most thoughtless girl in company, doing strange extravagant things; for instance making a wreath of flowers, then rushing with it into a grave and numerous party, and placing it on her patron's head."[44]

Landon's social circle now expanded to the 'blue-stocking' literary salon of the be-turbanned Miss Spence who, with her even more gloriously beturbanned co-hostess Miss Benger, attracted "litterateurs" to her gathering, despite living in two rooms in Quebec Street, "where tea was made in the bedroom, and where it was whispered the butter was kept cool in the wash-hand basin!"[45] Only those who had published were allowed to attend these gatherings, so Anna Maria Hall, whose literary career had not yet begun, was excluded. Samuel was invited, however and met there, amongst others, Lady Caroline Lamb and the beautiful wilful Rosina Wheeler, whom Lamb befriended. Landon warned Rosina not to let Lady Caroline get too close to her, good advice which went unheeded.[46] Landon and Rosina Wheeler became friends – although not, apparently, confidantes, as Wheeler wrote about Landon, "she never was in love in her life". Wheeler had not yet published anything, but was prized for her wit and conversation, so was an exception to the rule. Rosina Wheeler later married Edward Bulwer, whom she met at the salon in April 1826, a union with disastrous results.

Emma Roberts, an early memoirist of Landon's, was at the party, as was Jane Webb, later Loudon, a gentle author who subsequently wrote for Jerdan. On meeting Letitia Landon, Samuel Carter Hall liked her enough to arrange for his wife to call upon her the following day, when Anna Maria Hall recalled Landon as "a bright-eyed sparkling restless little girl in a pink gingham frock …". Landon was in fact twenty-three years old, and as "rapid as a squirrel". Jerdan must have enjoyed the witty, skittish side of his secret lover, quite contrasted with the poetry she produced. Although the Misses Spence and Benger's salon attracted mainly women writers, it was not exclusively sexist.[47] Bulwer was of aristocratic birth, so had access to far smarter gatherings, with better refreshments. However, the salon provided a sanctuary for him to meet his beloved Rosina Wheeler of whom his mother vastly disapproved. Jerdan would sometimes attend, always looking for a new writer and new material for the *Literary Gazette*. For him and Landon too, the salon would have been a sanctuary of sorts. Serving as a respectable place for unmarried women writers to socialize, the salon was also a kind of job market, where editors and compilers of annuals rubbed shoulders with writers seeking outlets for their work.

Editors of annuals were forever looking for suitable good quality contributions. In October 1825 Jerdan received a letter from Alaric Watts, reminding him that he had contributed to the *Literary Souvenir* the previous year, for which Watts was grateful, "and which I had reason to know was a service to the work".[48] He carefully explained that he had not approached Jerdan formally for another contribution this year, knowing how busy he was; but he had noticed "pieces from your pen" in many such volumes. His "delicacy" had delayed him approaching Southey, who would probably have sent a poem. Putting aside the question of a contribution, Watts asked Jerdan to give the *Literary Souvenir* a true review, favourable or otherwise. Jerdan responded to Watts's letter, and his verse, *The Three Kates*, appeared in the *Literary Souvenir* for 1825, which Watts claimed sold six thousand copies.[49] The narrator sees the beautiful Katherine, " … the limbs so finely formed / Round, polished soft and feminine" and hopes to make her his. Then he sees her mother, Kate, "plump, fair and forty", still attractive. Finally, he sees Kate's mother, her hand a bony claw, her hair thin and gray. This is his beloved's "upward line", but he understands this is the inevitable course of nature:

Yes, onward, onward flows the tide:
Love's raptures bless Youth's revel day;
The matron staid succeeds the bride,
And follows fast Eld's sad decay.
Why then rebel at the decree?
Come, ripe and bursting bud, be mine!
Three Kates, and thou the third I see –
To see a fourth I'll not repine.

At this time, when he had embarked upon his affair with Landon, Jerdan was still acquainted with her mother, (whose name was Catherine, a name often abbreviated to Kate), and more so with her grandmother at whose lodgings Landon was then living. He had ample opportunity, therefore, to study her "upward line", and had already taken the "bursting bud" as his own.

At Christmas 1825 William Jerdan was tempted to change his residence to one reflecting his successful position in society, and go "up-market". Moving only a stone's-throw away from their current home in Michael's Grove, he, his wife Frances and their seven children moved into the substantial and elegant Grove House in Brompton, also known as 11 Brompton Grove.[50] He later admitted this to be an error, as although he had a large enough income to run a smart establishment, he had not yet cleared his debts. The brother of George Twining, of the long-established tea business, whose new bank had opened on 12 November 1825, had changed his mind about taking a lease on Grove House. On the assumption that Jerdan's promotion of the bank to his large circle of colleagues and acquaintance would be good for business, Twining convinced him that to be seen to live in such a grand residence would increase sales of the *Literary Gazette*, on the basis that success breeds success. Jerdan subsequently noted "which it did, very considerably: worldly appearances go a great way in promoting success! What is a Physician without a carriage!"[51] To clinch the deal, Twining assured Jerdan that one thousand pounds would be credited to his bank account, an irresistible offer. This generosity turned out to have strings that Jerdan did not mention.

Grove House itself had an illustrious history which might have attracted Jerdan as much as the amenities it provided. It was the largest of three houses built in 1763, a handsome detached building having a one hundred foot frontage to the road. The house was five windows wide and three storeys high (see illustration no. 6). Next to the stables at the rear was "an unusual appendage", a 90' × 30' riding theatre, to allow exercise whatever the weather.[52] The first occupant of Grove House was Bartholomew Gallatin, Colonel of the 2nd Troop of Horse Grenadiers; he was followed by Sir George Savile, a politician. From 1794 to his death in 1821 Grove House was occupied by the larger-than-life figure of Sir John Macpherson, briefly Governor of India after Warren Hastings. (In

1805 Macpherson used Grove House as security for a mortgage of ten thousand pounds from the East India Company.) He added a single storey drawing room of 30x18' on the east side of the house, allegedly for entertaining the Prince Regent, a feature Jerdan would have greatly admired. Macpherson was known locally as the "gentle giant", "from his usually riding a very small pony and flourishing in a most determined manner a huge oak stick over the animal's head but never touching it with his club".[53] In complete contrast to this lively and eccentric occupant came the next tenant, William Wilberforce, who lived in Grove House from 1823 to 1825. Wilberforce resided in Grove House during the period in which he made his last speeches in the House of Commons in debates on the anti-slavery issue. Illness forced him to resign his seat and he moved to Highwood, Mill Hill, north of London.

The Jerdan family took over the house from Wilberforce. They were amazed to find so many comforts in the home "of a gentleman so pre-eminent in the religious world". There was a modern kitchen range, large enough to cater for fifty people a day and, to Jerdan's wonderment, a fascinating wine cellar. As the move had taken place in winter, an unpropitious time to move such treasures, Wilberforce had asked a favour of Jerdan, to leave the cellar of wine to be moved in the spring. As well as a curious selection of wines with some fine vintages, Wilberforce stored a collection of artefacts given to him as a consequence of his involvement with slavery issues. Jerdan invested a considerable part of the money Twining had supplied in furnishing his new home, and the family relished the grandeur of the house and enjoyed all the room for entertaining that it afforded. They gave many parties in Grove House and living in such a residence, with congenial neighbours, would have given Jerdan immense gratification, especially as his idol George Canning lived nearby.

Reminiscing years later, William Pitt, Lord Lennox, recalled:

During the time Jerdan lived at Brompton, his house was ever open to all the leading literary men, artists, dramatic authors and actors of the day. Nothing could be more delightful than his dinner parties, as I can vouch for, having often participated in his hospitality. Hook . . . Lord Normanby . . . Chief Baron Pollock . . . Judge Talfourd . . . were constant guests at his table. Jerdan was full of anecdote and his conversational powers were equal to his critical ones . . . he strenuously advocated the English, now almost obsolete, custom of sitting late after dinner, denouncing the foreign habit of quitting the table with the ladies as a dreadful innovation – a perfect abomination.[54]

This custom so impressed Lord Lennox that he quoted from Jerdan's own words on the subject, from [an unidentified] work Jerdan had written and which he was often in the habit of quoting:

We have always thought that the one English custom which raises us immeasureably above all other races and types of humanity, is that of sitting over our wine after dinner. In what other portion of the twenty-four hours have we either time or inclination for more talk? And is not the faculty of talk that which denotes the superiority of man over brutes? To talk, therefore, a certain part of the day must be devoted. Other nations mix up their talk with their business, and the consequence is, that neither talk nor business is done well. We, on the contrary, work while we are at it, and have all our talk out just at that very portion of our lives when it is physically, intellectually, and morally most beneficial to us. The pleasant talk promotes digestion, and prevents the mind from dwelling on the grinding of the digestive mill that is going on within us. The satisfaction and repose which follow a full meal tend to check a disposition to splenetic argument, or too much zeal in supporting an opinion; while the freedom and *abandon* of the intercourse which is thus kept up is eminently conducive to feelings of general benevolence. It is not too much, perhaps, to say that our 'glorious constitution' (not only as individuals, but as a body politic) is owing to the habit which the British Lion observes, 'of sitting over his wine after dinner'.

Another chronicler of the times noted that "Mr Jerdan was fond of eclât and fine company ... of him it was said he had been fond of running a wheelbarrow round the gravel in front of his house, to represent carriage visitors!" The author remarked that this anecdote was probably an envious '*jeu d'esprit*', "but it showed in what light it was possible to view him."[55] It is a wonderful image – even if it is imaginary.

This move into grandeur epitomized Jerdan's bad luck and bad timing as far as money matters were concerned. The industrial revolution was proceeding apace; the first railway line opened, and Brunel sank the first shaft of the Thames tunnel, while a chain suspension bridge appeared over the Menai Straits. In the financial world, however, all was not well. Jerdan was not unaware of the storm which was brewing. In the *Literary Gazette* of 19 November, under the heading of 'Politics', normally only one or two lines, appeared the paragraph: "The fall of the Funds is news which oddly enough seems to affect every body – those who have money, and those who have none. It is after all a riddle, and apparently quite inexplicable." It <u>was</u>, however, explicable, and led, over that winter and into the new year, to the Panic of 1826.

9

Financial 'Panic', Personal Attacks

Termed "the panic of 1826", it began at the end of the previous year, when Bank of England gold reserves fell dramatically. When its cash reserve fell below two million pounds, the Bank resolved to discontinue its credit facilities, and began to discriminate in the discounting of bills, and the making of loans. In December the house of Peter Pole & Co., agents for forty country banks, failed. The country banks then collapsed, suffering from stock market crashes which triggered commercial failures. The banks' failure was compounded by the fact that they were seen to have issued too many small denomination notes. The public panicked, and a run on gold ensued, almost entirely depleting the Bank of England reserve.[1] To alleviate the situation the Bank circulated one pound and two pound bank notes, and the Royal Mint increased production of sovereigns, moves that restored a measure of confidence in the Bank. The massive bank failures, stock crashes and recession in early 1826 were the impetus for a series of new Acts reorganizing the business of banking, but the English recession had far-reaching effects on Europe, and also on Latin America where so much had been invested in shareholdings. The fallout caused widespread economic hardship in Britain, with labour unrest in the factories and mills.

Much closer to home, Jerdan noted that at the Literary Club "Two or three absentees at a time were missing from their mess – their plates were empty, and so were their seats. Aldermen sent turtles no more; wealthy publishers forgot whence haunches came; stationers and printers, instead of baskets from their hot-houses, got a poor dessert in hot water; and as for the authors, they had to relinquish their feasting, and find themselves rather worse accommodated than they were before."[2] One of the hardest hit was Constable, publisher of Walter Scott, whose business collapsed on 14 January when a bill drawn by Constable on their London agent Hurst Robinson & Co. was dishonoured, leaving him, Ballantyne and Scott many thousands of pounds in debt. Colburn appears to have been the only publisher who managed to stay afloat during this terrible time, "the only man in the trade who continued to issue new books".[3]

In his memoir Jerdan was unusually clear about his own financial affairs at the time of the Panic. Scripps, printer of the *Literary Gazette*, had just erected "one of the most perfect printing houses in town" and was therefore short of funds to help him over the downturn. Those who would have helped him were suffering their own difficulties, and Jerdan somehow became caught up in Scripps's problems. "My bank credit was closed, and the advances reclaimed; and all around, everybody was urgent for everything due to them. It was fortunate I was in the flourishing condition I have stated; and yet it was with much loss and some difficulty that I succeeded in consolidating my incumbrances into a bond, with my share of the *Literary Gazette* as security for £3284 to be paid off by quarterly payments of £125, equal to £500 a year."[4] His seven years of famine, Jerdan noted, were supposed to be followed by seven years of plenty, but were now hampered by this considerable financial drain. His bond was held by Twinings (the Bank which had helped him to move into Grove House) and "to them and Messrs. Longmans some five-sixths of it were due". This was not Jerdan's only liability, as he had earlier raised the huge sum of £1600 "on an annuity in Rochdale" which, together with a life assurance, were costing him a "ruinous pitch" of £184.2.4 a year, payable half-yearly.[5] Over time, he paid off his bond, but let the insurance fall into arrears "at a late date when principal and fair interest had been paid over and over again". Coupled with these burdens, there was the expensive house to maintain and Jerdan had "the intense wish that I were in my cheap little box of a cottage again [and was] only aggravated by the impossibility of retreating thither". The Panic was far-reaching and was not the last time Jerdan's finances were affected by matters outside of his control.

Jerdan and John Trotter (of the Soho Bazaar), devised a scheme for placing the finances of the nation on a better footing. (That Jerdan, the most careless manager of his own money, should even consider this project, is ironic.) The two men worked strenuously on their plan, Trotter often interrupting Jerdan as he worked on *Literary Gazette* matters at home, far into the night. Jerdan was a night-owl, believing that "the most studious, and learned, and deeply pondered writings were produced by the sitters-up at night, and not by spinners in the sun".[6] He held to his earlier injunction: Sleeping will not do! The financial plan was devised to give a boost to the country and improve the value of currency. In the *Literary Gazette* of 30 April 1826 Jerdan told his readers that although the magazine normally touched only briefly on matters of religion, politics and finance, how much more secure Great Britain would be if:

A sound settled currency could be established liable to no fluctuation, but susceptible of easy and perpetual regulation as circumstances required, representing real property (the foundation being much more valuable than the representative) and preserving the precious metals and combining all the great interests of the country so intimately with the common weal, as to preclude the possibility of panic or consequential distress . . . The Editor of this journal does not assume to himself the capacity and knowledge which should entitle him to decide presumptuously on so vast a design; but he has to observe, that its simplicity is equal to its vastness.

The matter was revived at the end of September. Jerdan had been unable to persuade John Trotter to bring it forward, but he had permission to set the outline before the public. Lest this should look too serious for some readers, Jerdan assured his readers that "friends who look to the Gazette chiefly for the literature of the day and reading of a lighter class, need not apprehend any great encroachment upon our space with this discussion of a *political* tendency in the highest sense of the word. A column or two weekly, for a very few weeks, will suffice for it, extraordinary as we consider its bearing to be as regards every rank of society in the kingdom." The subject was followed up over several weeks. Jerdan received a good deal of response from his readers, as a result of which he announced that the various papers would be presented in a pamphlet "with the lines numbered and blank leaves for remarks, so that whatever objections are made, may be promptly and decisively answered by references to its declared principles and demonstrated practicabilities and advantages". They submitted the finished proposal to Sir Coutts Trotter, John Trotter's son and director of Coutts Bank, and also to various distinguished politicians and statesmen. Its ingenuity was acknowledged, but the "bullionist school" objected to the theory, whilst the opposite view held it to be a panacea for all monetary evil. Whilst nothing appeared to happen as a result of all Trotter's work and Jerdan's publicity, this was evidence of the latter's concern with a world wider than solely the literature for which his magazine was named. The following year Jerdan collected the *Literary Gazette* articles into a book, published by Longman, Rees, Orme, Brown and Green, entitled *National Polity and Finance: A Plan for establishing a sterling currency*.

With Jerdan's usual bad luck when it came to timing of financial matters, the family were now ensconsed in their smart too-expensive new mansion, Grove House. Landon was pregnant again, and decided it was time to move too. Leaving the comparatively sheltered environment of Sloane Street, she moved backwards, regressing it might be said, almost to the womb. She chose to take up residence in the boarding house of the Misses Lance at 22 Hans Place, the very house where she had briefly attended school many years previously, near to her erstwhile parental home, and birthplace. Here she lived in a sparsely furnished attic room for the next ten years. Another lodger in the house was the thirty-five year old Emma Roberts, also a writer, whose close first-hand observations of Landon have been much noted by those interested in Landon's poetry and life. It was not Roberts, however, who was criticized for living alone, but Landon. An unchaperoned single young woman, a professional author, caused rumours to start gathering. Landon had been accused of owing wages, by a servant who had left her employ some six years earlier. She set out her case in a clearly argued statement which she sent to Jerdan with a covering note, asking "Is there nothing I can do for you in the <u>live way</u>. I am still quite lame."[7] Jerdan sent her statement on to E. Dubois, the judge in the case, explaining that he had instructed his own solicitor to appear in court, and that if Dubois ruled for the Plaintiff, the money would be paid. Shrewdly, Jerdan noted in a postscript, "If you are an Autograph collector, the enclosure will reward you for the trouble." This incident demonstrated how Jerdan was Landon's advisor in business and in personal matters, as well as her secret lover.

Or not so secret. On 5 March 1826 the *Sunday Times*, under the heading 'Sapphics and Erotics', announced:

A well known English Sappho . . . famous for the amorous glow of her fancy, has just been detected in a *faux pas* with a literary man, the father of several children. The discovery happened when the *placens* . . . and brats were sent off . . . last September to the waterside, and was effected by means of a charwoman . . . Observing, that as often as the youthful Sappho arrived at the embowered recess of Love and the Muses, the blinds on the ground-floor study were *pulled down* and shutters *pulled up*; and wondering how *books* could be read in *the dark*, this female busybody stationed herself so ingeniously . . . as to see the whole poetical mystery, by which 'hearts throb with hearts,' and 'souls with souls unite.' This she expounded to the wife . . . Other truths then came out, from which it appeared that the 'virgin gentleness, the orphan muse' had honoured her *Benedict* (though not Benedictus) Phaon with a young chubby Terpander, or son of a *lyre*, two years before, and at Canterbury of all places, whither the gay deceiver cantered with her (so he gave out) on his way to Margate for the purpose of seeing his better half and seven fractions, like a good spouse, back to London.

Unless Landon had another child after Ella's birth in December 1823, the article surely refers to Ella's own birth and the newspaper got both the date and the gender wrong. The reference to the "seven fractions" is correct, as Jerdan and Frances had seven children. It is likely though, that it was during the autumn of 1826 that Jerdan and Landon's second child was born, a son they called Fred. Like his sister Ella, now about three years old, his surname was Stuart. Where he was born, and how he was fostered are, as yet, unsolved mysteries.

The satirical press had a field day. By this time L.E.L. was a celebrity, her face and figure well known in literary and artistic circles where she was often escorted by Jerdan, ostensibly in his professional capacity. The rumours turned to outright accusations, libellous had they not been true. *The Wasp* was one of the most outspoken and damaging.[8] On 7 October 1826 *The Wasp* remarked that Landon "in the course of a few months acquired so perceptible a degree of *embonpoint* as to induce her kind friend Jerdan to recommend a change of air . . . strange to say, such was the effect of even two months' absence from Brompton, that she returned as *thin* and poetical as ever".[9] In case this barb had missed its target, they tried again the following week, charging "L.E.L. (alias Letitia Languish) . . . with having written a sentimental elegy on the *Swellings of Jordan*. She pleaded that *the flood had gone off*; but the plea was overruled; and she was ordered into the country to gather *fruit*, and to *deliver* an account thereof on her return" (original italics). Landon had indeed been out of London, letters between June and September being dated as from Aberford, Yorkshire, the home of her uncle, an Anglican vicar and his family. Fred Stuart may well have been born on her way to Yorkshire, and left with a wet nurse while his mother recuperated at her uncle's house, her secret safe from her family. A close analysis of Landon's letters at this time has suggested the possibility that she travelled in the mail coach for Aberford, stopping at Royston, near Biggleswade in Hertfordshire, remaining there until late December, some two months after *The Wasp*'s reference to her being seen in London.[10] However, it is quite likely that Landon wrote about this to Katherine Thomson to cover her tracks, as a letter of early September to another friend said she would be staying in Aberford some more weeks. These anomalies will be resolved should a birth record for Fred Stuart ever be found, but this is unlikely as in those days no statutory registration was required.

It is more than possible that on one of those riotous nights with his friends, while Jerdan was on his third bottle of wine – a regular event – he might have let slip to Hook, or another tongue-wagger, that L.E.L. was carrying his child. Although boasting of his conquest does not seem to have been a practice of Jerdan's, he did not hesitate to blow his own trumpet when it came to his acquaintance with the high-powered of the land, such as Canning or Freeling. It is conceivable that he did unwisely tell someone about the expected child, and must have then been horrified to see it plastered all over *The Wasp* for anyone to deride. Another satirical journal of the gutter-press, the *Ass*, cruelly parodied Landon's own poetry, "False love, that like a mutton chop/ Is flung aside when cold."[11] In two other issues the *Ass* named Landon and Jerdan directly. The following day the accusation was picked up by the *Sunday Times* of 2 April: "The new publication called *The Ass*, in a letter to Mr William Jerdan of the *Literary Gazette,* says, he has . . . 'given the finishing stroke of inspiration to Miss Landon'. Is this banter or compliment?" Certainly, the *Sunday Times* did not mean it as a compliment, to reprint this tawdry accusation. Jerdan's response was mild in the extreme: The *Literary Gazette* of 2 May noted "A new periodical called *The Ass* has been going on these three weeks; it is seldom that proper names are so properly bestowed, by writers who are their own godfathers. There is, nevertheless, some humour in *The Ass* but if it wishes to succeed it must avoid indecency."

Jerdan was more hurt than this indicated. He kept copies of all these scurrilous periodicals for many years, "cherished by my vanity", although "they tickled me heinously at the time, and make me quite as sore now as they did then",[12] a quarter of a century earlier.

There is not a shred of available evidence that Frances Jerdan knew about her husband's affair with the famous poet, but once it became a matter of common suspicion, if not actual knowledge, it is hard to credit that some word did not reach her ears. Stuck at home, albeit a grand large home, with seven children, she had no choice but to keep up appearances and be his hostess when he chose to give one of his many parties. Landon, on the other hand, most definitely knew about these too-pointed references. Writing in June to her friend Katherine Thomson, wife of her Doctor, Landon informed her "I have taken some steps towards change", presumably concerning her change of residence, and then protested plaintively:

I also wished, if possible, to subdue the bitterness and indignation of feelings not to be expressed to one so kind as yourself. I must own I have succeeded better in the first than the last. I think of the treatment I have received until my very soul writhes under the powerlessness of its anger. It is only because I am poor, unprotected, and dependant on popularity, that I am a mark for all the gratuitous insolence and malice of idleness and ill-nature ... the only thing in the world I really feel an interest in..my writings . . . When my "Improvisatrice" came out, nobody discovered what is now alleged against it. I did not take up a review, a magazine, a newspaper, but if it named my book it was to praise 'the delicacy', 'the grace', 'the purity of feminine' it displayed . . . You must forgive this; I do not often speak of my own works, and I must say this was the first time it was ever done boastingly; but I must be allowed to place opinions of the many in opposition to the envious and illiberal cavillings of a few. As to the *report* you named, I know not which is greatest – the absurdity or the malice.[13]

To the end of her days Thomson either truly did not believe, or did not put her suspicions on paper, that Landon had been having an affair with Jerdan. If Dr Thomson had attended Landon for any of her several chronic ailments during any of her pregnancies, he could not have failed to take notice of her condition, and if he did so, then it is hard to believe he did not share his knowledge with his wife. Both of them, according to Blanchard, rarely let her out of their sight. Landon's concern seemed more about the taint to her work than about her personal reputation, and also that those who criticized her had never had to work for their living, as she did. Putting her works, and thus herself, on a high moral plane, Landon was both deceiving her friend, and attempting to divert her from the nub of the accusations centring on her relationship with Jerdan. Landon, in this letter at least, seemed to have no regard for telling the truth, nor any idea that this deception could undermine the trust her friend had in her. She continued this long complaint shamelessly seeking some sympathy: "The more I think of my past life, and of my future prospects, the more dreary do they seem. I have known little else than privation, disappointment, unkindness and harassment; from the time I was fifteen, my life has been one continual struggle in some shape or another against absolute poverty, and I must say not a tithe of my profits have I ever expended on myself." Much of this is patently untrue: she lived at home until she was twenty and although financially her family was not well off, she certainly never starved or lacked a roof over her head. Her grandmother showed her nothing but kindness, as did Jerdan who in one of his writings about her, corroborated that she did not spend much money on herself or her dress. Much of her income was still going towards the support of her mother, and her brother Whittington and likely, although we have nothing to evidence this supposition, upkeep of her children. Landon was, in fact, satisfied with her financial situation, telling Alaric Watts, "I think myself so rich I am delighted. First and last I have received between £900 and £1000, so I have full reason to be content."[14]

Jerdan, however, was still under attack. Westmacott was not alone in his overwrought reactions to perceived 'puffing' in the *Literary Gazette* and to Jerdan himself. *The Wasp*, *Scorpion* and the *Ass* all had their say. Jerdan quoted the second issue of *The Wasp* in his reminiscences, noting that its publisher, W. Jeffreys, patronizingly referring to him as Master Bill and Master Willie, said he was beaten as a child, a fact "altogether new" to Jerdan. With "equal truth and accuracy" Jeffreys claimed that Jerdan had bought a share in the *Literary Gazette* "as portable puffing machine" for Longmans. Jeffreys and Westmacott both piously asserted that their exposure of the alleged favouritism of the *Literary Gazette* and its Editor was to warn the public to be on their guard. They, and Jerdan's other persecutors, were desperate to challenge his authority as a literary critic, but could do so only on the basis of his past record, and the perception of the *Literary Gazette* as a promotional tool for its owners. Jerdan remarked that as he had not died of this assault, *The Wasp* tried again in issue number five, belabouring him and George Croly, accusing them of several instances of injustice, and qualities that "unfits this committee man of the Royal Society of Literature, this inquisitor of the Literary Fund etc. for any and every relation of literary and social life".[15] When *The Wasp* died, the *Scorpion* took up the cudgels, reiterating the same accusations, to be succeeded by the *Ass* which, said Jerdan, "was very filthy and indecent". Rumours and rumblings continued for some years, as background noise to the daily and weekly grind of turning out the *Literary Gazette*.

In April 1826 Jerdan's baby daughter Georgiana, his "little darling", fell ill and died. Jerdan's writings scarcely mention his family at all, so they remain shadowy figures in his story. Exceptionally, he became highly emotional relating the death of his little girl, aged sixteen months.[16] She contracted an infected mesenteric gland[17]. Watching his child dying was a horrific experience, knowing that no medicine could help her. It was clearly a traumatic time, as it would be for any doting parent, and Jerdan, with his self-confessed passion for children, was no exception. What went through his mind as his baby lay helpless, knowing that his other, secret daughter Ella Stuart, just two years older, was happily playing elsewhere, can only be left to the imagination.

The distraught father could not accept Georgiana's fate, and recalled that "In the enchanting light of a summer morning, my child about twelve months of age, turned upon her pillow, put her arms around my neck, touched my lips with one soft kiss and in that kiss breathed her soul to heaven". One must forgive him the melodramatic touches, and his minor factual errors: it was not summer, but April, and the child was not twelve but sixteen months old. The death-bed scene is nevertheless affecting and for Jerdan it was "the first mortal breach upon the integrity of my happiness". He had thought himself invulnerable, easily recovering from the many difficulties he had in life, but this loss was something greater, and he was utterly unmanned. He could not bear to part with the child, and kept her coffin in the house so that every morning he could kiss her, until her physical decay forced him to permit her burial, which took place on 26 April. All the griefs which he endured throughout his life, none had made him feel as this bereavement did, "a convincing sense of the utter helplessness of humanity".[18] To throw himself back into work was a blessing, and he found in literature a potent force for "soothing sorrows and blunting the stings of worldly troubles".

Worldly troubles, however, were never very far away; a 'Sketch of Society' in the series of 'Paul Pry on his travels' in the *Literary Gazette* of 30 July, observed:

> Many persons very wrongly imagine that the art of puffing is English: we are tolerably good hands at it as all readers of newspapers and posting bills know from Ross's wigs down to Rowland's Macassar Oil and Charles Wright's champagne (justly so called because he makes it all himself without the aid of the grower in France).

Wright was justifiably angry, and sued "Jerdan and Others" for libel. The matter was reported in the *Times* of 30 November 1826. Wright claimed damages of two thousand pounds. Fittingly, as the case opened, "the Court was at that moment placed under the extra obscuration of an eclipse of the sun". The prosecutor "had a tender regard for the liberty of the press", but was surprised that a literary journal should "taint their pages with the affairs of men in business and that a business not at all relating to literary works". The prosecutor himself had often enjoyed Wright's hospitality, and many a glass of his "delicious beverage . . . delightful drink". Because of his excellent wine Wright stood high with the public and enjoyed "the good opinion of the *bon ton*. The publisher of the libel must therefore have sought to injure Wright's reputation in order to "bring forward some more favoured and less deserving aspirant to public favour". Wright demanded that the *Literary Gazette* correct their statement in a future number of the *Gazette*. The defendants expressed regret, the notice had been an oversight, they would make every reparation in their power.

Their "reparation" was buried in a review of Parry's *Journal* on 26 August where, following a description of a masquerade devised to amuse the expedition to the North West Passage, when in their winter quarters, it read:

> Poor fellows! They had none of Charles Wright's Champagne, which we are induced to mention again, because, we are told, he is going to prosecute the Literary Gazette for a libel upon it – the Gazette we believe said that it was so good that it must be (as he advertized) his own, and not nasty French stuff . . .

The prosecuting lawyer was apoplectic: "This was the reparation – this was the recantation which had been promised – this was the refutation which was to appear in the journal." If the *Gazette* had made a proper apology, no case for libel would have been brought. Mr Wright paid tax of fourteen thousand pounds, proving that he imported great quantities of wine, and going "some way to prove that his champagne was not manufactured at home". Winding up his speech, the prosecutor advised the Court that Mr Wright traded from under the Colonnade in the Haymarket, "Where, if any of the gentlemen in the box, or any others, had a wish to purchase good and brilliant champagne," they would be so happy with it, they would repeat their orders, a blatant advertisement for his client's business. Wright's clerk was called as a witness: he had got one *Literary Gazette* from the publisher's office in Wellington Street, but was unable to get another. "Neither Jerdan nor Colburn live in the house in Wellington Street".

Jerdan's lawyer cross-examined the clerk as to whether he had seen Wright's advertisements in the *Sunday Times*:

> Tom Moore gaily says,
> That the best of all ways
> To lengthen our days
> Is to steal a few hours from the night.
> But deny it who can,
> A much better plan
> To lengthen life's span,
> Is to quaff the Champagne of Charles Wright.

Many other such advertisements were evidenced. The defendant's lawyer, Taddy, then said that as his colleague had admitted a "tender regard for the press", Taddy knew he also had a "tender regard for good wine". The accusation was not whether Wright's wine was good or not, but that he "professed to sell French champagne, and this at 5s6d a bottle, which is impossible". Better than press advertising, observed Taddy, was the puff his lawyer had just given him in Court. Taddy tore his opponent's speech to shreds, mocking his every point. Moreover, bringing this libel action had in fact advertised Wright's wines even more widely, and "in consequence it will be a benefit and not an injury to the plaintiff". Joking about the eclipse he suggested his "learned friend" felt oppressed, but whether from the eclipse of the sun or "from too liberal a draught of Mr Wright's champagne, he was unprepared to say". His wine could certainly be recommended to Captain Parry's expedition which "was placed under a permanent eclipse of the sun". Summing up, Taddy said that if the jury believed Wright had been truly injured they should find for him, but if they thought the action served to puff his wines and he would suffer no disadvantage, they should give a verdict for very small damages. The jury deliberated a short time, and returned a verdict for Wright. Damages were set at fifty pounds. This was a high price to pay and unnecessary, had Jerdan placed an apology into the *Gazette* rather than rub salt into Wright's wound with the second comment. Brushes with the law had already dogged Jerdan and would continue to do so. In this case his offence could be construed as careless rather than malicious.

With so many troubles and distractions, Jerdan had yet another upset to cope with. In the August issue of the *Examiner*, (which Leigh Hunt had started but of which he was no longer editor), was an unwarranted personal attack. The *Literary Gazette* had reviewed a novel entitled *Truth* (by W. P. Scargill) criticizing it severely, an unusual treatment from the usually kindly editor. The *Examiner* instantly took up the cudgels:

> Our readers know something already of the ignorance and malignity of the worthless hack who conducts the *Literary Gazette* . . . we have never thought it worth while to quarrel with criticisms which are inane and despised as they are notoriously corrupt: but when his venom overpours, and he goes out of his way to wound individuals by malicious falsehoods, we think he becomes of importance enough to warrant our holding him up to the scorn of society.

There was much more along the same lines, quoting Jerdan's contradictions, and holding them up to ridicule. There is an irony in the abusive treatment the paper, undoubtedly influenced by Leigh Hunt, gave to Jerdan in this and future issues of the *Examiner*, when in fact the two men had much in common throughout their lives.

The Bellingham assassination of Spencer Perceval highlighted their similarities: it had a strong influence on Leigh Hunt, who was eight years younger than Jerdan, and also a journalist; many circumstances and incidents throughout the lives of Jerdan and Hunt reflected those of the other man, and although they were acquainted were never close.[19] Like Jerdan, Hunt acknowledged that he had been over-indulged as a child, and thought this to have caused the flaws he saw in his own character. Hunt was more afflicted by the psychological reasons for Perceval's death, rather than the political. He was "preoccupied with the psychology of the murder, speculating on how madness and violence in adult life may be traced back to parental neglect or misdirected fondness".[20] His thoughts echoed Jerdan's reflection on his own childhood, how he grew up, "being pampered and petted with or without reason, I naturally grew up petulant and self-willed".[21] Whereas although Jerdan acknowledged such burdens and was generally able to shrug them off, Leigh Hunt suffered from them, and within three months of Perceval's assassination, "was afflicted by another upsurge of nervous illness".[22] Hunt's illness could also have been brought on by his troubles with the *Examiner*, for which he was jailed in 1812. Whilst he was imprisoned, he was visited by Byron, at a meeting that was to have consequences in later life for Hunt and, by literary association, for Jerdan too. Despite recurring parallels in the lives of the two writers, they never became friends but managed eventually to effect some measure of reconciliation, largely due to Jerdan's forgiveness for Hunt's vilification of him in various papers.

Samuel Maunder, whose brother-in-law Pinnock had ruined their publishing business, was helping the artist Richard Dagley to prepare a book entitled *Death's Doings*, for which Jerdan wrote a contribution in 1826. Maunder was delighted: "[I] think it gives variety and spirit to the work. It is an excellent baccanalian article – brisk and sparkling as champagne."[23] He doubted however that the Epitaph was entirely original and suggested an alternative. Not all contributors had pleased Maunder, as he told Jerdan: "I am afraid I shall be thought the Buffa of *Death's Doings*. But really some of the writers were so sober that I purposely got drunk – or more poetically, 'rapt, inspired!'", a state Jerdan could sympathise with. The book was a compilation of Dagley's drawings, verse by L.E.L. and others, and prose contributions from several writers. Jerdan's contribution was called *The Last Bottle*, a melange of prose and verse to accompany a macabre drawing of four people around a laden table, bottles rolling on the floor, and a skeleton, the figure of Death, putting the last bottle into a bowl. Jerdan's piece may have echoed his own thoughts at dark moments: "An' if it be the last bottle, Death is quite welcome; for then life has run to the very dregs and lees and there is nothing more in it which can be called enjoyment." He included drinking songs of the ancients, spoke of Herodotus and Plutarch, and ended with the friends of the deceased drinking their third bottle each, over an epitaph (presumably the alternative suggested by Maunder):

Habeas Corpus! Hic Jacet!
Here lies William Wassail, cut down by the Mower;
None ever drank faster or paid their debts slower –
Now quiet he lies as he sleeps with the *fast*,
He has drank his *last Bottle* and fast, fast he sped it o'er,
And paid his great debt to his principal creditor;
And compounded with all the rest, even with *Dust*.

Jerdan surely regretted Maunder's changes to his undoubtedly superior epitaph. In reviewing the book, the *Monthly Magazine* noted, regarding Jerdan's contribution, "There is something Rabelaisian in the style ... "[24] and the *Literary Gazette* gave *Death's Doings* an enthusiastic review over two issues with special emphasis on Dagley's drawings.[25] In neither review did Jerdan mention *The Last Bottle*, although he extracted copious quotations from the other contributors.[26] Richard Dagley was overwhelmingly grateful for the *Literary Gazette*'s notice of his work, such fervent praise bringing tears to the eyes of his family.[27] He sympathized, however, with the 'chagrin' Jerdan must have felt, seeing a notice on the same work in the *Literary Chronicle* on the same day. This race for first place was clearly of prime importance to editors, and the leak may have come, Dagley suspected, from the printers. Maunder, he felt, would have found it difficult to refuse a formal request from the *Chronicle*. Sycophantically, Dagley told Jerdan, "Of their favourable opinion I make little account, as it may have given vexation to you."

The race for first notices and the give and take between Jerdan and *Maga*'s Blackwood continued, more or less good-naturedly, each asking the other to review some pet writer. Blackwood had asked Jerdan to review a work by Gillies which he admired, and was delighted with the treatment it received in the *Literary Gazette*. Irritably, Jerdan advised him that the review had in fact been written

by a young lady for whom and for whose productions your *Magazine* has shown anything but partiality. Whether indeed as a friend brought before the world through the *Literary Gazette* or as a young female of very singular talent I do not think you have treated L.E.L. either with gallantry or justice – her publications have either not been noticed, or they have been slurred over; and even of herself you have permitted flippant and depreciating mention to be made. The public, however, have done her more justice, and so with all the faults of her compositions, will posterity, for she possesses genius.[28]

The *Literary Gazette* noted all major (and some minor) works of travel and exploration. The British were covering the globe, mapping and describing it for the benefit of those at home who went no further than their armchairs, to read about it. James Weddell sailed further into the Antarctic than anyone had been before, a record unsurpassed for ninety years. His feat was subsequently honoured by naming the sea, which he had called the King George IV Sea, for him, the Weddell Sea. He discovered a type of seal, since named the Weddell Seal, and his work was honoured with a Fellowship of the Royal Society of Edinburgh. His book recording this courageous and difficult voyage was published in 1825.[29] It gave details not only how to navigate these unfriendly waters, but the wildlife found there, and proposals for seal conservation, sealing having been the main purpose of the expedition.

Jerdan gave the book an enthusiastic and appreciative review in the *Literary Gazette* of 24 September, with further extracts in the two following weeks, drawing a grateful acknowledgement from the author, accompanied by "four dozen pints of the finest Malmsey Madeira brought from the Island".[30] Naturally, hospitality was offered in return and Weddell joined those from all walks of life whose company Jerdan enjoyed. Weddell had expressed his regard for Jerdan in a manner in which few have been so honoured, by naming an island after him.[31] Delighted as he was to receive such a mark of esteem, he was under no misapprehension about the benefits it may bring:

> I am proud of my name being given in his map to an Island, though at Cape Horn, and so desolate and unproductive, that even in my worst days, I have never thought of proceeding to that stormy region to take possession of my undoubted property, with its ice-bergs and pen-guins (such natural subjects for a pen-man), and, it might be, a native Patagonian or two, only I should have been afraid to attempt the rule over the females of so gigantic a people, however loyal and attached![32]

Weddell lost his vessel in a shipwreck and had to resort to employment on an Australian run. He died in London in poverty in 1834. Before this sad turn of events, however, there was a memorable party on board the ship that was to take Weddell to Australia. Jerdan was one of the guests and enjoyed an evening so unusual and merry that he recalled it in vivid detail years later. The company had dined, and were offering toasts to the prosperity of their host,

> when lo, a crash was heard, the broad cabin light above us was dashed into fragments, the shivered glass and frame-work descended in showers, and in the midst the cause of all this confusion, a huge black pig, objecting to the process, came tumbling through the skylight, not at all like Mercury alighting on a heaven-kissing hill. Some of us were knocked under the table, the upheld bumper glasses accompanying the fall of man, and we had no time to recover from our amazement, when a half-naked, and

much over-heated, huge negro rushed down the ladder into the cabin, and springing on the pig, the cause of all our woes, and clasping the also black monster in his arms, hugged it up to its destination in spite of struggles and shrieks the most swinishly desperate and deafening. The dénouement was followed, as we gathered ourselves up, with roars of uncontrollable laughter and, as none of us were seriously damaged, the jollity was renewed in a humour which did not tend to diminish the succeeding revels of the day.[33]

Jerdan's *joie de vivre*, his love of company and pleasure, is infectious in this account, and such a party would have been a great relief to him in a difficult year.

Another distraction, also involving an animal, occurred just over the road from the *Literary Gazette* office, so was an event for which Jerdan had a front-row seat. The Strand building of Exeter 'Change had, by this time, come to be synonymous with 'menagerie' (see illustration no. 6). Byron had visited it in 1813 to see Chunee, an elephant who had been retired there after performing for forty nights in pantomime at Covent Garden in 1811.[34] In 1825 Chunee accidentally killed his keeper, and a few months later went berserk in his upstairs cage, made of iron-bound oak bars, three feet in girth. Chunee's distress communicated itself to the other caged animals, and the army was called in to restore calm. Despite firing over one hundred rounds of ammunition into the frightened elephant, Chunee survived, and before the cannon arrived, "a keeper pierced Chunee's vitals with a harpoon. This wound, combined with the cumulative effect of 152 balls brought him down." The blood flooded the den to a considerable depth. Disposing of 10,000 pounds of elephant flesh was a massive problem, involving butchers and surgeons, and it was taken away in a long procession of carts. Chunee's skeleton went on display on tour, and then in the Egyptian Hall, and later to the Hunterian Museum; it was destroyed by bombing in World War II. (Exeter 'Change was closed in 1828 to make way for the creation of Trafalgar Square and the animals were eventually relocated to the new Regent's Park Zoo.)

Such an unusual event happening just outside his office window would have attracted Jerdan's curiosity, putting into perspective a petty and annoying occurrence which took place in September, when the *Literary Gazette* offices were broken into. Not much damage was done and Jerdan treated the affair humorously, advising his readers on 16 September under the exciting heading of "Robbery, Piracy, Plagiarism and Murder":

The melancholy accident which befel the LG last week, has not as yet been made known to the public through the usual means in such cases. There has neither been a police report upon the examination of the thieves, nor a coroners inquest upon our bodies in consequence of the suicide to which our misfortune has driven us. On the contrary our *Gazette* was published last Saturday as if nothing had happened, and we continue to write as if we were alive. But the fact is, that our new office in Wellington Street, in full view of the Thames and its police; under cognizance of the Strand and its nightly guardians; nay, within the very blaze of the gas-lit turnpike on Waterloo Bridge, was wickedly and feloniously broken open, and plundered to a very considerable amount, namely three shillings and fourpence, being the full and lawful price of two stamped and two unstamped *Literary* sheets. With regard to the literary tastes of our visitors, however, if we may judge from appearances, they were addicted to quick acquisitiveness, rather than to slow and patient study; for they took away with them every key in the place except a *Key to Hindu Mythology* in one vol. 8vo, which probably escaped their notice. But our doors, drawers and strong-box (as aforesaid) were all denuded. It seems as if these ingenious persons had been interrupted in their investigations, for various packages, evidently made up for removal, were left in most admired disorder; and whether in a hurry, or as a reproof to us for our abominable habit of punning occasionally, there was also left a crow-bar, indicating that they could crow over us without a dread of being brought to the bar.

Jerdan sounded relaxed about the disturbance at his office, but in the next week's *Gazette* his front page review was in a very different mood, most unusual for the invariably kind tone of the journal. *Reviewing A Word to the Members of the Mechanics Institute* by one R. Burnet of Devonport, he said:

this desultory and incoherent production . . . a meeting of the members and an assemblage of the inmates at Bedlam must be more alike than could be expected . . . such a gallimatias of sense and folly, of intelligence and rhapsody, of acuteness, incongruity, information and absurdity we never happened to peruse before . . . " there followed nearly 2 pages of extracts, then "But, with all this folly, it must not be thought that the author is an unmitigated ass; on the contrary, there are long portions of his book which may be read with gratification and instruction. Like Hamlet, he is only crazed nor-nor-west; when the wind is easterly at Plymouth he is mechanical enough to know a hand-saw from a steam engine . . .

and promised more the following week.

Stung, as well he might be, Burnet thanked him for the "excellent advertisement" and sent him ten shillings to put the publisher's name at the head of the article, "whether we go to a theatre to be amused by a Bedlam or read a work written by one amounts to the same thing provided we enjoy it," he told

Jerdan, who responded churlishly in the 'To Correspondents' column, saying he did not know what to do with half a sovereign and had sent it on to the Literary Fund, "a charity so excellent that even this sum must do some good". Despite his scorn of Burnet's work, the *Literary Gazette* carried another six columns of extracts from it.

Personal attacks continued. The *Atlas* printed a stinging one on Jerdan which was gleefully reprinted in the *Examiner* of October 1826. Jerdan was accused of falling into "fits of involuntary puffing" whereby, whilst he decried the practice, he was guilty of it. The article made fun of his protestations that "a fair meed of praise" was not a puff, and jeered at his practice of continuing reviews in subsequent issues matters he thought too heavy to complete in one, such as the *Plan for a National Currency*.

At the end of 1826 Jerdan wrote at least two contributions to annuals. *A Brother to his younger sister, on seeing her gather wild-flowers*, appeared in *The Amulet, A Christian and Literary Remembrancer*, a new venture edited for ten years by Samuel Carter Hall. This, with a few minor changes, was the poem Jerdan had written to his sister in 1802, when he was convalescing at home in Kelso.[35] In 1826 he was likely to have been far too busy with his own occupations to take the time to compose a poem especially for *The Amulet*, and so provided one that he had in his store. He reprinted it in his *Autobiography*, under the title of *The Nosegay*, indicating that for him it stood the test of time. The other contribution entitled *A Prayer and a Promise to Cupid* was made to *Friendship's Offering*, a tiny, thick annual. The four verses seem to reflect how he was feeling, torn between his wife and his mistress, needing always more time, more energy, more love:

Oh, lend me Love! A hundred hearts;
On thy Exchange I'll use the store,
Forgotten all the anguish smarts,
Suffered so oft – then felt no more.

The heart penurious nature gave,
Has been destroyed among the fair;
To every beauteous face a slave –
Giving to each fine form a share.

Then lend me, Love! A hundred hearts;
On thy Exchange I'll use the store;
Forgotten all the anguish smarts,
Endured so long, *then* felt no more.

Rich in the gift I'll hoard not one,
But, still, from bliss to bliss will rove;

> And, when my hundred hearts are gone –
> Lend me another hundred, Love!

This poem might also reflect the Jerdan who reputedly had several liaisons, not just with Landon but with other, unspecified women. No evidence has been found for this spiteful rumour, emanating mostly from Rosina Bulwer, who hated him. Perhaps it was about this time that Landon wrote her short poem, *Faith Destroyed*:

> Why did I love him? I looked up to him
> With earnest admiration, and sweet faith.
> I could forgive the miserable hours
> His falsehood, and his only, taught my heart;
> But I cannot forgive that for his sake,
> My faith in good is shaken, and my hopes
> Are pale and cold, for they have looked on death.
> Why should I love him? He no longer is
> That which I loved.[36]

If this was written about this time, Landon conquered her temporary despair, as the affair continued for several more years.

Generously, the *Literary Gazette* gave the *Forget-Me-Not* a long front page review on 28 October, referring to annuals as "exotics [which] have soon become naturalized in our genial literary climate. It would be in poor spirit to criticize them". However, he went on, clearly venting pent-up anger over the way he had been vilified in the gutter press,

A miserable trade in falsehood and calumny, may, perhaps, attract momentary notice to any disreputable journal; but it is vain to look either for public favour or endurance from a system of vulgar personality and corrupt depreciation. The petty talents required to be spiteful and malignant speedily find a correct estimate in public opinion: and like the noxious reptiles which, having ejected their poison, drop down harmless and die, the paltry revilers of all who fall in their way, having voided their slimy venom, become more impotent than before, confined, it is true, to the most obscure and wretched productions, whose only hope of getting to be known at all is the hope of attracting attention by slander and obscenity; and it is a strong example of the extent to which this vile and disgraceful traffic is carried, when even so pleasing and unexceptionable a volume as the *Forget me Not* could not escape the would-be bitterness of these crawling creatures.

But let us leave them to their unprofitable filth and unmanly acrimony, troubling their own little puddles of dirt, till a few short days or weeks sees them extinct and rotting; their dream that they have been inflicting pain on sensitive genius or humble worth vanished into thin air and the fond imagining that they were of mighty importance in the hour of their noisy gabbling dissipated for ever: "the rest is silence".

Having got this off his chest, Jerdan gave a much shorter, calmer review of *The Amulet* the following week, and in November one for the *Literary Souvenir*, singling out for admiring mention the poetry of Barry Cornwall and L.E.L. He did not forget to mention *Friendship's Offering*, calling it a "very pretty and elegant volume" which resembles the *Forget-Me-Not* and the *Souvenir*. "Upon the whole we think the latter superior to the former, and perhaps to anything of the same kind elsewhere. Some of the poetry is also of the highest beauty, but there are a few performances the mediocrity of which ought to have led to their exclusion."

In the midst of all this literary activity, Jerdan had to make time for his first family. His eldest son, John Stuart, aged nineteen, needed his help, and contacts. Worshipful as Jerdan was of George Canning, and fully aware of the politician's sensitivity towards charges that the press had undue influence on politics, Jerdan nevertheless attempted to use their friendship to further his family's interests. This is no more than fathers have done through the ages, and Jerdan would have seen nothing wrong in it. He sought a clerkship for his son in the Foreign Office, of which Canning was at that time Secretary for Foreign Affairs.

It was a week before Canning found time to reply frankly, explaining that he had many applications for such positions and had turned down requests from the Dukes of Cambridge and Gloucester. He thought, and believed, that on reflection Jerdan would agree, that because of his "connection with the *publick press*, however honourable, it would make the introduction of a son of yours into the Foreign Office liable to some objection".[37] In compensation however, he offered John Stuart a position to be available soon, in the Navy Pay Office under Mr Huskisson. Within a day or two Canning found time to speak personally to Jerdan on the matter, and in a subsequent letter explained his caution more fully. His objection was realistic; if Jerdan's son were in the Foreign Office, any indiscretion or leak of information would be blamed on him. Jerdan could only agree with this rationale, and considered it a kindness that the great man should take such trouble. John Stuart was quickly found a place as a clerk in the Board of Trade but this did not work out satisfactorily. With his father's encouragement he then became secretary for the Abbotsford subscription, to keep Sir Walter Scott's house as a living memorial for Scott's family.

At the end of the year a disgruntled Jerdan wished he could dispense with the annual custom of addressing his readers at this season. After ten years' labour, he said, "continually cheered by public approbation and progressive prosperity, we have but little to say". His independence in the conduct of the *Literary Gazette* had proved successful, and would continue, "our impartial spirit is directing that important power which this Journal has obtained for itself in the literature of the age".[38] Bentley's archives showed that in 1826, 5000 copies of the *Literary Gazette* were printed, of which about 4000 were sold.[39] This was an upbeat note on which to end a year which, for the nation, had proved so difficult in its financial transactions, and which for Jerdan himself had encompassed the personal tragedy of the loss of baby Georgiana.

Unfortunately, the next year, 1827, was to prove dreadful for Jerdan, causing him to muse that "there seems to be periods of fatality in the loss of those who are dear to us, as in the epochs of the falling stars, a series of our brilliant lights are extinguished and our firmament robbed of its beauty and lustre for ever".[40] The death this year that wrung his heart in early January was that of his brother Gilbert at forty-seven, two years older than William. They had been close as children; Jerdan remembered him as a youth, "sprightliest of the sprightly, wonderfully active, brave as a lion, fearless and kind-hearted".[41] Gilbert had been a clever boy, but had not been as lucky as William; he had not received an education at Dr Rutherford's establishment but had become a weaver in Glasgow. Dissatisfied, he turned to plumbing, but his unlucky streak persisted and his premature death was due to lead which poisoned his lungs. Jerdan mourned him deeply, reliving memories of his brother's humour and their shared boyhood. He had helped his brother often, even though Gilbert had sometimes drained his finances when Jerdan could afford to assist him, and even when he could not. Unlucky again, Gilbert had received his share of a family inheritance just a few months before his death, too late to be of any real use. A notice of Gilbert's death appeared in *The Times* of 17 January, and could only have been placed there by Jerdan himself: "On 15th last at Bronte Place, Walworth, Mr Gilbert Jerdan, second son of the late John Jerdan Esq. of Kelso N.B. and brother of the late Lieutenant-Colonel Jerdan of Bombay and of William Jerdan of Brompton". Jerdan took Gilbert's body back from London to Scotland. Jerdan missed his "cheerful, fondly-attached and affectionate brother" very much. Jerdan made no mention of Gilbert's family, but his brother left a wife Elizabeth, who died in Southwark, London, in 1851, aged 73 attended by Susannah Jerdan, probably their daughter.

On 18 June Jerdan's great friend and host of many enjoyable visits, Lord de Tabley died after an illness. Barely recovered from the loss of baby Georgiana, and Gilbert, this was a severe blow to Jerdan, who saw him as a "noble exemplar of refined taste and munificent patronage and native art".[42] A few years earlier de Tabley had tried to sell his collection of British art to create a National Gallery, but was refused by the Prime Minister. At the time of his death he and Jerdan were planning to coauthor a "British Ichthyology", the natural history of fishes, a mutual passion. The project had proceeded so far that it was advertised in the press as being "in preparation".[43] Over thirty years later Jerdan still considered this project "a desideratum, and a design likely to be highly prized, if executed in the accurate and superb style contemplated by Lord de Tabley".[44]

Jerdan's own interests were wider than literature and fish. He admired sculpture, and became a champion of the Northumbrian sculptor John Lough. He went to Lough's lodgings in London to see the giant figure of "Milo attacked by a Wolf", and hailed its creator as a "genius". He did not, however, mention that the frustrated sculptor had made a hole in the ceiling of his room in order to accommodate the statue's head! In the *Literary Gazette* of 12 May 1827, he devoted an entire column to "this young genius", and the following week L.E.L.'s poem *Genius* appeared, "inspired by a view of the sculpture designed by Mr Lough". Many years later, her poem *The Lost Pleiad* inspired one of Lough's own works.[45] When Lough married and moved to a more spacious lodging, Jerdan ensured that the *Literary Gazette* announced the new address of his gallery. He moved again and by 1846 was in a house where he remained for the rest of his life. The poetess Camilla Toulmin reported how she and about eight or ten chosen friends visited his studio to see a new work in clay, and were afterwards entertained to an informal meal. Jerdan was one of those "who professed to be art critics, [and] came to pass their opinion before it was too late to be of service".[46] In 1838 Lough unsuccessfully entered the competition for Nelson's monument, his design strongly supported by the *Literary Gazette*. Three years later Jerdan reviewed the sculpture exhibited at the Royal Academy and was indignant at Lough's failure to secure a commission from this, or any other competition. "What a commentary upon the state of the art of sculpture in England, its patronage and its appreciation!"[47] The following year Jerdan again expostulated that at the Royal Academy Exhibition there were only three busts by Lough, and called it "a national shame".

However, literary matters were always uppermost. A potential row flared up in the Spring of 1827 which took Jerdan's mind off his troubles for a while. Sir Walter Scott had completed his nine volumes of *The Life of Napoleon Buonaparte* under very difficult circumstances, as he had recently lost his wife, and his publisher Constable had collapsed leaving Scott with debts of one hundred and twenty one thousand pounds. This massive work of over a million words was published by Cadell in Edinburgh and by Longmans in London, the latter having paid 10,500 guineas for it, an astronomical sum. Lockhart had assured Jerdan that he would send him some volumes in the course of a week. This was at the end of April and Lockhart said that "The printer Mr Ballantyne tells me 'The work cannot appear before the end of the first week in June.'" On 19 and 27 May the *Literary Gazette* printed the first extracts from the book, acknowledging indebtedness to a North American Review for it, and vouching for its accuracy. On 2 June Jerdan wrote indignantly to either Lockhart or, more likely, to the publisher in Edinburgh, Cadell, advising them that he had cancelled a paper intended for that week's *Literary Gazette* and on the same date inserted a Notice which he hoped would satisfy Scott, Ballantyne and everyone concerned with the work. This read:

> We abstain from quoting (as we intended) any further portions of the Life of Napoleon in consequence of being, since our last Number, informed that what appeared in the American Review had been obtained in a surreptitious manner; though copies of that Review are in the hands of several persons in London as well as in ours, and consequently its contents may be (and have been) extracted by other Journals, we will not knowingly lend the LG to the propagation of what the author may not approve, and what indeed may be a very unfair example of the merits of the work.

He protested that other publications had noticed the work, "therefore if I had not printed what I did the *Literary Gazette* would have seemed inferior in information to other journals, instead of maintaining its character with the public . . . I never in my life, either as a man, or a writer, violated, to a hairbreadth, any confidence reposed in me . . . I hope it will not be forgotten that not merely a property on which I entirely depend but also a reputation which must be clear to every individual, are at stake."[48] Again, to be "first past the post" was of crucial importance to the status of the *Literary Gazette*.

Jerdan's troubles with Scott's work were not yet over. By October Cadell was ready to publish the two volumes of Scott's *Chronicles of the Canongate*, the first volume of which included a short story, "The Two Drovers". Somehow the text for this volume had been leaked en route to Paris, where Galignani was to publish a continental English-language edition. The pirated copy of "The Two Drovers" appeared in the *London Weekly Review* on 20 October, and the *Literary Gazette* published the Introduction to the book on 27 October. Self-righteously, Jerdan wrote to Cadell just before his issue appeared, "The piracy is assuredly one of the most rascally things I ever met with; and very injurious to you."[49] The "Drovers" had been touted around to the *Literary Chronicle* for twenty pounds and been rejected and it was then released to the *Weekly Review*, "the set connected with which appears to me to be of the most contemptible kind". Jerdan assured Cadell of his regard for the famous author: "I am surprised that any body should esteem me cold to the extraordinary genius of Sir Walter Scott. In all Great Britain he has not a warmer or more devoted admirer than myself. I even agree with my fair friend, L.E.L. that if she were a Queen she would be right in giving him a peerage of fifty thousand pounds a year, as the reward of the immeasureable delight he had given to his species . . . " Covering his back, his postscript divulged "I have printed the whole Introduction and trust <u>that</u> is not wrong. In fact it could not be compressed or described without gross injustice to its immortal writer."

Scott was not the only Scottish writer to be in financial difficulties. At the beginning of May 1827 Jerdan wrote to James Hogg, replying to what was evidently a request to be put forward to the Royal Society of Literature for a grant. Jerdan explained that Hogg's works of popular poetry and fiction stood no chance of success with that body. "It is rather for the encouragement of learning than of that kind of literature which may be sustained by making itself popular; and therefore authors of works requiring great labour and deep research (yet of a character not to attract general readers) come more distinctly within its sphere than authors of works of fancy and imagination."[50] Perhaps to sweeten the blow, Jerdan also mentioned that he had read Hogg's early works whilst a schoolboy in Kelso, and they had made a lasting impression upon him. At the same time Jerdan wrote to William Blackwood in Edinburgh, advising him of Hogg's plight and suggesting that an application be made to the Literary Fund. He was sensitive about not hurting Hogg's feelings, although "In my own judgment it ought not to do so – for every man is (and literary men most of all are) liable to depression, and need not be ashamed of sympathy and assistance."[51] He asked Blackwood to "smooth away any difficulties" in the matter. In May 1827 Jerdan apprised the Literary Fund Committee that Hogg was in an "embarrassed situation". Because Hogg had a "considerable reputation both as a Poet and as a writer of many popular works of fiction" the Fund granted him fifty pounds, "being on the largeish scale of the Society's grants" to be transmitted to Hogg through Jerdan.[52] Jerdan sent Hogg's acknowledgement to the Committee with a covering note saying that "from the nature of the letter that it would be unpleasant to my feelings to have it either read to the Committee or kept". The Fund's files do not include Hogg's letter, so they would appear to have honoured Jerdan's request.

However, his modesty may been disingenuous, as in his memoir he includes a most flattering letter from Hogg which is undated, but thanks Jerdan for the "valuable present", although uncertain as to what fund provided it.[53] Hogg remarked dryly, "I now see what hitherto I have sparingly believed, that it is not those who make the most glowing expressions of esteem or admiration etc. that are most to be depended on." Hogg mentioned the few days he had recently spent with Sir Walter Scott, who believed that Jerdan generally carried out what he undertook, and Hogg would confide only in Scott that Jerdan had indeed been of vital assistance to him. Hogg was at pains to explain that he was in financial difficulties not because of his own concerns, but because he had to take on the burdens of providing for three households of his family. Telling Jerdan that he had many manuscripts ready, he asked for some advice about publishing them, but apologized for selfishly taking up Jerdan's time; he was "really so proud at finding that I have a *real* and *sterling literary friend* which to my fondest estimations has hitherto proved rather equivocal . . . ". If this was indeed the letter enclosed to the Literary Fund, small wonder that Jerdan was embarrassed to have it read aloud to his co-committee members. An anonymous admirer of Hogg sent him a gift of twenty pounds, also using Jerdan as an intermediary.

With so many things on his mind, it was not perhaps surprising that in a note of July 1827 Jerdan wrote to the publisher Richard Bentley, that he had met with a severe accident and could not attend to much. He had had a narrow escape with his life but was in no danger. This might have been one of the many occasions when he was thrown from a carriage, or even the consequence of an accident arising from drinking too much. It may have been this accident, or a real ailment which caused Landon to comfort him:

> I am most truly sorry to hear of your illness – you will be quite knocked up, I wish you could go out of town for two or three days, a run down to Brighton would do you a world of good, leave the Gazette to me, would you trust it . . . I would call at your house, but I am afraid, for if any body here were to be ill six months hence, I should be thought to have brought hooping cough etc . . . Yours very pityingly, I should be so glad to do anything for you, to send you to Brighton would be the best service.[54]

Another undated letter in a December, told him, "I am very anxious to hear what you are doing – I think if you could manage it a run down to Clifton would do you a world of good. I want so to know if you approved my review of the 'Book of Beauty'. I miss so very much not being able to talk to you about my judgments before they become quite definite . . . I was so sorry to hear of your sore throat."[55]

Despite his illnesses and troubles with the *Literary Gazette*, Jerdan had not completely lost his sense of humour; he attended a 'conversazione' hosted by the Marquis of Northampton. Beards were not yet in fashion, and only two men at the gathering wore them. One was Mr Ward, a Royal Academician with failing eyesight, and the other the 'Blind Traveller' James Holman. Jerdan mirthfully recalled, "I took an opportunity to introduce them to each other, and as one was blind and the other could not see, advised the cultivation of a further intimacy by the mutual stroking of beards – a ceremony they performed with hearty laughter, and to the no small amusement of a little circle of admiring spectators."[56]

A small matter occurring in early April had unwelcome repercussions for Jerdan later that month. He let his admiration for Canning run away with him in a review of Ward's *De Vere*.[57] The book contained a portrayal of an ideal statesman, a god-like character, whom the Literary Gazette identified as Canning. Ward, pretending to be embarrassed by this, wrote at length to Canning distancing himself from such indelicacy, protesting about "the officiousness of the reviewer (whoever he may be, and however sincere in his admiration of yourself)". Canning reassured Ward that "While I concur with you in regretting the indiscretion of the editor of the Literary Gazette," he was not in the least offended. "I must be very sensitive if, after thirty-three years of Parliamentary life, any allusions of the press, in good or evil part, could seriously affect my equanimity."[58] The repercussions of the over-enthusiastic review were soon to become apparent.

With his vast network of acquaintances, writers and colleagues on a multitude of organizations. Jerdan was well placed to hear gossip and rumour. One occasion stood out far above all others. His friend Thomas Hunt, distinguished writer on architecture and a restorer of royal palaces, was working in St James Palace on 12 April 1827. Trapped unwittingly in a side room from which he could not escape without risking severe repercussions, Hunt was a hidden ear to a secret conversation. The King had just then invited Jerdan's hero, George Canning, to become Prime Minister, and retiring to the room adjacent to Hunt's, discussed this meeting with his confidante, the Marchioness of Conyngham. Hunt was terrified – he was eavesdropping on the King, too late to make his presence known. Once the King had moved away, Hunt left the Palace and went straight to Jerdan, who was delighted to learn from him that the King's impression of Canning was at least as high as his own, and that he believed the new Prime Minister would "conduct the affairs of the Kingdom to the heights of prosperity and glory".[59]

Overcome with emotion that his sovereign admired Canning as much as he did, Jerdan at once hastened the next morning to Downing Street, so that he could impart his privileged knowledge to the Prime Minister. Canning's private secretary, Stapleton, assured Jerdan that Canning could not possibly see him, burdened as he was with affairs of state and the appointment of ministers on this first morning in office. Jerdan persisted, insisting that his card be taken to Canning, on which he had written "Dear Sir – pray see me – if it were not of sufficient consequence I would not ask at such a time." To Stapleton's evident amazement Canning agreed. Jerdan was shown to a first floor room overlooking Downing Street where, waiting for his audience, he became "exceedingly agitated and worked up to so distressing a state of nervous tremor" that he sank into the nearest chair. In his highly charged state he could hardly believe his eyes when the bookcase in front of him swung open, and Canning entered the room. Struggling to his feet, Jerdan was overwhelmed to find that the Prime Minister was giving him his whole hand to shake, not just the one or two fingers usually proffered. For Jerdan, this was the surest sign of acceptance.

The interview which followed, as related in detail by Jerdan, was not only momentous for him, as sealing the tie of friendship between the holder of the highest office in the land, and the mere journalist/editor, but also throws light on how closely linked Jerdan was to the delicate political situation occurring on that day. Astonishingly, Canning seemed to have had time for a cosy chat, as

Jerdan described him placing two chairs with their backs to the window, and launching into a minute exposition about his interview with the King. Of course, we only have Jerdan's word for this extraordinary behaviour, but the wealth of detail and the fact that when he wrote about it thirty years later it was still so clear to him, tend to confirm that the meeting did take place in the way he related. Canning even showed him the manner in which the King extended his hand to be kissed, a nugget of play-acting that surely even the literary-minded Jerdan would not have invented. Canning divulged that the King had asked him what his intentions were, should the Protestant factions in Cabinet object to his appointment. Canning told him, in secrecy, that a prominent Whig had already promised the Opposition's support should this occur. Somehow the secret "oozed out", as Jerdan put it, and the consequence was that on this first day in office, seven members of the Cabinet resigned, and Canning found himself alone. Peel and Wellington, members of the Cabinet who may each have expected to be Prime Minister, were overlooked by the King, Peel as too junior and inexperienced, and Wellington because he had become commander-in-chief on the death of the Duke of York. Since the previous Prime Minister Lord Liverpool's illness and inability to continue in office since February, these two hopefuls "were not so much directly rejected by the King, as shelved during the course of a month of what Professor Aspinall has described as 'masterly inactivity'".[60]

Reluctant to appoint a Prime Minister once it was clear that a solidly Protestant government could not be formed, Canning was the obvious choice. Peel was violently against Roman Catholic concessions, whereas Canning was more liberally minded. (It was an irony, therefore, that within a few years Peel's views changed completely and he made the necessary concessions to Rome.) Over the previous two years the King had moved from an aversion to Canning to a liking: "the opposition of the great families of the country to a 'charlatan parvenu' only strengthened the King's belief that he was fighting the pretensions of the great aristocratic cliques which had tried to monopolize the office during his father's reign."[61] Sensitive to criticisms of Canning as a 'parvenu', Jerdan noted that the same could be said of Lord Eldon and the Duke of Wellington, who also rose from the ranks. Not everyone saw Canning's appointment merely as a revolt against paternal traditions. For the public and the press, his appointment was the most popular ever known.

No wonder then, that Canning on his first day, nervous and deserted by his ministers, found time and evident relief in discussing the situation with his old friend William Jerdan. Alternately flushed and pale, Canning's demeanour brought home to Jerdan "on how fragile a thread of human endurance the fate of a nation and the welfare or misery of millions may depend".[62] Jerdan was frightened for his friend's health. Bringing this unprecedented interview to a close, Canning asked Jerdan to attend the House of Commons every night, and make notes of his impressions, to be sent to the Prime Minister next morning, a task Jerdan could accomplish with ease because of his earlier journalistic experience on the *Sun* and other newspapers. Complying with this request gave Jerdan access to the Prime Minister whenever he wished.

Canning's political expertise overcame the split that his appointment had caused the Tory party, and he gathered a Cabinet which included moderate Whigs and the Hon. William Lamb (later Lord Melbourne). Canning faced violent hostility in the House, most notably from Earl Grey who denounced him "in one of the most personal invectives that ever was delivered in the Parliament of England",[63] an attack which Canning was unable to refute in his old articulate way, as his health declined under the strain. He was aware that Peel had not only resigned from the Cabinet, but was actively fomenting opposition – something Jerdan had forecast in one of his daily notes, which Canning had not yet had time to read. Upon doing so, he joked with Jerdan that he had inherited the second sight of his native country and was "an astute political prophet". In recalling these events, Jerdan forestalled any accusation of self-aggrandisement on the grounds that such intimate glimpses into the mind of a Prime Minister would not be of interest to future generations, an evidently ingenuous comment as he devoted many pages of his *Autobiography* to recounting them.

Mired as Jerdan was in charges of "puffing", despite the plethora of protests about editorial independence that pepper the *Autobiography*, he was quite prepared to use his considerable influence on behalf of his friends. The difference was that in the first instance he had pressure put upon him, but in the latter case he was in the driving seat, and wished to use his position at the *Literary Gazette* to promote those he admired. As always, there was a 'quid pro quo'. The most blatant example of this was Jerdan's letter to Prime Minister Canning in 1827; this was not concerned with 'puffing', but asked outright for some recognition in return for his services, albeit that it take the form of affording help in running the *Literary Gazette* to free him up to actively support Canning:

> I occupy a singular position in the literary world, and may claim the merit of some tact and discretion, if not of some talent, in having made my journal so widely influential. The result is that from the highest to almost the lowest class of public writers I am of sufficient importance to possess a very considerable weight with them. From book authors, through all gradations of the periodical press, it is not a boast to assert that I could do much to modify opinions, heat friends and cool enemies. I am on terms of personal intimacy with 49 out of 50 of those who direct the leading journals of the day; and I can from time to time oblige them all. Thus situated, I need not assure you that I have not failed to do what I could, where your interests were involved. But I am convinced that I could do

so much more; and without a compromise of any kind imperceptibly. I insensibly exercise a very desirable influence over these organs of public opinion.

Why I cannot do all I wish, without troubling you, is simply on account of my want of time and sufficient fortune to execute what I purpose. My Gazette nets nearly five thousand pounds a year, of which I have rather more than one-third; but every moment of my life is laboriously devoted to it. Should you think well of what I have stated, and find me eligible for any mark of favour which would enable me to associate an efficient coadjutor in the 'Literary Gazette' and take myself a somewhat higher status in society, I would without doubt or fear of success undertake to produce very beneficial consequences throughout the whole machinery of the press. It requires but cultivation.
I have etc. W Jerdan

I come even at this moment because I consider no time should be lost in meeting a bitter opposition and rallying supporters against it.

This appeal, written on 19 April 1827, appears to have gone unanswered. Canning no doubt had fresh in his mind Jerdan's indiscretion in the review of Ward's *De Vere* less than two weeks before, and his assurance to Ward that the press could not affect his equanimity. He had every reason to believe in Jerdan's loyal support, but little reason to believe in his powers of diplomacy and discretion. Jerdan tried again on 5 May, this time addressing himself to Canning's Secretary, Mr Stapleton. His letter was verbose, but his sincerity and enthusiasm to be of service to his idol Canning, are manifest. The letter referred back to the episode of his secret cipher used by the Foreign Office, and even his tiny part on the occasion of Perceval's assassination; he reiterated his request to Canning, continuing:

I trust it will be felt that this is not a selfish position, if in order to do what I wish I should give up a considerable portion of income, and risk the principal on which it is founded. But I am not, on the other hand, insensible to the benefit which might be to me and mine, if I were thought worthy to be brought forward at this stirring period . . .

I hope it may be anticipated that I would proceed with delicacy and discretion. My connections with the press being altogether literary renders me liable to no suspicion . . . My present situation in life is such that I flatter myself no objection could be urged against my eligibility for any payment, with which Mr Canning might think it right to honour me . . . I am persuaded that I could be essentially useful to his Administration and from the bottom of my soul I desire to be so. the present question can only be defeated if unfortunately deemed open to improper construction.

For myself, I am confident an arrangement might be effected without a scruple or a whisper ... It is painful to write about oneself, but the object contemplated is in my mind of infinite importance, and every hour delayed is a disadvantage. Pray pardon this letter and believe me to be etc.[64]

Two days later Jerdan received Stapleton's terse reply, advising him that Canning had commented that

considering one of the great grounds of attack on the Government is the influence possessed over it by the press, it is obviously necessary that he should have it in his power to deny in the House of Commons as distinctly as he now can do, and as Lord Goderich has desired in the House of Lords, that the influence of the Government has been employed to induce the press to support it. You will easily perceive how impossible it would be for Mr Canning to do this after consenting to adopt the project for which you recommend.

In the book of Canning's *Correspondence*, Stapleton mentioned that he was unaware of any previous friendship between Canning and Jerdan, so wrongly believed Jerdan to be opportunistic in approaching the Prime Minister. However, he also noted it to be his opinion that "Jerdan was a truly honest man", although he had "under-estimated the liability of the proposed transaction to suffer from malicious interpretation." Stapleton also believed that had an official promotion been conferred upon Jerdan as he requested, jealousy would "have dissolved nine-tenths of the influence on the strength of which he pleaded for the promotion". Wellington had been severe upon the matter of corruption in the press, thus giving Canning additional reasons for declining Jerdan's suggestion. On the same day as he received Stapleton's letter rejecting his help Jerdan wrote again, worried that the opposition already had its press support in place: "I am of the opinion that Lord Lowther has got the start in influencing the *John Bull*. The *Morning Post* I am inclined to believe, has some friend with the Duke of Wellington at its side." In the same note he asked if Canning would consent to take the chair at the forthcoming Literary Fund Dinner. Stapleton noted a little cynically, "This excellent and good litteraire writes more probably primarily with a view to bring his personality again before Mr Canning; secondly to mark his useful knowledge of the movements in the 'press' world ... " He may have been right, but it is indisputable that Jerdan's desire to be of service to Canning was heartfelt and genuine, and any benefit accruing to himself, although it would have been welcome, was of secondary importance. Certainly if he was receiving, as he mentioned in his first letter, "rather more than one-third" of the *Literary Gazette's* net profits, he was very well remunerated for his work and for his share in the journal; he was asking Canning primarily for preferment, not for money.

To Jerdan's surprise, in reply to his request, Canning agreed, finally, to join the Royal Society of Literature and, contrary to his principles five years previously, agreed to preside at the Literary Fund Anniversary Dinner the following month. On this memorable occasion Canning was accompanied by Chateaubriand, whom the Literary Fund had aided years previously, when he fled from the guillotine in the French Revolution. To repay this debt the famous visitor gave fifty pounds to the Fund. Jerdan was delighted that at last, after years of reluctance, Canning had finally made overt his desire to promote literature and the position of authors.

Just when Jerdan rejoiced that Canning had made public his support for literature, disaster struck. Following hard on the heels of Jerdan's recent bereavements, his dear friend George Canning fell ill and was taken to Chiswick where he died on 8 August 1827. It was said that he had caught cold when attending the midnight funeral of the Duke of York in January, in a bitterly cold St George's Chapel, Windsor.[65] Brooding about this a long time afterwards, Jerdan confessed that he never forgave himself for not offering Grove House for Canning's comfort. Brompton's air was so much better than Chiswick's and it was nearer to town. Jerdan remained convinced that he might have been the means of saving Canning's life. In the event, he requested and was granted a ticket to attend the funeral. Canning was buried in Westminster Abbey, commemorated by a statue in the Abbey and another, by Chantrey, in the garden of the House of Commons.

With Canning's death, Jerdan's hopes of using his influence for preferment for his sons and indeed for himself, died too. The accumulated loss was hard to bear. The earlier bereavements were bad enough, but for Jerdan, Canning's death was of another order: he had given the man his complete devotion for twenty years, and had shared many private as well as public experiences with him, and putting aside any differences they had had about press influence on politics, Jerdan had appreciated and relished the acknowledgement and friendship Canning had shown to him in return.[66]

Turning his attention back once more to literature, and using his experience and knowledge of the publishing business, Jerdan helped Landon to get good terms for her third book, *The Golden Violet with its Tales and Romance and Chivalry*. It was published by Longmans, forgetting their reluctance over *The Fate of Adelaide* and *The Improvisatrice*, ready to publish her now that she had established a following for her poetry. It was said that Landon received a thousand pounds for this volume.[67] Longmans printed two thousand copies, but six months later still had six hundred and forty in stock. These did not sell out for another ten years.[68] Another source agrees with the two thousand printed originally, but notes that Longman's archive shows a further five hundred printed in 1839, just after Landon's death, and another five hundred in 1844. A letter of 1 June from Longman to Jerdan agreed to half profits with an advance of two hundred pounds, "although it is contrary to the usual practice of the house".[69] Jerdan was clearly acting here as agent for Landon.

Jerdan reviewed *The Golden Violet* on the front page of the *Literary Gazette* of 16 December 1826. Before he got down to the book itself, he filled two columns with a discussion of the spirit of poesy in England, an Augustan epoch following the Elizabethan, a later epoch following the Augustan, each with a long and dreary time between. Now:

> There is a harvest of 'Beauties' for posterity to select, the extent of which, we who live in the midst of them are not able to estimate or appreciate. But still the mass of compositions was so over-whelming that three or four years ago, poetry became almost a drug – the glorious feast was over and the replete public had no taste, no appetite for more . . . In this state of languour the youthful poetess whose volume is now before us essayed her powers, and we have no doubt in tracing a potent revival of the influence of poetry to her enchanting pen . . . .it was reserved for a female in her teens, truly and gloriously to portray the tender affections, the sweet sympathies and the warmest emotions of feminine loveliness.

There was more, Jerdan praising L.E.L.'s poem *Erinna* as "perhaps the highest effort of L.E.L.'s genius" a perhaps inappropriately gushing effusion liable to call down scorn on his own head. Recalling his chiding of Blackwood for treating L.E.L. badly, Jerdan sent him a copy of the book with the heavy hint that "I am in great hopes to see a good review of *The Golden Violet* in your next No. Assuredly no writer of true poetic feeling but must desire to cherish genius like what is displayed in this Vol. and with the double recommendation of youth and sex."[70] *The Golden Violet* was not universally applauded. The *Monthly Review* criticized the other periodicals for praising L.E.L. so effusively, complaining that she spoke far too often of "love", at least on every second page, and once even using the word to rhyme with itself. Jerdan, whilst sometimes believing that she wrote too quickly and without time for revision, had no such scruples about her writing on the subject of "love", especially where much of it was so clearly addressed to him.

He received a manuscript which Blackwood had received from an unnamed writer, apparently a review of *The Golden Violet*. Blackwood had sent it to Jerdan for comment, and in rejecting it Jerdan evidently felt strongly that the writer was adversely criticizing his beloved L.E.L. and took the time to set out his objections at some length, an exercise which illuminates his protective attitude to his protégée:

> it certainly is not written in the spirit of kindness for the author. I do not object so much to the Criticisms on what is censureable; but surely it does

not do justice [to the] genius and multitude of natural beauties in the writer. The fairer way it seems to me of weighing a young and female candidate for poetical fame, is not to treat her as a matured and laborious author, but compare her with any other of her age and sex that ever existed, and see if there is any example of half so much talent. But I am a very partial judge in this particular instance, and may be wrong while your Critic is right . . . But look yourself at the noble composition Erinna and see if it deserves ridicule.[71]

Even though this now unknown critic had "power so great that the friends of the poet could not help being very anxious for your good word combined with truth and justice", Jerdan insisted on the superiority of his poet on the grounds of her talent, as well as her youth and sex.

This was the beginning of the hey-day of the annuals, Christmas gift books. Already having contributed to Ackermann's *Forget-Me-Not*, and Alaric Watts's *Literary Souvenir*, Landon now became involved with writing for a new one, the *Keepsake*. Her increasing output to satisfy the demand did not distract her from her major task of reviewing for the *Literary Gazette*, although the quantity of poetry she contributed to it decreased slightly. Jerdan too contributed to an annual in this year. One of his contributions to *Friendship's Offering* in 1827 was *Bagatelle Compliment*, sixteen lines, the first verse about ordinary people going to heaven needing to be changed into angels; the second verse addressed to his "peerless Fair", that now she is gone, she was an angel "ready-made". His other contribution was a short piece – not worthy of the word "poem", *The Proper Word; the idea taken from a French writer*. The bard sings about the 'house' that holds his beloved, but is challenged that 'house' is a poor word. Palace, castle or chateau would be loftier, but in the end it does not matter as

> " . . . they've sent, far, far, from me,
> To an *Hospital* the girl I love."

Landon had no reason to fear any competition from Jerdan in the matter of poetry composition.

This paltry offering of Jerdan's was but one of the many derogatory references made about him by Robert Montgomery, only nineteen years old, who did not like the way the country was going. Samuel Carter Hall recollected that Montgomery had shown him his satirical work and consulted him as to its publication. "It consisted of a series of assaults on all the leading poets and critics of the time: a David assailing a hundred Goliaths, without knowing how to use his sling."[72] Ignoring Hall's advice to throw it into the fire, the poem was duly published, "a wanton act of aggression," said Hall, "that, before long, no one had reason to lament more bitterly than its author." Montgomery vented his spleen, not only against the critics and poets, but against every aspect of society, in his verse satire, *The Age Reviewed*. Jerdan's name collected numerous mentions, which although painful to him, indicated the strength of his influence and high profile. Montgomery was not too subtle in his attack – most references to Jerdan are accompanied by an explanatory footnote, in case the full impact of his satire had passed the reader by. In the Introductory Dialogue we read, "Or jingling Jerdan paved the road to fame", with a note that "There is no one more capable of giving a new work a good introductory impetus than Mr W Jerdan, or to shew my respect for all HE says, 'The witty Mr J.'. – but let him not hear of your delinquencies in failing to admire him and his columns!"

This was mild stuff, and Montgomery picked up steam when he subjected Landon and Jerdan's relationship to his bile:

> Miss Thomas Moore (1) by Jerdan puff'd to fame,–
> Landon, or L.E.L. – whate'er thy name –
> So fervid, flowery, sparkling in thy page,
> Let school-girls trump thee, Sappho of the age!
> . . .
> Fie on the furious tongues that dare to speak
> 'Gainst thee, verse-fountain of the month and week
> While touchy Jerdan (2) hums a "Proper Word",
> Thy Sapphic moans shall balm the sighing herd;
> Did Crusca live, how would he pine to see,
> A burning Anna, realized in thee?

His footnote (1) stated:

"L.E.L. or Miss Landon, or Jerdan's Protégée, or the verse manufacturer for every magazine, review and journal, has dwindled into more superfineries than ever, since the publication of her 'Improvisatrice'. It is a great pity that she does not unshackle her mind from the controlling calculations of her mis-guided friend Jerdan. His glaring, enormous flatteries in the Literary Gazette will not *eventually* complete her fame, or gender improvement. Campbell says of her, 'She has turned her head into a cullendar, and all her brains are daily running out.' I trust Mrs Hemans will take the friendly hint, for she is becoming rather too common.

Footnote (2) was pointed, but not unjust:

Jerdan exposed himself very dangerously by printing 'The Proper Word' in *Friendship's Offering*. No one ever did him the justice to think him a poet, or a properly qualified critic; but such inharmonious doggerel was a sad *denouement* from the president – the poetical judge that sways the columns of the most popular Gazette in the Kingdom!! 'Pooh,' replies Jerdan, 'what care I for the opinions of the discerning? Seated round my port, I pronounce damnation or salvation on authors – just as the whim takes me – the weather affects me – or prejudice guides me.'

Elsewhere, Montgomery beat the same drum:

> Supremely blest! who, far from Jerdan's frown (1),
> Obtains a column for his week's renown;
> Like warbling Sappho, bends his pliant quill,
> To push a poem up Parnassus' hill; (2)
> Then, smooth that stream of praise, to authors dear –
> For tickled Jerdan lends a listening ear.

Montgomery must have thought he was risking too much by his damning comments on one of the most influential editors of the day. He used his foot-note (1) to mollify his target somewhat:

Mr William Jerdan is, "take him all in all", the most good-natured of those critics, not overburdened with discrimination and talent: perhaps it is somewhat creditable to him that he has brought his Gazette to such an unrivalled circulation as it now enjoys.

The country papers were castigated for merely copying the *Literary Gazette* without using their own judgment, saying which he was "aware that I am subjecting myself unto a bit of dirty DAMNATION ... but really I cannot resist writing a little truth ... " In his footnote (2) Montgomery fulminated:

It is rather audacious for Mr Jerdan to pronounce so positively on poetry, being himself so incapable of stringing a few decent verses together. Shaftesbury says 'every WRITING critic is bound to show himself capable of being a writer; for, if he be apparently impotent in this latter kind, he is to be denied all title or character in the other.' What says Mr Jerdan?

Alaric Watts was also vilified by the young satirist's vicious pen:

> Entranced, if Jerdan yield a barter'd page,
> Where, on young merit thou canst vomit rage ...
> ... Remorseful there, dissect thy feeble line,
> And print us all the tinsel, PURELY thine.(1)

Resuscitating the famous quarrel, Montgomery said, at (1):

Doubtless the reader must remember, that whilst all the rest of the world were pouring forth their homage to the genius of Byron, the *Literary Gazette* was making itself stupidly singular, by cavilling and pecking at his Lordship, in all manner of ways. In this respect, partial injustice has been done to Jerdan: the 'Plagiarisms' as they were called, of Lord Byron, were grabbed up by Alaric Watts, to whose envious despotism, Jerdan had, for a while, delivered the critical reins. Alaric Watts was never much esteemed before this – after this mean attempt, the littleness of his soul was too apparent to escape universal censure.

Montgomery even managed to include a gibe at the row between Jerdan and Wright over the "false champagne", with a footnote that "Mr Jerdan shows up this wine monger and his brotherhood with critical elegance". There were various other mentions of Jerdan's name, including the oft-quoted couplet "From them will Jerdan peck, and Colburn puff,/ Till all but author cry out, 'quantum suff!'" It is clear why Hall advised the satirist to throw his script into the fire, from these references to Jerdan alone, but the whole, more than sixty pages long, is equally, or more virulent about other notables in all fields of endeavour.

The *Literary Gazette* greeted *The Age Reviewed* with:

We have been tempted to bestow more exposure upon this empty coxcomb than he is worth; but as his impudence appeared to be on a par with his ignorance, his effrontery with his want of talent, and his baseness with his bad poetry, we trust we shall be pardoned for the castigation we have bestowed upon him... Many portions of the work ... so gross, offensive, and beastly as to be utterly unfit for any place but the stews ... altogether

By the time he came to write his *Autobiography*, Jerdan recalled that *The Age Reviewed* in which he had been so cruelly vilified by Montgomery, had been "lost sight of". It had received, he remarked, "strong and decided disapprobation at my hands, notwithstanding their author had been introduced and welcomed to very intimate terms and social attentions in my house, where he had opportunities of meeting persons to whom it was not undesirable that a rising bard should be known".[73]

In later life Montgomery calmed down and became a clergyman, but not before another literary offering, *The Omnipresence of the Deity* was published by Maunder in 1828 and reviewed in two instalments by the *Literary Gazette*. A second edition was swiftly printed, about which Jerdan generously stated:

True genius is a rare plant and we should be ashamed of ourselves and our station in the literary world if we permitted either a cold-heartedness as individuals, or a cold criticalness as public writers, to rob us of that sympathy and enthusiasm which the first efforts of struggling genius is so finely calculated to inspire . . .

In his reminiscences, Jerdan noted that at the time he had stood virtually alone in vindicating the writer's "poetic character", an opinion which was soon taken up generally. Montgomery became a poet celebrated by many, although now obscure, and often linked with Landon as two minor poets once famous but forgotten with time.[74] Jerdan also gave room to *Satan*, another poem of Montgomery's in January 1830, saying that he had not "the leisure to give it the attention its elevated character and importance demands" but devoted three pages to extracts, demonstrating yet again that he was not a man to bear a grudge. Montgomery's works went through many editions, although at the outset, "the whole Trade took only six copies! But the *Literary Gazette* reviews soon turned the scale and when the third edition was called, the publisher, in thanking me, stated that he had sold two thousand copies over the counter in ten days –a poetical sale unequalled since the days of 'Childe Harold' ".[75]

Jerdan's characteristic trait of not bearing a grudge was also evident in a note to Alaric Watts in December 1827. In addition to the *Literary Souvenir*, Watts was considering embarking on a new venture, possibly a right-wing newspaper *The Standard*. He had asked Jerdan's opinion and was told,

> You know the principles on which the *Literary Gazette* has been conducted, and my feelings with regard to fair and gentleman-like competition too entirely *in cute*, to doubt not only of my approving of your entering, should you see fit, on a weekly literary publication but of my wishing it to succeed in your hands. I must have been a consummate blockhead could I have fancied that it would be in my power to keep such a field for my own monopoly; and so far from thinking an honest rivalry injurious, I am persuaded it is the reverse.[76]

This generosity of spirit was not emulated by other journal editors. The *Age*, musing on "A Procession of Blues in Regent Street" noted "Miss Landon in swandown muff and tippet, acting *The Improvisatrice*, with a necklace of <u>Jerdan</u> mock brilliants; her appearance is more of the <u>gazelle</u> than the <u>gazette</u> although much puffed by the latter, a <u>man milliner</u>.[77] The *Literary Chronicle*, a look-alike imitation of the far more successful *Gazette*, sought opportunities to criticize Jerdan and his journal. In their issue of 5 April 1828 they created one out of odds and ends of literary matters, including quoting from the *Gazette*'s reception of *The Age Reviewed*, jeering about its critic's "style", and pointing out that "in some dozen lines of his satire [Montgomery] dared to speak derisively of a certain sacred person named Jerdan. What could be more wicked! Such a circumstance could not but contaminate the whole poem, and acting the reverse of the philosopher's stone, convert gold into rubbish. Such conduct was intolerable; and all the thunders of criticism were called into action, to annihilate the audacious satirist. They have however, proved mere 'bruta fulmina'."[78] The *Chronicle* wrongly noted that *The Omnipresence of the Deity* was Montgomery's first work, and called him "one of our greatest poets".

The *Chronicle's* article had been inspired by a comment in the *Edinburgh Review*, that "The success of some late literary journals only proves the demand for such matter, not, we fear, the capacity of their conductors adequately and worthily to supply it; the scissors being in truth the mechanical power mainly brought into play by these humble, though very useful personages." Jerdan had taken this attack personally, giving rise to the *Chronicle* sarcastically calling him "the illustrious editor", and observing, "The most offensive thing about the *Edinburgh Review* appears to be, however, its indulgence in puffs. This is too much for the sensitive nerves of the editor of the *Literary Gazette* – puff being a word absolutely wanting to his own vocabulary. He never speaks contemptuously of his neighbours, he never praises the superiority of his own journal which 'Like Aaron's serpent swallows all the rest.'" They chided him for comparing Landon to Sappho, and his partiality for the poetess, and others from Colburn's stable. However much this article may have upset him at the time, Jerdan had the last laugh, as the *Literary Chronicle* folded three months later, and became absorbed into the *Athenaeum*. Always regarded as inseparable, Jerdan and the *Literary Gazette* were both attacked in *The Inspector, Literary Magazine and Review* (Vol. II, 1827). *The Plan for a National Currency* was criticized at some length and in the same issue the *Gazette* was lampooned in a feature entitled 'Saturnalia'.

Although Jerdan purported not to care about these barbed comments, their cumulative effect would have wounded him, but not enough to make him wary of praising to an excessive degree everything Letitia Landon wrote.

Part III

The Editor's Life,
1828–1840

10

Athenaeum Competition and Challenging Projects

aving sailed through the choppy seas of Westmacott's vilification of himself and his journal, Jerdan now faced a greater challenge. After all the flattering and not-so-flattering imitators of the *Literary Gazette* which had appeared and disappeared over the course of nearly ten years, another now arrived on the scene. This one was to prove impossible to dislodge, and was eventually to topple the *Literary Gazette* from its pedestal. One of its chief weapons was the resuscitation of the old complaint against Jerdan, that of 'puffing'.

The *Athenaeum* was started by James Silk Buckingham in 1828, in equal partnership with the ubiquitous Henry Colburn. Jerdan's recollection of the circumstances surrounding Colburn's interest in the new periodical was that Colburn was so offended by the *Literary Gazette*'s impartiality in reviewing books produced under his imprint that he supported the *Athenaeum* at the expense of his interest in Jerdan's *Gazette*. Colburn's own words confirm this. He wrote to Jerdan and Longmans on 31 December 1827:[1]

> As my partners in the *Literary Gazette* I think it is right to apprise you that I have joined Mr Buckingham in the new literary journal, the *Athenaeum*.
>
> I have determined in adopting this step in consequence of the injustice done to *my authors* generally (who are on the liberal side) by the *Literary Gazette*. I cannot any longer consent to see my best authors unfairly reviewed, and my own property injured, and often sacrificed to the politics of that paper.
>
> At the same time I may state, that the step I am now taking does not seem likely to injure the sale of the *L.G*. The *Athenaeum* will be published on another day in the week; it will address persons of other politics, and *when likely to be treated with impartiality* in the *L.G.*, early copies shall be supplied to both publications on the same day, leaving it to chance which shall anticipate the other in its notices of them.

Colburn was trying to hedge his bets by part-owning both periodicals, assuming that if not both, at least one of them would 'puff' or favourably review the books he published. Jerdan called it a "little suicidal act of pique and folly". He was piqued himself enough to take the time to re-examine copies of the *Literary Gazette* for 1827, analyzing the reviews that Colburn protested about. He dismissed the jibe about politics – the *Gazette* didn't go in for politics, having been warned off the subject by Canning, although Jerdan himself was an ardent Tory; Colburn was not a political man, being motivated solely by profit. Jerdan found that all the publisher's books had received praise, to the extent that the *Literary Gazette* had been reproached for its "good nature and being indiscriminately favourable to everybody".

One of the exceptions to the good reviews given to Colburn's books had tipped the publisher over into the *Athenaeum* camp. His feelings had been hurt by a critical review of Lady Morgan's novel, *O'Brien's and O'Flaherty's* for which he had paid a generous thirteen hundred pounds. Jerdan had not known at the time that this author was to Colburn "an idol of his Heroine worship".[2] Worse, Jerdan admitted that "there was no love lost" between Lady Morgan and himself: he had been presented to her at a soirée, and later heard that she had complained to a friend at "the idea of presenting that odious man to Me!" (He may well have been odious that night as, telling the tale against himself, he had been asked to stand in for the absent host. Excited by the company, he "contrived, through toast, sentiment, and the eliciting of interesting conversation, to do justice to my position and astonish the fine old butler by the frequency of his intercourse with the Bacchanalian regions".)[3] Jerdan concluded that Colburn's anger, far from the reasons set out in his letter, was in fact purely personal: the *Literary Gazette* had not praised an author whom the publisher especially admired, especially as in Jerdan's eyes the book was not suitable for young ladies. In a nice twist of irony, Colburn eventually sold off his interest in the *Athenaeum* and lost Lady Morgan's next book, *Review of France 1829–30*, to rival publishers Saunders and Otley.[4]

Throwing a more objective light on Jerdan's poor review of Lady Morgan's book, and on Jerdan himself, was a letter discussing the matter from one of his close friends, Crofton Croker, to another, William Blackwood:

Poor Lady Morgan! Her 'O'Briens and O'Flaherties' seems to have fallen dead, completely dead, from the press. The book is decidely dull, but still her name ought to have carried an edition through. Colburn, I hear, swears that Jerdan's having discovered it was an improper book for ladies to read has cost him £500 and really this is not impossible. The man of New Burlington Street [Colburn] is therefor (sic) very angry with the moral editor of the *Literary Gazette* and to this has been attributed the taking up of the *Athenaeum*. Jerdan smarts, but nevertheless chuckles at his own impartiality – just criticism and duty to the public etc. etc. I believe too, from my soul, that Jerdan fancies all this; but the fact is he is naturally of the disposition that in the very face of truth he is continually doing flattering if not kind things to the set of literary midges which buzz about him and consider his commendations as sufficient to establish their reputation as wits, scholars and poets.[5]

There were other *Literary Gazette* reviews of Colburn's publications during 1827 which angered him, such as the review of *Hyde Nugent* which included an attack on puffery, and called the work "a commonplace story . . . offensive to good taste and always frivolous".[6] A comment on another of Colburn's books called it "very silly, full of ridiculous opinions".[7] Yet another was "too verbose, too desultory . . . all the love history is bad".[8] Such instances show that Jerdan was not as entirely under Colburn's thumb as his enemies accused and, ready as he had been to use his influence for Canning's benefit, Jerdan was still careful about promoting works he had not read, even for close friends. In November he wrote to Allan Cunningham:

> There is no judgment (in <u>this</u> world) that I would rely on more than your's, and if I do not insert your notice of the Ant till I see something of the Ant, you are not to impute it to scepticism – for I am orthodox in what I have just proposed. But my rule has been to see, where possible, and confirm by my own knowledge, that I have gratefully admitted from any other quarter. <u>You</u> will readily perceive that by this means alone I could play the difficult cards (dirty paper!) I have to play. I stand the brunt of L.G. and <u>no</u> body has <u>no</u> claims from my being friendly to my friends.[9]

Although Landon was always an exception, a letter like this and a few surviving similar ones, reinforce Jerdan's frequent claims at the time, and all through his *Autobiography*, that he did not show favour to his friends unless it was deserved – his influence could not be taken for granted.

Jerdan recalled that Buckingham had offered to sell the *Athenaeum* to him, before Colburn bought his share in it. However, as the *Literary Gazette* was then so superior, Jerdan's co-partners thought it was not a worthwhile purchase, a decision later to be regretted. The *Athenaeum* was losing money and Colburn was as unhappy with the *Athenaeum* for failing to routinely puff his books as he had been with the *Literary Gazette*. His complaints were unfounded in both journals: the *Athenaeum* favourably reviewed the books Colburn advertised in their pages; in September 1828 "there was a leading article on the Colburn publications as a whole, not extravagantly puffing, but still serving to advertise Colburn books."[10] Dissatisfied with the attention given to his books Colburn quickly sold his share in the *Athenaeum*.

Jerdan quoted a reader's letter as saying that the *Athenaeum* was "sad stuff –

heavy as unleavened bread – it cannot rise".[11] This view was not an isolated one. "The charge of dullness was a frequent one at this time (1827–8) though often in the pages of rival publications it sprang from envy or malice."[12] Support for the *Literary Gazette* came from a surprising source. John Wilson of Blackwood's, writing in his persona as Christopher North, noted the advent of the *Athenaeum* in No. XXXVI of 'Noctes Ambrosianae' but gave it as his opinion that none of the weekly periodicals would ever oust the *Literary Gazette*, "simply for one reason – Mr Jerdan is a gentleman, and is assisted by none but gentlemen". A year later he had not changed his mind: the *Literary Gazette* "stands beyond dispute at the head of its own class".[13] Seemingly, the public agreed with him, even though the *Athenaeum*'s format closely resembled that of the *Literary Gazette,* and it followed the established journal's content too, printing substantial extracts from the books it reviewed. Marchand suggests that the circulation of the *Athenaeum* was about 500–600, low even by the standards of the day.[14]

At the end of its second year therefore, with such a low circulation, the *Athenaeum* seemed to be going the same way as other imitators of the *Literary Gazette*. Buckingham's share was bought by a consortium of friends, who quickly sold it on to Charles Wentworth Dilke. He became its editor, and changed its fortunes. At the outset of Dilke's connection however, the *Athenaeum* was still dull and heavily moralistic. Jerdan's *Autobiography* quoted a 'squib' received by the *Literary Gazette*, allegedly from a supportive reader:[15]

> Mr Dilke, Mr Dilke,
> Though the novice you bilk,
> Be not hasty to sing the Te Deum,
> No reader will quit
> A print that has wit,
> For your prosy and dull Athenaeum.

Jerdan was not yet worried about the competition: the *Literary Gazette* was still on an upward trajectory. Based upon the calculation that circulation of the *Literary Gazette* in 1817 was 3000[16] and had grown substantially in the following decade, it has been suggested that it reached seven to eight thousand a week by 1829,[17] far superior to the upstart *Athenaeum*.

One of Jerdan's many correspondents was Chauncey Hare Townshend, whose letter of 3 March 1828[18] Jerdan annotated as 'highly amusing', as it detailed Townshend's tribulations in rebuilding and preparing an old mansion, Baynards in Sevenoaks. Perhaps because he knew of Jerdan's affair with Landon, or maybe because of her association with the *Literary Gazette*, Townshend commented "I hope that Miss Landon is well, and that her unusual silence in the Muses' chair forebodes a more meditated and a longer strain than any with which she has lately delighted us. Mrs Townshend often speaks of her with interest and we plan to induce her to visit our miniature Knole, when it is completed, and to give her the carved bed in the tapestry chamber, where dreams of the olden day may flit about her head . . ." Townshend was himself a writer, and in the midst of his chatty letter requested Jerdan to put in a few weeks of 'advertisements' for his work *The Reigning Vice*, with notices from the reviews, "as now, being the springtime of literature, it may be well to remind the world that there is such a poem". He had just read "that scurrilous book, Leigh Hunt's *Lord Byron*", which inspired him to write a poem he enclosed. "If you should honour my indignation by giving it publicity in your Gazette I shall feel gratified, as I really think that fellow requires a trimming."

Hunt had been contributing to the *New Monthly Magazine*, and taking advantage of his urgent need for income to return to England from Italy, Colburn commissioned Hunt to write a book on Byron. Hunt had been a guest of Byron's in Italy for two years, but at the end felt Byron had abandoned him. Colburn had published the "scurrilous" book Townshend complained of, *Lord Byron and some of his Contemporaries*. In some circles it was considered a breach of honour, and gave rise to a verse attack by Thomas Moore called *The 'Living Dog' and the 'Dead Lion'*, to which Hunt, or a friend of his, replied with another verse entitled *The Giant and the Dwarf*. Colburn had been shrewd as ever, and Hunt's book went into a second edition in the first year. In the *Literary Gazette* review of 26 January 1828, Jerdan objected to Hunt's exposure of private quarrels with Byron, now unanswerable after Byron's death, calling Hunt's behaviour "base and unworthy . . . these personal and posthumous injuries are a disgrace to their perpetrators, and to the press of the country". In calmer vein, Jerdan also reviewed *The Works of Lord Byron* (with the exception of the "licentious" *Don Juan*), published by Murray. Jerdan praised the cheap and neat edition, of which six thousand copies were sold on the first day. He particularly approved of affordable editions which "are well calculated to balk, if not to destroy that piratical system of pillaging British authors and publishers which is so extensively and shamefully carried on in France". (In Paris, Galignani had published an edition at the same time and Jerdan naturally supported a British publisher over a foreign one.) Murray's edition reawakened Jerdan's old ambivalent feelings about Byron:

> We always admired his genius, and we always entered our protest against his evil principles. The tomb has modified these feelings but has not altered them. We perhaps admire his genius more highly and we perhaps feel more charity towards his errors. We were often condemned as his enemies for pointing out his faults as a man and as a poet the sources whence he unquestionably borrowed many of his ideas; but because we would not shut our eyes to these facts, were we blind to the extraordinary merits of this gifted individual?

The notion of Jerdan, in the throes of his affair with Landon, setting up the *Literary Gazette* as a moral judge of Byron, could be thought hypocritical until we recall that for him, a guiding principle of the *Gazette* was to provide reading material suitable for respectable young ladies and thus could not be seen to accept Byron's more licentious writings. In the *Quarterly* Lockhart jeered that Hunt's was "the miserable book of a miserable man: the little airy fopperies of its manner are like the fantastic trip and compulsive simpers of some poor worn-out wanton, struggling between famine and remorse, leering through her tears".[19] How much more of a gentleman Jerdan sounded.

In the summer of 1828 Landon and Jerdan paid a visit, at the same time, to the Woodcot home of the now married Edward and Rosina Bulwer. The visit lasted some days according to Mary Greene, who lived much of the time with the Bulwers. Observing relaxed banter between Landon and her host, she assumed that they were philandering. In view of what is now known about Landon and Jerdan's relationship, it is unlikely that Landon would have trifled with Bulwer under Jerdan's nose, and doubly unlikely as Rosina Bulwer was at this time still her friend and ever watchful. Inviting Landon and Jerdan together, Bulwer may have changed his mind about their sexual involvement. A year or so earlier he had told his wife, "Mr Jerdan is awful! Poor Miss Landon ought not to go home in a hackney coach alone with him. The ill-natured who have read Miss Landon and *not seen* Mr Jerdan will talk."[20] Bulwer clearly thought that Landon's poems were transparently addressed to Jerdan, but found it hard to understand his attraction for her. By the end of the year however, Bulwer wrote to Jerdan from Weymouth, thanking him for a glowing review of *The Disowned*. Jerdan printed this letter in his *Autobiography* and included Bulwer's postcript: "We hope Miss Landon is recovered. Should you see her, may we request you to remember us kindly to her."[21] This conventional note could be decoded in the light of what is now known – that by December 1828 Landon was three months pregnant with her third child, and suffering the common symptoms of nausea. Bulwer's "should you see her" could be construed as a cloak for his knowledge of Jerdan's paternity, and understanding that he did indeed see her very often. In the *Autobiography* Jerdan could not resist adding a footnote, confiding to his readers, "Of this charming being a note of nearly the same date says 'It is impossible for any one acquainted as we are, with her many good and fine qualities not to feel greatly interested in her'." If, as rumour had it, Bulwer was romantically involved with Landon, he was hardly likely to sing her praises to his rival, quite so openly.

Still occasionally caught up in bickering between his literary colleagues, in May Jerdan was asked to sympathize with a friend who was deeply offended by a review in *The Court Journal*, another of Colburn's publications. The review was by Croly (already in trouble with Alaric Watts). G.P.R. James, whose book was the subject of the review, declared Croly was unfit to be a critic and had, moreover, given away his whole plot in bald detail, and made errors of fact. The *Literary Gazette* review, on the other hand, was "a delightful little paragraph [which] came most soothingly . . . and instantly took away the burning sensation which this <u>Court Plaster</u> had occasioned".[22]

Such praise often came Jerdan's way, earned by what was widely perceived as his kindness to writers. One of the *Literary Gazette's* favourite authors, W.H. Pyne, was another of Jerdan's contributors who fell upon difficult times, and had to apply to the Literary Fund for money to survive. In May 1828 Jerdan wrote to Snow of the Literary Fund, asking for forty pounds for his friend who was in "very distressed circumstances".[23] Jerdan was to pay the grant by instalments, as he thought expedient. This he did, and in July the Fund received a note from Pyne acknowledging the sum. He was forced to make other applications, right up until his death in 1843.

More positively, Jerdan was sitting for his portrait, to an artist named John Moore, evidenced by a note from Moore asking to postpone that week's sitting, although the canvas had already been sent. The resulting painting was engraved by Woolnoth and published by Fisher in 1830 (see illustration no. 3). Around this time too, a marble bust of Jerdan was made by F. W. Smith, a pupil of Chantrey, and exhibited at the Royal Academy, the second time a sculpture of Jerdan had been on show there. It also appears that Jerdan was sitting for a portrait to the artist John Isaac Lilley. He apologized to Jerdan for the "folly of my servant", and asked for one sitting "before you leave town . . . as after that I can forward the picture very much without you".[24] An undated letter to Lilley from Jerdan offered to come on two days in the same week "if you desire another sitting, as I wish you much to make a good picture and the last sitting was very effective".[25] No trace of this portrait has come to light.

Jerdan sent a contribution to Alaric Watts's *Poetical Album*, which he also included in his *Autobiography*. This was *Lines Written by the Seaside*, and commenced grandly, "Hastings, upon thy coast I stood -/ Still onward, onward rolled the flood." His uneven two pages of verse analogised the waves with Man and his life, the roaring surge being like a warrior, gentle waves like the grave; rock pools and splashing water like joy, endlessly ebbing and flowing, leaving no trade. He ended:

> And Man, whence springs thy senseless pride?
> 'Tis but a CENTURY or a TIDE.

His melancholic verse may have owed something to Landon's influence, or to the prevailing poetic mood of the times.

At the end of the year Jerdan also made two other contributions to annuals. A three-verse scrap for the 1828 *Friendship's Offering* was signed with Jerdan's pseudonym, 'Teutha', his usual signature when he did not wish to be easily identified with a work. This was a *Ballad* with a first and last line to every verse, "'Tis heigh-ho, with a garland" to crown a lover's brow when he returns from battle, or, if he is not a victor he will have been killed, in which case it will decorate a maiden's grave. This may have been a Scottish ballad of which Jerdan knew many, but he does not claim it to be other than his own words. The second contribution was to *The Amulet*. *The Poet and the Glow-worm* is a brief narrative, in which the poet, taking a night-time walk, observes a glow-worm. Sorry for its vulnerability to predators because its light signals its presence, he gives utterance to his thoughts. The glow-worm, "The first with human speech supplied", explains how wrong the poet is, comparing his own self-knowledge with the vanity of Man, who thinks himself above the rest of nature. "Man sees all dangers but his own", he says. The glow-worm's fire inhibits predators, he tells the poet, therefore his light is his "pride and safeguard too". The next lines speak directly to the gossip and rumours surrounding Jerdan and his lover:

> But what avails in modern days
> The splendour of the poet's blaze?
> Say, shields it from the woes of life,
> From envy, malice, slander, strife,
> Insult, oppression, scorn and hate,
> The frowns of fortune and of fate?
> Or rather does it not expose
> To other ills and add to those?

The poet, withdraws, sadly acknowledging the truth of the glow-worm's analogy.

Jerdan, by his own admittance, was useless at keeping track of money. Accounts and book-keeping were a foreign language to him. "[m]y blunders in attempting numbers, reckonings, or accounts have been so ludicrous, that a schoolboy of ten years old would have been whipt for making them . . . "[26]. Fortunately however, his business partners in the *Literary Gazette* were more methodical, and some records survive showing the *Gazette* accounts with Longman Rees & Co. for the years 1826–1829.[27] Jerdan had two income streams from the *Literary Gazette*. He pocketed one-third of the profits made by the magazine, the other thirds going to Colburn, and to Longman & Co. This profit share was paid quarterly; in 1826, the first year he was in Grove House, he earned a total of £1075 17s 0d for 467 issues of the *Literary Gazette*. His 1827 share was £1,032 12s 5d, and in 1828 it rose to a hefty £1,444 17s 0d, reflecting increased circulation. In addition to this profit share he was paid separately as Editor, mostly, but not always, on a regular weekly basis. His fee was seven guineas per issue from January 1826 to the end of 1827, when it became ten guineas per issue. Two entries of five pounds each were shown in October and December

1826 for "balance" payments, possibly for extra work. During these lucrative years, Jerdan banked with Drummonds. He recorded his 'intromissions' (deposits) as £2,110 2s 7d in 1826, £3,275 19s 4d in 1827, £2,349 5s 9d in 1818 and £2,593 10s 9d in 1829 – "in four years £10,328.18.5 all my own fair earning."[28]

In 1828 Jerdan, Crofton Croker and some other Fellows of the Society of Antiquaries travelled to Keston in Kent, to excavate a site thought to be the Roman station of Noviomagus. "They discovered the foundations of a temple, and several ancient stone coffins, Roman remains etc."[29] Jerdan was always unsure whether these items were truly "taken from the bosom of the earth or carried there by some humorist of the party".[30] Crofton Croker and another of the Fellows read papers on these finds to the Society of Antiquaries on 27 November. A few weeks later Crofton Croker was elected "Lord High President" of an offshoot of the Society of Antiquaries, known as the "Society of Noviomagus", after the Roman station. The new society was a social club, more to the taste of the break-away group than the learned and serious Antiquarians. Members however, had to be FSAs, and Jerdan was happy to be among their number. The Noviomagians dined together six times a year, initially at Wood's Hotel in Portugal Street, and later at the Freemasons' Tavern. Crofton Croker remained Lord High President until his death. Other officials bore titles such as "Father-Confessor", "Poet-Laureate" or "Keeper of the Records". Samuel Carter Hall, who joined later, recalled that a "country outing" was held on the first Saturday in July, when ladies were also invited. On such occasions a brief historical and antiquarian paper was read by one of the members.

The Noviomagians were bent on fun as well as learning, and their principles were "topsy-turvy". To pass a resolution, there had to be a preponderance of 'Noes'; in giving a toast to honour a guest, the speaker had to say what he did not mean, and mean what he did not say. This led "to keen and happy contests of wit between assailant and assailed". The Minutes had to record the jokes, to misrepresent what anyone said, and carefully note the objects of antiquarian interest which were handed round and examined at each dinner. Jerdan recalled the meetings as "often exceedingly instructive and always entertaining [but] in the midst of these high-jink enjoyments, it must not be thought that the real business of Archaeological inquiry and science was quite neglected".[31]

Jerdan's one-third partner and founder of the *Literary Gazette,* Henry Colburn, was a thoroughly commercial man, interested only in the profitability of his investments, using them to promote the books he published. He already had the *New Monthly Magazine* in addition to the *Literary Gazette*. In January 1829 he purchased the *London Weekly Review*. This had been founded two years earlier by D. L. Richardson and was initially so successful that John Murray offered to take a half-share in it. To Richardson's eternal regret, he declined Murray's offer, and his paper soon folded. Colburn's transaction over the *Weekly*

Review stirred Jerdan and the Longmans into action, fearing a rival to the *Literary Gazette*, even though Colburn still held one-third of its shares. Writing from Longmans' offices in Paternoster Row, declaring that he was authorized by the publisher to speak on their behalf, Jerdan advised Colburn in a businesslike and clear letter of their decision, in a spirit of "zealous, cordial and friendly co-oper-ation in future". They were "ready to charge £750 on the *Literary Gazette* as a maximum to keep you harmless of loss in your speculation with the *Weekly Review*. Leaving it to your honour, should less have been incurred, to make any deduction necessary."[32] Colburn was to promise to sell on the *Review* "to a person in my confidence" so that the *Literary Gazette* did not appear to be buying up its rivals; Colburn should withdraw completely from the *Review,* and when it was sold, it should be discontinued. Jerdan's last stipulation was that no partner in the *Literary Gazette* was to be "connected with any Reviewing or Literary Weekly publication similar to the *Literary Gazette*". Agreement from Colburn was requested within the week, and the matter was to be kept confidential. It is surprising that Longmans left such a legalistic letter to Jerdan, rather than to one of their own directors more used to drafting agreements, but they may have felt that any rival to the *Literary Gazette* would be better quashed by one who had a more heavily vested interest in its success. To avoid all of Jerdan's restrictions however, and to sidestep the agreement he had made with Richardson to share future profits in the *London Weekly Review*, Colburn merely closed down the periodical and in May 1829 re-started it under the name of the *Court Journal.* For a brief period P.G. Patmore was editor, succeeded eventually by Laman Blanchard for a longer time.

In October 1829 whilst he was already very busy, Jerdan agreed to take on writing twenty-four pages a month for Fisher's *National Portrait Gallery of Illustrious and Eminent Personages of the Nineteenth Century.* Each twenty-four pages earned him twenty-five pounds, and he was paid in arrears. Fisher's letter of 7 October enclosed "a Bill for £105 at five months", as the first payment.[33] He agreed with terms Jerdan had proposed to him, except for the mode of payment. Fisher was not a man to pay in advance, so covered himself by terms that paid Jerdan this first £105 to be cashed in March 1830, to cover the first four numbers of the *Gallery*. The second payment for the same sum for the following four numbers would be paid as a Bill for encashment four months later, and so on. The agreement was to bind both parties for twelve months, unless dissolved by mutual consent. Fisher was very precise as to his require-ments: "Copy for three Memoirs that we name to you, to be forwarded to us monthly, and every month, not later than the 15th of each month; each number to contain not less than three half sheets of letter press . . . " If Jerdan did not perform, there would be a penalty of £100.

Jerdan considered his fee liberal, and although he was not in financial need at this time, he later mused that it would have been all the same if he had relied upon it, as the agreement would have been withdrawn eventually, leaving him destitute: he used this as an example of the uncertainty of literary pursuits, one of his main themes of his *Autobiography*. However, he accepted the commission of this work, and dedicated it to George IV, but it was an onus which lay "like a load" upon him, and he "would rather have written ten times as much of any other kind of literature".[34] For a man with his amount of journalistic output, and with experience of many years of editing and reviewing for his *Literary Gazette*, it is surprising to learn how difficult Jerdan found this new commission. He explained the reason behind his difficulty:

> Of all species of authorship, faithful and satisfactory biography is the most difficult. The impossibility of being perfectly certain of facts is the first stumbling block; the risk of drawing right conclusions from those you are fortunate enough to obtain is the next; and the delicacy required for steering by the lamp of truth, without flattery or offence, consummates the obstacles to authentic personal history. In the case of living individuals, the responsibility is increased, and the dilemmas multiplied tenfold;[35]

Each individual included in the *National Portrait Gallery* was depicted in an engraving, using a variety of artists. The accompanying text, for which Jerdan was responsible, varied in length between four and fourteen pages. Exceptionally, he devoted no less than twenty-eight pages to George Canning, the entry being written less than three years after Canning's death, his memory still dear to Jerdan. The personal link between the two men is evident in the language Jerdan uses; the entry is more of a hagiography than a biography, emotion running off the page. Having described the ancestry of his subject and the historic events with which he was concerned on his political path to the Premiership, Jerdan moved on to the multitude of memorabilia – monuments, sculptures and paintings – which abounded following Canning's death. None, Jerdan said, are truly a satisfactory likeness. Reviewing the King's Edition of the *National Portrait Gallery* in the *Literary Gazette* of 15 May 1830, Jerdan quoted extracts from his own memoir of Canning as "they cannot fail to be interesting to our readers" – a puff if ever there was one. Unfortunately for Jerdan, few of his subjects came as easily to him as Canning, and required much research and discussion to acquire the facts that he needed.

An entry in Volume I was on Spencer Perceval and, as he described, Jerdan was "a close eye-witness of, and an agitated actor in, the scene that deprived England of her distinguished ornament and principal Minister". More than four of the thirteen pages on the subject of the former Prime Minister went into great detail about the Bellingham assassination and Jerdan's part in it, complete with a diagram of the position of the participants. However, as Jerdan said, this was an unparalleled event in the history of the country, causing "extraordinary agitation which every where prevailed, looked more like the convulsion of an empire, that the loss of one man, however exalted and beloved".[36]

Jerdan regarded some of the biographies on which he worked as of high historical value, because of the intrinsic integrity of the material. Others were more commonplace; he found some living subjects more co-operative and amusing than others when asked to proof read their entry. One example of this was his memoir of Lord Chancellor Eldon who caused him so much extra work in checking minute facts that in compensation he sent Jerdan a brace of birds shot by his own hand. However, Eldon "ruthlessly struck out" Jerdan's torrid account of his runaway marriage, giving Jerdan "the only specimen that I am aware of, of the manner in which a really great and distinguished man would write his autobiography".[37] Besides Canning and Perceval, other subjects with whom Jerdan was personally acquainted were Huskisson, Palmerston, Goderich and Aberdeen – the Tory great and good, and others in the world of literature and the arts.

The series in the *National Portrait Gallery* was much admired and achieved successful sales for Fisher. However, as with all successful plans, copyists were not far behind. Jerdan's acquaintances Lord Brougham and Charles Knight set up in the literary business and amongst many other types of publications produced a *Portrait Gallery*, "the plan copied from, and in direct competition with Messrs. Fishers'".[38] Supported by subscription, they undersold Fisher's publication, and cut costs by using old engravings, and advertising widely at moderate expense, utilising their literary contacts. In the light of this competition Fisher asked Jerdan to accept a reduction in his fee of one-third; whilst being sympathetic to his employer's problem, Jerdan declined, not only for the financial reduction, but because the tedium and pressure after four years' continuous monthly production was uncongenial and he was glad to find an excuse to terminate his commission.

Astonishingly, Jerdan found time between his work on Fisher's *Gallery*, the *Literary Gazette*, his family and his affair with Landon, to write a burlesque upon the fashionable travel books popular at this time. Twelve years earlier he had exploited the explosion of books on Paris with his *Six Weeks in Paris, or a Cure for the Gallomania*. This time his target was nearer home, a spoof upon such books as Richard Phillips's *A Morning's Walk from London to Kew* (1817) and his *A Personal Tour Through the United Kingdom* (1828). The very title page gives the game away, in its absurd amount of detail: *Personal Narrative of a Journey Over-Land from The Bank to Barnes, by way of Piccadilly, Knightsbridge, Brentford, Tossbury, Putney Bridge and the Countries West of London, as you approach Mortlake, Kew, Richmond, and other Royalties on the Banks of the Thames, with some Account of the Inhabitants and Customs of the regions East of Kensington, by an Inside Passenger. To which is appended A Model for a Magazine being the product of the author's sojourn at the village of Barnes during five rainy days.* The volume was published by Jerdan's

Literary Gazette partners Longman, Rees, Orme, Brown & Green. It falls into two quite distinct sections, the "travel" part taking up fifty pages, and the Magazine Model one hundred and sixteen pages, although billed as a mere appendage. Longman & Co. must have realized that a 'model for a magazine' would not sell books, but a travel book was always popular, and a skit even more so.

The 'Prefatory Admonition' discussed the problems confronting the traveller at home; whilst writing of adventures in a foreign land, even the gouty can "bound from crag over ravine with the fleetness of the chamois". At home, an encounter with "an amorous bull might serve to diversify, but it sadly wants dignity of situation". The seven chapters which follow adopted the language of travel writers. The 'adventures' of the journey included a pretty girl to whom the narrator made advances, a young man destined for the university and his silly scientific pretensions; observations on horse troughs and pumps by the roadside, and a disquisition on the archives at Tossbury, where Jerdan could not resist a jibe at do-gooders, relating how Squire Gubbins left eighteen pounds to the parish on condition it was to accumulate in the funds until there was a sufficiency to "cloath, feed, educate and apprentice ten boys and ten girls of the village". The 'travel' book is full of such absurdities, culminating when the stage drew near to Kew:

> We saw about half-a-dozen cows galloping furiously towards the river's brink; flirting their tails, and indeed, conducting themselves with a vivacity perfectly inconsistent with the acknowledged sobriety of that useful animal. He [the young university man] calmed our apprehensions by informing us that they were intended for the East Indies. Every other day they are fed with best rock-salt, instead of green-meat; which, by chemical agency renders them fat and fit to be killed, and sent on ship-board at a moment's notice; the trouble and delay of salting down being totally unnecessary. These cows, he assured us, had just finished their thirst-inducing meal.

Jerdan created many opportunities like this to make fun of the pontificating tone of the travel book genre, and of the abundance of pseudo-scientific experiments ubiquitous at the time. It made an amusing light read, and could not possibly be taken as a serious travel book, especially when teamed with the 'Model for a Magazine'.

It is possible that this section of the volume was written either with, or by, Theodore Hook, but the style is Jerdan's, especially salient as it started by insisting that "'Prospectus' and 'Puff' are not synonymes". The 'Model' is divided into categories such as any general magazine might offer: Original Communications, Biographiana, Politics, Original Poetry, Musical Reviews and so on, with a brief paragraph on each. The humour is heavy-handed: the Chinese correspondent offered an "Infallible Recipe for Restoring the Teeth to an Inimitable Jet-Black" by applying a mixture of black tea, Indian ink and 'as much indigo as will cover a Chinese foot', and not eating or drinking for three days. A 'Plan for the Total Abolition of Accidents' proposed punishment for every accident suffered; Reviews of Literature noted 'The Four Bloody Monks or the Court of Thunderumbo', a grand Gothic romance in which "the greatest possible number of murders will be compressed into the least possible quantity of letter-press." Other views were similarly jocular, and one can imagine Jerdan chuckling to himself, or with Hook, inventing spoofs on every aspect of current culture as fast as they could. It must have been a welcome relief from the more serious business of their working lives.[39]

Jerdan's dangerous juggling with his two lives was once more risked when Landon hazarded disclosure in her fourth book, *The Venetian Bracelet*, again published by Longmans. She received one hundred and fifty pounds for this work; 1500 copies were printed, and a further 500 were published in 1844. This collection included *Lines of Life*, which, read with the knowledge of the gossip gathering around the poet, sounds like a cry from her heart:

> . . . .
> I live among the cold, the false,
> And I must seem like them;
> And such I am, for I am false
> As those I most condemn.
>
> I teach my lip its sweetest smile,
> My tongue its softest tone;
> I borrow others' likeness, till
> Almost I lose my own.
>
> I pass through flattery's gilded sieve,
> Whatever I would say;
> In social life, all, like the blind,
> Must learn to feel their way.

and so on for another twenty-two verses. She is saying here what her own friends remember clearly about her in their memoirs, that she wore a different face in society from her poetical self. In the same volume, *A Summer Evening's Tale* asks, "Am I not better by my love for you?/ At least I am less selfish." Having had an affair with Jerdan for around five years, borne him two children with another on the way, one can but marvel at her question, as if adultery were something virtuous.

Jerdan's reviews of *The Venetian Bracelet* appeared before publication and were designed to encourage sales of the book and of the magazine.[40] Hailing L.E.L. as usual as a "genius", he nevertheless drew attention to her "apparent moods and sentiment of self-condemnation", a complaint taken up by later reviewers.

The splits between Landon's private life with Jerdan, her own sparse domestic life, the social face for parties, and her poetic persona were all there in her poetry, but general enough – like horoscopes – for her readers to see in them anything they wanted to see. James Hogg, the Ettrick Shepherd commented in 'Noctes Ambrosianae', that Landon in society was "a brilliant creature . . . none of your lachrymose muses . . . that's the character o' real geniuses, baith males and females. They're ae thing wi' a pen in their haun, at a green desk, wi' only an ink bottle on't and a sheet o' paper – and anither thing entirely at a white table a' covered wi' plates and trenchers, soup in the middle, sawmon at the head . . . "[41] This claim could not be made for Jerdan himself, who was the same genial, company-loving, literature-loving man whether at his desk or at table – but then neither he, nor posterity, made any claim that he was a "genius".

Writers of some celebrity, like Landon, were taken up by society hostesses as 'catches' or adornments to their parties. The same was true for artists of all kinds, such as actors, painters and musicians. Jerdan too would have been asked to social evenings on his own account, not merely as an escort for Landon. She would have been sought after for her charm and famously witty, sometimes sharp, conversation, as an 'entertainer' for the higher echelons of society. That she herself did not especially enjoy such gatherings was made clear in *Lines of Life*, but refusal to attend would have diminished her attraction for her middle-class readers, who liked to know that their muse frequented high-class society. The emptiness and vapidity of many such gatherings was caught very clearly in a sketch by Jerdan, most of which has survived.

This sketch, which does not appear to have been published, was entitled "The Conversazione". It satirized these vacuous social get-togethers where the participants were bored with themselves and with each other, and the predictable conversations. The surviving manuscript runs to nineteen large pages, and is annotated that four pages are missing.[42] Judging from the handwriting, Jerdan tossed this off in great haste, with much crossing out and overwriting, rendering some of the words illegible. However, there is quite enough to give a strong flavour of the fun Jerdan is making of polite society.

At an evening gathering, expected guests are discussed with much back-biting and criticism, only for them to be met with unctuous flattery when they enter the room. A writer wishes to read his latest play, but they whittle down his performance until they reach "at least this first page". He gets as far as declaiming the first two lines when the company is saved by the arrival of a singer. The writer concedes defeat, muttering as he packs away his manuscript, "Such confounded, silly, tasteless, chattering set never man got into." The singer is swiftly interrupted by the hostess who invites everyone to gather around and inspect a newcomer's "delightful drawings" and to hear his ridiculous ideas about buildings. He bores the company at length with his proposal to remove half of Waterloo Bridge to make the river navigable for boats up to Oxford. In the background of all these performances a certain amount of flirting is carried on, oblivious of manners or morals. The evening ends at last, everyone dissatisfied, but doubtless prepared to repeat the experience again the next night.

Jerdan's irony is not nearly as caustic as it might have been, suggesting that this piece might have been dashed off for an amateur dramatic production as private entertainment, rather than for print. If even half of the ennui he implied was the tenor of these gatherings, they would indeed have been a trial, especially for Landon who knew that her reputation was being torn to pieces at this time.

Much more to his liking were the sort of evenings he described with glee, such as the first time he dined with Coleridge. Frederic Mansell Reynolds, editor of *The Keepsake*, invited Jerdan as the cornerstone of a party of eight, to the two small rooms he rented for the autumn months upstairs in a gardener's cottage in Highgate. Fine wines were served, and in the absence of port, black-strap was obtained from a nearby inn. The brilliant punster Hook toasted their host, amazing Coleridge with his cleverness and quickness. Another guest distrusted Hook's extemporizing, challenging him to declaim a verse on 'Cocoanut Oil', then advertised as the best flame feeder. Hook obliged instantly, giving the whole story in verse, "polished enough for instant publication". Many toasts followed and Coleridge instigated a game of 'tumblershying', involving smashing all the drinking glasses. The noise and merriment so upset the cook, the gardener's wife (who was also the subject of Hook's last song), that she fled for protection to her sister. Walking home later, in company with the hired waiter, scenes in the kitchen were described so vividly that Jerdan, laughing helplessly, had to hang on to the railings in Piccadilly for support. He was pulled up by a 'Charley', a nightwatchman, and managed to get home without further incident. "Evenings such as this shed a bright halo over the clouds of life," he recalled.[43]

Jerdan's entertainments continued to include the 'shows' he so enjoyed, and which continued to provide material for the *Literary Gazette*. The Colosseum, completed in late 1832 in Regents Park, where the Royal College of Physicians now stands, featured the first passenger elevator in London worked by hydraulic power. Ten or twelve people a time were taken to the top of the building to appreciate the huge panorama of London as if from the pinnacle of St Paul's Cathedral. Thomas Horner, who owned the building (and invented the elevator in 1826), had been left in dire straits when his partner absconded with a fortune. "Horner's manifold connections with the London press were never more useful than now. In immediate response to the crisis, the *Literary Gazette* came out with a two-part article on 17 and 31 January 1829. The *London Magazine,* the *Athenaeum* and the *Mirror of Literature* also carried articles."[44] The Colosseum was bought two years later by the singer Braham (of the Melodists Club), after

Horner had fled to America, where he died in 1844. In an adjectival orgy, the *Literary Gazette* noticed a recurring panorama of Constantinople, displayed in Leicester Square and, in 1829, in the Strand; the review drew crowds to the show: "the present critical situation of the Turkish Empire, when no one can tell how soon this magnificent city, with its splendid palaces, superb kiosks, swelling domes, extensive terraces, lofty mosques, pointed minarets, glittering crescents, and populous seraglios, may be exposed to the ravages of an almost barbarous army."[45]

Freaks continued to be popular: the *Literary Gazette* reported on Siamese twins at the Egyptian Hall[46] and a child with two heads, "a disagreeable mass in a glass jar of spirits" which disgruntled visitors had expected to see alive.[47] One of the most absurd exhibits was supposedly a three year old French girl with the words 'Napoleon Empereur' in her left iris and 'Empereur Napoleon' in her right iris. Similar claims were immediately made for other children, and the *Literary Gazette* of 23 August 1828 commented caustically, "We should not be surprised to see it become the (inconvenient) fashion for every baby to have its papa's initials at least on one of its peepers." Jerdan, at least, would be relieved that this was only a joke. Scientific inventions enabled the microbes in a single drop of London water to be examined, at the aptly named Microcosm in Regent Street. At another venue the *Literary Gazette* tartly noted, "To see a flea as large as a camel must gratify every flea-bitten observer, by inducing a satisfaction and sense of security at not having been devoured by the attack of such an animal."[48]

Jerdan was still using Grove House frequently for literary gatherings and his associates thus became acquainted, and often friends with Frances Jerdan and her daughters. Edward Blaquiere, the author and scholar on Greece, and Bulwer both mentioned the family in letters in mid-1829. Bulwer's greeting came with a gift which meant a great deal to the emotional and sentimental Jerdan:

> Happening to call at my silversmith's I was struck with the oddity and workmanship of a little inkstand, and on enquiry learnt that it had once been ordered by Mr Canning, but never sent home to him on account of his death. Upon hearing this, I remembered your friendship for that remarkable man, and imagined that the circumstance might give the inkstand that value, which in itself is too mere a trifle to possess.[49]

With such a sensitive gesture, Bulwer proved himself a genuine friend to Jerdan. Not everyone took such a view. Dilke's grandson interpreted the gift as a bribe.[50]

Dickens's future father-in-law, George Hogarth and his wife also sent greetings to Mrs Jerdan, with "a delightful recollection of the great kindness we received from you when in London a few years ago, and have often wished to have the pleasure of seeing you among us here. I beg also to be remembered to Miss Landon, who probably has no remembrance of us – but you may remind her of a very pleasant day we spent along with her and you in seeing a great many <u>lions</u>. At that time she was just beginning to acquire that name which has become so celebrated."[51] The purpose of Hogarth's letter was to request Jerdan and Landon's permission to insert a song he wrote to an old verse of L.E.L.'s into Chappell's music annual, but from his memories it is clear that he associated Jerdan with both his wife and Landon, whose poetic influence by this time had crossed the Atlantic. This influence was confirmed in February 1829 when the *Literary Gazette* reviewed *The Token*, an literary annual published in America and in England. The poetry it carried was strikingly imitative of L.E.L.'s work.

At the end of the year Jerdan sent a verse, *Bells* to the *Gem* for 1830, which probably took him fewer moments to write than the eight lines it comprised would take to recite. He also contributed to *The Keepsake* for 1829, a poem called *Life's Day*. Many of his verses for annuals take the journey through life as their motif; he was to compare life stages to footsteps and to the sea. Here he spoke of morning, noon, evening and night as friends are lost, love has fled, and death beckons:

> Where the morn's tints shall all be forgot,
> Where the noon's heat shall penetrate not,
> Where the eve's gather'd harvest shall rot –
> Untroubled the rest of the tomb.

In his over-stretched life, Jerdan seems to have sent this poem in without much revision.

On 29 June 1829, (according to her baptismal record of 17 March 1850[52]), Landon gave birth in Clerkenwell to a daughter, and called her Laura, as a reflection of her admiration for Petrarch's Laura. This time the surname was Landon, not Stuart as the two earlier children had been named. This is a curious change, and might be construed as Laura being not Jerdan's daughter, but fathered by one of the other men with whom Landon was widely rumoured to have a relationship, although no evidence for any such affairs has yet been found. The list included Maginn, Maclise and Edward Bulwer. Whoever was Laura's biological father, Jerdan assumed she was his, writing to his daughter Ella in his old age, "Laura is a dear creature, and I love her beyond expression."[53]

The publisher Henry Colburn had taken Richard Bentley into partnership in his publishing house in 1829. Bentley was "short, pink-faced, heavily whiskered and bristly-haired. He had a strong character and was daring in his plans which usually succeeded."[54] Their arrangement lasted only three years at which time Colburn sold his share of the business to Bentley, but retained his interest in the magazines, including the *Literary Gazette*. Ignoring his agreement not to compete with Bentley, Colburn set up in business again and became a fierce rival to Bentley who eventually paid him to dissolve the agreement. They and their rivalry were famously portrayed as Bacon and Bungay by Thackeray in *Pendennis*. Colburn returned to London where his puffing practice grew in earnest.

Jerdan wrote an uncharacteristically testy note to Richard Bentley on 4 December, requesting the response which Colburn had assured him would be "immediate", to a proposition concerning a new novel by L.E.L. Ollier, their man of business, thought it would be a good idea and Jerdan was sure it would be profitable. Relations between Jerdan and Colburn were yet again at a low ebb, as he told Bentley: "My letter from Mr Colburn being in other respects an unpleasant one, as he seems to think I have charged him with injustice and illiberality, whereas I only accused him of delays and want of decision which have done me considerable injury, besides keeping my mind unsettled – I venture to hope that you will meet my friendly (however misconstrued) (sic) more promptly and in a better spirit."[55] To urge a speedy reply Jerdan noted that Miss Landon was leaving town in a day or two. Bentley was usually more amenable than Colburn, and most people preferred to deal with him rather than with his aggressive partner. Shortly afterwards, not having received a response, Jerdan pressed again saying that he was "coaching down" to visit the friends where Landon was staying and wished to conclude the business of the novel, as delays and uncertainties divert the mind. It seemed that the publishers had agreed to take her novel. Acting as her agent, Jerdan said that if they wished it to be completed by May, they could do so, and "I will ratify (as authorized) my agreement in her name, if done at once."[56] Landon had wanted to divide profits at Longmans, which Jerdan agreed would be most profitable, but she was prepared to deal with Bentley as her circumstances demanded immediate resources. Bulwer concurred and Jerdan reported that the popular novelist "said he thought it madness not to secure this writer at a much higher cost".[57] The proposed novel was likely to have been Landon's first, *Romance and Reality*, published at the beginning of 1831.

It is obvious from his comments above that Jerdan was acting on behalf of Landon as her agent, in dealings with the publisher, and he has been identified as the 'first agent' in the field of literature, a topic to be considered later.[58] At least one Edinburgh publisher wished to appoint an agent in London. Jerdan spent what was plainly a merry evening with Blackwood, when the Edinburgh editor was in London in May 1829. Dropping him a note next morning, Jerdan remarked that if he had had his wits about him when they spoke of Blackwood's London Agency, he would have recommended his "worthy frere James Duncan".[59] Should Blackwood contemplate other arrangements, he offered his own services. He forgot to tell Blackwood at the time that he had recommended him as "the publisher of able and successful works of this description" for a translation from the German of a two-volume novel, *The Early Days of Count Eugene*. "What do you give for such an affair: i.e. if you relish the offer at all? I think the writer might be in other ways useful to C. North Esq."[60] Sitting where he was, in the centre of a vast web of writers of all sorts, booksellers, publishers, politicians, institutional directors and socialites, Jerdan was ideally placed to act as facilitator or mediator in any number of ways. He could have made himself a comfortable additional income from such work, but it was more in keeping with his character that he did such tasks out of kindness and a willingness to be helpful to everyone.

11

'Wing-spreading' Editor

In the midst of the extra burden imposed by writing a huge number of biographies for Fisher's *National Portrait Gallery*, Jerdan became immersed in developing a new project, an idea for a *Foreign Literary Gazette*. He had a financial and active partner in this venture, a Captain Williams, later to become an Inspector of Prisons. (Always keen to take any credit he could, Jerdan speculated that Williams's experience on the *Foreign Literary Gazette* cultivated his mind, produced sagacity in the performance of his duties, and lucidity in writing his Blue Book Reports.[1] He was serious about this, believing that "There are few schools superior to the school of literary reviewing and miscellaneous essay for developing the intellectual faculties and enlarging the understanding.") There were other staff assisting in producing the new journal; a Mr Smith, who became Secretary to King's College London, and the faithful Mr Lloyd of the Foreign Post Office who had worked with Jerdan since he started with the *Literary Gazette*.

An enormous amount of "correspondence, research and application" ensued, resulting in appointment of correspondents "from Petersburgh to Naples", and publishers in every corner. Jerdan sent Smith off to Belgium, Holland and Germany. Williams went to France, and Jerdan stayed in London pulling whatever strings he could. He canvassed his contacts abroad, and at the end of October 1829 wrote to Lord Burghersh in Florence, reminding him that they had met in Paris in 1814, and that his Lordship's work had been noticed from time to time in the columns of the *Literary Gazette*.[2] Jerdan outlined his plan to "make this new journal to Foreign what the Literary is to English literature". He asked his Lordship's assistance in garnering information concerning "interesting works – correspondence of able men – Reports of learned and Scientific Institutions – notice of what is <u>new</u> in Antiquities, the drama, music, the fine arts etc. etc.". The plan had been approved throughout the Continent, he explained, but he needed co-operation in Italy, which he hoped Burghersh could help to procure with his influence.

Jerdan tried to interest John Murray in joining him in this venture, but without success. Murray had asked Longmans if they intended to participate, but receiving no satisfactory reply, declined Jerdan's offer, saying that he would be "a restless and teasing partner" preferring to act alone.[3] Jerdan also approached his partners in the *Literary Gazette,* the Longmans and Colburn, who debated for a long time about investing £500 each. They eventually declined. Jerdan thought it was because they were concerned that it would distract him from his duties on the *Literary Gazette,* which was then "a very lucrative investment".[4] This was probably a correct surmise as the printer Scripps wrote to Jerdan telling him that Mr Orme of Longmans was very displeased to see the Scripps name connected with advertisements and bills for the *Foreign Literary Gazette*, and asked for this to be discontinued.[5]

All Jerdan's plans were in place, his overseas agents ready to send in their contributions and he still did not know how he was to produce the new journal. His failure to attract investment contributed largely to the failure of the project, but somehow thirteen issues were produced, between January and March 1830. The *Age*, never a friend to Jerdan, nevertheless remarked that the new publication reflected "great credit on the Editor Mr Jerdan, not only for the originality of the information it conveys, but for the excellent style in which the various articles are written".[6] Carlyle commented to a German correspondent that Britain had already two Foreign <u>Reviews</u> which were prospering, and there was now a third. "We have a *Foreign Literary Gazette* published weekly in London and which tho' it is a mere steam-engine concern, managed by an utter *Dummkopf* solely for lucre, appears to meet with sale. So great is the curiosity, so boundless is the ignorance of men."[7] Carlyle's optimism was misplaced, as was his unkind remark about Jerdan, who was working hard on the project, but it was not enough. The *Literary Gazette* of 6 March declared that as the publication's first two months had been completed, "it would be a sacrifice of our opinion to ultra-delicacy were we to altogether avoid calling our readers' attention to it". Jerdan did so in a brief paragraph, saying that the mass of information in its pages was "both instructive and entertaining". As well as a lack of investment from his partners, Jerdan blamed the stamp for defeating his project; he also blamed the public for being unwilling to pay two shillings a week for two literary journals, the *Foreign* on Wednesday and the *Literary* on Saturday; he blamed too the lack of advertising, especially from the house of Colburn. The whole enterprise had been very expensive – translations from several languages had been costly – and although the issues which did appear had met with approbation, it was not enough to keep the thing afloat:

> Thus situated, though we might suppose that a great outlay of capital and a long course of persevering industry would raise this Periodical to that degree of circulation which should reward the proprietors; we are not inclined to resort to the expedients which now seem so necessary to bring any work into general notice. Our public is self-occupied, and nothing

but a system of extravagant puffing seems adequate to awaken attention to any literary performance; and rather than resort to *that system*, we, thanking our friends for their many kindnesses, have resolved to close our well-intentioned labours.[8]

Jerdan reckoned that he and Williams had lost a hundred pounds a week, but comforted himself that it was the best lesson his colleague ever learnt.

The pressure on Jerdan's time and attention was considerable: the *Foreign Literary Gazette* had created much work, in addition to the mammoth task he had undertaken for Fisher's *National Portrait Gallery*, and his frequent contributions to the fashionable Annuals, all this to be fitted in around his main occupation of producing the *Literary Gazette*. As editor of the foremost weekly literary review, Jerdan inevitably got embroiled in various squabbles, some with lasting effect, others petty, blown up out of all proportion.

His leading review of 16 January 1830 featured a book published by Murray, an instance when Jerdan's choice trumped a Colburn publication. Volume I of Thomas Moore's *Letters and Journals of Lord Byron with Notices of his Life* was given seven pages, mainly extracts, with the eulogy that "Under this modest title we have now before us – whether we consider the subject, the writer, or the performance itself – one of the most interesting pieces of biography that has ever adorned the literature of England." Lady Byron took offence and on 20 March the *Literary Gazette* printed 'Remarks occasioned by Mr Moore's Notices of Lord Byron's Life', reproducing her letter to Moore, which objected to his publishing domestic details prior to her separation from Byron. She maintained that if such details were printed, persons affected had a right to refute injurious charges; she especially resented that her parents were spoken of badly. Jerdan believed that the 'Remarks' were legitimate prize to be printed, though 'unpublished', and promised to explain his views in the next week's *Gazette*. His rather evasive and nit-picking response duly appeared; vindicating his editorial decision in 'Sketches of Society' of 27 March, Jerdan informed his readers that "the *Literary Gazette* is the last Journal to be looked to, either for controversy or for such news as is merely calculated to gratify prurient appetites". By using italics, he claimed, the *Gazette* showed that it was incapable of intruding on anyone's privacy and had merely reprinted a document already in circulation. It was absurd to suppose that Lady Byron's printed 'Remarks' were intended to be kept secret. Triumphantly, the *Literary Gazette* asserted:

Our sheet, with this exclusive paper, was not dry from the press, when a would-be fashionable contemporary, called in mockery we suppose, The Court Journal, thought fit to attract the public attention by covering London with placards of a second edition, "containing Lady Byron's *Letter* to Mr Moore, stolen, within a few hours, from the *Literary Gazette*

– for if the plagiarist had seen the original, he would have discovered that the title was not *Letter* but *Remarks* ... Now that the *Literary Gazette* stands so high, that it can very well afford to be plundered in this way (and we never complain of the hundreds of our columns taken daily and weekly into other periodicals, in the ordinary course without acknowledgement) ...

By 3 April the quarrel had spread, and under 'Sketches of Society' the *Literary Gazette* noted that "this subject continues to be discussed in almost every society and a new filip has been given to it by a determined attack upon Mr Moore and his biography by Mr T Campbell, as a friend to Lady Byron, in the *New Monthly Magazine*". Campbell had accused Byron of "some dark crime" and Moore of "screening his hero by disparaging his exemplar lady and her relatives". Primly, Jerdan remarked that such information had come too late for considered comment, "the matter is too serious and indelicate, not to say disgusting, of being treated of hastily". He insisted that the *Gazette's* publishing of the "Remarks" was fully justified. Pressing his point on 10 April, he again protested against Campbell's "odious imputations . . . in the name of all that is honourable in human nature." Colburn had two of his journals at each other's throats, so he could not lose as long as readers were kept enthralled by the squabble.

Clearly out of sorts, and contrary to his habitual practice of kindly reviews, or no review at all, Jerdan and the *Literary Gazette* vented spleen in the issue of July 10, on Charles Lamb's *Album Verses*. It accused Lamb of vanity and egotism for printing verses he wrote in young ladies' albums, whilst he had called them "the proverbial receptacles for trash!" Lamb had said in his dedication that his motive was to benefit his publishers by showing their skills, and accordingly the *Gazette's* slashing comments ended with a final rapier thrust, "the title page is especially pretty". The *Athenaeum* maintained that this harshness was solely because the book was published by Moxon, not by Colburn and, predictably, talked of "a Lamb offering itself for the sacrifice".[9] It was believed that Jerdan disliked Lamb for taunting "his hero William Gifford", and furthermore, an object of Jerdan's displeasure, Samuel Rogers the Banker Poet, was named in the dedication of *Album Verses*.[10] Such vituperation was unusual for Jerdan, giving rise to another theory that it was Landon who wrote the cruel review, as it was too personal to be in Jerdan's style, and Jerdan had reviewed Lamb kindly some years earlier, in August 1819.[11] Landon would have objected to albums being denigrated, as she was so closely involved with them; furthermore, as others like Chorley complained, she could be biting in her reviews. Chorley said, "For years the amount of gibing sarcasm and imputation to which I was exposed was largely swelled by this poor woman's commanded spite"[12] – commanded, he meant, by Jerdan.

Southey came out in defence of Lamb in *The Times* of 6 August, a gracious act as it was his first public utterance on his old school-friend since "Elia's" famous letter to him some time earlier. Southey's verse, *To Charles Lamb: On the Reviewal of his 'Album Verses' in the 'Literary Gazette'* spoke of Lamb's "genius", his "sterling worth", his lasting name when those of his critics would be forgotten. For good measure Southey attacked not only Jerdan but also Jeffrey, founder, and until July 1829 editor, of the *Edinburgh Review*. His defence of Lamb ended:

> Matter it is of mirthful memory
> To think, when thou wert early in the field,
> How doughtily small Jeffrey ran at thee
> A-tilt, and broke a bulrush on thy shield.
> And now, a veteran in the lists of fame,
> I ween, old Friend! Thou are not worse bested
> When with a maudlin eye and drunken aim
> Dulness hath thrown a "jerdan" at thy head.★

★ (a pun, 'jordan' being an Elizabethan term for chamber-pot)

The *Athenaeum* praised Southey for picking up the cudgels, especially as his name was distinguished and influential. It warned, "unless there be more discretion both in the praise and censure of the *Literary Gazette*, not all the interest of Messrs. Longman and Co. and Colburn and Bentley, whose property it is, can uphold that paper."[13]

Leigh Hunt's old paper, *The Examiner*, was also unhappy with Jerdan. In 'Rejected Epigrams, offered to, but not accepted by the editor of a weekly publication' signed T.A.[14] The first and second of these, published in the issue of 15 August 1830 were of two lines each and were heavy-handed and not witty. The third Epigram, although longer, was vicious:

> In lanes and at the corners of the streets,
> The eye of passengers a caution greets,
> Advising them that at that sacred spot
> The laws of decency be not forgot,
> In terms so plain, the most unletter'd lurdan
> Can scarce mistake – save Literary J——n,
> Who thinks he hits the meaning, and the true sense
> While in his writing he commits no *new sense*.

The next attack was even more personal:

> If we believe St. Paul and Scripture sense
> There are, and must be, "Vessels of Offence":

And such is *one,* whose name would dirt our pen,
That casts its water upon blameless men,
Replenished to the brim with stalest ware,
Yet, strange to tell, a favourite with the fair;
And for perversion, with an eye to pelf,
Makes of good things a handle for itself.

Lest Jerdan think this was the worst damage *The Examiner* could do to him, the paper noted that the Epigrams were "To be continued weekly, till the proprietors of the publication in question shall dismiss their present editor for incompetency and imbecility – an event which is calculated as probable to happen about the first week of October."

The following week, the fifth epigram addressed itself to L.E.L. advised her to "Come from that unclean cage", and that her genius " . . . should scorn – O servile tax/ To be the hack to booksellers vile hacks". T.A. warmed to his task, and the sixth epigram warned:

In Merry England I computed once
The number of the dunces, dunce by dunce;
There were four hundred, if I don't forget,
The readers of the *Literary Gazette*:
But if the author to himself keep true
In some short months they'll be reduced to *two.*

Several more Jerdan-attacking squibs followed, including one on 12 September, poking fun at Jerdan's attribution to Shakespeare of a modern poem, a trap into which Jerdan had readily fallen: "To shew what Shakespeare did *not* write is easy/But what he *did*! J——n I see you're queasy."

Leigh Hunt printed an 'Inquest Extraordinary' in the first issue of his *Tatler* on 4 October:

1830: Last week a porter died beneath his burden;
    Verdict: Found carrying a *Gazette* from Jerdan.[15]

Same day: Two gentlewomen died of vapours,
    Verdict: Hair curl'd with Mr Jerdan's papers.[16]

The next issue carried Objections to the Lines on Jerdan:

Why, Mr TATLER, should you tell
The world a truth it knows so well?
That JERDAN is a dunce we know,
For every week he tells us so.

> Sure, Mr TATLER, you conferred an
> Honour unmerited on JERDAN,
> Saying his intellect was small;
> 'Twas thought that he had none at all.

Hunt's *Tatler* was short-lived, closing in February 1832.

Lamb received a note of comfort from Bernard Barton following the *Literary Gazette* review, and replying on 30 August assured him that the sight of annuals made him sick, and further, that "They are all rogues who edit them, and something else who write in them." His ire was excited by Jerdan's unnecessarily cruel review, especially in a journal so renowned for its habitual kindness. Jerdan was, apparently, not in his usual generous frame of mind and had created a row over a trifle that a respectable literary journal might have been well advised to ignore. He mentioned nothing of all this furore in his *Autobiography*, neither did he take it further in the *Literary Gazette*, possibly because Landon had written the offending review, or because he generally tried to avoid personal controversy, especially as in this case he must have felt outnumbered and outgunned.

Another rare glimpse of his irritability is apparent in a letter he wrote to William Blackwood in Edinburgh requesting his friend and rival to reconsider a book sent to him for review three months earlier;[17] he followed this with "I dare not do more than suggest to such a Wizard as Ebony, but I think if he will look at . . . he will find quotations fit for his various page; and he will oblige me by paying as early an attention to this recommendation as I am always inclined to pay to any from him." He must have felt the fates conspiring against him, although he was at the peak of his powers at this time: he told 'Ebony' that "LEL is also shelved I fear – so that I fear it will be fearful for you to venture to London this Spring" . He does not explain why L.E.L. was "shelved" but if she was indisposed, he would have had an extra burden of work to get through on the *Literary Gazette*, which would not have improved his temper, and at the same time, the great issue of 'puffing' was gathering steam. He was in need of all the support he could get. Crossly, he told 'Ebony' in his postscript: "By the bye, why do your Editors fling at me – the ill-will is but slight and I regard it not; but it should not appear in a friend's publication. Instead therefore I have contributed to the Annuals (fairly enough for a busy body – have put my name to the National Gallery of Portraits, and have set up a New (Foreign) Lit Gazette in all of which you might have given me a good office." He presumably meant 'puffs' in *Maga*, which were not forthcoming.

One of his contributions to an annual was to *The Keepsake* of 1830, a poem entitled *The Time Was – And Is*, a clumsy title for a sad poem about drinking and singing with friends in earlier days; they are now dead, and wine has no power to restore feelings and friends of youth. Jerdan took some time off to accompany Wordsworth to the Royal Academy exhibition; they inspected Turner's painting of 'Jessica', Shylock's daughter, which Jerdan thought "an outrageous slapdash". The future Poet Laureate went further: "She looks as if she had supped off underdone pork, and been unable to digest it in the morning."[18]

There was considerable financial pressure on Jerdan at this time and he was driven to repeat a sacrifice which had cost him dear the first time around. On 27 November 1829 he assigned his one-third share in the *Literary Gazette* to Longmans for £1000; this was part of a complex arrangement negotiated with Twinings, to whom Jerdan owed a considerable sum, and Roby who held his insurance policy. Jerdan agreed to pay interest to Longmans at two pounds per cent per annum on a quarterly basis, and if he failed to pay it, Longmans was authorized to withhold it from monies due to him as Editor.[19]

Despite grumbling about the volume of work he was getting through, Jerdan seemed to thrive on it. "Activity of mind seems to grow with the utmost stretch of employment," he remarked, continuing with the memory that "The *Literary Gazette* gave me incessant occupation, I may say night and day. On returning from the gayest party, I was usually at my books and desk writing for reviews, or scribbling down some *disjuncta membra* to remind me of passing original thoughts. To use a much-abused phrase, my imagination was much more 'suggestive' in *post-prandial* and nocturnal than in breakfasting and matitudinal hours."[20] Here, he lightly touched upon the subject for which he was most noted in contemporary memoirs, that of a man who enjoyed a bottle or two, but for Jerdan the stimulation gained from partying was the lubricant he needed to accomplish his work. Then to be productive, "to enjoy the needful quietude and sedateness, the busy world must be shut out and asleep, and then you may glide from all the philosophies of letters and life, to revel in stranger abstractions and the fantastic delirium of dreamland. Castles in the air are delicious buildings; unreal? No! they are real cities, temples, sanctuaries of refuge from the cares, the troubles, the anxieties of the material lump-world." Small wonder that Jerdan, with all his professional, domestic and extra-curricular cares, welcomed the "fantastic delirium of dreamland".

Given his concerns, it was remarkable that Jerdan's interests were far wider than solely the promulgation and review of literature; his active interest in the Royal Society of Literature and the Literary Fund were part and parcel of his primary focus, but he also used the *Literary Gazette* as an instrument to lay the foundation for the (later Royal) Geographical Society. The seed had been sown in the issue of 24 May 1828 when, responding to a letter from 'A.C.C.' identified later as a clerk or librarian in the India House,[21] he agreed that a Geographical Society "would be an excellent institution in England . . . It is a great desideratum among our literary and scientific associations . . . it only needs three or four active and influential persons to originate such a plan. We trust to see this matter taken up by efficient hands." "From the egg thus dropt", said Jerdan, "the Royal Geographical Society was hatched."[22] He received, and published on 20 September, a letter from W. Huttman, of the Asiatic Society, enthusiastically supporting and elaborating the idea. More than a year passed, during which meetings were held by Huttman, with John Britton, Jerdan, and a few others, a Captain, a Colonel and a Lieutenant. Eventually, after their various deliberations, Jerdan received an uncorrected proof of a Prospectus, which he published in the *Literary Gazette* of 8 May 1830. Jerdan made some amendment to the prospectus which mentioned only Britton's name. This was then printed and circulated amongst interested parties. Jerdan reprinted this Prospectus in the Appendix to Volume IV of his *Autobiography*, plainly delighted to have had such an influential part in the establishment of an august institution.

Understandably keen for his journal to take full credit for initiating such an important new Society so in keeping with the exploring and discovering spirit of the age, Jerdan wrote again in the *Literary Gazette*:

We are happy to see the suggestions, first promulgated in the Literary Gazette, respecting the formation of a Geographical Society in London, at length so highly and powerfully adopted as to leave no doubt either as to the formation of such an Institution, or as to its efficiency. In England we move slowly – *perhaps*, but if the cause be good, *perhaps* not the less surely. The hints we have thrown out during the last two years did not immediately fructify, but they made their impression; or, not to spoil our metaphor, they took root; and when we lately intimated that they were about to produce the desired return, the statement seems to have stimulated those most competent to realise the harvest into the activity which was, alone, requisite to the occasion.

In the summer of 1830 a meeting occurred at the Raleigh (Travelling Club) where Captain Smyth proposed his own draft prospectus. John (afterwards Sir John) Barrow, Secretary of the Admiralty, was in the chair, and resolutions were agreed for the establishment of a Geographical Society. Britton sent the rival prospectus to Jerdan who saw its marked similarities to his own draft. He "confessed to a feeling of mortification at the supercession of the plan at which he and his friends had been working for two years, but he made the best of the situation".[23] Formally invited to become a Member of the Society, Jerdan wrote to Barrow on 10 June:

I am very much obliged by the Prospectus of the Geographic Society, which being first suggested in the Literary Gazette is naturally a favourite with me.

I should be proud of the honour of being a Member of the Society; and happy to promote its interests by every means in my power, tho' with such names as I now see associated with it, and under such influence as yours, it can need very little from the humble efforts of an individual like me.[24]

Jerdan did as he promised, and kept the public informed about the Geographical Society through the columns of his magazine. The consequence of this publicity, Jerdan claimed, was that "above five hundred adhesions were announced of noblemen and gentleman of distinction in life and literature, such as I never knew combined before at the commencement of any undertaking of any kind ...". Before the end of the season Lord Goderich (Earl of Ripon and lately Prime Minister) "was elected President, and the Society entered fairly and fully upon the career of its imperial usefulness ... somewhat *in loco parentis*, I take a papa's pride in believing that it is at the present day in as flourishing and beneficial a condition as ever it was at any preceding date".[25] In February, probably of the following year, he wrote again to Barrow, offering the services of a correspondent who wished to travel in Paraguay and was seeking a grant for the purpose. There was no suggestion of this approach being of any financial advantage to himself, so it would seem to be another instance of Jerdan's kindness in using his network to help anyone who needed assistance. Although one of the original Fellows of the RGS, Jerdan took on no official role, but retained a great interest in the Society throughout his life.

Neither the *Literary Gazette* nor the *Athenaeum*, in common with other similar journals of the time, named their reviewers. In the *Literary Gazette* the leading reviews were likely to have been largely written by Jerdan himself, assisted by L.E.L., although it is probable that her input was in poetry reviews rather than prose. As far as the *Literary Gazette's* rival, the *Athenaeum* was concerned, its editor Charles Dilke insisted not only on anonymity in the printed publication, but he also "never signed anything that he himself wrote, and he carefully refrained from putting the names of reviewers of books written by members of the *Athenaeum* staff in the marked office file".[26] Jerdan's failure to keep an office file at all avoided this difficulty. (Unfortunately, it was an omission which now renders it impossible to identify many contributors with certainty.) Dilke's insistence on impartiality was of a piece with the highly moral stance for which the *Athenaeum* had, by this time, become well known; it was, however, at odds with the practices common in journals which had business links with publishers, like the *Literary Gazette*, the *New Monthly Magazine, Court Journal* and *United Services Journal,* all part of Henry Colburn's stable. Dilke pursued this moral stance to an obsessive degree, even demonstrating a "reluctance to go into society in order to avoid making literary acquaintances".[27] What a contrast to the excessively sociable editor of the *Literary Gazette*, for whom society in all its forms provided the materials and enthusiasm for his work and even, it may be said, for his life.

Decisions whether or not to review works by friends and colleagues was of a different order from decisions about reviewing works published by those with a financial interest in the journal, making the "reviews" look like impartial criticism, when they were in fact paid paragraphs. This was the "puffing" that the *Athenaeum* so despised, and of which Jerdan had been so violently accused – notably by Westmacott, and again in the pages of the *Athenaeum*. The latter made the charge very openly:

> The deceptive influence, against which the public should be put on their guard, is that of book publishers; we have no doubt, that if Mr Watts will examine five hundred columns of reviews in the *Literary Gazette*, one half will be found filled with the praise of works published by Colburn.[28]

From this distance in time it could be suggested that frequent mention of the works emanating from Colburn's publishing house was almost unavoidable. The *Literary Gazette* was aimed at the middle-class family, whose taste in fiction was, at this period, for the 'silver-fork' school in which Colburn specialized. It has been pointed out, in fact, that "It is hardly an exaggeration to say that nine-tenths of the fashionable novels bear the colophon of Henry Colburn."[29] Colburn's list for 1828 showed sixty-five new books in addition to his back list.[30] His authors included Hazlitt, Disraeli, Hook and Bulwer. Therefore, if Jerdan had refused to review the output of Colburn's silver-fork fiction and the flood of other novels under this publisher's imprint in order to avoid the charge of partiality, the *Literary Gazette* could have been accused to failing to review the popular fiction of the day. Jerdan was between a rock and a hard place. Edward Bulwer stood up for Jerdan, although without naming him, claiming that as far as Colburn was concerned,

> it was a matter of the most rankling complaint in his mind, that the editor of the journal, (who had an equal share himself in the journal, and could not be removed), was so anxious not to deserve the reproach as to be unduly harsh to the books he was accused of unduly favouring . . . I certainly calculated that a greater proportion of books belonging to the bookseller in question had been severely treated than was consistent with the ratio of praise and censure accorded to the works appertaining to any other publisher.[31]

However, it has been noted that "the majority of readers of the *New Monthly* or the *Literary Gazette* and newspaper 'paid paragraphs' accepted the judgments as opinions of impartial critics of literature".[32] There were occasional exceptions: in the issue of 30 January 1830 appears a notice of a book published by Colburn and Bentley. "*Random Records* deserves a random review and these volumes are not entitled to more than desultory notice". In the same issue, *Adventures of an*

Irish Gentleman, also published by Colburn and Bentley, was harshly reviewed: "The 'adventures' are improbable and absurd, as well as coarse and of a style and school quite departed, as the Americans say, 'slick right away'."

The *Court Journal*, (the reincarnated *London Weekly Review*) another of Colburn's publications, had revealed that a novel by Lady Charlotte Bury, published by Colburn, was a revision of another book which had appeared fifteen or twenty years earlier. The *Literary Gazette* defended Colburn & Bentley, asserting that they did not know of this deception. The *Athenaeum* was delighted to have a real target:

> 'We are convinced', says the Editor of the Literary Gazette, 'that Mr Colburn must have been unconscious of this trick, for we find the following preparatory announcement in the *New Monthly Magazine* for August, *which is also his publication and would not have sanctioned the utterance of such a paragraph had he been aware of the truth.*' Here is the admission of the Editor of the *Literary Gazette* that Mr Colburn is in the habit of *sanctioning* and *approving* (of inserting, for that is the plain English), paragraphs in *his own papers* and the *newspapers* which are so worded as to pass for the honest judgment of the Editor of the work; – and the Editor of the *Literary Gazette* speaks with authority, seeing that *Colburn is a large shareholder* in his own paper.[33]

Jerdan could not win, at the behest of such a man as Colburn.

The other side of the puffing coin was one that did not directly involve Jerdan and the other editors at all, but was crucial to the publishers. They, and most notably Colburn, used their skill in advertising books to tempt authors to choose them above rival publishers to produce their works. Reputedly, around 1830 Colburn was spending on average £9000 a year on advertising.[34] Advertisements containing excellent reviews, whether 'puffed' or genuine, might persuade a potential best-seller writer to select one house over another. Colburn had a reputation for paying high prices and achieving substantial sales, benefits which, for writers, overcame his other reputation for "unsavoury or at least undignified methods of advertising (which) grew into something of a byword in the trade".[35] Jerdan fought back.

In a rare example of writing a Leader or Editorial for the *Literary Gazette*, Jerdan used his journal's front page and half a column of the next, on 17 April 1830, for an article he called 'The Cut-and-Dry System of Criticism!' It is a method, he pronounced, "growing into great force and magnitude, is individually and patriotically odious in our eyes. It affects us and it injures literature: it is founded on selfish motives and abuses the public mind." The practice referred to was the selection of twenty or so striking passages from a book about to be published, made by the writer or the publisher. These extracts were printed on to a separate sheet and sent out with review copies of the book to newspapers and magazines. The reviewer was thus relieved of the task of reading the book, but could merely quote from the suggested passages. Jerdan acknowledged his ingratitude in exposing this "cut-and-dry" method, which was designed to make his, and other reviewers' lives easier. He noted ironically that they were not only saved from "wading through lots of dulness and trash", but the system also put reviewers on excellent terms with authors and publishers, as they just had to praise them and give the selected extracts, thereby avoiding the abuse often hurled at them for not praising enough. Even remote provincial journals could thus be reached by publishers, resulting in the rapid spread of unanimous good opinion of the cut-and-dry promoted books. The consequences of this abysmal practice, said Jerdan, are "humbug and imposition". The public were gulled into buying, were disappointed, felt cheated, until the next reviews, when the cycle started again.

This was merely the tip of the iceberg. "The great wrong lies deeper", he declared. "It is by the protrusion of what is worthless that real merit and talent are stifled. The voice of modest Genius cannot be heard amid the din of clamorous puffing . . ." Jerdan believed, furthermore, that the practice of cut-and-dry had a deleterious effect upon the national literature, because learned volumes, beautifully produced poetry and original research, were too expensive for publishers to produce good quality for a limited number of readers, whereas the Circulating Libraries bought quantities of "the ephemerides of the hour, which, by being puffed into notoriety, attract the multitude, are disposed of, repay the outlay, disgrace our literature, deprave the public taste, and are forgotten". The newspapers were devoted mainly to political news and were content to fill their other columns with paid paragraphs and advertising, the one ensuring the other, so that all newspapers were alike, because they used the same material. The *Literary Gazette*, promised Jerdan, would "adhere to the opposite course . . . and deliver its own opinions". He pointed out that the practice he abhorred was so widespread, no personal allusions had been made. "If the English reader wants a book calculated for future times, he must go to Germany, or France or Russia! For in England there are nothing but reprints, compilations, annuals, periodicals and the old species of machinery of the druggists' bottles mingling the contents of several and shewing off the mixtures of every colour of the rainbow". His readers would now recognize the "cut-and-dry" method, and know that such reviews were "not the dicta of literary independence and justice". This was a startling and daring article, and Jerdan was taking a considerable risk. A large part of the *Literary Gazette*'s income emanated from the pages of advertising for new books and annuals, as well as the compilations of which he complained. To risk cutting off the hands which fed his journal, he would have had to feel very strongly on the matter, which, as well as an attack on publishers in general, was a more specific attack on Colburn, whose puffing activities were notorious. Such a serious and responsible attitude to his profession belies the story told of Jerdan that he cut the pages of a book and smelled the paper knife for matter on which to base a review.[36]

The charge of puffery was one that continued to bedevil Jerdan. George Whittaker threatened him with withdrawing advertising in the *Literary Gazette* unless reviews of his works improved, even though he maintained that sales would remain the same with good or bad reviews. This was a threat to be taken seriously, as Whittaker's publishing house was second only to Longmans in the number of new titles listed in the English Catalogue of Books for this period. When he was thirty years old in 1823 Whittaker had been elected sheriff of London and Middlesex, so was a man who wielded some considerable clout in many circles and it took courage to stand up to him. Jerdan protested to Cosmo Orme, a partner in Longmans, that nine of the ten reviews of Whittaker's works in the previous month had been favourable, and that "It is utterly impossible to produce a review which shall always be puffing: and every person of common sense must feel that individual pretensions . . . must be contemned if we mean to cultivate an honest reputation with the general reader."[37] Jerdan followed this up with a spirited response to Whittaker himself: "be assured that indiscriminate praise is not the course to serve any publisher; at any rate, I will not sacrifice my independence and integrity by making the *Gazette* its organ . . . I will not give up one jot of its fairness, impartiality or justice, to conciliate all the publishers in London."[38] (An examination of the ten reviews disclosed "that of the nine works Jerdan claimed had received 'praise', five were met with qualifications which would have made buyers hesitate and booksellers, who expected enthusiastic puffs, uneasy."[39]) In his *Autobiography* Jerdan offered his correspondence with Whittaker as proof of his clear intention to keep the *Literary Gazette* impartial. To do so, he had to fight not only outside publishers, but also his own partners, a heroic but ultimately impossible task. In self-defence he wrote:

> In vindicating the *Gazette* from the aspersions with which it was so insidiously assailed and misrepresented, till a pretty general belief was obtained for the falsehoods, I do not mean to say that it, or any journal of its class, can be carried on with perfect freedom, and uninfluenced by any circumstances. On the contrary, personal regards and attachments, literary connections, and friendly interferences must have an effect in enhancing praise, and moderating blame; and, in a baser manner, rivalry, envy, and malignity will, in some instances, have the opposite effect in producing damning faint praise, or undue commendation, and abusive censure. To the former I plead very partially guilty – the latter I utterly repudiate and deny. I never penned a malevolent article during the whole of my long career; and, to the best of my knowledge, I never concealed or perverted

a truth, even when noticing the performances of those I knew to be my unscrupulous enemies.[40]

Despite his best endeavours to maintain high principles, he was still perceived as the publishers' hack, leading him to protest "I do not believe that any periodical and its editor were ever exposed to the industrious circulation of systematic falsehood in a greater degree than the *Literary Gazette* and myself for many years."[41] There is a degree of naivety in his protestations: the practice of puffing was expected by the publishers, and compliance was a form of mutual back-scratching. In return, journal editors were favoured with early copies of books for review. William Maginn, editor of *Fraser's* magazine wrote to Jerdan in 1825, "I write to you – for there is no use of talking humbug – to ask you for a favourable critique, or a puff, or any other *thing* of the kind – the *word* being no matter . . . You will oblige me by giving it a favourable and early review in your 'Gazette'."[42] Maginn may have been squeamish about using the 'puffing' word, but his request was clear.

Jerdan had an almost impossible task in struggling to keep the *Literary Gazette* impartial. Colburn was remorseless in demands to 'puff' the books he published, and became so synonymous with the practice that jokes and jibes at his expense appeared in the popular press, and were encouraged by writers who were not part of his stable. Commercial rivalry and professional jealousy would be primary motivators for such attacks, as well as a fairly universal dislike of Colburn's self-promoting personality. Dilke's *Athenaeum* was in the forefront of fighting the practice of puffery, and the target of Dilke's opening barrage was the 'Juvenile Library' published by Colburn and Bentley.

Only a month after the demise of the ill-fated *Foreign Literary Gazette*, Colburn and Bentley came up with a plan. Seeing the success of a series of good works in cheap editions pioneered a few years earlier by Constable's 'Miscellany of Original and Selected Publications', they proposed to publish four distinct series of their own. A printed Prospectus[43] for 'The Library of Modern Travels, Voyages and Discoveries' did not proceed past the planning stage; 'The Standard Novels', "a reprint series, was profitable enough to appear from 1831 into the 60s. A third series, 'The National Library' "produced seven original books in late 1830 and early 1831, before harsh but well-deserved reviews halted it".[44] The fourth in the proposed series was the 'Juvenile Library'.

Jerdan worked hard, producing a four-page list of suggestions for this project, the puffing of which was to cause the *Athenaeum* such fury.[45] His suggested subjects ranged from a History of Christianity including the Accounts of Massacres and Martyrdoms, to Dress and Costume, the Medici, a History of Trees, and many other topics. He slipped in a line for "Jerdan's Cyclopaedia" to be 24 volumes, commencing two years hence. He also suggested a few possible writers, including Mrs Hofland, Miss Edgeworth and Bulwer. It has been noted that "Jerdan's selection of authors was safe, for he took the easy course of engaging writers who had contributed to other serial works".[46] It seems natural that he would indeed choose authors who had a proven track record, and whose names would be well enough known to attract the buying public to the new series. Jerdan mentioned his ideas to a few people who thought well of the plan.

At the end of April 1830 he drafted a Memorandum of Agreement[47] asking for three hundred pounds per annum for twelve volumes,[48] twenty-five pounds for any extra volumes, and fifty pounds extra per annum for the sale of every thousand copies above four thousand. The agreement to be for one hundred volumes (i.e. over eight years' work), to be continued thereafter by mutual consent or, if unsuccessful, to be discontinued after twenty volumes. His draft stated, "The discretion in the choice of subjects and writers to be vested in the Editor". He wished to clarify payments to his writers at one hundred pounds per volume for eight, and seventy-five pounds per volume for four within the year, anything larger to be agreed with Colburn and Bentley. He substantiated his suggestion of three hundred pounds per annum, saying that twenty-five pounds per volume was a fair price. "I have the same for writing 24 pages of the *National Gallery*, which has risen in thousands within the five months of my superintendance, the labour of the Library must be much more − infinitely more." He assured Colburn and Bentley that "writers will make fairest bargains with <u>me</u> than with you. They will press less greedily". On payments, he may pay some fifty pounds, others one hundred and fifty pounds, but the total would remain as agreed. Jerdan urged that the project be started at once, and that writers should be engaged for the first twelve to fifteen volumes. To hasten their decision he told them that Mr Whittaker (of the rival publishing house) had been to see him, and had agreed to abandon his plan for a similar Library in favour of Jerdan's.

The following day, 30 April 1830, a revised contract was drawn up between Jerdan and Henry Colburn and Richard Bentley Publishers of New Burlington Street.[49] Jerdan was to "edit, revise and prepare the said work for publication in the most careful manner" and to acquire the best writers on reasonable terms, and promote the sale of the work. His remuneration was that "so long as the work shall be regularly published and continued at one volume per month" Jerdan would receive three hundred pounds per annum. Should any monthly part reach sales of five thousand copies (this revision increased the original suggestion by one thousand copies per month), Jerdan's salary would rise to three hundred and fifty pounds per annum, and so on, adding fifty pounds per annum for every additional thousand copies sold monthly. Colburn and Bentley agreed to the extra twenty-five pounds to edit and prepare any additional volumes. A clause that underwent a fundamental change was the one which stated "The choice of subjects and the writers and the sums to be paid to them to be mutually agreed upon between the said parties − that is to say neither party to be at liberty to enforce the writing purchases or publication of any work against the reasonable advice of the others." Jerdan was thus kept in tight control under the thumb of the publishers, who further inserted into their contract a clause to the effect that "the work to be continued only so long as the said Colburn and Bentley find it sufficiently advantageous to them to do so" differing again from Jerdan's original suggestion of a minimum of twenty volumes, and a rethink after one hundred. No security then for Jerdan, who was under enormous pressure to perform well in this new project, in addition to his already arduous duties on the *Literary Gazette*. A postcript to the contract noted that Bentley and Colburn "will not object to the sum of from Fifty to One hundred pounds per volume being given when the interest of the Work and the influence of the writers shall warrant the same", again taking from Jerdan control of what was paid to an individual writer.

The several changes to his draft agreement, all reducing his control and power over subjects and writers, drew an angry letter from Jerdan.[50] So indignant was he at the lack of trust, that he declined the editorship of the Juvenile Library, explaining carefully that it was specifically the fourth clause to which he objected, the one in which there was to be mutual agreement over writers, subjects, and fees. Jerdan's letter is the clearest contemporary surviving statement of his professionalism, his self-esteem and self-confidence in his editorial abilities. He may justifiably have been outraged by the cavalier treatment of his potential employers; he had, after all, been associated with Colburn for better or worse, for the previous thirteen years, and felt that his credentials had been impugned: "Upon the editing of this work I must stake my whole literary credit . . . " Under the redrawn terms Colburn and Bentley could end the Library, and Jerdan's employment in it, at any time; it was thus obviously in his own interest, Jerdan pointed out, to put in the work necessary to ensure its success. "I therefore hold myself entitled to the whole trust and to your perfect confidence, in the selection of works and writers." In addition – and this was brave, considering Colburn's monopoly of the popular market for fiction – Jerdan continued: "I should desire to keep myself distinct from your particular class of writers, without meaning the slightest disrespect to them . . . to be monthly discussing which is best or worst would I fear led to misunderstandings, and I cannot go on with a work unless I give my heart and soul to it in my own way." He went on to insist that he should pay what he saw as necessary to specific writers as long as the total did not exceed the sum agreed. He demanded that his would-be employers look "to me and not to my means for the proper execution of my work". If the scheme did not work, he wrote, he would step down, with six months' notice on either side. Tacitly acknowledging his bad record with figures, he concluded, "The simplification of operations and accounts the whole being reduced to twelve entries per annum is a powerful recommendation of the task."

That Colburn and Bentley finally agreed to his terms seems apparent, as within a very short time, a scant two months, the first issue of the 'Juvenile Library' was published. This was *Lives of Remarkable Youth of Both Sexes*, by D. S. Williams and Don J. Telesforo de Trueba y Cosio, the first of two volumes. It seems to have been a case of 'more haste less speed'. Jerdan wrote to Richard Bentley that he was "much chagrined to see a Volume so full of errors as the first of the Juvenile Library to go forth to the world as sanctioned by me, and I certainly cannot permit my name to be so abused".[51] He also objected to the price being raised from three shillings and sixpence to four shillings. Prophetically, he remarked "I am not a grumbler, but we must proceed fairly together, with a good understanding, or evil will come of it." For once, the *Athenaeum* agreed with him, declaring, "we do not know how the young of both sexes could be better employed, for the improvement of their minds, than in correcting the sentences in the first volume of the Juvenile Library."[52]

The *Literary Gazette* of 26 June 1830 noted the arrival of the new volume, but had not time to review it. The "puff" highlighted the four portraits and suggested the book as a "holyday gift". The following week it reluctantly reviewed the book. Sensitive to the ongoing accusations of 'puffing' the reviewer claimed to be embarrassed as to how to deal with the book. If he wished to dispraise it, that "would be an effort of stern virtue scarcely to be expected from human nature; to eulogise it, however deserving we may consider it of eulogium, would be inevitably to expose ourselves to the sneers and ridicule of all our 'good-natured friends'; entirely to abstain from noticing it, would be signally to fail in our duty both to the public and the publishers". He compromised by letting the book speak for itself, and selecting one life of the nine lives it contained and quoting the extract in full over about one and a half pages. There is also a comment that three thousand copies were 'disposed of' on the first day the book appeared. The 'review' ended by promising a further extract from one of the other lives in the next issue of the *Literary Gazette*. In the same issue, under the heading 'To Our Correspondents', Jerdan proclaimed that:

> Our review of this work, to a certain degree explains the difficulty of our position with regard to it; . . . the volume was submitted for criticism to a gentleman as independent of the *Literary Gazette* as the *Literary Gazette* is itself independent. A man of firmness, talent and integrity, he was assured that our invariable rule was to know neither friend nor adversary in these pages; and that therefore he should exercise in this and every similar case, his unbiased judgment.

This declaration conflicts somewhat with the "embarrassment" mentioned by the reviewer, but it served to bring the 'Juvenile Library' to the notice of the reader once again. In all, it received six mentions in the *Literary Gazette*; Jerdan was clearly not so embarrassed that he did not make full use of his position to promote this project of his own, at a time when the death of King George IV, briefly mentioned under 'Politics' in the stamped edition of the *Literary Gazette*, was likely to be uppermost in the minds of his readers, together with the accession of his sixty-five year old brother, William IV.

The second volume in the new series was Samuel Carter Hall's *Historic Anecdotes of France*. Hall recollected how Jerdan, in a state of harassed apprehension, came to him on the ninth day of a month and explained that a history of France promised for the first day of the next month was not forthcoming. Jerdan declared that it was a case of producing the book or closing the series, and he asked Hall to undertake the task. Agreeing to do so, Hall spent one day surrounding himself with a hundred books on France. He then had only eighteen days in which to produce a book of four hundred pages. During one stretch of twelve days he never went to bed, and the result was "a brain-fever" and a wretched book. Hall naïvely concluded: 'it is somewhat strange that Jerdan in his *Autobiography* has made no mention of this series, or of his engagement with Colburn and Bentley, as its editor.'"[53] There is no reason to doubt Hall's account of the pressure Jerdan put him under, although his concluding remark is inaccurate. He was by then a man of eighty-three years old, recalling events of several decades earlier.

Learning from past experience, Jerdan took his time producing the third volume of the 'Juvenile Library', which appeared on 4 October 1830. It was by Miss Jane Webb,[54] and titled *Africa: its History*. Sending Jerdan the concluding pages, Jane Webb told him that Colburn had advanced her ten pounds three weeks earlier, but the money was now gone. She had written two or three times to Bentley. "He however is not as fascinating as the dear little man for he has never replied to my letters."[55] The *Examiner*, although it devoted several columns to extracts from the book, was vicious about its editor: "We know not . . . why the instruction of little folks must be superintended by Mr Jerdan, who knows nothing, little or great"; and went on to point out grammatical errors which had slipped past his notice.[56] The *Athenaeum* remarked meanly that *Africa* was "in a less pretending style than that of its melancholy predecessors", hinted at hostility between Jerdan and his publishers, and concluded "it is not very improbable but that this juvenile expedition to the Timbuctoo of knowledge may utterly perish in Africa".[57]

They were right. The 'Juvenile Library' was not a success. In desperation, Jerdan wrote to Bentley at the beginning of October

I think you are not truly keeping faith with me respecting the Juvenile Library; but on the contrary are sacrificing it to the National Series. After what we agreed to I could not expect that you would depreciate this work by statements that it was to be immediately dropt, as has been done to Mrs Hall – rumours of this kind leave no fair chance for the publication, and are very painful as well as injurious to me – my name and literary character being made mere sports of on the occasion. I think it only right to let you know my sentiments on this business in which I embarked at your own pressing instance and through which you are in honour bound to hear me respectably.[58]

Money was always an issue with Jerdan. He had agreed to pay seventy-five pounds to the writer of the fourth volume, *Greece*, due in November, and asked Bentley for a cheque to cover this. He again had to write to Bentley telling him that he was "obliged to anticipate fifty guineas at Messrs. Longmans in order to meet my draft on Drummonds tomorrow on account of the Juvenile Library. I think it is very hard."[59] Another note, written with great urgency, instructing the bearer to wait for a reply, asked Bentley for a 'note' of fifty pounds payable in two months, to cover the next two volumes of the Juvenile editorship; his reason was· that he in turn was having to give advances to writers and was "dry as a chip" for a few days.[60] Dated only 'Monday night' and annotated 1830, another letter from Jerdan to Bentley referred to money, but also to another matter which is now not clear. This may have referred to L.E.L., Dr Thomson being her physician and friend. It read:

> I am much obliged by your letter and exceedingly vexed that we should correspond on so unpleasant a subject. I fear the real gist of the matter is evaded, or not seen in what has been done. From Dr Thomson's I have the most degrading representations – it is (myself out of the question) the most vexatious thing that could occur for the credit of C & B – All that I shall do is to clear myself – I am no beggar off of engagements and I dread being held up even by the worst of periodicals in so miserable a light . . . I have today borrowed money again to give for the honour of the concern, while much put about myself. I hope to hear tomorrow, but after the delays I have seen, will proceed as declared.

He added, squeezed into a corner, "I had not room to sign W. Jerdan but I shall not allow another day to pass without taking steps to set myself right with all concerned."[61]

Far from puffing the new project as he was widely accused of doing with all his productions, Colburn was, in Jerdan's estimation, "liberally damning it". Jerdan informed Bentley that he would be "glad to release you from an undertaking prosecuted with so little cordiality".[62] Two weeks later the relationship between Jerdan and the publishers had deteriorated to the point of no return. Jerdan claimed to have put his own feelings aside, in the matter of the 'Juvenile Library', only to find that Colburn and Bentley had gone behind his back, trying to negotiate secretly and separately with the writers with whom he had already made arrangements. Speaking of his "disappointment and mortification" Jerdan protested vehemently that all his own efforts had been counteracted and that

> you seem bent on incurring the evils pecuniary and literary I have been so anxious to prevent by very fruitless, and I think not very creditable or high-spirited negociations with each in their turn. You will find this fail, and you are provoking hostilities of the most irritating and injurious kind. Cost in the end, and public attacks upon your characters to boot are inevitable . . . .my position appears to be utterly forgotten, and every individual whom I have engaged with to write is treated separately in a manner I deeply disapprove, and without reference to what has passed between them and me – placing me in a light so ridiculous and contemptible that I neither can nor will endure.[63]

A scrawled list in Jerdan's handwriting probably relates to the commissions he handed out for the 'Juvenile Library'.[64] His 'Absolute' list of five writers totalled £375; the second group of four, "may be stopped at (say £25)", and included Landon; the third, six writers who should share £100 between them. The total owed was £534. A few more names came under the heading 'Doubtful'.

To salvage what he could from the impossible situation Jerdan offered Colburn and Bentley "more in pity than in anger" a choice of two courses: one, that for five hundred pounds he would continue his original negotiations, and take any claims upon himself; alternatively, that he would send all writers a circular letter (a copy of which he enclosed for their information) absolving himself from all responsibility and informing the writers that they were now answerable to Colburn and Bentley directly. This would cost them far more: "I believe that £1000 and much odium must be the price and result of this alternative." He gave them the weekend to make up their minds. The note which he appended to the copy of his letter circulated to the writers, announced that they chose the second option, and "I have therefore to request you will not proceed farther with the work you engaged to write, but furnish them with the amount of your demand for what you may have done, which they have assured me will be immediately and honourably discharged." They were possibly not quite as immediate as they promised: in December Jerdan received a request from his friend James Robinson Planché for a formal letter stating that he had been engaged to write a volume on Costume for the Juvenile Library for a fee of one hundred pounds, confirming that this had been sanctioned by Colburn and Bentley, together with ten similar engagements. The possibility of a second volume had not been discussed with the publishers. Had the publishers paid their debts on time, Planché would not have needed this formality from Jerdan.

Barely on speaking terms with his publishers, Jerdan's eyes and ears at New

Burlington Street were those of Charles Ollier, the partners' general assistant, who drew up a list of works in progress when the 'Juvenile Library' was abandoned.[65] This named titles and authors, with a note of the status of each work. It corroborated the letter Jerdan wrote to Bentley asking for seventy-five pounds for the manuscript of a *History of the Children of Israel* for which he held the writer's discharge, noting "besides a further advance". The list itemised which works were "in progress", "nearly complete", or "hardly begun", and stated that Planché's work on Dress, which they were slow to remunerate, was in a state of "considerable progress". Planché sued Colburn for failure to accept and pay for his commissioned work, and won. According to a report in the *Athenaeum*, Jerdan said he thought that Planché and the other writers would have accepted twenty-five pounds because they were his personal friends, and "he had the power of obliging them".[66] The *Athenaeum* believed they were each due double that amount, but the journal had every reason to belittle their rival, Jerdan. On the other hand, the writers *were* Jerdan's friends, and he may well have made such an ill-considered statement, to rile Colburn. *The Times* was more objective, stating that Jerdan had contracted to pay one hundred guineas for the volume, and thought fifty pounds only a fair remuneration for his trouble. "He had never said £25 was sufficient. A paper was, however, produced in Mr Jerdan's writing", saying that Planché and others might be satisfied with one hundred pounds between them. "Mr Jerdan said this was on the footing of an arrangement personally with himself, as friend of the parties, but he thought the plaintiff's claim against the booksellers, of £50 was quite fair."[67]

Jerdan and his writers were not the only ones to lose by the abandonment of the 'Juvenile Library'. Colburn and Bentley bore a financial loss, as itemised in this statement of the project amongst the Bentley papers which also shows how quickly sales declined with each volume produced:[68]

Jerdan editing	£125	sale no. 1	3300		
Copyrights	400	sale no. 2		2000	
Advertising	500	sale no. 3		1300	
Illustration	50		6600	£875	
Binding	180	stock	3600	£160	
Printing	180			£1035	
Paper	300	Loss		£ 900	

If Jerdan's claim that the first volume sold three thousand on the first day is true, then the additional three hundred indicates the poor reception of the book once it was in circulation. Jerdan's dissatisfaction seems to have been only with Colburn, as he wrote to Bentley that he believed it was not *his* fault things had gone so badly wrong, and he would not add another complaint to all the unpleasantness which the publisher must be experiencing. Jerdan mentioned that he had already been censured for the debacle "in a high quarter". Colburn tried to make Bentley pay two hundred pounds for three books intended for the Juvenile Library, a claim Bentley stoutly refuted. Three other books were salvaged and published later.[69]

Jerdan's only reference to this fiasco in his four-volume *Autobiography* was in the concluding chapter of Volume Four, indicating either its insignificance to him or, more likely, that over twenty years later he was still so hurt by the treatment he had received he could hardly bear to mention it. "[a]fter some progress", he recalled, "the design was abandoned by the publishers; in consequence of which several annoying disputes arose between them and the contributors, led to considerable expense, and vexed me extremely . . . it is yet an excellent plan, and might be carried into effect."[70]

Abandonment of the project was hardly surprising in the light of the *Athenaeum*'s attack on the puffing Colburn lavished upon it. The issue of 17 July 1830 sneered:

> No-one will have the hardihood to say that the 'Juvenile Library' is not become a positive nuisance in the newspapers; for it is scarcely possible to get through a single column of *Chronicle* or *Herald* without having to suffer a Burlington Street paragraph. Nothing can be so moral and edifying as the 'Juvenile Library'; nothing so pure and pleasant as its style; nothing so disinterested and generous as its object. The paragraphs, which are paid for, say all this; . . .

(This accusation is at odds with Jerdan's perception that Colburn was 'liberally damning' the project, but perhaps the 'damning' was merely verbal to those in Colburn's circle.) The *Athenaeum* and, in Jerdan's eyes at least, the *Literary Gazette* set out to bring literature into public notice and encourage readers. However, for Colburn and others like him a book was a commodity to be advertised and regarded no differently from boot polish or potatoes. It was this mercantile approach and the onslaught of advertising, as well as its poor opinion of the 'Juvenile Library', that goaded the *Athenaeum* into complaining: "It is the duty of an independent journal to protect as far as possible the credulous, confiding and unwary, from the wily arts of the insidious advertiser. And as we honestly think that the 'Juvenile Library', judging it from the volume before us, is a hasty, pretending, ill-written work . . . we hold it right to strike out of the path which our contemporaries have pursued, and to devote to it a candid column instead of a paid paragraph."[71] Three weeks later it referred again to "one of the most hasty, inaccurate and contemptible books ever published – the first number of the 'Juvenile Library'.[72] Unsurprisingly, Colburn withdrew his advertising for the 'Juvenile Library' from the *Athenaeum*. When the fledgling project failed, the *Athenaeum* jibed: "By the bye, we have not seen even one little pleasant paragraph paying gentleman-usher to the <u>third</u> volume of the 'Juvenile'." Jerdan's hope of extra income had died with it.

The *Athenaeum* now had the bit firmly between its teeth, and regularly attacked the practice of puffery. Although its ire was directed mainly at the publishers the *Literary Gazette*, perceived as a lackey of Colburn's, did not escape its barbs. The issue of 4 September 1830 devoted a whole article to the *Literary Gazette*, noting that twenty-one columns concerned books published by Colburn and Bentley, but only one-eighth of a column to a book from John Murray's 'Family Library'. This observation is true,[73] and it is easy to imagine the forceful demands that the aggressive, publicity hungry Colburn made upon his partner, the editor of the *Literary Gazette*. On one notable occasion, however, Jerdan refused to toe the party line, causing the startled *Athenaeum* praisingly to remark that "The Literary Gazette has out-heroded Herod . . . it has honestly slaughtered Mr Williams (The Life and Correspondence of Sir Thomas Lawrence); but the attack on 'book-making' – 'the tricks of the trade' – 'puffing' and 'paid paragraphs' is really so like a column out of the *Athenaeum*, that we imagined we had mistaken the paper, and, feared we had been repeating ourselves."[74]

Unfortunately for Jerdan, who must have felt besieged by the strength and regularity of attacks on his journal, he was linked in business to the odious Colburn and thus laid himself open to the *Athenaeum*'s scorn. The *Athenaeum* had another of Colburn's journals in its sights too: it noted that in his *New Monthly Magazine*, a list of forthcoming books comprised 95 percent from the publishing house of Colburn and Bentley, the remaining 5 percent being books published by every other publisher in the kingdom. The note concluded ironically "Commend us to the announcements in the *New Monthly*, but above all, to the criticisms in the *Literary Gazette*!!!"[75]

Determined to avoid any possibility of the *Athenaeum* being found guilty of 'puffing', it was made quite clear that it would accept only advertisements which were indisputably advertisements, and would reject anything smacking of a 'paid paragraph'. Lest any reader should doubt its intention or confuse its ethos with other literary journals, Dilke announced loudly in January 1831 that: "It surely ought to be enough for one house to have property in, and therefore influence over, the *Literary Gazette,* the *Sunday Times*, the *Court Journal*, the *New Monthly Magazine,* and the *United Service Journal* without shaking the public faith in every other journal in the kingdom by criticisms, which, we again repeat, *were all paid for.*"

In addition to inserting his 'paid paragraphs' into as many papers as he could, Colburn also sent free extracts from his books to country papers who were often glad of such material to fill their pages. This was the practice Jerdan had discussed in his 'Cut-and-Dry' article, and of course, this practice was also not to the *Athenaeum*'s liking. Neither was Colburn's habit of sending review copies to his favoured journals pre-publication. As the *Athenaeum* was obviously not on his list at this time, they reacted badly to a letter from the publishers "asking them not to print a review until *due notice* of publication had been given".[76] This was a gift to their satiric pen:

> this honest testimony to our integrity by Messrs. Colburn and Bentley deserves our best thanks., When did they ever serve a like notice on the Editor of the Literary Gazette? We ask Mr Bentley if he interfered *to prevent* the review of the first number of the Juvenile Library from appearing in that paper previous to the publication of the work itself?[77]

The following issue again complained that the *Literary Gazette* had prior information, (and indeed, Hood quipped that 'Jerdan does not review books, he previews them'[78]) and enthusiastically praised a book which the *Athenaeum* and other independent literary papers had been embargoed to discuss until a later publication date. Jerdan did not have it all his own way, however. He wrote to Colburn and Bentley in August 1831 complaining: "The next time you send me an early publication in common with the *Athenaeum*, however little you may care for the *Gazette*, I will be obliged by its being mentioned in order that I may avoid similarity of appearance, so injurious as today between an 8vo and a 4vo publication."[79] Colburn's partly illegible scrawl on this note is something to the effect that "I have frequently pointed out the necessity of a better management so as to give the LG the priority interest . . . totally to give advantage to Mr Jerdan . . . " Trying to hedge his bets by supplying more than one journal with an early publication, he succeeded in alienating them all. The problem did not disappear, although the preference turned towards the *Athenaeum*. In 1832 Jerdan wrote to Bentley an uncharacteristically furious letter pointedly marked "not private", in which he chided:

> As I perceive you coquette so entirely with the Athenaeum while you pretend to give me a priority, I beg to say that my only objection is to be mystified in this manner. You are as welcome as you can be to be exclusive where you think fit and all I ask is (1) not be told <u>Clouds</u>, and (2) not to be induced to make the LG in its contents the like of any other publication, so that a heedless reader of a puff might not tell the one from the other.
>
> If you chuse to whore your favours you will find that virtue would be better than prostitution.
>
> As it is, I do not know how to treat your <u>early</u> favours. One does not like to be laught at for boasting of a preference in such consarns.
>
> My rule is, if unpublished I will not blame where I cannot praise – the issue is with you, and I would rather not have common copies upon which I may not justly exercise my discretion.[80]

His fight was always for a degree of independence that Colburn, in particular, was not prepared to permit. The *Athenaeum* was not alone in fighting Colburn and his fellow publishers. According to Marchand, *Blackwood's* disliked Colburn not so much for his puffing, but for his vulgarity in "encouraging broken down roués to write memoirs of the society from which they had been cast".[81]

A change in literary tastes occurring at this time was marked by the debut in February 1830 of *Fraser's Magazine*. Poetry, personified by the Romantics including Landon, had lost much of its popularity, replaced by the 'silver-fork' novels, and the era of what has come to be known as classic Victorian fiction had not yet quite begun. The change was not clear-cut. One analyst noted that at the end of the 'romantic period', the oft-quoted shift from verse to novel was based on evidence from catalogues and advertisements, and does not take into account the fact that a book might have sold only a tiny number. Verse still came from the aristocracy or gentry, often privately printed and attributed by name. Poetry by others, moved down socially and materially, was published in smaller books and needed to be pushed onto the market, whereas purchase of novels became demand-led.[82] The advent of stereotype rather than the slow and tedious moveable hand setting meant that editions did not vary as they had previously, and that popular books never went out of print. Authors and would-be authors were constantly on the look-out for publications to take their work, and *Fraser's* came along to fulfil their need.

The new monthly publication promoted reality against romanticism, launching "a merciless assault on the lesser disciples of Scott and Byron, on the pretentious Edward Bulwer and the 'satanic' Robert Montgomery. They flayed alike the rhetorical bombast of Mrs Hemans and the lachrymose nostalgia of Tom Moore."[83] *Fraser's* politics were Tory, a sworn rival to Colburn's Whiggish *New Monthly Magazine*. The largest part of the new periodical was written by Maginn, recognizable by his biting satiric tone. He was the nominal editor of *Fraser's* between 1830 and 1836 assisted by Thackeray. Although it was immensely popular, selling about 8700 copies at a cover price of two shillings and sixpence in its first year, its proprietor James Fraser, did not make a profit that year. He paid well, although not so much as Colburn who reputedly paid twenty guineas per sheet (sixteen pages) for the *New Monthly Magazine*; the *Quarterly* paid about sixteen guineas, but Fraser paid according to the value of the contributor, offering Carlyle fifteen guineas a sheet, rising to twenty pounds, and Thackeray ten pounds, equal to twelve shillings and sixpence per page.[84] These payments were comparable with those Jerdan offered Griffin (a guinea a page) and Pyne for 'Wine and Walnuts' (three pounds for three pages) but possibly less than he paid for *Literary Gazette* reviews reflecting the decline in the *Gazette's* circulation, at this time calculated to be about seven thousand.[85] Maginn earned about six hundred pounds a year for his editing and contributions to *Fraser's*,[86] less than Jerdan was making for his comparable work on the *Literary Gazette*.

Fraser's flung itself into the 'puffing' controversy, hitting out at Colburn's practices, calling him the "Prince Paramount of Puffers and Quacks".[87] They included in their opprobrium all his editors, with the single exception of "honest Mr Jerdan". Jerdan was a member of the twenty-seven strong group of Fraserians, famously drawn by Daniel Maclise carousing around the table in Fraser's office at Regent Street. Members included *Fraser's* editor, William Maginn, Thackeray, Galt, Hogg, Coleridge and other luminaries. However, it has been pointed out that of the twenty-seven men pictured, eight, including Jerdan, wrote nothing or only once for *Fraser's*, but were included to enhance the prestige of the publication.[88]

Fraser's began their 'Gallery of Illustrious Literary Characters', eighty-one portraits and groups over nearly seven years; five, including that of L.E.L. were written by Prout,[89] the remainder by Maginn, originally published in the magazine between June 1830 and 1838. Despite its title, many of the subjects were not 'literary' at all, but included scientists such as Faraday and politicians like Lord Russell. Every portrait was sketched by Daniel Maclise, and they were "capital as likenesses". S.C. Hall knew Maclise as he created the portraits, and reported that "there was an affectation of secrecy about the procedure and certainly few or none of the 'sitters' sat for a portrait; they were all done from memory, possibly aided by a few stolen memoranda; but he had a wonderful faculty for 'catching a likeness'".[90] Hall's allegation was corroborated by Alaric Watts's son who noted that when his father appeared in *Fraser's* 'Gallery', "The artist was evidently not personally acquainted with the face of his sitter and the caricature was probably derived from a portrait of my father ... suitably idealized from a humorous and sarcastic point of view."[91] Maclise depicted Watts apparently stealing paintings, and Maginn's article on him was scurrilous, asserting that Watts had libelled everyone who had helped him in his career, including Jerdan. Watts sued for libel, amassing letters of support from all Maginn had named, and was awarded one hundred and fifty pounds damages.

However, the place of honour, their No. 1 Illustrious Literary Character, went to Jerdan (see illustration no. 1). Maclise's portrait shows him well-dressed, sitting upright, reading by the light of a large candle which throws his shadow on to the wall behind. This image of strong masculinity, "the manly man", has been contrasted with the "effeminate man" shown in the portrait of Thomas Campbell, then nominally editor of the *New Monthly Magazine*. Campbell could not stand up to the owner of his paper, whereas "sturdy" William Jerdan maintained his independence from Colburn.[92]

Reviewing their endeavour, the magazine commented that the project had been started "in mere jocularity, and trusting to his well-known good nature and long-tried good temper, selected Jerdan as our opening portrait. There was nothing in what we said that could annoy a man for whom we had so sincere a regard."[93] Maginn wrote the entry on Jerdan, commenting first on the "wonderful likeness" of the accompanying portrait, then explaining his selection in prime position of the series: " . . . because upon him depends judicially, in the first instance, the fates and fortunes of literary works. He is the grand jury, the publisher being only the committing magistrate." Despite such sycophancy, from the first words Maginn made fun of Jerdan, saying he was born in 1730, which would have made him a hundred years old. Passing quickly over his youthful follies to arrival in London, and employment in journalism, Maginn stated that "Afterwards, filled with a just indignation against the vices of society, his name occurs among those who determined to tear off their deceitful mask, and to expose, by name, to the public scorn, culprits whom they deemed unworthy of being concealed from the penalties of their turpitude." Vice being triumphant, Jerdan moved to the *Sun*, Maginn naturally mentioning his controversy with Taylor, the Perceval assassination, translation of *The Hermit in Paris*, and finally, becoming editor of the *Literary Gazette,* "and there he sits still enthroned, high arbiter of wit".

Maginn's "Johnsonian notice" done, he had little else to say, "except that he is the best of good fellows, convivial abroad, hospitable at home . . . he manages his *Literary Gazette* admirably well – that he gives the earliest literary news – chooses the fairest specimens from new books – does not encumber us with criticism and is wholly free from spite and rivalry". It sounded more like an obituary than a journalistic feature. Reference was made to a joke played on Jerdan a few years earlier, by "some foolish Cockneys" passing off a Shakespearean sonnet as a modern composition;[94] if he makes no worse critical lapse, "he may set his heart at ease, and drink his third bottle in quietness." Jerdan may not be a brilliant critic, Maginn went on, he is no Dr Johnson, but "with opportunity of being smart and caustic, of inflicting hurt and injury to shew his wit and his spleen, he has taken the other course – that of aiding the efforts of early genius, of encouraging the hopes of neglected talent." The niggardly payments for which the *Literary Gazette* was known, were not Jerdan's fault, but of "others'". His article concluded:

> If to his fault some critic errors fall,
> Look in his face, and you'll forget them all.

But we allow that the best time for looking at it is not that chosen by our Rembrandt – the favourable hour is ten o'clock at night, and his position at the head of a table, firmly seated behind an entrenchment of decanters.

On the remaining portion of *Fraser's* page there follows a poem *The Youngest* by L.E.L. – a juxtaposition possibly more than coincidental.

Jerdan needed the boost to his morale that *Fraser's* and Maginn provided. The *Athenaeum's* relentless attacks on the *Literary Gazette* for puffing Colburn's books were beginning to adversely affect sales. The rival journal's boast of complete independence from any publisher, and its much-advertised refusal to accept 'paid paragraphs' began to eke support from the *Literary Gazette* and increase sales of the *Athenaeum*.

Whilst Jerdan had been strenuously involved in the failed *Foreign Literary Gazette* and the struggling 'Juvenile Library', Landon had sat for her portrait to Daniel Maclise. He wrote to ask Jerdan's permission, along with Landon's, to send it to the Royal Academy Exhibition in the Spring of 1830, at the same time as his portrait of Thomas Campbell.[95] He also asked Jerdan where he might send it to be measured for a frame, an odd question from a successful painter who could be expected to have his own sources. It is curious that he should have asked Jerdan about these matters, unless it was Jerdan who had commissioned him to paint Landon's portrait.

Even in the throes of all his extra work, Jerdan did not fail to promote Landon. The *Literary Gazette* of 19 June 1830 was up to its old tricks, publishing a praising poem. *To the author of The Improvisatrice* by an American writer, J. Greenleaf Whittier. Disingenuously, Jerdan inserted a coy Note:

> We do not often admit personal tributes into our columns; but the poet-ical beauties of this composition, and its gratifying character, as confirming, from another hemisphere, the fame attached to the writings of LEL, our long-valued and especial favourite in this country, have induced us to give it insertion. The author is described to us, in a letter from Philadelphia, to be a 'young American poet-editor of great promise' in the U.S.; and these lines afford high proofs of talent.

Over the years Landon had contributed over three hundred poems to the *Literary Gazette*. Now her contributions to it declined as she changed her focus, but still continued to write reviews for the magazine. Public taste had moved away from poetry to prose, and Colburn and Bentley entered into their greatly popular and profitable era of "silver-fork" fiction. In this genre authors, usually promoted as belonging to the aristocracy, laid open their fashionable world to less-fortunate, middle-class readers. They, in turn, were enabled to feel superior, more worthy, than the shallow, trivial frivolities portrayed within the pages of their novels. The "silver-fork" novels played to this dichotomy, often satirising the foppish world to such an extent that they seemed to celebrate it in a heavily ironic way, as an ideal. Few were as overtly satirical as Landon, in her next venture.

Climbing onto the bandwagon, and pressed by the contract she had signed to "produce a mountain of prose", Landon wrote *Romance and Reality* which appeared the following year. Jerdan read the entire manuscript before Landon submitted it to the publishers. He had been negotiating with Bentley on Landon's behalf for most of the year. In February 1830 he had sent Bentley

Landon's signed agreement, together with a note from her appointing Jerdan as her "Treasurer and Agent on this occasion". A fee of three hundred pounds had been agreed, (compared with fifteen hundred pounds for Bulwer's *Devereux* around the same time), and Jerdan, trading on his relationship with Bentley, asked him for a favour. "I am afraid it is out of order, but if you cd make the date of the bill three months, it wd facilitate what I am asked to do, and at three months end I wd redraw it for three more – the same in the end – but if this is not right business, make it at six, and oblige me with it by the bearer, as I have a chance of a country banker dining with me tomorrow."[96] Somehow, Jerdan was forever living hand-to-mouth, the expenses of Grove House draining his resources. He was forced to apply to Bentley again, once *Romance and Reality* had been put at least partly into type; Edward and Rosina Bulwer had suggested some changes to Volume I, which Jerdan was anxious to make before the volume appeared.[97]

At the end of 1830 Jerdan approached Bulwer directly, asking openly for his friend's help.[98] "I suppose that troubling a friend on one's private affairs is something like the confession of a lady's love – after the first blush is over, there is no stint." He explained that in endeavouring to secure his future prospects he had "fairly inconvenienced my present ... I require quietness of mind, little of interruption, and as far as possible, abstraction from any but literary business". He wished to borrow one hundred pounds, and set out his financial situation to Bulwer:

> With regard to securities I am unfortunate in having copyright instead of Houses and Land; but when it is seen that my L.G. share is worth about £8000★ at 5 years purchase, that my personal estate is good, and that my death would realize from ten to twelve thousand pounds, I think my responsibility might be considered amply sufficient.
> ★I shd mention that in purchasing and furnishing etc at Grove House I got about £4000 into debt – above £2000 of which I have paid off at £500 a year to Twining & Co. being still about £1000 in their debt and £1000 due to Longman & Co.

Bulwer annotated this letter "Jerdan, ci–devant Editor of LG. He was always kind to me – more so in this paper than any other critic." However, there is no evidence as to whether Bulwer agreed to help Jerdan out of his present financial difficulties.

Jerdan's own troubles never diverted him from the wider issue of helping his fellow literary men. After the death of George IV on 26 June 1830, the generous annual sum granted to the Royal Society of Literature by the King ceased, as William IV declined to continue the endowment. It had been used to pension ten Royal Associates with an honorarium, on which some had come to rely. Jerdan renewed his slight acquaintance with Lord Melbourne (initiated at that infamous party when Jerdan was found with his head in Lady Caroline Lamb's lap), and told him of the hardship caused. Melbourne rose to the occasion and provided funds from national sources to offset the deficit.

Whilst the Royal Society of Literature gave grants to already distinguished writers, the Literary Fund had continued to dispense small amounts to destitute, and often unknown writers, giving out £6160 to four hundred and eight cases. In the present year, fifty-six cases were receiving grants.[99] One such was Nathaniel Carrington, a teacher in Plymouth by day and a poet by night, whose works were admired by Jerdan and published by Murray. Carrington's first applications to the Fund had been made in 1823. A proud man suffering from consumption, he had been reluctant to name a referee, deeming it a humiliation, but he was sponsored by Lord John Russell and received small grants. He eventually had to leave London to live with his son in Dorset. The son, who edited a small local paper, wrote to Jerdan that he had to provide for his family of eight on an income of one hundred and fifty pounds per annum, so his father's grants were vitally necessary. Jerdan had persuaded some annuals to include Carrington's poems, but for these he was "never thanked and from none of which did he reap reward". In May 1830 Jerdan heard from him that "I am unable to creep into the sunshine without assistance. I am reduced to a skeleton. I have had no school for the last quarter and subsist entirely from my son's scanty income."[100] In the summer of 1830 Jerdan met with what a correspondent termed a "a very serious accident" although no details were forthcoming. He was laid up, rendering him more than ten days late in sending Carrington's money. The Literary Fund received urgent letters from Carrington's son, asking for the funds, and on being pressed, Jerdan wrote to Snow, of the Fund on 22 August, "I am very far from well, and can hardly get through the indispensable things before me. I will of course attend instantly to poor Carrington, my worthy friend whose relief and comfort has always been an object near my breast."[101] Carrington died on 2 September, hopefully not as a direct result of Jerdan's tardiness.

Jerdan's contribution to *The Iris* of 1830 reflected the struggle he saw all around him. *The Iris* was a literary and religious publication, and *The Footsteps' Fall* the sole time Jerdan wrote for it. He prefaced the seven four-line stanzas by noting how individuals could be recognized by their footsteps, and how their joy or sadness affects the tread. He knew this was a familiar subject, and apologized that "the novelty of the application (if it has even that slightest merit), is all it has to recommend it". His stanzas followed life through from infancy to the grave, noting how footsteps fall swiftly – merrily – heavy – slowly, as life passes through its stages. This was, he must have considered, a suitably serious subject for a religious publication.

In completely different mood was his contribution to the *Juvenile Keepsake* of 1830. *The End of the Holidays*, four verses celebrating the child's return to school after the tedium of having nothing to do but play:

> Therefore, goodbye Papa, Mamma!
> Goodbye to life in clover,
> Goodbye to everlasting play
> There must be toil to make it gay –
> To school again!
> We're wondrous glad the holidays are over!

With children at home, Jerdan himself was probably glad the holidays were over. He had matters of state on his mind, but also matters concerning schooling.

It was about this time that he took an active interest in the education of the two youngest sons of his marriage, William Freeling, now aged 13 and George, aged 11. The Western Grammar School had been founded in Alexander Square nearby, one of several new independent proprietary schools financed by the sale of shares. The shareholders were the proprietors of the school and were usually parents of those attending; they controlled the curriculum. Shares cost fifteen pounds each and proprietors were each permitted to hold up to three of the one hundred shares originally available, and had the right to nominate one pupil to the school in respect of each share. They also had to pay nine guineas annually towards running expenses. Jerdan became a shareholder, and a member of the elected committee of proprietors and honorary officers who managed the school. Initially, the school was free of any religious bias, but in 1836 was taken into union with King's College, when it had to adopt the doctrines of the Church of England. It is not certain how long Jerdan served on this committee, but his membership highlights his active interest in his sons' education, perhaps more so as he was unlikely to have much influence on that of Fred Stuart, his son with Landon.

This period was one of close friendship between Jerdan and Edward Bulwer, whose widely varied novels enjoyed popular success and were much praised by the *Literary Gazette*. On a visit to the Bulwers at Woodcot Jerdan suggested an idea for a novel, which Bulwer liked; this was to be a satire upon what he called the "worthless ephemerae" of the "common practice of inferior publishers to catch and gull the public by pseudo-personal characters, sadly misdrawn and vilely represented". Jerdan's idea was to turn this on its head, by providing the 'Key' founded not upon real people, but upon dramatic personae from the 'Beggar's Opera'.[102] Adopting this notion, Bulwer started enthusiastically on *Paul Clifford*; after some time however he could not continue with the book on that basis, and changed it into a novel on prison reform, the thesis of which was in its last line: "The very worst use to which you can put a man is to hang him". He sent Jerdan proofs of the first volume, generously telling him, "You see that I have very imperfectly caught your idea; but wherever it is in the smallest degree caught, I think you will find the most amusing parts of the book. I wish you had struck off yourself your own conception . . . "[103]

The political temperature of the country was heating up, and the government of Wellington, who had become Prime Minister on Canning's death, fell as a result of widespread agitation for constitutional and parliamentary reform. The Whig administration of Earl Grey came into power, and the House of Commons attempted to deal with the unfair anomalies of rotten boroughs and under-representation, by passing a Reform Bill. The House of Lords was reluctant to pass the Bill, but Grey prevailed by advising the King to overwhelm the House by creating pro-Reform peers. In July 1830 Bulwer was campaigning as an ultra-Reform candidate in St Ives, Cornwall. Hearing of Jerdan's accident he wrote to sympathise, and tried to joke that "it wd not however prevent my witnessing the usual flirtation which takes place between you and Mrs Bulwer when ever – which is to say truth not very often – you meet".[104] Bulwer's anonymous novel *Pelham*, published in 1828, was still enjoying popular success, but he needed Jerdan's help in his political campaign. He wrote from Truro, asking for letters of introduction, telling Jerdan he was having "all manner of 'fun' seemly for a grave man – I only envy your spirits and youth of mind – to double my present single enjoyments."[105] His postcript announced: "They have found out the Author!!! All I hope is they will forget the election scene in *Pelham* or at least interpret it rightly." Bulwer won his seat, but it was to be a short-lived victory, as the reforms for which he fought were embodied in the Reform Act the following year, and his seat of St Ives, Huntingdonshire, vanished in the ensuing reorganization. However, Bulwer later gained a seat for Lincoln, and campaigned hard for a reduction in tax on newspapers.

12

The *Literary Gazette* Teeters

The year 1831 opened with Jerdan's announcement that it had been fifteen years since he began editing the *Literary Gazette*; he proudly told his readers:

> The *Gazette* enjoys, by many thousands, the greatest circulation of any purely literary journal ever published in England; and it has risen to this eminence under the <u>absolute</u> control and direction of its editor, who is also the proprietor of the <u>largest</u> proportion of the entire emoluments derived from this widely extended sale.

There was no mistaking his claim that the *Literary Gazette* was making him wealthy, a claim later to come back to haunt him when he wanted to warn young people that the literary life would not bring them financial security. He was proud of doing extraordinarily well, but it was the pride which came before his fall.

He was always interested in national matters, in every aspect of life, although refraining from political comment in his journal, in obedience to Canning's dictum. Even so Jerdan clung to his Tory heritage, whilst his friend Bulwer was campaigning for Reform. Four years after Canning's death, Jerdan was still in favour with the government, sufficiently so for Viscount Goderich (whose five-month premiership had ended ignominiously) to select him as Tory candidate for Weymouth in the general election of May 1831. The idea appealed enormously to Jerdan. He was fifty years old, with what he called "a large and not overpoweringly encumbered income . . . neither deficient in mental nor bodily vigour".[1] He threw himself enthusiastically into the campaign, as he always did whatever his current project might be.

At that time a would-be Member of Parliament needed a certain amount of property, of which Jerdan had some, "subject to family arrangements", but not enough. This may mean that Grove House was mortgaged, or that property in Scotland was shared with his siblings. He fortunately had a good friend and neighbour, a Dr. Anderson of Brompton, who assigned to Jerdan several houses in Alexander Square and some land and tenements on the river near Richmond. This meant that Jerdan was the owner of sufficient property to enable him to become a candidate. He kept a chaise and horses in readiness at livery stables by Fulham Bridge, and ensured that his household always knew where to find him, in case of a summons from the Treasury in the person of Edward Ellice who lived in Pall Mall, where Jerdan visited him every day. Throughout May he was in contact with people of influence in Weymouth, resulting in such encouragement that he decided to visit the town and start canvassing.

Before leaving Jerdan sent a note to his old friend Barnes, editor of *The Times*, telling of his intentions and asking for such assistance as he could conscientiously give. He misjudged his man. His confidence was abused. Jerdan thought it might have been due to the paper's heated support of the Reform question, but whatever was Barnes's reason, the next day's *Times* carried a vituperative leader denouncing the pretensions of literary men standing for Parliament, and threatening ministers with popular odium if they upheld such a state of affairs. Jerdan ruefully acknowledged that he was hoist with his own petard. Calling as usual on Ellice it was agreed that he would not proceed with his candidacy; the chaise and horses were stood down, and Jerdan's dream of a parliamentary career came to a sudden end. He somehow maintained a civil relationship with the editor of *The Times*, and was touched to receive a long and sympathetic letter from John Murray.

The postscript to this episode is pure Jerdan: no-one remembered to re-assign the properties that had been given to him, and it was not until ten years later that he came across the legal papers showing that he was still their proprietor. This could have been the cause of much wrangling in the interim, but fortunately the rightful owner was still alive, aged ninety-two, and the documents were safely restored to him.

Fraser's had no respect for anyone, so even had Jerdan succeeded in becoming an MP, the magazine would still have made fun of him. In *A Long Song of Ecstasy* in May 1831, *Fraser's* sang its own praises, and mocked its rivals, giving a line or two to all the current literary luminaries. Letitia Landon's "thrilling lute" gave way to:

> With <u>Portraits</u> of our learned men
> It makes the world acquainted;
> To see their Phizzes pencilled there
> Is next to being sainted!
> <u>Jerdan</u> was drawn as Jerdan is
> When evening dews are falling!

(implying his usual condition, with a drink in front of him)

Jerdan's full schedule appeared to have distracted his attention from Landon;

she wrote to him about Bentley's insistence that she find mottoes as chapter headings for her novel, and also that she was asking Maginn to put in a good word for her brother when he saw the Bishop of Exeter; she mentioned that Lady Stepney had called Jerdan "that charmant person" and ended with "I want so to hear from you."[2] Her tone suggested that he had been neglecting her, but she, of all people, must have understood the vast quantity of reading and writing that Jerdan had to get through each and every day.

As an 'Inhabitant Householder' of Grove House, Jerdan was entitled to become a vestryman at the newly built Church of Holy Trinity, Brompton, consecrated in 1829. His family had been members of the Presbyterian Church of Scotland, so Jerdan would have had to make some adjustments to the more decorative aspects of the new church when he became a member of the Church of England. His education at the parochial school in Kelso had taught him to accept all types of religious practice, so that "converting" to the English Church would not have caused him difficulty; many friends and colleagues would have made a similar move, to ease social relations when they moved away from home. The new Holy Trinity could seat 1505 people (606 free, 899 rented seats).[3] Jerdan did not take his vestry duties too seriously, calling them "rather droll affairs", with some of his colleagues "though parochially well-to-do, not over-stocked with the fruits of education".[4] He relished the time when he pointed out that a comma in the wrong place had changed the sense of a local act; another vestryman, a builder, was infuriated by this display of erudition, exclaiming, "Pray, Sir, don't talk to me of a comma: I don't care for fifty commas!". Ever after, Jerdan moved amendments consisting of fifty commas. After the "amusing enough" vestry meetings, Jerdan adjourned with two or three old friends "to a welcome parlour, a sober rubber, or a game at Boston, a slight refection, a glass of toddy, a merry family chat and to bed". Although he dismissed this activity so lightly, in fact Jerdan took his duties seriously, at least at the outset. The first Select Vestry Meeting was held on 8 February 1830 and Jerdan joined the following month. He was present at seven of the eleven meetings that year, and at five of the eight held in 1831. In 1832 he attended only four out of ten meetings, and one of the two held in 1833. By March 1834 he had moved away and his seat was declared vacant.[5] The Vestry Minutes disclose quite tedious matters of appointing officers of the church such as pew openers, selecting an organist, and dealing with clogged drains and clock cleaning; it was therefore clearly the social aspect which drew Jerdan to spend some of his free time there.

Some of the authors whom Jerdan reviewed in the *Literary Gazette* became family friends. It is through one such that we have a rare glimpse of Jerdan *en famille*. The traveller and writer John Carne and his wife Ellen were good friends of the Jerdans. In 1826 Carne's *Letters from the East* which had been published in the *New Monthly Magazine* were gathered into a volume dedicated to Sir

Walter Scott and published by Colburn. He and his wife went to live in Penzance, and a joint letter from each of them to Jerdan in the summer of 1831 was warm and affectionate. Ellen recalled the many happy hours spent with the Jerdan family and hoped that the "charming daughters" had recovered from their sickness. The girls were encouraged to visit the Carnes in Cornwall, where Ellen was starved for intelligent company. She anxiously awaited the weekly delivery of the *Literary Gazette* which was "like conversing with an old friend".[6] Two comments in this letter relate directly to Jerdan's activities: Ellen was "very glad you have at last resented the attack made at you by those who would be Critics", and she asked him to use his influence with Carne's publishers Saunders and Otley, to make a settlement to her husband, as she suspected they had sold more than they admitted. Carne's part of the letter responded to an account Jerdan had given of a dinner at Grove House, which "revived many a pleasant remembrance", especially Jerdan's "splendid Hock Grave and Champagne". He too asked Jerdan to intercede for him, this time with Lockhart, who was tardy in returning proof sheets. Carne reiterated his wife's invitation that the Jerdans should visit them, it would be like "Manna in the desert", or "a well of water to a thirsty man", and tempted Jerdan with "sea trips, mines, minerals and picnics". Jerdan did eventually make the trip and enjoyed his visits to mines and museums, especially the well known scientific mineral and natural collections at Falmouth and Penzance. He stored up the wealth of information gleaned on this visit, and used it to some effect in a story he wrote a little later in *Bentley's Miscellany*.

Within a few months of his announcement that he was profiting handsomely from the *Literary Gazette,* Jerdan's sense of financial security had vanished. He asked his *Gazette* partner Longmans for an advance, and received a withering response from Owen Rees:

> my partners feel that so little attention has been given to the interest of our house in the *Literary Gazette* (but indeed quite the reverse) that they do not consider you have any claim to their favourable consideration; besides Twinings [bank] have given us notice not to pay you any money till you have repaid them the money they have paid on your policy of Insurance; and we have told them that we shall expect our claim to be first liquidated.[7]

The following day brought worse news for Jerdan as the publishers told him that "finding the sale of the *Literary Gazette* declining and being already £1200 in advance to you, they do not feel themselves warranted on making the advance you now desire".[8]

His funds had diminished so quickly, beyond his normal expenditure, it seems probable that he had to meet a number of demands. He may have had to make some considerable provision for his and Landon's children, maybe putting some funds into trust for them, or giving capital amounts to those who were taking care of them. This is only supposition; he could as easily have been overspending his income on good living at Grove House and elsewhere, on entertaining Landon and maybe other women too, but whatever was causing him financial hardship was draining his resources enough to force him to go cap in hand to his partners, who turned him down.

In 1831 Jerdan contributed 'The Sleepless Woman', a short story in three chapters, to Volume 2 of *The Club Book*, which was a collection of tales by various authors edited by another Scot, Andrew Picken, who included one of his own stories. The Introduction to this publication remarked that "since the clubs have come *in*, marriage has entirely *gone out*" as the Clubs offered young men more luxurious surroundings and services than they could afford at home. "How can it be expected," asked the editor with his tongue almost in his cheek, "that a gentleman should marry for the old-fashioned motives of comfort and society when the clubs and their appendages supply all this at a tenth of the cost?" Mrs S. C. Hall disagreed, having "a truly feminine antipathy to clubs". Her home was her club; clubmen would eventually go one way, their wives another. "I don't like them – I never shall like them: the club is the axe at the root of domestic happiness."[9] Some twenty years later Jerdan evidently remained satisfied with his *Club Book* story, as it appeared in Volume 1 of his *Autobiography*, as one continuous narrative.

The tale opened atmospherically, in a dark and gloomy castle at the death bed of the Baron. Adolphe, his handsome and dashing nephew and heir arrived in time to hear his uncle's dying words. The Baron had seen into the future and warned Adolphe that "evil came into the world with woman, and in her is bound up the evil of your destiny". After the Baron's death, the gloominess of the castle weighed on the young man, who turned his thoughts ever more frequently towards Paris and bright lights. However, in true fairy-tale tradition, he passed a rich coach in which he espied a beautiful young girl with bewitching eyes, "radiant orbs", "bright and piercing". Of course, she is rich and high-born, and Jerdan's story quickly passed over the courtship, to their marriage, despite dire warnings from the old Baron's servants.

Here the fairy-tale turned to gothic horror, as the bridegroom was woken night after night by his bride gazing at him with those radiant orbs . Horrified, he realized that she never slept – an idea she found abhorrent. "Sleep! One of my noble race, sleep? I never slept in my life." He took her to live in Paris where, with her beautiful eyes, she is the toast of the town, whilst the erstwhile handsome bridegroom became sallow and emaciated. Slipping away from a party at their country chateau, he found himself in an avenue of dark cedar trees leading to a still lake. Consumed with exhaustion he was deluded into believing that a stray sunbeam was his wife still gazing at him. Unable to bear her sleeplessness any longer, he plunged into the lake and drowned. Instead of stopping at the climax of his story, Jerdan misguidedly added a final paragraph in which he stepped away from the narrative, to observe that whilst some believe the story to be accurate, others think it is an "ingenious allegory – and that the real secret of the Sleepless Lady was jealousy". He concluded by remarking "Now, if a jealous wife can't drive a man out of his mind and into a lake, we do not know what can!"

This story is more fanciful than some of Jerdan's later efforts, and appears influenced by the ubiquity of gothic novels saturated with the sublime and supernatural so parodied by Austen and Peacock only ten years previously. He could also have been feeling overwhelmed by the demands of his family and rather sour about women in general, (and Frances certainly had reason to be jealous), but it could be none of these factors, and he merely produced what he considered suitable for *The Club Book* readership, a traditional adventure tale, but without a happy ending.

Clubs were an important element of a gentleman's life, and a new one had been formed in August 1831. The first gathering of the Garrick Club, named after the eighteenth-century century actor David Garrick, met in the committee room of the Drury Lane Theatre, and in the following three weeks, one hundred men had joined. Jerdan was one of the original members, invited by Lord Mulgrave, the Club's President. The Garrick's avowed purpose was for the "promotion of drama and general interest of the stage". Jerdan was elected to the Committee on 22 October and a few days later Probatt's Hotel in King Street had been acquired for the Club's premises. Two temporary committees were then established, one for 'furnishing' and one for 'providing', both to report to the General Committee. Jerdan, even though arriving an hour late for the meeting on 2 November, was appointed Chair of the Providing Committee, which was responsible for recruiting servants and setting prices etc. They set up a wine committee, to which Jerdan was appointed. Records of the Garrick reveal that Jerdan was a very active member at this time.[10] "He is recorded as undertaking tasks such as selecting glasses for the Committee's approval, and was always present for discussions about livery, number of servants, type of silver, selecting a cook etc., all those tasks required to get the Club house opened, which it did on February 1, 1832." Jerdan stepped down according to committee rules, in 1834, but remained a member until he resigned in 1862, unable to pay his dues.

Getting things ready for the new Club was a busy and happy time for him, most especially his duties in the selection of wines. He recorded that Grove House was the most convenient place to sample and judge wines for the Garrick, and his colleagues dined with him frequently for the purpose of wine-tasting.[11] "The specialities of the occasion induced much merriment and relished the more on account of its difference from the formalities of set entertainment", he wrote, describing how the floor on one side of the dining room was arranged with phials and bottles. Whatever was left remained in Grove House, and was doubtless afterwards consumed by Jerdan. He was "astonished" to receive bills from the wine merchants for these samples, listing from a surviving bill the port, claret, whisky, brandy, champagne and so on which the Wine Committee had sampled, "the sum total of which caused my eyes to water (after my mouth had)," he recalled, "and a certain exchange of gold to pass from my pocket into that of the acute dealer".

He thought he had been inspired by such revelry to triumph in designing the symbol of the Garrick Club, which is used to this day. The Club's Minutes of 30 November noted that "Mr Jerdan proposed that the seal, or emblem of the Club, be a globe encircled with a ribband with the words 'All the World's A Stage' . . . ." The words 'Garrick Club' and '1831' appear on the encircling ribbon. Jerdan was so delighted that his design had been accepted, that with the approval of the President and Committee, he printed it on sixteen issues of the *Literary Gazette* during the first six months of the Club's existence. Reciprocally, a box was placed in the Club's library where members could deposit contributions of dramatic and theatrical matters for the *Literary Gazette*.

Then, as now, membership of the Garrick was closely guarded, and Jerdan found himself in the awkward position of answering a complaint from his old friend Edward Bulwer, who pressed for the selection of a Mr Ryde. Jerdan advised Bulwer that as Ryde had never paid his membership subscription, he had not actually joined the Garrick. Jerdan said that he had nothing against Ryde, "except the expression of a hint that he was a writer in some of those periodicals which most Gentlemen seem to consider injurious to the enjoyments of private and social life. In fact, unless a man is extremely guarded in this respect every one connected with the press must feel that his society is neither wished nor courted by the better orders."[12] Jerdan obviously put himself on a far superior level to that of such a questionable journalist. There could have been another reason why Ryde was unacceptable. A contemporary observer noted that "the electing committee is compelled to exercise very vigilant care, for it is clear that it would be better that ten unobjectionable men should be excluded than that one terrible bore should be admitted".[13]

Not a club, but the foundation of a great scientific society, the British Association, also occurred in 1831. Jerdan assiduously attended every Annual Meeting (except the one held in Belfast) and kept *Literary Gazette* readers informed of the activities of the Association, even at the expense of circulation dropping at the sight of these long and detailed reports, "its leaves like those of the trees falling in Autumn".[14]

London literary society was epitomized by Jerdan and his *Literary Gazette*, a fact celebrated even by the *Edinburgh Literary Journal* which published *A London Soirée, Being a letter from Emily in town to her aunt in the country*.[15] The first verse of this rather long poem was:

> I'll give you a sketch, my dear aunt,
> Of a party I've been to in London,
> Where poets and wits were not scant,
> Whom Jerdan delightfully punn'd on –
> He edits, as you know, the Gazette,
> Which, though rivalled by Dilke's Athenaeum,
> Is read, they say, everywhere yet,
> In Paris, Calcutta and Siam.

The literary public were clearly familiar with the foremost magazines and, more surprisingly compared to our own times, their editors. This verse was at least not denigrating Jerdan for alleged puffing and merely mentioned his name as one which would doubtless be familiar to all readers of the *Journal*.

Away from Clubs and scientific activities, literature was still Jerdan's first concern. With him acting as her agent, Landon's first foray into three-volume fiction appeared at the end of 1831. *Romance and Reality* was published by Colburn and Bentley, paying her "£300, in Bills when the work was ready or within 2–3 weeks of it being ready for press".[16] The first print run was to be 1250 copies, and if a second edition was required, they would print a further 750 copies.[17] Their reason for limiting the editions was that most middle-class readers would not afford to purchase the three volumes outright, and that Colburn's unsurpassable talents for puffing in the periodicals would ensure that the book would be in great demand through libraries, his targeted market for sales. Knowing that Landon had already requested her copies for reviewers and friends, Jerdan asked Bentley for " a copy neatly bound by Wednesday to be on my Table, having a largish party".[18] Jerdan was concerned that the "political ferment is not in its favour",[19] a reference to the unrest which resulted in the 1832 Reform Act.

The *Literary Gazette* reviewed the book on its front pages on 26 November 1831, asking rhetorically whether admirers of L.E.L.'s poetry would find the same qualities in her prose. Whilst it was "totally different from the writer's poetry", said the reviewer, "it displays altogether various faculties and powers hitherto undeveloped by her publications." "We think *Romance and Reality* a perfectly original specimen of fictitious narrative; there is no performance of the class, within our knowledge, which it resembles." The reviewer analyzed, with examples, several "classes" of novels, including the Romantic, Historical, Fashionable, Satirical and many others, explaining that in *Romance and Reality* "we have glimpses of most of the ingredients we have enumerated . . . ". No mention was made of Landon's evident weariness with her own story, dismissing it in her final chapter with "Luckily in the closing chapter a little explanation goes a long way, and a character, like a rule of morality, may be dismissed in a sentence." The reviewer, certainly Jerdan, is clearly at a loss to know what to make of the work. Landon was gently rebuked for a "few unimportant errors", for introducing characters who could be easily recognized in real life. "This is not done ill-naturedly, but the thing itself is below the standard of the writer's genius." As always, the "review" then became a page or two of extracts from the novel. Mary Howitt, who met "Daddy Jerdan" and Landon at The Rosery in Brompton, home of Samuel Carter and Mrs Hall, reported that "Miss Landon chattered hard all the time, was using her round eyes that evening; in her forthcoming book *Romance and Reality* some of her friends were given ridiculous 'puffs' and she introduced the present company."[20] Landon did portray Mary Howitt, as well as an instantly recognizable and complimentary portrait of Edward and Rosina Bulwer. It was hardly surprising then that Bulwer gave Landon's book a glowing review in the *New Monthly Magazine* of which he was then editor,[21] a review which he introduced with the anecdote, since much quoted, of the Cambridge undergraduates scrambling for a glimpse of the latest L.E.L. poem in the *Literary Gazette*. His praise was in part a reciprocation for Landon's article on his own work, which had been published in May of the same year in the *New Monthly Magazine*, an article so fulsome that *Fraser's* affected to believe it had been written by Bulwer himself.[22]

The *Athenaeum* was quick to complain that the *Literary Gazette* had given the book twelve columns of puffing before it was made available to other reviewers. This attack was clearly against the periodical and Colburn, not against Jerdan personally; the following week the *Athenaeum* gave a lead position to a praising review which nevertheless concluded that Landon had not yet fully used her powers.[23] Other reviews complained that *Romance and Reality* was not a novel. Landon used the first two volumes as a vehicle for discussing society's foibles, the state of literature, and politics, with authorial asides on any other subjects that took her fancy. The plot line was subservient to all these 'messages', and it was not until the third volume that much action occurred at all. The book was not a success. Portraits of some writers were highly unflattering. Those who believed they had suffered from Landon's reviews in the *Literary Gazette* took the opportunity to return the compliment in their critical reviews and comments. However, Landon's explicit portrait of her radical friend Edward Bulwer was a dangerous indulgence, drawing down insinuations about her relationship with him. Mischievously, in his text for *Fraser's* 'Gallery of Illustrious Literary Characters' Maginn would not describe Bulwer, saying only "L.E.L. in her *Romance and Reality* has so completely depicted Bulwer (we shall not say *con amore* lest that purely technical phrase should be construed literally) . . . that it would be useless . . . ".[24]

Although Landon penned this distinct portrait of Bulwer, any portrait of Jerdan is altogether absent. There are small clues which definitely refer to him, here and there, and some passages where Landon may have had him in mind. In Volume 1, a character says that "the excitement of a literary career is so great, that most sentiments seem tame by its side. Homage you have from the many – praise is familiar to your ear, and your lover's compliment seems cold when weighed against that of your reviewer. Besides, a lover is chiefly valued for the consequence he gives; he loses one great charm when you have it without him." The speaker here was described as "good-looking and singularly tall". Whilst this may depict Jerdan, it could as well be another Scottish friend of Landon's, Allan Cunningham, or merely a figment of her imagination. However, Landon was not now so much in need of Jerdan's "consequence" as she had been at the outset of her career, and this comment may be a small indication that for her, he was losing "one great charm".

In another chapter she quoted a couplet from Scott's *Lay of the Last Minstrel*, with a footnote coyly stating "I find this remark previously made in the *National Portrait Gallery*; and I am glad to observe the opinion confirmed by such authority as the author of those biographical sketches." She could simply have named Jerdan, but chose not to do so. Elsewhere she began a chapter with a quotation attributed to the 'Juvenile Library,' a little unkindly perhaps, considering what a failure this was for Jerdan. In another chapter she attributes an "elaborate essay" on the relative intelligence of geese and turkeys to the *Foreign Literary Gazette*. This was either playful or unkind, as no such article appeared in any of the few issues of this, another of Jerdan's ill-fated ventures. Several of the literary works mentioned in the novel had been reviewed in the *Literary Gazette* between 1824 and 1831, written either by Landon herself, or by Jerdan.

Landon remarked that the pleasures of childhood are more satisfying than those of later days, as they "suffice unto themselves. The race is run without an eye to a prize . . . Hope destroys pleasure" as life darkens around us. Landon inserted a footnote to her phrase "Hope destroys pleasure", most likely referring to Jerdan as she had previously used terminology about deferring to his judgment:

This remark having been questioned by one to whose judgment I exceedingly defer, may I be permitted not to retract, but to defend my assertion? Hope is like constancy, the country, or solitude – all of which owe their reputation to the pretty things that have been said about them. Hope is but the poetical name for that feverish restlessness which hurries over today for the sake of to-morrow. Who among us pauses upon the actual moment, to own "Now, even now, am I happy?" The wisest of men has said, that hope deferred is sickness to the heart: yet what hope have we that is not deferred? For my part, I believe that there are two spirits who preside over this feeling, and that hope, like love, has its Eros and Anteros. Its Eros, that reposes on fancy, and creates rather than calculates; while its Anteros lives on expectation, and is dissatisfied with all that is, in vague longing for what may be.

This refutation of Jerdan's objection to her phrase reads as a message directly to him. Landon had spent quite a few years in "feverish restlessness", and possibly in expectation, and she may easily have been at the stage of being "dissatisfied with all that is". Jerdan, in contrast, found pleasure almost everywhere, and apart from his financial worries, appeared to live life very much in the present, with little attention to "Hope".

In Chapter IX of Volume 3 of *Romance and Reality* Landon appeared remorseful, sorry for the situation in which she found herself, with no protective husband and, somewhere out of sight, three small children:

> Alas, for human sagacity! And that which is to depend on it – human conduct! Look back on all the past occurrences of our lives; – who are there that, on reflection, would not act diametrically opposite to what they formerly acted on impulse? No one would do the same thing twice over. Experience teaches, it is true; but she never teaches in time. Each event brings its lesson, and the lesson is remembered; but the same event never occurs again.

Except, of course, that for Landon it *had* occurred again, and then again. Landon's pervasive air of melancholy in the poems, and in this first novel, did not find favour with readers. Her perpetual fascination with sorrows, deaths and suicides was not in accord with popular taste.

In addition to taking care of Landon's literary endeavours, Jerdan helped her in family matters. Her younger brother Whittington had completed his studies at Worcester College Oxford; after a year's curacy he was seeking employment. Jerdan inserted an advertisement into the *Literary Gazette* on 23 April 1831, to the effect that "A young clergyman M.A. of Oxford, residing in London, would be glad to engage as Classical Tutor in preparing One or Two Pupils for the University or to read with them during the vacations." He received at least one reply, asking for a reference, to whom he divulged the name of the would-be Tutor.[25] Jerdan was again to offer a helping hand to Whittington when he sought employment at the Literary Fund Society.

One small activity which briefly engaged him in the summer of 1831 was to join forces with fourteen other literary men in a touching tribute to Goethe. They included Carlyle, Maginn, Wilson, Scott, Lockhart, Southey, Wordsworth and Barry Cornwall.[26] A gold seal was made to celebrate Goethe's birthday on 28 August, to a design by Jane Carlyle, representing the serpent of eternity encircling a star, with the words 'Ohne Hast aber Ohne Rast'[27] in allusion to Goethe's verses. They sent their gift "To the German Master: From Friends in England" with an accompanying letter of tribute to which Goethe warmly responded. In his *Autobiography* Jerdan made no mention of this kindly gesture, as it had probably slipped his mind twenty years later.

The event which, more than any other, was to mark a significant moment in the affairs of the *Literary Gazette*, occurred in the autumn of 1831. The *Athenaeum* had now reached a circulation of about 3000; hoping to double it, Dilke halved the price of his paper from eightpence (also the price of the *Literary Gazette*), to fourpence. Jerdan refused to accept their advertisement announcing the price reduction, a refusal which gave the *Athenaeum* a golden opportunity to goad the *Literary Gazette* yet again:

> While friends, known and unknown, take such interest in the success of an independent literary paper, what avails the miserable policy of the Publishing Proprietors of the *Literary Gazette* in refusing to insert our Advertisements? The truth will be known, though it be shut out even from the advertising columns of that paper . . . the old orthodox belief in all that is in print is shaken – the day for booksellers' Reviews, and for booksellers reviewing their own books, is gone; the public generally now know well enough, that the everlasting songs of praise in the *Literary Gazette* are but mystic hymns to their breeches pockets, and therefore button them the tighter; and the readers of the *Gazette* will learn this truth; though it be but the echo of public opinion that shall disturb their slumbers.[28]

Sales of the *Athenaeum* rose six-fold on the second day of this experiment, making this the turning-point in its ascendancy and in the decline of the *Literary Gazette*.[29] Jerdan himself recalled the moment his rival struck the fatal blow:

> The *Athenaeum* held on in fruitless efforts and with some curious accidents, till the lucky idea of cheap literature suggested the expedient of lowering the price of the publication one half, and the plan, seconded by clever and not over-literary business and publishing devices, worked its way to popular success. It gradually took the wind out of the sails of the *Gazette* and possessed quite ability enough to account for the change especially in a commercial country, where, whatever else may be misunderstood, the difference between fourpence and eightpence cannot be mistaken.[30]

This was written with hindsight, but it is extraordinary that at the time Jerdan and his partners did not follow the *Athenaeum*'s lead and reduce the price of the *Literary Gazette*. Jerdan might have tried to persuade his partners to match the halved price of the *Athenaeum* although there is no evidence that he did so. Longmans would have done the arithmetic and found, as did Dilke, that selling a journal for fourpence instead of eightpence necessitated doubling its sales; the *Athenaeum* had stolen a march on them, the advantage in such a competition being always on the side of the initiator. Moreover, the *Athenaeum* operated at a loss for some years after its price reduction, despite a rise in circulation. Dilke could bear the loss as he had a private income, but the commercially-minded partners of the *Literary Gazette* could not contemplate such a sudden drop in profit, nor would Jerdan have welcomed so obviously playing second fiddle to the *Athenaeum's* lead. The *Literary Gazette* had led the field for so many years, and he had so relished its superior position, that he would resist change for a commercial reason. Furthermore, the policies of the *Literary Gazette* remained the same as ever, and would have needed reinvigorating to attract new readers to choose the *Gazette* over the *Athenaeum*; also, the *Athenaeum's* relentless attacks on puffery had lowered respect for the *Gazette*. All of these factors combined to push the *Literary Gazette* further and further down the path of lower circulation, so that although it still had many years ahead, it never again recovered the peak it reached before the *Athenaeum* halved its price and vastly increased its readership. It was to be fifteen years before the price of the *Literary Gazette* was lowered.

Jerdan found some small solace in the *Athenaeum* occasionally seeking guidance from the *Literary Gazette*, and offering to reciprocate, something Jerdan thought "what ought to exist where literary men and gentlemen are concerned. When the press falls into the hands of persons who are neither, the degradation is pitiable."[31] Here is the core of Jerdan's problem: he still clung to the idea of publishing being a gentleman's occupation, and was unable to see that it had become a commercial business. His inability to change with the times was to have a serious effect upon the *Literary Gazette*. His personality too, affected his success. "He was popular, but hardly admired, windy, cheerful, bibulous and not very discriminating," it has been observed, noting that these qualities combined with Jerdan's considerable energy "were adequate for popular and commercial success in the 1820s. They would not be adequate for the more rigorous demands of the next decade."[32]

Perhaps in an effort to forget the huge blow struck by the *Athenaeum*, Jerdan still enthusiastically pursued his non-literary interests, which served as a relaxation from the relentless daily and weekly routines of reading a mass of journals and newspapers from home and abroad, as well as the mountain of manuscripts from hopeful writers. He still took an active interest in the Society of Antiquaries. A gold earring had been found in Athens, with a bulls head decoration, other designs corresponding with a ring Jerdan had discussed at some length, illustrated by Greek quotations, and scholarly references, printed with a drawing in the Society's *Archaeologia*[33] and also reported in the *Gentleman's Magazine*.[34] However, far more than the stuffy Society of Antiquaries he enjoyed the convivial company of the break-away group of Noviomagians, with whom he dined and occasionally went on archaeological trips.

Not all of Jerdan's expeditions were for reasons of archaeology or antiquity hunting. One, of which a long and jovial account remains, took place in the winter of 1830–31.[35] It portrayed glimpses of Jerdan at play, relaxing from his daily labours and displaying that glee in life which he enjoyed so seldom. A group of friends escaped "the murky atmosphere of this pestiferous metropolis" and went fishing near Shoreham. A fictional Tom Manumitter,[36] with Campbell and Moore were of the party, with Jerdan and Croly, and a "free black" of Manumitter's, and other servants. *Fraser's Magazine* irreverently described the Reverend Croly's appearance and appurtenances, his "green shalloon jacket with duck trowsers, white as driven snow and wide and magnificent as the interminable gulf, yawning for the avalanche . . . ". Thomas Moore wore white-buttoned pantaloons and slippers of pale brown leather with an orange waistcoat and jacket, in the pocket of which was a stash of maggots carefully wrapped in a page from his *Life of Byron*. Manumitter and Campbell were similarly scrutinized and mocked for their strange attire.

> But no-one excelled in outward man our peculiar friend Jerdan. Furze and bramble bushes are great enemies to comfort; he therefore drew on a pair of good doe skin sad-coloured breeches, with leggins of tough fustian. His jacket was tightly bound round the waist with a black glazed leathern belt, a willow hat sat jauntily cocked on one side of the head; a netted bag was suspended from the girdle, and a natty imitation Indian cane stick curiously contained his rod. In his pocket lay our Magazine (for he could not for love or money recover a number of the *Literary*,) to hold all his good things, either for man or fish.

Squeezed into a closed carriage for their departure from London, Mungo,[37] the black servant, complained of the heat. His master swatted him. " 'Nay, blackey's in the right', interrupted Jerdan, 'it is infernally hot, and something else besides; and although all the fish that ever clove the Tweed were to be the reward, I shall travel no farther like a potted char in rank grease and fetid abomination. So here I go'. And our friend, springing out, rushed to a stand, and ordered immediate delivery of four score oysters, and a dozen of ginger beer." They disembarked after a skirmish between Mungo and the driver over a sixpence. The skies darkened, and on a bleak road, a stage-coach appeared. " 'We had better get in here', said Jerdan. 'We are going to have an evening that would revivify all the ducks and toads that have expired since the creation of the world. Four wheels for me.'" Jerdan leapt into the coach, joined by 'Oliver Yorke', (the embodiment of *Fraser's Magazine*). The others walked on, Manumitter calling in vain for Mungo, who was nowhere to be seen. The skies opened, the rain poured down.

> Jerdan hastily endeavouring to pull up the window exposed to the storm, felt his foot rest on something warm and soft, and yielding. He had once

sat down on a haggis, and almost thought the same accident had occurred again. "Ged," he involuntarily muttered, "I hope it will not burst!" "Me hope so too," came an answer from under the straw, "for me squeezed like poor pig when him tumble in sugar mill. Oh, massa, take away foot." "Who the devil are you?" exclaimed Jerdan. "Me? Me, Mungo." "And what brought you there, you imp of ebony?" "Ah, massa, keep sixpence dry. Him tizzy no love wet."

Whilst the rest of the party trudged on in the rain, finally getting a lift in a cart half full of cheese and onions, Jerdan and Yorke passed a comfortable night at the Red Lion of Farningham. At daybreak, the cart full of their friends arrived, causing much commotion. "'God be praised, they have reached this safe at last', exclaimed Jerdan, stretching out his neck out of the window, his head surmounted with a tapering red nightcap, (which having got entangled with the bell pull, every nod he gave filled the house with noise and confusion)."

After a mountainous breakfast, Tom Moore went fishing in the noxious pond opposite the hostelry and with much to-do, fished out a dog the land-lord had drowned the previous night. The group left instantly, climbing the hills above the Tarrant, getting overheated with the effort. ""No wonder," remarked Jerdan dryly, "considering these are the dog days." Stopping for refreshment at the house of Mr and Mrs Day in Shoreham, they stripped the place of ale and hams. "In a trice Croly's face was hidden in foam, and Jerdan was gnawing a pork shin-bone of a flavour which would have corrupted the purity of Hyam Barnet himself." Having eaten his fill, Jerdan (so said *Fraser's*), was ready to hold forth:

> "But I'm astonished," continued our friend, wiping his lips, and folding half a cold fowl in an old *John Bull*, and depositing it in one of his wallet looking pockets, "I am ashamed to see you devote the glory of the morn to the indulgence of the grosser appetites, especially in these times of unprecedented distress and suffering, when the poor, even with the sweat of their brows, and the heart-wringing agonies of sleepless nights and overwrought days . . . Landlady, I'll trouble you for a thimble full of Hollands, and let the claret be iced into a delicious coolness by the time we return. Mrs Day, may I be permitted a salute? By Heavens, there's that inconceivable varlet, Ebony, pressing his large gluey lips upon the cadav-erous cheek of the scullion! But let us to the war, my ancients. Here I hoist my pennon . . . "

Many more pages were devoted to the fishing adventures of the party, uproar-ious and amusing, including an encounter with Hogg, who had not previously been mentioned, an opportunity for Maginn, the author, to indulge in some

Scottish dialect, and more wild adventures. Jerdan was not mentioned again until Hogg, believing he was dying from having swallowed poison (which was only cold punch), spoke to "Maister Jergun" telling him

> "Farewell, also, thou son of mirth, and grandson of pun! I leave to thee a legacy. When I am no more, if perchance sorrow reaches the bosom of my friends when they turn their ee and see my place vacant, dash awa the tear. Solace them wi' your wit, your humour; and, in the *Literary*, dinna be ower severe on their warks or mine, Maister Jergun – or mine. *De mortuis*, ye ken, is a Christian maxim." "Your works can never die," said Mr Jerdan impressively; "they are imperishable while memory lives. – Bonny Kilmeny has wreathed your brow with unfading laurel." "Ah!" murmured the dying man, a smile for a moment lighting up his pallid countenance, "ye are ower favourable, but it's kindly meant."

The sixteen pages of this rumbustious story may have been entirely a figment of the writer's imagination, but the participants are so clearly delineated that it is more likely to be a highly embroidered version of an actual excursion. In either event, it depicts this group of influential literary men at play, in a manner that makes them more present and alive than even their own writings can achieve.

The joyful (if possibly fictional) cameraderie portrayed in this story renders all the more puzzling an advertisement for *Fraser's Magazine*, for which they took a full page in the *Literary Gazette* of 30 July 1831. The on-going accusations of puffery turned extremely vicious and personal through this unexpected medium. Jerdan was on good terms with all the Fraserians, and was indeed one of their number in social terms, so why *Fraser's* chose to attack the *Literary Gazette*, synonymous with its Editor, as well as attacking Colburn, is a puzzle. The full-page advertisement was a mass of small type, part of which was comprised of complimentary quotes on *Fraser's* from London and provincial papers. Publicity was given to their 'Gallery of Illustrious Literary Characters', naming Jerdan as one of those featured, and they also plugged their Panoramic Plan of London.

However, a block of this advertisement in even smaller type, quoted a long paragraph from the *Aberdeen Observer*, mentioning the

> inanity, folly, filthiness and obscenity of the trashy novels issuing from Burlington Street and elsewhere . . . critical publications entered into an unholy alliance with the booksellers . . . To say that Frasers Magazine has wholly subverted this tyranny of evil, were to go too far, so long as we see the New Monthly is still zealous to puff and instant to praise the grossest trash of its publishers – and so long as the atmosphere is tainted by the corruption of the London Literary Gazette, a publication which our

contemporary, the Aberdeen Magazine, has justly designated "the common sewer of the vilest bibliopolical corruption.

In his 'To Correspondents' column in the same issue, Jerdan attacked back at some length, and with strong feeling:

While the falsehood and scurrility of low periodicals respecting the Literary Gazette are confined to their own small spheres, we leave them to the obscure contempt which alone they have the power to provoke; but having admitted into our pages today (in the way of business) an advertisement which will thus afford to such abuse a publicity otherwise unattainable, we deem it right to accompany it with a few words of remark. Belonging to that class of the press which finds it easier to struggle into a narrow and ephemeral notoriety by the shameful means of slander and personalities, than to prefer a widespread and permanent claim to the public regard by meritorious efforts in the cause of literature and improvement, we might well leave the Magazine in question, and the impudent lies it has intruded into our own columns, to the degradation earned by the one, and the speedy oblivion which is sure to overtake the other. But we will publicly tell the propagator of these attacks upon us (which he knows to be utterly false and which are rendered personal by a preceding part of the advertisement) that the individual who can so readily violate the least burdensome, though not the least imperative of human virtues, gratitude to a benefactor, is not the best calculated to inform or benefit mankind as the editor of a periodical work: but his voca-tion, like that of this fellows, is not to promote any good or useful purpose. Entitled as we feel we are, to the general confidence and rewarded by a circulation far beyond any literary Journal that ever was published, we shall continue to despise the base detractions of unsuccessful envy. [To guard against misapprehension we should say, that a private friend of ours, a gentleman whose name is frequently mentioned as editor of this Magazine, but who denies that responsibility, is not in the slightest degree alluded to in this notice of a stupid and worthless calumny.]

This seemed to be the end of the sudden squall. However, the matter again reared its ugly head six months later in January 1832, when *Fraser's* printed an article headed "The Literary Gazette, the Court Journal, the Spectator and REGINA". Harking back to their July advertisement, *Fraser's* said that the Aberdeen quote was merely "some casual remarks upon the manifold sins of the *Literary Gazette*, which called forth the following indignant remonstrance from that worthy print". They quoted in full (omitting the final sentence) Jerdan's riposte given above, noting that the *Age* of the following day had outrageously declared this "magnanimous burst to be a specimen of the 'puff reverberative', and had accused *Fraser's* of paying Jerdan to insert his comments as a "guide-post or index" to their advertisement. In the persona of Oliver Yorke, *Fraser's* denied knowing anything about that; if their proprietor did pay, "it is a matter wholly out of our province". The notion of Jerdan accepting a fee for an insertion which attacked his own journal is simply absurd, but this was not the main thrust of *Fraser's* article.

It asked, "Who the deuce is it Jerdan alludes to, when he talks of gratitude being due to him? We, Oliver Yorke, owe him none; and upon looking through the list of persons who, justly or unjustly, are considered to be competitors of ours, we find several to whom Jerdan has many, many reasons to be grateful – not one who owes him any favour. We therefore purge ourselves of the accusation of ingratitude altogether." Yorke then turned his spleen on to the Court Journal and the Spectator, having finished with Jerdan for the time being. If this warmed-over argument was intended as a serious attack on the *Literary Gazette* one wonders why *Fraser's* waited six months before resurrecting it; if it was meant to be humorous, there was nothing in it to indicate this intention. A possible explanation could be that it was revived because Jerdan had personally offended someone of influence at *Fraser's*, maybe Maginn, but if this was the case, no corroborative evidence has come to light to support this supposition.

Maginn, through the pages of *Fraser's*, also impugned Alaric Watts, his motivation being just as mysterious, there having been no ill-feeling, only friendship, between the two men.[38] Watts found some retaliation by composing "The Conversazione" in his *Literary Souvenir* of 1832, hitting back, amongst others, directly at Maginn. *Fraser's*, under the guise of 'biography' in the 'Gallery of Literary Characters', remarked "There is not a man to whom he has not been under an obligation from Jerdan to Lockhart . . . etc. etc." The accompanying drawing was sarcastic and not drawn by Maclise from life, but from a portrait of Watts then on exhibition at the Royal Academy. (This corroborates S. C. Hall's observation that Maclise seldom drew from life for his *Fraser's* portraits.) Unlike Watts, Jerdan did not sue *Fraser's*, which may be interpreted as his having no case to answer, or simply that he was too busy to take the time to refute the accusations. He was still showing signs of anxiety a few months later, rejecting some Essays of an unknown contributor:

> The LG has been so very guarded, that matters which would be unobjected to in almost any other publication provoke severe animadversion in it. I am not myself inclined to be either too hypercritical or prudish, but having established a periodical upon certain principles, one is forced to be rather over-delicate than to risk censure on points, which if they could be defended there is no place wherein to defend them.[39]

On Christmas Day 1831, the *Satirist, or Censor of the Times* printed a squib with a title which would have made Jerdan and Landon very nervous indeed, *The Baby: A Dialogue between W. Jerdan Esq. and L.E.L.* The scene was set in a Back Parlour in Colburn's Shop.

Jerdan: O wondrous woman, pretty L.E.L!
To meet you gives me infinite delight.
My baby you've not seen, you'd like it well:
Lo! I'll produce it, little darling wight!

L.E.L. O Jer! Your works, they say, do equal Brougham,
But think how all our enemies would sneer,
Should we be overheard in this back room
Talking about a little baby dear.

Jerdan: Charming L.E.L! Be not so coy;
My baby's in the Keepsake, splendid book!
And not a word of either *girl* or *boy* –
You'll nurse it now? I read it in that look.

L.E.L. Your baby I'll not own; and, in addition,
I'll tell you truly what I told *A-ram*
Bulwer, that, if writing's your ambition,
Nothing you've ever penned is worth a d—n!

The following week, as a *New Year Wish*, another verse appeared. Buried amongst other stanzas it said:

> To Jerdan the ability
> A 'baby' to produce
> That LEL deign to own
> And nurse would not refuse.

Finding that the 'Baby' referred to was Jerdan's contribution to *The Keepsake* for 1832, published in November or December 1831, rather than one of their flesh and blood babies, would have come as a huge relief to the secret parents of Ella, Fred and Laura.

'Baby! An Autobiographical Memoir' also appeared in two parts in *The Mirror*, under the heading 'Spirit of the Annuals'. Jerdan chose as its epigraph a quotation from Landon's novel *Romance and Reality*: "Death sends Truth before it as its messenger", not a subject generally considered uplifting or cheerful enough for the annuals. It also raised the ire of the *Royal Lady's Magazine* who noted that the novel was not due for publication for a further three months, and called Jerdan's quotation "the puff-preliminary-extraordinary". But they didn't like his story either, calling it "intensely gross, filthy, nauseous, vulgar and indecent", selecting those tid-bits they found especially distasteful so that they could share their spleen with readers.

Jerdan's story was the twenty-four hours of a new-born's life told by the baby himself, from the moment he emerged into the world roughly handled by a disgusting hag he perceived as trying to kill him. The harridan swigged gin, then fiercely rubbed some into his skull, scorching his brain. As this did not finish him off, she plunged him headfirst into a pan of water; he kicked and yelled, and "to gratify her hellish spite" she scraped him "from head to foot more in the manner of a dead pig than a living boy". The next torment was to be tightly swaddled as an Egyptian mummy, finally tying a bonnet on his head, the ribbons of which were tight enough to strangle him. Having, as Baby saw it, had three attempts upon his life in the first thirty minutes of existence, he was left to himself to contemplate his sorry situation. The Nurse ("Curse would have been a juster title"), returned and poured a spoonful of something bitter down his throat from a bottle marked 'Ol Ricini', castor oil. "A sense of sickness took possession of me. I asked myself, Is this the food of human beings? Is it for the enjoyment of such delicacies as this that gourmandism and sensuality fill so prodigious an extent in the existence of men?" Defeated and exhausted, Baby fell asleep. When he awoke he was again assailed by Nurse who spooned a revolting substance called pap or gruel into his mouth – "whoever sent the meat, the devil inspired the cook." Wrapped in warming flannel he was again allowed to sleep. Later, on Nurse's knee, he looked around the room, "so untidy that I could well under-stand why it was called a sick-room; it was enough to make any body sick". He was carried to the window where Nurse tried to blind him by opening the curtains onto the glare of morning.

A small pantomime followed wherein the Baby's father ("another ruthless enemy of mine") entered, paid the doctor his fee, ("the bribe"), bent to kiss his wife in bed, ("putting his face close to hers gave her a smack which, though partially concealed, was perfectly audible to my ear"). Baby, full of rage and hatred, longed to protect his ailing mother, especially from the villain's chin, which was "armed all over with sharp spears and short but cutting knives". Desolate that his only hope of rescue, his mother, was also in the power of the Nurse, Baby's soul died within him. Various females came to inspect him as the day drew on, one "a very old female whom they styled grandmamma, because she was dressed in a stately guise; this hideous person disguised herself by putting two round glasses over her eyes then came close to me ... ". It was insufferable, her powder drifted over Baby, causing him to sneeze and the company to laugh – "my curse be upon them for their inhumanity".

Baby was so debilitated by his dreadful experience of life that he stopped fighting. "Flayed, drowned, insulted, incapacitated, smothered, abused, tortured, poisoned, is it to be wondered at that I resigned myself quietly to the prospect of a release?" A man dressed as from a masquerade read a prayer over him, while the parents argued about a name for him. His last moments were of heavenly peace upon the soft bosom of his mother.

Unable to just leave the end of any story without interposing his authorial voice, Jerdan added that, not wanting to interrupt the "pathos and elegant connexion" of his tale, he had left until the end that Baby had stated during the course of his life that he "was a genius and born with a natural taste for literature". Asked for a definition of Man, which even Plato could not provide, Baby replied, "Man is a writing animal". Overcome by this "immortal answer" Baby is asked how his memory may be venerated. With humility he requested that upon his monument be engraved:

> Since I have been so quickly done for,
> What on earth was I begun for !!!

The notion of Man's lifetime condensed into a single day of sorrows and disappointments and death is treated with some dark humour by Jerdan; it does not seem to have been provoked by any such dismal feelings in his own life at this point. On re-reading it twenty years later, he still thought it worthy of including it as an Appendix in his *Autobiography*.

For his second contribution to *The Keepsake* of 1832 he wrote *Scan.-Mag*, a lively piece about society's delight in a scandal magazine. Reynolds, the editor of *The Keepsake*, appended a note to the effect that Jerdan had written it "in less than half an hour, in order to meet an exigency occasioned by the sudden and inevitable exclusion of a very able but long article on the same subject". Whether the article itself was due from Jerdan, he did not clarify. Despite its haste, this verse seems more Jerdan's natural style than the many melancholy poems he usually provided for the annuals; one of its five stanzas read:

> You've heard of poor Miss M's affair,
> 'Twas at the Oratory;
> Upon my life I do declare
> I crimson at that story
> I told it to her aunt Mill Poll,
> But she made sham to pout,
> And call'd it silly rigmarole,
> I knew 'twas roundabout
> And so long as tongues can wag.
> I'll tell it, fearless of scan.-mag.

Reynolds accompanied this hasty and amusing offering of Jerdan's by an engraving of a painting by Smirke called Scandal, showing two women deep in exchanging gossip whilst a boy and dog play beside them. The *Royal Lady's*

1

Yours ever
W. Jerdan

THE EDITOR OF THE LITERARY GAZETTE.

THE LITERARY GAZETTE,
AND
Journal of Belles Lettres, Arts, Sciences, &c.

No. 389. SATURDAY, JULY 3, 1824. PRICE 1s.

REVIEW OF NEW BOOKS.

The Improvisatrice; and other Poems. By
L. E. L. 12mo. pp. 327. London 1824.
Hurst, Robinson, & Co.; Edinburgh, Constable & Co.

It will be expected from us that we speak of
this volume in terms of the warmest admiration; because, if we had not thought very
highly of the genius of its author, the pages
of the *Literary Gazette* would not have been
enriched with so many of her compositions.
But indeed we are enthusiastic in this respect; and as far as our poetical taste and
critical judgment enable us to form an opinion, we can adduce no instance, ancient or
modern, of similar talent and excellence.
That the *Improvisatrice* is the work of a young
female, may, at the outset, lessen its importance in the eyes of those who judge by
analogy, without fairly examining individual
merits; but it will ultimately enhance the
value and augment the celebrity of this delightful production.*

If true poetry consist in originality of conception, fineness of imagination, beautiful
fitness and glow of expression, genuine feeling, and the outpourings of fresh and natural
thoughts in all the force of fresh and natural
language, it is pre-eminently conspicuous in
the writings of L. E. L. Neither are her subjects nor mode of treating them, borrowed
from others; but simplicity, gracefulness,
fancy, and pathos, seem to gush forth in spontaneous and sweet union, whatever may be
the theme. And, especially for a youthful
author, her poems possess one rare and almost
peculiar quality—their style is purely English.
In the whole volume before us we do not
meet with one ambitious word, one extraneous
idiom, or one affected phrase. The effect is
correspondingly great; and never did accustomed English words more distinctly prove
their high poetical powers. It seems as if by
some magic touch mean and household things
were changed into the rarest and most brilliant ornaments; and in reality it is that the
spell of native genius throws a splendour over
the common, and imparts a new degree of
energy and beauty to the simple and plain.

Having offered these general remarks, we
shall proceed to illustrate them by a view of
the principal poem—*The Improvisatrice*, which
would, alone, entitle the fair author to the
name of the English Sappho. It is an exquisite story of unfortunate love; and extremely
ingenious in its frame or construction. The
Improvisatrice is an impassioned daughter of
sunny Italy, gifted with those powers of song

which the name implies, and supposed to
utter her extemporaneous effusions, as occasions are presented in her chequered life.
Her career is represented as alternately bright
and clouded; her perceptions are always
vivid, and her feelings intense. All fire, and
heart, and soul, the chords of her existence
vibrate to the slightest impressions, and send
forth tones of various and striking melody
when swept by the stronger impulses of her
excitable and sensitive nature. Endowed with
all the characteristic tenderness, fragility,
and loveliness of woman, she is the very creature of inspiration; and her being may be
said to be divided between the finest sense of
external beauty and the deepest consciousness
of moral emotions. "I am," she abruptly
but charmingly exclaims, describing herself
at the opening of the poem,—

I am a daughter of that land,
Where the poet's lip and the painter's hand
Are most divine,—where earth and sky
Are picture both and poetry—
I am of Florence. 'Mid the chill
Of hope and feeling, oh! I still
Am proud to think to where I owe
My birth, though but the dawn of woe!
My childhood pass'd 'mid radiant things,
Glorious as Hope's imaginings;
Statues but known from shapes of the earth,
By being too lovely for mortal birth;
Paintings whose colours of life were caught
From the fairy tints in the rainbow wrought;
Music whose sighs had a spell like those
That float on the sea at the evening's close;
Language so silvery, that every word
Was like the lute's awakening chord;
Skies half sunshine, and half starlight;
Flowers whose lives were a breath of delight;
Leaves whose green pomp knew no withering;
Fountains bright as the skies of our Spring;
And songs whose wild and passionate line
Suited a soul of romance like mine.
My power was but a woman's power;
Yet, in that great and glorious dower
Which Genius gives, I had my part:
I poured my full and burning heart
In song, and on the canvass made
My dreams of beauty visible:
I know not which I loved the most—
Pencil or lute,—both loved so well.

This spirited commencement is however
but an unfavourable example of the poem.
It proceeds to depict the Improvisatrice's
sensations on beholding the first produce of
her pencil. Her next painting is of the immortal Poetess of Lesbos, to whom, in her
genius, we have ventured to compare our
own charming contemporary. The portrait is
worthy of Raphael:

- - - - Her head was bending down,
As if in weariness, and near,
But unworn, was a laurel crown.
She was not beautiful, if bloom
And smiles form beauty; for, like death,
Her brow was ghastly; and her lip
Was parched, *as fever were its breath.*
There was a shade upon her dark,
Large, floating eyes, as if each spark
Of minstrel ecstasy was fled,
Yet, leaving them no tears to shed;
Fixed in their hopelessness of care,
And reckless in their *great despair.*

She sat beneath a cypress tree,
A little fountain ran beside.
And, in the distance, one dark rock
Threw its long shadow o'er the tide;
And to the west, where the nightfall
Was darkening day's gemm'd coronal,
Its *white shafts* crimsoning in the sky,
Arose the sun-god's sanctuary.
I deemed, that of lyre, life, and love
She was a long, last farewell taking;—
That, from her pale and parched lips,
Her latest, wildest song was breaking.

To this delicious personation (a few words
of which we have marked in italics, to point
their application to our introductory observations on the author's felicitous choice of
epithets and true poetry of expression,) is
added the improvised death-song of Sappho;
than which we are acquainted with nothing
more beautiful in our language:

Farewell, my lute!—and would that I
Had never waked thy burning chords!
Poison has been upon thy sigh,
And fever has breathed in thy words.
Yet wherefore, wherefore should I blame
Thy power, thy spell, my gentlest lute?
I should have been the wretch I am,
Had every chord of thine been mute.
It was my evil star above,
Not my sweet lute, that wrought me wrong;
It was not song that taught me love,
But it was love that taught me song.
If song be past, and hope undone,
And pulse, and head, and heart, are flame;
It is thy work, thou faithless one!
But, no!—I will not name thy name!
Sun-god, lute, wreath, are vowed to thee!
Long be their light upon my grave:
My glorious grave—yon deep blue sea:
I shall sleep calm beneath its wave!

Returning to herself, the Improvisatrice
says—

As yet I loved not;—but each wild,
High thought I nourished raised a pyre
For love to light; and lighted once
By love, it would be like the fire,
The burning lava floods, that dwell
In Etna's cave unquenchable.

That moment, so fearful for such a heart,
comes too soon. But before we go to that
epocha, we would fain pause to extract " a
Moorish Romance," which the scene suggests
to memory; our limits, however, debar us
from the gratification.

Leaving this sweet example of diversified
talent, we can only find space for one feature
of *his* portrait who has the glory of inspiring
the Improvisatrice's bosom with love:

Such a lip!—oh, poured from thence
Lava floods of eloquence
Would come with fiery energy,
Like those words that cannot die.
Words the Grecian warrior spoke
When the Persian's chain he broke;
Or that low and honey tone,
Making woman's heart his own;
Such as should be heard at night,
In the dim and sweet starlight;
Sounds that haunt a beauty's sleep,
Treasures for her heart to keep.

PORTRAITS OF WILLIAM JERDAN

William Jerdan aged 48.

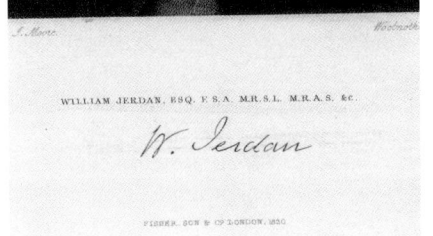

William Jerdan aged about 78

Edward Bulwer

George Canning

L.E.L. aged 25, c.1827.

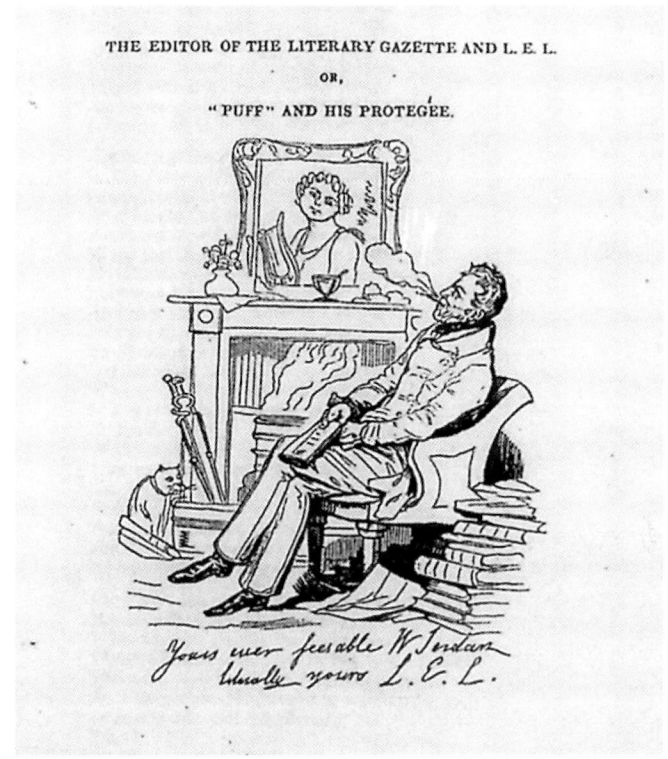

"A Few of the F.S.A.s" (William Jerdan and Crofton Croker, on left)

GROVE HOUSE, 1844.

Statue of George III

Exeter 'Change in the Strand. The offices of the 'Literary Gazette' were on the left side of the street.

7

Ella Stuart, Melbourne, Australia.

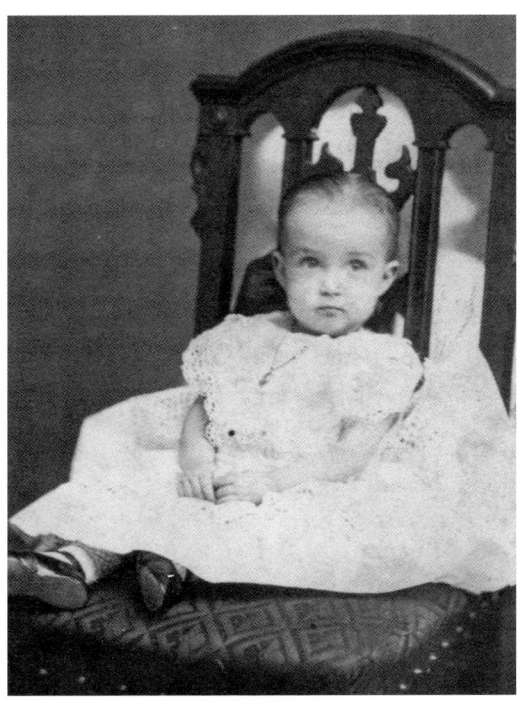

Emily Ella Stuart,
Port-of-Spain, Trinidad.

Charles Stuart Jerdan

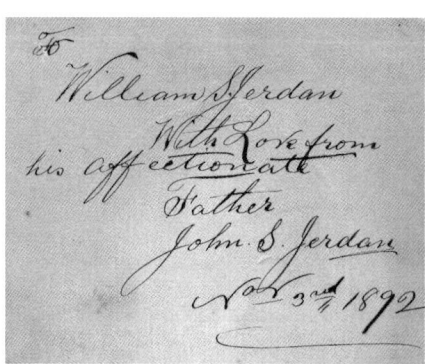

John Jerdan, 1892, and dedication on reverse of portrait

Magazine was unhappy with this offering as well, penning their own satirical verse in sixty-five seconds, not the half hour that Jerdan claimed to have taken, advising readers that "Well – such poetry as this, / We never read before;/ It's really worse than L.E.L.'s,/ And what can we say more?" etc.

Jerdan overcame his discomfiture over allegations of puffing, and despite rumbling rumours over his affair with Landon, he was either invited, or more likely applied for, a position of Commissioner of the Peace and Deputy Lieutenant of Middlesex. Writing in January to the Lord Lieutenant the Duke of Portland, Jerdan acknowledged his request for a testimonial of his fitness to be a Magistrate, and apologized that in response he had merely mentioned a few "noble and distinguished persons" who would give him a reference. Since then it had been pointed out that he should have taken the trouble himself to acquire such documentation, and he was now doing so.[40] A few days later he asked Lord Goderich (who had encouraged him to stand as Tory candidate for Weymouth) to sign a paper which he enclosed, recommending Jerdan to the Duke of Portland. In this same letter Jerdan had a bigger favour to ask. His son John Stuart had been working for the Abbotsford Subscription, but now Jerdan wanted a better position for him.[41] Having tried to see the Duke of Portland three times the previous week, Jerdan apologised for his intrusion, but

> I can only rely for my excuse upon the same goodness which principally led to my visit, namely your Lordship's kind intuitions towards my son; the assurance of which has rendered both him and me very anxious, though truly feeling that your Lordship would not forget the hope you had created. Amid the cares and overwhelming fatigues of Office, may I beg gratefully to remind your Lordship of this.

He gently jogged the great man's sense of obligation by remarking "I hope your Lordship received a very small book about six weeks ago which I offered for Lady Goderich's acceptance."[42] More than two months passed without news of a job for his son, so Jerdan tried again in April, having noticed in the newspaper that a diplomat was retiring from the Buenos Aires Consulate, thus presumably creating a vacancy lower down. "Should it place aught in your Lordship's power, I should be most grateful, for Stuart's being unoccupied and unprovided for is a heavy weight on the mind of, My Lord, your faithful servant . . ."[43] Humiliatingly, he was forced to beg again in July, saying how much of his welfare and happiness depended on Goderich's kind promise to his son. John Stuart was at this time twenty-five years old, still apparently reliant on his father finding him a job. Jerdan's persistence eventually paid off and his son was sent out to Jamaica as a Stipendiary Magistrate, a move Jerdan would come to deeply regret. No more was said about his own application to become a Magistrate, and he did not mention this episode in his *Autobiography*. This indicates that the testimonials he sought were hard to come by, or else that he had second thoughts about taking a position in which expense would be incurred. The very fact that Portland had even considered Jerdan for a position of Magistrate suggests that Jerdan had reached a certain status in society, entirely based on his editorship of the *Literary Gazette*. When he first made his application, he was extremely busy in another, more enjoyable, direction.

The more enjoyable activity in the winter of 1831–32 was the arrival in London of the celebrated Scottish poet, James Hogg the Ettrick Shepherd. Many of the "better classes of its Scottish residents"[44] wished to honour him, and the task was undertaken chiefly by Jerdan and Lockhart. There was little time to organize the Dinner and Burns' Night, 25 January, was chosen as an appropriate time. It was a hectic time for Hogg; he was being lionized, and partying every night. He wrote to his wife about the great Dinner being planned. It "will be such a meeting as was never in London . . . But do not be afraid, for vain as I am, it will not turn my head; on the contrary it has made me melancholy, and I wish it were fairly over . . . And all this to do honour to a poor old shepherd."[45]

More people than were expected wanted to honour the "poor old shepherd". The organizers were taken unawares by the huge rush for admission. Nearly two hundred people crushed into the Freemasons Tavern, causing a chaotic delay whilst tables were lengthened. In Jerdan's memoir twenty years later recollection of the Dinner was muted, concentrating mostly on the names of the titled and famous who were present. He also mentioned the presence of the sons of Robert Burns, the many toasts that were sung, and the "good laugh at the toast-master's proclaiming silence for the pleasure of a song from *Mr Shepherd* – Ettrick was *terra incognita* to him!" This account of what was clearly a noisy and riotous evening, just the kind of revelry Jerdan loved, pales next to the contemporary account in *Fraser's Magazine* of February 1832. Their article ran to fourteen pages, purportedly to correct the inaccuracies in a long list of newspapers and magazines (including the *Literary Gazette*) which reported on the great event. In true Fraserian style all these publications were lambasted for reports which "have been coloured by base adulation on the one hand, and by the still more abominable spirit of personality and the existing age".

Fraser's listed the great and the good who attended, drawing them up in military formation: Booksellers Murray and Colburn, then "authors arraying according to the size of their works", down to pamphleteers, then the "gentlemen of the press", unshaven and predatory in habit. Finally, "the Magazine men lay on the flanks and came out, as Magazines usually do, in numbers" headed by Campbell and Bulwer. Jerdan was named too, taking the place of his friend Jack Mitford, a prolific writer but penniless alcoholic who had died in the workhouse just a month earlier. This assembly of literary men collected Hogg at his lodgings and paraded him down the intricate byways to the Freemasons Tavern, many stopping off at public houses along the way. *Fraser's* reported that Cuff, the hosteller of the Freemasons, was overwhelmed by

> the literature of London let loose upon him. Anxiety for his spoons first seized on his soul – then the horrible apprehensions of the fate of his viands under the ravenous grinders of the Scotchmen, hungry from the hills, and, as was evident from the appearance of their jaws, the generality of them having fasted for a couple of days, in order to be prepared for this dinner.

Quoting from the *Morning Advertiser*, the *Fraser's* account reported how everyone except the sixty or seventy seated at the centre table were served with food, and that these starving guests set up a clattering and banging of cutlery against plates, silenced only by the arrival not of food, but of bagpipes. Having paid their twenty-five shillings admission, and still unfed, they were given leftovers from the other tables and had to make do with that. Paganini fainted away at the sound of bagpipes, and fun was made of the gargantuan appetite of Sir John Malcolm who told his neighbour not to bother carving the duck, just put the whole thing on his plate, from whence it was quickly eaten. Toasts to the King and the Queen followed, and, controversially by one to "The Duke!" first called forth huge cheers, but then,

> ceasing for a while, there came a shabby hiss, issuing from lips too cowardly to express any sentiment not worthy of the snake, very audible in one or two quarters of the room. It was the paltriest hiss that ever was ventured upon; it sounded like the filthiest fizzing of the filthiest water flung into the filthiest of fires.

Hogg's response to his health being drunk was given by *Fraser's* in full, starting in a broad Scots dialect quickly reverting to normal English – perhaps so that it could be more easily enjoyed by the readers. Hogg announced that he was born on Burns's birthday, ascribing to this coincidence his own "undoubted talents" as a Poet. Tears of emotion and other toasts followed. All through this rumbustious dinner Hogg, according to Jerdan, "brewed sundry bowls of punch in Burns's bowl, kept sacred for such anniversaries".[46] Picken, a fellow Scot, gave a long and patriotic speech upon the superiority of all things Scottish, citing famous Scots like James Watt inventor of the steam engine, James Patterson who established the bank of England, Walter Scott writer of the Waverley Novels, leading journalists and editors of magazines, "And who writes the *Literary Gazette* (another great work) but a Kelso Scotchman? [immense applause]." One can almost feel Jerdan's happy blush, to be included in such an august collection. Hogg reminded the roisterers there were ladies in the room, albeit up in the gallery. Clearing his throat, he sang a song about "luve o' bonnie lasses". Yet more speeches and toasts were followed by another Scottish ballad sung by Allan Cunningham as a compliment to the ladies. Bulwer then responded to Sir John Malcolm's toast to his health, announcing that he "loved a lord; and it is my delight to be a tuft-hunter". He had prepared and practised a song for the occasion, playing with words commencing with "ass", which he had been called previously by *Fraser's Magazine*. One of several verses was:

> Let. Landon declares I'm an ass-
> onant to love and to beauty;
> Cries Mrs. B. 'O what an ass-
> ociate in conjugal duty!'
> There's Jerdan exclaims, I'm an ass-
> ayer of poesy's pinions;
> And I, too, affirm, I'm an ass-
> enter to all their opinions.[47]

Replete with "copious draughts of rude port" Bulwer jumped on to the table, dancing to the bagpipes, "to the amusement of the whole company, puffing being, he said, his business". His capering broke several decanters and glasses. When he admitted to Cuff that he had no money to pay for them, Cuff threatened to call the police, refusing any credit to literary men. At the last moment Colburn came to his rescue, drawing a bill for almost five pounds to be paid to Cuff at six months. The altercation caused much noise and confusion, in the midst of which Allan Cunningham thought his pocket was being picked and punched his neighbour. Crofton Croker joyfully joined in, hitting anybody in range, Bulwer hid behind Colburn, "Jerdan and Patmore engaged in mortal combat, but we did not hear the result", and Hogg judiciously departed the scene of his and Burns's Dinner.

Jerdan saw a great deal of Hogg on this visit to London and they met often at various houses and entertainments, as well as at Jerdan's home. Hogg took a fancy to Jerdan's eighteen-year-old daughter Mary. He thought her beauty resembled a portrait of Mary Queen of Scots. On his eventual return home, Hogg sent her a formal proposal of marriage on behalf of his nephew, a surgeon leaving London to return to India. In a letter concerned mainly with a Whig election victory at Selkirk, and deep anxieties over Sir Walter Scott's Monument, Hogg regretted that his suit "had been so equivocally received by the lovely Mary". He didn't know how to go about getting Mary and his nephew together, but insisted "There never was a match my heart was so much set on as that, not even my own marriage, and I got a very lovely and amiable lady, for I regard William as quite a treasure . . . "[48] Hogg sold his nephew hard, he had come home to find a wife, his future was secure, he required no dowry. Hogg urged

Jerdan not to let Mary, "the wild sly-looking gypsy" decide, but that he and Jerdan should plan between themselves. Mary never met the surgeon and the matter was dropped. Jerdan thought perhaps such practices were more common in the quiet part of deeply rural Scotland where Hogg lived.[49]

The Ettrick Shepherd made himself well liked in the fine society of the capital, and charmed all who met him. Jerdan remarked that this was due to Hogg's "manners and joviality, combined with his shrewdness, discretion and ready wit",[50] no small accomplishment for a man unused to 'society'. He was, however, an outspoken blunt man, and in recording several anecdotes about Hogg's reactions to London society, Jerdan mentioned one especially memorable evening. He and Hogg were dining at Sir George Warrender's, where Hogg enticed everyone away from the excellent claret and made them whisky toddies. From there they attended an evening party at the home of Mr and Mrs Samuel Carter Hall, Landon's close friends. According to Jerdan, Hogg "was in his glory, crushed within a circle of fine women, like an Apollo, he sang song after song to their intense delight, and was in fact as great as Moore, or more". Mrs Hall remembered that Hogg "shouted forth in an untunable voice, songs that were his own especial favourites, giving us some account of each at its conclusion".[51] It was on this evening that Hogg was introduced to Letitia Landon, of whose sullied reputation he had already heard and participated in spreading. Delighted with her charm, he declared that he "never thought she could have been sie a bonny sweet lassie".[52] Samuel Carter Hall recalled this meeting slightly differently. Being the uptight moralist that he was, Hall was shocked at Landon's decolletage, and was highly and vocally critical of Jerdan's drinking habits. His recollection of Hogg's impulsive reaction to Landon "in his rich and manly Scottish voice" was "I've said many hard things aboot ye. I'll do so nae mair. I didna think ye'd been sae bonnie!"[53] The feeling is the same, only the words are a little changed.

In a book about Hogg Jerdan was referred to as Hogg's "malicious deevil", but without attribution or giving reasons.[54] Perhaps this was a phrase used by Hogg at an earlier time as, in 1824, the *Literary Gazette* reviewed Hogg's *Confessions of a Justified Sinner* as "strange . . . mystical and extravagant (and what we dislike still more, allegorical) . . . a work of irregular genius . . .".[55] Of Hogg's *Queen Hynde* the *Gazette* observed, "Here is as much to censure as to praise . . . it is made tiresomely long . . . it defies our penetration to tell whether he means it to be serious or burlesque."[56] They may have had their differences over these reviews, but Jerdan's accounts of their close friendship on Hogg's visit to London, Hogg's desire to join their two families in matrimony, and Jerdan's repeated efforts to get Literary Fund support for Hogg, belie this cruel epithet.

Jerdan missed Hogg when he finally left London, and found that "Grove House seemed to have lost its life, seeing his honest face look in daily no more, no laughing at his jokes, no listening with admiration and delight to his songs, nor hearing his most original descriptions of all he had seen ... " Hogg's powers of description in his poetry had always been a source of wonder to Jerdan. They had been talking about his poetry one day, and Jerdan "observed that he had put two exquisite rural images into a single line, quite equal to anything in Theocritus, or the most celebrated in Greek pastoral composition ... ".[57] Hogg's response was impatient, as on a similar occasion when he told Jerdan irritably, "Surely ye're daft; it's only joost true about the wee burdies, and the cows at e'en, and the wild flowers, and the sunset and clouds, and things and the feelings they create. 'A canna fathom what ye're making a' this fuss about. It's joost a plain description of what everybody can see: there's nae grand poetry in it."[58] The literary critic in Jerdan wondered "was this beautiful passage suggested by unconscious inspiration? Or did he think that pure invention alone, and not an actual perception of beauties in nature, was poetry – imagination, not appreciation?"[59] Wishing to avoid the danger (as he saw it) of being knighted, with its attendant expenses, Hogg returned home to Scotland in March. A few months after this successful visit to London, Hogg again got into financial troubles. In June Jerdan once more applied to the Literary Fund on his behalf but without Hogg's knowledge. This time the Fund provided forty pounds for which Hogg was grateful.

Jerdan had a small skirmish with the law, reported in *The Times* of 18 April 1832. Scripps, the printer of the *Literary Gazette*, had an 'information' preferred against him by a Mr Judge, for not duly stamping the issue of the *Gazette* dated 7 April, rendering himself liable to a fine of twenty pounds. Jerdan was present at the hearing before the Bow Street magistrate, but he was represented by his solicitor who got Scripps off on a technicality, based upon Mr Judge not being an officer of stamps. Jerdan's lawyer remarked testily that the law had been framed "to clip the wings of common informers and prevent printers and publishers from being subject to vexatious informations". Such actions were to become a thing of the past when, in June 1832, Bulwer Lytton opened a debate in the House of Commons which resulted, in 1836, in lowering the hated stamp duty from fourpence to one penny, and that on advertisements from three shillings and sixpence to one shilling and sixpence. These taxes were finally abolished in 1855, but it was not until 1861 that the heavy duty on paper was repealed.

Landon and Jerdan were seen together so often, and worked together so much on the *Literary Gazette*, it was inevitable that their names should be linked in print. A small thirty-two page booklet appeared in 1832, published by James Gilbert. It was called *The Poetical March of Humbug! By the Great Unmentionable, being burlesque imitations of the principal poets of the day after the manner of 'Rejected Addresses'*. Amongst those it made fun of were Jerdan and the poetess. "Well, reader, what do you think of Jerdan and his 'own delightful minstrel L.E.L?" it asked. Accompanying this was a sketch of Jerdan in his armchair, puffing a cigar, a pile of books at his side, with a roaring fire, above which is a framed picture at which he gazes, of a muse holding a lyre. The title of the sketch is 'The Editor of the Literary Gazette and L.E.L. or, "Puff" and his protégée.'[60] (See illustration no. 5.) The identity of the author, "The Great Unmentionable", has not been revealed, but it has been suggested that Hook is the likeliest candidate, as he was in the habit of sketching in pen and ink on his letters and would have relished the discomfiture such a sketch would have caused Jerdan and L.E.L.[61] who were in no position to sue over the innuendo implicit in this sketch. Beneath the sketch are supposed signatures, reading "Yours ever feesable (sic) W. Jerdan" and "Literally yours L.E.L.", the latter a daring and blatant statement. The text explained, "The room before you is the Editor's study, where he is generally to be found puffing morning and evening at a rapid and voluminous rate. His breathings of course, occasionally end in smoke, and such is the force of example, that several of L.E.L's late effusions have terminated their career in a similar manner, by being thrown into the fire after a first perusal . . . " A narrative verse called *The False Hussar* and purporting to be "by L.E.L" followed – the tale of a young woman dazzled by the hussar, sitting on his knee and allowing him to kiss her; she later sees news of his marriage and dies of a broken heart.

Undeterred by being the butt of such a prank, Landon was as busy as ever. She believed some of her finest work appeared in the annuals, especially in *Fisher's Drawing-Room Scrap Book*. She told Crofton Croker that the work came at a good time for her: "a week ago Messrs. Fisher's (sic) proposal would have been a matter of comparative indifference, but from some recent family events it is a perfect fairy-gift."[62] The 'family events' may have been demands on her purse from her mother, brother, or upkeep for her children. She edited the *Drawing-Room Scrap Book* from 1832 until 1839, the final issue appearing after her death. It was distributed not only in London, but also in New York, Paris, Berlin and St. Petersburg. She was much more than editor: she was almost the sole author of all eight volumes of what has been termed "one of the most impressive annuals".[63] Jerdan remembered that "she had no assistance from any hand", but contrary to this accepted view Maginn "used to repeat those poems which he had given to the fair editress, laughing heartily all the time at the little hoax they were playing off on the public".[64] From 1825 until the end of her life Landon wrote poems for many other annuals, including the *Forget Me Not* and its Juvenile version, *Friendship's Offering, Literary Souvenir*, the *Amulet, Pledge of Friendship*, the *Bijou*, and *The Keepsake*. In 1833 she contributed all the articles and verse to the first volume of Heath's *Book of Beauty*. Some writers and reviewers derided the annuals. When Thackeray wrote *Pendennis* in 1850 he satirized them quite savagely, but by that time, their day had long since ended. However, they were a welcome source of income for Landon, as well as providing her with many outlets for her particular brand of poetry. Jerdan reported that she received thirty pounds for *The Easter Gift*, which was in the form of an annual. About this time, Landon proposed a plan for a new type of annual, describing it in detail to Jerdan, and suggesting it be called *The Choice*. She left the scheme in his hands "as you know far better than I do what publishers might be likely to act upon the scheme".[65] No such annual appeared.

Editing an annual was a coveted occupation, one not below the attention of the titled, albeit financially embarrassed Lady Blessington, who edited and wrote for Heath's *Book of Beauty* and for *The Keepsake*. Her career was to intertwine with both Jerdan and Landon at various points, whilst her connection ensured that "persons of fashion" vied to be included in her annuals. Marguerite, Countess of Blessington, had had a turbulent past, born in Ireland, sold at sixteen by her father to an abusive husband whom she quickly left. Another, kinder man took her under his protection, and she eventually married Lord Blessington, a wealthy Irish landlord with whom she lived for many years. She was reviled in England for her past alliances, making life in London impossible, so she and her husband lived in great luxury in France and in Italy where she met and spent much time with Byron, an experience on which she later traded. Lord Blessington's only legitimate son by his first marriage died unexpectedly; perhaps unhinged by this tragedy Lord Blessington became closely attached to Alfred, Count d'Orsay, changing his will in favour of the young Frenchman on condition that he marry one of Blessington's two daughters, then aged eleven and twelve, and leaving his wife an annuity of only two thousand pounds. This action laid the foundation for her later troubles. Blessington's younger daughter Harriet Gardiner was the bride d'Orsay chose from the two on offer, although he showed no interest in her, or in most other women. Despite his apparent predilections, rumours later abounded that he had an affair with Lady Blessington. Lord Burghersh (to whom Jerdan had applied for contributions to the *Foreign Literary Gazette)*, was the English Minister in Florence, and put so many obstacles in the way of the discreditable match, (Harriet was only fifteen-and-a-half, at this point), that the marriage was finally performed in Rome in 1828. A few months later Lord Blessington died, leaving his estates in chaos.

Lady Blessington understood that she had to find a way to earn her own money, as the annuity was insufficient for her accustomed life style. Revolution was brewing in Paris and she returned to London, setting up home in Seamore Place, Park Lane, determined to create the relaxed and intellectual atmosphere of her salon in Paris. She was in fierce competition with other society hostesses, but aimed for a different group, for "men of taste", in a club-like ambience where literature and the arts would be discussed openly, not solely politics which was on everyone's lips at the time. Her visitors were mainly bourgeois, such as Dickens, Thackeray and Disraeli, "who were prepared to turn a withering satire upon all whose arrogance rested on mere accident of birth. To many of these spokesmen of the new culture, private passions came ultimately to count for less than public ills."[66] Lady Blessington's house was soon the centre of a lively group of clever men, enjoying her renowned beauty and her witty conversation. Some women made calls on her in the daytime, others were appalled at her presence in London, and she was not welcome to return calls anywhere, lest she offend high society. Her evenings were thus attended solely by men; d'Orsay was usually present, his child-wife out of sight elsewhere in the house. Up to this time Lady Blessington's fortunes were dependent on d'Orsay's legacy from her late husband, earned on his marriage to Harriet. He was a profligate gambler and spendthrift, running up enormous debts with gay abandon.

Lady Blessington was determined to satisfy her desire to fill her house with the kind of men she valued for their talk, to offer them a place to meet under the guidance of a sympathetic hostess of great beauty and social skill. Edward Bulwer came to her evenings, as did Jerdan, Disraeli and that moralizing teetotaller, Samuel Carter Hall. Deciding that to make money she should become an author, Bulwer, then editor of the *New Monthly Magazine*, agreed to serialize her *Conversations with Lord Byron*, from notes she had kept during her Italian travels. These appeared from time to time between July 1832 and December 1833. In the meantime, she asked Bulwer's advice on writing novels. He was now a successful author and took her proposal to Bentley, who was to publish his next three books. Bentley offered Lady Blessington four hundred pounds for the copyright of her first book, a generous offer; in response, she produced six hundred pages in four weeks, of the total nine hundred and eight pages of *The Repealers*, published in three volumes in June 1833. This work contained thinly veiled references to her enemies in Ireland, but also directly complimented L.E.L.'s *Romance and Reality*. The success of her *Conversations with Lord Byron* and her novel obtained an offer for her to edit Heath's *Book of Beauty*, the first volume of which Landon had produced. For Heath, the snob appeal of a Countess was more attractive than that of a mere poetess, however famous. She prepared her first issue during the summer of 1833 and it was published in November, to enable it to be shipped to America, India and the Colonies, but dated 1834. Contributors to this issue were her dear friends Walter Savage Landor and Bulwer, as well as Henry Bulwer and John Galt, and seven contributions from her own pen. Heath raised Lady Blessington's salary when the *Book of Beauty* beat Landon's popular *Drawing Room Scrapbook* by two thousand copies, a sore fact for Landon.[67]

In the midst of all Landon's workload of reviewing, poetry composition, editing and considering another novel, her grandmother Letitia Bishop died on 10 November 1832 at the age of eighty-two. According to Samuel Carter Hall, she was buried in the third grave in the new churchyard of Holy Trinity, Brompton. (This was not quite accurate; several burials took place before her own.) Hall quoted the letter Landon wrote to his wife:

I have had time to recover the first shock, and it was great weakness to feel so sorry, though even now I do not like to think of her very sudden death. I am thankful for its giving her so little confinement or pain. She had never known illness, and would have borne it impatiently – a great addition to suffering. I am so very grateful to Mr Hall, for I really did not know what to do. Her funeral is fixed for Friday; the hour will be arranged to his and Mr Jerdan's convenience.[68]

Jerdan was therefore still much in evidence as her friend and colleague, possibly still as her lover, but it seems probable that their affair had run its course; he was certainly not her only admirer. Landon did not benefit financially as much as she had hoped from her grandmother's death. Katherine Thomson recorded that the bulk of Mrs Bishop's money had gone into an annuity, but that Landon received the residue of her estate. "£350 was every farthing she ever received after the age of seventeen, independently of her own exertions."[69] Thomson estimated Landon's annual income to be £250 of which she retained £120 for herself, the rest going on the upkeep of her family. Thomson took her information from Jerdan's *Autobiography*, just as she had already quoted his figures on Landon's earnings for specific books. Jerdan received "the good old lady's good old watch", which was stolen from his pocket one night at the theatre.[70]

During this year, Landon was at one of the gatherings at the home of Rosina and Edward Bulwer Lytton where Disraeli was also present. He snobbishly commented that he had "avoided L.E.L. who looked the very personification of Brompton – pink satin dress and white satin shoes, red cheeks, snub nose, and her hair *à la Sappho*".[71] He was in no position to be critical, having been described at Lady Blessington's salon "with the last rays of the sunlight reflected from the gorgeous gold flowers of a splendidly embroidered waistcoat, a quantity of gold chains about his neck and pockets, a white stick with a black cord and tassel in his hand, and a thick mass of jet-black ringlets falling over his left cheek almost to his collarless stock".[72] Such gatherings were the brighter side of London life in 1832, when cholera was raging through the city.

One victim was David Blaikie, a Scotsman staying with family in Kensington. Blaikie had started the *Edinburgh Evening Post* and on selling it in 1829 purchased the copyright of the *Edinburgh Weekly Chronicle*. He also tried for two years to publish the *Edinburgh Literary Gazette* but ultimately found no call for it in Scotland. He and Jerdan knew each other well, and when Blaikie fell ill, Jerdan went to comfort him and his pregnant wife. The Liberal paper the *True Sun*, (an offshoot of Jerdan's old paper the *Sun*), published an account of Jerdan's actions which the *New Monthly Magazine* reprinted, Jerdan himself being too modest to divulge what had happened (begging the question of how the *True Sun* learnt of the story).[73] "He found his friend Blaikie ill of this appalling, and perhaps infectious disease and he stuck by him nevertheless to the last. Mr Blaikie, we understand, died in his arms. He then takes the widow home to his house . . . "

Mrs Blaikie gave birth to a daughter twelve hours after her husband was buried. The *True Sun* went on to admit that

> the writer of this article has had occasion, in the course of his life, to differ much with Mr Jerdan and to be differed with by him. All idea of ill-will has long been done away, we trust, on either side, from a knowledge that on neither side was there any real ill-blood. But an instance of genuine feeling like this, with or without the numerous testimonies we have heard to this gentleman's natural kind-heartedness, places him at once, we beg leave to say, in a high rank in our respect ... Mr Jerdan, in all probability, is not exempt from the trouble common to most of us, he has assuredly this consolation within him – that he must believe in the existence of what is good and kind, because he has it in his own heart.

The author of the article was possibly Laman Blanchard who was writing for the *True Sun* at this time. Jerdan had put himself in danger by his kindness to Blaikie. A day or so later a mutual friend, a fine young man from Aberdeen, came to Grove House at 10 in the morning, to accompany Jerdan to Blaikie's funeral. He looked ill, and Jerdan suggested he go home and call for a doctor. By five in the afternoon the young man was dead. A bereavement closer to Jerdan occurred at Grove House on 6 December 1832 when his sister Agnes, who had been staying with him, died at the age of 58.

Even disasters such as cholera did not halt Jerdan's enemies from making opportunities to attack him. The *Age*, which had long had Jerdan as its target, also disliked the exclusive Garrick Club and its members. They created their own tid-bit of scandal, reporting that Mr D lost his black gloves at the Garrick. "Mr D begs further to observe that Mr Jerdan has lately adopted black gloves. He used not to wear any."[74] A petty matter, but another stone to add to the mountain of scandal that attached to Jerdan over the years.

Still occasionally active in the Society of Antiquarians, Jerdan exhibited a drawing and impression of a seal found in a field near Winchester; it was a stamp for woollen cloths for Southampton, dating from the time of Edward III.[75] He would have been amused to see that in May 1832 the always irreverent *Fraser's Magazine* bestowed upon "The Antiquaries" the honour of a place in their 'Gallery of Literary Characters'. Maginn, who was the author of the long-running feature, referred to a sketch by Croquis (pseudonym of Maclise) depicting the Society of Antiquaries at their meetings, having dispensed with business, enjoying their cakes and coffee. "Here stand and sit the A.S.S.es, great and small, long and short; in witness whereof behold the lengthy Jerdan, peering through his glass at every thing and person around him; while the five-feet noth-ingness of Crofty Croker has taken up a position under Jerdan's elbow, sipping his coffee in the blessed unconsciousness of the fairyhood of his situation." (See illustration no. 5.) The rest of the article was in the same vein, noting, for instance, "Why the Society has two secretaries, is a question that has been asked in these reforming times. The necessity is obvious — because one can't read, and the other can't write." For a popular journal to select such a subject throws an interesting light upon the level of public interest in, and awareness of, the learned societies, which could not be emulated today.

Having been baulked at the beginning of the year in his wish to become a Magistrate, Jerdan turned his attention to other public matters. In October he was approached to offer his services to the Scott Committee, formed to memorialise the great novelist who had died the previous month. He replied enthusiastically:

The meeting which has so promptly and patriotically undertaken to devise the best means of testifying the national sense of our lamented loss in Sir Walter Scott, having done me the honour to invite my humble co-operation, I beg to say that I shall enter with very strong feelings into every plan for the promotion of this object. I lived on friendly terms with my immortal Countryman, and my family with his family; and I consequently have a deep private sympathy added to my sense of a public duty on this mournful occasion.[76]

✌︎13✌︎

Financial Ruin

Given Jerdan's fascination with shows of all kinds, and particularly the theatre, it was natural that he should first admire and then befriend the great tragic actor of the day, William Charles Macready. An Irishman without a sense of humour, he was ill-tempered and "had a hearty and ill-concealed contempt for his calling".[1] Macready crossed swords with his rival actor Charles Kemble who, in 1822, took over Covent Garden Theatre and moved in 1823 to Drury Lane. His failings were to give "far too much rein to over-sensitiveness and a disposition to manufacture grievances". As time went on he did not need to manufacture the grievances he had against Jerdan; he had all too much reason for them. Macready entered into a long-running battle with Alfred Bunn, the stage manager at Drury Lane, which had been taken over in 1831 by a Captain Frederick Polhill. The vendetta against Bunn played out in Macready's Diaries which commenced in 1833.

In May of that year Macready received a visit from Thomas Gaspey, an acquaintance of Jerdan's, and occasional contributor to the *Literary Gazette*. Gaspey warned Macready of "Jerdan's habit of laying his friends under contribution"; this warning was "kind but needless", Macready noted, and was to come to wish he had listened more carefully. In August 1833 he dined with Jerdan at the Garrick, and they went together to the Victoria Theatre; he invited Jerdan to visit him at his country home at Elstree the following week.

Jerdan's friend Edward Bulwer was instrumental in getting a Bill passed in Parliament to establish copyright for drama. In light-hearted mood, Jerdan wrote as 'Teutha' from the Garrick Club, making fun of the politician:

> The Drama: A Squib
> Bulwer, my friend, you've framed a bill –
> I fear 'tis all bow-wow –
> To regulate the Drama's course,
> For where's the Drama now?

To Covent Garden should you pass,
The doors are shut, I vow,
And all the actors sent to grass,
So where's the Drama now?

And more, thirteen verses in all.[2]

Jerdan's private life was changing as Landon had been seeing John Forster, editor of *The Examiner*, later biographer of Charles Dickens and Walter Savage Landor. He was ten years younger than Landon, and somewhat of a social climber. L.E.L. was the perfect wife to complement his ambitions, and they eventually became engaged. Jerdan liked Forster and it is impossible to know what his feelings were upon hearing this news. The engagement triggered a revival of the old scandals. Landon's name was linked with Jerdan and also, as before, with Maginn, Maclise and Bulwer Lytton. There was further scandal concerning letters from Landon. Maginn's biographer explained what had transpired:[3]

> Finally, it is said, Mr Forster received in a blank envelope, several letters written by L.E.L. addressed to Dr Maginn, familiarly commencing with the words 'My dearest William' and written in a tone of affectionate friendship which the quick jealousy of a lover interpreted as confirming the worst report which anonymous slander had breathed into his mind . . . in a paroxysm of rage and suspicion Mr Forster enclosed the letter to L.E.L., with one line saying that they were 'parted for ever', that the love-epistles which he had sent back explained why.

Forster had been sent these letters by Maginn's wife in a fit of pique when she discovered them in her husband's desk. She confessed her action to Forster and believed that she had wronged Landon, but by then it was too late to remedy the situation.

Another variation of what happened suggested by a biographer of Bulwer, was that Maginn wrote several anonymous letters to Landon's friends, accusing her of being the mistress of a married man.[4] She was, of course, but Jerdan was not the married man rumour lit upon, but Maginn himself who, in the 1830s, was living contentedly with his wife. Maginn had a history of baiting Bulwer in *Fraser's*, and in the *Age*, quite probably with the connivance of Westmacott. His hatred of Bulwer may have arisen from his perception that Landon had rejected his own advances, whilst being intimate with Bulwer and his wife, and the anonymous letters were his revenge upon her.

Maginn was widely considered brilliant, but fatally flawed in his love of drink and women. Certainly, S.C. Hall clearly despised him, saying that "A man less likely to have gained the affections of any woman could not easily have been found. To say nothing of his being a married man – dirty in his dress and habits, revolting in manners, and rarely sober, he might have been pointed out as one from whom a woman of refinement would have turned with loathing rather than have approached with love."[5] In further vindication of Landon's behaviour, Hall published her letter to his wife, vehemently attacking Mrs Maginn as spiteful for accusing Landon of having written twenty-four love letters to Maclise, and of "sheer envy, operating upon a weak, vulgar, but cunning nature".[6] Landon utterly denied any wrongdoing with Maginn, claiming to have been so afraid of him that she had to force herself to be civil.

When the rumours reached the ears of John Forster, he asked Landon to refute the stories. She told him to ask her friends for their opinion. He did so, and was satisfied as to her innocence, at which point Landon broke off their engagement. Her friend Laman Blanchard later printed her letter to Forster in which she said she could not allow him to marry a woman whose honour had been called into question – it would not be fair to him. Blanchard approved of this sentiment, calling it "the self-sacrifice she deemed herself called on by duty to make".[7] This was the reason that was allowed to circulate as to why the engagement was at an end. However, privately Landon wrote to her good friend Edward Bulwer in a very different tone:

> If his future protection is to harass and humiliate me as much as his present – God keep me from it – I cannot get over the entire want of delicacy to me which could repeat such slander to myself. The whole of his late conduct to me personally has left behind almost dislike – certainly fear of his imperious and overbearing temper. I am sure we could never be happy together.[8]

This tone of self-righteous indignation would be amusing, given the known facts of her affair, were it not yet another of Landon's masks, hiding the truth, maybe even from herself. From a perspective of time it seems rather odd that she broke her engagement to a highly respectable, suitable man whom she must at least have liked initially, thus necessitating continuing the hard-working, fairly Spartan life she was leading. However, taking the measure of the man and her times, she could never have divulged to him the existence of her children, having once convinced him of her innocence and purity. If the truth became known and she was one day exposed as their mother, it would have created a situation untenable both for her and for Forster.

Katherine Thomson remembered that following the break-up of the engagement Landon became "morbid, desperate, hopeless . . . Happily, her friend, her first friend Mr Jerdan and his daughters, did not forsake her on account of the coarse and cruel manner in which the name of L.E.L. had been traduced on his account. They were devoted to her to the last."[9] Was Thomson really as hood-winked as she appeared to be, or was the passing reference to Jerdan's daughters a way of hiding what she knew of the illicit relationship behind a cloak of respectability?

In this year Landon wrote a short story called "The Head", which highlighted the unwritten rules of fashionable society where it was tacitly accepted that a married woman may have lovers without the slightest intention of giving up her wealth and position to run away with them. The frustrated lover in Landon's story groans "Curse on these social laws! Which are made for the convenience of the few and the degradation of the many."[10] That was the crucial difference which bedevilled Landon: she was not a married woman, but a single, independent, professional woman, for whom it was unthinkable to take even one lover, let alone more.

Her real and putative lovers crossed swords in April 1833. As a critic, Jerdan tried always to be kind and positive, especially towards the work of colleagues and associates. It must then have been difficult for him to write to Richard Bentley concerning an anonymous new novel *Godolphin* which was by Edward Bulwer, although Jerdan may have only suspected this when he wrote his letter:

> Finding it impossible to meet your idea of Godolphin, I was most reluctantly compelled to omit the Review of it yesterday. A work of great talent it unquestionably is; but the able author has taken a wrong and perverted twist, which infects his whole story, and spoils what, with a sounder view, would have done credit to any writer now living.
>
> I am very sorry for this on every ground; and especially because I am sure that what springs from private and individual feeling will scarcely meet with general success. It is impossible indeed to make other characters and the action of a fiction conform to such a feeling; and this induces inconsistency throughout. I look upon Godolphin therefore altogether to be the mistake of a person as capable of writing successfully as any of our time.[11]

This was a hard-hitting critique, particularly since Bulwer had six earlier novels published, several, including *Pelham*, being best-sellers. He was to be hailed the following year by the *American Quarterly Review* as "without doubt, the most popular writer now living".[12] The faults Jerdan found in *Godolphin* were ones Bulwer knew himself. Having been the target of furious attacks by Maginn, Thackeray and others for his previous book *Eugene Aram*, which made a hero out of a murderer, *Godolphin* was published anonymously. Jerdan, or possibly Landon, reviewed it in the *Literary Gazette* of 11 May, in similar vein to his letter to Bentley, devoting in all five and a half columns to comment and extracts. Other periodicals gave it a lukewarm reception, even the *New Monthly Magazine* of which Bulwer himself was editor. The strain of vituperation and the consequences of his huge output of writings over the past decade told on

Bulwer's health. In the summer he resigned from the editorship of the *New Monthly Magazine* and travelled with his wife to Italy in an attempt to save their marriage, after his indiscreet liaison with a society beauty. How Jerdan must sometimes have envied Bulwer's economic independence, to be able to relinquish his duties so easily, relying confidently on the income that his writing brought him, as well as hoping that his mother would eventually accept his marriage, and thus raise expectations of his family connections.

A clue that Jerdan was not as happy as he could be is found in a letter from his old family friends Ellen and John Carne. They wrote thanking Jerdan for his kindness, sending warm wishes to Mrs Jerdan, Agnes and Mary, inviting them again to visit Cornwall. Their letter hoped for Jerdan "much more happiness than you have at present be your portion".[13] The unhappiness to which they referred could have been caused by the ongoing rumours about Landon and her imminent engagement, or more probably, the rough time he was getting from the gutter press. The Carnes's letter indicates that on family matters nothing was amiss – Frances and the daughters were still at home in Grove House.

Jerdan was embattled on another front besides his association with Bentley. He was still in financial trouble and received a terse letter from Longmans who had been approached by Twinings for one hundred and twenty-five pounds Jerdan owed to them.[14] Jerdan had made an agreement to pay the bank but had not complied, and Longmans warned him that they would have to release the funds unless he did so himself. Five days later Longmans told him that as he had not replied, the money had been paid to Twinings.[15] This sum was presumably added to the advances already made to Jerdan. Another probable cause for Jerdan's unhappiness was the continual struggle to keep control of the *Literary Gazette* as he fought against interference from his partners and from Richard Bentley, who wanted him to "puff" their productions, and even to dictate the placement of important reviews. In June he had occasion to protest to Bentley:

> As you have departed from the old and wonted course which you assured me you would always follow, it is less in my power to do all I could wish in regard to your publications. But you may rely upon it, I shall ever be happy to do my best for you; tho' I decline running in common and equal harness with inferior periodicals – you must see that it would not do for the Gazette at its price to have too much of the same external features and appearance as the cheaper papers. I perceive today how right I was in not putting Beckford first review; but in all these matters I wish to be clearly understood – I object to nothing done for others to wean them from the system of attack and abuse which a publisher might fear; nor do I court any favour for myself. My course under every circumstance is unbiased and founded on principles not to be shaken; only I must shape it somewhat differently as the case requires.[16]

A few months later Jerdan again complained to Bentley, "I must also repeat my other standing objection to be made the organ of common communications – it wd destroy the whole character and power of the Gazette to serve you and any one; by showing that it was the vehicle of the opinions of others and not of its own unbiased judgment."[17] Jerdan did not anticipate these private letters becoming public, so he was not grand-standing his repeated claims of independence. When he came to write his *Autobiography* twenty years later, such claims were for public consumption and for posterity, and were only to be expected. His private correspondence therefore is more convincing, setting out the ethos as to how he believed the *Literary Gazette* should be conducted.

A new magazine, the *National Standard*, burst upon the scene in January 1833. Jerdan warned of " cheap periodicals" in *Literary Gazette* articles even before it appeared. Its price was two pence. The front page of the first issue of the *Standard* noted sententiously that it "contained the same quantity of material as the eight-pence *Literary Gazette* and considerably more matter than the fourpence *Athenaeum*". On an inside page, Thomas Hood made Jerdan and Dilke figures of fun, portraying them as desperately anxious about the new competition:

Jerdan, for instance, has been crying before our office door: aye, actually dropping
 An Editor's Tear

Before the door he stood
To take his first sad look
At the page as large as his *Gazette*,
And the *twopence* in the nook.
He paused till "*Oh how cheap*," grew quite
Familiar to his ear,
Then thought of eight-pence for his own,
And wiped away a tear.

Beside that office door
Poor Dilke was on his knees,
He held an *Athenaeum* sheet,
That fluttered in the breeze.
He cried out "That can never last,
It's cheaper than this here," –
But when men shouted "*Yes, it will*"
He wiped away a tear.

They turned to leave the spot,
Yes, Jerdan did – and Dilke,
Both saying that, "a sow's ear next

Would make a purse of silk."
Go – wait another month or two,
You'll find it pretty clear,
That when we talk of our success,
They'll wipe away a tear.

The first editor of the *National Standard* was F.W.N. Bayley; five months after it began, the paper was bought by Thackeray and lasted only until February 1834 when Thackeray was confronted by financial disasters. Jerdan and Dilke had the last laugh, this time.

Jerdan used the *Literary Gazette* as a platform for various campaigns, one of which was a fight against the building of the National Gallery in Trafalgar Square, "the perpetration of which unseemly job I in vain endeavoured to prevent, brought on a fracas and complaints and hostilities of a rather bitter description", he said.[18] He ran a determined campaign, setting out several cogent reasons for objecting to the proposed building. He approved, at least, of the site:"The site assigned is most eligible; with every local capability, central, convenient and obvious to view."[19] But, he thought, such a public building should "stand single and alone in grandeur and grace, rather than see it cabined, cribbed, confined – a masked battery for soldiery, with gateways through which to debouch, should occasion require it".[20] Moreover, the dirty London air would ruin the pictures. A serious objection was the capacity of the proposed building to house the national art collection; no extension was possible with the barracks on one side and a poor house in the rear. This would surely discourage future benefactors from leaving collections to the National Gallery. Wilkins's building would partially obscure the church of St. Martin's, cutting in half the view of it from Pall Mall. The Royal Academy which, under the present proposal, would be housed in the middle of the National Gallery, should "be placed where it ought to be, by itself; it gives up, it is said, the worth of £50,000 in Somerset House, and ought in return to have an adequate provision made for it. Do not let us drivel away our means and our character together for a worthless folly, and lose this almost last chance of excellence by niggardly dabbling in fantastic theories."[21] The architecture itself came in for damning criticism; Wilkins's "pure Greek" style may not be suitable in London.

The difference between a Grecian plain and Charing Cross; between an ever-bright sky and our smoky atmosphere; between insulation and architectural confusion, does not seem to have been considered in a theory which would bend every thing to an idea of abstract grace. Mr Wilkins's other buildings, Downing College Cambridge, the London University and St. Georges Hospital, are samples – the new work will be the least elevated of them all.[22]

Various changes were made to the design, some of which answered Jerdan's complaints. By September, Jerdan admitted that he was beaten: "Wilkins's Greek job . . . IS ACTUALLY IN PROGRESS". He followed up with a dozen reasons why "We lament" this decision, "but above all, we lament it on account of its being done in the face of the disapprobation of the country, of every man of taste and judgment in art and after the blinding mock discussion in the House of Commons, in order to get the vote of a sum of money upon other provisos and pretences . . . but complaint seems useless as a reason and we shall only add a pithy quotation: IT IS TOO BAD!"[23]

Better-qualified men than Jerdan also objected to the design of the Gallery; Pugin and Cockerell wrote against it "as the epitome of a debased and demoralized architecture".[24] The Gallery did expand however, when the barracks and the poor house were demolished, and in 1869 the Royal Academy found another home in Burlington House and in 1895 the National Portrait Gallery moved to its own building. The National Gallery itself, both as an institution and a building, has a long and detailed history,[25] the latest incarnation being Prince Charles's rejection in 2004 of the proposed extension as "a monstrous carbuncle on the face of a much-loved and elegant friend", in favour of what is now known as the Sainsbury Wing, an addition which would surely have earned Jerdan's renewed disapproval.

Jerdan never allowed himself to be so distracted that he forgot his charitable interests. The Literary Fund continued its work of donations to needy writers, but still came under occasional attack. One writer, R. H. Horne, asked in 1833 whether it had enabled anyone to write a fine work, and wondered how many 'men of genius' had been relieved from distress. It was not the Fund's purpose to sponsor literary works, "though in fact it did so on several occasions . . . the Literary Fund had given grants to some twenty men and women of distinction and at least six hundred other authors, and was to recognize Horne's own literary merit by granting him a total of £430 in his declining years".[26] Reviewing Horne's work *Exposition of False Medium and Barriers Excluding Men of Genius* in which his accusation was made, Jerdan had taken the trouble to consult the Fund's records and could refute Horne's allegation in the case of a Mr Heron in 1807. The Fund was flourishing, and had increased its bounties; "were it possible for its presence to be generally known, there would be found very many cases of such exquisite misery turned into joy and gladness as would shame all the invented pathos of romance, and we are convinced, excite thousands to contribute to the increase of so patriotic, so interesting and so nobly benevolent a resource, where the destitute and deserving never seek help in vain and where judgment and pity ever go hand in hand in lifting up the oppressed and saving the broken-hearted."[27] Jerdan's evident passion for the Literary Fund clearly overrode his objectivity in assessing the worth of Horne's work, although in line with his usual practice of being "fair" gave the book (which was dedicated to Bulwer), three instalments in the *Literary Gazette*.

Jerdan was always alert for those in real need, and claimed to send to the Literary Fund any monies received by the *Literary Gazette* incorrectly. "From this source frequent and considerable subscriptions were derived."[28] He cited £50 from the Marquis of Normanby and £67 from the well-known novelist G.P.R. James as Jerdan's fee for negotiating the sale of some manuscripts for publication.[29] He related an anecdote in which he met an old man, feeble and poorly clothed, walking near Grove House. Touched, Jerdan spoke to him and proferred half a crown, which was declined. The shabby old man turned out to be wealthy, and thenceforward donated £20 annually to the Literary Fund because of Jerdan's kindness and his connection to the Fund.

Even whilst revelling in the good living and parties at Grove House, Jerdan was still painfully aware of others' poverty. He heard of a sad case just nearby and, on visiting the writer who had produced some creditable work, found him sitting stupefied, a dead three-year old in a corner, and the mother with another child on a makeshift bed on the floor. Jerdan immediately arranged for the child's burial, for the family to get food, and for the rent arrears to be paid. In such a case he conceded that those who criticized the Literary Fund for giving too little too late were right. He gave this man some assistance for years, horribly aware that he could not fill the needs of all penniless writers. Such straits were painful to behold, and strengthened the view that became a theme of his memoirs, that writing was a chancy business and could not be relied upon for a living.

In January 1834 Jerdan began a series of eleven articles on "The Publishing Trade". His main target was the Society for the Diffusion of Useful Knowledge and its "Superintending Committee" whose Chairman was the Lord Chancellor; the list of its members featured many in exalted public office. Jerdan's first front-page article drew on support from Colburn's other journal, the *New Monthly Magazine* which had dealt with the same matter in its January issue. Jerdan attacked the current "low estate" of literature and the cheap publication of compilations and "monthly epitomes of every sort" in which "the beauty of the arts, and the utility, not to say the dignity of letters, are utterly sacrificed". What really upset him though, was the "false pretence" of the Society. The Committee of "high names" raised subscriptions for the Society's range of publications "(Almanacs, Magazines, Cookery, History, Penny Cyclopaedias etc.)" under the guise of diffusing useful knowledge among the poorer classes of the people. Jerdan insisted that this was "a shameful violation of just principles, a gross invasion of private property, and an odious monopoly most injurious to the true interests of learning and the freedom of the press". He challenged the notion that the men on the Committee actually "superintended" any of the publications, asking rhetorically if the Lord Chancellor's official duties could be neglected so as to oversee fourpenny maps and tenpenny portraits. He believed "the whole matter is fallacy and fudge; that they have not even seen the works sanctioned by their names". Moreover, in addition to this deception, Jerdan stated that such public officials "have no right to impose upon the people by lending their names to subterfuge and falsehood . . . Is it proper that the highest dignitaries of the law and state should be at the head of a publishing club?"

Jerdan's article then turned to the old question of puffing, listing examples which were designed, he said, to mislead the public and ultimately to disappoint purchasers of the books so puffed. He deplored "the new method of manufac-turing books merely for the ready market of the day", the pursuit of profit with no regard for the quality of information or content. Promotion of the worth-less, he maintained, shut out the worthy. "They load the public with the poor and injurious production of the venal and profligate, while they exclude from the press such works as would improve the age, and reflect an honour upon our national literature." In a direct attack on Colburn, with his staff of paid "puff" writers, Jerdan made a pointed reference to "the clever project of having a band of hacks in regular pay, organised to tell readers what they ought to think of other hacks also in regular pay – the aforesaid hacks, as need arose, changing places at a wave of the conjuror's *golden* wand . . . ".

The remaining articles in the series of "The Publishing Trade" expounded at greater length on the matters set out in the first. Jerdan looked back and claimed some credit for the *Literary Gazette* "for having, in a considerable degree, checked the career of what were miscalled *fashionable novels*, of which not one in forty ought ever to have affronted the public taste and judgment". Jerdan was not against dissemination of knowledge, whether useful or merely entertaining, but in these articles he insisted that books should be of a high standard, other-wise they were

> proportionately injurious to the growth of human intellect . . . when we begin with inaccuracy and trumpery, the desire created is for the same sort of ignorance and trifling; the readers have made no real acquisition to their means of comfort or enjoyment, and having only learnt what is wrong, the end, instead of improvement, is dissatisfaction; instead of content, presumption; instead of moral and religious truth, restlessness of disposition, and vicious indulgence.

Jerdan's agenda was to raise awareness of the low standard of the books put out by unscrupulous publishers, in which he included the Society for the Diffusion of Useful Knowledge, as being interested solely in profit, but under the cloak of educating the poor. Henry Vizetelly agreed with him saying that the Society was "bent upon teaching the working classes something of every-thing, if not everything of something".[30] Jerdan accused the Society of being a monopoly with unwarranted power to injure fair booksellers and publishers, "(individual competition forming the mass of national wealth and prosperity)"; he reproduced a letter which had appeared in *The Times*, asking Lord Brougham the Lord Chancellor and Chairman of the Society, to consider his position should the Society face an injunction for literary piracy – as many of their compilations merely copied from other works without acknowledgement. The Chairman would have to defend the Society before the Lord Chancellor – that is, himself. Jerdan called upon these "eminent men" to resign from their book-selling concern and "leave the publishing trade as they found it, open". The following week he listed those who had left the Committee since its inception and those who remained.

He then turned his fire on to another Society which, thinking the Useful Knowledge diffused by the first one was not sufficiently religious, formed The Society for Promoting Christian Knowledge, supported by voluntary contributions. Jerdan called this "unwarrantable competition", the contributions paying for printing and publishing religious tracts and bibles, risking the funds subscribed, and by implication, taking work from genuine publishers and booksellers. In an effort to be fair, Jerdan printed a letter supporting cheap reprints of original old books, which would otherwise be beyond the reach of most people's pockets. He had no objection to this type of cheap publication but every objection to piracy and plagiarism. He devoted his fifth article to this, naming works so pirated. So that there should be no misunderstanding his reasoning, he clarified "It is the principle which we denounce and reprobate. We care not one farthing for any publisher existing; but it is unjust to every private interest, unfavourable to the pursuits of literature, and injurious to the country, that these scandalous monopolies should be established and supported under false pretence."

In the seventh of his series, Jerdan reproduced extracts from "The Printing Machine: a Review for the Many", an attempted rebuttal by the Society for the Diffusion of Useful Knowledge against his earlier articles. He selected their attack on the *Literary Gazette*'s own position as a "cheap paper", to which Jerdan parried that "Dearness and cheapness are not merely comparative but convertible terms. One sheet may be dear at a penny – another cheap at half a crown. It is the merits, not the bulk of periodicals, that we contend for . . . " He held their detailed accusations to ridicule, letting them be hung by their own words, generously conceding, "To be sure it is but bread and water after all; but then consider the quantity – as much as you can drink and all for the small sum of One Penny."

The fight became personal, Jerdan accusing the writers for the Society of being careless of "one grand element of knowledge – namely, Truth". He spoke highly of Charles Knight, publisher of "The Printing Machine" and of most of the Society's works, absolving him from the errors and untruths of the other writers. If they had only asked Knight's opinion, Jerdan said, they would have avoided "some of their negligent or wilful misrepresentations". The *Literary Gazette* had been accused of encouraging young, and sometimes indifferent writers, a charge to which Jerdan pleaded guilty; his "leaning was decidedly to cherish the youthful to higher efforts . . . Our chiefest boast is having done precisely what is here alleged as a fault." He confronted other criticisms in the same tone of patient explanation, ending by repeating his core philosophy, from which he did not waver his whole life: "truth and kindness and mercy are the best canons of criticism."

Jerdan was sensitive to the allegation in "The Printing Machine" that because of the vast numbers of new books pouring off the presses, it was impossible for a weekly periodical to offer a valuable criticism, joking that it was like sticking a bodkin into a ham and smelling it to see if the meat was cooked – a joke reflecting the one from his detractors, that Jerdan cut the pages of a new book with a paper knife and smelled it for the book's contents. He vigorously refuted such allegations, turning the attack towards the "essay writing" of the monthly and quarterly reviews, and insisting that if there were "more of mere judicious reporting, in every periodical devoted to these pursuits, we should deem it a very essential gain and benefit to the public". He had read three hundred pages of a review, he complained, without learning anything about the book it purported to discuss.

Stung by the suggestion that his attacks on the cheap mass productions of the publishing societies were in effect support of a "tax on knowledge" Jerdan was crystal clear:

> The Literary Gazette is, and has ever been, as warm and sincere an advo-
> cate as the Penny Magazine for the unlimited instruction of every class
> of the people. We hold education to be the staff of life to the mind, as
> much as bread itself is the staff of life to the body; and we should as soon
> think of desiring the former to be stinted as the latter. God forbid that
> we should do either!

It was the quality of mass publishing he decried, and even more, the self-congrat-ulation of those eminent men who promulgated it. It was not because of the cheapness of the publications "that we dislike them; but because they are BAD".

His final article in this series on "The Publishing Trade" was in April, and noted that the articles had made people realize the dangers of the "inferiority . . . like an insidious weed [which has] been creeping over the fair and fruitful class of literature". Dismissing the old chestnut that the *Literary Gazette* always gave Colburn's books undeserving praise, Jerdan said that he was not going to defend all Colburn's novels, but that along with "the many bad ones, he also published many of the best in our day", and reminded readers that the *Literary*

Gazette's reviews of the bad ones had driven Colburn to take a share in the *Athenaeum.*

The whole series of Jerdan's articles can be taken as his creed for the publishing industry at the time, for his personal philosophy, and even for his political views. Some points were personal, like his grievance against the "worthies" of a subscription body who did not, as they claimed, superintend the works put out in their name. Other arguments he made were clearly deeply felt and genuine, but with hindsight read like the protests of a man embattled against the oncoming tide.

Whilst he was formulating his campaign against the societies, Landon was preparing for a visit overseas. She asked Jerdan to approach Bentley "in the most forcible light" for an advance; she planned to set her next novel "in Paris during the latter end of the Revolution" and needed local colour.[31] She wanted new ideas and to escape for a while from money worries. Only a very few letters between Landon and Jerdan seem to have survived, and most of those that have are printed by Jerdan in his *Autobiography*. They are from Landon on her trip to Paris in the summer of 1834 and from their often affectionate and playful tone indicate the close relationship between the two correspondents who, if they were no longer in the throes of a sexual relationship, were still good friends and colleagues. Jerdan's alleged rationale for printing these missives was the interest of comparing his own trip to Paris in 1814 to the city Landon was experiencing twenty years later and his *Autobiography* was written almost twenty years after that. However, whereas Jerdan's writings from Paris had been extensive journal- istic observations, destined for daily publication in the *Sun* newspaper of which he was then editor, Landon's letters are chiefly concerned with herself, and her trials and disappointments in the city. Jerdan, clearly blinded by emotion, calls her correspondence "sprightly pictures", not noticing how self-centred they are.

Landon had decided to visit Paris for three reasons, she told Jerdan: scenes from her next novel were set there and it would be helpful to see the city for herself; she needed fresh ideas, and also needed a change of scene as relief from her money worries. She acquired as companion a Miss Turin, many years her senior and of independent means. "We parted on Thursday," she reminded him, "though not at all too soon, much as I regretted it. You cannot think how I missed you. I really thought the morning would never pass."[32] Taking to her bed, exhausted by the crossing, she recovered sufficiently to confess that "The sun has scorched my face to such a hideous degree – forehead, nose and cheeks are all a 'lively crimson' and swelled till I do not know myself in the glass." Signing off, she sent regards to her friends, "and hoping that you are missing me very much". Despite Jerdan's self-consciously offering "an excuse for the tone of reliance on me in regard to literary projects and business which had not lessened with the passage of time", the feelings in this first letter are entirely personal and warm.

Keeping Jerdan informed at every step of her journey, Landon wrote again the moment she arrived in Paris, confessing "Never was there a worse traveller!" Ever worried about the cost of letters, Landon warned Jerdan, "Be sure, wafer, and thin paper." Even publishing these letters so long after they were written, Jerdan was embarrassed about Landon's penny-pinching: "In the second letter of the same day there is a terrible economising about franks and postage – evidently concerns of no small weight . . . "[33] In this note she wished she could send letters via the ambassador's bag, and thus avoid the two-franc cost and the trek to the post office. Paris was looking better to her, now that she had recovered from the journey: "How much I like the avenues. They were so crowded, the people looking so gay; but Paris is very empty . . . "These apparently contradictory observations referred to the usual French habit of the aristocracy and upper classes, her natural habitat, leaving the city in the summer – the crowds that were left behind being the lower and working classes, with whom Landon did not socialize.

The next letter that Jerdan kept for posterity was again very concerned about the cost of postage, castigating him for including a copy of the *Literary Gazette* with his letter. She tried to smuggle home a decorative waistcoat as a gift for Jerdan, wearing it under her clothes, but at Dover was "stript to the skin" and the gift, with other items, was confiscated. Even whilst visiting the Louvre and strolling in the Tuileries, business was never far from Landon's mind. She told Jerdan that she thought interesting papers might be written on modern French authors, and would need to buy some to do the work. She was missing him more than usual, as this letter was signed "Your affectionate . . . " instead of the more common "Yours truly . . . "

Taking advantage of sending letters with an acquaintance leaving for London the next day, Landon recounted for Jerdan an incident which amused her. Heinrich Heine called and she took a while, she said, to conquer her shyness in speaking with a stranger. By way of conversation he asked her how she amused herself in Paris: had she been shopping? No. To the Jardin des Plantes? No. The opera? Theatres? No. Taken a walk? No. Read a great deal, or written, perhaps? No. But Mademoiselle, he asked in despair, what have you done? "I looked out of the window" was all she could manage. "Was there ever anything *si bete*?" she asked Jerdan. Quickly, Landon was back to business, telling him that a "most delightful series of articles" could be written on French literature, which "would require an immense deal of softening and adaptation to suit it to English taste".

Another note berated Jerdan for not sending her the *Literary Gazette* and for not writing to her. She named several people who called on her, and invited her out to various entertainments, but nevertheless "it is impossible for me to go out by myself, or accept the attendance of any gentleman alone, so that I am surrounded with all sorts of little difficulties and embarrassments". For a strong-minded independent woman who had a life of her own in London where everyone knew her, these claims to be so helpless sound false, as if she were both assuring Jerdan that she was behaving herself and showing herself as incapable of functioning without him. Jerdan seemed to have been a little envious of the good time he suspected she was having, despite her frequent complaints; she assured him "You seem very much to over-rate my gaiety".

She saw a giraffe for the first time, describing it to Jerdan as "if nature had been making two creatures at once, and not having time to finish both, joined them together in a hurry, being about as well matched as marriages in general". This could be construed as an oblique reference to her broken engagement to John Forster, or to Jerdan's own marriage. He appended a footnote commenting on this analogy, saying "Unequal marriages are, it is true, seldom happy, but some-times those which appear to be equal at the outset, turn out no better." Although he followed this with an amusing little illustrative anecdote, he could well be referring to his own union with Frances, with whom he had shared a life for nearly thirty years.

In a business-like letter which she requested he read "with all due attention", Landon enthused about her project of translating "with judgement" French liter-ature, proposing to make an annual consisting entirely of translations of French prose and verse. She was aware of the costs involved in such a production, proposing to use existing prints on general subjects, rather than commissioning new ones to illustrate the book. She asked Jerdan to find her a publisher, as she could be ready in six weeks. Closer to her heart, he had not overwhelmed her with instant praise on her newest work. "How odd you should tell me that you had read the end of *Francesca*, and not say what you think of it. How can you justify such an omission?"

Landon's second novel, a historical romance, *Francesca Carrara* had just been published in three volumes by Bentley. According to Jerdan she earned £300 for this book. The *Literary Gazette* mentioned first the recent proliferation of novels, then moved on to Landon's earlier work, *Romance and Reality*, described here as [though] "deficient in connected story, is a sparkling and brilliant performance". In the new work "the fair writer, however, has evinced a still more perfect command of her subject. The story is sufficiently involved, continuous, marked by incident and full of deep interest". The review also noted that "we have never perused a more varied, excellent and delightful production".[34] These vague generic terms are far from Jerdan's usual florid praise of Landon's work and may reflect the distance he felt between them, and was the reason why he did not comment on the book in his letters to Landon.

Landon's constant complaints did not, at least in retrospect, irritate Jerdan. Instead, he declared that her letter

affords an idea of that feature of character which is often painted in her poetry; an excess of feminine timidity which, much as it might distress her and intensely as it might long for protection, yet ever led her rather to suffer absolute agony, than trouble, or encroach upon the good offices of others; for though she was as complete a coward as could be imagined, (and often suffered in great concerns and small, from want of common resolution,) the asking or accepting of an ordinary civility, which would have averted the evil, was a difficulty which, I suppose, none but splendid female poltroons could account for.[35]

He seemed to relish the notion of Landon as a martyr to her feminine sensibilities, especially as she had turned down his offer to come across the Channel to escort her home, on the grounds that it would not be prudent. Did it strike him as comic that she worried about this, at such a late stage of their relationship? He could, she allowed, meet her at the Dover customs house. She had second thoughts, though, and her final letter before departure told him "You quite misunderstood what I said about coming to Boulogne. As regarded myself, it is both a convenience and a pleasure. I spoke entirely with reference to yourself, and if I see you there, I shall be as glad as it is possible to be." It is not known whether Jerdan did come to meet Landon at Boulogne or, more likely, at Dover, but that he proposed to take the time to do so indicates a continuing close friendship, if nothing more.

These few letters from Paris are the only indication of Landon's easy, familiar communication with Jerdan, the consequence of a secret affair over twelve years. Their very familiarity suggests that the relationship was ongoing. Clearly, the letters meant a great deal to Jerdan, notorious for losing papers and even his own writings, as he kept them safe for nearly twenty years until he came to write his *Autobiography*. He explained why:

I have no comment to offer on these natural and unaffected reminiscences. To my mind they combine the wonderfully mixed qualities of every-day sense and observation, the peculiarities of sex, the love of nature and the beautiful in all things, the playfulness of fancy, and the innate charm of genius. Out of them I, at least, can re-create a vivid portrait of the lamented writer.[36]

But there may well have been more than friendship at this time, despite the interruption of Landon's engagement to Forster. In *Unpublished Letters of Lady Bulwer Lytton to A. E. Chalon* in 1914 was a letter concerning an incident in the mid-1830s, told from a perspective of twenty years after the event.

According to Rosina's husband, 'that loathsome satyr, old Jerdan, in one of his drunken fits at some dinner let out all his liaison with Miss Landon and gave her name coupled with some disgusting toast.' Rosina Bulwer Lytton says that she then warned Landon not to admit Jerdan, and Landon promised not to, but not long afterwards, making a surprise visit to the poet's room at the boarding house, she found 'Miss Landon on old Jerdan's knee, with her arm around his neck!' This moved her to end her long friendship with Landon. No one has ever paid much attention to the allegations made in her letter to Chalon.[37]

However, it has been noted that by the time this letter was written, Rosina "was so far gone in hysterical loathing of Bulwer and everything connected with him, that to throw filth at his friends had become a form of indulgence of her hatred of himself".[38] Rosina's hatred for Jerdan was an old story, probably simply for the reason that he was a friend of her husband's, but if there is any truth in her account of surprising Jerdan dangling Landon on his knee around the mid-1830s, it seems quite likely that the affair was not yet over.

Jerdan was, as always, trying to help Landon's family. In July her brother urgently asked Jerdan to meet a bill of fifteen pounds. Whittington had not had a successful career, but his letter claimed that he was attempting to improve. "I have done all I could for the last three years to recover the effects of former errors and faults by my conduct." He had been advised to publish a few sermons, "it must do me good – it will shew the authorities, tho' unhired, I have not been idle, positive failure cannot lower me in opinion because opinion never raised me."[39] His sister had paid his way through Oxford and was probably still supporting their mother, so Whittington may not have felt able to face asking her to meet his debt. It is somewhat ironic that he turned to Jerdan for help, a man equally bad at managing his own finances. Jerdan did what he could to help, reviewing Landon's *Ten Sermons Preached in the Parish Church of Tavistock*, linking him with his "association with the poetry and imaginative literature of our age and country as Mr Landon is through the same of his gifted sister L.E.L.". A brief but favourable review followed.[40] This did not please L.E.L. who, three days later, berated Jerdan: "I cannot get over my dissappointment (sic) about Whittington's book. You should have made one or two quotations . . . can you not say you omitted last week by mistake? And give a column or two?"[41]

Driven by the need to keep money coming in, both for her own and her mother's support, as well as the perennially needy Whittington, and more than likely having to contribute in whole or in part towards the three children she and Jerdan had fostered on to others to care for, Landon's next book of poetry, *The Zenana*, appeared in *Fisher's Drawing-Room Scrapbook* of 1834. She had been given sixteen engravings on which to compose poetic responses on Indian themes, and she also included footnotes providing commentary on her story.

She continued to review for the *Literary Gazette*, earning the vilification of Henry Fothergill Chorley, who had recently joined the editorial staff of the *Athenaeum* as music critic and literary reviewer. "It would not be easy to sum up the iniquities of criticism (the word is not too strong) perpetrated at the instance of publishers," fulminated Chorley, "by a young woman writer who was in the grasp of Mr Jerdan, and who gilt or blackened all writers of the time as he ordained . . . It is hard to conceive anyone who by flimsiness and flippancy was made more distasteful to those who did not know her than was Miss Landon."[42] Clearly, Landon had written something critical of Chorley's work, and he was intent on getting his revenge.

As previously noted, public taste in reading was changing rapidly. Musing on the 1830s from the perspective of fifty years later, Walter Besant noted a turning away from the glut of popular, and often poor novels of the 1820s, when everyone wanted to be a second Walter Scott.[43] Where publishers had printed two thousand copies, they sold only fifty, and at the same time "The drop in poetry was even more terrible than that of novels. Suddenly, and without any warning, the people of Great Britain left off reading poetry." Dickens, Thackeray and Eliot redeemed the novel by their huge success, but otherwise the public turned to books of non-fiction: travel, exploration and science. Besant noted that for instance, James Holman's 'Round the World' (1834) and Lamartine's 'Pilgrimage', sold at least a thousand copies each. Landon had been just in time in producing her novels, although she was still churning out poetry for the annuals. Besant's opinion was that "one of the causes of the decay of trade as regards poetry and fiction may have been the badness of the annuals". Beautifully printed and bound, the engravings were interesting, but the literary content was of much lower quality.

The *Literary Gazette*, however, remained consistent to its pattern of the last twenty years, Jerdan failing to notice, or to acknowledge, the changing tastes of his readers. This was by no means his only problem at this time. According to one opinion, another factor was that the *Literary Gazette* "continued to review the fashionable novels seriously, while almost all the other reviews . . . were decrying them without mercy . . . the *Literary Gazette* was still addressing those who were ambitious to move above the salt, or at least dream about it".[44] *Fraser's* was still on the attack: "To say that the *Literary Gazette* is feeble, is certainly not being very original; it should be called the <u>Laudatory</u> rather than the *Literary Gazette*. With it 'all is fish that comes to net'."[45]

No stranger to finding himself in a Court of Law, Jerdan was again dragged into a case heard in the Lord Mayor's Court in July 1834. He was not a principal in the action, which was *Chambers v. Longman & Co.*, but it was a case of "attachment". Chambers was a tailor who claimed that Jerdan owed him £315, a huge sum. He knew that Longmans held money of Jerdan's, paid him a salary as editor of the *Literary Gazette*, and also a share of the profits. Longmans denied they held any money belonging to Jerdan. The publisher Scripps was questioned and explained that proceeds from the sale of the *Literary Gazette* and its advertisements were paid directly to Longmans. A clerk from Longmans was then called to confirm that he handed *Literary Gazette* money to Longmans every week, and knew nothing of any money belonging to Mr Jerdan. The unfortunate tailor lost his case, having failed to make a claim which convinced the Recorder.[46]

In 1834 the seeds of yet another financial disaster were sown for Jerdan. This time it was of his own making, not due to collapsing banks as had previously been the case. This was a disaster of immense consequences for him, and he felt the pain long afterwards, devoting only a few pages to the incident in his *Autobiography*, but no other mention or reference to it is made in surviving letters. There is thus only Jerdan's own account and this is guarded as even twenty years later he divulged no names or corroborative details.

Jerdan related how a wealthy man had returned from India with two sons; they lived in a handsome square in high style. The sons were gifted and had literary ambitions, swiftly establishing a place in society. They became intimate friends of Jerdan's and he watched them for years as they rose in literary repute and reward. "The foundations were hollow", he wrote, and despite their gains in reputation, "the whole superstructure fell miserably to the ground, and the sunny times were lost in painful darkness."[47] Jerdan had participated in some of their endeavours, more as a friend than on a formal basis, as he admired their cleverness and abilities. Jerdan was induced, "for certain reasons" which he did not disclose, to negotiate a contract with one of the brothers, for him to take over a portion of Jerdan's work in the *Literary Gazette*. The partners were brought into the negotiations. Whilst talks were proceeding, the other brother "entered into a copartnery with one of a reputedly very rich Jewish family in the city". Dazzled by this alliance, Jerdan "in an evil hour" put his name to several large bills, "to enable him to <u>show</u> something against the Leviathan fortune in the administration of which he was about to participate as a broker". It does not seem to have occurred to Jerdan that the father of the two brothers, reputedly so wealthy, would have been the man to guarantee his son's investment, but he clearly believed he was running no risk in doing so himself.

Things fell apart; the negotiation concerning the *Literary Gazette* failed, as did the promising brokerage. Jerdan was sued for between three and four thousand pounds. He was ruined. Looking back to this time, he sought to find a moral in the story. The brother with whom he was closest was a happy, spirited individual, welcomed everywhere. He had not a vicious or evil disposition. "What then," asked Jerdan, "caused his downfall? Vanity! Vanity alone led to boasts and falsehoods", to an extent that the young man could no longer distinguish truth from lie. Jerdan approached the bankers who held his bills, apprising them of the "real state of the case", and that he had personally received absolutely nothing in exchange for his guarantees. The bankers offered to forgo their claims on him – all he had to do was to get a letter stating this fact from the brother for whom he had signed the bills. Relieved and elated to be so close to salvation, Jerdan requested such a note from his friend. The man had, however, told so many lies on such a scale when depositing the bills at the bank, he could not bring himself to do as Jerdan asked, which would have shown himself to be a liar. Accordingly, he fled to the Continent, leaving Jerdan "to bide the brunt of my unpardonable imprudence".

In his account, it must be to Jerdan's credit that he did not try to whitewash his own vanity or greed, but noted it for what it was, the character flaw that had dogged him always, imprudence and a misplaced faith that as in his childhood 'spoiling', things would work out well despite his behaviour. The consequences of this incident were catastrophic. Jerdan was forced to sell his beloved Grove House, scene of so many happy parties and home to his large family. The contents went to auction, fetching less than he had paid Wilberforce for the fixtures alone, and adding a further thousand pounds to his losses. He was obliged to take up residence in the Westminster Bridge Road. His long-suffering wife would have had to bear the strain not only of moving from a grand house to lodgings, but of having to cope with a husband whose bad judgment alone had brought such disaster down upon them.

Focused by the recent introduction of workhouses in the Poor Law Amendment Act, Jerdan said that "by every possible sacrifice" he met all his debts, but in doing so he incurred other "incumbrances". The *Literary Gazette* was falling in circulation, as a direct result of the *Athenaeum* halving its price. This in turn led to Longmans losing interest in the *Gazette*. The publisher too was older and overworked, causing errors to creep in. Jerdan was frustrated to hear that "while I was losing more and more from week to week, one of my *employés*, at a guinea-a-week wages contrived, as I am informed, to save enough to purchase houses!!"[48] All this misfortune was the beginning of the long and slippery slope that was the remainder of his life.

In an undated letter to Bentley, Jerdan told him, "I have exposed myself to be swindled out of a ruinous sum, which however I am assured can be avoided by an immediate payment of no very large amount, but at present out of my power. What to do for about £100 I know not, and if I do not find them, I dread the consequences of a law suit with a scoundrel attorney at the head of a conspiracy to defraud me."[49] Undated as this letter is, its contents could have applied to several occasions in Jerdan's life from this time onwards. He also told Bentley that he was involved in a "soap concern" which could be used as collateral. Benjamin Hawes's successful soapworks was a prominent landmark at the Temple, near to Jerdan's office, and perhaps this gave him the idea to go into the business. No more was said about the enterprise.

On 23 April 1834 Macready gathered some friends for a private supper at the Garrick, including Forster and Talfourd. The number of guests increased, some were even strangers to him. Then he noted, "Jerdan was amongst us! And I thought (not, I hope, uncharitably) that it would have been more graceful to have absented himself from a festive meeting under his peculiar circumstances which he evidently cannot feel very strongly."[50] Most probably Macready referred to Jerdan's downfall although he did not know any details, merely surmising that they were "probably of a financial nature".

The Literary Fund had sent Macready an invitation which he did not quite understand, and he called at the Literary Fund's office for clarification. The Secretary, Snow, told him that a compliment was intended, but they would not even drink his health if he preferred. On that basis Macready accepted their invitation and spent the following week in a state of nerves, writing his speech. On the day of the Dinner, Jerdan presented him to the Duke of Somerset, President of the Fund, and he enjoyed the company and the dinner, overshadowed only by worries over his speech which, in the end, he was not called upon to make. On 18 August Jerdan and Landon shared a box at the Opera House for one of Macready's performances, and were joined afterwards by the actor and John Forster.

Fraser's Magazine still ran its series, 'Gallery of Illustrious Literary Characters', of which Jerdan had been the first. It now featured the hitherto derided author and publisher Leigh Hunt, on the occasion of his 50th birthday. "He has been an excessively ill-used man in many respects, and by none more than by Lord Byron, and those who panegyrise his lordship", said *Fraser's*.[51] Even Blackwood's *Maga*, penitent over 'Z's scathing attacks on the 'Cockney School' years earlier, praised Hunt's new periodical the *London Journal*.[52] This, as so many of Hunt's publishing ventures, lasted for only a year, despite, or maybe because, "it was still well ahead of its time in its appreciation of Keats's significance [in the 'Eve of St Agnes]".[53]

In the first issue of his new *London Journal*, Hunt wrote an obituary for his schoolfriend Charles Lamb, who died in December 1834. Bryan Procter, whose poetry had first been published in the *Literary Gazette* and subsequently in Hunt's own journals, complained that Hunt's treatment of his friend was scanty and cold. A public row ensued, which was overwhelmed by the country's concern about an increasingly belligerent Russia, with the British Mediterranean Squadron on standby-by to defend Constantinople in the event of a Russian attack. The peace was a fragile one.[54]

A few weeks earlier, in October, a terrible fire had engulfed the Houses of Parliament, scene of Jerdan's early journalistic endeavours. It was caused by the burning of a large amount of wooden Exchequer tallies in the stoves of the House of Lords. Jerdan was seen in the crowd valiantly trying to dowse the flames. Only Westminster Hall remained, but on the positive side, the conflagration inspired Turner to paint two famous pictures of the event. During the year, within sight of several of the *Literary Gazette's* former offices, on the corner of Wellington Street and the Strand, the Lyceum Theatre was built. A special room was included in the building for meetings of the elite Beefsteak Club, about which Jerdan was to write in the last article of his life.

⚡14⚡

Notoriety and a New Family

The year 1835 began with the worst possible news for Jerdan. His first-born son John Stuart, on whose behalf he had importuned the Duke of Portland for a job, had died aged twenty-six. In response to Jerdan's persistent requests that a post be found for him, he had been sent as a stipendiary magistrate to Jamaica. His death occurred on Christmas Day 1834, and his obituary in the *Jamaica Dispatch* was copied in the *Gentleman's Magazine* of March 1835.

> To an active and enterprising character he added a zeal in the execution of his arduous duties, which rendered him respected and beloved both by master and servant; he tempered justice with mercy.

John Stuart's previous work as Secretary of the Abbotsford Subscription was also mentioned, "seconding the ardent wish of his father for its success". It was also noted that he was attached to the study of natural history and had made his fine collections in entomology in England, the Netherlands and Jamaica. Jerdan probably had a hand in the obituary in the *Gentleman's Magazine*, which ended proudly, "He was nephew to Colonel John Stuart Jerdan, whose remains lie at the Cape of Good Hope." The just deceased John Stuart had married the elder daughter of distinguished engraver, John Vendramini;[1] it is not known if they had any issue.

The eldest child at home was Frances-Agnes, now almost twenty-six; Mary aged twenty-one, soon to be married; William Freeling, nineteen, running errands for his father and generally assisting with the *Literary Gazette*; George Canning, only seventeen, not yet out in the world; and finally the baby of the family since Georgiana's death, Elizabeth aged fifteen. All these, plus his wife Frances, were a heavy responsibility for Jerdan, presumably in addition to the upkeep of the three children he had with Landon who were still aged only thirteen, nine and six. Grove House had gone, and with it the fine lifestyle of parties and dinners, and the visible, tangible evidence that he was a man of some status in society. With all these burdens and anxieties the marriage with Frances was under strain, if not entirely broken down. Jerdan would have heard of the scandalous rumours about Landon, and maybe harboured some doubts as to their foundation as far as the other men gossiped about were concerned. Despite all this, during the next couple of years he was to complicate and burden his life still further.

More than a hint of Jerdan's despondent mood could be found in a poem he wrote in February 1835, published in *Friendship's Offering* for 1836, and entitled *On My Grey Hairs*. Recalling how at the beginning, each grey hair was plucked as it appeared, his second verse said:

> Those years are fled, I greet you now
> The dearest guests to me; –
> Why should the stem live when the bough
> Falls withered from the tree?
> When keen afflictions piercing blast
> Hath nipt the foliage free;
> And when the storm hath torn the hopes
> Of blossomings to be!

The poem concluded,

> But loves, and fears, and griefs, and tears,
> All centre in the grave.

With the death of his son, and troubles with Landon, Jerdan's life was clearly unhappy, and this poem comes across as more true than his earlier melancholic L.E.L.-type offerings in other annuals.

In early 1835 Jerdan's downturn in fortunes was making him short-tempered. He had disagreements with Bentley over some of the novels that came from the publisher, and was not afraid to state his opinion:

> I am sorry to notice that I do not think you can be led by <u>their merits</u> to some of your Novels; and it is bad policy to be induced to publish indifferent ones, with only a star now and then. Nothing short of superior class will do now; and the mediocre must serve to pull down the high.
>
> I wish you were better advised, but you publishers are almost all alike obstinate fellows! It may be however in this case as in others that lookers on do no more than fancy they know the game better than the player.[2]

Wishing to be free for Ascot Week, Jerdan asked Bentley for any novels he wished to be noticed to be sent quickly. He could not resist giving the publisher some advice: "Only beware of poor and bad works as much as you can and rely upon it you may place yourself at the head of the publishing trade. <u>Also be very direct with all those</u> you have to treat with about MSS etc. etc. Pardon my advising."[3] In Jerdan's opinion Bentley did not always follow this well-meant advice. Notwithstanding Jerdan's warnings, Bentley's publishing house continued with some success, and Bentley himself was to become the recipient of many of Jerdan's anguished letters pleading for financial help.

Despite the trend away from poetry to prose, 1835 saw the publication of another volume of Landon's poems, *The Vow of the Peacock and Other Poems*, published by Saunders and Otley. Many of the poems had been previously printed in the *Literary Gazette*, and the theme of the title poem came from a painting by Daniel Maclise. The *Literary Gazette* of 24 October reviewed the new book, vilifying complaints that pseudo-Utilitarians made against the 'school' of L.E.L. The reviewer, if it was not Jerdan, could well have been Landon herself:

> Pseudo-Utilitarians tell us that the love of poetry is over; and that, under their auspices, the human kind have become a mere shrewd, calculating, sordid, work-o'-day race. That to toil, and to spin, to draw water, and cleave wood, to gather and amass, to drudge and hoard, and never to enjoy, is the wisdom, the only wisdom of life. We are ready to believe their doctrines when we shall be convinced that the love of gracefulness and beauty, the fine moral perception, the sense which gives a tear to sorrow, the noble enthusiasm awakened by illustrious deeds – when natural feeling, sympathy, generosity, and heroic aspiring, have all departed from among the children of men. And not till then.

The passionate refutation of this so-called pseudo-Utilitarianism continued, the very passion suggesting that the writer was Landon herself, defending her poetry. Jerdan, as usual, urged Blackwood to review the book: "I do not remember if you have noticed Miss Landon's last Novel (sic) *The Vow of the Peacock*. I am sure you have not; shall I transmit a copy or copies."[4]

Daniel Maclise had made a portrait of Landon for the frontispiece of *The Vow of the Peacock*. He had also made one for *Fraser's* 'Gallery', but it is likely the former which became the subject of his note to Jerdan that the price for such a drawing was ten guineas.[5] Landon told Jerdan that she was "much surprised about the portrait but Mr Maclise may I am sure keep it since he takes it back again".[6] Jerdan sent this note on to Crofton Croker, complaining that he had sent the portrait to Saunders and Otley (publishers of *The Vow of the Peacock*), "and though our friend M'Clise (sic) misliked the Engraving it does seem too bad that he shd like my picture and keep it. Miss L. of course will not ask him for it <u>again</u> and I am between the stools unless I make a row with Saunders and

Otley. Pray take an opportunity of mentioning this matter in a friendly way to M'Clise, from who I do not think that I deserve any wrong."[7]

In September 1835 Jerdan's story "The Line of Beauty: or, Les Noces de Nose" appeared in the *New Monthly Magazine*. It was the story of Ned Redmund, "almost a universal genius; that is, he knew a little of everything and in our days very little serves". Of independent means, Redmund was a connoisseur in the fine arts, but anything outside of the Line of Beauty was "error and abomination". He followed a woman, bewitched by her figure, and then he examined her face. Jerdan's sense of humour is apparent as he described her nose which: "took its rise between a pair of eyebrows ... not wholly joined; nor yet just quite apart", and descended in a straight line towards the upper lips; "neither too short nor too long, neither cocked up impertinently, nor drooping disagreeably; neither pinched in avariciously, nor dilating passionately ... it was the *juste milieu* of noses!"

Plans were made for marriage, but disaster struck, as they rode their horses towards Regent's Park. Jerdan could not resist a bit of harmless fun when he chose his location. "Just opposite Lockhart's house a dirty-looking boy ran hastily past, and the creature started, fell and threw its rider; which was not surprising, as it happened to be a printer's devil carrying the copy of an article on Melton Mowbray for the *Quarterly Review*." On rushing to help Betsy, Ned's horse came too near to her prostrate form and his iron shoe struck her face, mutilating it horribly: "after weeks of darkness and bandaging and suffering, it was found that her nose, that temple of beauty worshipped by the disconsolate Redmund, was irrecoverably gone", and it was all Ned's fault that the Line of Beauty had been annihilated.

Having set the stage of the tragedy, Jerdan brought into his story the celebrated Scottish surgeon Robert Liston, who had reconstructed noses in Edinburgh, and to whom he had dedicated his tale. He was now in London, and Ned consulted him. Hope instantly improved Ned's health and outlook, giving Jerdan the opportunity to satirise the florid language so beloved of L.E.L. and other contemporary novelists:

Hope, that takes its seat on our nature's throne, and issues its decrees to all the vassal vessels round, till brightness gleams from the dull eye, smiles dimple on the languid cheek, breath flows freely from the choken throat, the red blood circulates briskly in the stagnate veins, the heart beats lightly, the foot treads firmly, and every look and motion bespeak the balmy influence of the rosy and god-like monarch who reigns when 'Hope told a flattering tale'.

Though frightened, Betsy agreed to an operation because, as Jerdan remarked, "nobody likes to be without a nose and few girls to be without a husband". Ned had told Liston that "a mere nose" would be an acquisition but for him to be happy, it needed to be Greco-Roman and consistent with the line of beauty. When Betsy healed, the result was almost perfect except for a slight dip at the tip. Another operation was performed, and the happy couple were duly married.

Jerdan's postcript to his story was an acknowledgement that he had witnessed a similar operation in London's University Hospital a few months earlier, and hoped that Mr Liston would not take offence at the freedom taken with his name and skill in the story. Pleased with the reception given to the tale by the *Courier* and elsewhere, Jerdan approached Blackwood mentioning it, as it had "inspired a desire to write a few papers in some Maga for the ensuing year". He sent a sample, promising that his contributions would be better, and leaving the 'reward' to Blackwood, "as I have promised proceeds to a destined purpose, and not of a selfish kind".[8] However, no contributions of Jerdan's appear to ever have been published in *Blackwood's*.

Jerdan continued his life as normally as possibly, retaining his great love of the theatre, and his friendship with the actor Macready, who recorded in his Diary that Jerdan came to his room three times in four days in August. They discussed the breakdown of Byron's marriage, and Jerdan agreed to accompany Macready to Wicklow. They met up again in September when they saw a five-act comedy at the Haymarket, and thought it dull and commonplace. On 20 November Macready went to call on John Forster "and stayed some time listening to a tale of wretched abandonment to passion that surprised and depressed me". This was the breaking off of Forster's engagement to Landon, having apparently heard that she had twice "made an abrupt and passionate declaration of love to Maclise". Macready also heard the story of the Maginn letters. He had never met Maginn, but had heard he was "a beastly biped". The fastidious Macready was revolted by the whole affair: "I felt quite concerned that a women of such splendid genius and such agreeable manners should be so depraved in taste and so lost to a sense of what was due to her high reputation. She is fallen." Fortunately for Macready's sensibilities, he had no idea of the truth about L.E.L. He was not the only one to have heard about Landon and Maginn. A later writer recalled that Grantley Berkeley (who had famously duelled with Maginn), reported that: "Before his duel with Maginn, Miss Landon (L.E.L.) had appealed to him for protection against the doctor's persistent persecution, asserting that, although a married man, he had made much too ardent love to her, and not meeting with the encouragement he expected, had then endeavoured to extort money from her."[9] One wonders why, if Landon was truly troubled by Maginn, she did not go to Jerdan for some "protection", rather than to a man with whom she had little to do.

Rumours abounded about Landon, many suggesting a liaison with Jerdan, with Maginn and Maclise. The possibility has also been discussed that Landon was being blackmailed which would account for her shortage of money. Who the blackmailer was, or what hold he had over her, is not certain, but it has been suggested that the motive for sending anonymous accusatory letters to Forster was to prevent Landon entering into marriage and thus possibly cease being susceptible to the blackmail. The secret may have had to do with disclosure of Landon's and Jerdan's three children, although there is no evidence that Jerdan himself was subjected to blackmail, or it may have been related to a suggestion that Landon herself was illegitimate.[10]

Jerdan's bank account for 1835[11] opened with a debit of £4178, reflecting his dire situation as a consequence of his imprudent investment and the loss of Grove House. No details of transactions have survived after January until July, when his debit had been reduced to £72.10 probably by the sale of house contents. This substantial improvement goes far to corroborate Jerdan's claim that he eventually paid off his debt. Transactions on his account between July and December 1835 reveal eleven withdrawals for himself, mostly around five to six pounds, with an unusual thirty-five pounds in August, perhaps for holiday expenses. Payments to "Mr Jerdan" are likely to refer to William Freeling, possibly for his assistance on the *Literary Gazette*. In August, October and December these were for five pounds and in November for five guineas. There are disbursements too to "Mrs Jerdan", and others to "Home" or "House" at five pounds a time, at irregular intervals. Names recurring are those of Biffin, Chambers and Grant, but to what these payments refer is not known, although they are quite possibly instalments to clear loans. The total of Jerdan's debits in this six-month period amounted to about £480. On the credit side, this exactly balanced his income, which comprised deposits of sums varying between £5 and £100. Where the payments came from is not listed, but Jerdan was drawing his regular salary from Longmans as *Literary Gazette* editor, and being paid for contributions to other journals, such as the *New Monthly Magazine* for his story of "The Line of Beauty". The sum of one hundred pounds paid in December may have been his partnership share in the *Literary Gazette*, but the precise reasons for his payments and receipts can only be the subject of speculation.

In November 1835 James Hogg died and was buried in Ettrick. The sad event would have brought mixed memories to Jerdan's mind: the famous Burns Dinner, Hogg's desire to bind their two families by marriage, and the dire poverty that had necessitated Literary Fund donations, even for so successful an author. Writing to his brother, Carlyle recalled the last time he had seen Hogg, and went on to remark how glad he was that John Carlyle had met with William Fraser. He had himself been enquiring about Fraser, but without result; "the monster Jerdan of the *Gazette* had not 'heard a word of him' two months ago and was and remained a satyr-cannibal Literary Gazetteer; who shall live (leben hoch [live high] if he like and can), only far from me . . . "[12] Carlyle disliked Jerdan for his huge energies and love of life, drink and women, contrasting strongly with his own straitlaced personality.

Dilke shared Carlyle's dislike of Jerdan, the latter for his personal traits and the former for his perceived 'puffing' in the *Literary Gazette* and subservience to Colburn. Dilke received a very long letter from Thomas Hood, written from Coblenz in January 1836, and referring to some news Dilke had recently sent to him:

> By the bye the Jerdan story – his application to you for character etc. is astounding! The net is plain, a plan to entrap same [some] easy rich man into marriage with his daughter – but the application to you reads to me like a drunken audacious Garrick Club or Beefsteak Joke!!! Are you sure it is not one of your own on an innocent at Coblenz? After that, come any thing. Is the day fixed when Wentworth and Agnes Jerdan are to be united? I will come to that wedding anyhow. I must believe you – but after that I think I can play the Boa with a whole rabbit.[13]

In a footnote the editor noted:

> Wentworth was Dilke's son, Charles Wentworth Dilke II, born in 1810. Is he the "easy rich man" whom Jerdan wished to entrap into marriage with his daughter? It seems hardly likely. The greater probability is that he merely wanted to make use of Dilke's good name to further his interest with another, and that Hood's suggestion of a union between Wentworth and Agnes Jerdan was only his jesting way of indicating how ridiculously absurd he considered Jerdan's proposal, whatever it was.

Jerdan considered Hood his friend, a regard that does not seem, from the tone of Hood's letter, to have been reciprocated.

Since 1820 Jerdan had been trying to popularize the idea of a fitting monument in London in memory of George III. The wildly ambitious proposal by Matthew Wyatt of the king on a car drawn by four horses attended by angels had not been practicable as insufficient subscriptions had been raised to meet the cost. All these years later a much more modest monument came to fruition. Jerdan heralded it in the *Literary Gazette* of 27 February 1836 announcing that it would be erected on 4 June, the late King's birthday. More money was needed, and to grip his readers' attention the *Literary Gazette* article included a large engraving of the horse's head, and referred to, but did not explain, an accident which had befallen the project but had been surmounted by Wyatt. Nearer to the great day, the *Literary Gazette* of 28 May 1836, said of the Committee, "Their labours and exertions, and the public can hardly surmise how great they have been, are now on the eve of a triumphant termination." The statue was to be erected that week, in the presence of royalty and nobility. More in hope than expectation, Jerdan wrote "we think may promise the opening of an Equestrian

Group which no age or artist has ever surpassed." Subscriptions had amounted to £3130 4s.1d. (The figure given in 1822 was already £5000 but perhaps this reflected the changed value of the Pound.) It was hoped that additional subscriptions would be forthcoming, "to reward the talent and exertions of the artist in a more suitable manner". Far from the elaborate and allegorical statue first designed, the nation's memorial to King George III was a twelve-foot high granite pedestal surmounted by a sculpture of the King, wearing a pigtail, seated on his horse – not quite the "Equestrian Group" of which Jerdan spoke (see illustration no. 6). The pigtail was much derided at the time and even the site chosen caused objections, which were overridden by the Lord Chancellor. The statue is still there, in the triangle between Cockspur Street and Pall Mall East, now sadly isolated by streams of traffic, and ignored by throngs of tourists hurrying into Trafalgar Square.

If failure to provide a suitably elaborate memorial to his beloved King disappointed Jerdan, it was only the beginning; 1836 was to prove an emotionally roller-coaster year. The volatile marriage of his friends Edward and Rosina Bulwer came to an embittered end in April, when they formally separated after Rosina had raided her husband's Albany apartments, publicly accusing him of entertaining his mistress there. The fall-out continued for many years, Rosina becoming ever more hysterical and abusive. As one marriage ended, another was just about to begin. Jerdan's second daughter, Mary Felicity Dawn (whom Hogg had wanted to marry off to his nephew), was twenty-two years old. She met Edward Rawdon Power, three years older. With a marriage looming, and the need to keep up a suitably lavish lifestyle, at least until the ceremonies were over, Jerdan was seriously pressed for money. In January he asked Longmans for the funds he was owed, but received an unsatisfactory note that the book-keeper had "not yet made any progress in the account". A few days later he approached Bentley in a more ingratiating tone than he had hitherto adopted:

> The great kindness you expressed the other morning has seduced me to ask a favour which I am sure if not inconvenient you will grant. The family matters I mentioned pulls my pursestrings hard and there is little in it, and it is of consequence to me to go through with arrangements in a rather liberal style. Well, by the enclosed [probably the letter from Longmans], you may guess that my friends are in no hurry with the quarterly dividends, and they are not called on to send the accounts in till the beginning of February. If you could therefore till then (say a month hence) be my banker from sixty to a hundred pounds and the more the better, I will send you my faithful cheque for it payable at that time. I told the girls of your kind intents and they say you are a nice man and was (sic) very kind to them at Hastings.[14]

This was not the first letter Jerdan was forced to write asking for a loan, and was by no means the last. From this time on, his fortunes declined rapidly, but for now, the crucial thing was to keep up appearances until Mary was safely married. Bentley seems to have assented, as on 7 March Jerdan added a note to a business letter, telling him, "Tomorrow from 1–3 o'clock there will be a breakfast on table at 21 Grosvenor Street for any <u>friends</u> after the marriage ceremony. You would be welcome." (One would hope so, as it was Bentley's money paying for the breakfast!) The following day Mary and Edward Power were married at St George's, Hanover Square, a short stroll from the new *Literary Gazette* offices where the wedding breakfast was held. The couple moved out to Ceylon where their son Edmund was born in 1842, in the palace at Candy of Sir Robert Wilmot Horton, the Governor of Ceylon, to whom Power was Private Secretary. Power rose to senior appointments in the Ceylon Civil Service, becoming Assistant Colonial Secretary and Government Agent of Candy. He edited one of the earliest periodicals in Ceylon, starting the quarterly magazine, "The Ceylon Miscellany" in which Mary took a great interest. Power introduced a system of shorthand to Ceylon, and also seemed to have been a good athlete, with "a very expressive face and a large head with curly black hair".[15]

A few weeks after the wedding, Jerdan wrote a personal note to the Governor, asking him and Lady Horton to be kind to his daughter: "She has been a home bird all her days till now, and must feel, as I shall do, the more grateful for any attention you are good enough to bestow upon her."[16] He sent a copy of Back's *Journal* as a token of his esteem.[17] His letter, dated 23 May, brought him to Horton's notice as someone who could act as his agent, and would be pleased to do anything for the man who could make his daughter's new life more pleasant. This, of course, was never spelled out.

Horton had a long history of passionate pamphleteering and campaigning on pauperism and emigration, seeing mass emigration as a solution to poverty and overpopulation at home, and a shortage of labour in the colonies, mainly in Canada; he had strong pro-Catholic views, which made him unpopular in some circles. He had been made Governor of Ceylon in 1831 and served until 1837, overseeing the final abolition of slavery in the country and the development of a free press. In November 1836, shortly after Mary and Edward Power's arrival in Ceylon, Horton wrote a long letter to Jerdan explaining that he had erroneously entrusted all his writings to be published by his Bookseller, Mr Lloyd. The books had not succeeded because Horton had refused to allow them to be advertised and Lloyd thus had no means of making them known. He told Jerdan that although he had contributed articles to the *Quarterly Review*, he had fallen out with John Murray which was why he had turned to Lloyd. He suggested to Jerdan that maybe Longmans would be interested in republishing his works. He now wanted Jerdan to arrange publication of *Letters from the Dead*, correspondence he had received from eminent men, including several Bishops, on the topic of poverty in Ireland. His instructions were detailed and verbose, discussing Notes and Appendices, a 'Motto' and a dedication and a long 'Prefatory Chapter'. He promised to send the manuscript in December, so that it should arrive in England in April, and be published in June. He gave the project into Jerdan's hands: "I name no other person because you must be far better acquainted than I am as to expediency of selection".[18] He gave Jerdan the name of his solicitors, but nowhere in his long letter did he mention or suggest that Jerdan would receive any remuneration for the arduous tasks he expected of him, from re-writing, editing, finding a publisher, rearranging the title page and negotiating the terms of payment to Horton.

In February 1837 Horton sent the original of his book, noting changes, dele-tions and additions not yet ready. He bade Jerdan get a copy of a Government "Report of a Committee on Emigration" of 1827 and make substantial extracts from this, although a few days later, by the next ship, he had changed his mind and the Report was to be published in full. "The Table of Contents must, I am sorry to say, be drawn up in England" – presumably another task Jerdan was supposed to undertake gratis. Another month passed and Horton sent an urgent note instructing Jerdan to omit a certain passage from a letter to the Bishop of Limerick, because "it may perhaps be considered objectionable by the friends of the late Bishop to have it published". However, he wanted it extracted and sent to another correspondent, enclosing a covering letter which he told Jerdan to "read and act upon". This tacit assumption that Jerdan would jump to his command reflected Horton's obsessive passion for his causes, oblivious to the fact that Jerdan had other tasks to perform, like running his weekly journal. Jerdan, however, would have been in no position to refuse the Governor anything, reliant as the young Powers were on his good will. No book by Horton with the title of *Letters from the Dead* seems to have been published among the plethora of pamphlets, books and letters with which he deluged politicians and public alike.

Not long after his daughter's marriage, Jerdan embroiled himself in a major occurrence which made news in the *Times* and doubtless, much discussion amongst his friends. In 1834, Daniel Maclise[19] volunteered, at the request of Crofton Croker who was also a member of the Committee of the Literary Fund, to paint a portrait of Sir John Soane, in recognition of his "liberal patronage". When completed in May 1835 it was framed and hung on the walls of the Committee Room. As far as the Committee was aware Soane had seen and approved the portrait. However, in November it was intimated to the Committee, verbally, that Soane was dissatisfied with the picture, "deeming it a libel and caricature",[20] and after long debate it was resolved to take the problem to Maclise. He proved willing to take back the portrait, as Soane had not indi-cated any desire to have it. The Committee wrote officially to Soane to explain the situation, as did Maclise, but neither received any response.

John Britton took up the cudgels on Soane's behalf, telling Jerdan that he had been hurt by language used by Dilke, Foss, and Barham at a meeting of the Literary Fund; if there was a repetition, Britton would resign in favour of some other Society who would treat him better. "I shall be <u>compelled</u> to bring forward Soane's poor portrait again – I wish <u>you</u> could prevail on Maclise to give up his unfinished daub for the fine specimen from Lawrence – Sir John will not live or die in peace with the Society unless it be exchanged – he is <u>violent</u> on the subject," he told Jerdan.[21] At the Fund's Committee meeting in March "a person claiming to represent Soane" (namely John Britton) announced that unless Soane "obtained the picture immediately and unreservedly he would withdrawn his patronage from the institution, without an intended bequest and appeal to the public."[22] Information about this was gleaned from letters in the *Times* written on behalf of the Literary Fund by W.C. Taylor.[23] This spokesman reported that he intended to table a motion marking the Committee's notice of such a threat. However, "on the Saturday night before my motion could be discussed, a Mr Jerdan gained admission to the rooms and destroyed the picture". He had in fact slashed it to ribbons. In an effort to pre-empt the inevitable furore, Jerdan wrote to the *Times* newspaper on 11 May, putting a light gloss on events: Soane had become older since his flattering earlier portrait by Sir Thomas Lawrence, and disliked his present appearance, "sans teeth, sans taste", depicted by Maclise. Soane wished the Maclise portrait returned, and would present the Fund with the one by Lawrence, making this a condition of his future benefaction. Jerdan wrote that many agreed to

> humour the veteran architect and return the picture. but Radicalism and Opposition creeps in everywhere. A certain faction stoutly resisted the proposal . . . when lo! A certain literary reviewer and member of the Council of the Fund well known for his social kindness and humanity as well as his heedless eccentricities, put an end to all contention by entering the Committee Room, and cutting the caricature of Sir John (as the latter considered it) in pieces with his penknife! The Radical faction are again in arms and are taking secret counsel together whether the said summary settler of contentions has not committed an act of felony which may subject him to being hanged!

Taylor's first furious reaction was to loudly deny Jerdan's accusation: "I am not a Radical and that I belong to no faction". As for the felony charge, he had taken legal advice and merely meant that illegal entry and wilful destruction were felonious acts. In his letter to *The Times* of 13 May Taylor protested, "The few observations I made have been strangely perverted into an anxiety to fix a charge of felony on Mr Jerdan; I feel too much respect for that gentleman on public and private grounds to dream of any such thing." However, Taylor wished the public to know the story to prove that the Literary Fund would not "stoop to accept money by the sacrifice of principle", by which he may have meant that they would spurn any further gifts from Soane if they were conditional on having the portrait destroyed or returned to him.

There are no surviving diaries of Soane for 1836, so it is not possible to know from that source whether he asked Jerdan to act on his behalf to destroy the picture or whether Jerdan acted on his own initiative. That Jerdan had pre-determined his act, and it had not been impulsive, was mentioned by Charles Macready. On reading the account of Jerdan's act of destruction in the *Morning Chronicle*, Macready noted in his Diary that, when visiting his house at Elstree, Jerdan had expressed his intention to destroy the picture and Macready also stated that Soane "has been absurdly and tetchily desirous of destroying that too faithful record of his personal appearance".[24] However, the archives of the Literary Fund are rather more informative than Jerdan's own memoir, which treats the affair jocularly. At the Committee Meeting of 11 May 1836 Jerdan explained his motives for having destroying the picture a few days earlier.[25] He then absented himself from the meeting, leaving behind a letter to be read out, deemed sufficiently important by the Society to be copied into the Minutes Book. In this he paid tribute to the generosity of Sir John Soane as a benefactor and Vice President of the Literary Fund, and to the "young and rising Artist of the highest talents" who had volunteered to make the portrait. Jerdan pointed to the failure of the Committee to submit the portrait "for the approbation of Sir John Soane in the first instance", especially as it was to honour him. What had been intended as a compliment was in fact an object of "strong aversion and disgust" to the subject.

"Our dilemma was complete", Jerdan went on. The Committee could not affront the Painter, nor did it wish to upset Sir John, who was of an advanced age. Jerdan complained that "One portion of the Committee looked one way, and another the contrary way to get as best we could out of this perplexity, none expressing a desire to retain the portrait", but all wishing the cause of division to be removed. This he had taken upon himself to do, he explained, but only after consulting the artist first. Referring to Maclise in high-flown language extolling his "liberality which belongs to true genius", Jerdan told the Committee that the painter's desire was to contribute to the interests of the Literary Fund, and if destroying his work achieved this end, he agreed that it should be done, and for this "he is entitled to the ever-lasting thanks of the Literary Fund Society". Having done his best to ensure that the artist was exonerated from any censure, Jerdan concluded by acquiescing that "In the hope of doing a great good, I am sensible that I have boldly ventured to do no small wrong". If he was forgiven, he would be "highly gratified", and if censured, would instantly resign from the Committee, but loving the Fund as he did, would continue to work for it in a private capacity. Jerdan's submission was followed by a brief note from Maclise, addressed to Nichols, Senior Registrar of the Literary Fund, noting that it had been at Nichols's house that he had discussed the matter with Crofton Croker, a member of the Committee, telling Croker that disposal of the portrait was acceptable to him, if it was in the Society's interest. Maclise believed that Jerdan had been told this by his good friend Croker, and had acted accordingly.

The anti-Jerdan faction of the Committee, fronted by Messrs Woodfall and Duncan, immediately gave notice of a motion which was discussed the following week. They moved that Jerdan's conduct be referred to a public meeting of Literary Fund members, but this motion was defeated. Dr Taylor proposed a Resolution acknowledging that Jerdan's act was "wholly unjustifiable in itself" but that no dangerous precedent had been established. As Soane had disliked the portrait and the artist had agreed to its destruction no further action should be taken. The Committee carried this Resolution unanimously, so Jerdan was "off the hook" for his escapade.

Jerdan himself related only that the Literary Fund's newly appointed Secretary, whose election he had supported, was a young Irishman named Cusack P. Roney, (later Sir), who, on the night of the destruction, was enjoying an evening of ballet at the Opera House. He was intercepted by Jerdan, who showed him a strip of canvas which had been the eyes of Soane's portrait. This had the instant effect of Roney leaving the ballet to remonstrate with him. Roney was understandably furious and threatened Jerdan with vengeance, for what Jerdan himself later called a "half-crazy deed". The episode was possibly why Roney stayed in the post for only a year. Perhaps he did not want to be associated with an institution which harboured such a hot-head. Eventually the furore died down and an unrepentant Jerdan made fun of the episode when he came to write his memoirs, quoting a 'squib' about the affair:

> Ochone! Ochone![26]
> For the portrait of Soane!
> Jerdan! You ought to have let it alone,
> Don't you see that instead of "removing the bone
> Of contention," the apple of discord you've thrown?
> One general moan,
> Like a tragedy groan,
> Burst forth when the picturecide deed became known.
> When the story got blown,
> From the Thames to the Rhone,
> Folks were calling for ether and Eau de Cologne,
> All shocked at the want of discretion you've shown.
> If your heart's not a stone,
> You will forthwith atone,

> The best way to do that is to ask Mr Rone-
> -y to sew up the slits; the Committee you'll own,
> When it's once stitched together, must see that it's SOANE★
> ★Qu. SEWN? – Print. Dev. (a very Jerdanish pun)

There is a postscript to this act of vandalism: a fragment of Maclise's portrait of Soane was found in 2006 in the Victoria and Albert Museum.[27] The fragment shows Sir John's thumb, and is accompanied by a note setting out the story of the portrait and its destruction. It has been suggested that the note was by Maclise himself, but this is unlikely as it refers to the Committee "being embarrassed how to act, as sending to Sir John would offend the artist, and withholding it would give umbrage to Sir John"; Maclise may not have referred to himself as "the artist". (The identification was possible as an etching of the portrait appeared in *Fraser's Magazine* in 1836.) Maybe Soane had been told that it was unflattering, as the note indicated that "Sir John being blind or nearly so could not judge of its merits himself." The etching accompanied No. 75 in *Fraser's* 'Gallery of Literary Characters'. The text called Jerdan "the iconoclast", teasing him that his action "had not even the merit of originality: the experiment of rejuvenating a tough old subject, by the process of cutting up, was long ago tried on Pelias, King of Colchis, at the suggestion of Medea the witch, and was not found to answer". The article chided Soane for forgetting his own indebtedness to charity at the start of his career, and insisted that literature survives longer than stone and mortar: "a MS may be destroyed, but EDITIONS defy Torch and Turk".

Undeterred by Jerdan's notorious activities over the Soane portrait, Thackeray wrote to Jerdan on 22 April 1836, asking, "Will you give me a little puff for the accompanying caricatures? As to their merits, being a modest man, I am dumb; but that is no reason why my friends should be silent – Besides this is my first appearance before the public and I trust that my wages and my character will improve, by the judicious praise which I hope to receive from you."[28] He declined Jerdan's invitation to the Garrick, saying he had "better keep the six guineas." The *Literary Gazette* was often the first public appearance of writers who subsequently became well-known, even famous, a legacy for which Jerdan was solely responsible. Also undeterred by the Soane incident was Richard Bentley, who asked Jerdan to promote his election to the Literary Fund. Jerdan agreed to do so, but warned Bentley that objections might be raised by one of the members to yet another publisher, "as he thought there were more than a fair proportion of them in the Committee".[29] Bentley was elected to the Committee in November 1836.

The well-known historical novelist G.P.R. James also asked a favour of Jerdan, to review a friend's book: "I am anxious too to get a review pretty early in the Gazette because as you well know there are many of our good critical friends that will abuse the book first because it is written by a lady, and secondly because she is a friend of mine. I who am an abomination unto them!"[30] He complained of having lost Jerdan's Grosvenor Street address, so was forced to write to "your inhospitable office in Wellington Street, where I think it is a rule to take in nothing un-post paid". That old problem of postage was still relevant, but James sweetened his complaint by repeating his previous invitations to Blackheath: "there is a bed and knife and fork, a bottle of claret and a hearty welcome at your service." Making most literary quarrels seem quite tame was the enraged reaction of the Hon. Grantley Berkeley to an adverse review of his novel in *Fraser's Magazine*. He brutally attacked the publisher, injuring him seriously. On hearing this Maginn, who had written the review, accepted Berkeley's challenge to a duel, which both survived.

In May 1836 Jerdan dropped the prefix "London" from the *Literary Gazette* title, responding to changes in the law which no longer required him to publish two separate editions, one for London and the other for the provinces and overseas.[31]

Jerdan's editorship of the journal had given him access to virtually anyone he wished to see in all walks of life, even now as the *Literary Gazette* declined in influence and circulation. His circumstances were getting "cold and colder", initiated by the reduction to half price of the *Athenaeum*, and also the rise and affordability of popular novels, so that long extracts in the *Gazette* were no longer so important. Mary Russell Mitford noted the changes afoot, writing to a friend, "Do you ever see the London weekly literary journal called the *Athenaeum*. It is the fashionable paper now, having superseded the *Literary Gazette*. It has such a circulation that, although published at the small price of fourpence the income derived from it by the proprietor is said to be more than £4000 per annum."[32] Jerdan tried to put a good face on his problems, and Planché recalled in his memoirs, "His buoyant spirits enabled him to bear up against 'a sea of troubles' which would have overwhelmed an ordinary man. Mr Moyes, his printer, a 'canny Scot', being asked by a mutual acquaintance, 'Has our friend Jerdan got through his difficulties?' characteristically exclaimed, 'Difficulties! I never knew he was in any!'"[33] In this respect Jerdan had inherited his father's easy-going laid-back attitude to life.

With his fortunes going downhill, Jerdan would have been cheered to see *Foster's Cabinet Miscellany* by Theodore Foster, published in 1836. The chapter on weekly periodicals naturally featured the *Literary Gazette* as the oldest of these. He had no compunction in discussing the money Jerdan was rumoured to be making, noting that some said he got £1000 a year for the editorship, others thought £800, plus a share of the profits. These, he said, at one time averaged £5000 per annum, and were still very considerable. He explained how business was done: "Contributors receive a written order for the amount of their remuneration from Mr Jerdan on Messrs. Longman and Co. who immediately pay it.... literary men have received as high as one guinea per column, or twenty-four guineas per sheet." Foster put the *Literary Gazette*'s circulation for many years at over 5000 a week; a special issue containing the review of "A Key to Almack's" pushed it to 7000. The *Gazette* was still a "good property", he felt. The remainder of the section praised Jerdan for bringing on individual authors, naming L.E.L. and Robert Montgomery. He insisted that charges against the *Literary Gazette* for its "want of independence" were unjust: three or four out of every five of Colburn's books, he calculated, "have been most liberally condemned". If Jerdan were guilty at all, it was of an unconscious "feeling of friendship towards the authors rather than from solicitations or understood wishes of any publishing house". As if to prove his point, Foster added a note to reassure his readers that he had no "personal inducement" to speak in support of Jerdan; indeed, the *Literary Gazette*'s review of his own last work "exceeded the limits of temperate criticism". Jerdan needed all the champions he could muster at this challenging time, and Foster's voluntary contribution must have been most welcome.

Readers were attracted to serialised novels, and the year 1836 saw the start of one of the greatest of these, published by Chapman and Hall. At the end of March the first instalment of *Pickwick Papers* appeared, priced at one shilling with a print run of a thousand copies. Sales were modest, so the next instalment a month later was reduced to five hundred copies, but the third instalment rose again to one thousand. Jerdan was as entranced as everyone else with Dickens's tale. He was especially charmed by the story of Sam Weller in the fourth episode, extracting this and reprinting it in the *Literary Gazette* without acknowledgement. His friendship with Dickens was linked to their mutual support of the Literary Fund, so he felt that he could write to the author about the new serial, and urged him to develop Sam Weller's character "largely – to the utmost", advice which Dickens accepted in good part and which proved to be so important for *Pickwick*'s success. Sales soared and orders for back numbers poured in. Dickens deleted an aside in Chapter 11 of later editions, about an "unflattering portrait of Sir John Soane destroyed by Soane's friend and subsequently Sam Weller's champion, William Jerdan".[34] Jerdan could thus be hailed as one who made *Pickwick* famous, thereby ensuring the gratitude and success of Dickens.

At the same time Dickens had a job as reporter on the *Morning Chronicle*, and between the appearance of the third and fourth episodes of *Pickwick* had to cover the trial of Lord Melbourne. Taking advantage of Dickens's rising popularity, Bentley offered him a contract for two novels, with no time limit. Dickens requested a higher fee and it was agreed that he would receive five hundred pounds for each; the contract was signed in August. Another contract between the two was signed in November. Dickens agreed to edit the new *Bentley's Miscellany* for twenty pounds a month, plus twenty guineas for contributing sixteen pages of his own writing, the copyright belonging to Bentley. This new task, with income from the *Chronicle* and *Pickwick*, raised his income to almost £800 a year, but he quickly resigned from the *Chronicle* to concentrate on the *Miscellany* and his own writing. Jerdan was to contribute several articles to the *Miscellany* in the years ahead.

In low spirits for a variety of reasons, the actor William Macready dined alone at the Garrick at the beginning of May, and noted that Jerdan, amongst others, came to his table to greet him. Calling on John Forster, Macready learnt that Jerdan had done as he had threatened, and destroyed the Soane portrait. By 3 June, Jerdan had put the portrait débâcle behind him, and dined at the Garrick, where he and Forster were toasted by Macready as "uniform and earnest supporters of the cause of the drama . . . Jerdan made a good speech, if at all to be questioned, only for his too much kindness to me".[35]

Jerdan's domestic life was still weighing heavily upon him when he met a woman named Mary Maxwell, and began a new affair which resulted in a large family. Nothing is known about her, save that she was born in Somerset. At nineteen, she was thirty-five years younger than Jerdan and eight years younger than his daughter Frances-Agnes. When exactly this new relationship started is unsure, as records are unavailable. However, Mary Maxwell became pregnant and in about 1836 gave birth to Marion, nicknamed Mop, who was quickly followed by Matilda Maxwell Jerdan (originally named Stewart), and familiarly known as Tilly. The two girls were soon followed by a son, Henry.

With this third family to support it is astonishing that Jerdan kept going both financially and physically, but on the surface at least his work for the *Literary Gazette*, his other writings, meetings, dinners and activities, kept up the same pace as always. Nothing survives to indicate his feelings at this time – or any time – so one can only speculate how he managed his extremely complicated life. Mary and her children would most likely have been a secret at this point, but Frances must have known about her husband's financial and moral dilemmas, if she was at all interested in him any longer. They would have had to put a good public face on their union, at least until Mary's marriage to Edward Power had been safely accomplished.

Whether Landon was aware of Jerdan's new affair cannot be known; it raises the question as to whether Jerdan embarked on his new relationship as a backlash to Landon's albeit failed engagement to John Forster, or whether Landon engaged, and then disengaged herself to Forster, and contracted marriage with the man she was about to meet, in the face of what she may have seen as Jerdan's abandonment of her in favour of Mary Maxwell. With rumours flying about Landon's alleged affairs with several men, and Jerdan's (now-revealed) affairs with at least Landon and Maxwell, and maybe others, the atmosphere was a hothouse of jealousy, passion and deception. All this took its toll on her. Henry Vizetelly saw her around this time and recalled:

I am ignorant of what L.E.L.'s pretensions to beauty may have been in the days when she captivated the too amorous Maginn after the susceptible Jerdan had been enamoured of her; but when I saw her on one occasion no very long time afterwards, prior to her ill-fated marriage, she was certainly most unattractive, and I failed to recognize any resemblance to the flattering portrait that formed the frontispiece to one of her books. The recollection I have preserved is of a pale-faced, plain-looking little woman with lustreless eyes, and somewhat dowdily dressed, whom no amount of enthusiasm could have idealized into a sentimental poetess.[36]

In the meantime, that same year Landon published a book of children's stories, *Traits and Trials of Early Life*. The *Literary Gazette*'s review on 30 July, (significantly, not on the usual front page position of Landon's other works), compared the writer to an elephant, meant as a compliment – wise, strong, gentle. It was a charming book, thought the reviewer, addressed to younger readers in "an affecting tone of moral inculcation". Written about the same time, another of Landon's stories "First Love; or, Constancy in the Nineteenth Century" began by observing "Now, a love affair . . . is, of all others, a thing apart – an enchanted dream where 'common griefs and cares come not' . . . it is a sweet and subtle language, 'that none understand but the speakers;' and yet this fine and delicate spirit is most especially the object of public curiosity."[37] Their affair had ever been "a thing apart". Landon's spirits improved, and she told Crofton Croker, "I have been fêted and carressed (sic) to the last degree, till, what with dinners, dances, praises and presents I begin to think life is, after all, not so bad."[38] In spite of this show of Landon's bravado, Jerdan's newest family could not but have been a source of envy and grief to one whose own three children were being brought up elsewhere, and with a recent very publicly failed engagement behind her.

These thoughts could have been in her mind when, in October, she accepted an invitation to visit the home of Matthew Forster, no relation to her ex-fiancé, but a partner in Forster and Smith, a shipping company importing goods from the Gold Coast. Before the dinner party, Forster gave Landon some papers to read to prepare her to meet one of the guests. This was a despatch about an expedition against the King of Nzema (Appollonia, to Europeans), an exciting read and just one of the brave exploits of the guest of honour, George Maclean. He had a career in the Colonial Service, having been sent to Africa when young. He had risen to become "Governor"[39] of Cape Coast Castle, in what we now know as Ghana. He had fulfilled her childhood dream of travelling to Africa, and she was avid to hear about it. Landon's biographer noted, "there was at least one subject of deep interest to both, one ready topic of delightful conversation – African habits, African horrors, and African wonders – the sea, the coast, the desert, the climate, and the people."[40] Maclean was Othello to Landon's

Desdemona: "She loved me for the dangers I had passed/ And I loved her that she did pity them."

Landon no longer felt "independent", recalled Katherine Thomson, " ... and hers was an independent mind. All these circumstances made her wish to have a claim, a home somewhere, and Mr Maclean soon offered to her these sighed-for objects of her heart."[41] Thomson did not approve of her friend's choice. Apart from the "Scotch" speech, (which would have reminded her of her former lover's Border accent), Maclean could not have been more different from the witty, sociable, and often foolish Jerdan, a difference which may, at this stage of her life, have appealed to Landon, who wanted a new start, in a new country. The pair met frequently and, astonishing her friends by the speed at which she made up her mind, an engagement was agreed. Blanchard thought that Landon at that point had no reason to think she would have to return with him to Africa, but once it was clear that was expected of her, she "courageously assented" to it.

15

Conflict and Loss

Following his acrimonious parting of the ways from Henry Colburn, Richard Bentley had decided to start a new magazine to rival Colburn's *New Monthly Magazine*, but with more humour. Bentley first settled on the title *The Wit's Miscellany*, then changed it to *Bentley's Miscellany*. On being told of the change, Jerdan is said to have remarked "what need was there to have gone to the opposite extreme?"[1] Not to be outdone, Colburn immediately secured Theodore Hook as editor of another new magazine to take the wind out of Bentley's sails. He gave Hook a much-needed four hundred pounds in bills as advance payment of his first year's salary. S. C. Hall, then acting editor of the *New Monthly Magazine*, protested that such a move would ruin the *New Monthly*, and Colburn abandoned his plans for another publication. Hook had already spent his advance, suggesting that he would work it out as editor of the *New Monthly* and it was agreed that he and Hall would be joint-editors, an arrangement which was short-lived, Hall being paid off by Colburn shortly afterwards. This knee-jerk reaction to Bentley's planned *Miscellany* cost Colburn dearly, in money and in the running of the *New Monthly*. John Forster could not work with Hook either, and he severed his connection with the paper. In an ironic twist of fate, Henry Colburn's widow married John Forster in 1856.

Bentley must have watched these to-ings and fro-ings with amusement. In November 1836 he asked Jerdan to call on him to discuss the matter, being too ill to leave his room. The first issue of *Bentley's Miscellany* appeared on 31 January 1837 and was an immediate success, mainly because it carried the first instalment of Dickens's *Oliver Twist*, with illustrations by Cruikshank. Dickens's novel was not in the spirit of the *Miscellany*, which avowed to be non-political and humorous, but it was immensely popular. The Prologue to the first issue was written by Maginn, as Bentley hired him and other writers from *Fraser's* for his new venture.

A note from Jerdan to Bentley, undated, but about December 1837, acknowledged two advances of twenty pounds each, but, said Jerdan, he had "no idea what your scale of allowances is for my articles. Whatever it is I shall be well pleased and shall continue regularly as long as you and CD think they benefit the Magazine."[2] Unblushingly, he asked Bentley for another advance of twenty-five "or rather thirty"; "it is for a pressing purpose in which parties for whom I am much concerned have all at stake, and I am unable to do what I could wish." Bentley's accounts show that an advance of twenty pounds was made in February 1838. Jerdan wrote a number of contributions for *Bentley's Miscellany*, for which he was paid one guinea per page. Between 1837 and 1846 he produced fifteen articles for a total of eighty-six pounds fifteen shillings. However, he had drawn advances from 1837–1840 of twenty to twenty-five pounds a time, totalling one hundred and fifty pounds, so ended his labours for the *Miscellany* by owing Bentley sixty-three pounds five shillings.[3]

In 1837 Jerdan's work appeared in the February, March and June issues. The first, a "Biographical Sketch of Richardson the Showman", who had died three months earlier, ran to eight pages. Dickens had returned the proofs to Jerdan apologising for having "cut it a little here and there", having had to do the same with his own articles the previous month. The subject of the Showman was close to Jerdan's heart, loving as he did all manner of shows, theatres, freaks and exhibitions. Even though he revered Richardson, Jerdan could not resist the temptation as "a scribbler for hire", to branch off into a disquisition on the history of Bartholomew Fair from its inception in 1641. It was at this Fair that Richardson's independent career as a showman commenced in 1798, when he opened his first booth as manager of an itinerant theatrical show. Taking some information from an earlier writer, Jerdan described Richardson's theatre of 1825, housing nearly one thousand people, "continually emptying and filling, and the performances were got over in about quarter of an hour!", the show thus being repeated over twenty times a day.

When Bartholomew Fair was not in season, Richardson and his troupe travelled around the country in a caravan, and "for nearly forty years his show was the most prominent attraction of the English fairground".[4] Jerdan designated Richardson "the National Theatre" and described in detail some of the individuals in his company, including the famous actor Edmund Kean and, in this age of freak shows, the "Spotted Boy" (a black child with pigmentation defects caused by vitiligo) who "was a fortune to him". Fortune or not, the Spotted Boy was treated like a son by Richardson, who was childless. The boy died very young, and on Richardson's own death he was buried in the same grave as his golden goose.

Jerdan's biography included some direct quotes from Richardson's store of puns and quips, and tributes to his generosity to impoverished actors, noting that Richardson's own fortunes had swung from rags to riches. Jerdan's admiration for his subject shines through even his tangential account of Bartholomew Fair, and he sourly observed that fairs in general were "sinking under the march of intellect, the diffusion of knowledge, and the confusion of reform". He asked plaintively, "Who shall now open the gates of the temple to dramatic fame? The

Janitor is gone for ever." This biography in *Bentley's Miscellany* is perhaps one of Jerdan's most sincere and heartfelt writings, even including the *Autobiography* that he wrote some fifteen years later. Shows of all kinds were the spice of his life, and Richardson had been the showman *par excellence*. Jerdan felt that his passing marked the end of an era, a sadness that is unmistakeable in his tribute, written at a time when his own affairs were in trouble, and the years of his own success seemed to be fast receding.

Jerdan had to carry on providing manuscripts for Bentley's *Miscellany*, and in March his six page story "Hippothanasia; or, the Last of Tails" appeared. Noting the plethora of railway companies recently formed, Jerdan's amusing conceit was that all the horses in the empire were horrified at this development, as they had been superseded by rail and were no longer needed. Jerdan cited Gulliver's Houyhnhms which showed man the intelligence and habits of this noble species. Nevertheless, his fictional government ordered all and every horse to be slaughtered as they no longer served any purpose and were too expensive to feed. "Wherefore should they live? Steam-boats had thrown the wayfaring tracks out of hay; steam-ploughs, the agricultural labours out of oats ... the military out of service ... the mechanics out of mills and factories ... " In the ensuing chaos following the great killing, asses became highly prized, and cows, pigs and dogs were tried in place of the absent horses; it was the higher orders who suffered the loss most – no horses were available to draw the King's carriage from Windsor to London: Eton boys were not strong enough, the river route was too slow. No-one knew what to do: Ministers sat around playing cards, mails did not arrive; Masters of Hounds committed suicide, the parks were deserted. At Ascot, not all was lost: sack races and wheelbarrow races were run. Jerdan gleefully described the plight of the elite Royal Horse Guards in their splendid uniforms, turning into the Royal Ass Guards, mounted upon donkeys – in short, the complete breakdown of society at every level. His dénoument is – for Jerdan – subtle. The learned societies puzzle over the "sudden and enormous rise in the price of German, Strasburg and Bologna sausages", and to solve the mystery one must travel to the fabled land of the Houyhnhms, "and at all events, make our finale like Trojans, by trusting to the horse!"

Although this is plainly a political satire, Jerdan was no Luddite, seeming to relish the new ease of travel made possible by the railways, and there is no evidence that he felt particularly strongly about the increased industrialization of the country. Indeed, a few years later he was to write a Railway Guide. However, the Prime Minister of the time was the Whig, Lord Melbourne, formerly William Lamb – perhaps this attack on government short-sightedness was Jerdan's revenge on Lamb's scolding at a long-ago party, a dish by now very cold indeed.

It was not of much immediate interest to Jerdan when, in February 1837, the boarding house of the Misses Lance at 22 Hans Place was given up. Landon had lived there, in her barely furnished room, since December 1826, but in 1834 the Lances themselves had moved out and the new tenant was a Mrs Sheldon.[5] When this tenant left Hans Place, Landon went with her, to 28 Upper Berkeley Street West, London. Later, Landon told her confidante, Katherine Thomson, that initially Mrs Sheldon had been prejudiced against her, but after they had lived together for two years, she had been treated with affection, "almost as if I were a child of her own". Nevertheless, Landon moved again within a few months. Jerdan did, however, become involved in Landon's affairs yet again, soon after her removal to the new lodging.

The Secretaryship of the Literary Fund was vacant, and Landon wrote to ask Crofton Croker to support her brother Whittington's application for the post: "It would be perfect salvation for him and me". However, Croker explained that at an earlier election when Octavian Blewett had been unsuccessful, he had promised to vote for him on the next occasion, and suggested that Landon apply to Jerdan without delay, as a very active and influential member of the council and committee.[6] Landon wrote letters to everyone she thought could assist her brother's election. Despite Crofton Croker's earlier refusal to Landon, in March Jerdan wrote to him, asking for his help. Unusually, his letter was marked "Private" and, also unusually, he addressed his friend by his first name. This was clearly a letter of grave importance to him.

> My dear Crofton, I am sure that not only as a _most_ esteemed personal friend of mine, but as one much attached to our L.E.L., you must have felt great regret at considering yourself pledged against us at the Election. It is a matter of vital consequence.
>
> I know your honour and principles too well to have said a word before; but I merely suggest _now_ does not Mahoney's offer afford you a just and fair opportunity for being neutral, and the same with other friends of, Yours truly . . . [7]

On 8 March Landon wrote on the same matter to Jerdan:

> Lord John Russell, Lord Francis Egerton and Lord Munster have all promised their support in the kindest manner – that with Sir John makes four – I hope to God the election will not come on about Easter, for then these people are all going out of town . . . I hope we shall get the three new council.

Held after Easter the vote was equal, until the late arrival of Lord John Russell and Sir Robert Peel who swung the vote in Landon's favour. The result delighted and excited his sister so much that she reported "When I heard of our success the blood rushed from my nose and mouth in torrents".[8]

Although probably pleased for Landon that her brother had won the position she wanted for him, Jerdan was in a sour mood at this time because of an article on the Literary Fund in the April issue of *Fraser's Magazine*, which billed it as a conflict between the Editor of the *Literary Gazette* and the Editor of the *Athenaeum*. As *Fraser's* agreed with the *Gazette*, in the interests of fairness they quoted at length the *Athenaeum's* argument. This rested upon the blurring of distinction between the Literary Fund Club and the Literary Fund Society, promulgated by "certain paragraphs" which had been sent to the papers. The idea that these two were identical, believed the *Athenaeum*, was prejudicial to the interests of any benevolent institution. Mr Dilke agreed with their view (naturally, as he <u>was</u> the *Athenaeum)* and especially resisted the proposal to elect members of the Club to the Committee, which would tighten the bonds between the two. The *Athenaeum* reported that re-election of the committee was about to proceed when Crofton Croker opposed the re-election of Mr Dilke. Asked for his reasons, he remained silent. Jerdan stated that in his opinion the club had benefited the institution, so a person who opposed one could not be a friend to the other, and he supported Crofton Croker's objection. When the vote was taken, only four people objected to Dilke: Jerdan, Croker, Britton and Moyes. The *Athenaeum* jeered that "to determine the brain sympathies" of the parties, it should be noted that Jerdan was the editor of the *Literary Gazette*, Britton and Croker had written for it for years, and Moyes printed it. The *Athenaeum* believed that "some change must take place in the committee – whether they have selected the person who ought to retire remains for proof".

Having quoted for a full page the *Athenaeum's* position on the matter, *Fraser's* revealed that they <u>could</u> say a great deal about the Literary Fund, but would restrict themselves to merely estimating the other paper's points instead. The argument was simply whether the Literary Fund Institution benefited or otherwise from the Literary Fund Club. The Institution dined together once a year, "on which occasions very bad speeches and very good subscriptions are furnished with a 'continual giving' liberality", and they administer the distribution of funds to the needy. The Literary Fund Club were all members and most were promoters of the Literary Fund Institution. The *Athenaeum's* "horror" concerning eating and drinking made them duller than usual for not understanding that club dinners aided the Institution. "What, we would ask, keeps together every benevolent institution in this metropolis? Dinners, dinners, dinners." The *Athenaeum* was talking nonsense to say the Club was not mixed up with the Institution, and put this pettiness down to personal jealousies. Although belonging to a temperance society, joked *Fraser's*, they recommended these two "talented editors to hob-nob together . . . a rivalry but not feeling it – animated, in short, by one heart and soul in the noble endeavour of humbugging his Majesty's subjects . . .". Jerdan and Dilke were never going to "hob-nob" and they crossed swords again, immediately.

Despite his seemingly tireless work on behalf of authors desperate for help from the Literary Fund, Jerdan was attacked by Dilke, at a meeting of the Committee on 12 April 1837, most probably as a direct result of Jerdan's vote against his re-election. Dilke wished the meeting to consider "the conduct of a member in respect to monies voted to him for the relief of applicants". Although his Motion was seconded and carried, Jerdan's reliable friend Croly moved an Amendment that the Committee proceed no further in the business, a motion that was also carried. Although Jerdan's name did not appear in the Minutes, it was clearly he who was Dilke's target, as on 10 May it was noted that "Mr Jerdan was heard by the Committee in explanation of the subject noticed in the Minutes of the last Meeting".

During the course of his association with the Literary Fund, Jerdan person-ally sponsored some thirty applicants, many of whom made multiple applications to the Fund, each requiring separate forms and letters and, if successful, acknowl-edgements. He was no doubt instrumental in guiding many more destitute writers to the charity of the Fund, to be sponsored by others. Letters in the files of the Fund are full of heartbreaking descriptions of the poverty assailing writers and their families, and make plain how very precarious it was to rely upon writing for an income. Jerdan, luckier than so many, felt a deep sympathy with these men and women, and did everything he could to give them the support they needed. Veiled accusations of misconduct from Dilke, who had come from a privileged background and known nothing of hardship, must have been anathema to Jerdan's ears. He knew enough hard luck stories to fill a book, he remarked in his memoirs, but preferred other witnesses to offer evidence "whose sentiments on the subject of literary distress and the futile nature of literary pursuits will not, perhaps, be so angrily impugned as, in certain quarters, mine have been".[9] He cited as "witnesses" the advice that Charles Lamb gave to the Quaker poet Bernard Barton, when the latter thought of giving up employment at the Bank in order to write: "Throw yourself rather, my dear Sir, from the Tarpeian Rock, slap down headlong upon iron spikes . . . Oh, you know not, may you never know, the miseries of subsisting by authorship! . . . keep to your Bank and your Bank will keep you." Barton got the same advice from Byron: "You know what ills the author's life assail,/ Toil, envy, want, the patron and the jail." Nevertheless, Jerdan's friends were still producing successful books, Bulwer publishing *Ernest Maltravers* and two others, Lady Blessington's *Victims of Society* and Disraeli's *Venetia*, all giving the lie to Byron's advice. Leigh Hunt published his poem 'Blue Stocking Revels' in yet another of his ventures, the *Monthly Repository*, and asked Jerdan to notice it in the *Literary Gazette*, a clear indication that a highly experienced writer still believed the *Gazette* to have influence. In the poem he celebrated female poets such as Elizabeth Barrett, Felicia Hemans, Anna Barbauld and, of course, L.E.L.[10] Lady Blessington also did her best for the *Repository*, but it failed within a year. About this time Jerdan received a note from Thackeray, whose periodical *The Constitutional* had recently failed. "Is it fair to ask whether the *Literary Gazette* is for sale? I should like to treat; and thought it best to apply to the fountain-head of whom I am always, the obligated W.M.T."[11] Nothing came of this proposal.

Jerdan and Dickens were at this time socializing in much the same circles, and the bright spot of the year as far as the Literary Fund association was concerned was the attendance of Charles Dickens as guest of honour at the Anniversary Dinner, an occasion on which he made his first public speech for the organization. Dickens had been introduced by William Harrison Ainsworth to Maclise, Cruikshank, and the young publisher John Macrone. John Forster, recently dis-engaged from Landon, took Dickens in June to see 'Othello' at the Haymarket Theatre, and introduced him to the famous tragic actor William Macready, Jerdan's friend. Forster acted as Dickens's agent, negotiating new agreements with Bentley, increasing his salary to thirty pounds a month for editing the *Miscellany*, and five hundred pounds for the remainder of *Oliver Twist*, which had given Bentley's journal such a flying start. In September Bentley had acquired the *Memoirs of Joseph Grimaldi* who had died in May, and had given Dickens the task of editing them. The arrangements concerning the *Memoirs* and *Oliver Twist* had repercussions which were to involve Jerdan.

Pickwick Papers was finally completed in November 1837, celebrated by a banquet on the 18th for a select group of Talfourd, Forster, Ainsworth, Jerdan, the publisher and Macready, at the Prince of Wales in Leicester Place.[12] Having played such an important part by his suggestion to develop the character of Sam Weller, Jerdan was invited to the "semi-business, Pickwickian sort of dinner", by a letter from the author saying "I depend upon you above everybody."[13] Jerdan was delighted and noted with pleasure that "author, printer, artist and publisher had all proceeded on simply verbal assurances, and that there never had arisen a word to interrupt or prevent the complete satisfaction of everyone". Collegial himself, but too often involved in quarrels, he would have preferred to live in a world of gentleman's agreements. Dickens's affairs were more business-like, especially while Forster was managing them.

Hard up for ready money, Jerdan wrote constantly to Bentley asking for help. On 10 June (with no year noted), a letter rather more explicit than many other such letters, told Bentley that Jerdan had always found him friendly, and before plunging in with his request, warned him to "not be startled by its first aspect, but look to its real features and extent". Jerdan explained that a loan had been recalled, and he needed to reborrow the amount. The principal was secured, but he wished Bentley to act as co-guarantor with Crofton Croker, for his "punctual payment of an Insurance Policy and the interest". He had paid premiums on the Policy for thirteen years, so it was only for the interest that he needed guarantors. In return, he offered Bentley "a Novel for next Season from a party from whom you are very desirous to have a work of that sort".[14] Jerdan later mentioned that he had been forced to let his insurance policies lapse, so it appears unlikely that Bentley and Croker agreed to stand as guarantors for him.

In an attempt to earn more, the *Miscellany* of June 1837 saw the publication of Jerdan's longest contribution so far, nine and a half pages earning him £9 19s. 6d. The story was entitled "John Pouledoune, the Victim of Improvements!" Jerdan was late with his story. Dickens chided him, "I feared you were not going to introduce me to the victim at all, so long have I expected him without avail."[15] Dickens complained that Jerdan should not have blamed him for errors in the last story, as there was no time for corrections, an indication of the hectic speed at which Jerdan was turning out all the work he was committed to. "John Pouledoune" was another thinly veiled attack on the state of modern society, its heartlessness and disregard for the individual. The protagonist, son of a hosier of self-made wealth, was told his fortune by gipsies in terms that seemed incomprehensible to him. On inheriting his father's considerable wealth, John Pooledoune endeavoured to create many 'improvements', each more absurd than the last, and each causing him serious physical harm. One such, recalling Jerdan's earlier tale, "Hippothanasia", was the sale of his farm horse and purchase of a steam plough which, as he demonstrated its use to his farm labourers, over-turned, covering him with steam and burning coals. Another 'improvement' fractured his arm, another left him bald and facially scarred. His fortune vanished and he took to drink, finally trying to drown himself in the Thames. However he was rescued and taken to the poor house as a pauper, dying before reaching it. His funeral was a sham, the coffin was empty. His emaciated body was displayed for medical students and lectured upon. Jerdan could not resist poking fun at the popular interest in phrenology; the bumps on the corpse's skull inflicted by the grappling irons that pulled him from the Thames were interpreted as "organs of philoprogenitiveness, amativeness and destructiveness". Pooledoune's skeleton was eventually displayed in a glass case in the hospital's museum. Thus were the gipsies' prophecies fulfilled, the last of which was that he will be "Dead; resembling Death, yet keeping thy place among the dead and the living; thy end shall not be an ending, and every one shall know that thou art and art not!" Jerdan again spoilt the climax of his tale by needlessly observing that as *Bentley's Miscellany* was a "moral magazine", the point of his story was "May we all be preserved from the fascination of Gipsies!"

Macready's glow about Jerdan's kind speech at the Garrick had worn off a year later when, on 13 May, he saw a copy of the *Literary Gazette*'s review of Miss Martineau's *Society in America*. Jerdan, like many Britons, would have had feelings of antipathy towards America which waged war when England was threatened by Napoleon; at this time, although he changed later, he found nothing to admire and wanted nothing to do with the new republic. (His view of American literature, however, was more favourable, such as his early praise of Washington Irving and later, Fenimore Cooper.) The Martineau review was, in truth, on the light side for such an erudite book. As if at a loss for an opinion on the content of the work, the reviewer (probably Jerdan) took issue with the wording of the title, while noting that the work

stands upon higher grounds. Miss Martineau is a decided politician, political economist and philosopher. Her book is redolent of all the profundities of speculation connected with these grand questions: then why give a flippant commonplace name to an article of much higher order? Miss Martineau writes like a man, and she ought not, thus, to be treated as a woman. Saunders and Otley have to answer for it.

Both Colburn and Bentley had vied for Martineau's book, offering her extravagant sums. That Saunders and Otley were successful is likely to have caused a furious Colburn to insist on the *Literary Gazette's* finding fault with it, on whatever grounds it could fabricate. Small wonder then that Macready wrote in his Diary, "Jerdan is not a man of sufficient intelligence, extent of view, probity or philanthropy enough to estimate such a work – his notice is in my mind a disgrace to himself. He does not understand, nor can he feel the truth contained in the book." His criticism was indeed merited, but Jerdan could not possibly have had time to read Martineau's book in any detail and still get out a review at the earliest opportunity; nevertheless, to take issue with its title in place of any serious comment, was not up to Jerdan's usual standards, even when pushed by his irate partner Colburn. Full of righteous indignation, Macready spent the evening at Miss Martineau's, where he knew no-one but passed a cheerful time. His disgust with Jerdan did not last long, as the following week he invited him to some entertainment. That Christmas, Macready and Kemble acted in a pantomime, where Jerdan was also on the stage, as happy to participate in a play as to watch one.

In June 1837 King William IV died, and the young Princess Victoria came to the throne to begin her long reign. The country's celebrations were not shared by Jerdan, who had troubles on his mind. In July he wrote a brief and poignant note to Mr Burn,[16] solicitor, of Raymonds Buildings, Grays Inn, who was probably acting on behalf of a creditor. His letter encapsulated his situation and his emotions.

Mr Jerdan assures Mr Burn that he is most unwilling to provoke either trouble or expence, being ill prepared for either. But at this moment he cannot help himself and must be at the mercy of any one who has a claim upon him which he cannot immediately satisfy. Several concurrent circumstances have exhausted his resources, and tho' only for a short breathing time, he is for the instant utterly defenceless.[17]

Although their paths had diverged widely by this time, Jerdan could not have helped but know about Landon's every action, of significance to him as it would affect the upkeep and care of their children. Now, according to Landon's first biographer Laman Blanchard, the behaviour of Landon's intended was giving cause for concern. In the summer of 1837, a few months after first meeting his betrothed, Maclean went up to see his family in Scotland. He appeared to be having second thoughts about the marriage, failed to write to Landon, or to respond to her letters. Blanchard did not know that at this time Maclean had been sent to Holland on a diplomatic mission, which would have absorbed his time and interest and possibly made corresponding with Landon more difficult.[18] She fell ill under the strain, convinced that the old scandals had come to the notice of Maclean and his family. He was absent for six months, suddenly reappearing. Whatever explanations he gave to Landon were private, Maclean not being a man to take any notice of rumour and gossip, and the engagement was intact. Landon, however, had heard rumours about him, that he already had a native wife living in Cape Coast Castle. Shocked and alarmed, she confronted him, and after his explanation that no such person was at the Castle, that any such connection was long over, she agreed to continue with preparations for the marriage, and for her departure for Africa.

Blanchard believed that her terror of breaking off a second engagement would unleash upon her head the judgment that all the slanders must have been correct, and "this old familiar thought occasioned far more pain than any fear of consequences likely to ensue from the bygone domestic arrangement of her intended husband".[19] Much of Blanchard's information in his *Life of L.E.L.* was given to him by Landon herself for an article in the *New Monthly Magazine*, for which they both worked from time to time; he knew her well, and his view on this emotional matter may well be accurate. In Lady Blessington's recent epistolary novel *Victims of Society*, she wrote "In London, any woman in a brilliant position may lose her reputation in a week, without even having imagined a dereliction from honour."[20] She would have been painfully conscious of the scandals that had earlier surrounded her friend, Letitia Landon.

Landon's health improved, and she became much happier. She published another historical novel, *Ethel Churchill or The Two Brides*, which was well received, and later translated into Dutch and German. Restoring Landon to its front page, the *Literary Gazette* of 7 October 1837 noted that the book was the result of moral investigation. Landon's poetry was luxuriant in imagery, impassioned, but her prose was "marked by analysis and purpose". *Ethel Churchill* was "far superior to any of Miss Landon's former works". The absence of Jerdan's usual over-exuberant praise of her work is striking, but Jerdan's feelings must have been torn between losing Landon, the demands and needs of his wife Frances and her grown children, and his new family with Mary Maxwell.

Writing to Bentley at the end of the year, Jerdan was uncharacteristically circumspect. He enclosed two short contributions to the *Miscellany*, to be forwarded to "our friend Boz, suitable to the season and of no value at any other time, if of any now". If accepted, they should not give the author's name. He also enclosed a manuscript of Landon's which he did not recall previously appearing in print, but was not sure. "If you like to risk it, we might put in a doubtful note."[21]

Jerdan planned to submit several contributions to *Bentley's Miscellany* during 1838, but at the very beginning of the year was again out of funds. The long-suffering Bentley had once again come to his rescue, earning himself another heartfelt letter:

> What you were good enough to advance as a 'Miscellany account' will be so long of repayment that it looks more like a donation to be without return, than a friendly aid to help through a great temporary danger. Indeed I am bound to say that for the latter it would be so ineffectual that I am wavering upon its enclosure to you, and will certainly hesitate to employ it beyond placing it at my bankers.[22]

Jerdan's first of five appearances in the *Miscellany* for 1838 was in March, entitled "Life" and signed with his pseudonym 'Teutha'. The scrappy haste of this piece might be his reason for using an alias. It opened with a meeting of the "Nothing New Under the Sun" Society, at which a member declared that "Life is like a week". The members gabble "It may be like a day, like a play, like stubble, like a bubble, like a vomit, like a comet" and so on for a paragraph. The remainder of the piece described each day's characteristics in terms of human development, Friday being personified as Avarice, Saturday with stiffened limbs and Sunday as the rest of the grave. As so often, Jerdan ended awkwardly, saying that the "Nothing New Under the Sun" Society considered the article as a novelty and worthy of the Society, and as Bentley's *Miscellany* was only one year old, it was still a novelty itself. It is a short piece, and hardly worthy of Jerdan's ability; there is no indication that Bentley made any complaint about either its brevity or its quality, but he was paying a flat page rate for Jerdan's work, and this was mercifully brief .

Considering this to be a "rather grave article", Jerdan sent Bentley a more humorous one for the April issue, " likely perhaps to serve the *Miscellany* in Cornwall and Wales".[23] He told Bentley rather plaintively, "I will faithfully go on every month if you do not make any lapses between, which discourage me as much as if I were a novice in writing." He was ashamed, he acknowledged, to come to the point of his letter, asking for a hundred pounds, as money he was expecting was delayed. Lord Willoughby was due in town and would repay the loan. Jerdan sent this letter with his son, who was to return with Bentley's answer.

The story he sent, which he hoped would appeal to the *Miscellany's* Cornish and Welsh readers, was "The Snuff Box – A Tale of Wales", which appeared in April. This odd story appears at first to be Jerdan showing off his detailed knowledge of Cornish mining, as his hero travels to Cornwall on the way to Wales, filling his hampers with samples of ore. Jerdan's list of minerals covered a long paragraph, and included quite a number of exclusively Cornish words. This makes for a tedious reading of lists, but it is an impressive show of knowledge. He had, a little earlier, visited his old friend John Carne in Penzance and had been taken to visit mines and museums in the area. He found these of great interest and clearly remembered, or noted, many items of which he made good use in the opening lines of this story. All this erudition merely paved the way for his hero to ingratiate himself into Swansea society. Once known and respected, at a dinner party he exhibited a fabulously jewelled snuffbox, modestly displaying an inscription inside declaring it as a gift to him from King Louis First of Bavaria, for discovering an inexhaustible silver mine, and promising him a huge annuity.

Thus marked out as a desirable catch, he had his pick of potential brides, settling on one who, though not very attractive, was endowed with £30,000. The following week, a party given by the newly-weds was rudely interrupted by two rough and dirty men bursting in and seizing the jewelled snuff box, claiming it against a bad debt of eight guineas. The snuff box was a fake, and the bride's only hope was that her husband would turn into a honest gentleman, which would be a "wonderful change and worthy of award more real than the fine Bavarian royal box". This cynical tale of avarice and deception weighs poorly in the balance against the opening promise of learned information on mines and mining, and ends with a rather flat moral.

The strains of his depleted finances made Jerdan quite ill. In May, Crofton Croker suggested he come to his home, Rosamund's Bower, to be nursed back to health. He was worried that Jerdan's incapacity would have a serious effect upon arrangements for the Literary Fund Dinner, "for really I know not who could take your place in directing the needful to be done".[24] There was a genuine friendship between the two men, and despite his recent illness and accruing financial problems, it was typical of Jerdan's thoughtfulness and affectionate regard for his friend that he proposed that the tenth anniversary of the Society of Noviomagus be marked by a presentation to their Chairman. He suggested to J. B. Nichols "What say you to a subscription tribute from the Club, to be presented on 2 July. If you approve, keep the secret from Crofton, and let us buy some pretty little thing of <u>old</u> plate or what you might think better, and give it at the Anniversary."[25] Nichols responded favourably, agreeing that old plate, "the older the better", was an ideal gift. Jerdan then approached other Noviomagians, including John Bruce,[26] reminding him to keep the matter secret until the day of presentation.

Jerdan had confided to Nichols that he had "bestowed much pains" on the presentation he was making that week to the Society of Antiquaries, and Nichols assured him that he would be there to listen. Jerdan's offering was of two "remarkable armlets . . . of great beauty and workmanship" which had been found at Drummond Castle, the home of Lord and Lady Willoughby de Eresby, when the land was being ploughed. The armlets were made of brass, respectively sixteen and fifteen inches in circumference, weighing over three pounds apiece. The Society's journal *Archaelogia* described them in great detail, noting that Jerdan had consulted various references, and had dated these finds at "soon after the Christian era; in the time of Agricola and Galgacus".[27] A letter to Jerdan from Henry Ellis, Director of the British Museum, indicated that these Armlets had been gifted to the Museum by Lord and Lady de Eresby.[28] At the same meeting as he displayed the Perthshire armlets, Jerdan also exhibited a fragment specimen of painting from the walls of a room in Pompeii. It is not known how he came by this fragment, but it was minuted as "an interesting example of the type and composition of their ancient Frescoes".

Reflecting Jerdan's illness and lack of energy were the next two stories which appeared in the *Miscellany*, both signed with his pseudonym 'Teutha', which often indicated a work that Jerdan was not anxious to acknowledge as his own. The May contribution, "Thomas Noddy Esq."[29] was in the style of a biography, listing absurdly improbable lineage for the ancestry of his eponymous hero. Jerdan gave spurious and amusing references playing upon the name of Noddy, such as a Bishop Noddy: "It was from this holy man and pious divine that assemblies of the clergy were styled *sy-nods*. Vide Archaeologia Vol. I, p. 1." As an infant his hero was dropped by his mother and trampled by a pony, resulting in a twisted head, with involuntary winking and nodding. The remainder of the tale related the dire consequences of the misunderstandings caused by this affliction, such as the night he took the stage box at a performance of Hamlet, causing roars of laughter by his nodding and winking in inappropriate places. Being a man of wealth, he paid a huge compensation to the theatre; he visited an auction and predictably found himself the owner of large amounts of china, pictures and jewels; he fell down an open hole in the street, went to a levee and nodded and winked at Queen Victoria; and finally, so upset a lady who interpreted his affliction as unwelcome attention, that her lover challenged him to a duel. He was killed and his second, who was his heir, inherited all his property. This story seems to have no moral point or deeper meaning other than as a mere amusement, and perhaps that is why Jerdan chose to sign himself as Teutha. The piece certainly does not show Jerdan at his best, nor does it contain any elements of his knowledge that can be found in other stories appearing in Bentley's *Miscellany*.

The following month saw the publication of "A Windsor Ball of the Latest Fashion". Two women and two men sharing a house threw a party to celebrate their achieving a total of 191 years. Reminiscent of his earlier "Conversazione", Jerdan recounted the banal conversations of their similarly elderly guests, their hopes and plans for whatever future remained to them, but always with a cynical or sarcastic edge. The party was a success, some even carefully walking through a minuet. On the stroke of midnight a horrifying apparition appeared, hideous and misshapen, ghoulishly depicted with a noxious smell and blue flames. Most frightening, the 'monster' wore a sign on its back with the word "Influenza". The party broke up in chaos, people fleeing the dread figure. Never one to leave well enough alone, Jerdan explained that the local 'wags' had costumed a dwarf and obtained the awful smells and blue fire from a chemist to terrify the party-goers. He remarked that six years later the four old friends still lived happily together, so no lasting damage was done.

This story may well have been symbolic of the way he felt in the Spring and Summer of 1838. It was a terrible year for him as Landon's marriage loomed, circulation of the *Literary Gazette* kept dropping, and he was always short of money. Bentley had helped him out countless times before, but that well was running dry. In a brief letter annotated 1838, it appears that Jerdan had been rebuffed by his colleague and was deeply hurt:

> my disappointment yesterday was great; so great that I must write a few lines, the last on the subject, and at least with one good quality, because they are to assure you that I will never again allude to this or broach anything of the kind again.
>
> Of course I know that you could have rendered me the service if you had thought it right; and at the same time I am free to acknowledge that you had a perfect right to refuse, and that circumstances of various kinds might exist in your mind to warrant that refusal, and so cogent that I must simply confess their preponderence. So let the matter rest, and let me indulge in the hope that it may not occur again when so much may depend on so little. At all events you shall dismiss all fear of being trou-bled.[30]

Although Jerdan was always verbose, the tone of this letter is more garbled than usual, indicating his frantic state of mind.

Another reason for Jerdan's distracted state of mind was that on 28 July 1838 a son, Charles, was born to 'William Stuart Jerdan' (annexing his mother's surname) and 'Mary Ann Jerdan, formerly Maxwell'.[31] Mary was living at 87 Hercules Buildings, Lambeth, which had been constructed by Philip Astley as workers' houses, around 1818. William Blake had lived on the same site, and in a cyclical reminder of Jerdan's boyhood memory of seeing the balloonist Lunardi, another resident of Hercules Buildings was G. P. Harding, publisher of prints of Charles Green, Aeronaut, another famous balloonist.

For ten years after Jerdan had lost Grove House the only addresses on his letters were those of the *Literary Gazette* office; there could have been some form of accommodation at these premises as well, but it is more probable that he had gone to live with Mary Maxwell in Hercules Buildings. Although on the baby Charles's birth certificate she is styled as 'Mary Ann Jerdan formerly Maxwell', Jerdan was still married to Frances. By December 1839 another son, John, arrived, called merely "Boy" on his birth certificate, as they had not yet decided on his name.[32] This new, fast-expanding family was a drain not only on Jerdan's energy but on his resources, stretched to the limit as the *Literary Gazette* declined.

He still had faithful contributors, however. One, the poet Charles Swain, sent him a humorous verse entitled *The Leek*, telling him "I think the Cambrians might to elect me their Poet Laureate for my patriotic song."[33] His other offerings were *To Gaglioni*, a famous Italian ballerina, and *Ode to a Coal Fire (found near Rydal Mount)*. This latter piece, he explained to Jerdan, had been intended as a "pleasant squib upon certain <u>imitators</u> of Wordsworth". He had thought of destroying it – but left it to Jerdan to decide upon its merits. "I look upon you as my literary parent – what you burn is best burnt", he declared. Jerdan did not burn it, but printed it in the *Literary Gazette* of May 1838.

In the world of drama, so fascinating to Jerdan, Macready had been collaborating with Bulwer on a new play, 'The Lady of Lyons', which opened in February 1838. It was successful and Bulwer, reflecting his commitment to the enterprise, refused to accept his royalties, returning to Macready his cheque for two hundred guineas. This was accompanied by a letter which, noted Macready, was "recompense for much ill-requited labour and unpitied suffering; it is an honour to him, and a subject of pride to myself". Macready called Jerdan in and told him that Bulwer's kindness should be made public. In the *Literary Gazette* of 31 March readers were advised of Bulwer's generosity, and told that

> To estimate Mr Macready's exertions and sacrifice is something, but to lay so noble a testimony of that estimation on the altar of personal sympathies and a public cause – is alike honourable to the receiver and the giver – we know no praise too high for it. With such an example, who will doubt the ultimate issue of the struggle to reclaim the stage and the drama of England.

Jerdan would have been delighted at the opportunity to extol two of his dear friends in one paragraph. In April, Macready was incensed that his sworn enemy Bunn was elected to the Garrick Club. He resigned in protest but was begged to return and did so. Jerdan wrote in sympathy for his predicament.

By December Jerdan was in dire straits and called upon Macready for assistance. The actor confided to his Diary:

> A note from Jerdan asking me to withhold the cheque for £70, upon the faith of which he had borrowed that sum from me. The fact cannot be

disguised; he is a man who has no conscience obtaining the means of other men. The money is gone! Wrote notes to Ransom's to withhold Jerdan's cheque. It is useless to make strife with a man who has it in his power to cheat you. And is determined to do so. One's mind must be made up. He has sold me, as others have done!

The following day his entry was brief and to the point: "Letter from Jerdan. More frivolous excuses. He has robbed me and there is an end."

What Jerdan said or thought about Landon's imminent marriage can only be imagined as he did not write about it in any known document. What Landon privately thought about leaving him and their children when she moved to another continent can also only be the subject of speculation. Whether he or she made the necessary arrangements to take care of their offspring, to house, feed, clothe and educate them, cannot be known, but she must have been prepared to face the fact that as her new life was in Africa, she might never see them again.

Landon's choice of future husband was not universally welcomed by her friends or even by her enemies. The *Age* noted, "Alas! 'tis true Miss Landon is about to be married to Mr Maclean, the governor of the British settlements on the Gold Coast, whither they sail in three or four weeks. To think of 'L'Improvisatrice' amongst the negroes!! 'It's too bad'."[34] As well as Katherine Thomson who disliked Maclean's dourness, Samuel Carter Hall also had strong misgivings. He believed that Maclean "neither knew, felt, nor estimated her value: He wedded her, I am sure, only because he was vain of her celebrity . . . There was, in this case, no love, no esteem, no respect and there could have been no discharge of duty that was not thankless and irksome."[35] In fairness, he admitted that Bulwer Lytton did not agree with him about Maclean's character; he wrote to Hall about the bridegroom "in terms of consideration and respect".

On 7 June 1838, in a strictly private ceremony, Landon and Maclean were married in St Mary's, Bryanston Square, London. Whittington Landon officiated, and after the ceremony there was no celebration of any sort. In *Queens of Society* Katherine Thomson related that the newly weds went to the Sackville Street Hotel for one night, after which Landon returned to her friends the Liddiards at Hyde Park Street, kept her maiden name, and went on with her life as usual. One reason for this secrecy was posited by Thomson who suspected it was to avoid news of the marriage reaching Cape Coast Castle before Maclean could give instructions for his 'other wife' to be moved out. Maclean's reason was that he was very busy at the Colonial Office, and did not like celebrations and festivities.[36]

Three weeks later, on 28 June, Queen Victoria was crowned. Landon watched the Coronation procession, but suddenly, she stepped back and was gone from sight. This was the last day on which the famous poet was seen in public. That evening all of London was ablaze with lights, bells were ringing and the streets were full of happy crowds. There was a farewell party for the newly-weds but Jerdan did not come to say a last goodbye to his erstwhile dearly loved L.E.L. Samuel Carter Hall was naturally emotional, knowing it was unlikely he would ever see his friend again. He made a warm speech, referring to Landon as his wife's valued friend, and spoke of the affection and respect of her many other friends. His evident strength of feelings drew tears from some of the company present. What happened next was unexpected and painful:

> The reader may imagine the chill which came over that party when McLean had risen to 'return thanks'. He merely said, 'If Mrs. McLean has as many friends as Mr Hall says she has, I only wonder they allow her to leave them.' That was all: it was more than a chill – it was a blight. A gloomy foreboding as to the future of that doomed woman came to all the guests, as one by one they rose and departed, with a brief and mournful farewell.[37]

The following morning Whittington, who escorted the couple to Portsmouth and on to the ship, asked his sister how she would manage without her friends to talk to. "I shall talk to them through my books", she replied.

On 5 July they sailed for Africa on the brig 'Maclean', fitted up especially for the comfort of the new Mrs. Maclean. On 15 August, the day after her 36th birthday, they arrived at Cape Coast Castle. On 15 October Landon was found dead, holding an empty vial of prussic acid. The circumstances surrounding this untoward death were reported, skewed, twisted, gossiped over and analyzed immediately the news reached England, and again more recently as interest in Landon's poetry has revived. There were conflicting reports from those at the Castle, unreliable as they were frequently influenced by personal and business grudges against Maclean. The talk centered around whether she had taken her own life, been poisoned, or had become ill and collapsed. Samuel Carter Hall, for instance, was certain he knew, and had not changed his mind when he reviewed Landon's death many years later: "Her marriage wrecked her life . . . For my part, that unhappy L.E.L. was murdered, I never had a doubt."[38] Because of the extreme heat Maclean had her buried immediately, which precluded any medical examination that might have helped to determine the cause of death.[39]

Recent research on Landon's death has pointed to the possibility that the cause was Stokes-Adams Syndrome, a chronic condition only then recently identified, in which the patient suffers a series of collapses due to a stoppage of the heart, likely to be the cause of symptoms which Landon had displayed for years – spasms, migraines, fainting fits and other complaints.[40] In all probability the truth will never be known, but the suddenness and the circumstances surrounding her death gave rise to a contemporary small industry of memoirs of the poet, both biographical and fictional. Even in 1928 a romanticized biography stated unequivocally that "There can be little doubt that Letitia remained to the day of her marriage, a stainless virgin."[41] Another later writer was of the opinion that between Jerdan and Maginn was "uninterrupted kindliness and understanding [which] becomes in a way a surety for the right relations between Maginn and L.E.L. Both men professed the deepest attachment for L.E.L . . . she presumably treated them as good companions, granting no undue favours to either."[42] This same author decried the treatment of Landon and Maginn in another book[43] published around the same time. Many factual errors in two other semi-fictional biographies have been pointed out in some detail by Duncan.[44] Such blatant errors illuminate the many misunderstandings that crept into all the so-called biographies of L.E.L. and highlights the caution necessary in using them as sources. Interpretations of interpretations rolled on and on for years after Landon's death. A recent addition to these fictionalized biographies is one published in 2009 by the great-great-great-grandson of L.E.L. and William Jerdan.[45]

News of Landon's death was first published in *The Courier* on 1 January 1839, and followed by other newspapers in the ensuing days. One of the earliest notices was, of course, in the *Literary Gazette* of 5 January 1839, where Jerdan observed:

> Whether after ages look at the glowing purity and nature of her first poems, or the more sustained thoughtfulness and vigour of her later works, in prose or in verse, they will cherish her memory as that of one of the most beloved female authors, the pride and glory of our country while she lived, and the undying delight of succeeding generations.

When Jerdan came to write his *Autobiography* in 1852–53, he left any mention of Landon's death until almost the last page of the final volume, as if he could not bear to put it into words. All that he said then was, "Of the shock received by the death of L.E.L. I dare not trust my pen to write. The news stunned me at the time it was told – I fell down insensate – and the memory is too painful for even a line to bewail the sacrifice. No more."[46] His pain is palpable, even fourteen years after the event. The only other record of his feelings immediately after hearing of her death is an eloquent emotional letter he sent to the always sympathetic Lady Blessington on 5 January, in reply to hers:

> Dear Lady Blessington,
> Your note but too truly expresses what I was sure you would feel for the miserable calamity which has closed the earthly carreer [sic] of our wonderfully gifted friend. Could her life be told what a history would be there of Womans fated wretchedness and of the woes which genius must endure. A life of self sacrifice from infancy to the grave – of sufferings vainly concealed under mocking brilliancy and assumed mirth – of a heart

broken by mortification, of spirits always forced, of the finest of human chords ever crushed and lacerated by the rudest handling, of sensitiveness subjected to perpetual injury – in features such as these are to be read the sad story of L.E.L. – Men are exposed to unhappiness, but alas what else is there for their beautiful and gentle companions?

Hard is the fate of Womankind; and the serpent whose curse contends with the heel of the one, gnaws the heart and drains the life-blood of the other. My poor, dear, all but adored L.E.L. – the creature whose earliest and precocious aspirations it was mine to cherish and improve, whose mind unfolded its marvellous stores as drawn forth and encouraged by me – well did she sweetly paint it when she said "We love the bird we taught to sing", and truly and devotedly did I love her for fifteen eventful years. Deeply did I deprecate her fateful union with a man altogether unfitted for her, because I foresaw nothing but that misery which she, annoyed and depressed by the inconvenience and humiliations of her own position, could not or would not see.

Dear Lady Blessington, since writing these lines I have marked my letter private; for I know not how it is, I have been led to unbosom myself to you in a manner that would not do for many in our own bad world. Yes, I do know how it is! It is because I am writing to one, every emotion in whose breast is attuned to the dearest and loveliest sympathies of our Nature.

May Heaven give her many happy moments.[47]

This is Jerdan at his best, not putting on any disguise, not trying to "keep a stiff upper lip", but just talking to an old and trusted friend, who also was close to his beloved and was all but certain to have been privy to the truth of their situation. There were few, if any, that he could trust with their secret, and except for the occasion when Edward Bulwer reported his drunken boast, had no confidante to whom he could unburden his sorrow at Landon's too-early and mysterious death. Lady Blessington gave what support she could, but this was a dreadful time in her life too; she was weary with overwork and struggling to appear vital and interesting, especially when Louis Napoleon came to call whilst waiting his chance to claim the French throne. Anna Maria Hall condoled Jerdan on L.E.L.'s death, and he responded more cautiously than to Lady Blessington: "I am in truth bewildered by this frightful calamity and feel altogether unequal to think or dwell upon the subject. Heaven knows how deeply I deprecated this fatal African marriage; but poor L.E.L. was a sacrifice through all her life, and if to continue so, it is almost well it has ended."[48]

Maginn too was appalled by Landon's death, "and almost lost his senses for two days. In his own last hours, when he fancied that he saw visions, he said to one who watched by his bedside, 'I have just been talking to Letitia – she has been here an hour, she sat there, just opposite.'"[49] Maginn blamed himself for her death – had he not received those incriminating letters which his wife sent to Forster, Landon might never have married Maclean, with such tragic consequences.

The report of her burial place, given by Dr Madden, who visited Cape Coast in 1841, caused grief to her friends at home. Madden was no friend of Maclean, and probably relished the opportunity of painting him as black as possible. Appalled by his account of Landon's burial place under the feet of drilling soldiers, Lady Blessington told Madden to have erected, at her cost, a suitable monument over the grave. She was immediately bombarded with begging letters from Whittington Landon.[50] Maclean told Madden this was unnecessary as he had already ordered a mural slab with a suitable inscription to be erected, which was done shortly afterwards. Landon's friends thought to make a subscription for a tablet to be erected to the memory of "L.E.L." in Holy Trinity, Brompton, where her grandmother was buried, and of which she had written a poem, *The First Grave*. However, it quickly became clear that Landon's death had left her mother even more poverty-stricken, and the subscription that was collected went instead for her support. Maclean had offered to double the fifty pounds a year which his wife had given to her mother. Mrs Landon replied that if her daughter had been happy with him, she would accept it. No more was ever said, neither did Maclean send back to England any of Landon's possessions. He does appear to have sent her manuscripts to Laman Blanchard whom Landon had appointed as her literary executor. Bulwer Lytton paid Mrs Landon a generous annual amount until her death in 1854 and in a letter of February 1840 asked Macready to contribute too. She was also awarded a small pension of fifteen pounds from a fund by Sir Robert Peel. Whittington helped as much as he could, which was not much. Katherine Thomson told Jerdan in 1846 that Mrs Landon had a government annuity of fifteen pounds, twenty pounds from the N. Benevolent, twenty-five pounds from Whittington, ten pounds from Mrs. [illegible], fifteen pounds from herself and sundry contributions from friends of L.E.L. bringing a total of eighty-five pounds. Her own contribution had dwindled from thirty pounds to fifteen pounds and was still not very secure.[51]

Two months after Landon married, and whilst she was at sea on the way to her new life, Jerdan produced another tale for *Bentley's Miscellany*, "Nonsense! A Miscellany about Love" this time signed with his own name. Landon would inevitably have been on Jerdan's mind, and in ruminating on the nature of love he remarked, "Perhaps it is that not being quite as young as one was, the same matter which formerly was deemed the main business, aim, scope and material, may have changed its hue, and so become to be looked upon as the Nonsense of Life." He was clearly feeling his fifty-six years and his three families weighing heavily.

He described Love as invoked by a picture in his study, by a fictional Genoese artist Cangiaggio. His poem is in the lush romantic style of L.E.L., ending as her own verse so often did, on a note of death. Jerdan wrote fondly of love as a fledgling bird, soft and downy, full of promise, but Time passes, the bird sickens, pines, decays and dies, whilst one watched in horror. The sadness and feeling of ageing evident in this section of his article changed suddenly, as if Jerdan became aware of being too solemn. To liven up his tone, he told a story of Isaac Newton whose friends thought it was time should be married. On sitting with a candidate for the post, he absent-mindedly took her hand, using her finger in his pipe as a tobacco tamper. Her scream confirmed him in his belief that he should remain a bachelor. This, Jerdan noted, is the "comedy of love; better, perhaps, than the melodrama, serious opera or tragedy". This anecdote was followed by another, seemingly unconnected with his topic, about a Sicilian Queen in 1347 regulating unlicensed intrigues, relating how a Jew was whipped through the streets for an infringement of the rules. Jerdan awkwardly twists this to moralize that ladies should attend to their scarfs, boas and jewels in public places, so they are not lost – a meaningless inclusion even into a "miscellany" about love. Jerdan seemed to realise this, and returned in serious vein to his theme of love: "No adverse fate, no storm, no danger, not death itself, can alter its destiny. It is high above fate; it is deeper than the storm can reach; it is safe from danger, it is beyond the victory of the grave." He continued in this vein with metaphors about oceans, tides and boats – doubtless thinking of L.E.L. at that moment on her sea voyage to Cape Coast Castle. "The passion of love," he wrote, "ought never to be supplanted by the passion of hate, not even of anger." He thought that "a Quaker-like sorrow and regret" better reflected past happiness, and mentioned the Quaker poet, Bernard Barton. This is yet another clue that his mind was on L.E.L., as it was Barton who had penned a tribute to L.E.L. in those long-ago early days when she first appeared in the *Literary Gazette*. The verse that followed this thought is a further reinforcement of the strong impression he gave that she was uppermost in his thoughts.[52] The fourth stanza read:

> Everything fails, everything flies;
> The very light of Ella's eyes,
> Even while I gaze upon it, seems
> Melting away, like joy in dreams.

Ella, of course, was the name he and L.E.L. gave to their first child who, at the time of Jerdan's writing, was about sixteen years old.

In case his readers missed his point – which in such an odd collection of writing would be easily done – Jerdan explained that his moral was that "The readers who did not understand what love is before they began to peruse this paper, will not understand it a bit the better now they have finished it." He insisted that, "it is quite impossible for me to pen any thing without conferring a benefit on my kind", but spoilt the altruistic effect by deciding at the last minute to include a verse of fourteen four-line stanzas entitled *Cupid Couched!*, a vulgar piece making fun of mothers bringing their daughters "to market", ancient maiden ladies and the "ugly, consumptive, scorbutic, monstrous gathering" who seek love. At the close of this contribution to *Bentley's Miscellany*, Jerdan referred to his "desultory and miscellaneous" chapter on love. It is a miscellany in that he mixed prose and poetry, but there are parts that seem heartfelt and true, and not mere column-fillers, as were some of his earlier efforts for that magazine.

~16~
Encouraging Authors –
Creating Fiction

T he friendly connection between Jerdan and Dickens was to involve him in some of the author's business arrangements. Bentley had given Dickens the task of editing the memoirs of Grimaldi the clown, which he had worked on reluctantly at the beginning of 1838. In February of that year the Memoir was published, and Dickens received one hundred pounds for his editorial work. In September he signed a further agreement with Bentley concerning the *Miscellany*, and also concerning the publication of *Barnaby Rudge*. Overwhelmed by work, in January 1839 Dickens asked Bentley for a six-month postponement of the novel, and angry correspondence ensued;[1] the outcome was that in February Dickens resigned from editing the *Miscellany*, and Bentley gave him until the end of the year to complete *Barnaby Rudge*. Harrison Ainsworth, who succeeded him as Editor of the *Miscellany*, invited Dickens to dinner; other guests included Jerdan, Forster, Cruikshank and Leigh Hunt.

Throughout 1839 Dickens became ever closer to Macready, telling the actor that he was going to dedicate *Nicholas Nickleby* to him, and accepting Macready's request to be godfather to his son. In October, Dickens noted that he dined with Macready, Forster, Maclise and Jerdan, indicating that despite his penurious condition, Jerdan was still accepted into his accustomed social circles and also that although Dickens had severed his connection with the *Miscellany*, this did not affect his acquaintance with Jerdan.

Rather out of season, Jerdan's contribution, "Dead Man's Race – a Christmas Story" appeared in the February 1839 issue *of Bentley's Miscellany*. It drew a picture of a traditional fireside in a great hall; master, family, servants and visitors gathered around. Games were played, toasts drunk, songs sung, until it was time for the host's own contribution, The Dead Man's Race, a horror story designed to raise the hair on the necks of the assembled company, and contrasting vividly with the cosy scene. A drunken farmer, robbed on an unsuccessful visit to the fair, loses his way home in wild countryside. He finds a hut to shelter in, but is appalled to see it contains only a dead man in his coffin. Riding quickly away he is chased by the coffin mounted on wheels complete with its occupant. As he slowed or sped up so did the coffin. Terrified into insensibility he fell off his horse. Found next day, he told his awful story and was thought to be raving; he died a few days later. Some believed his tale to be true. The fireside listeners were so scared by the story the maids refused to sleep alone that night. On the same page in the *Miscellany* that this tale ended was printed Camilla Toulmin's poem, *On the Death of Mrs MacLean (L.E.L.)*, a placement that was surely not a coincidence.

In this year 1839, Charles Dickens was elected to the Committee of the Literary Fund, which already included Jerdan and Dickens's enemy and former publisher Richard Bentley. Dickens attended very few meetings and was not eligible for re-election when his term ended in 1841. He was on the Committee however when the Rev. Whittington Landon resigned the Secretaryship of the Literary Fund in February, with effect from 24 June that year, a resignation forced by the fact that he failed to account for ten pounds five shillings. Jerdan's son, William Freeling, applied for the job, as did Octavian Blewitt who had previously lost the election to Whittington Landon two years earlier. Anxious that his membership of the Committee should not adversely affect his son's chances, Jerdan wrote formally to the Literary Fund, offering to resign if his son was appointed Secretary. He had taken soundings from older members of the Committee who saw no impropriety in his remaining, but others had expressed concerns about possible conflict of interest. Seldom too subtle, Jerdan put his son's case all too plainly: "I trust that my past exertions in the cause will not be deemed a sufficient ground to put a relative out of the pale of employment, and at all events as I have for many years procured the Fund as much as its Secretary's Annual Salary, that such a source of service may not provoke either uncourteous remark or unmerited hostility".[2] Writing on 11 March to Crofton Croker, Jerdan was very concerned that "William is very unlucky in having Lords Munster and Mountnorris, Sir J Swinburne and Sir P Joddrell and perhaps Brandreth all absent from Town; so that I fear only you, our friends, Mr Nichols and another or two be active instead of passive, our chance is O."[3] William Freeling Jerdan's application was supported by testimonials from M C Wyatt, Crofton Croker and Walter Henry Watts. A ballot was held on 13 March, in which young Jerdan got 14 votes, and Blewitt 31. Details of the voting were not disclosed but it is highly likely that his father's chequered reputation with the Fund, (such as destroying Soane's portrait and questions over handling some monies entrusted to him), were a grave disadvantage to his son. The decision to appoint Blewitt was to prove invaluable for the Society. He was an excellent organizer and administrator and benefited posterity by keeping the papers of the Fund in impeccable order. One poignant application to the Fund in 1839 was from Leigh Hunt, in dire poverty, coping with many children and a wife driven to alcoholism. He received fifty pounds. His plight would have reminded Jerdan just how precarious was a life in literature.

On the receiving end of so many hundreds of letters, most of them wanting something of him, Jerdan would have been happy to receive one from the distinguished painter Thomas Uwins. Ostensibly to correct attribution of a painting mentioned in the *Literary Gazette* from himself to his nephew, Uwins gave Jerdan a well-timed and unsolicited testimonial of appreciation:

I cannot refuse myself the pleasure of thanking you, Sir, for the kind manner in which you have spoken of my works through the whole of my career – the more, as kindness is so much opposed to the fashion of the times. Goldsmith's disabled soldier says 'two fellows belonging to a press-gang knocked me down and then told me to stand'. This is the line of action generally pursued by the British Press towards the art and artists of England. At the conclusion of your labours you will have to reflect on a different course – you have tried to do good in your day and generation, and at least you will not lose the reward of gratitude from those who, like me, have been stimulated by your encouragement and have derived benefit from your praise.[4]

Such sentiments were meat and drink to Jerdan whose abiding philosophy had been to give kindness and praise whenever possible, and the kindness of omission where it was not. There had, of course, been exceptions in his long career, but this was the touchstone he tried to adhere to.

Another tribute came from a writer, Simon Gray. Longman, Orme & Co. published a book by him in 1839, containing two works. One was "The Spaniard, or Relvindez and Elzora, a Tragedy" and the other a comedy written in 1789, "The Young Country Widow". Noticing the book, the *Gentleman's Magazine* remarked that "the comedy is dedicated to another great critic, Mr Jerdan".[5] Gray's Dedication was in the form of a letter addressed to "William Jerdan Esq. Croupier to the A Club",[6] and began:

If I thought our very worthy chairman would smile on having a tragedy put into his hands by one who paid so much attention to so dry, heavy – how shall we epithetise it? – a subject or science as statistics or political economy, surely I cannot expect less from our very worthy croupier, on having a comedy, forsooth, put into his hands by the same student of the dry, or heavy, but that he should laugh fairly and broadly out.

There was much more of this heavy-handed attempt at humour, a dig at Jerdan's "dabbling with the currency", a reference to his work with John Trotter on the national finances, and finally an apology for not having "punning personae" in his comedy, recalling Jerdan's statement at some previous meeting in a club, "that it was barely possible for any man, on average, to create a truly good, unsought for pun, above once a fortnight". Jerdan, inveterate punster that he was, could surely not have meant what he said. No response from Jerdan survives to inform us whether he was pleased or otherwise at this verbose tribute.

Jerdan's relationship with Bentley had taken a knock since Bentley's refusal of another loan. This may have been the reason for Jerdan's unusually peevish note in May 1839, having sent a story in to the *Miscellany*:

> I am much chagrined at not having had a proof of the Legacies of Intellect agreeably to your promise. Perhaps you will return the MS of which I have only to say that I refused a guinea a page for it, in consequence of the friendly terms on which you and I have long gone on. I am not one of the captious or easily affronted writers; but feel such things to be very discouraging, and also that a monthly certainty to the amount I am offered would be very convenient were I to write elsewhere . . . I literally locked myself up nearly two whole days to supply the article now thrown aside.[7]

Bentley must have reconsidered the story, as "The Legacies of Intellect – a Philosophical Vagary" appeared in the June issue. This long contribution was said by Jerdan to be an allegory on the perils of too much knowledge – this at a time when he himself was promoting in the pages of the *Literary Gazette* information from all the Royal Societies and other scientific and arts institutions and celebrating the seemingly endless discoveries and inventions of the age. He did "not mean to write in praise of Ignorance", he declared, but quoted Pope that a single pursuit is more suited to man's intellect.

His allegory centred around a long-ago hero, Alfric Athelwerd, whose thirst for knowledge was encouraged by his gifted and wealthy parents. He became renowned for all he knew and was called "The Happy Man". Jerdan's penchant for fairy tales allowed him to change the laws of nature so that individuals could bequeath the sum of their own knowledge to someone else. In a cynical aside Jerdan noted how the more one has the more one gets, and so Alfric became the heir to many people's understanding of science, poetry, mechanics and so on. Alfric coped with all this information, "But at Length came the fatal Legacies of Intellect, and he was advanced a hundred years beyond the age in which he lived." He could out-strategy Wellington, make the achievements of Newton and Faraday insignificant, and was in sum "a vast and single instance of pre-human intelligence".

Bringing his story right up to date Jerdan said that in July 18__ war was declared, and a "mighty armament" was ordered to sail for the Mediterranean. Alfric begged the government to delay as, using his superhuman powers, he knew that fatal storms were due in the Bay of Biscay. He was laughed at and ignored. The inevitable occurred and thirty thousand men were lost at sea. The following year he foresaw crop failure would cause a famine in England and devised a way to avert catastrophe. Again he was derided and ignored, and famine and many deaths followed.

Rejected and repelled, Alfric decided to marry, choosing a bride who knew nothing, but was attracted by his wealth. Returning to his studies he became infatuated by astronomy, and here the story took off into the realms of the surreal. He built a telescope billions of times stronger than any known, with which he could watch planetary worlds, finding their beings more corpulent the nearer they were to the sun, and noting other characteristics specific to certain planets. Jerdan surmised that Alfric's observations might not be understood until the year 2839, "when the human race may have proceeded to a similar extent of intelligence". Alfric invented balloons to visit other planets and a language which might be universally understood. Whilst he worked on a theory that the world was informed by one soul, which was divisible into an eternity of parts and communicated by sparks, his wife presented him with a daughter.

Jerdan's examples of his hero's hypotheses were sometimes credible, sometimes absurd: at one time he announced "There is no such thing in creation as inorganic matter" and later, that "Shadows are real beings, not less substantial than the men and women they had been supposed to copy", differing only in that they can elongate or shorten themselves.

Alfric's apogee was his experiment with the human soul: he wanted to go further than the current obsession with phrenology and mesmerism (both of which fascinated Jerdan), and believed that the soul resided in the brain. By removing part of the skull and passing his hands in one direction, he watched the soul take wing and leave the skull. Passing his hands the opposite way Alfric rehoused the soul which, he found on interrogation, had conversed with pre-Adamite angels. Overcome by the immensity of his discovery, Alfric confided to his wife his intention to send their baby daughter's soul on a similar journey. Terrified, she secretly arranged for him to be restrained and charged with insanity. Here, Jerdan observed that "to be once charged with insanity is so indubitable a presumption of the fact, that it is next to impossible to persuade any one to believe the contrary. If you are angry, it is furiousness, if you are quiet, it is sulkiness; if you are silent, you are morbid; and if you speak you are misunderstood." Despite his earlier prophecies proving accurate, Alfric's pleas as to the truth of his discoveries were in vain, and he was sent to an asylum, "a woeful example", concluded Jerdan, "of the danger of being wiser than the generation in which he lived, to be declared, instead of 'The Happy Man', a *Monomaniac!!!*"

Jerdan's frame of mind seems to have been no lighter in May, when "The Bridegroom's Star" appeared in *Bentley's Miscellany*. His bridegroom, Henry, counted the days until his marriage with the peerless Marion; his joyful anticipation turned to fear as the day drew nearer. Jerdan's thoughts were given to Henry: "Ah! how like to far travel is the journey of life! . . . The last brief tide *is* the voyage round the world – the last few hours *is* the sum and history of human existence." As the day came closer, Marion asked to be alone on the day preceding the wedding, and on the penultimate night they revisited the places dear to them. The wedding day dawned, but Marion was deathly ill with plague and died in agony. Mad with grief, Henry did not attend her burial and lost his reason for a time. Recovering slightly, he saw "a new and dazzling Star", and believed it to be his Marion, who was not, after all, alone; they were at last together. Suddenly the star burst from the sky, and Henry fell dead and was buried with his love. Their inscription read only "A Falling Star". This story may signify Jerdan's feelings on the quick marriage, followed by the unexplained untimely death of L.E.L. – his star had vanished and even in his chaotic and hectic life he would have missed her brilliance and her company, and been at a loss to comprehend why she should have been so untimely wrenched from the world.

Obviously distracted, Jerdan sent Bentley another article dashed off in a hurry, clear from the internal evidence, and therefore signed with Jerdan's pseudonym. He explained that the term "Hatchment" is an adaption of "Achievement", and described a tablet displaying the coat of arms of a deceased person. This odd article took the form of a letter to the Countess of B[lessington], telling her he had been inspired by the previous night's party at her home, G[ore] House, to pen a poem about a Hatchment seen at another mansion. Six stanzas, each of eleven lines, indifferently rhymed, (one carrying Jerdan's footnote that he had "to apologize for the difference of construction in this stanza; but I have not time to amend it). The poem illustrated the sentiments in Jerdan's opening letter, that at the happiest of times we sometimes fall into melancholy and a Hatchment overlooking scenes of revelry is a reminder of mortality. This gloomy piece was unlikely to give much cheer to readers of this issue of Bentley's *Miscellany*.

Encouraged by Bentley's acceptance of the long story "Legacies of Intellect" and perhaps to make up for the scrappiness of "The Hatchment", Jerdan sent Bentley his next offering, following it up with a note that he could either adopt it whole or with omissions Jerdan had marked. Jerdan thought this story might "attract some notice from a new class of readers belonging to the various Societies named". Bentley had softened a little in the matter of advances, and mentioned money to Jerdan, laying himself open to receive another pleading note: "I must greatly depend on you for my Autumn Excursion, on which I move on Friday", wrote Jerdan, asking for an advance "towards fifty, on the *Miscellany* score . . . "[8] The new story, "Baron Von Dullbrainz", appeared in the September issue.

The title immediately indicated that Jerdan's sombre mood had lifted some-what, and he was back to his old tricks, satirical and word-playing. His foreign hero was "fated to be fêted" and was introduced into fashionable London society, proof said Jerdan "of the extreme readiness with which the people of Great

Britain confess the superiority of foreigners, whilst native talents are left to be their own reward". There followed an account of an assembly of the Royal Society when, after a talk on "improvements in photogenic drawings" by "Mr Talbot Foxhound",[9] Von Dullbrainz gave a speech on the subject, in excruciating English, portrayed with gusto by Jerdan full of "dat" and "dere". He ended by insulting the assembled Fellows by saying his host had told him that FRS meant "Fellow Remarkable Stupide" and the President was therefore well suited to be at the head of such a Society. Despite this, or perhaps because of it, he was lionized by all and in great demand, his opinions sought on every topic.

Jerdan enjoyed himself on Von Dullbrainz's next disquisition on Balls – hand-balls, footballs, golf balls, St Paul's, dancing Balls, voting balls – all in the phonetic foreign accent: an avalanche of unintelligible nonsense, which merely served to confirm his brilliance in the eyes of his hosts. Similar events occurred at the Geological and Astronomical Societies, and many others. At the Mechanics Institute, Jerdan allowed Von Dullbrainz to speak about "a cleber mechanicien call Babbleage"[10] and pointed out that it is easy to make a machine more clever than the maker. "For example, I make a vheel; dat vheel is more cleber dan me, for he can roll a hunder mile, and I gannot roll one!" Von Dullbrainz intended to improve Babbleage's machine and incorporate "Mr Veetstone's" speaking machine[11] that would "speak more plainter and better English as me".

Jerdan's creativity and sense of mischief then invented Von Dullbrainz's most biting and entertaining exploit. At the Statistical Society he disputed the benefits of censuses, and statistical tables on population and social classes. His table was to calculate the "Lies, Fibs, Misrepresents and Mistyficasions" of various trades and professions, and Jerdan set out the statistics in tabular form. In one thousand MPs, for example, were 84,118 lies, "18 ½% to be added during Election time". He calculated how many gold or silver watches were owned by each class of person, and that laid side by side they would measure over fifty-seven miles. This last pronouncement was clearly influenced by an occasion Jerdan wrote about many years later; he had been present at an event when Sir Mark Isambard Brunel "ended with an estimate showing how many gold and silver watches were worn by particular members belonging to the several classes of people and how, if laid down on the road, touching each other, they would reach from London to Portsmouth . . .".[12]

Considering that it was time to leave England whilst his reputation was high, Von Dullbrainz made a final appearance at the British Association in Birmingham, where a grand dinner was given in his honour. His farewell speech noted how in his own land he had been derided but that the English had known how to value him. "You know notting of de sciences, de lierature, or de arts; but you are amable peoples and ven cleber foreigner of genus come to you, you savey to appreciate him." His speech was interrupted by a Chartist attack, during which the orator fled from the room and was last heard of in another country, where he was writing about his travels. Jerdan's intimate acquaintance with the proceedings of all the societies and institutions, both because of their inclusion in the *Literary Gazette* and for his own personal interests, gave him the material for this convincing story and allowed him to make fun of them, and of the English proclivity to admire foreign "intellectuals".

Dullbrainz's "Mr Talbot Foxhound" was, of course, William Henry Fox Talbot, an early pioneer of photography. Jerdan's original intention when he took over the *Literary Gazette* was that it should become a resource wherein future generations could trace the history of literature. In fact, it became a source of information about many other things too: art, music, drama and science. Of particular interest is the correspondence from Fox Talbot to Jerdan,[13] beginning in response to a request for details about his invention on which he addressed the Royal Society on 31 January 1839, on "the art of photogenic drawing". Fox Talbot's lengthy reply appeared in the *Gazette* of 2 February. He explained that he had worked on his invention for a long time, and at the exact moment he was preparing his presentation to the Royal Society, Daguerre in Paris came out with a very similar, but not identical system. In the race for pre-eminence, Fox Talbot had been urged to exhibit his materials at the Royal Institution's Friday evening lecture led by Michael Faraday on 25 January, before reading his paper at the Royal Society. His letter explained how his invention was an improvement on the *camera obscura* and *camera lucida*, familiar to most persons. In his invention, "it is not the artist who makes the picture, but the picture which makes itself".

In March, Fox Talbot offered Jerdan a choice of various documents for the *Literary Gazette*, but the following week on 30 March Jerdan printed another letter from him, dissenting from a statement in the previous week's paper, challenging the claim made that his process had been improved upon, and that the discovery was made by several persons simultaneously. This printed letter contained many details in support of Fox Talbot's pre-eminence. A draft letter to Jerdan, with many crossings-out indicated the inventor's impatience in trying to set out his case, followed a few days later by a letter in which he declared that he disliked controversy, and had already stated in the *Literary Gazette* that as long ago as 1834 he had "discovered the art of obtaining photogenic pictures from glass", and pressing his point that Daguerre's sudden intervention had precipitated him into presenting a paper more "imperfect and hasty" than he would otherwise have done. In June, Fox Talbot sent Jerdan a packet of photogenic drawings. Not everyone was happy with the new inventions. Jerdan remarked that some referred to it punningly as "The Foe To Graphic Art".[14]

Fox Talbot found in Jerdan's *Literary Gazette* a popular channel by which he could spread the word about his invention, thus reaching many more than might read transactions of the Royal Society. Two years later he wrote to Jerdan again, in a letter published in the *Literary Gazette* of 13 February 1841, revealing a discovery made a few months earlier, "of a chemical process by which paper may be made far more sensitive to light than by any means hitherto known". This meant vastly quicker pictures could be achieved. He called this new process Calotype, to distinguish it from Daguerreotype. Noting the *Gazette*'s earlier support for Fox Talbot, Jerdan appended an Editor's note to this letter: "See *Literary Gazette* of that period in which we exposed foreign pretensions and established just rights and British claims." Patriotic and clearly fascinated by the new technology, Jerdan gave considerable space to more detailed letters from Fox Talbot in the *Literary Gazette* of February and July 1841. When the photographer's serial "The Pencil of Nature" was published by Longmans in 1844, Fox Talbot sent Jerdan a copy for review. These strictly scientific exchanges merged, as they often did with Jerdan, into a more friendly relationship a few years later when Jerdan was able to offer Fox Talbot the support of the *Literary Gazette* in an erupting quarrel.

In his personal life Jerdan was still upsetting his friend Macready. Having, at Jerdan's request, withheld his cheque for £70 in December, in February he now received Jerdan's dishonoured note or draught on Longmans for his debt. "Oh, Jerdan! Jerdan!" moaned the long-suffering Macready to his Diary. For all the quick temper for which Macready was renowned, his patience with his debtor was amazing, but not so amazing as Jerdan's evident thick skin and unabashedness at facing him. When Macready performed in Bulwer's 'Richelieu' on 7 March, Jerdan was amongst the group who came afterwards to his room, and at the end of the month Macready invited him to dinner with others. The following day the Shakespeare Club was honouring the actor, and he spent the morning fretting, as usual, over his speech. Dickens was in the Chair, with Jerdan and Blanchard as joint Vice-Presidents. There were over two hundred guests including Leigh Hunt, Maclise and Thackeray. After an excellent dinner songs were sung and "Jerdan spoke very well". The financial transactions between them evidently did not affect their basic friendship. Jerdan visited back stage during that summer, and attended Macready's Testimonial Dinner at the Freemasons Tavern in July, when the actor "proclaimed that his poverty not his will, had obliged him to desist from management" (of Covent Garden). Jerdan's non-payment of his debt was clearly a serious matter to Macready at this precarious time in his life.

A major celebration on 5 October was Charles Dickens's dinner at the Albion, Aldersgate, to mark the completion of *Nicholas Nickleby*. It fell to Macready to propose Dickens's health, and it took him all morning to work on his speech. "We sat down to a <u>too</u> splendid dinner", he noted; "the portrait of Dickens by Maclise was in the room."[15] Jerdan recalled being given the "post of honour at the bottom of the table, and am happy to remember that I acquitted myself so creditably of its onerous duties, as to receive the approbation of the giver of the feast, his better half and the *oi polloi* unanimously".[16]

Maclise had made a portrait of Jerdan as well as of Dickens, this being the one used by *Fraser's* for their 'Gallery of Illustrious Literary Characters' in 1830. Two more portraits of Jerdan were made; one dated 20 October 1839 was by Count d'Orsay, a delicate pencil study of Jerdan in profile, wearing tiny spectacles, a high stock and a coat with deep lapels. In addition to d'Orsay's signature, Jerdan added his own beneath his portrait. A few months later Alexander Craig painted Jerdan in oils on board; his subject wore a similar, or probably the same, coat, but now buttoned closely. He was in a relaxed pose, facing forwards. Neither of these images shows a man significantly more aged than the Maclise portrait ten years earlier, despite the emotional and financial turmoils that Jerdan endured in the intervening years.

Jerdan had a new scheme hatching which was taking up a good deal of his time and attention, a welcome diversion from grieving about Landon's untimely death and concerns for his new expanding family. He had always given support to those whose life was dedicated to literature, as his efforts on behalf of the Royal Society of Literature and more effectively the Literary Fund Society showed. After expending a considerable amount of work, he assembled a committee to progress his big idea, the formulation of "A Plan of a National Association for the Encouragement and Protection of Authors and Men of Talent and Genius".

At the time, he was unaware of two previous attempts at creating a similar association. When apprised on the first of these by Sir Henry Ellis of the British Museum, Jerdan hurried there to examine the archive. This plan was a century old, had been well funded and impressively supported by men from all professions. Their Proceedings had been published, but at the point in Jerdan's *Autobiography* where he mentions this, he had almost reached his allotted number of pages and did not go into any detail. This old association lasted for thirteen years, and when it ceased the remaining funds were donated to the Foundling Hospital.

The second such idea was much more recent. It seems odd that Jerdan had not been asked to participate when, only seven years previously, under the patronage of the Duke of Somerset President of the Royal Institution, Thomas Campbell and others had promoted a similar scheme. They tried it for a short while, but gave up in the face of insurmountable difficulties when their Bankers became bankrupt losing all of the collected subscriptions.

Jerdan knew nothing of these earlier attempts when, in the autumn of 1839, he used all his influence and contacts to obtain patronage and subscriptions for his great Plan. The Duke of Rutland and Lord Willoughby de Eresby each subscribed one hundred guineas, various Marquises, Earls and Lords followed; Jerdan's friend Frederick Pollock joined in, as did some authors who had achieved great success, such as Captain Marryat and G. P. R. James. He wrote to Sir Thomas Noon Talfourd that he had a "Committee of much distinction to aid in launching it in a manner to assure the public of its high, benevolent, just and patriotic character. It is closely allied to your Copyright measure, and would give that which it will secure and perpetuate."[17] He urged Talfourd as the Plan's "natural ally" to rally to its support. Confiding to Crofton Croker that he had also persuaded Sir Martin Archer Shee to join the committee, Jerdan told his friend, "I only want the sinews of war to put the Plan on its feet and let it march on. I am trying hard for them."[18] A Prospectus was prepared, setting out in detail the financial aspects of the Plan. Discovering now the earlier efforts to create an Association to encourage literary men, Jerdan believed it useful to put the whole idea into context, writing an "Illustration" of his Plan in which he set out the information relating to these two earlier efforts.

For his brave new Plan, Jerdan gave himself the titles "F.S.A., M.R.S.L. and Corresponding Member of the Real Academia de la Historia of Spain etc."[19] befitting his status as Secretary of the proposed new Association. Noting that "The wants and complaints of Authors are not of modern birth: they are co-eval with the annals of literary labour, and, certainly, have not decreased with the increase of publication, or, as it is whimsically styled, the Spread of Knowledge." The new Plan was two-fold: to encourage the production of good literature and to benefit authors. Jerdan was especially pleased to note that several of the current benefactors had ancestors who had supported the original Plan in 1738, a coincidence which aroused in him "strange emotions", the great and the good working together for "the same pure and beneficent purpose".

In his Prospectus, Jerdan acknowledged that the two earlier associations had ended for quite understandable reasons, but set out his "hope that, taught by experience and belonging to an age of far more universal cultivation and extended intellectual pursuits, the Establishment of the Undertaking . . . will become an effectual and permanent resource against the evils that oppress literary merit and talent, and a fountain whence the national literature may gush out afresh in purer and more abundant affluence than has for years attended its turbid and polluted course." He listed the first patrons, explaining that it was intended to bring in also heads of "the highest institutions for instruction and refinement", lawyers, eminent artists, popular writers and "independent and liberal men of every creed, class, occupation, pursuit and character". Seizing a chance to establish his own place amongst such exalted company, Jerdan inserted a few lines about himself:

With regard to the Secretary we have but one word to say: for many years intimately connected with every ramification of the literary and publishing world, he has seen enough to induce him to devote all the energy he possesses to the furtherance of this undertaking; and he does so in pure and good faith, because he is convinced it will be a great and lasting blessing to those whose sufferings he has during all that period, deeply commiserated, and tend to establish a superior order of National publication.

The Prospectus then turned to the formal business of the Association, proposing capital of 200,000 shares, being 2000 of ten pounds each and 9000 of twenty pounds each.[20] There were to be two classes of shareholders, one being of Patron Proprietors who would contribute the whole of their investment at the outset and earn dividends on their shares. Some had agreed to forgo any dividends and these would be consolidated, the profits thus accrued paid into the Literary Fund. Patron Proprietors were to be protected from any further liability. The second class was of Subscribing Shareholders who could also earn dividends, this class being able to purchase the lower value shares and thus extend membership of the Association to the less affluent. The total capital mentioned was a huge sum, but the Prospectus explained that the "Experiment" could proceed once £50,000 had been raised and a Deed of Settlement executed.

Jerdan set out three ways that publication was at present achieved: the first was self-publishing, very expensive, with a large percentage going to agents; secondly, established authors sold their copyright to publishers, who then took a disproportionately large share of the proceeds; and the third, and by far the most common method, was that of authors "who write for bread", and who are at the mercy of publishers doling out to them "often under circumstances painfully humiliating, a scanty and uncertain pay". The purpose of the Association was to "rescue the intellectual character of the nation from these degrading and deteriorating circumstances, by providing Capital for the less wealthy, ready access to fair competition for the deserving, adequate compensation for the skilful and industrious, diminished cost and increased emolument to all". This was to be achieved by authors submitting their work to a properly constituted committee called a "College", and if a decision was taken that the work had merit it would be published by the Association at its own cost and risk, or it would assist the writers in publishing, or it would purchase the manuscript "at such prices as may be deemed advisable". The College would be remunerated by a small percentage on profit of successful works, from which a deduction would be made from those with poor sales. By this system, Jerdan asserted, the College's "decision must be confessedly far superior to the existing system, in which superficiality and ignorance, instead of learning and intellect, almost always decide the question of publication, and no element enters into the calculation but the trading methods for most rapidly realizing the pounds, shillings, and pence".

Premises were to be taken from which to run the scheme, publishers would not suffer as the books published by the Association would be high-priced works which most publishers would not undertake, and the Association would benefit from profits which would otherwise "go into the pocket of the *mere* Capitalist".

The current practice of publishers to turn a quick profit, and an unwillingness to take on books of superior quality, "is one of the great causes of the superficial and debased state of our national literature; from which, it is anticipated, this Association will retrieve it, and place England on a level with Foreign countries". The Prospectus included much more detail, setting out precise allotments of shares, together with addresses at which applications could be made. The "National Association Office" was for the time being at 13 Parliament Street, Jerdan's own office, from which he sent out handsomely written letters to accompany the Prospectus, which was printed by James Moyes of Leicester Square and published by W. Stephenson of 12 and 13 Parliament Street.[21] These letters put forward the Prospectus as a work in progress and invited "expedient amendments".

The Plan was then set afoot with high hopes for the benefits it offered to literature and the men who wrote it. The Council were indeed noble and titled, but that did not necessarily make them good businessmen. Jerdan later compared Campbell's plan of 1831 being defeated by the bankruptcy of the Bank to his own Plan, "wrecked by the introduction into it of several City men of business, who were to undertake the issuing of shares and other matters, of which I and my literary colleagues were profoundly ignorant. The result was, that they did manage the affairs into a ruin."[22] A house had been taken in Charing Cross, other expenses incurred and, like so many of Jerdan's encounters with the world of finance, "the whole fabric fell smash to the ground". He was somehow left several hundred pounds the worse, "no one thanked me, that some laughed at me, and that my friends the publishers said it served me right". His record of financial disasters was unfortunate, not always due to his own carelessness and ignorance. The crash of Whiteheads Bank at the beginning of his career, and the Panic of 1826 were both outside of his control. However, in handling such large sums of donated money as were subscribed for the Association, one would have expected others more experienced and capable to be jointly responsible for its care. This was unfortunately not the last time that Jerdan was to be the victim of financial skulduggery.

A dozen or so importuning letters survive from Jerdan to Bentley, all undated by year. One, on 16 December, asked the long-suffering publisher for money. Jerdan had been ill for three weeks, he said, and "would esteem him a good fellow and friend who would lend me £20 or £25 till I could send a cheque about the middle of January or before".[23] Another, dated 19 December, so likely to refer to Bentley's response, complained that "being ill and depressed by pain" he had hoped for an earlier reply. Bentley had not sent the requested funds, and Jerdan was hurt and indignant: "I have no right to find fault either with the spirit or wording of it; though between you and me I <u>wd</u> rather have had you say straightforwardly I wd rather not than speak to a man of common understanding of a disposition to serve, in an independent gentleman, prevented by 'adherence to a strict rule of business', which he had known not to interfere in a hundred instances."[24] Jerdan's hasty handwriting and lack of punctuation betray the desperation he felt at Bentley's refusal to help on this occasion.

For twenty-two years the *Literary Gazette* had dispensed what Jerdan insisted were independent opinions of the books it reviewed; the *Gazette*, with its imitators and followers, had been influential in guiding all aspects of the publishing profession from writers through printers and publishers, to booksellers, libraries and the reading public. Such influence set Laman Blanchard to considering what was "The Influence of Periodical Literature on the State of the Fine Arts" in the *Monthly Chronicle* of 4 December 1839. His article was chiefly concerned with drama, which had been in a low state until Macready took over Covent Garden Theatre, but the actor could have done better, Blanchard thought, by turning "his resources to a nobler purpose than that of pampering the prevailing taste for spectacle". Turning to criticism of books, Blanchard understood that a balance had to be achieved between honesty and affording "the requisite amount of satisfaction to an advertising bookseller", (a reference of the old topic of puffing). Advances in this respect, he felt, "appears rather to have been owing to the influences of private friendships than to a thoroughly awakened sense of public duty . . . the tone of personal partiality is too obvious in some – that of personal hostility still more disagreeably striking in others". He called for more conscientiousness in newspapers and periodicals, standing as they did midway between professional writers and artists, and the public. He suggested that reviewers should not be swayed by friendship alone, that they should not merely succumb to "a desire to conciliate the givers of agreeable parties, encourage the willing contributions of engravers and publishers, or, return the small but convenient patronage of numerous free admissions". Blanchard did not name any names and Jerdan would doubtless deny this as a description of himself, but he was as susceptible as anyone to any benefits that his position would bring him, short of compromising his literary judgment.

On 30 December a great party took Jerdan's mind off more serious matters. Pryor's Bank Fulham was the home of Thomas Baylis and William Lechmere Whitmore, both Fellows of the Society of Antiquaries. Their house was overflowing with curious objects, art and furniture, and on this day they held a masque. It was written for the occasion by Theodore Hook; the text was printed and sold in the rooms to the one hundred and fifty guests, for the benefit of the Royal Literary Fund, raising three pounds twelve shillings and sixpence. Hook played the part of the Great Frost; Crofton Croker was Father Christmas and there was a Grand Tournament in which the hosts, mounted on hobby horses, jousted fiercely. The fun became "fast and furious, and to which an impudent but most amusing jester (Mr Jerdan) mainly contributed, was checked only by the announcement of supper".[25] Jerdan's resilience in the face of ongoing struggles and disappointments seemed unquenchable.

By 1840 Bentley was prospering as a publisher on his own account; he had received £1500 for his share in his printing business, plus a £3500 penalty from Colburn for breaking their partnership. He had also received £750 from Bulwer who wished to regain copyright of three of his novels.[26] With Jerdan's help, Bentley was about to make even more money. The *Literary Gazette* of 4 April 1840 gave a short but enthusiastic reception to Dickens's new work, *Master Humphrey's Clock*. Jerdan became closely involved in the affairs of the popular author, acting on Bentley's behalf, whilst John Forster acted for Dickens, in negotiating a final agreement. On 2 June Dickens wrote to his solicitor, Thomas Mitton, "I shall be anxious to know what Forster and Jerdan do, and I hope and trust that they may be able to arrange that matter and set it at rest for ever. You have heard from Forster, I dare say, of Jerdan's admission that it was intended as a settlement of the *Barnaby* question? That's a great point, I know you will think, as I do."[27] There were several matters in dispute: *The Memoirs of Grimaldi*, *Barnaby Rudge* and *Oliver Twist*, as well as copyright in Dickens's writings in Bentley's *Miscellany*. On the last of these, Dickens told Mitton, "Let *Miscellany* papers go. They are of no great worth and when one has the Devil on one's shoulder it is best to shake him off, tho' he has one's cloak on." Both Forster and Jerdan agreed that it was not worth disputing the copyright in the five papers concerned, and Jerdan so advised Bentley on the 19 June that Dickens could include these "slight papers" in any future collection of his writings, although the copyright remained with Bentley.

The major matter was *Oliver Twist*, the first of Dickens's novels to be published under his own name, his other writings having been signed 'Boz'. Jerdan's negotiations were set out in his letter to Bentley of 19 June 1840 for his publisher to ratify or reject.[28] Dickens was to pay Bentley £1500 for relinquishing the copyright of *Oliver Twist* and release from the contract for *Barnaby Rudge*; £750 for Bentley's unsold stock of 1002 copies of *Oliver Twist*, together with Cruikshank's plates of the illustrations. Jerdan advised Bentley that should he ever require an impression from the plates for the *Miscellany*, he was entitled to it. Dickens was to be advanced the £2250 he had to pay to Bentley by Chapman and Hall. Bentley responded favourably, telling Jerdan that "I am so perfectly convinced that you did all that could be done under the circumstances . . . "[29] that he ratified the agreement with only petty amendments about the cost of striking off a Cruikshank plate, and that he should receive the money for the stock within a week of signing the agreement which was concluded on 2 July. With regard to the Grimaldi *Memoir*, Jerdan suggested that it was not worth much; Bentley should give Dickens fifty pounds to give up any claim to it, and there was no point in keeping past papers now that the matter was settled.[30] These negotiations were revealed by Jerdan in his *Autobiography* several years later, causing Bentley great offence.

Jerdan's interventions on Bentley's behalf were unusual in that he had no

formal role in Bentley's business but the two had been intertwined professionally for many years, both through Colburn and latterly because of the *Miscellany*.
Jerdan was also morally obligated to Bentley, on whose patience and generosity
he so frequently called. Dickens did not take it amiss that Jerdan had represented
Bentley against him, rather that he had helped to smooth the difficulties that
had arisen. In March Jerdan was one of a group who dined with Dickens and
Forster, but on 16 August Dickens and Forster quarrelled at dinner at Dickens's
home, where Maclise and Macready were also present. Forster was asked to leave
the house, but apologized for the offence he had given, causing Dickens to write
the following day to Macready, "There is no man, alive or dead, who tries his
friends as [Forster] does."[31] Macready probably thought that Jerdan came in a
close second.

Jerdan frequently called in to see Macready at the theatre during the year,
but Macready's Diary made no more mention of any financial exchanges
between them. However, Jerdan still contrived to incur his friend's considerable
displeasure when, on 7 November, Macready recorded:

> Looked at the newspapers and was especially disgusted to see Jerdan
> yielding a sort of assent to the pretension of character on the part of that
> wretched fellow Bunn – actually recommending him to make another
> essay!!! What a thing this Press is – all that is brutal, base and blackguard
> is concentrated in its trade, and with the rare exception of Fonblanque
> and a few others, there is not a gentleman to be found throughout the
> mass of them.

This was a case of letting his personal animosity for Bunn override his judgment of the Press as a whole. He was himself indebted to the newspapers for
good reviews. A few days after this Macready's daughter Joan died, and he was
involved in another, more public personal matter. This closely mirrored Jerdan
and Landon's early relationship and must have brought back many memories to
Jerdan. Macready's young female lead in most of his plays, Helen Faucit, visited
his room nightly after performances, supposedly so that he could help her with
her studies, just as Landon originally went to Jerdan for tuition. Macready was
susceptible to such evident adoration as his young pupil offered him.

Jerdan knew that the *Literary Gazette* was running into difficulties; in yet
another undated letter, probably of this time, he wrote to Bentley being "vexed
and disappointed" that he had called three times that day without success. He
had three urgent matters to discuss: he was leaving town and needed some
money as "a small arrangement and very temporary but of consequence to me
to be done"; he was to "do a jocular 'Journal of a British Ass' for the *Miscellany*
in strict confidence, and finally, the most crucial matter for Jerdan: "I wish to
speak with you on an important crise (sic) which may open a share in the LG

(most confidential)."[32] From subsequent events, it appears that Bentley was not amenable to taking a share in Jerdan's periodical.

"The year 1840 marks a turning point in the rewards of authorship",[33] according to the records of the Literary Fund. Before this date distinguished authors were more likely to be applicants than sponsors. Such famous but ill-rewarded authors included Coleridge, Hogg, Peacock, Hunt and Hood. There were writers such as Wordsworth, Lamb and Shelley who also earned little, but had a private income or paid employment, so had no need to apply to the Literary Fund. After the 1840 point authors like Dickens, Thackeray, Tennyson and Trollope earned good incomes from their work, and became subscribers to the Literary Fund. The organisation itself saw some changes in this year, two of which were particularly unhappy events for their participants.

The Rev. Whittington Landon's apparent misconduct concerning the missing £10 5s, for which he had been forced to resign his Secretaryship, was referred for a meeting of the sub committee of the Literary Fund in March 1840. By November Landon had applied for a post in the Church, and the Committee was asked for a reference by the Rector of All Hallows, Lombard Street. Without giving him any details the Committee replied that "the motives which led to the rescinding of Mr Landon's testimonial were not such as to diminish his utility as a parish priest" and that he was merely inefficient as a Secretary.[34]

At the same meeting that pushed Landon to resign, a question was raised as to whether any member of the Committee or Council was disqualified by reason of their arrears. Blewitt reported that Mr Jerdan's subscription had been unpaid since 1835. Jerdan protested that he had paid, and could produce receipts to prove it. Coming as he often did to his friend's rescue, Croly seconded by Nichols proposed to refer the matter to a sub-committee, pending which Jerdan's re-election to the Council should stand, but that if he could not produce receipts for his subscriptions, he would resign. On 8 April a letter from Jerdan was read to the Chairman of the Meeting, resigning his place on both the General Committee and the Council of the Literary Fund. Jerdan's old enemy, Charles Dilke of the *Athenaeum*, did not let matters lie. He moved that the Committee look more closely at two donations in particular which had involved Jerdan as intermediary. These donations had been made ten months previously but Dilke seems to have waited until Jerdan was already under fire before raising the matter. It would be charitable to believe that he had the good interests of the Fund at heart rather than rejoicing at an opportunity to kick his victim whilst he was down.

At a subsequent meeting of the Fund it became clear that at the last Anniversary Dinner a John Howell had pledged money to the Fund in the form of a cheque handed to Jerdan and that a Mr Baily had also given his draft for ten guineas donation to the Fund to Jerdan. Upon investigation it was revealed that Jerdan had given Howell's cheque for eleven guineas to Stevenson, "a

Bookseller of Parliament Street . . . for the rent of chambers in his house occupied by the 'National Association for the Encouragement of Authors'".[35] Jerdan had owed five pounds for the rent and Stevenson had paid him the difference in cash. Baily's cheque had been cashed by Jerdan on 9 May 1839. It was not explained why it had taken ten months for these misappropriations to come to light. Jerdan wrote to John Britton in June to say that he was considering writing to the Fund, "to prevent the grounds of my retirement either being misrepresented now or on the books hereafter . . . ". He asked Britton to call on him "with Mr Howell's partner, who knows you, and has some fancy that he might have handed a cheque to you for the Fund by which means it might come to me, At present how it could do so, as I believe it did, is the most incomprehensible puzzle I ever had in my life."[36] Whatever the outcome, Jerdan was required to pay the missing twenty-two pounds one shilling to the Fund, "or give such an explanation as he may think proper". Even Jerdan's friend Thomas Hood, was appalled by the turn of events, writing to his wife in April, "I did not tell you there has been strange work in the Literary Fund – embezzling of money etc. People who had given £10 and so forth at the anniversary said not to have paid – but on being applied to, <u>had</u> paid – and some of their cheques I believe paid in to Jerdan's banker – traced. <u>Jerdan has resigned his seat there</u> so we may presume Verdict Guilty. What a set they are."[37]

Jerdan repaid the missing money in June, asking the Committee to include names of intermediaries in their Printed Lists as well as the names of donors. This was rejected by the Committee. Another letter from Jerdan was read at this meeting, concerning his resignation from the Council, and yet a third letter, the contents of which were not disclosed in the Minutes but were simply "passed over." At the same meeting, as he had been unable to produce receipts for his membership subscriptions, he was removed from membership of the Society and his election to the Council was null and void. Thus ignominiously ended an association of over twenty years which had given Jerdan much pleasure and brought relief to many struggling writers. In writing his memoirs Jerdan restrained himself until the fourth volume before referring to it, merely as "A dislike to new principles in the grants, a cabal, and a paltry insult, which I thought the official authorities ought to have taken up, caused me to retire from it; yet with every warm wish for its increase and liberal and humane management." Jerdan thought the Fund should support equally the 'distinguished' and the struggling writer, a distinction he felt had been lost in favour of the former.[38]

Jerdan seems to have been unable to accept that his removal from the Council of the Literary Fund was a *fait accompli*. In February (the year was not given, but likely to have been 1841), he wrote to Snow of the Fund reluctantly tendering his resignation from the Council and was pained to see an advertisement for the pre-Anniversary meeting. "I am sure I need not say," he wrote, "that my wish in this respect arises from no abatement of zeal or affection for the Institution; but

I have allowed myself, by misplaced confidence, to be driven into a position in which I can be of no use to the Society; and I can only hope that no longer period will elapse before I am enabled to prove my regard for it as usual even without official oblyphons."[39] At the same time Jerdan was forced to leave the Literary Fund, Queen Victoria married Prince Albert, that enthusiastic supporter of the arts to whom Jerdan may well have applied for royal patronage for his many charitable interests, had the timing of his resignation not been so unfortunate.

Even as he was under such a dark cloud and risking his reputation with the Literary Fund and possibly even the public, should the rumours be leaked, Jerdan had to keep producing work. *The Mirror* of July 1840 noted that the staple of Bentley's *Miscellany* was "jocularity and light reading", and that it frequently had "papers of fine wit and brilliant satire. That which chiefly sparkles on its front this month is 'The Sleeping Beauty in our Time', a marvellous tale . . . ." written by Jerdan.

Jerdan's device for this story was to update an old fairy tale as a vehicle for considering how England has changed over the preceding century. He looked back at one of the Frost Fairs for which London had been famous since the mid-seventeenth century, choosing the fair of 1740 as a convenient comparison with the present day. A young princess vanished from the festivities, never to be found. A hundred years later, as Jerdan wrote the story, a whaler returned to port from the Arctic bringing ashore a young woman. She had been discovered when a harpoon split open an iceberg, and she was found perfectly preserved inside. Gradually thawed she returned to life, and the remainder of the story concerned her conversations with the ship's captain, each of course thinking the other insane, not comprehending that a century separated their worlds. She enquired about the people and politics of 1740, of which the captain knew nothing, but told her instead of contemporary equivalents, such as that since the Reform Bill, Lord Melbourne had been the premier, "but they say that he, rather than guard and uphold, likes to deal heavy blows and sore discouragement on the Protestant church . . . .".

Seeing the Hamburgh steamer sailing past, the princess screamed in terror for the captain to save the people on board, not knowing about steam, and that ships were no longer reliant on wind:" . . . you would have me believe that, by means of a kettle of water put on to boil, you could force great ships to move against wind, and tide, and stream, wherever they wish to go. Fie! To treat me as if I were a fool or a simpleton." The princess demanded to know the progress of many things that were happening in England at the time of her disappearance, and was told about the founding of the British Museum with its wonders, the establishment of the United States, development of London around the old Foundling Hospital, which was just raising subscriptions in 1740, and the many changes of alliances in the wider world. Mutually puzzled about foreign affairs, the princess and the captain could find no common ground as they neared England. Sighting Dover Castle the princess looked forward to a welcome from "Mr Weller the deputy governor." Jerdan, shamelessly stealing from Dickens, has the captain tell her: "Mr Weller, Madam, is not the governor. Mr Pickwick is, and Samivell is his servant." She was amazed to be told that London streets were safe from robbers, that a police force had reduced murders, dinner was at eight and not at two, and that Chelsea Fields were now Belgrave and Eaton Squares. Demanding a sedan chair she was escorted to a train, the wonder and vapour and rattling of which sent her into a swoon. Roused to consciousness she caught sight of London Bridge: "not the London Bridge of her memory, with its incumbrances and mouldering buildings, but a splendid edifice spanning the flood of Thames in two or three prodigious strides, whilst immediately above a greater miracle still presented itself, a bridge of iron! And hundreds of demon steamers were plying in every direction, some of wood, some of iron, and all crowded with busy thousands."

Jerdan remarked that one could point out millions of changes, but would pick out a few that occurred to him; one was the printing of Parliamentary debates with the names of speakers – an imprisonable offence a century earlier – no franking, no lottery, and coffee houses superseded by clubs. Looking back to the literary luminaries of the princess's day, Jerdan listed Dryden, Pope and Thomson, reserving Swift for a "bonne bouche". This was an account of Dean Swift creating a huge bonfire in Dublin to mark the anniversary of the Battle of the Boyne, but Jerdan remarked that the Ireland of a century ago was "too like the Ireland of today – stained with rapine, murders and banded combinations riding roughshod over the laws". However, in England things were better: manners had become more refined, the administration of justice vastly improved, as demonstrated by the fact that hangings and floggings were not so common or barbaric as had been the practice.

Bringing himself up short from his long catalogue of the century's changes, he commented that he had intended to pen a *jeu d'esprit*, and not an essay, saying at last that in bygone days charity was more abundant than in present times. In the days of the old Frost Fair, the rich took care of the poor. His story ended rather abruptly, and inconsequentially, as if he had run out of steam, or space. However, this last comparison, the only one in which earlier days were better than the present, reflected his abiding concern for the dire poverty around him, especially amongst writers, and through the Literary Fund he had done what he could to alleviate it.

Part IV

Times of Change,
1841–1851

17

Sole Possession – Serious Pursuits

Much to his dismay, in February 1841 Jerdan received a letter requesting arrears of twenty-three pounds to the Royal Geographical Society, under penalty of being named a defaulter. He wrote to Barrow, with whom he had formed the society so eagerly back in 1830, protesting that had he been asked agreeably he might have paid the amount or retired from the expense. He had not attended more than ten meetings nor received the transactions. He had understood that there was a tacit agreement that annual subscriptions were not asked of him as he rendered "superior support" by promoting the Society through publicity in the *Literary Gazette*. "On other Societies", he explained, not altogether accurately, "I have been elected an Honorary member under the notion that it was inexpedient to impose upon a friend whose press was devoted to their interests, the burthen of an expence which tho' trifling in particulars, is a heavy charge in the aggregate."[1] Hoping the Society would not disrespect him he left the matter in Barrow's hands. His letter was annotated, presumably by Barrow, "ordered to be taken no notice of", and there the matter stayed.

Jerdan was no longer a member of his beloved Literary Fund, and now was expelled from the Royal Geographical Society but he still, nominally at least, retained his membership of the Society of Antiquaries. His final presentation to them was in November 1841, when he exhibited a "specimen of money from Ceylon, in the form of a double hook. Its name in the language of the Kandians is *Andoo* which means a hook. It is of silver, weighing about ten pence of our current coin, though its value in Kandy, where it is stated to have been in use for more than three centuries, is only four pence."[2] This specimen was probably sent to Jerdan by Edward Power, his son-in-law who was then living in Ceylon.

Jerdan's family affairs were in some disarray. The Census for 1841 poses more questions than it provides answers. Of Frances Jerdan and the children who remained with her, no trace can be found, neither is there any mention of Ella and Fred Stuart or Laura Landon, the children of Jerdan and Letitia Landon. Jerdan and Mary Maxwell had, in accordance with the statutory regulations introduced in 1837, duly registered the birth of Charles and John, but those of

Marion and Matilda were pre-1837 and as they were not christened, no record was made of their births. Having given their real names on their sons' birth registrations, it is surprising that when the census-taker came to the door of 87 Hercules Buildings, he found there William Stewart, age 50, of independent means, born in Scotland; Maria Stewart age 25, Maria Stewart age 5, Matilda Stewart age 4, Charles age 3 and John, 18 months. There was also a female servant in the household. The underquoting of nine years in Jerdan's age could perhaps be because he had told Mary that he was younger than his real age, or because of vanity, as he would have had to complete the householder's schedule, the first time such forms were issued for every household in the country The 1841 census required less information than future ones concerning relationships, birthplaces or ages, but was supposed to cover every family in the country, except that it apparently omitted Jerdans, Stuarts and Landons. William and Mary's sixth child, another son, was born on 28 July and named William,[3] too late to be included in the census.

In 1841 the publisher John Reid sent a questionnaire to editors of all stamped papers, asking them to specify the politics of their publications. He published the responses, adding information on the number of stamps bought in 1839.[4] This showed that the *Literary Gazette,* listed under "Stamped Papers, in which Politics are excluded, neutral or of secondary interest", had purchased 27,030 stamps, whilst the liberal *Athenaeum* purchased 63,500. Assuming the ratio of stamped and unstamped copies was the same for both journals, the *Athenaeum's* total sales were more than twice those of the *Gazette.* Taking into account fluctuations resulting from changes to the stamp tax, it has been calculated that in 1840 the *Gazette's* circulation was about 2000 copies per week, about a third of sales a decade earlier.

In the Spring of 1841 Jerdan decided to make a last ditch attempt to pull the *Literary Gazette* back out of the mire. Presumably completely out of funds himself he used what he called "family connexions", and proposed to buy out the shares held by Longman and Colburn. He received a partially illegible note from Colburn dated 11 May 1841, saying that he would "await the result of the valuation of Longman's share to us both . . . I think Mr Thomas of the *Court Journal* would be a very proper person to undertake the office".[5] As the *Court Journal* was one of Colburn's publications, Mr Thomas might not be quite as impartial as Colburn suggested. Nevertheless negotiations were completed and Jerdan became sole proprietor of the ailing *Literary Gazette.* Now he "set out again, sanguine, hopeful, uncontradicted and uncontrolled, on my own capital".[6] He had some degree of success, but admitted that "the counting by thousands which had been reduced to hundreds, did not rise to thousands again."

Jerdan acquired total ownership of the *Literary Gazette* on 21 July 1841. We know the date as he wrote excitedly to Wright: "Are you alive or dead? If dead, write to me immediately – I leave Town on Monday and am this day sole owner of the *Literary Gazette*, having bought both Longman's and Colburn's shares."[7] He announced the change of proprietor in the issue of 7 August. Determined to finally quash the old allegations he went on to declare:

> Though [the editor] has exercised a despotic and independent control over the *Gazette's* literature during all that period, it has been difficult to disabuse the public of a certain degree of belief in interested and inimical representations, – that, being connected with eminent publishers, it was sometimes biased in its views by prepossessions in their favour. There was not a particle of truth in this industriously circulated rumour; but it had, like all often-repeated falsehoods, a partial effect, which we take this opportunity to remove for ever, since the Literary Gazette is now entirely unconnected with "the trade."[8]

The same notice was repeated in the *Gazette* of 21 August, and again on 4 September, when Jerdan added a response to the *Athenaeum's* reaction to news of his sole ownership. "The *Athenaeum* has had the bad taste to step out of its way in order to comment on that with which it could have nothing to do, and the impertinence to misrepresent private transactions of the nature of which it could know nothing. To puff itself and depreciate the *Literary Gazette* seems to be the intent of this foolish exhibition." Stung by the *Athenaeum's* attribution of "a pining atrophy" as the cause of ownership change, Jerdan mentioned the "singular increase of circulation" which had recently occurred; and he went on to explain that Longmans had had a change in their own partnership, in consequence of which the firm was prepared to give up their share in the *Literary Gazette*; as for Colburn, "it is enough to state that he retired with great reluctance and on the ground alone that he took an economic and retrenching view". There had thus been an "honourable separation" with no bad feelings. Had Jerdan left his argument here it might have been convincing, but he continued for another half-column to berate the *Athenaeum* for trumpeting its price reduction as the *Literary Gazette* "would rather supply a grain of gold or silver than a whole pit of lead, a column of pith, rather than a sheet of verbiage". Winding up, Jerdan tried to take the high moral ground: "We will not be further provoked to trespass on our readers with controversy about our merits or defects." At the same time that Jerdan took over the *Gazette*, there was a change of printer, and Messrs Robson, Levey and Franklyn who had worked on the *Gazette* for a number of years as employees of Moyes, now became its printers in their own names, while William Armiger Scripps remained as publisher for a further six years.

Jerdan's sympathy was aroused by the premature death of John Macrone, Dickens's first publisher, leaving his young family unprovided for. Dickens decided to produce a publication to benefit Macrone's family and Jerdan's contribution to this duly appeared in *Pic Nic Papers* published by Henry Colburn.[9] Jerdan's covering letter was also printed, noting that the story was "a simple and curious sketch of Scottish manners, belonging to a not very distant time, yet so completely erased by 'the march' of modern ideas and changes, as to seem a tale of centuries gone by rather than of yesterday . . . ". The story, 'Aidy Eddie', was not original to Jerdan, but related to him by his "loved and venerated father . . . whom he has often heard repeat the anecdote in that style of rich quiet humour for which he was so noted". The punchline of the story was that Jerdan's father, sitting as the magistrate at Kelso, tried the case of a man who had been arrested for begging. The culprit protested that he was merely singing to the landlady of a pub, hoping for a morsel for himself and his dog. Baillie Jerdan demanded to know who had most recently given the beggar alms, as it was then believed that the donor was as culpable as the recipient. Reluctantly the beggar replied, "I dinna like to do that, but if it maun be, it maun be; the last amous I got was frae yer ain sel; yer worship gae me sax-pence, yue'll mind when we foregathered yestereen at Maxwell-heugh". Baillie Jerdan saw the joke, joining in the roars of laughter which filled his courtroom, and freed the beggar, who was given alms by everyone present. Jerdan chose this story for Macrone's benefit publication, thinking it was "not inappropriate to a work on behalf of a worthy Scotsman's bereaved relatives". It is also an illuminating glimpse of the character of his father, and the severe social conditions of his childhood.

The *Literary Gazette* still attempted to review all important new books, but did not always select those which have stood the test of time. Jerdan had found Carlyle's *Sartor Resartus* too challenging when it appeared in 1838, passing lightly over it, describing it as "the oddest patchwork . . . a huge mass of imagination . . . made repulsive by form and manner". Several other literary journals failed to give it even so much notice at the time of its publication. When it reappeared, Jerdan considered it "somewhat too German and Transcendental for our taste (for we, alas! have not time for books that require much poring over and speculation to be well understood)".[10] Carlyle's style and content was apparently too dense and inaccessible to tempt Jerdan's interest, perhaps more especially at this time when he had such a huge drain on his resources and energies, now that he was sole proprietor of the *Gazette*. It is easy to criticise his superficial treatment of difficult literature as implying Jerdan's lack of intellect; one writer decided that "At no time did Jerdan make a serious effort to understand Carlyle himself, or to interpret him to readers."[11] In similar vein Jerdan reviewed the *Essays* of Emerson when they were published in England with an introduction by Carlyle. He sidestepped having to come to terms with Emerson's transcendentalism by jovially, pseudo-intellectually, noting:

Mr Carlyle approves of this book; and no wonder for it out-Carlyle's Carlyle himself, exaggerates all his peculiarities and faults and possesses very slight glimpses of his excellencies. It imitates his inflations, his verbiage, his Germanico-Kantian abstractions, his metaphysics and mysticism; but wants the originality, the soul, the high and searching intellect, which, in spite of these 'pribbles and prabbles, look ye' ever and anon burst out with something to fill the reader with admiration and set the mind to work upon noble expressions and striking and grand ideas.[12]

Jerdan made little or no attempt to understand Emerson's work. He knew enough to use the jargon or language of a serious review, but fell back upon his usual recourse of generalisations to fill columns. In spite of his difficulties, he somehow recognized that Emerson was an author whose work the *Gazette* should review, and must have considered that it had sufficient interest to his readership to choose it in the first place. This was Jerdan's journalist's instinct taking over, as it often did, from his intellectual instincts which could be submerged by "difficult" writers.

Even though the *Literary Gazette* no longer had the magical aura it had once enjoyed, Jerdan's opinion was still believed by some to carry weight. The prolific historical novelist G.P.R. James asked him to "make much" of his latest work, *Morley Ernstein, or The Tenants of the Heart*. James had recently left Longmans who had been his publishers for years, explaining to Jerdan that he had reason to suspect them of bad-mouthing a book he had published elsewhere; he was not so concerned about his "old enemy, the *Athenaeum*", but assured Jerdan that he had taken great pains with the present book, and that Jerdan should "not let it be injured if you can help it – which you can entirely if you like".[13] In the same letter James brought Jerdan up to date with the campaign he had been waging for five years, to exclude French piracies of literature from England by regulating Customs, "and secondly the active prosecution of negociations for international treaties for the security of copyright". These were matters that anyone involved in literature had to be interested in, as cheap foreign reprints could ruin business for English publishers. The copyright question was still unresolved, but James told Jerdan that his campaign on the first issue had been successful, so that "even single copies of foreign reprints to pass in travellers luggage must now be old and used. No more cutting of leaves and writing names on the outside will do . . . "[14] He urged Jerdan to mention this in the *Gazette* as "Galignani, Baudry and their agents are zealously assuring all English Travellers abroad that the reprints pass without difficulty". One wonders how James responded to Galignani's publishing of a foreign edition of *Morley Ernstein* at the same time as the English edition.

James planned to see Jerdan at the Literary Fund dinner in March but was unsure what the situation now was: "I forget whether you have had anything to say to that Institution after the ungrateful manner in which some of the people connected with it treated you, but I know you still wish well to it whether you take any share in its proceedings or not." In his *Autobiography* Jerdan spoke highly of James, recalling twenty-five years of happy memories. James enjoyed a private income, so did not fall within Jerdan's theme of writers relying on literature for survival. James, observed Jerdan, had a nobility of nature and was admired for his high morals, practising in private life what he preached in his books. Jerdan could not have failed to notice the difference between his friend and himself.

Jerdan was thinking now not of morals but of his own busy plans. Money was still a problem. On 13 February, probably of 1842, Jerdan offered Bentley a "half laugh Valentine", and the balance of his debt the following week, as "it will save my decency at the bankers".[15] Despite this, to celebrate the 25th anniversary of the *Literary Gazette* he held a dinner party for "a brilliant intellectual company of about sixty" of its friends, at the Freemasons Tavern. Dickens postponed a planned trip to Yorkshire so that he could attend, assuring Jerdan that of all the congratulations he would receive, "there will be none more cordial and warm-hearted than mine" and he looked forward to the *Gazette's* 50th birthday. Jerdan reported that the party was agreeable and satisfactory.[16]

In July 1842 Forster organized a welcome home dinner for Dickens at Greenwich, following the author's unhappy American tour. Hood was too ill to take the Chair although he was present, so Captain Marryat presided with Jerdan as Vice-Chair. Hood recalled much singing, toasting of 'the Boz', a response from Dickens, and more singing; he also remarked on "Jerdan, as Jerdanish as usual on such occasions – you know how paradoxically he is QUITE AT HOME IN DINING OUT".[17] Certainly it seems that 'dining out' was a prerequisite for any man who wished to be seen about town and known for his connections which were, in Jerdan's case at least, vital for the content of his *Literary Gazette*.

The grumpy actor Macready noted another occasion when Jerdan "dined out". In May a dinner party of journalists and critics were invited to Bulwer's home at Fulham; Jerdan, Forster, Ainsworth, Leigh Hunt and others were included in the group. Macready complained to his Diary that it was "One of the dullest, most uncomfortable days I have spent for some years. I asked Quin once the time; he said, 'A quarter-past nine; you thought it was eleven'. I was not very well pleased with Bulwer inviting me to indifferent company and a very bad dinner . . . "[18] As several of the company were Macready's chosen acquaintance and his frequent guests, it is possible that he was merely in a bad mood and no company would have satisfied him on that occasion.

The time-honoured habit of 'salons' was continued by Anna Maria Hall, who entertained literary and artistic guests on Thursday afternoons at 'The Rosery', her home in Old Brompton, adjacent to Landon's home when Jerdan first saw her. He does not mention attending one of these modest gatherings, and perhaps fought shy of them, feeling that his reputation had waned so far as to be embarrassing.

Jerdan's path crossed so often now with Forster's, usually because of some association with Dickens, it is tempting to speculate whether either of them mentioned the dangerous name of L.E.L; one had been her lover for several years, the other had broken his engagement because of the rumours surrounding her, Jerdan's name being one of these. By now, four years after her death, any awkwardness would likely have worn off and they had both moved on with their lives. Jerdan, certainly, was fully occupied on the domestic front as his home with Mary Maxwell was now busy with six small children.

On 21 November 1842 William Jerdan wrote his Preface to the *Rutland Papers*, which he had edited. These were "original documents illustrative of the Courts and times of Henry VII and Henry VIII, selected from the Private Archives of His Grace the Duke of Rutland". This was a project he undertook for the Camden Society, which had been founded four years earlier and named after an early English historian, William Camden. Its purpose was to publish early historical and literary remains, unedited manuscripts and to republish selected scarce printed books. The parliamentary printer and proprietor of the *Gentleman's Magazine*, John Bowyer Nichols, had initiated the Society and printed its publications. Its first secretary was Thomas Wright, an editor of early texts. Membership soared and in 1843 Prince Albert joined the Society and remained a member until his death. By March 1840 the limit on membership had risen to one thousand two hundred and fifty, with a list waiting for deaths and resignations, although ten years later membership had dropped considerably. Each publication was sent to every member and to the five major libraries. Jerdan's work in 1842 was therefore seen by well over a thousand knowledgeable and interested people, and was a task which combined his love of antiquarianism with his lifelong interest in literature. It also brought him into contact with men he already knew, some his close friends like Crofton Croker, and others with whom closer ties developed such as James Orchard Halliwell, Thomas Wright, and Sir Henry Ellis, Director of the British Museum, all also members of the Society of Antiquaries, as well as on the Council of the Camden Society in 1842–43.

Jerdan's Preface thanked the Duke of Rutland for access to his papers and, contrary to Jerdan's frequent practice, said that he had no apology to make for his editorial work, as having had the expert assistance of John Bruce and Thomas Wright, he was assured of their integrity, and also was (probably only very slightly) ashamed at being named the principal author of the work. The *Rutland Papers* is 130 quarto pages, bound as a book, the forerunner, Jerdan hoped, of future projects from the same fertile source. One document he included was 'A Device for the Coronation of King Henry VII', a detailed schedule of arrangements, ceremonies and dress for the occasion; another was a list of those present at the Field of the Cloth of Gold, followed by an account of the meeting between Henry VIII and Emperor Charles V. The collection contained other historical sixteenth-century documents, each with brief editorial notations. The book's review in *The Mirror* of January 1843 commented that "it is a collection of great interest and the editor has well performed his task by directing attention to many of the items which are most worthy of notice". This was a work of serious historical scholarship, akin to Jerdan's occasional presentations to the Society of Antiquaries, and shows a side of his character which was not often evident in his daily labours.

His association on the Camden Society with Halliwell and Wright developed into friendship, especially as all three men were also members of the first Council of the Percy Society, for which Wright was secretary and treasurer. This scholarly book club was founded in 1840 and lasted for twelve years. The Percy produced bound books of text, carefully copied from original sources in the Bodleian, British Museum and other collections, with special emphasis on Elizabethan ballads, for which they attempted to find the appropriate tunes, plays, poetry and popular literature. Jerdan had intended to produce 'Jacobite Ballads and Fragments' for the Percy, but this does not appear to have been published. Jerdan's old crony Crofton Croker was also a member of both these scholarly societies and still friendly, despite the débâcle at the Literary Fund. Halliwell married in November, and Jerdan wrote to congratulate him. Three weeks later he corresponded again with Halliwell on a more prosaic matter. A row had erupted at the Percy Society:

> In our friend Wright's absence, I attended the Percy on Thursday when there was something of a stormy discusson and the general question of your rather lengthy letter was postponed till next month. Meanwhile I should be glad if you have kept and could send me any letters from the Secretary or Treasurer to you especially one requiring you in the name of the Council to return the transcripts made for intended publications. Is there a letter from you to the Treasurer saying you would see the Society or the Council damned first, and if so, what provoked it?[19]

A further letter the following week put him firmly on Halliwell's side in the argument, and discussed yet another society:

> I have no objection to be a Council Man on the Shakspere; and shall probably be on the Camden having finished one Volume for it and begun another. But I fear it will be nearly all for the honour of the thing, as my time. By the by, we <u>aught</u> to have an elaborate article on the Shakspere and Shakesperiansy of Knight, Collier and Halliwell. Your letter is very satisfactory – I think it is probable enough that both Wright and I may bid the Percy goodnight. Nous verrons. . . .[20]

The Shakspere (sic) Society had been founded the previous year by John

Payne Collier, also one of the twelve founders of the Percy. Jerdan's name was on a 'London Committee for the purchase of Shakespeare's House', so his association with the Shakspere Society continued for several years.[21] He did not bid the Percy "goodnight", but continued his connection for a few more years. The Percy's search for genuine old ballads from Scotland may have inspired Jerdan to write a song of his own, 'Go Along at the Time'. He sent it to the composer Herbert Rodwell to set to music. He received a disappointing response: "I have returned your very clever lines, not because I do not admire them, for I really do, and think the idea excellent, but because my ass of a genius is a stubborn beast and will not always trot along as he is bidden . . . "[22]

Jerdan wanted the *Literary Gazette* to represent every aspect of contemporary life – except politics. All cultural activities formed part of the regular content of the magazine, but there was one topic of great interest to everybody which formed the focus of 'Sketches of Society' in 1843.[23] This was the adulteration of food, brought to the forefront some years earlier by Frederick Accum a chemist of Soho, whose treatise on the subject was known colloquially as "Death in the Pot". The *Literary Gazette* 'Sketches' came under the heading of 'Cockney Catechism' and were in the format of a play initiated by "the great increase of sudden deaths in London . . . complaints of the heart are often induced by unwholesome provisions taken into the system and affecting the vital fluid and its grand receptacle". The subject, however, was anything but playful: the characters discussed the corruption of coffee and especially of sugar: "This Muscovado sugar, for instance, you would hardly believe that in bad hands it will take from 20 to 25 per cent of salt, without being detected; and is very often mixed to that extent!" Coffee could be made from "burnt or scorched beans, of roasted peas and other grain. Occasionally the sweepings of real coffee are thrown into the mess; but it sells very generally as coffee without the addition." The noxious practices of butchery were the topic of another instalment, and the contents of a bottle of soda-water a further episode. "Here, it is ____'s! The bottles are theirs but the contents are not. This imitation is advertised to cost fourpence per dozen, and not to have a single grain of soda in the whole composition . . . cheating you of what you want and furnishing a noxious instead of a beneficial beverage." The *Literary Gazette* was by no means the first or only paper to raise public awareness of the practices of food manufacturers but nothing was done about the problem for many years; it took until 1855 when articles in *The Lancet* sparked a huge response and calls for reform and legislation, which eventually became effective in 1875. Jerdan was to take up the cudgels on this subject again in 1860.

Jerdan's long association with the Royal Society of Literature, and his present affiliations in various societies with Thomas Wright, combined when he reviewed a book of Wright's which had been published under the superintendence of the RSL. Jerdan had sent his manuscript to the editor of the *Edinburgh*

Review (Macvey Napier), in August, suggesting that if it could be published in October "it would be a great consideration as in that case the *Review* would prelude the winter session and Meeting of the Society in November".[24] Running to more than seventeen pages, the review duly appeared in the October 1843 issue of the *Edinburgh Review*. Jerdan discussed Wright's *Biography of Literary Characters of Great Britain and Ireland, arranged in Chronological Order. Anglo-Saxon Period*. Before approaching the work itself Jerdan took the opportunity of recounting the history of the RSL in great detail including the prizes which were awarded initially. Amongst the many names listed as members of the new Society was Jerdan's, appearing four times. The delays and postponements were carefully noted culminating with the current situation of the Society, its premises and its library. The article then linked this history, which consumed nine full pages, with the speech made by the President in his address of 1838, recommending a biographical undertaking of Anglo-Saxon and Anglo-Norman works, the first of which was now, finally, to be reviewed, whilst the second, also by Wright, was in preparation. An extract from the President's speech filled another page, until Jerdan had at last to confront his task of reviewing Wright's *Biography*.

Sketching in the previous absence of any such literary history of England, Jerdan, following Wright, mentioned the earliest attempts in the sixteenth century and others which followed. He praised Wright for not merely copying older texts but for checking on their authenticity. True to his *Literary Gazette* practice, Jerdan quoted long extracts from the book as this "affords a fair example of the author's style, reasoning and learning", followed by a further lengthy extract on King Alfred. The review went on to mention dozens of the names in Wright's book, commenting that the whole "exhibits the greatness and energy of the Anglo-Saxon character". In his overview of the work, Jerdan concluded that it was a credit to the RSL and to the scholarship of Mr Wright, as would, no doubt, be the Anglo-Norman volume to come.

Jerdan's name as reviewer did not appear in print, but it is clearly his work from the emphasis on the foundation of the Royal Society of Literature, which he reprised in his *Autobiography* a decade later, and his literary style. Macvey Napier sent Jerdan a generous twenty guineas for his contribution, remarking that he would be interested in any literary news Jerdan could not use in the *Literary Gazette*.[25] The venerated *Edinburgh Review* had a more serious literary tone than his own paper and Jerdan did his utmost in this review to come up to the high standard expected. He had the education and interest to have become an expert in many different fields of learning, but his nature was not that of an academic, preferring as he so reliably demonstrated, the more social life of a literary editor. This was more superficial perhaps, skimming over all topics rather than diving in, but he was able nevertheless to participate in matters of especial interest such as archaeology and the more arcane reaches of literary endeavour.

Writers were never shy of taking advantage of Jerdan's famous kindness. A note from Thackeray promoting a friend's work sycophantically asked, "If you delight in performing good actions (as you notoriously do) pray insert the inclosed para about a really clever novel ... and count on the gratitude of your Titmarsh."[26] Dickens felt some affection for Jerdan, although the wordly affairs of the two were so different, one at his peak, the other on a decline. Possibly in response to a note from Jerdan praising *Martin Chuzzlewit*, Dickens replied:

> A thousand thanks for your kind and genial letter ... it is not a weak cheer, but good cheer, strong cheer, heart cheer, and cheer I love to have. It satisfied me more than I can tell you, My Dear Jerdan. Faithfully, your friend. ...[27]

Bentley asked Jerdan to assist him at the Literary Fund's General Meeting to re-elect officers.[28] He also used Jerdan to mediate with one of his authors, Anna Eliza Bray, whom he believed should return to him £25 advanced for her book *Henry de Pomeroy*. "I shall still be a great loser by the publication", he moaned.[29] Mrs Bray was struggling with illness, and her husband was also ailing. Jerdan was acting as her agent, and she told him that she hoped Bentley would reprint her former novels.

> By having one now, I trust, so likely to do well in his hands ... I would consent to the terms he offered you on my account – namely to publicize my new work on the principle of 'Holy Pupils' allowing him to deduct from my share of the same the £25 in question. This £25 (unsolicited by him), I told him, I had offered to repay him if "Henry de Pomeroy" sold for only twenty-seven shillings. That work, however, sold for twenty-eight shillings and sixpence. I could not therefore feel that I was in his debt. But rather than he should be disappointed, I was willing to accede to the terms named. To this I added he must allow me 25 copies of my new work, gratis, on publication.

Plainly, Bentley drove a hard bargain, but times were unfavourable to him: sales of the *Miscellany* had dropped to one-third of the original level and he was forced to sell "huge numbers" of his books to the dealer Tegg; moreover, he could no longer pay his printers in cash so that his costs rose and his profits fell.[30] Mrs Bray was "disappointed ... that Bentley has offered me such poor terms – but I feel not the less thankful to you, because I know you would have done better for me if you could. ..." She hoped that Jerdan was recovered from his illness, and wished "Mrs Jerdan, yourself and the family many happy years." She was presumably referring to the real Mrs Jerdan, Frances, and not to his new "wife", Mary Maxwell; many literary figures had attended parties at Grove House in the good years, and it was unlikely that Jerdan would have brought Mary Maxwell into his established literary circles. Mrs Bray may not have known that his circumstances had changed so dramatically since the days of Grove House parties, and was merely being courteous in her good wishes.

Another son had been born on 20 January 1843 and named Walter.[31] On his registration on 8 March, Mary's residence was given as 1 Melina Place, in St John's, Marylebone, where a 'Mrs. Stuart' was listed at No. 1 in a Directory of 1844. None of Jerdan's surviving correspondence used this address, so it is unclear whether he lived there with his family. Mary and Jerdan now had seven mouths to feed as well as their own. Jerdan's perpetual state of penury was counterbalanced by flattering notes from friends and authors, but Jerdan was once again forced to turn to Bentley for help:

> I write this lest I should not find you at home. Whilst I feel so greatly obliged by your kind help three weeks ago, I am the more unwilling to trespass farther, but I have been most vexatiously delayed in money matters, and if you will oblige me still more by holding over my draught till I can see you towards the end of the week, it will be a favour (like the rest) not to be forgotten.[32]

His more cautious friend Macready had directed a play in February called 'Blot on the 'Scutcheon'. Jerdan visited him in his room afterwards to tell him he had not liked it. Macready himself made his final stage appearance in June, as Macbeth, and was fêted at a triumphant dinner a few days later. The year closed with a birthday party for his daughter Nina, which he was unable to attend. Although feeling ill Jane Carlyle went along, dreading the event. As she wrote to Jeannie Welsh on 28 December, it proved however "the very most agreeable party that ever I was at in London – everybody there seemed animated with one purpose to make up to Mrs Macready and her children for the absence of 'the tragic actor' . . . " Dickens and Forster performed magic tricks. Then began the dancing: "Old Jerdan of the *Literary Gazette* (escaped out of the Rules of the Queen's Bench for the great occasion!),[33] the gigantic Thackeray etc. etc. all capering like Maenades!!" The party was full of wild dancing, finishing at midnight. Jane Carlyle's account gives a glimpse of Jerdan bent on enjoying himself, despite the problems which beset him on all sides.

His troubles made him slightly cynical and sour. Nearly four years had elapsed since his previous contribution to Bentley's *Miscellany* but in February 1844 appeared "The Happy Family – A Tale of the Town". He took as his theme the ancient tale (at least since Chaucer's time) of the Dunmow Flitch. This is an award of a side of bacon offered to a married couple who can convince a jury of six maidens and six bachelors that in a year and a day they have not quarrelled or wished themselves unmarried. Jerdan noted that for the past eighty years the Flitch had not been claimed, leading him to muse on the reasons for this sad state of affairs. His researches led him to be told that there was only one Happy Family in all of London. Repudiating this idea he said he knew at least a dozen, but his opponent challenged this claim.

The first noble pair given as an example were in reality bored with each other and longed for any disturbance to their tedious, privileged lives. A step down the social scale, a merchant banker's family were held up as an example of happiness. No, said the challenger. "They are about the most wretched in the metropolis." The banker was incapable of feeling happiness as his sole interest was his fortune. Such a deadening lack of emotion had stifled his wife's affections, and their children neither esteemed their father nor loved their mother. Moreover the male offspring were gamblers and villains, whilst the girls had formed most unsuitable and low attachments. Within six months all their troubles would be public and their only consolation in disgrace would be their money. A further example of happy parents with six beautiful children was shown to be a sham: the children drove the parents to distraction, leaving the wife a nervous wreck and the husband unwilling to be at home. Balancing this was a childless couple in easy circumstances, sharing affection and mutual interests. However, their apparent happiness was blighted by the absence of children.

Bewildered, seeking in vain for a happy family amongst the rich, attention turned to the shopkeeper, clerk or mechanic. Each example was refuted: one was careworn in providing for his family; another worked away from home so much that his wife was lonely and sought company of whom he disapproved, and the third was so attached to his Institute that his neglected wife, although a member of the Total Abstinence Society, turned to secret drinking. Even a "millionaire millocrat" was in despair, wishing he were a pauper who could be taken to the Union (poor house) and thus separated from his wife. Next, the Queen was offered as an example of happiness, but "fatigues and ceremonies and cares of royalty were never allied with human happiness".

However, said the challenger, there is one happy family, but not of humans. These were animals caged in Trafalgar Square. They exemplified different needs living together in a symbiotic relationship: "three rats, three owls, three guineapigs, a hare, rabbits, pigeons, starlings, daws, hawks and mice." The secret was in their different tastes, so there was no fighting. Each animal in Jerdan's story represented one of the major sources of strife in humans and if people followed their example, they would be happier. He posited that if all shrill "tabby aunts" were doped with opium, they would become calm and purr like cats; ratty political men should have their teeth drawn and become harmless and live in harmony with others; guineapigs represented sybarites whose only function was to cushion collisions of others; owls should be trusted only in the day and hawks at night, when they sleep.

The story concluded that Charles Fourier's system of association was folly as it did not provide against dissension by eradicating causes of evil or allow scope for weakness.[34] Jerdan's moral was that the only 'happy family' had beastly habits, and happiness in human society can be achieved only by beastly means, such as "drugging, removing instruments of force, separating and governing with a discretion unknown to the social or family compacts of man". This allegorical and thoughtful article represented a more serious side of Jerdan's concerns, although he still needed to wrap his social comment in the guise of anecdotal episodes. Bentley may have found this contribution altogether too serious or too vulgar, as it was to be nearly two years before Jerdan's next article appeared in the *Miscellany*.

He still had his finger in various pies, such as involvement with the sculptor Matthew Cotes Wyatt, for an enormous statue of the Duke of Wellington to be placed on top of the arch opposite Apsley House. He had received a note – almost illegible – from the Duke of Rutland, thanking him for a description of the statue,[35] and one from Wyatt, suggesting that Jerdan write to the Duke of Rutland asking that an application be made for surplus metal required for making the statue. Sir Francis Chantry sent over four tons of cannon; Jerdan, Rutland and a group of officers acquired about forty tons of cannon at a time when there was a shortage of metal;[36] Wyatt urged him to hurry and get his request in "before Sir Peter".[37] Jerdan was present when the forequarters of the massive horse were cast in September 1845. He reported excitedly,

> The flow of so large a quantity of molten metal from the furnace to the receptacle whence it descends to fill the mould is a very grand and remarkable phenomenon . . . The dazzling red stream throws up clouds of vapour of every prismatic hue, the green tinges prevailing; but blues, yellows and various gradations of red, rolling along both in these clouds and in flames emitted from, accompanying and hovering over the lava torrent.[38]

Another extra-curricular activity was Jerdan's membership of the London committee attempting to raise funds to complete the monument to Sir Walter Scott in Edinburgh. £3000 was needed, but subscriptions had been slow to accumulate and only £269 had been raised. A grand Waverley Ball was held in Willis's Rooms on 8 July 1844, and £1100 was raised. The official unveiling of the Monument took place in August 1846, but fund-raising continued until the final thirty-two statuettes adorning the Monument were completed in 1882. Bulwer Lytton declined to join the committee, as did Dickens who maintained "that there is an idea abroad that the Edinburgh people, or Scotch people at all events, should finish their own monument, and that some prejudice is created by the incompleteness of the testimonials to their two great men, Scott and Burns".[39]

The *Literary Gazette* was still influential enough that the major Societies wished to be represented in the journal. Despite having expelled Jerdan for not paying his membership fees, the Royal Geographical Society invited him to a Dinner;[40] Prince Albert was considering becoming a Vice-Patron and a notice in the *Literary Gazette* would be helpful.

In April Sir Peter Laurie, his friend from youth who was now a magistrate and on his way to becoming Lord Mayor, suggested that Jerdan arbitrate in a dispute between a writer and the man to whom he had entrusted his autobiography for editing, on the basis of friendship. After two years the so-called editor refused to return the manuscript, demanding fifty pounds for work done, or one hundred pounds to complete it. As the magistrate himself then offered to act as "a friend between them", it is unlikely that Jerdan's services were utilized.

Jerdan's eldest daughter Frances-Agnes, at the advanced age of thirty-five, married on 30 April 1844.[41] Her husband was Thomas Irwin, a year younger and styled as "Gentleman". He was employed as a Clerk in the Audit Office, and lived at 12 Montpelier Square Brompton, but the marriage took place in Bentley, Hampshire, witnessed by the bride's parents, her brother William Freeling Jerdan and by John Eggar. John Eggar was probably grandfather of the bride, if the clue in the story of *The Hermit of Aroostook* is correct, saying that Robert Eggar was the brother of Jerdan's wife Frances. The newly married pair lost no time in having a family, and by 1852 had five children. In 1851 they lived at Park Walk Chelsea but ten years later had moved to Childs Hill in Middlesex, to have cleaner air and more space for their growing family.

Jerdan was satisfied with his new son-in-law, and together they attended many meetings of the British Association for the Advancement of Science. He enjoyed all aspects of his attendances at these annual meetings held each year at a different place: "A multitude of useful and pleasant connections were formed during a score of meetings, new scenes were visited, and new attractions of antiquities, arts and nature explored . . ."[42] Only one incident marred this delightful occupation. It concerned Dr Whewell who, according to Jerdan, had climbed the ladder of the British Association to become Master of Trinity College Cambridge. Jerdan admired his learning but found him arrogant. Once in post as Master, Whewell described the BA as "declining and unable to support itself, and proposed biennial or triennial meetings, that it might drop off gradually and die a decent and unmasked death".[43] Jerdan printed some "free remarks" upon this view which offended Whewell but the two glossed over their differences at the next meetings, with the intervention of the Marquis of Northampton. Whewell however had not forgiven Jerdan and created a scene at a College Dinner to which Jerdan and his son-in-law Irwin had been invited by another Professor. As they were seated in places of honour, a lackey sent by Whewell asked them whose guests they were; Jerdan prepared to reply when he became aware, from his neighbours, "that the communication was not such as could be tolerated by gentlemen belonging to the College". On withdrawing to another room for dessert, Jerdan was again elevated near to Whewell at the top table, inciting the Master to fury. This was, as Jerdan said, "a silly matter", but it had the consequence that "perfect turmoil ensued". The next evening the college members boycotted the Master's invitations, deserting his rooms, and congregating instead in the common-hall. Jerdan sent him a note: "Understanding that a question put to me from you in Trinity Hall on Friday must (from the customs of the place with which I was at the time unacquainted), be considered an offensive personality, I have to request from you, and as early as possible, an explanation of the matter . . . "[44] Whewell was not a popular figure; indeed "it was wittily said that science was his forte and omniscience his foible, [he] was notorious for his bearish ways".[45] Only after much correspondence with "leading men" did he ungraciously apologize to Jerdan: "I am sorry that such representations have been made to you as to [show?] you when anything offensive in the message sent to you in College Hall on Friday. The question was put as the only obvious way of ascertaining a point which it was fit the College should know; and in my opinion could not reasonably be considered offensive by any one."[46] Thereafter whenever the two met Whewell would scowl angrily, so that Jerdan observed, "I have ever rejoiced that his *caput* did not possess the powers of the head of Medusa, for if it had, I should have been a paving stone and perhaps Macadamised long ago."[47] The whole sorry affair gave rise to squibs and epigrams from anonymous people who disliked the Master, but showed that Jerdan had enough confidence and support to stand his ground against such an eminent figure.

As sole proprietor of the *Literary Gazette* Jerdan now had to watch the financial side of his journal instead of leaving it all to Longmans as previously. Annoyed that the Royal Academy had not submitted paid advertising but had relied upon his good will he wrote to the organisation. In response, he heard on 4 April from its President, Sir Martin Archer Shee: "I always understood that your Paper was considered by the Academy as friendly to the Arts, and I was therefore surprised at the intimation conveyed in your note. To prevent however mistake or omission hereafter, the Council have given precise instruction that all the advertisements of the Academy shall be sent for insertion in the *Literary Gazette*."[48] On the other side of the fence, the Statistical Society requested that the *Literary Gazette* pay for copies of their Papers for insertion into the journal. Jerdan scrawled a note on their letter: "Scandalous. Dun for contributions to benefit Society."[49]

More enjoyable correspondence came in an invitation from John Forster to a dinner at the Trafalgar Tavern, Greenwich, where Lord Normanby was to take the Chair. The dinner was to say 'Farewell' to Dickens as he left for Italy. "You know the pleasure it will give Dickens to see you among his entertainers . . . ",[50] wrote Forster. Over forty people attended and the *Literary Gazette* duly reported that there were "many speeches" but gave no details.

To posterity, Dickens was Jerdan's most famous friend, but he felt closer to John and Ellen Carne, the family friends whom he had visited years earlier in Penzance. Carne died on 19 April 1844 aged 55, and in thanking Jerdan for his letter of condolence, Ellen in her turn consoled him: "and above all when you are yourself suffering from an almost sudden loss and one so nearly related to you. I who know the strong affection you have to all who are related or connected to you know how deeply you feel these things."[51] It is not clear whose death she meant; it does not appear to be a member of any one of Jerdan's immediate families, and therefore, being "nearly related" might be an infant death of a grandchild, perhaps a child of Mary Power's in Ceylon, or even one of Jerdan's sisters. Ellen Carne went on to give Jerdan some information which would have touched him deeply:

> And now, my dear kind friend, in regard to the Memoranda of my dear husband's life about which I am most anxious merely from some words he dropped about six weeks ago. He was reading the *Gazette* and I don't know what struck him at the moment, but he said if dear Jerdan should outlive me, I know no more hands I should most like to fall into so much for he knows the human heart! He had been talking much of you lately and saying what delight he should feel in shewing by the kindness of his manner when he met you, to make up for angry or irritable tempers he had ever shewn towards you at any time . . . it was curious that the last thing he read was the *Gazette*, and the last word was your name.

To assist Jerdan, she set out a brief biography of her husband. A four-line notice of Carne's death was in the *Literary Gazette* of 27 April, with an obituary in the issue of 4 May.[52]

Perhaps it was the loss of a cherished friend which made him reflective, or simply selecting a work to review in the journal, Jerdan decided to address *Imagination and Fancy* by his old enemy of the 'Cockney School', Leigh Hunt. He referred to the jibes Hunt had published against him in the *Tatler* back in 1830, stating that he had long forgiven them. He believed that Hunt's writing had improved in the interval, praised the preface of the new book and his choice of poets.[53] Jerdan's overture for peace was immediately rewarded by a letter from Hunt, published in the *Literary Gazette* the following week, gladly accepting the hand of friendship, and recalling that back in those days of literary in-fighting they had both been "squibbed and squibbified in our turn". They had both "survived a period of violent political warfare, during which to think differently was to feel angrily; and if all the writers of that period had the courage and good-nature of yourself and one or two more, I believe there is not one of us who would not find himself impelled to make similar acknowledgements". Hunt, having only recently learnt about the troubles Byron suffered at the time he stayed with him in Italy, deeply regretted the book he had written which Jerdan had so denigrated in the *Literary Gazette* of the time. Had he known, said Hunt, "I would rather have had my hand cut off than ever written a syllable against him, but I would have devoted the best part of my time and faculties (such as they were) to whatsoever could have done him service." Thus did Hunt make his peace with the dead Byron and the still very much alive William Jerdan.

Jerdan's interest in the Percy Society was an incentive to introduce his friend Peter Buchan to Thomas Wright and others. Buchan was a collector of ballads, something which Jerdan himself had done as a youth encouraged by his father. His introductions and subsequent correspondence with the Percy assisted Buchan. In June 1845 the Percy Society published a book based on

> two folio volumes of ballads, songs and poems taken down by Mr P Buchan of Peterhead, from the oral recitation of the peasantry of his country . . . .[these volumes were] finally by a vote of the Council . . . placed in the hands of the Editor [J. H. Dixon] and his friend W. Jerdan Esq. for them to decide on the authenticity and general merit of the Ballad portion of the volumes . . . in preparing the Ballads for the press, the editor's labours have been pleasantly relieved by the assistance he has derived at the hands of Mr Jerdan, a gentleman on whose high scholastic attainments and sound critical taste, it were needless to expatiate.[54]

Jerdan apparently suffered "a long and severe illness" in the autumn of 1844 and was absent from town.[55] On his return he arranged for the Percy Society to send Buchan £10 for his contribution. The warm relationship which had developed over this mutually beneficial collaboration did not last. Jerdan hung on to Buchan's manuscript folios for two years. He claimed that the parcel had been ready to return but that Buchan had not sent him an address. Finally, he wrote angrily:

> I have sent your MS addressed to Messrs Buchan Bros, 153 Queen Street Glasgow; and will offer no other reply to your scurrilous and ungrateful letter of the 6th than to say that I took much trouble and wasted much valuable time in my endeavours to serve you, and that I now almost rejoice in which I regretted before, viz. that I had not succeeded to a greater amount than I did accomplish for your benefit.[56]

(The "almost rejoice" betrays Jerdan's innate good-heartedness – he could not bring himself to entirely rejoice that he had not succeeded more on Buchan's behalf.)

Another hand, possibly Buchan's own, noted on this letter that Jerdan had "kept possession of several volumes of valuable MS Ballads for many years, and although written at least twenty times would not deliver them up till legal steps were about to be taken for the purpose – and this is the answer". Jerdan clearly had kept the manuscripts long after he should have returned them, but his dereliction was more likely to have been carelessness and mislaying them in his heaps of papers, than malice in retaining them at no profit to himself.

Jerdan himself felt the passing of an era not just by his rapprochement with Leigh Hunt, but also in the fundamental changes that had taken place since he took up his editorial chair at the *Literary Gazette:*

> That this is not the age of poetry and imagination is asserted on all hands, and we should think with no small degree of truth, though the general mislike may rather apply to the vast mass of imitation and mediocrity, than to originality and the true ore where it exists. But if we were to judge by the number of volumes published, some of them sumptuous, many exceedingly neat and ornamental, a portion of huge dimensions (out-epicking epics), and thousands of less ambitious-looking efforts besides, we should believe that there never was an age of poetry and imagination so prolific as our own.
>
> To the shame, or the credit, of the *Literary Gazette* be it spoken, that periodical, so long the hot-bed and nurse of poetic genius, has of late been almost utilitarianised; and has forsaken much of the dutiful service of the Nine. What shall we say in our defence: Truly the affluence of the Muses hath not been altogether so rich as of yore; and there has been more of common metal than we could wish. We cannot, with relish, descend from gold to copper; and perhaps this feeling may have caused a neglect of some not unworthy silver. We must look about us, now that the bustle of the season is over, and we have a few weeks to spare.[57]

Jerdan was mourning not only the passing of the glorious poetry of his youth and early years of the *Literary Gazette*, but implicitly mourning the passing of L.E.L. who had embodied the poetic values he held so dear.

18

Struggle for Financial Survival

The first part of 1845 was marked by three deaths: in February came the shocking news of Laman Blanchard's suicide; the following week Jerdan wrote to comfort William Francis Ainsworth on the death of his son and received detailed directions how to travel by omnibus to reach Hammersmith for the funeral. He was urged to arrive early, as his "presence would bring me much comfort", and "I have now put my reliance in you, I know you will not disappoint me."[1] Despite his own domestic upheavals Jerdan was valued by a few discerning friends who saw beyond his 'good fellow' exterior to the emotional and sympathetic man within; he was indeed referred to by William Harrison Ainsworth as "the friend of all who struggle in the thorny way of literature".[2] The third death was of a literary friend Richard Barham, contributor to the *Literary Gazette* and author of the 'Ingoldsby Legends'. These popular tales appeared in *Bentley's Miscellany* from 1837 until 1843, when they moved to the rival *New Monthly Magazine* under Thomas Hood. Barham nevertheless remained friends with Bentley, who asked Jerdan to prepare an article on him after Barham's death in June. Jerdan replied that he had been "looking out for data to write a right and proper memoir of our regretted friend Barham and think I shall be able to do what you ask".[3] His tribute appeared in the July issue of the *Miscellany*, along with Barham's last lyric poem.

Difficulties were rife in the literary world. The popularity of annuals declined. Heath, publisher of the *Book of Beauty* amongst others, was almost bankrupt, causing Lady Blessington's health to suffer from the worry and endless drudgery which she undertook in order to support herself and the profligate Count D'Orsay. It has been said that literary visitors to her dinners wearied of her cadging contributions to her annuals and, that to add insult to injury, she was vilified for her connection to the annuals by those whom a short time before were clamouring to be allowed to contribute to them.[4] Women writers were the target of an anonymous book which Jerdan reviewed favourably. *Tracts for the Improvement of our Popular Literature* opined that a women "thrusting her name and sentiments before the world in the pages of a book is a violation of the delicacy and beautiful silence which should attend her being. No woman, even the most successful in authorship, has added to her dignity by her writings."[5] Like hundreds of other women, Lady Blessington and the late L.E.L. wrote for their daily bread, and hung on to as much "dignity" as possible while so doing. The fact that Jerdan chose to extract from and review this book suggests that he was in agreement with its tenets and thus at odds with his own important support of women writers.

The handful of Jerdan's surviving correspondence at this period was sent from the '*Literary Gazette* Office'. Mrs Bray asked him in March 1845 whether he still resided in Surrey Street, or was only there occasionally, as she was unsure where to send a review of her work she wished him to include in the *Gazette*. Jerdan may easily have wanted to cover his tracks, between his legal wife and his present and growing family in Lambeth. He might have used his office premises as a place to sleep on occasion.

Jerdan's bank account details of 1845 have survived, and show on the credit side only "Receipts" but, with a single exception, do not identify who was paying him.[6] Over the course of the year twenty-six deposits were made, ranging between £5 and £262 10s, totalling just over £1352. His expenses were a little over £50 less than this, several to a variety of unfamiliar names, the reasons for which are not known. He paid £11 7s to Christies and Manson, precursors of the art auctioneers Christies, and £7 19s 10d to Swan & Edgar, a fashion store. Such payments suggest purchases of non-essentials, surprising as Jerdan's affairs were in a precarious state. He also made fifteen payments at irregular dates and of varying amounts to a Mr. Stuart, totalling £174 1s 9d. The identity of 'Mr. Stuart' is not certain, but there are two main possibilities: one is that Jerdan was sending money to Fred Stuart, his son by Landon now about twenty years old; the other, and stronger, possibility is that when Jerdan had borrowed money from, as he had called it, a "family connexion" in 1841, this is quite likely to have been his mother's wealthy brother John Stuart, gentleman farmer of Ednam near Kelso. Jerdan had needed the money to buy up Longman's and Colburn's shares in the *Literary Gazette* and these payments were probably made to reduce his loan. In 1845 Jerdan also made three payments to the Garrick Club, ten pounds to (Masonic) Lodge No. 1 and in June, sixteen pounds to the British Association, indicating that he considered that he was still in a position to pay his subscriptions to these institutions. However, he could not manage to keep up his subscriptions to every organisation as money was still in short supply. On 17 April 1845 William Jerdan was expelled from the Society of Antiquaries for being sixteen years in arrears with his subscription. It was the old familiar story – an echo of what had happened with the Geographical Society. In his *Autobiography* Jerdan explained, "As years accrued, I found that my eight guineas entrance and four guineas per annum subscription met with no adequate return or inducement to continue a member; for not having time to hunt him up, I never could get papers or volumes of the *Archaeology* from the then fat, contented and rosy official of the name of Martin, and I therefore discontinued my attendance."[7] It does not seem to have occurred to him that he did not receive these documents as he had not paid his dues. Nevertheless, he still faithfully inserted reports of the Society's meetings in the *Literary Gazette*.

On the same day as his expulsion from the Antiquaries, Jerdan was cheered by attending a meeting of the Metropolitan Red Lions at the 'Cheshire Cheese' in Fleet Street. He enjoyed "an evening ever memorable for the brilliancy and pungency of the songs, anecdotes and jokes, at which we shall find the following grave philosophers assisting in the mysteries of the brotherhood . . ."[8]. The Red Lions were formed in 1839 as an offshoot of the British Association; they were, continued the article in the *Edinburgh Magazine*, "the younger tribe of naturalists, disliking the irksomeness of the established ordinary", in the same spirit as the Noviomagians who split from the staid Society of Antiquaries. Jerdan was always ready to join the group which had less formality and more fun, and had been elected as a member in York in September 1844. He received an offer of two Silver Tickets for the Royal Orthopaedic Hospital Festival with a letter exhorting him to choose a companion "worthy of the occasion", as the charity had been distinguished by a Royal Title and a Royal President. Quarles Harris, who wrote this letter, must have been well aware of the boisterous company Jerdan enjoyed keeping even though he softened his stricture by noting that "My Brother was much gratified by your favourable notice of his Poem. It has been very ill treated by many."[9] Quarles's fears were unfounded. As much as Jerdan enjoyed an evening singing and drinking with his circle of mainly Irish and Scottish friends, he had also mixed with Prime Ministers, and many Lords and nobles, and knew how to comport himself in high society.

Jerdan wrote an obituary for his late dear friend Thomas Hood, who had died in misery and penury:

[a] spirit of true philanthropy has departed from its earthly tenement; the light of a curious and peculiar wit has been extinguished; the feeling and pathos of a natural poet have descended into the grave; and left those who knew, admired and loved these qualities to feel and deplore the loss of him in whom they were so pre-eminently united.

Yet we can hardly say that we deplore his death. Poor Hood! His sportive humour, like the rays from a crackling fire in a dilapidated building, had long played among the fractures of a ruined constitution, and flashed upon the world through the flaws and rents of a shattered wreck. Yet infirm as was the fabric, the equal mind was never disturbed to the last. He contemplated the approach of death with a composed philosophy and a resigned soul. It had no terrors for him.[10]

Jerdan revealed that Hood was helped at the last by Sir Robert Peel, who organised a pension for Hood's widow of one hundred pounds per annum. The *Literary Gazette* was once again a way in which Jerdan could make known to the public the kindnesses and generosity given and received by those he considered friends, as he had done earlier at the time Bulwer refused to take royalties from Macready when the actor could scarcely support his family.

Jerdan's own finances were still on a knife-edge. He was unwell in the summer and sent his long-suffering son William Freeling to Bentley with a note enclosing a draft for more than the thirty pounds he already owed Bentley, urgently requesting a cheque for the difference. He also owed money to a Mr Smith, and had heard from Gibbs, Smith's agent, that the terms of acceptable payment were twenty pounds down plus Gibbs's expenses and "the remainder in quarterly payments with 5% added from dishonour of the Bills".[11] This seems as if it were a substantial debt, and Jerdan had to earn fast just to stand still.

Some time between acquiring the sole property of the *Literary Gazette* in 1841 and the summer of 1847, Jerdan took on two dormant partners. One was his son-in-law Thomas Irwin and the other was Irwin's brother. Given the parlous state of Jerdan's finances the Irwins presumably paid Jerdan something for their shares;[12] their partnership with him ended in December 1847 but was to land them in Court despite this precaution.

In May 1845 a Testimonial was proposed for John Britton, who had risen from a penniless childhood to a respected place as antiquarian and topographer. His books on English cathedrals had been rendered uncompetitive by the advent of steel engraving rather than copperplate, and although Britton switched to the new medium he was still dependent on private subsidies. For forty years he had been an adviser to the Literary Fund; he campaigned for government protection of ancient monuments, and was a keen supporter of what was to become the Royal Institute of British Architects.[13] However, he was now facing bankruptcy, hence the Testimonial. He wrote to ask Jerdan's advice how to make it a special occasion, and thanked him for the "constant and reiterated acts of courtesy and kindness you have ever evinced for the works and characters of those authors and artists who have come under cognizance".[14] He would have become aware of this through their joint efforts at the Literary Fund. A few years later Britton, like Jerdan, could not afford his membership of the Society of Antiquaries; he died of bronchitis in 1857. Britton's portrait had been painted in 1845 by John Wood who, a few months earlier, had himself written to Jerdan. His plaintive letter said that his son had died and he asked Jerdan to exert his "powerful influence" to get his surviving son a place at Christ's Hospital School, "the best testimonial you could pay to the memory of your departed friend".[15] (This possibly referred to the recent death of Hood.) Wood evidently placed a great deal of faith in the spheres of Jerdan's influence, but Jerdan may not have responded too favourably to such blatant emotional pleading.

In September Jerdan went to Miss Kelly's Theatre with Macready, Maclise and others, to see an amateur performance of Ben Jonson's 'Every Man in his Humour'. Forster and Dickens played the leading parts. Macready had a dreadful cold and waiting in the pouring rain afterwards to gather his party together did not improve *his* humour. He griped, "I read Jerdan's notice in the *Literary Gazette* of the performance of the amateur play. It was written in a false spirit and will do harm to the persons engaged in the play."[16] Jerdan's review acknowledged that the theatricals were supposed to be a private affair, "but it is not easy to keep from the press secrets entrusted to ten or fifteen score of confidants, especially within the walls of a theatre".[17] He praised the scenery, and the skill of the actors: "There was visible at once a self-possession and earnestness, which seemed far more like long practice and experience than first attempts, however well rehearsed, to embody the admirably drawn creations of the dramatist . . . Mr Forster threw himself into it with a perfect *abandon*, and executed his task as if he had trod the boards for years, with perhaps only a little more freshness both in conception and delineation. It was impossible to fancy it a *debut* . . . Mr Dickens makes the 'stricken deer' the veriest hang-dog and craven that can be imagined; a sneaking, pitiful fellow." Why Macready thought such enthusiastic praise would "do harm" to those in the play could only be a matter of professional jealousy at their excellent performances.

One of Jerdan's favourite projects made a step forward in September when the 6th Earl of Clarendon laid the foundation stone for the Booksellers' Provident Retreat.[18] John Dickinson, eminent papermaker of Apsley Mills, had given three acres of land at Abbots Langley Hertfordshire, to the Booksellers' Provident Society to build accommodation for their members, who had to have subscribed for a minimum of seven years to the Booksellers' Provident Fund, or for members' widows.[19] Jerdan proudly made the formal introduction of the Earl to the assembled company. The cost of building was estimated at two thousand six hundred pounds, and although seven hundred pounds short, the deficit was made up by those present. A commemorative scroll together with silver and copper coins was buried in a crystal bottle according to custom. Although Jerdan's name did not appear on the Committee for 1845,[20] he was one of a number who made toasts at this important event. By the following March the project was well under way and the *Literary Gazette* reported that an official 'opening' was planned when it was completed.[21]

This occurred in July 1846, and Jerdan participated in this formal opening of the Booksellers' Provident Retreat. At noon a special train took about two hundred people from London to Abbots Langley. There were heavy showers and when these had passed the company was shown over and around the building, listened to an address from the architect and a prayer from the Vicar. Finally, with the addition of local worthies, two hundred and fifty people sat down to luncheon. Edward Bulwer Lytton was in the Chair and many toasts were made including one by Jerdan. It was a long day as the London train to take the party home did not leave until seven in the evening, but it was a good cause and one with which Jerdan was proud to be associated.

The desperate plight of so many even well-educated people – such as the booksellers – as well as the many without that advantage prompted Disraeli, in his novel *Sybil*, to observe the contrast between rich and poor: "Two nations between whom there is no intercourse and no sympathy; who are as ignorant of each other's habits, thoughts and feelings as if they were . . . inhabitants of different planets." This was not entirely true, as the age was marked by an explosion of private charities, such as those which Jerdan so actively supported.

During 1846 Jerdan edited a second volume for the Camden Society, following the success of his book on the *Rutland Papers* four years earlier. The new volume was *Letters from James Earl of Perth, Lord Chancellor of Scotland to his sister the Countess of Errol and other members of his family*. The original documents had been loaned to Jerdan by Lady Willoughby de Eresby. He prefaced the volume with a letter to his benefactor thanking her and referring to "grateful recollections of the beautiful country perilled and lost by your ancestors in what they deemed a sacred cause, and justly and happily restored to their descendants". The hope that her descendants would continue to enjoy "this noble possession is not mine alone, but the fervent and heartfelt wish of all who have had the good fortune to partake of the refined hospitalities of Drummond Castle; and whilst delighting in its social and intellectual intercourse, to revel in those glorious Highland sports which, with health and excitement in their train, give a zest to life it would be difficult to surpass within the sphere of humanity". Jerdan thus managed, in the space of a few lines, to impress his readers about his familiarity with Drummond Castle and its lordly inhabitants, and at the same time to be suitably grateful to the Lady of the Castle.

His introduction to the Perth Papers showed a detailed knowledge of the Drummond clan history over five hundred years; he gave a brief history of the Stuart kings, partisan in a way that has been called "annoyingly sentimental"[22] but this was only to be expected considering Jerdan's Borders background and his politics, especially his mother's claim to be descended from the Stuart kings. He attempted a balanced view of the Stuarts, asking rhetorically:

Were they faultless? No! Were they inferior to or more vicious than their contemporary sovereigns in the civilized world? Certainly the reverse! Who couples with the name of any one of them the epithets cruel, savage, barbarous, perfidious, bloodthirsty or tyrannical? None! Adversaries inspired by religious differences and conflicting politics have endeavoured to point out weaknesses and errors in the characters of some of them, and prove that they were – fallible human beings; but the glance we have cast hurriedly over their melancholy fates, varieties of premature and appalling deaths, by assassination, by rebellion, by war, or by the executioner's axe, will demonstrate that they were indeed more sinned against than sinning, and admit us to the understanding of the grounds upon which they were almost adored by the thousands and tens of thousand who were ready to lay down their lives, and did die for them in many a gory bed, and in many an ignominious and more horrible sacrifice.

Jerdan went on to set out the story of the three Thanes of Perth, the Drummonds, whose true sense of patriotism and loyalty led them to risk all of their fortune and property. The letters he edited for this volume were dated from December 1688 when the Earl of Perth tried to escape to France to follow James II. He was in disguise, with his pregnant wife, but was apprehended and imprisoned in Stirling Castle, not released until 1693 upon a bond of five thousand pounds that he would leave the Kingdom. He went to Rotterdam and on to Italy, writing vividly descriptive letters to his brother and sister at home of which twenty-six were reprinted in Jerdan's work. The letters told of the customs, religious observances, landscapes and politics of those he met on his travels. Many of his references to people and places were carefully annotated by "Ed.", Jerdan drawing on his personal knowledge or consulting books for the relevant information.

The resulting book was reviewed in depth in the *Gentleman's Magazine* of January 1846, interesting in that while it reported the letters themselves accurately, (even correcting one of Jerdan's transcriptions), the reviewer took quite the opposite view to Jerdan's wholehearted support for the Stuart cause:

Mr Jerdan's Dedication and Introduction are very lively and interesting, but we totally disagree with him in his estimate of the worth of the princes of the house of Stewart (sic). We think too, he is altogether mistaken in endeavouring to explain or defend Scottish loyalty to that house by a consideration of the presumed excellence of its several members as princes. No! The partisans of the Stewarts in Scotland had read history with different eyes to Mr Jerdan and were too wise to rest their cause upon any such perilous foundation.

Despite this controversy, the reviewer concluded that "The whole book indeed is one of the most readable and interesting the Camden Society has issued." The *Athenaeum* also reviewed the publication, taking a leaf out of the *Literary Gazette*'s book by printing substantial extracts from the letters. Having edited the successful *Rutland Papers*, and now the *Perth Papers*, Jerdan could have reasonably expected some mark of recognition from the Camden Society. It was not to be. "I perceived that I was not treated with the consideration due to me; *ex.gr.* by the Camden Society, to which I contributed two of as interesting and popular volumes as it has published. The private hostility, indorsed, as I was told, by Mr. A. Way, was so great, that I never had the compliment paid to me to be placed upon the Council. So much for affronted Humbug." [23] Jerdan, it seemed, had upset at least one of the Council members, who blackballed him from being elevated to the position he coveted.

There was at this period an unprecedented rise in availability of news and information. In London alone it has been said, "there were nearly two thousand [coffee and tea houses], all well-stocked with the organs of 'useful knowledge'. One ... subscribed to 43 London daily papers, 7 country papers, 6 foreign papers, 24 monthly magazines, 4 quarterlies and 11 weeklies."[24] This easy access competed with the value of the *Literary Gazette* as a digest and adviser of what was new in the cultural sphere (although of course a large part of the *Gazette*'s readership was female, and read the journal at home, not in coffee houses). Even closer to the heart of Jerdan's difficulties was the half-price *Athenaeum*, which continued to make life difficult for him as he struggled to keep the *Literary Gazette* afloat. In the first issue of the new year he referred to "the great change we have made BY NEARLY DOUBLING THE SIZE AND QUITE HALVING THE PRICE OF THE LITERARY GAZETTE". Its usual sixteen pages became twenty-four, and the price dropped to fourpence unstamped, fivepence stamped; it had taken him about fifteen years to follow the *Athenaeum*'s lead, in which period the rival paper had out-stripped his own. Book reviews remained the *Literary Gazette*'s primary focus, but it was becoming increasingly hard to keep up with the flood of new works. In 1843 the *Gazette* commented in reviews or notices on about 630 of 1900 works published, and in 1847 on 700 of over 2000 published works.[25] Whilst the buying public bought fewer *Literary Gazettes*, the magazine's influence was still considerable, and sought after by publishers and authors. A contemporary source, the *Newspaper Press Directory* of 1846, commented that the *Literary Gazette* "has long sustained its reputation and is too well known to need much description: when it reigned without a rival, its decisions had almost as much of authority as official announcements in the *Gazette* [the London Gazette] ... but the old original [Literary] *Gazette,* yet maintains 'high place' in literature, and, with the present year, a more popular character has been given to it by increase in size".[26]

The paper thus continued on its plan, Jerdan said, "for encouraging all that can tend to special good and harmony, cheering on the labourers in every part of their course, and only condemning (without asperity) such things as threaten the progress of the truth, intelligence, prosperity and happiness among our fellow men". Such high-mindedness was hard to keep up. Gleefully he noted on a letter from William Nicol, "The Athenaeum shown up".[27] Nicol had highlighted errors made in the rival paper, calling their reviewer an "ignoramus". Any crumb of comfort at the discomfiture of the journal which had usurped his *Gazette* was welcome to Jerdan. However, the *Literary Gazette* still had enough influence for Bentley to send Jerdan early sheets from his newest book, a life of the Marquis

Wellesley, a week prior to its publication, requesting that it be 'noticed' as Bentley considered it his most important work of the season.[28]

In April, the *Literary Gazette* announced the acquisition of a new steam printing press; Jerdan thought that circulation of his larger, cheaper journal had increased dramatically enough to merit investment in the latest technology. This proved to be a poor financial decision.

Keeping up a good face on his declining paper even though he had halved its price, Jerdan commented to Halliwell, "I hope you see the *Gazette*: it is getting on famously."[29] Strenuous efforts appear to have been afoot to gain new readers for the *Literary Gazette*. In October 1846 Jerdan heard from a C. Smith of the City that:

> I should have liked a much larger number of Lit Gaz circulars. I find I continually get members to take it, and especially new and sincere ones, but (as I always feared) when we decided upon the annual subscription, we have an immense number down as associates who never give us either literary or pecuniary aid and from whom we ought to relieve ourselves. I hope to bring in 200 or 300 more respectable associates from different towns and places, and am printing new circulars for our friends to persuade them with. Hitherto people have been elected too carelessly. The Lord Mayor about whom such a fuss was made, (like many more) has never noticed his Election! Now with all such persons we have no hopes for the Gazette, but as our lists get purified so I think your excellent periodical will increase in circulation.[30]

Jerdan told Halliwell "Nice rows getting up in the R. Soc of Antiquaries! There will be a good bit of fun yet." In this case it was about the resignation of the President, the Earl of Aberdeen, and the creation without consultation of a new office of Assistant Secretary at one hundred and fifty pounds per annum. The *Literary Gazette* covered the row in issues of 21 and 28 March. Halliwell and Wright were in a tussle too, and Jerdan told Halliwell, "This day's number is a great sheet on our side – for the Archaeological Association, for Wright and for yourself. It shows what a set of inimical underhand intrigues and intriguers have been at work against what is right, upright, honest and Wright."[31] Jerdan would never let a punning opportunity pass him by.

In January 1846 the Council of the Royal Society of Literature had adopted Jerdan's notion to repeal certain bye-laws, and a special general meeting was called which agreed to reduce admission and subscription fees which had been set since 1826. Coincidentally, at the same meeting seven new members were elected including Jerdan's son William Freeling, who had married Louisa Richards on 30 December 1845.[32] The Society was having its own troubles, reported in the *Literary Gazette* of 14 March, centering on the allegedly illegal award of a Gold Medal, illegal because the paper for which it had been awarded had not been included in the Philosophical Transactions of the Society for 1845. The Society stood firm on its award, causing the *Literary Gazette* to pontificate "it is hoped that the irresponsible committees would be abolished, with their sooner or later jealousies, selfishness and favouritism".

The March and April 1846 issues of *Tait's Edinburgh Magazine* carried a lengthy review by Jerdan of John Hill Burton's *Life of David Hume. Tait's* was founded in 1832 and grew to rival *Blackwood's* in popularity and sales. The review commenced with a question: "What is Biography?" and answered it: "For our present purposes it is sufficient to assume that the great end of biography is to convey a complete and accurate idea of the individual who forms its subject in his inner, and in his external life; especially as that is shaped and coloured by the society and circumstances in which he is placed."[33] The tone of Jerdan's review was positive and he discussed Hume as portrayed by Burton. He offered a few short extracts and was critical that too much time had been spent on Hume's first work which the philosopher himself disclaimed. Retelling the main points of Hume's life Jerdan then selected anecdotes from Burton's book on topics he himself was interested in: people, marriages, money. He concluded by remarking that he could give only a "very imperfect idea" of a work of a thousand pages, "containing so much rare and wholly original matter".

The *Literary Gazette* noted the major work on 14 and 21 March; a reader wrote to the *Gazette* drawing the Editor's attention to a quotation from Hume's letter containing the expression "You seem to be relapsing into barbarism and Christianity in England", and asking whether Burton had actually seen such a document. "A little controversy will not hurt the work", commented this reader whose letter, perplexingly, was signed "W. Jerdan" and is in Jerdan's handwriting, a brave effort to stir up interest. Jerdan received a long letter from Burton following a public one printed in the *Literary Gazette*. Jerdan had also written to Tait who had shown his letter to Burton. There had been such a passage in one of Hume's letters, Burton confirmed, but he had decided to omit it and explained his reasons at some length. Although he would prefer nothing more said on the subject, if Jerdan thought it useful he would give a public explanation. He thought Jerdan's review had been in a "very liberal and kind spirit" and left it to him to decide, feeling "that I am in the hands of a man of honour and discretion".[34]

Even with the usual drudgery of filling the *Literary Gazette* every week Jerdan appeared to have time – and need – for extra work, such as this long review in *Tait's*. He approached Bentley with a proposal that he should edit Theodore Hook's productions and posthumous papers. He and Hook had been friends from 1808 until Hook's death in 1841, and Jerdan believed that "if properly done it wd redound to the honour of his memory and exhibit him to the world as a far superior being to its common apprehension of his character".[35] This was a project Jerdan really wanted to undertake. "If confided to me, I can promise to do my best, con amore, for I dearly loved Hook and spent hundreds and thousands of happy hours in his brilliant and delightful society, admiring his wonderful variety, promptness and extent of his genius. To do some justice to them would be a pleasure, tho' of a mournful nature." This letter was dated 4 April with no year given, and in another of 4 February, also with no year given, Jerdan asked Bentley "Aught of the Hookiana?" It would seem that Bentley could not be persuaded to commission Jerdan to memorialise his friend as he wished.[36]

In the meantime, Jerdan's social life continued in much the same way. Macready noted that on 28 April 1846 he dined with Lady Blessington and the company included Jerdan, Dickens, Forster, Landseer and Lord Chesterfield. The Countess was in deep financial difficulties because of D'Orsay's wild spending and because of the debts she had incurred when moving into Gore House in 1835.[37] Dickens tried to help by making her "Society Correspondent" for his *Daily News* at two hundred and fifty pounds for a six-month trial, but he resigned after only three weeks and her contract was not renewed. The money problem seemed universal. In his Diary Macready recorded on 15 May that Jerdan was still up to his old habits; "Note from Jerdan, again asking me, in a confidential note, to lend him money; he has already £100 of mine. I cannot afford to – *risk* is a foolish word – to *lose* any more. I wrote very kindly stating my inability to accommodate him."

A lively outing was just the thing to cheer Jerdan up. The Society of Noviomagus had been in existence for eighteen years but their members clearly never outgrew their need for fun. On 11 May the *Times* newspaper reprinted an account from the *Dover Chronicle* of their latest antics in which Jerdan naturally participated. The account is so much in the spirit of the excursion that it is given here in full:

AN ANTIQUARIAN VISITATION

On Monday last, a village near this place was invaded by a troop of outlandish-looking beings. What they were, who they were, or whence they came, was a problem too difficult to be at once solved. The first impression of the inhabitants at the mysterious proceedings of the strangers was that they were spies from the Prince de Jonville, sounding the banks of the Ottenham creek, because, after leaving a weird craft in two boats, as soon as they had rounded the cant, they ever and anon recklessly jumped into the soft mud, in which they sank to their middles, and began pricking the banks with iron rods, hazel or divining wands, wooden spades, broken sword sticks, and other queer instruments; whilst some, dropping upon their knees in the tenacious stuff, appeared to invoke the blessing of the gods for having successfully arrived at such adhesive land as the Kent coast presented. The costume of the creatures was wonderful; how the boots in which their lower limbs were encased had been affixed was marvellous; some had helmets on their heads of strange shape; others the red cap of liberty; the commander of the crew had a silver whistle and a cap with a gold band. After two or three hours' plunging, tumbling, screaming, and digging now and then one of them out of the bed of the creek, they took their departure. It was afterwards discovered that the suspicious-looking fellows were a party of distinguished British archae-ologists, searching after Roman pots and pans, accompanied by Mr Hulkes of Rochester, who had brought them in his splendid yacht the Gnome. The gentlemen consisted of Mr Jerdan the editor of the Literary Gazette; Mr Wright the editor of the Archaeological Album, and the Journal; Mr C Roach Smith, the founder of the association, and author of Collecteana Antiqua; Mr Fairholt, the draughtsman to the association; Mr A J Dunkin, the editor of the Canterbury Report; and Mr Wickham. Some very pretty specimens were dug up out of the mud, and heaps of fragments of futile ware. It is evident, from the amazing quantities which extend along the coast for six miles, that the spot was a famous mart for crockery during the Roman era.

In this period, a few letters from Jerdan carry the address of 'Kilburn Priory'. The author William Harrison Ainsworth lived there and for about a year Jerdan found lodgings near to his friend; a Directory of 1847 lists him as a resident.[38]

Jerdan's family with Mary was expanding yet again. Agnes Maxwell Jerdan was born in 1846,[39] bringing the total of this third family to eight, with more to come. Agnes had been Jerdan's mother's name, but also the name of his elder daughter by Frances, so it seems curious that he chose this name for another daughter. Writing in September to Macvey Napier of the *Edinburgh Review* suggesting that he publish some reviews by Thomas Wright, Jerdan mentioned that he had been in indifferent health with severe bronchitis which he was anxious would go before winter or he would have a hard time of it. Nevertheless, he still had to meet his commitments and his contribution to the *Miscellany* in November was "Titular Confusion: The Borough-Title Terminus". This was an amusing light confection on the comedies of errors arising from three Lords with almost identical titles staying at the same hotel. Cases of mistaken identity, missed dinners, letters wrongly opened, giving away secrets of cheating at horse-racing and other things the real addressee would rather not have made public, and every possible mishap cram this farcical story. Jerdan ended with a paragraph starting 'Moral'. He asked the Queen to confer titles from India or China, to avoid such confusion in future, rather "than run the risk of any accidental mischance among the aristocracy, to whose example we are all bound to look up for the purest morality and correctness of conduct". If the reader was unsure about the moral until the end, Jerdan's tongue firmly in his cheek removed all doubt.

Short of funds yet again Jerdan tried Bentley, shrewdly reminding him that the *Literary Gazette* was awaiting Bentley's latest book, and then coaxed, "if you think my *Miscellany* contributions worth anything and will favour me with it, now will oblige me. I have a share call which I need all I can muster to make up, or lose a considerable deposit."[40] Bentley scrawled across this letter his computation that far from owing Jerdan anything, the debt was on Jerdan's side, having been advanced £150 and earned only £86 15s and he therefore owed Bentley £63 5s.[41] Furious, Jerdan fired back:

> I think if you yourself take a look at the account sent in to me you will <u>repudiate</u> all the statements 1837–40 never mentioned to me in any way during now six years. As for myself I have no memory, check nor notion about them; and only think that what appears as a debt due by me must have been your kindly accommodating me, for short periods with cash for cheques which were either at once or eventually paid. However determine as you think proper. I am not one of the cantankerous grumblers.

Trying to turn the knife, he reminded Bentley:

> I have been consulted about the only worthy life and correspondence of T Campbell – if you have any wishes in that direction, you will do well to talk it over with me soon. Remember Borneo. You might have had – and a huge prize to its publishers. There is nothing like plainness and straightforward decision – and no varying afterwards.

This angry communication ended with some business concerning Landon's works, with Jerdan trying to lay down the law:

> With regard to the matter of our last conversation, I have the power to cover or guarantee you against any demand; but I must do the whole entirely in my own way, acting upon circumstances only known to myself. If you are agreeable to this, and will give £25 per Work, so guaranteed, I will trust my picture to the Engraver for that purpose only, and if you desire it write you a brief Sketch or Memoir. as the picture matter will cost me money down, I have only to add that your decision at once and a draught wd be the answer expected by Dear Bentley, Yrs faithfully, W Jerdan.[42]

Stung, Bentley responded immediately:

Well! it is really a fine joke to call upon me to assist you in repudiating your debt to me in regard to the Miscellany.

On a little reflection you must confess that this is asking <u>rather</u> too much of my complaisance. As to the way we may hereafter agree upon arranging that account is another affair.

With respect to the Novels of L.E.L., Romance & Reality, Francesca Carrara and Ethel Churchill, I am willing, upon being guaranteed the undisturbed and sole remaining copyright in the three works to take them at your own valuation, namely £25 each.[43]

Jerdan responded that

My guarantee would be founded on the affairs many years before Mr Maclean appeared, which are amply sufficient for a hundred times the possible Contingency. But as you appear doubtful, I can only say that my offer was for the benefit of all parties, and that I have not the slightest desire to interfere with my responsibility.[44]

This bad-tempered exchange may have been the cause of one of the shortest contributions Jerdan made to Bentley's *Miscellany* in December 1846. The story was entitled "The Reasoning Schoolmaster – a real character". Surprisingly, given its brevity and content, it was signed with his name and not his pseudonym. It took the form of a dialogue between a strict teacher and a pupil being caned for a minor offence. The beatings continued until the pupil thanked the teacher for the punishment. The teacher was then satisfied that justice had been done and acknowledged. Maybe Jerdan was thinking back to his own schooldays, or possibly this was an incident which one of his own children suffered. The sub-title indicates that it had the nub of a true story. It is not an entertaining piece especially in an issue around Christmas time, neither does it have an explicated moral as many of Jerdan's stories did. It has the hallmark of haste and carelessness as if Jerdan had promised Bentley something and this was what came most easily to hand.

In the angry exchange between Jerdan and Bentley, Jerdan had alluded to a portrait and a memoir or sketch; these relate to two items Bentley was to publish within the next year or so, one being a "Biographical Sketch of L.E.L." and the other, a new edition of *Romance and Reality*. Jerdan's offer to Bentley of selling him the copyright in Landon's three novels raises the question of his entitlement so to do. Laman Blanchard, who was her literary executor, had taken his own life in February 1845. Landon had died intestate, and it would appear that as Jerdan had been acting as her agent ever since her first works appeared in print there was now no-one else who had a greater claim to interest in her literary executorship. William Jerdan has been identified by Harry Ransom as an early literary agent, a claim based upon comments in Jerdan's *Autobiography*, and in an archive of letters held at the University of Texas, consisting mainly of letters from Jerdan to Richard Bentley.[45] Twenty years later a page appeared in *Notes & Queries* entitled "William Jerdan: early literary agent".[46] The author of this piece (who had also written his PhD thesis on Jerdan and the *Literary Gazette* in the same year), used the same sources as the first writer on the subject, with the addition of correspondence files concerning Jerdan held at the Bodleian Library Oxford and, of course, Ransom's published paper. Forty years later, much more material has become available, none of which confirms or refutes absolutely the labelling of Jerdan as a literary agent.[47]

In his position as editor of the *Literary Gazette*, and being a man of legendary kindness and willingness to help authors, Jerdan was constantly asked for assistance in getting work published, for much of which help he appears to have been unpaid. In the first fifteen years of the *Literary Gazette* it (and therefore Jerdan), had great influence: he sat in the centre of a web of authors, printers, publishers, booksellers, engravers and artists, as well as scientists of all kinds, so was inevitably a facilitator between all these different interests. Many of Jerdan's interventions between author and publisher have been noted in this present work as they arose, starting as far back as 1818,[48] when he negotiated publication of Fitzclarence's *Journey from India to England* with John Murray, who paid him seventy-five pounds, and another fifty pounds for Col. Hippesley's *Voyage to the Orinoko*. Jerdan earned another one hundred pounds for negotiating the copyright to Hippesley (and a gift from the grateful author). He procured Alexander Fisher's *Journal of a Voyage of Discovery to the Arctic Regions* and "saw it through the press".[49] He implied that this last action was for friendship; it was published by his *Literary Gazette* partner Longman & Co., and ran to several editions; it is possible that Longmans made Jerdan some payment for his services, although this is not known. He performed agent-type functions on many other occasions, including helping a writer, W. L. Bryan "prepare something for the press" in 1821, and after lengthy discussion succeeded in arranging for Longmans to publish *Calthorpe* for Thomas Gaspey, having been unsuccessful in interesting John Murray first. "Has any body, who reads this, ever had any experience of what it is to treat with a publisher for the publication of a new work by a little known author?" he asked plaintively, going on to print the anguished letters he received from Gaspey, before Longmans were persuaded to publish his work.[50]

The part that Jerdan played as literary agent is most marked in the crucial role he played for Letitia Landon. Quite apart from his whole-hearted enthusiastic promotion of her poetry in the *Literary Gazette*, fired by her adoration and their long love affair, Jerdan took a central and active role when Landon published her books of poetry and prose. It has already been noted how he negotiated with Hurst and Robinson to pay Landon three hundred pounds for *The*

Improvisatrice, arranging that he would undertake proof-reading and discussing the frontispiece design, the best way to advertise the book, and how Landon was to be paid. When *The Troubadour* was ready he went into great detail with Robinson to get Landon the best possible return. *Romance and Reality*, published by Jerdan's partner Colburn together with Bentley, occasioned correspondence in which Jerdan discussed the financial aspect of the deal on Landon's behalf, and after Blanchard's death he took on the role of her literary executor, negotiating the sale of her copyrights to Bentley. Other authors wanted his help too; one asked him to handle drafting a contract with publishers, and another to polish her work and try to get it published.[51] He acted as agent between a Miss Landau and Longmans in 1820, the publishers advising him that they agreed to divide profits on her book of poems, and contrary to usual practice, would advance her two hundred pounds on the day of publication. Miss Landau, as a woman, plainly felt that she could not negotiate such terms with Longmans without help.[52]

Occasions where Jerdan tried to smooth over disagreements which involved his friends have been interpreted as evidence of his acting as 'agent'; however, it seems much more likely that he was acting merely as a friendly moderator, with no financial involvement whatsoever. Twice there were disputes between the novelist G.P.R. James and Bentley; in 1838, following James's failure to produce Romances promised the previous year, Bentley had made an unreasonable demand for a three volume book to be ready within three months, and another three months later. The two parties could not agree and James turned to Jerdan for help, complaining that he had worked solidly for Bentley, unpaid, for several months. Bentley did not welcome Jerdan's interference complaining bitterly to him, "what appeared to me both parties required was a <u>mediator</u>, not an arbitrator. By being put in possession of the view of both Mr James and myself, you would be best able to give <u>advice</u> in the matter and best serve both parties".[53] James thanked Jerdan "most sincerely for all the exertion, all the zeal, and all the interest you have displayed in this business. Knowing well the immensity you have to do, I can appreciate fully the sacrifice of time that you must have made. I need not tell you that I appreciate no less the friendship which prompted that sacrifice, or the judgment that brought it to a good result."[54] Jerdan's personal friendship was with James, but his business relationship was with Bentley, and he tried to do his best for both parties. In the end he put the manuscript into Bentley's hands, "and the affair was quietly finished". On another occasion he told Bentley, "I have seen Mr Weld today and he says he is sure Mr James would willingly refer the matter between you and him to <u>be settled by me</u> . . . I have moved in this business on your saying that if I cd manage it, it wd be the greatest service I cd render you – I merely mention the grounds that there may be no mistake hereafter."[55] Jerdan certainly owed Bentley a favour, in return for his constant drain on Bentley's finances, but in the end the dispute was not solved.

Bentley was also involved in a difficulty with Anna Eliza Bray over the poor sale of her works, and his intention to reduce her payments; she turned to Jerdan to intervene on her behalf. Here again, it is questionable whether the intervention was as a 'friend' or an 'agent' and although she promised that "one day you will find me really grateful in <u>deeds</u> as well as <u>words</u>"[56] given that she was a middle-aged lady married to a clergyman, her 'deeds' could only refer to future acts of kindness to Jerdan, to reciprocate the kindness she requested of him. Jerdan reported a more business-like episode when the Misses Spence and Webb asked him and Landon to join them in a project, "The Tabby's Magazine", as they did not feel it was possible for them to find and negotiate with publishers directly, and Jerdan had the necessary contacts and experience.[57]

In August of an unknown year, Jerdan approached Bentley in a clear role as agent for unnamed authors:

> Are you inclined to speculate on my judgment for a novel on a very popular and interesting subject – written by more than one person high in literary reputation – but to be utterly secret . . . the price of a hundred pounds down and hundred on receiving all the MSS and a hundred on publishing a 750 Edition.
>
> Now there is a pig in a poke for you, which in my opinion wd turn out a good fat sow; but you must judge for yourself what my judgment is worth.[58]

It is unlikely that Bentley agreed to this "pig" without seeing a manuscript, and Jerdan's fee, if there was to be one from the aspiring authors, would have been lost.

Involvement in the ill-fated 'Juvenile Library' has been cited as evidence that Jerdan was an 'agent', as he was to select authors and titles, and agree their rates of pay. In the event as mentioned earlier, to Jerdan's disgust Bentley tried to negotiate directly with the authors and the series soon failed.

Many of the surviving letters are not the business correspondence of a 'literary agent' but are typical of Jerdan's goodwill and kindness, full of good advice and introductions that might prove beneficial. There was no such profession as 'literary agent' in Jerdan's time, and he clearly assumed the activities of that role as part of his daily routine; there is little surviving evidence that he profited financially by these kindnesses, although as he admitted, he was never averse to receiving "gifts" from grateful friends.

One commentator noted John Forster (and T. Watts-Dunton who was active from 1880), as "two of the most notable informal agents in the whole century".[59] The activities noted for Forster, mainly in connection with his work for Dickens, were similar to those of Jerdan in the same period, although possibly Forster was held in higher esteem by some. Thackeray observed of Forster, "Whenever anybody is in a scrape we all fly to him for refuge – he is omniscient and works miracles."[60] Jerdan and Forster worked together for their disputing principals Bentley and Dickens, coming to an amicable and gentlemanly agreement over copyrights. Like Jerdan, Forster was not paid for such a function – it was all part of the day's work.

Sir Walter Scott apparently employed paid agents, the Ballantyne brothers, and if this was their role, rather than 'merely' printers and publishers of Scott's work, then they pre-date the period of Jerdan's activity by a few years; the Ballantynes' function after 1813 was also to handle Scott's dealings with publishers; they "suggested terms, played off John Murray against Constable, and concluded agreements".[61] If Ballantyne acted as Scott's 'literary agent' it was not, at the outset, in a commercial sense; he insisted that Scott rewrite the first twenty-four pages of *St Ronan's Well*, "to keep the Waverley novels the moral model acceptable by all". Subsequently he was, with Constable, Scott's partner in the "close vertical and horizontal concentration of media ownership". When the whole elaborate edifice built around Scott came crashing down in 1826, Scott's lawyer became his agent, negotiating successfully with Longman's for *Woodstock*. This merging of the job of 'literary agent' with the functions of printer, publisher or lawyer serves to highlight the accepted practice of, in today's jargon, "multi-tasking", and nowhere was this more true than in the case of William Jerdan, whose vast web of contacts facilitated his involvement at all stages of the business of publishing.

19

Leading to Bankruptcy

William Jerdan's reputation for kindness must sometimes have been a burden to him; he constantly heard hard-luck stories, tales of real tragedy, and endless requests to notice or publish work in the *Literary Gazette*. In the space of a few months between January and August 1847, even bearing in mind that Jerdan's professional star was waning, he was begged for help by one friend who was convalescing from throat cancer, another who claimed to be owed fifteen thousand pounds salary and wanted Jerdan to assist him in getting his plight noticed in *The Times*; from Mrs Bray whose brother had died (she was continually ill and Colburn offered her only half profits on her next book); along with requests to insert three sonnets about pictures in the Royal Academy Exhibition; a review of a book on *The Law of Costs*; and to visit an artist's studio to review his latest work.[1]

Towards the end of 1847 Bentley was preparing to republish Landon's *Romance and Reality*. In a February letter, likely to have been in 1847, Jerdan had told him, "My Pickersgill portrait of L.E.L., if you have any idea of an engraving from it, might be in Burlington Street for your judgment, and pledge for £25 which it would cost to have it from <u>deposit</u> with other pictures (not <u>pawn</u> mind you!) Be that as you please: I think it wd largely increase the sale of her Novels."[2] By November he was again corresponding with Bentley: "I shall be very happy to co-operate with you in producing *Romance and Reality* or any other novel of L.E.L. you may wish to publish ... and I think I offered you, for a small expence, the use of a fine portrait by Pickersgill, if you wished an Engraving, or thought it would largely promote the sale."[3] Bentley republished *Romance and Reality* in 1848, with a 'Memoir of L.E.L'. by Jerdan. In the 'Memoir' Jerdan explained how he had made time to encourage Landon's writing, a role that he now related, with some self-congratulation, and no fear of contradiction:

> Cherishing the ruling passion, there was an incessant community of thought; every line and every motion of a soul imbued with a quench-less thirst for literary distinction and poetic glory was submitted for my advice; mine was the counsel that pointed the course and the hand that

steered the bark, and the breath that filled the sail: was it then to be wondered at that the conscious progress towards the fruit of this engrossing ambition should resolve and extend itself into an enthusiastic feeling, even on such feeble foundations of affection for the guide and the hyperbolical estimate, which magnified and illuminated every trivial and common feature till very slight, if any, resemblance to the original remained? The world was only opening and unknown to her, and she might – even holding her child-like gratitude in view – both feel and say, "For almost every pleasure I can remember I am indebted to one friend. I love poetry; who taught me to love it but he? I love praise; to whom do I owe so much of it as to him? I love paintings; I have rarely seen them but with him. I love the theatre, and there I have seldom gone but with him. I love the acquisition of ideas; he had conducted me to their attainment. Thus his image has become associated with my enjoyments and the public admiration already accorded to my efforts, and he must be all I picture of kindness, talents and excellence."
Gratitude is prone to such illusions, and especially where combined with the fire and fervour of genius; and if

> We love the bird we taught to sing,

how much more intensely must we cherish the love of the bird that sings in such a strain?[4]

Even ten years after Landon's untimely death, and his involvement in a recent and expanding family of his own, (Gilbert, the ninth child, was born in 1848),[5] Jerdan's emotional memories over-rode his sense of propriety. Pressed for time he wrote irritably to Bentley, "I was not aware of the exact desire for L.E.L. correspondence this month and you gave me very short notice . . . I have hardly known which way to turn to get well through. Could you postpone the matter till June and do my uttermost to have something good for you? Might a short notice do, just referring to the republication of *Romance and Reality*?"[6] This short-tempered protest may relate to a "Biographical Sketch of L.E.L." which appeared in Bentley's Miscellany of 1848, on pages 532–34, with an accompanying portrait of the poet, an engraving after Pickersgill, therefore apparently the portrait to which Jerdan had referred earlier. This "Sketch" is unsigned and it is by no means certain that Jerdan was the author, but as Bentley had commissioned him to write the "Memoir of L.E.L." in his new edition of *Romance and Reality* it would seem highly probable that he also asked Jerdan for this biographical sketch as a means of promoting the new edition.[7] It is indeed a sketchy piece, even to the extent of relying on a quotation from Laman Blanchard's biography for a description of L.E.L.'s physical appearance, which could well reflect the pressure Jerdan felt he was under at this time.

Possibly suggesting an investment in the *Literary Gazette* as the Irwin brothers were on the verge of dissolving their partnership with him, or maybe the idea of a Scottish edition, Jerdan seems to have proposed some sort of arrangement to his friend Halliwell. Whatever the plan was, Halliwell thought better of it. Disappointed, Jerdan wrote to him in May 1847:

> I regret <u>extremely</u> that we cannot see a means to the union we both desire. I wd help it by every way in my power, but a certain amount is directly needful. I am quite sure that it wd be a most eligible thing for you in a literary point of view as furnishing an object for regular pursuit, and I am equally certain that it would be very profitable for all parties.[8]

Jerdan had expected Halliwell to make an investment in his project but Halliwell, knowing his friend's track record, decided against it. Some aspect of the financial proposal offended him, as Jerdan remarked:

> I have read your letter with very sincere regret and am sorry indeed that any circumstances should appear to you incompatible with the function I had hoped to effect. The arrangement I wished to try might probably have been merged into that of the reversion you spoke of; and was, even without that, so simple and safe that I fancied I had hit on the readiest of means if the bankers agreed.

Reflecting his apparent financial difficulties, the *Literary Gazette* office moved yet again in August 1847 to 300 Strand, and the long-time publisher Scripps retired. The printing of the *Literary Gazette* was then undertaken by a Mr Silverlock of Doctors' Commons, an arrangement which led to a law suit three years later. Jerdan wrote to Bentley that his IOU which his son, probably William Freeling, had given Bentley, was on Jerdan's behalf and "comes with the [cancel?] of all pecuniary obligations between us when we agreed about the L.E.L. copyrights At all events (<u>under circumstances</u>) I rely on your so considering and letting him have account clear, in full, today as he wants it specially for Somerset House".[9] Somerset House was then home to three learned Societies, the Navy Office and the Inland Revenue. One might speculate that it was with the latter that Jerdan's son so urgently had business with Bentley's money.

Jerdan was not alone in his constant financial problems. By this time Lady Blessington, although still occasionally holding her salons at Gore House, was in increasing difficulties. The Irish potato famine had a direct impact on her annuity, which had dwindled over the last few years then ceased as people fled Ireland, and no funds were forthcoming. She turned to Bulwer, who helped her get part of the income due from the trustees, but she was forced to pledge her jewellery for loans. A further blow struck when, in the autumn, Heath the financier of the *Keepsake* and the *Book of Beauty* died bankrupt, owing her seven hundred pounds for her work. His administrators reduced her salary for editing the two annuals which hung on a little longer, but the craze for annuals had subsided and they did not continue.

Although not suffering the fate of the annuals, Bentley dropped Jerdan from his contributors to the *Miscellany*. His contribution had anyway been sparse in this decade, one in 1840, one in 1844, and the last scrappy offering in November 1846. Grieved at the tone of a note from Bentley, in January (letter carries no year but likely to have been 1847) Jerdan protested,

> I know not how it is, but the least trifle on my part seems to be taken as a high offence, whilst I see others rewarded for years of wrong and hostility. I have been the first and best friend to literature and publishers – and for you certainly among the foremost have felt an anxious wish to promote your interests by every friendly act both of service and forbearing . . . To conciliate foes is perhaps more prudent than to favour friends who will not neglect or forsake you on any grounds. It is too much the way of the world, and I have no right to expect being made an exception.[10]

Jerdan was obviously hurt by what he saw as Bentley's lack of trust in him, and this letter set out as clearly as any of the statements in his later *Autobiography*, what his philosophy was. Bentley seems not to have responded, and in June Jerdan wanted the last word: "As you have cut me and my offering for the *Miscellany* I am sure you will not be displeased to learn that my literary amour propre has carried me elsewhere. My vanity whispers that the rejected of Bentley may be popular enough in other quarters, but I would not change my beat without telling you."[11] This letter was undated as most of Jerdan's letters were, and may refer to his recent review of Wright's biography of Hume in *Tait's Edinburgh Magazine* or to some other plan he had in mind. Relations with Bentley were again, or still, at a low ebb.

Jerdan's *Literary Gazette* was often the first journal to review a new book or a new translation. He greatly admired the fairy tales and stories of the Danish writer Hans Christian Andersen, many of which had become available in English translation by 1846, and he gave Andersen's work glowing reviews. Andersen loved to travel and was planning another tour when, in the autumn of 1846, he received a letter from Jerdan suggesting that he visit England where he would be warmly received. Andersen's long reply in Danish,[12] which has been partially translated in a biography,[13] mentioned his interest in Shakespeare, and especially in Walter Scott whose novels had helped him to forget hunger and poverty. "How dear do I not hold Bulwer," he continued, "how fervently do I not wish to press Boz's hand . . . " Jerdan sent it on to Dickens, who returned it with a note: "His spirit shines through him in all he does. It is the most single-hearted, innocent, captivating letter I have ever read in my life."[14] Charles Beckwith Lohmeyer, Andersen's friend, and translator of his travel sketches, *A Poet's Bazaar*, wrote to Jerdan assuring him that Andersen "considers your journal the principal medium through which his writings have been made known to the English public".[15] Jerdan was not Andersen's only fan in England: Dickens admired his writings, and Robert Browning and Elizabeth Barrett wrote about his work *Improvisatore* in their love letters, whilst Thackeray told a friend, "I am wild about him, having only just discovered that delightful, fanciful creature."[16]

Jerdan wrote again to Andersen in March 1847 apologizing for the long delay in replying to his letter. "I hope you will think of me and the matter, as of a horse in a mill, so incessantly engaged in drudging round and round, that it never has any time to look out for a bit of pleasure like other beasts of burden . . . "[17] He assured Andersen that only ten days previously he had told Dickens "how warmly you spoke of him, and he was exceedingly flattered by your good opinion . . . no one will be more desirous to give you warm welcome than he will be". At this time Andersen had a poor grasp of English, although he was taking lessons and, knowing this, it is rather strange that Jerdan's letter went on to a wider discussion about the state of the country:

At present our literary world is very dull. Irish Famine, like Pharaoh's lean kine, seems to eat up all that is worth anything, physically, morally, or intellectually. The failure of potatoes has led to the failure of mental culture, and the arts and literature may fast without a royal proclamation. The mechanical sciences alone continue in full activity; for they bring money, direct as cause and effect and money is the mighty idol to which all bow the knee in a Commercial Country.

This is a fascinating idiosyncratic light on an aspect of the terrible potato famine. Jerdan's apparent disdain for "money" can only be simulated – it was a commodity that for him was in increasingly short supply. However, he was excited at Andersen's imminent visit as the Danish author arrived in London on 23 June 1847. He was fêted at the houses of Lord Palmerston, Lord Castlereagh, Lord Willoughby de Eresby (introduced by Jerdan), and Count Reventlow, the Danish Minister. He was quickly taken up and lionized by London society, and was soon writing back to his friend in Denmark that he was exhausted by the relentless round of parties, reigniting his anger that he was not properly recognized at home in Denmark. There had not even been time to meet with Jerdan who wrote on 29 June, "I grieved to leave London without seeing you; but I hope you have received an invitation to a City feast tomorrow and are free to accept it, as I shall run up by rail from Oxford on purpose to call on you . . . "[18] Although Andersen was gratified by the high society who entertained him, he was not meeting some of the writers he wanted to see. Jerdan tried to make a dinner party for him to meet Bulwer, Dickens, Macready and Harrison Ainsworth, but it was not possible to arrange this. Dickens, however, sent a parcel to Andersen containing "twelve marvellously bound volumes of stories by Dickens with the even more marvellous dedication: 'To Hans Christian Andersen from his Friend and Admirer Charles Dickens'".[19] Jerdan sent Andersen a note that he would call at 7 o'clock on Friday to take him to Lady Blessington's to dinner. Blessington, of course, was not "received" in the higher echelons of society, but the literary men and artists she gathered at Gore House were precisely the milieu that Andersen sought. Jerdan took Andersen to see her on 6 July, and she invited them to a dinner party she planned in Andersen's honour ten days later. Dickens would be there too. He told Jerdan: "I dine at the Gore House on Friday, when we will discuss our great question. Tell Andersen not to let the nimrods of London kill him, but to live and write more books. I mean, if I can, to live and read 'em."[20]

The day of Lady Blessington's dinner party finally dawned, and Andersen described the occasion in a letter to a friend, telling how there was a portrait of Napoleon in nearly every room and that his neighbour at dinner was the Duke of Wellington. The Emperor of the French was also present, and Jerdan was amused that "the bewildered author could by no means reconcile himself to the fact that the nephew of the mighty Napoleon, and the son of the conquering hero could sit down, even with a lady between them, without fighting *a l'outrance*".[21] Lady Blessington herself was wreathed in splendour and magnificence. As Andersen was signing a copy of his book for her,

a man came into the room, exactly like the portrait we have all seen, a man who had come to town on my account and had written 'I must see Andersen!' When he had greeted the company, I ran from the writing table over to him, we took each other by both hands, gazed in each other's eyes, laughed and rejoiced. We knew one another so well, although we were meeting for the first time – it was Charles Dickens. He comes up to the highest expectations I had of him.[22]

Now that the two great writers had met, through Jerdan's introduction, their relationship blossomed for a time. In the *Literary Gazette* of 17 July 1847 Jerdan reviewed *The True Story of my Life,* which had been translated by Mary Howitt, but he began with a eulogy of Andersen:

Herr Andersen has now been three weeks amongst us, in the literary and refined society of London, converting that admiration and popularity into warm personal regard, affectionate esteem, and cherished friendship. Every one who has met him is delighted with his character, in which is united to acknowledged originality of genius and poetic imagination, a simplicity the most captivating, and a candour and truth of that rare nature which lays the individual soul, as it were, open to the view of the most heedless observer.

He ended by noting that Andersen was "this truly excellent man, delightful poet and original and fertile author". He also called him the counterpart of Jenny Lind, the Swedish singer known as 'the nightingale', with whom Andersen had fallen platonically in love.[23] The young sculptor Joseph Durham wanted to make portrait busts of each of them and he asked Jerdan to arrange a visit. "I wish to bring my young Artist friend to call on you", he told Andersen. "He will just take your physiognomical dimensions with the Callipen and then prepare his clay for modelling . . . ."[24] A week later Jerdan reported how delighted he was with the bust: "The man and the Poet are there." To persuade Jenny Lind to grant Durham another brief sitting "to finish the mouth", Jerdan urged Andersen to tell her that "the plot for taking her was mine, and that my *Literary Gazette* was the first publication in England which made her rare endowments known to the public".[25]

Andersen stayed now and again with his countryman, Joseph Hambro, founder of the eponymous Bank, at whose house in Kilburn he was invited to rest and relax. Discovering this, Jerdan wrote in July from his new home at 21 Beaufoy Terrace, Edgware Road, "My residence is a hundred yards removed from Kilburn which I only left in June, and had I known you were so near me, I might have been tempted to disturb your repose."[26] He invited Andersen to stop in at his "humble cottage" when he passed that way. Jerdan did not explain why he had moved house, but it was likely that he needed a cheaper rent than at Kilburn Priory.

Andersen travelled to Scotland, armed with a letter of introduction from Jerdan to Jeffrey, previously editor of the *Edinburgh Review*. Jerdan also asked him to take a letter to his brother at Kelso and sang the praises of his homeland's attractions. He received a letter from Andersen from Edinburgh thanking him for all his "friendly attentions", and asking Jerdan to arrange for him to meet Bulwer and Dickens on the only two days he could spend in London before leaving England. On his return from Scotland he called on Jerdan, who immediately sent a note combining the personal with the commercial:

I was much affected by your visit this morning – a sad pleasure I shall never forget. I did not tell you how I thanked you for, and valued, your portrait. It shall be one of my Loves. . . . I send you six Lit. Gazettes of today and hope you will like the account of my much-loved Busts. I shall always be proud of having procured such treasures to be made – it will link my name hereafter with those of Andersen and Lind! If convenient, please present one of my Journals to your Ambassador, and others to any friends in London, Germany or Denmark. I shd. much like to have the Column about your's and Lind's likeness translated into the publications of those countries.[27]

Richard Bentley had published Andersen's novels, and *A Poet's Bazaar*, but not his *Tales*. Andersen spent a couple of days with Bentley at his home in Sevenoaks, Kent, and was impressed with his "wonderful house, very elegant, footmen in silk stockings waiting on the guests – that's what I call a publisher!"[28] Andersen did not manage to meet Bulwer, who was busy electioneering, but he met other writers, including Leigh Hunt. In response to Andersen's plea to see Dickens before he left, Jerdan advised him that Dickens was staying with his family at Broadstairs in Kent. Andersen wrote to Dickens that he would be arriving in Ramsgate the following day, prior to taking the steamboat for Ostend. Dickens invited him to supper and the following day walked from Broadstairs to Ramsgate to say goodbye. Andersen confided to his Diary, "He swung his hat and finally raised one hand up toward the sky; I wonder if that meant, we won't see each other again until up there."[29] It was to be ten years before Andersen visited England again, but he continued his correspondence with William Jerdan, as well as with Dickens.

Strangely, despite his evident admiration for the Danish writer and their personal friendship, Jerdan did not mention Andersen in his own *Autobiography*, written only five years after Andersen's visit to England. This is doubly curious, given Jerdan's penchant for name-dropping and Andersen's ever-increasing fame and popularity. One can only speculate on the reason for this omission, perhaps caused by events which occurred between the visit and the book's publication, which caused Jerdan much heartache and changed his circumstances.

American authors were increasingly popular in England. Jerdan was keen to promote them, recalling his success with Washington Irving's *Sketchbook* over twenty years earlier. Fenimore Cooper, prolific author of books such as *The Deerslayer*, and *Last of the Mohicans*, wrote to Jerdan in July 1847. Jerdan's reply told Cooper that he was gratified by his letter and by his new work. This was *Mark's Reef, or The Crater*, which was reviewed on the front page of the *Literary Gazette* on 9 October 1847. Cooper seemed to have made Jerdan a proposition, to which the response came, "I will with pleasure negotiate an arrangement with a London publisher for your next production and hope the notice of the last will facilitate that process and be to your advantage."[30] Jerdan was once again willing to act as agent for a writer. Richard Bentley had published Cooper's *The Pathfinder* and *The Deerslayer* in 1843 and had undertaken to publish *The Bee Hunter* and *Captain Spike* in 1848. In 1854 *The Sea Lions* was published by Routledge. Possibly Jerdan was instrumental in this change of publisher, having just at that time written the introduction to a book Routledge published, so he may have had a hand in it. Referring to a mutual acquaintance, Jerdan told

Cooper "Robert Egar (sic) is a bit of character, and I hardly know what had become of him. He once bought me an alotment of land in New Brunswick, I don't know what became of that?!!" How like Jerdan not to follow up an investment which could have proved lucrative, especially as this Robert Egar was his brother-in-law, according to Lanman's story.[31]

The end of the year note 'To Readers' of the *Literary Gazette* revealed Jerdan's disappointment and frustration that his journal, now reverted to sixteen pages, had not grown in circulation since he became sole owner:

> We confess, it strikes us, that the distinct class of periodical writing most nearly allied to such a paper as the *Literary Gazette*, has not acquired that extent of circulation which it ought to reach in a community desirous of knowledge. When we see statements of 40 or 50,000 copies being issued by very commonplace miscellanies, mixtures of all sorts, we consider it strange and unfortunate that a similar fortune should not attend those which by mature systematic arrangement, increasing diligence, large expenditure, and the employment of eminent talent, aim at supplying, and do supply, a continuous stream of intelligence worthy of every inquiring mind.[32]

Jerdan's dig at "commonplace miscellanies" was probably aimed at Bentley; his portrayal of his own journal, which had barely changed for thirty years, was the way he perceived it, though his claim to employ "eminent talent" may be questioned as income from the *Gazette* at this point could not have afforded "eminent talent" fees. Indeed, in December Irwin and his brother withdrew from the *Literary Gazette*, having a Dissolution of Partnership drawn up, making official a break which had already occurred.

In the same Christmas Day issue, Jerdan set out his unchanged editorial policy. He compared – favourably of course – the education young people could derive from "the truly instructive Periodicals" to those who did not have the advantage of reading them. He made a large and unprovable generalisation: "Provision, advancement, and honours, are gained or lost to thousands upon this single ground." Regretting the proliferation of cheap magazines, available on every street corner, he commented,

> The very low prices, alas, of several very respectable papers, are their just and deserving recommendation. But still, for effects worthy the grave attention we have, in these remarks, endeavoured to incite, we must adhere to our opinion, that the habitual cultivation of the youthful mind by such easy and attractive means is a desideratum of much private and national consequence.

The cultivation of young readers by giving them a weekly paper full of the latest literature (as long as it was 'moral'), arts and science news, had ever been Jerdan's object, one that it is hard to quarrel with, even a century and a half later.

In pursuance of the science aspect of contemporary activity, the *Literary Gazette* had devoted considerable attention to Fox Talbot's photographic invention and also to his later developments. Jerdan was clearly fascinated by the process and aware of its importance. By 1848 his acquaintance with the inventor had gone beyond the solely professional stage. In a letter of 1 December 1847 he told Fox Talbot: "I have kept a space open for you in the *Literary Gazette* to the latest day every week for some weeks past. Have you given up the idea of setting the *Quarterly* right?"[33] He advised that he had signed the proposal form for the Royal Society of Literature and Fox Talbot would be elected at the next meeting; indeed, Fox Talbot's name is on the list of Members for 1847–48 where Jerdan's name appears on the Council. Three weeks later, complaining of suffering severely from gout, Jerdan enthusiastically told Fox Talbot that he had been delighted with the latter's manuscript which he had just read:

> To my mind it is precisely what the literary world and the public in general will enjoy. It is as if a professed Bruiser, having assaulted a Gentleman, had met with a queer Customer in an unexpected stand-up encounter, and been handsomely punished and floored, to the great gratification of the lookers on – I am convinced this will be the universal feeling on the perusal of your masterly exposition.[34]

The manuscript in question was the one "to set the *Quarterly* right", and appeared in the *Literary Gazette* of 1 January 1848. It filled six pages and was a good-humoured, sarcastic, scholarly debunking of the highly critical review of Fox Talbot's *English Etymologies* which had appeared in the *Quarterly*. The reviewer was jovially shown up as not having done his homework, by Talbot quoting his sources going back centuries, and demonstrating his familiarity with Latin, Greek, French, German and Italian. It was just the kind of witty yet erudite rebuttal which would have delighted Jerdan in its own right, and allowing the *Literary Gazette* to be the mouthpiece of Talbot's riposte to the august *Quarterly* would have been the icing on the cake. The *Gazette's* own review of Talbot's book had been warmly enthusiastic so to support Talbot's own response Jerdan added an Editor's note. Conscious that his paper was frequently accused of being too kind, he said he had taken the trouble to verify many of Talbot's etymologies and to check out those which the *Quarterly* had challenged. In every instance Talbot proved correct. This being the case "we must plead guilty to the critical offence of being too good-natured, instead of infusing the proper abuse, and indiscriminating, instead of righteously bitter in the detection or misapprehension of errors". Rubbing salt into the wounds of the *Quarterly*'s reviewer, Jerdan pompously observed:

> [Talbot's] high position in the social and literary scale, and his remarkable discoveries in science (honourable to his country), ought to have saved him from rude assault; and the censor would remember that at least decent language was due to one who, in one scientific pursuit alone, had made a name that would never perish . . .

Standing firm for a friend whose invention or work he championed was one aspect of Jerdan's editorial duties; another, as mentioned earlier, was the expectation that he would act as arbitrator in authorial quarrels. In 1848 John Forster published his *Life and Adventures of Oliver Goldsmith*. Eleven years earlier James Prior had published his own *Life of Goldsmith*, and was enraged at what he alleged was Forster's piracy of his work. He lobbied Jerdan:

> Of course I do not know whether you have touched upon Mr John Forster or not. I do not wish to hamper you with him in any way disagreeable to yourself, and therefore beg you to choose your own way of treating the matter. Only I think in an independent journal of Criticism, a gross piracy and specimen of book-making the most egregious should not pass unnoticed and uncensured.[35]

Prior backed up his allegation with evidence of the piracy, claiming that of the whole of Forster's work only one and a half pages was original. A few days later the *Literary Gazette*'s review appeared. Jerdan sat firmly upon the fence, declining to enter the fray, but explaining the reason for the lateness of the review:

> Our difficulty, therefore, has not been with the nature of the work, but with a vexatious literary quarrel which has sprung up out of it, between two persons with whom we have lived in friendly intimacy for many years. We hate all feuds, and especially where our being involved as umpires, either publicly or privately, does not promise to be productive of any good.
>
> Therefore, liking this book much per se, it has distressed us to find the question raised by Mr Prior, on the propriety or impropriety of using the materials he gave to the world eleven years ago, and, no matter in however able or graceful a form, reconstructing them into a rival publication. What is the time within which it is just and fair for an author to avail himself of the labours of another? Is eleven years a sufficient length of protecting copyright, either partially or entirely? This Mr Prior denies, and a correspondence has ensued upon the subject, which, as it is likely to come

before the public, we have considered it most fit to mention, and from its unpleasantness excuse ourselves for the delays in reviewing Mr Forster's handsomely embellished performance. The Question, on personal grounds, we must leave, without an opinion.[36]

Jerdan was unwilling to take sides in such a contentious matter, although saying that Forster's book was "a very attractive and ably written volume, beautifully and characteristically illustrated and every way calculated to gratify popular taste" was an indication of his true sympathies. This was not good enough for James Prior who, the following year, published an open letter accusing Forster and Washington Irving of pirating his book.

The *Literary Gazette* of 3 June 1848 listed Jerdan as both printer and publisher, but within a few months Jerdan changed the printers of the *Literary Gazette* to Messrs Savill and Edwards, who did a reliable job in producing the magazine "without accident . . . before six o'clock every Saturday morning".[37] There was much work involved in printing the *Literary Gazette*. Jerdan, as was the practice in the first half of the nineteenth century, calculated the amount of letterpress he provided for the readers. The first issue of 1848 calculated the output for the previous year as 910 pages containing 2730 columns, of which 530 columns were advertisements, the remaining 2200 columns of text averaging 680 words each.

Besides the change of printers, the *Literary Gazette* was undergoing financial and other pressures. Jerdan seemed distracted. The *Gazette* had always prided itself on its early reviews – in the old days often before the book was published – but now Jerdan found himself a whole year behindhand in reviewing Tennyson's *The Princess*. The magazine's treatment of the poet had varied wildly in the preceding years, labelling his works as "eminently disagreeable", "intolerable", in "perpetual discord". Tennyson had been accused of belonging to the "Baa-Lamb" school by which was meant, "a preposterous inclination to engraft antique phraseology upon commonplace notions which occur to everybody".[38] However, ten years later the *Literary Gazette* admitted that Tennyson had poetical genius, was "foremost of our young poets", but was often "too grand".[39] Jerdan acknowledged his inconsistencies in his tardy review of *The Princess,* unusual for his candour and uncertainty:

That we are behind most even of our heaviest and slowest contemporaries in the notice of this volume, is a fact for which we cannot satisfactorily account to ourselves, and can therefore hardly hope to be able to make a valid excuse to our readers. The truth is, that whenever we turned to it we became like the needle between positive and negative electric poles, so attracted and repelled, that we vibrated too much to settle to any fixed condition. Vacillation prevented criticism, and we had to try the experiment again and again before we could arrive at the necessary equipoise to indicate the right direction of taste and opinion.[40]

His metaphor of the needle was an apt one for his own life at this point, pulled hither and thither by the many demands of family and the *Literary Gazette.*

Jerdan's lack of understanding of Tennyson, as earlier of Wordsworth and Coleridge, can be seen as evidence that he failed to grow or to change with the times. "He is patently inadequate in the face of new forms and new ideas", charged one writer. "The editor avoided the difficult task of dealing with ideas, by concentrating on a line-by-line and passage by passage dissection, on diction and style. When the forest was impenetrable, he contented himself with a close study of the trees."[41] The charge has some basis in truth, and Jerdan's difficulties with modern poetry may have had their roots in his early alliances with harmonic poetry, with the safe and comfortable world of Landon's mythological, sentimental poetry, and the "new" poets seemed to him discordant and difficult.

If he was distracted by changes he could not easily cope with, some help was at hand. William Freeling, Jerdan's son, wrote to Halliwell in July, sending him the second volume of *Pepys* for review in the *Literary Gazette.* "My father says that the *Athenaeum* review (I enclose it) is too carping and nasty and he would like you (without at all fettering or biasing your judgment) to take a more liberal view of Lord Braybrooke's volume . . . "[42] The following month, however, William Freeling was back to his usual task of raising money. Macready noted, "Mr Jerdan Junior called with a note from his father who has been taken in execution, asking my assistance. I told him my means would not allow me to advance money. I read his note and asked the amount of his liability; he told me £50 odd, of which he had part, and wanted only £15. I therefore wrote him a cheque for the money."[43] With help, Jerdan managed to stay out of debtors' prison, but his friend Alaric Watts was not so fortunate, spending months incarcerated during 1848, with little effort to secure his release being made by the Peelites for whose cause he had long worked, at huge cost to himself. It was not until the premiership of Lord Aberdeen in 1854 that Watts was granted a pension of £100 per annum.

Jerdan and Hans Christian Andersen continued to correspond once the Dane had returned home, and the 8 January 1847 issue of the *Literary Gazette* favourably reviewed Andersen's *Christmas Greeting to my English Friends* published by Bentley. About Andersen's tales, Jerdan observed astutely:

> subjects which to ordinary minds would not suggest a single idea beyond their external form or use, become in his alembic, profuse of matter and reflective illustration, and his invention invests them with human vitality and superhuman interest; out of both which result the purest sentiments, the purest morality, and the sagest advice. And to contemplate the charm, the radiant colours of poetry are thrown over the whole with a lavish

hand, so that we are at a loss to tell whether we are most benefited by the real, or delighted by the imaginative.

On 17 March 1848, more than six months after his visit, Andersen wrote to Jerdan:

My happy stay in England, where you in particular, contributed so much to my comfort, stand so vividly in my thoughts that it almost appears to me as if it were but a few weeks since I was there; if however I look into the almanac it shows me that it is months since, and I reproach myself for not having written to you, not thanked you for the indescribably hearty reception you gave me, and that good feeling you have show towards me.[44]

Andersen's beloved King Christian had died, he told Jerdan, and he was deeply concerned at events unfolding in France. Two "sunbeams" however had fallen on him, a letter from Dickens and one from Jenny Lind who was about to return to London. Andersen asked Jerdan to remind Durham of his promise to send casts of his and Lind's busts and was anxious to receive them in time for the opening of the Danish Gallery of Art. Charging Jerdan with giving his compliments to Lady Blessington and to Dickens, Andersen asked him also to "Give my heartfelt greeting to your lady and children." The "lady" could only have been Mary Maxwell and the "children", the nine she and Jerdan had at that time. This is a very infrequent reference to Jerdan's latest family being introduced to any of his literary friends. He may have made an exception in Andersen's case as his visit was fleeting, and he may never have even known of the existence of Jerdan's first and second families with Frances and L.E.L.

Jerdan reassured Andersen that the precious busts were safely packed and on their way to him. He told Andersen wryly that Durham "has just finished one of me; but is wroth with my 'flexible countenance' as he calls it, and cannot satisfy himself with the likeness".[45] He had passed on greetings to Dickens and they would drink to Andersen at the next week's Dombey Dinner.[46] He had also greeted Lady Blessington on Andersen's behalf, and told Andersen that in reply she had written, "I have seldom felt so strong an interest in a person of whom I saw so little; for he interested me as being quite as good as he is clever, and of how few authors can we say this!"[47] Andersen had promised to send her a story for *The Keepsake* which she needed by the end of June. Having brought his friend up to date, Jerdan told him, " the impression you left in my little domicile does not wear out at all, but yr. portrait, your looks, your kindly and affectionate manners are stored in a manner that years will not efface. We all love you."

A week or so later Jerdan made a rare exception to Canning's dictum about eschewing politics. Just before the decisive, but ultimately fatal, battle of Schleswig, against more than 20,000 Prussians who had crossed the border into Jutland, Andersen wrote a long letter to Jerdan concerning the political situation in Denmark. Jerdan printed his letter in the *Literary Gazette* of 29 April 1848. It was a brave attempt on Andersen's part to call for peace and understanding across all of Europe, and he had been asked to write this letter by his government, in his role as an internationally renowned and respected Dane who was known for his innocence and pacifism. His letter, sent to other publications as well as the *Literary Gazette*, showed Andersen's belief in Europe, and his faith in an intercultural community.[48] The goal of peace should be achieved by calling the enemy to order in an unwarlike manner:

> In our time the storm of change passes through all lands; but there is One above who changes not – it is the just God. He is for Denmark, which only demands its rights; and they will and must be acknowledged, for truth is the conquering power for all people and all nations. May every nationality obtain its rights, and all that is truly good have its progress! This is and ought to be Europe's watchword, and with this I look consolingly forward. The Germans are an honest, truth-loving people; they will get a clear view of the state of affairs here, and their exasperation will be transformed to esteem and friendship. May that hour soon arrive! And may God let the light of his countenance shine on all lands.

It is a measure of Jerdan's respect and admiration for Andersen that he used the *Literary Gazette* for political ends, something he had been careful to avoid throughout the thirty-one years of his editorship. Unfortunately for Denmark the Prussians occupied Jutland; Andersen wrote to Richard Bentley, "Denmark is a small country, she is being overpowered, she is suffering the greatest injustice; she is bleeding to death. Britain has guaranteed us Schleswig, we have looked confidently towards Britain. Noble, high-minded Britain! Oh, that help might come. Just from there I should like to see it coming, there where my heart has grown firm by the friends I have there and by the spiritual nationality I have acquired there."[49]

Britain had its problems at home, struggling to recover from the crisis of the Irish potato famine. Parliament had finally voted ten million pounds to help Ireland, by passing the "Soup Kitchen Act" in 1847, but this aid stopped long before it should have done.[50] Horrified by 53,000 deaths from cholera in this year alone, Parliament had also passed a Public Health Act under which Sir Edwin Chadwick set up the Board of Health. This enforced proper buried sewage systems, dramatically increasing life expectancy. The Chartists' final petition was delivered without demonstrations, and revolutions on the Continent were not reflected in Britain. Samuel Smiles 'Self help' doctrines became popular and the country's trading supremacy was unparalleled. The novels of the Brontë sisters appeared and women writers such as Elizabeth Barrett Browning, Harriet Martineau and Mrs Gaskell raised eyebrows and awareness with their passionate representations of women's aspirations and the realism of their social and political situations. A new world was opening before his eyes, but it was one to which Jerdan seemed oblivious.

In the *Literary Gazette* of 27 January 1849 William Freeling Jerdan was listed as printer and publisher, perhaps a final attempt to breathe some life into the dying journal, or to dissociate it from the aging editor.

On the surface, life went on as usual. Jerdan still served on the Council of the Royal Society of Literature, signing the certificate electing Austen Henry Layard as an Honorary Member of the Society.[51] He still received some requests – but by no means as often as before – to 'notice' new books in the *Literary Gazette*. The poet Eliza Cook, who was to write a tribute poem on his death, asked him for the favour of printing a review of her *Journal*. This was a miscellany directed mainly at women and the working classes, encouraging education and opportunities for expanding the mind. It ran for 291 issues until 1854. "I promise you my *Journal* shall not disgrace your mention of it", she told Jerdan. "I am preparing in a very steady and business-like way . . . and your great credit for the 'judgment' I evince (don't laugh) and everything promises well . . . I shall be right glad if I can get your word of praise for my endeavours."[52] Jerdan had earlier praised many of Cook's poems which had been published in the *New Monthly Magazine* and other publications, and must therefore have admired her political, reforming stance, and been flattered that his opinion and blessing was still sought.

Another reformer, but with a capital R, was the highly successful novelist and politician, Jerdan's friend Edward Bulwer, who sent him " 'the child of my love' – later portions better than earlier, the whole the best thing I have ever done".[53] In his *Autobiography* Jerdan printed a letter from Bulwer which asked for his opinion on the work, flatteringly relying on Jerdan's good judgement on matters of poetry, as Bulwer knew that his prose works had met with general approbation.[54] These letters appear to refer to a poetic work *King Arthur*, as a review of three and a half columns appeared in the *Literary Gazette* of 3 February 1849. The reviewer thought that although the book had many merits and superior qualities, these would preclude the chance of popularity as the world was too busy for epics.

Although to Jerdan's great disappointment Halliwell had declined to enter into a financial arrangement with the *Literary Gazette* the two continued to correspond quite vigorously, with Jerdan encouraging his friend to review the volumes of Pepys and others. Jerdan was only too glad now of contributions from other people, whereas in the heyday of the *Gazette* he had more material than he could cope with. "I assure you," he wrote to Halliwell, "I never think half so well of an *Literary Gazette* as when I see contributions of my esteemed and able friends in it. When there is too much of Mr J. in the We, I get very fidgety and dissatisfied."[55] He had been away in the country to recover his health and was now much improved and optimistic. "I flatter me that the *Gazette* has been very much to the purpose for some months, and I am glad to tell you that 'my pensive public' seems to be of the same opinion . . . with good help we bid fair to mount now a few hundreds in 1849 then all wd be velvetty." This was a far cry from the numbers of two decades previously, and he was still in difficulties. In June he tried Halliwell again, following a furious row between Halliwell and the British Museum: "Do recent matters make any change with you to incline you to take up a regular trade in LG? I am and it is kept sadly back for want of a free and impulsive Capital. Within the last six months it has been regularly extending in circulation and needs only liberal outlay to bring rapid and large returns. However, I merely repeat the suggestion as you formerly thought well of attaching yourself to a regular literary pursuit."[56] Jerdan may have been more optimistic than accurate in his claim of growing circulation, struggling as he was to keep the paper afloat.

Jerdan went off to Oxford for a few days, and on his return corresponded again with Halliwell:"(Isn't it nice to be in the Bodleian at quarter to 4 of c. and dining in Russell Square at 6?) . . . I regret you do not see the way to a connection which I think might be very pleasant and advantageous – affording me ease, and to an extent, a medium and object for employing your literary talents, profitably to LG and JOH"[57] [*Literary Gazette* and James Orchard Halliwell]. Desperate as he was for matter to fill his paper Jerdan maintained his usual standards, telling his Edinburgh friend, "I like your Rev[iew] of PC very much, but as it resembles that style which we condemn and repudiate, i.e. the finding out all the blemishes, and not discovering merits, I wish much to quote a column or two of the matters you generally praise, so that we may show the laudable as well as the defective together. Will you pick me out such fair balancing . . . "[58] Halliwell's review of Peter Cunningham's *A Handbook for London Past and Present*, published by Murray, duly appeared in the *Literary Gazette* of 28 July. Despite Jerdan's request it was a highly critical but scholarly review, objecting to the indiscriminate mixing of information about ancient and modern London. Halliwell could not bring himself to find much to "balance" his poor opinion. A few weeks later things had not improved: Jerdan told him, "I am nearly at my wit's end and there is such a scarcity of matter to work on at present. I shall therefore be very glad of a long review of Pepys . . . "[59]

Jerdan's friend, the author and society hostess Lady Blessington, was at a crucial time in her life also. Creditors were baying for payment and Gore House was in a state of siege. She realised that d'Orsay would be sent to prison because of his own huge debts, so she arranged for him to leave the country quickly. Arrangements were made for the sale of all her belongings and the lease of Gore House. Lady Blessington wrote farewell letters to Bulwer, Disraeli, Forster and Landor. In mid-April she left England. The sale enabled all her and d'Orsay's creditors to be paid. The Gore House lease was to bring her a surplus of £1500, but her lawyers waited in vain for instructions. Lady Blessington had died suddenly, at the age of fifty-eight, from an apoplectic seizure and heart disease. A heartbroken d'Orsay built his benefactor a huge monument in Chambourcy; Landor wrote the Latin epitaph (altered when it was engraved on the stone), and Barry Cornwall an English one. D'Orsay died two years later, aged fifty-one, and was buried alongside Lady Blessington. So ended the mercurial life of one of the few friends in whom Jerdan could confide his feelings about Landon, and at whose house so many literary alliances had been made. His own tribute to her said:

> I visited her constantly in St James Square Mayfair, and Gore House; and the more I saw and knew of her, the more I loved her kind and generous nature, her disposition to be good to all and her faithful energy to serve her friends. Full of fine tastes, intelligence, and animation, she was indeed a lovable woman; and, by a wide circle, she was regarded as the centre of a highly intellectual and brilliant society.[60]

A little light relief came Jerdan's way on 10 June 1849 when the 'Britton Club' met at the house of Mr Hill, once Sheriff of London. "Mr Jerdan (the veteran editor of the *Literary Gazette*) was complimented in connection with the Periodical Press, to which toast he made a reply, replete with erudition, acute criticism, and witty comment."[61] His speech went down so well that he was asked to commit it to paper. After some jocularity and raillery, Jerdan spoke about the Club's founder, John Britton, likening his literary life to a small boat tossed on the waves, finding at last a safe mooring – the little boat metamorphosing by stages to a splendid ship. At another meeting, recalled Britton, Jerdan produced a series of verses "not only specifying the names of all its members, but intimating some of their characteristics. Near the end, he included himself:

> What think ye of such Club? – There yet remain
> The Scribe, so oft reproved for wretched jest,
> To whom ye owe this load of doggrel strain,
> Proof that more ways than one he is a pest.[62]

The following month the Britton Club reassembled at Norbury Park, home of High Sheriff Grissell, to plant a cedar tree marking Britton's 78th birthday. Jerdan told the company that many temples and idols of the Chinese were made of cedar, a sacred tree, no less sacred on British soil, where it was so laudably dedicated to hospitality and friendship. This lively gathering took place on 10 July, just before the storm broke over Jerdan's head. Whilst the clouds gathered, the following day he attended an entertainment at the Mansion House where the Lord Mayor welcomed members of the Royal Society, Royal Academy and men distinguished in literature, including Dickens and Thackeray. The gap between Jerdan's public and private life was about to become a chasm.

At the same time as Jerdan was struggling valiantly with his failing finances, he also became embroiled in a legal dispute which was instigated by HRH Prince Albert. The case concerned some etchings made by Queen Victoria and Prince Albert, which had somehow fallen into the hands of a Mr Judge. This came to light when Judge asked the Royal couple's permission to exhibit these etchings and was refused on the grounds that they had been stolen from their private apartments. Judge contended that he had bought them as 'waste' from a printer in Windsor, and the case had gone on for some time. Jerdan became involved, and swore an affidavit, because he had caught wind of the proposed exhibition and said on oath that he had asked the publisher of the etchings, William Strange, to allow the *Literary Gazette* to have a list of the exhibits and requested that he should be invited to attend a private view. Judge published a 74-page pamphlet setting out his case and in July 1849 this pamphlet was 'reviewed' on the front page of the *Literary Gazette*; it included considerable extracts of those sections naming Jerdan as guilty of inserting a notice of the forthcoming exhibition into his paper before Judge had received the Queen's permission. The matter had caught the public's attention because the *Literary Gazette* was so widely copied by country papers that the news had quickly spread. Jerdan refuted all of Judge's accusations point by point, concentrating on how he acquired his information in the first place. Jerdan's affidavit referred to his meeting with Strange, but Judge pointed out that he had in fact met with Strange Junior, while his father was two hundred miles away. He argued that Strange Junior had been merely polite to Jerdan and had no knowledge of a proposed catalogue or exhibition. In his 'review' of the pamphlet, Jerdan dismissed this detail as an 'oversight' of no consequence to the case. Judge insisted that he had bought the unauthorised proofs in good faith and only wished to demonstrate the Royal talents to the British public; he had received no permissions but several law suits. Jerdan's involvement, although seemingly central in promoting Judge's plan by publicising the list of etchings and promising an exhibition, was in reality no more than an Editor doing his job of giving eager readers news hot off the press; unfortunately for him, it was off an illegal press. No penalty appears to have been incurred by Jerdan or the *Literary Gazette* as a result of the Royal ire, which was heaped solely on the shoulders of Judge and Strange.

It was fortunate for Jerdan that the proceedings did not prove worse for him, as he had quite enough to cope with at this time. On 28 July 1849 his solicitor, Benham of Essex Street, Strand, filed a declaration of Jerdan's insolvency.[63] The notice was printed in the *London Gazette* of 31 July where Jerdan's address was given as 62 Milton Road, Milton-next-Gravesend, an address that does not appear on any other surviving document, and noted that he was "late of" 21 Beaufoy Terrace, Edgware Road, where he had moved in June 1847. He was instructed to appear before the Court of Bankruptcy at Basinghall Street on 9

August to "make a full discovery and disclosure of his estate and effects". He was also told to appear on 18 September when his creditors should make their claims and the procedure would be completed. No record of the hearing on 9 August exists, but the second hearing on 18 September was reported in the *Times* on the following day. An adjournment was agreed to give Jerdan time to explain certain details, "particularly as regards an alleged partnership". A balance sheet had been filed, covering two years, showing that on 2 July 1847 Jerdan's deficit was £6,104. Some of his affairs were listed, showing:

Unsecured creditors	£5790
Secured creditors	£5378
Profit, about	£3167
Credit side, debtors	£ 351
Bad debts	£ 100
House expenses	£1184
Law charges	£ 237
Estimated value of property held by creditors	£3060
Payment of annuities etc.	£ 602

The adjournment offered Jerdan a little breathing space, as the next meeting was postponed until February 1850. An editor's footnote to a letter of Charles Dickens dated 4 November 1850 says that Jerdan came before the Bankruptcy Court with debts of £11,000, and that he had sold the *Literary Gazette* to his son in 1849. It is not clear how either of these facts were substantiated, although the fact that William Freeling's name had been listed as printer and publisher in the January *Literary Gazette* may have been the source of this assumption. Jerdan's financial difficulties probably included the fact that he had not kept his own account books for the *Literary Gazette*, having relied on Longmans for nearly thirty years; his losses, and the measures he took back in 1826 to avert disaster then, came home to haunt him now as he had no resources to fall back on.

Struggling under this blow, trying to maintain his ailing *Literary Gazette*, and mourning the loss of his dear friend Lady Blessington, Jerdan was faced with another disaster when, in October, his younger brother George died, aged 65. "So near and dear to us, it is not in these pages that we would indulge in the expression of our sorrows," he wrote in the *Gazette* after quoting the bare facts from the newspaper obituary, "but a few words are due to the literary antecedents and position of the deceased." A brief history of the *Kelso Mail* followed, crediting his father John Jerdan with influencing its creation, together with a footnote about his father's weekly court and his encouragement of the schoolboy Walter Scott. George's continual efforts on behalf of local agriculture and his presentation on retirement with "a handsome piece of plate" were mentioned, and then Jerdan allowed himself a more personal note:

> In private life we believe, we may truly say that no individual of his station was ever more generally esteemed. His judgment was acute and sound, and Scottish hospitality had in him a pattern, when his abode was favoured with the visits of authors or artists of southern fame. His delight in them was evinced by every attention which could lead to their enjoyment of the lovely and interesting country around his native place, and friendships were consequently formed with many of the distinguished ornaments of our literature and arts. An affectionately attached family, still more sensibly, lament his loss.[64]

His extended family life caused Jerdan his usual roller-coaster of emotions: Mary Maxwell's tenth child was born and called George after Jerdan's brother.[65] At the very end of the year Jerdan's daughter Mary Felicity Power, who was on a visit to England from Ceylon, died in London at the home of her brother William Freeling, and his wife Louisa Richards at 10 Grafton Street, St Pancras. Mary was only 35 years old, and left her husband with a son, Edmund, and at least one other child.[66] Her husband who was in the Civil Service in Ceylon had not accompanied her on her journey to England. Her death certificate noted that she died of "Dysentery 4 years ulceration of bowels, Anasarca 1 month", indicating that perhaps she returned to England for treatment of her chronic condition.[67] "I grieve to think of all she must have felt in leaving her little ones in this cold world with their father far away", wrote a consoling friend to Jerdan.[68]

It was perhaps around this time that Jerdan's wife Frances had had enough of her wayward husband. She moved out of her home and, with her youngest daughter Elizabeth Hall Dare, went back to her childhood home of Bentley in Hampshire. They moved into Whiteley Cottage, where the 1851 census shows them as neighbours to the Bull Inn on one side, and a large family of agricultural labourers on the other. Frances's sisters Mary and Ann, now aged seventy-four and sixty-seven, shared another cottage in Bentley village; perhaps here, in the quiet countryside, Frances found the peace of mind of which she had been deprived throughout the long years of Jerdan's infidelities and financial upheavals. Certainly, he was now in the throes of the worst of these.

20

Losing the *Literary Gazette*

As the year opened, Jerdan was on the point of losing his beloved *Literary Gazette*. On 15 February 1850 he made another appearance in the Bankruptcy Court. He was told to bring proof of his debts before Commissioner Holroyd on 18 June. This worry, and the recent deaths of his younger brother and of his daughter, must have somewhat overshadowed the birth on 6 March of another boy, their eleventh child, born to Mary Maxwell.[1] They called him John, suggesting that the first John, born ten years earlier, had died in the interim.[2] Now, "Mary Ann Jerdan, formerly Maxwell" was living at 2 Richmond Place, St George's Road, Southwark, and on registering his son, Jerdan styled himself in the nick of time, as "Editor of Literary Gazette" – the last time he was able to proudly put this on an official document.

Another significant event occurred for one of Jerdan's children on 17 March 1850. Laura Landon, daughter of L.E.L., was almost twenty-one when she had herself christened which her parents had seemingly failed to do at her birth. Laura had been brought up from an early age by Theophilus and Mary Goodwin. By 1851 Goodwin was a Master Silk Manufacturer employing three hundred and twenty people people, and the family lived in Islington, at Alford Cottage, Roseberry Place, where Laura appeared in the Census as 'Niece'. The christening took place at St Michael's, Queenhithe, City of London.[3] Errors on the baptism certificate suggest that she regarded Goodwin as her father, as his name was first written, but then heavily over-written by "Jerdan". In the space for "Occupation of Father" was first written "Silk Manufacturer", subsequently crossed through and "Gentleman" written instead. It could be concluded from these changes that Laura had only recently been told about her real parentage, perhaps as she approached her 21st birthday, and although she certainly had contact with Jerdan in subsequent years, his was not the name she instantly thought of as her Father when asked for information at her christening. It is not known whether Jerdan was invited to witness this important event in his daughter's life, nor is it known how the Goodwins came to adopt her as their own, or whether Laura's brother and sister had similar good fortune in their foster-parents. Jerdan's life poses many unanswered questions.

Despite Jerdan's best endeavours he must by this time have been despondent and weary, as the *Literary Gazette* "dwindled, became small by degrees, and beautifully less".[4] He was struggling to keep it alive; in the first few months of 1850, and indeed until October when Charles Swain sent him a note, this and other surviving letters show that Jerdan was still receiving submissions, welcoming contributions, and sending books for review. He kept Halliwell busy, asking him for a second article on Dyce. "I should not like to pass it or him so lightly as one single notice",[5] Jerdan said, remembering his long connection with Dyce, to whom he had inscribed a copy of his biography of the poet James Thomson, written in his youth. Dyce had also edited several publications for the Camden and Percy Societies, and so they were more recently acquainted. Jerdan's letters to Halliwell came from an address of "Briars, Forest Hill", but he later moved to Swanscombe, Kent.

As Jerdan's journal declined, Charles Dickens started one of his own. The first number of *Household Words* appeared on 30 March and cost two pence. Dickens's purpose was to have a journal "in which he could speak personally to the large circle of readers whom his name had drawn to him."[6] Agreeing with Jerdan's moral standard for the *Literary Gazette,* and in common with his own novels, Dickens would publish nothing which, in the words of Mr Podsnap, "would bring a blush to the cheek of a young person". Unlike the *Literary Gazette* however, the new journal did not review books, nor discuss them as literature, but it did summarize them and quote selections. Dickens's direct competitors were *Eliza Cook's Journal* and *Douglas Jerrold's Shilling Magazine* which, like *Household Words*, were also concerned with social issues. Leigh Hunt contributed prolifically to the new magazine, and his articles were published as a book in 1855. Jerdan, however, did not contribute to *Household Words* for several years, until 1857.

In *Tait's Edinburgh Magazine* of May 1850 was a long review entitled "The Papacy under Napoleon", signed with the initials W.J. (and attributed by the Wellesley Index to Jerdan). The subject was one with which there is no other indication that Jerdan was familiar, books on religious matters having played little part in his literary life. He was, however, always interested in history and this may have been the aspect that attracted him. *Tait's* made no distinction between Jerdan's own words and what appears to be a lengthy extract from the book under 'review', *Historical Memoirs of Cardinal Pacca, Prime Minister to Pius VII.* Jerdan praised the translator Sir George Head, and the first paragraphs gave a brief introduction to Cardinal Pacca, presumably culled by Jerdan from the book. With no quotation marks or other evidence that the body of the review was directly extracted from the book, the final paragraph seemed to revert to the reviewer, commenting that the memoirs were of much general interest and of historical value. "They have some bearing on questions now affecting Rome and the Papacy; above all, they are important to teach vain-glorious Frenchmen, sighing for empire, what France may gain and lose under a Bonaparte empire." Jerdan, hater of Napoleon, steered a neutral course avoiding direct political comment, as advised so long ago by George Canning.

It was finally the end of the road for his beloved *Literary Gazette*. Jerdan would not describe the actions of another by which he was "finally and foully <u>done</u>, not only out of the property, but out of the editing and income attached to it by a regular written agreement".[7] Tales of wrongs would not interest his readers, he said. Death and retirement necessitated new arrangements for printing and publishing. As Jerdan told the story he was – yet again – the unfortunate victim of someone else's fault. His account was decidedly murky and lacking in particulars; he claimed that he was betrayed by "the best intentions of one of my best and dearest friends, into contracts with parties who proved every way unworthy of trust. An aim to attain an ulterior object and supplant me in my copyright property, was from the beginning cunningly and systematically pursued." Such scheming was exacerbated by Jerdan's old nemesis – not taking care of the accounts. He sank into "the lower still" and was confused and muddled. This made him vulnerable, he said, to intrigue and plotting and there was a "final contest, from which the much-changed *Gazette* was rescued, but I fell a victim to as gross malignity as ever was foully resorted to in revenge for disappointed roguery". Jerdan seemed more offended by being taken to task for not keeping adequate account books than for any other failings, inserting a note into his record of events that "An envenomed injury was done me, not as a gentleman, a man of honour, but as a <u>trader</u> . . . " This was construed as an insult to the essentially eighteenth-century literary man who had nevertheless guided much of the reading public throughout three decades in the first half of the nineteenth century. The kind and decent man Jerdan was, (setting aside some of his personal life), did not seem able to grasp the necessity in the fast, new, changed world in which he found himself, that business had to be attended to according to rules and law, even when one had no liking or aptitude for such work. The exact circumstances of the *Literary Gazette's* fate were vague, and Jerdan was no more explicit in his personal correspondence. A letter dated 15 January, probably of 1851, from Blenheim Villas, gave no indication of his addressee, but it might have been Halliwell, because of the reference to their mutual friend Wright:

My dear Sir,
My head is so confused that I do not know that I have written to you since yours of the 11th.

The utter rascality of the persons now holding the LG by a succession of gross swindling is amost incredible; but that may rest for exposure and I need not trouble friends with the distress into which it has plunged me.

I would to heaven another Journal could be brought on on the original plan with some improvements, and I think it wd soon succeed – <u>but</u>

– <u>but</u> the capital is wanting among us all, though there are learning, talent and ability enough for an excellent publication.

It might be an efficient organ of Archaeology and bright general literature. But where is the Maecaenas, or the Trader, who wd be content with a fair share? Your ideas are good, <u>but</u>. I have left the Quarterly to be returned to you in the city.

In a scheme I scratched out and gave to Wright, I included your name as a valuable contributor – we could be very strong.

I have a very long explanatory letter from the Marquis which I shd like to show you – "private".
Most truly yours,[8]

Jerdan's unwillingness to explain what happened may indicate his own failings in the matter, but this letter shows his eagerness to bounce back with another journal, surely not least because of his urgent need for income.

Jerdan's *Literary Gazette* had enjoyed success for more than twenty years, and some reasons for its subsequent failure have been suggested as they occurred: he stuck firmly to his own rules of reviewing books of good morals and good taste, suitable for young ladies and family reading; he swam almost always with the tide of public opinion, not against it; he discovered, promoted and was loyal to many young writers, not only Landon, but Procter, Montgomery and others, and enjoyed to the utmost the social contacts his editorship offered. Some of these "positives" were also "negatives", to use Jerdan's own metaphor of the vacillating needle: his loyalty and personal taste for moral works blinkered him to changes in popular taste, as in his inability to understand such as Wordsworth, Coleridge or Carlyle, and to his continued enthusiastic support of minor poets such as Hemans and Joanna Baillie because he admired their piety in precedence over their poetic skills.

What is certain is that Jerdan had, for four decades, a huge energy and output of work, the ability to produce a lively and detailed paper on a regular weekly basis, sometimes in the face of tremendous difficulties when printer or publisher failed; he was active in raising three separate families, in membership of several learned societies, in pursuing his interests in archaeology, history and antiquities, in theatre and shows of all kinds, and generally in keeping all of these balls in the air over long periods, with frequent financial disasters, some but not all, of his own making. His ultimate failure was, perhaps, exacerbated by his refusal through vanity or penury to hire others more equipped than he to deal with such authors and works that he found unpalatable or difficult. However, he was so closely identified with the *Literary Gazette*, and so closely did he identify himself with it, that he would have found such passing-off most unpleasant, always excepting the invaluable help that he acknowledged he had received from Landon, their close relationship at that time making them almost inseparable. In short, the very characteristics of morality, sentimentality and closeness to the public taste, which had made the *Literary Gazette* so popular and successful in the 1820s and 1830s, were those same characteristics which Jerdan did not, or could not change, and which caused its decline throughout the 1840s.

On the financial side, given Jerdan's history of defaulting on loans, or of borrowing from Peter to pay Paul, it is probable that he had put the *Gazette* up as security against loans which he was unable to repay. The paper would thus fall into the hands of those who held his pledges, either directly or were sold on to other interested parties, who became the new owners of Jerdan's journal. That he had finally lost control of the *Literary Gazette* is evident from an announcement in the paper on 30 November 1850 that the price would drop from 4d to 3d on 1 January, and that it would henceforth be confined to literature, dropping all other departments, and that from January, all "Order and Advertisements will in future be received by Messrs Reeve and Benham, 5 Henrietta Street, Covent Garden, where, after the 1ˢᵗ January 1851, the *Literary Gazette* will be published."

The first *Literary Gazette* of 1851, published now by Reeve and Benham, announced a new Editor,[9] an extended circle of contributors and a reduced price, in "the hope of regaining the position it once held in the periodical literature of this country". Cold comfort to Jerdan who was now, after nearly half a century, out of work. Of his first family two children were dead, two married, one in India and the last, William Freeling, working with him. Two of Landon's children were living abroad, although Laura was still in London. Jerdan and Mary Maxwell were still producing children and living in difficult circumstances. In one considerable way it was the end of an era, but in Jerdan's domestic life, things were very much the same as ever. He had a note from the Rev. William Bruce Robertson who had heard him read a paper somewhere and wished to know him better, warmly inviting him to Edinburgh. He requested Jerdan to give his "special regards to Mrs Jerdan and warmest remembrances of course to the yr 10 old with so much of the dew of his youth upon him . . . ".[10] From this it is evident that Jerdan's current family was by now public knowledge. The ten-year old boy could have been Charles, William or Walter, but as the letter is undated, one cannot be sure; what is clear is that Mary Maxwell was known as Mrs Jerdan and was, by now, meeting at least some of Jerdan's acquaintance.

The news quickly spread that Jerdan "had been violently and disgracefully terminated" from his thirty-three year connection with the *Literary Gazette*, and had fallen upon hard times.[11] His friends did not desert him. William Francis Ainsworth loyally wrote to him at Christmas, "I hope you are making arrangements about a new Gazette. It is evident you ought to do so as the old one will soon not be worth picking up in the streets."[12] Other friends set about two projects to alleviate his predicament. One was to lobby for a pension for him, the other to open a subscription for a public testimonial on his behalf.

The petition for a pension for "the literary labours of Mr Jerdan . . . in token of our approbation of his meritorious efforts during a long series of years . . . " was signed by several Lords and a bishop who added a note "with special reference to the conduct of the *Literary Gazette* as regards its moral tendencies during a long course of years". This would have pleased Jerdan, who had set much store by his journal's moral integrity. The 'Memorial' or petition was sent to Lord John Russell, the Prime Minister in July 1850, with a covering note from Jerdan's life-long friend the Lord Chief Baron Frederick Pollock. The fund was dry, however, and Russell suggested another application be made the following year.

With time to spare, Jerdan made the first of his many contributions to the magazine *Notes & Queries*, which had been launched the previous year by the antiquary W. J. Thorns. Its object was for readers to ask and answer questions primarily concerned with English language, literature and lexicography, history and antiquarianism. Jerdan's foray was about a notice of a paraphrase of the Bible which he had examined and found the manuscript to be "utterly unfit for decent perusal". Having delivered himself of this opinion, Jerdan made no further published contributions to *Notes & Queries* for another five years, although several entries mentioned his name, usually in connection with quotations from the *Literary Gazette*.

He would have noted with interest the publication of Leigh Hunt's autobiography, aware of the many parallels in their respective lives. Hunt received excellent reviews, except from John Forster who complained that he had not been mentioned enough.[13] Hunt had hoped to be made Poet Laureate but, in 1843 on the death of Southey, had been passed over in favour of Wordsworth, who had himself now just died; Hunt's bid for the honour was opposed by the *Athenaeum* and Hunt accepted that Tennyson was the worthy holder of the post. The plaudits that Hunt received for his autobiography may well have given Jerdan the idea to write his own book, which appeared two years later.

The year 1851 saw Turner's death and burial in St. Paul's; the Pre-Raphaelite brotherhood, founded three years earlier, got into its stride and, more significantly, it was the year of the Great Exhibition at Crystal Palace. Jerdan made no mention of going to see this, but it is inconceivable that he failed to do so, loving as he did all kinds of 'shows'. He was surely one of the six million who attended, travelling on one of the three thousand omnibuses which London now boasted, each with ten horses, carrying three hundred people a day. The year marked the juncture between the discontents of the 'Condition of England' period and what has been called 'the age of equipoise'.[14] Engel's *Condition of the Working Classes in England* had been published seven years earlier. Popular literature had left behind Romantic poetry and silver fork novels, and embraced the tales of Dickens, then turned to Trollope, Thackeray and George Eliot. Carlyle's 'heroic' books of the 1830s had seized the Victorian mind, although this terminology is applied with hindsight, his works straddling Victoria's accession to the throne.

The turning-point of the year in the context of British history, from years of war and tumult to comparative calm and prosperity, reflected a time of change in Jerdan's own life, from a busy journalist and editor of the *Literary Gazette*, to an unemployed and almost unemployable, unhappy, impoverished man. How fortunes had changed from twenty years earlier when Jerdan was at the peak of his career, in love with Landon, and a valued member of the learned societies. Now he was reduced to asking Macready for a stall at the theatre. "Poor fellow", Macready wrote in his Diary.[15] He himself was suffering – the previous day his eldest daughter Nina had died, the second of his children to pre-decease him. Jerdan wanted the seat for Macready's farewell performance on the following day, when he played Macbeth. Jerdan was amongst the usual crowd including Dickens and Bulwer, who came to his room after the performance.

Jerdan's bankruptcy proceedings had culminated on 18 June when he appeared with proof of his debts. He must have then been officially declared bankrupt as, when he found himself in Court yet again, he was described as "insolvent". This Court appearance was in an action taken by Silverlock, the printer of the *Literary Gazette* against Thomas Irwin, husband of Frances-Agnes, Jerdan's eldest daughter. The case concerned a number of bills of exchange drawn by the printer and accepted by Jerdan, and also for work done for Irwin for which he had paid £168 into Court. The *Times* report noted that Jerdan was, in August 1847, the registered proprietor of the *Literary Gazette* but that he had two dormant partners, the brothers Irwin.[16] Silverlock knew of this partnership and believing the *Literary Gazette* to be solvent had invested in new types and commenced work at £13 12s.0d. a week. His bills were paid by Jerdan initially but by the end of November 1847 they were in arrears. He then applied to Irwin at his place of work, the Audit Office, and was told that Irwin denied liability and had severed his connection with the *Literary Gazette*. He was therefore free of any liability incurred by the journal especially as the bills had been accepted by Jerdan alone. The jury had to determine whether Silverlock had already known about the dissolution of the partnership; they could not decide the point, and "it was agreed that the printer should have the verdict for the balance of £400 if the Court were of opinion there was any evidence of the plaintiff's knowledge of the dissolution". This affair, together with the no doubt unpleasant situation of dissolving their brief partnership, must have strained relations between Jerdan and his son-in-law who had probably entered into such an agreement in an attempt to help Jerdan in troubled times.

Dickens was elected to the Council of the Royal Literary Fund in 1851. Dissatisfied with the management of the Fund Dickens attempted reform on two fronts, and spent the next year trying to reform the administration of the Fund, in the face of increasing opposition from the more conservative members. He wanted to ensure that authors applying for aid were not treated as beggars but could retain some dignity. He also protested that the administration costs were out of all proportion to the funds distributed to applicants.[17] He also wanted to empower the Council which, due to an error in the amended Charter of 1847, had lost any power over the Committee and the work of the Royal Literary Fund. Failing to persuade the Royal Literary Fund, Dickens and Bulwer Lytton, started a Guild of Literature and Art. Jerdan believed that the Guild "was an enlarged and probably more skilfully modelled adoption" of his earlier plan. The Guild's principle was to honour professional writers by granting pensions and, if necessary, accommodation. Outraged by Dickens's unmistakeable portrait of him as Skimpole in *Bleak House*, Leigh Hunt refused to join the Guild, but Charles Dilke of the *Athenaeum* and John Forster did join it. It was a success for a short time, but was outlasted by the Royal Literary Fund which is still in existence.

In the face of Dickens's prolonged campaign the Royal Literary Fund set up a Special Committee to look into reform, which itself set up a sub-committee to recommend extensions to the Fund's policies. These extensions sound very much like the proposals Jerdan had claimed to put forward a couple of years earlier: granting of pensions and loans to authors, the Fund's premises to be a literary club and hotel, and the founding of a college. There was money for this, as the Permanent Fund had accrued £21,000 since 1802, and subscriptions could be raised from a public appeal. A further proposal of the sub-committee was to rename the fund the "Literary Institution of Great Britain".[18] Predictably, other committee members vetoed the proposals, horrified at the notion of spending funds on providing a literary club and using the Fund's premises as a hotel for literary men. Dickens fought on for the next few years.

Jerdan claimed to have made a proposal to the Royal Literary Fund to provide housing for "unsuccessful and worn out authors".[19] He said he had a promise of Crown lands for free, in Essex, a list of donations over one thousand pounds and volunteer gifts of manuscripts for publication, the fees for which were to be added to the Fund. Some on the Committee opposed him and his plan was not adopted.

There were troubles afoot in another charity connected with literature. In May 1852 John Chapman, publisher of 'free-thinking' books and new owner of the *Westminster Review*, mounted a campaign against the Booksellers' Association, a price-fixing cartel which prevented small publishers offering discounts of more than 10% on the published price. Dickens chaired the meeting and letters of support from Leigh Hunt, Gladstone, Mill and others were read out. Jerdan, whose interests lay with the Booksellers Provident Society and their Retreat, was not noted as being present at this meeting. His presence was felt, however, at a meeting of the Royal Society of Literature on 27 February, when a memoir he had written was read. This was on *An Interesting Passage in the Life of Mary Queen of Scots during the time of her Imprisonment in England*. The *Athenaeum* reported that this was an abstract of correspondence between Philip II of Spain and the Duke of Alva during 1569–71; the letters were preserved in an archive in Brussels.[20]

Whilst the application for Jerdan's pension was initially rejected, the proposed Testimonial was drawn up. Jerdan told a friend that it far exceeded his "most sanguine expectations; there are fifty members and every name of public note and value: some of the highest in every walk of life and literature. I am gratified beyond expression."[21] He had some personal problems, however; "a painful face ache and face so swollen and distorted that you would not have recognized me – so out of drawing and drawing out – except teeth." He had also been "run down by a street cab and a narrow escape with life and limb". Taking his mind off these troubles he heard from Dickens who, accepting his invitation to serve on the Testimonial Committee, urged Jerdan, "I strongly advise this – that there be no public notification of, or allusion to, the design, until that committee shall have been formed and shall have met and decided on their course. It seems to me exceedingly important, for many reasons, to be strict in observing this rule."[22] Disillusioned, Crofton Croker declined to serve on the Committee telling Balmanno, "it was very painful for me to refuse, but it was due to my own character as a man of integrity to do so".[23] Although sympathetic to Jerdan, Croker believed "he certainly has much to blame himself for and has ship-wrecked his character with respect to his utter wrecklessness respecting money matters . . . This is a sad thing – but that it would come to this was foreseen by everyone twenty years ago or even more." Everyone, he meant, except Jerdan.

The Committee's first meeting took place on 14 April, and was duly reported in the *Times*. By the meeting in August, at the Royal Society of Literature, there were an impressive sixty-eight members whom Jerdan proudly listed in his *Autobiography*. He had reason to be proud as his list began with the illustrious Lord Brougham, included his old friends the Lord Chief Baron and Lord Warren de Tabley, many from the worlds of art and literature, and even the actor Macready who had been so exasperated by Jerdan's constant borrowing and non-repayment of loans. Jerdan quoted from the *Globe* newspaper of April 1851 the grounds for raising the subscription:

'That the literary labours of such a man are well deserving of *a special mark of public estimation*' and that it had been 'resolved to open a subscription for *the expression of this opinion by all friends of Literature, Arts, ad Sciences,* who may have appreciated the devotedness of the Editor of the 'Literary Gazette' and the influence of his writings during this long period' (thirty-four years); and farther, 'To acknowledge his services in *a gratifying and suitable manner by presenting him with a lasting token of the esteem in which he is held by the literary world.*'

And to this the editor of the journal liberally added:–

This task so honourable to all concerned, has been undertaken by a committee of nearly seventy noblemen and gentlemen, representing every high order and class of intellectual society, and especially by Mr Jerdan's distinguished literary contemporaries, who thus unanimously unite in recommending his services in the Press to the notice of the country which has profited by them. In few words we may assert that the example of the 'Literary Gazette' opened the way to, and effected a complete revolution in, periodical publications. Previous to its appearance, literature, the fine arts, and the sciences were very rarely mentioned in the journals; but now they have not only separate organs, but form prominent parts and portions of every periodical throughout the British Empire. Need we stop to observe the consequences of this system on their diffusion, encouragement and improvement.

Entirely in accord with the quarrels and problems Jerdan had encountered in his literary life, according to his own account the committee quarrelled amongst themselves, did not publish the list of subscribers as was the norm, and failed to accept voluntary offers of co-operation from towns and provinces. Jerdan was flattered that committee meetings were held at the premises of the Royal Society of Literature, and despite the subscription list not being published, he set it out in his *Autobiography*, showing the contributions of 142 people, ranging from fifty pounds to five shillings. Names of several *Literary Gazette* contributors were on his list, such as the poets Bryan Procter and Charles Swain, George Croly and Thomas Gaspey; Maclise subscribed, as did Dickens and Thackeray, and his old friend Edward Bulwer, now Sir Edward Bulwer Lytton, Bart. Jerdan himself took an active part causing Crofton Croker to tell Balmanno that "Jerdan is now reduced to the humiliating position of soliciting a subscription for his support".[24] The magazine *Notes & Queries* published a subscription list as an incentive to their readers to make their own contribution in appreciation of Jerdan's long years as Editor of the *Literary Gazette*, following this up with a further notice two weeks later.[25] The total amounted to £900. Jerdan was "proud and grateful" for this tribute, but noted sadly that:

It might be deemed an involuntary compliment to the honour and independence of the *Gazette*, that this tributary testimonial to its services to literature has not been signed by a number of publishers; but I am forced by truth to say that their public abstinence is of a different colour from their private assurances. I have quires of letters asking favours, and piles of letters returning thanks for them when they could be granted, from nearly every member of 'the Trade'; but Messrs Longman and Co., and John Murray, in London and Blackwood and Robert Chambers in Edinburgh, are the only exceptions to the rule of economic oblivion. I confess that I looked for many a token, and that the slightest would have been the most agreeable to me; but I reconcile myself to the condition of the world by re-perusing a few of the olden epistles, expressive of such everlasting gratitude. They are very edifying, and would make an amusing olio for publication.[26]

Blackwood had subscribed £20, Longmans £50, and Murray £25. By casually mentioning a possible publication of an 'olio' (a 'miscellany') Jerdan may have been holding out a veiled threat to all those whom he deemed ungrateful – ingratitude being one of the worst sins, in his opinion.

Jerdan did his best to carry on with life as normally as possible with no employment and no income. He was still a committee member of the Statistical Section of the British Association for the Advancement of Science, and in June attended its 21st meeting, in Ipswich. He wrote to his host, "With regard to myself and the British Association, I believe I am the only individual who has attended every meeting since the first; and been, besides, a faithful historian of them all. This is some merit and not unworthy of acknowledgement. Forgive the egotism, of which I am rarely guilty."[27] Jerdan could well be forgiven for trying to salvage some remnant of merit from the fiasco that was now his life.

The Census of 1851 revealed that William Freeling Jerdan and his wife Louisa had left Grafton Street, where Mary Power had died two years earlier, and were now living at 10 East Street, St Georges, Southwark, with Louisa's parents, a sure sign that economically life was as tough for William the son as it was for William the father. Louisa's father was unemployed and her mother a needlewoman; they shared their home with four other children and a servant. By the time of this Census Jerdan saw no more need for the pseudonym of Stewart, behind which he hid in the previous Census in Hercules Buildings. Now briefly resident at Blenheim Villas, Charlton, in Kent, he was in plain view, (although wrongly spelled by the census transcription as Jerdon), aged sixty-seven, with Mary, thirty-four. From this census we learn that Mary was born in Bath, Somerset and that her mother Ann was living with them, no doubt helping to care for a growing family. The two eldest girls, Marion and Matilda, aged 15 and 14, were still at home; Charles and John, children listed on the 1841 census disappeared from this one, John having presumably died and been replaced by the second John aged one year. Agnes Maxwell Jerdan did not appear on this Census, although on the following one in 1861 her age is given as fifteen.[28] William, Walter, Emma, Gilbert and George, aged between 7 and 3 had been added to the family in the last ten years, all the children born in "Middlesex, London". Mary Maxwell had given birth to at least eleven children in fifteen years. The Census entry also recorded a Thomas Stewart, an unmarried relation of 22, a School Assistant.

The family at Blenheim Villas were living next door to Francis Bennoch, aged thirty-eight and his wife Margaret and her mother. Jerdan told the childless

Bennoch, "I don't know how you manage, but every one of my children gets as attached to you as yours truly."[29] The son of the American writer and US Consul Nathaniel Hawthorne, who was a close friend of Bennoch's, recalled him as "a superb specimen of a human being . . . sparkling black eyes full of hearty sunshine and kindness, a broad and high forehead over bushy brows, and black wavy hair . . . he was the kindest, jolliest, most hospitable, most generous and chivalrous of men, and his affection and admiration for my father were also of the superlative kind".[30] A few years later Nathaniel Hawthorne visited Bennoch at his home: "Reaching Mr Bennoch's house, we found it a pretty and comfortable one, and adorned with many works of art; for he seems to be a patron of art and literature, and a warm hearted man, of active benevolence and vivid sympathies in many directions. His face shows this. I have never seen eyes of a warmer glow than his."[31] The Jerdan children evidently had good instincts as far as their neighbour was concerned. The Bennochs proved to be good and supportive friends throughout this difficult time for Jerdan. In his best hand-writing and, unusually, dating his letter, "Gloomy November the First A.D. 1851" Jerdan wrote to Mrs Bennoch, "Your hospitalities have so cheered me with poetic society of late that I think it must have re-lighted my old feeble rushlight and tempted me again to try versification."[32] He told her of the robin redbreast which sang at Blackheath railway station, inspiring the seven verses he wrote on the train, set out for her delight. The robin's life was more free than man's, he believed:

> What is't to you whose golden breast
> Still marks that happy age,
> Ere toil the youthful world opprest,
> Or Care filled life's next page!

The verse was no worse than many Jerdan had published in the *Literary Gazette* or the various annual over the years, but he did not take his effort too seriously: "Say let Charles Swain read this in his best manner and weep . . . I defy any of them, including Mr Fields, to spoil the 'Poetry'!?!"

Mrs Bennoch enjoyed his verse and restored Jerdan's self-confidence. He promised to bring her one of his *'jeux d'esprits'*, when he next came to visit, a celebration of Lord Mayor's Day published in the *Literary Gazette* of 1830. "It is as full of puns as Hood could have stuck it, and consequently a disgrace to the 'solidarity' (I do love new words)", he joked.[33] Jerdan told her that he had enjoyed the volume of Fields's poetry she had lent to him, and was pleased to have the American's favourable opinion. The volume had been published by Fields's partner Ticknor in 1849. Jerdan, sadly noting " Sat. night and no grog", returned the book to Bennoch, with a note of his five preferences. As Fields was a "friend and admirer of [Samuel] Lover's" Jerdan would "be glad to have a meet in my humble <u>willa</u>".[34]

In December Jerdan moved to Parkwood House in Swanscombe, Kent, from where he wrote to Bennoch, "The Weekly Paper suggestion if entertained had better be thought of at once – my notion is that it won't keep intact, and if <u>we</u> do not intrude, somebody else will. I think it safe now, as it is capable of being raised to a superb position both for profit and as a powerful organ – and unless J. is unreasonable, suspectible of an excellent practical arrangement, good for All."[35] He hoped "Hookey Walker[36] could be made easy . . . for I faint when I look round me, and the whole tribe of Israel gaping up to My dear Bennoch, (no, not to you, but to) yours most truly, W. Jerdan." His "tribe of Israel" was an apt metaphor: Mary and eleven children relied on him for everything. He desperately needed to create some income, and from the content of this letter seems to have tried to persuade Bennoch to finance a new paper.

Some relief was imminent, as he had been negotiating with Hall and Virtue to write his *Autobiography*. He confided to the sculptor Durham that he expected "a fair partition of the profits; and I am not without hopes that my Publisher wd have nothing to regret in the issue. Expedite this if opportunity offers. From what I have seen I am firmly persuaded that Mr.V. is well placed to take a foremost place in 'the Trade'. Few of our leading booksellers have any claims to their positions – they are intellectually poor."[37] Jerdan also told Bennoch that Virtue "is rather warm upon the Autobiography which would, for divers reasons, be very eligible".[38] He was about to spend a few days near Aylesbury and asked Bennoch or his wife to keep an eye on the family in his absence. "The expectation will be a cause of order where there is no supreme or effective authority." He did not, apparently, consider Mary capable of maintaining discipline over her large brood of children, possibly because she was showing signs of mental illness by this time. Jerdan was so poor now that he even asked for an advance on Mrs Bennoch's contribution to his Testimonial, even though Bennoch had already given him money to tide him over until Christmas. He was finding it difficult to get started on the *Autobiography*. "My Life worries me to death", he told Bennoch in his usual punning style. "I have not been able to begin it yet."[39] One distraction had been the illness of his son Henry whom he went to see in Clapham; scarlatina was feared, but it was not so serious and Henry recovered after a few days in bed. Jerdan, however, had got soaked on his journey and was feeling unwell although on his arrival home, "I whiskeyed and it did restore me for the time". It was not a cheery Christmas.

Part V
Life After the *Gazette,*
1851–1869

❧21❧

Publication of Autobiography

inally free from his years of labour, Jerdan had plenty of time but no income. The first of several poems he contributed to *Fraser's Magazine* was in the issue of December 1851; it was called *Prospero* and like some of those which followed, indicated Jerdan's sombre mood. His poem ended:

> Away! I hear your little voices sinking
> Into the wood – notes of the breeze –
> I hear you say – "Enough, enough of thinking!"
> Love lies beyond the seas.

Life beyond the seas was to be the choice of several of Jerdan's offspring. In 1852 Ella, his and Landon's eldest daughter, now aged 25, decided to emigrate to Australia. Her life is known solely through memories of her own daughter and grand-daughter, which mention that in the late 1840s Ella stayed with Jerdan's children in London and had noted how many he had. There was also a notation that in about 1848 Ella had been a governess in the family of the British Ambassador in Paris. (In 1848 this was Lord Normanby, whose son had married in 1844, and started his family.) She spoke fluent French, an indication of having been educated in a good family, and had the presence to conduct herself well in high society. Her decision to sail for Australia may have been linked to her desire to find a better life and climate, both for herself and for her brother Fred, who had always suffered from chest complaints. Knowing she was leaving England (and therefore apparently familiar with her whereabouts and circumstances) Jerdan presented her with his *Autobiography*, inscribed "A prosperous and happy journey in the distant world to which she is now going". He did not mention such an incriminating word as "daughter". However, in a note written by her great-granddaughter, Ella is alleged to have said that her father's voice was "ringing in her ears that she would never be welcomed back".[1] Some caution should be used in accepting the family lore that has been handed down by Ella's descendants: they were told, or believed, that L.E.L. and Jerdan had been married in France, overlooking the fact that Jerdan was already married to Frances, (presumably, even in the absence of documentary evidence), and also over-looking that even if L.E.L. had been married to Jerdan, she could not then have married Maclean. The note also claims that Landon was "murdered by one of the servants" at Cape Coast Castle, another unfounded rumour, but one that the family may have thought added to the glamour of their famous ancestor.

The voyage to Australia took six months, during which time Ella and the ship's Captain, James Gregson, formed a close relationship. On arriving in Melbourne Ella, possibly aided by letters of introduction from Lord Normanby, moved in Government House circles and indeed, Captain Gregson's love letters were addressed to her there.[2] On 23 June 1852 in Richmond, Victoria, Ella married James Gregson. He retired from shipping shortly afterwards and invested in land. They lived well, and Ella became a keen huntswoman, owning hunting horses and riding to hounds,[3] (see illustration no. 7). She started the first girls' school in Melbourne. Of course no one, espe-cially a woman making her way in a new country, could be expected to admit to her illegitimacy, although it would appear, because of the existence of a por-trait of L.E.L. in the family's possession, that Ella was proud to acknowledge her mother's identity. She may have been less eager to acknowledge Jerdan as her father, but Ella's feelings for her father have been coloured by the written and handed-down reminiscences of her granddaughter Ethel. Ella seems to have remained close to her brother Fred, taking responsibility for his welfare, but she was reputedly cold towards her sister Laura for reasons only to be guessed at. Ella and James Gregson had five children, one named Laura Landon Gregson, after Ella's sister. This conflicts with the family story that Ella and her sister Laura were never friends and disliked each other, yet another instance where the family mythology does not square with known facts.[4] Ella Stuart Gregson lived to the age of 87, and died in 1910.

Jerdan had now arranged with Arthur Hall, Virtue & Co of Paternoster Row, to publish his *Autobiography*. To heighten anticipation, hints were dropped to the press. The *Critic* of December 1851[5] noted under the heading of 'Gossip of the Literary World', that "Mr Jerdan is, we are assured, proceeding . . . with his *Autobiography and Reminiscences* the commencement of which will relate to the youth of some of the highest dignitaries of the law now living and the sequel will illustrate, from forty years of intimacy, the character and acts of George Canning and nearly all the leading statesmen, politicians, literati and artists who have flourished within that period." This could indicate, by reference to 'the sequel' that only two volumes were originally intended, but Jerdan had many memories and the *Autobiography*, subtitled *with his Literary, Political and Social Reminiscences and Correspondence* finally ran to four volumes. His publishers had been created in 1849 by a merger between Arthur Hall, publisher of *Sharpe's London Magazine* and George Virtue. This latter also published *The Art Journal*, edited by S. C. Hall, which rose to become a highly successful publication. The newly merged company had then expanded into book production, with Jerdan's *Autobiography* being one of its early titles.

The first volume was completed on Jerdan's seventieth birthday, 16 April 1852, and was dedicated to his long-time and influential friend the Lord Chief Baron, the Rt. Hon. Sir Frederick Pollock, with a brief but emotional reference to the length of their friendship and Jerdan's esteem and regard for his dedicatee. Of the four volumes the first is the most recognizable as autobiography, being in more or less chronological order, commencing with some background of his parents, following his activities through to his visit to Paris in 1814, with a sprinkling of anecdotes of poets and writers of that time.

In his Introduction, Jerdan acknowledged the difficulty of writing about 'Self'. He was an experienced biographer, having written dozens of such articles for Fisher's *National Portrait Gallery*, but "had not the faintest conception of the embarrassments and obstacles which stood in the way of a satisfactory performance of the altered task". He felt repugnance at casting himself as hero, but had been for so long connected with the great men of the nation, and his work was so diffused in many periodicals, this was an opportunity to leave an "enduring monument". His main purpose however, he stated, was to warn would-be writers of the perils of a literary life. His own life had been one of "much vicissitude, of infinite struggle and latterly of very grave misfortune", although he admitted that "much that has been owing to mistakes, to errors, to faults, and to improvidence on my own side". He was not willing to take all the blame however, and pointed to "misconceptions, injustice, wrongs and persecutions, unprovoked by any act of mine, on the part of others". Literature was less profitable than felony, he claimed.

Jerdan foresaw that his narrative would be of a "very mixed and almost incongruous character", his life having been a rapid alternation of pain and pleasure. "I have drained the Circe-cup to the lees," he confessed, "but I still gratefully acknowledge the enchanting draught of its exquisite and transporting sweetness, in spite of the emptiness of its froth and the bitterness of its dregs." He mourned all his departed friends, and quoted a long passage from L.E.L. written in 1833, on the theme of man's destruction of what should be held dear to him. Such an early appearance of Landon, in the very Introduction to his *Autobiography*, demonstrates that she was seldom far from his thoughts. In contrast, his marriage was barely mentioned. As before and later in the lives of Jerdan and Hunt, this omission reflected Leigh Hunt's own autobiography, published two years earlier where, in nine hundred and sixty eight pages, he mentioned his wife only once. Perhaps Jerdan had read Hunt's book, and taken note of his virtual silence on the matter, even though, as a biographer of Hunt's noted, such omission was "remarkable even in those reticent times".[6]

Much of Jerdan's early history from Volume I has been incorporated into the present biography, but even in this early stage of his *Autobiography*, he showed a disregard for dating his information. What was irritating to readers of this volume became a real frustration in those which followed, as he seldom indicated with any clarity to what year his memories related. He made some excuse for this in the Postscript to Volume I, where he rejoiced that the printers had sufficient quantity for this volume, but he was concerned about the quality, trying perhaps to pre-empt criticism of errors and inaccuracies. A private matter, he said, "had occurred to break hurtfully" into his time, and he had been surprised to discovered that his forty to fifty years of papers had been dissipated, "no one knew whither!" What this hurtful private matter was can only be conjectured. Mary Maxwell, at home with at least some of her eleven children was probably by now showing signs of the mental distress which was later to confine her to an asylum. Although the printers were satisfied with the two hundred pages he had produced, Jerdan added a further eighty pages of Appendices, one being his story of 'The Sleepless Woman'. He also reprinted Southey's *March to Moscow*, and revealed a previously unpublished poem of the late Thomas Hood's, written in 1827, entitled *Lamia*. This first volume ended with his plan of the House of Commons lobby, showing the position of the various people in it, when Perceval was assassinated. Jerdan had wanted to include the outline of the fatal pistol, but the page size was too small. Jerdan told his dear friend Francis Bennoch, "I have wrought like a Galley Slave, and as the printers have galleys, I suppose it must be just and right."[7]

The sense of purpose and energy in this early book, and its usefulness in tracing events in Jerdan's life, diminished in the volumes that followed. This may have been largely due to the mixed reception given by the press to Volume I. Reviews appeared from 8 May, only three weeks after Jerdan had finished writing it. His old foe the *Athenaeum* devoted four columns to it, acknowledging Jerdan's long association with famous literary, political and professional figures. However, as Jerdan had feared, the *Athenaeum* noted the disconnection of the narrative and how Jerdan was "sparing in dates and altogether careless of the order of time". A few of the lighter anecdotes were then extracted, followed by a remark that "the only subject on which Mr Jerdan quits his gossiping chit-chat style is that of the adoption by young men of literature as a profession. To this topic he returns again and again", quoting one of Jerdan's more bitter pieces of advice:

I earnestly advise every enthusiastic thinker, every fair scholar, every ambitious author, every inspired poet, without independent fortune, to fortify themselves with a something more worldly to do. A living in the Church is not uncongenial with the pursuits of the thinker and scholar, the practice of medicine is not inconsistent with the labours of the author, and the chinking of fees in the law is almost in tuning with the harmony of the poet's verse. Let no man be bred to literature alone, for, as has been far less truly said of another occupation, it will not be bread to him. Fallacious hopes, bitter disappointments, uncertain rewards, vile impositions, and censure and slander from oppressors are their lot, as sure as ever they put pen to paper for publication, or risk their peace of mind on the black, black sea of printer's ink. With a fortune to sustain, or a profession to stand by, it may still be bad enough; but without one or the other, it is as foolish as alchemy, as desperate as suicide.

Poor as he was at this time, Jerdan was not necessarily thinking here of himself alone; over the years of working for the Literary Fund he had seen scores of writers falling upon times of dire poverty and this warning could be seen for exactly what he claimed: a warning to young men to equip themselves more fully for the world if they wished to write, as it was an unreliable occupation.

The *Spectator* of 15 May quoted the same extract and noted: "It is not the calling but the man that produces the success . . . the life which Mr Jerdan describes himself as having led . . . would have been fatal in any profession." This perceptive observation did not prevent the *Spectator*'s review of the *Autobiography* from being favourable to the work, remarking that there "is a solid and sustained interest . . . they are very well written . . . [it has] a good deal of matter". Its emphasis was on Jerdan's *Autobiography* representing the class of "littérateurs . . . persons who . . . are drawn to writing by circumstances, or a failure in vocations of drier and more sustained labour". Despite its mainly positive review, the *Spectator* leaves one feeling that its judgment of Jerdan was as somewhat of a dilettante figure, a judgment which disregarded his huge literary output as editor of the *Literary Gazette*, and his other reviews and stories.

Tait's Edinburgh Magazine took an opposing view of Jerdan the man. "Mr Jerdan tells us he was a spoiled child . . . the wonder is that so petted a juvenile should ever have been transformed into such a dogged and indefatigable worker as he has shown himself to be for nearly half a century."[8] Jerdan's ubiquitously quoted passage mystified *Tait's*, who pointed out that poverty is felt at very different levels by different people. Apart from this quibble, however, *Tait's* advised their readers that "there is not an atom of spleen" in Volume 1,

> which is filled with good things . . . The writer has moved in the best company in the true sense of the term – men of genius, men of enterprise, men of valour . . . Mr Jerdan can delineate subjects the reverse of aristocratic with the graphic power of Boz, though he but rarely condescends to do it.

Such a warm reception would have given Jerdan great encouragement for his second volume.

Chambers' Edinburgh Journal of 12 June also gave Jerdan's book a friendly review: "It will be found to be one of the most amusing books of the day, and also not without a moral of its own kind . . . we at least feel pretty sure that the lives and characters of living men could scarcely be in gentler or more genial hands than those of William Jerdan." Noting the generally sympathetic tone of Jerdan's *Literary Gazette* over the years, in contrast with that of its rivals, the editor was now,

> at seventy, relieved from his cares, with little tangible result from his long and active career; but for this the readers of his autobiography will be at no loss to account. Jerdan has evidently been a kind-hearted, mirth-making, tomorrow-defying mortal all his days, as if he had patriotically set himself from the beginning to prove that Scotland could produce something different from those hosts of staid, sober, calculating men for which it has become so much distinguished.

The New Quarterly Review followed much the same argument as the *Spectator*, referring to the success of Jerdan's boyhood friends, which he had said was because they chose professions while he chose literature.[9] The *New Quarterly* was pitiless: "No such thing: it was because they minded the shop and he did not." More charitably, the review concluded that the volume was amusing and the public should buy it. To draw the sting out of their sharp remarks they ended on a humane note:

> We have been, in truth, not a little moved to take his part by a furious onslaught made upon him by a periodical upon which delicacy and good taste should have imposed silence if they could not dictate applause. Mr Jerdan is not quite an eagle, but we do not like to see him wounded by a shaft feathered by his own goose-quill. Such ungenerous assaults remind one of those prudent savages who, when their fathers grow old and unfit for work, made them contribute to the family economy by roasting and eating them.

The assault to which this paper referred was in fact the one review which Jerdan could justifiably have expected to celebrate his first volume: that in the *Literary Gazette*, the journal on which he had expended so much effort and warmth for thirty-four years but which was now in other hands. If he looked here for some sympathetic and encouraging mention to stimulate sales of his book, he would have been sorely disappointed. On 15 May the reviewer, who was of course not named, purported to regret his inability to produce a favourable review. Indeed, it was with "unaffected pain" that he noticed the work, and would have preferred to let it pass unremarked, but Jerdan's close association with the *Literary Gazette* made this impossible. The "old man . . . writing in the evening of his life, as we fear for his daily bread . . . should receive from every critic charitable consideration and the tenderest treatment," especially from his old paper. This was the tone Jerdan himself might have taken in reviewing an old friend. Instead, the reviewer was merciless, attacking Jerdan far more personally than any of the other reviews, with a ferocity that suggests revenge for some perceived offence. His insinuations also strongly suggested a knowledge of Jerdan's personal domestic arrangements which, even if known to the other critics, they had the decency to avoid mentioning. Jerdan was roundly criticized at some length for saying that literature was a profession to be avoided unless in possession of independent means. Were his accusations true, that society was culpable for his misfortunes, then he would be justified in his opinion; however, challenged the reviewer, "Investigate the matter fairly, and it shall be found that not one real grievance can Mr Jerdan bring before any tribunal competent to judge between man and man, whilst society has a thousand charges to lay at the door of this unhappy man of letters, to every one of which, for very shame, he cannot choose but plead guilty." Jerdan had no-one to blame but himself, "when the only thing really worth mourning over has been his own wilful and wicked flinging away of the finest opportunities".

Jerdan's *Autobiography* was briefly compared with Leigh Hunt's. Both had suffered financial hardships, both blamed others for their misfortunes, both decried the status of literature, both, according to the reviewer, had been well paid for their efforts but had carelessly disregarded their good fortunes. (What the reviewer did not note was that coincidentally both men had blamed the indulgence they had been given as children for their inability to control their lives more effectively.) Further, both had apologized for the disconnected nature of their memoirs, as Jerdan had done in his Postscript which, the *Literary Gazette* critic pointed out, "may be taken as a sample of Mr Jerdan's life . . . He is not a man of substance at this moment; he is thrown from the social eminence upon which his abilities well entitled him to be placed – not because he took to letters in his youth as the substantial pursuit of his life – but because, from beginning to end, wherever and howsoever employed, and with whomsoever engaged, it was the curse of William Jerdan to have 'private circumstances occurring to break hurtfully into his work'." This reviewer certainly seems to have known more about Jerdan's life than a casual critic would have done. He went on to stress the "high capabilities wilfully wasted", and wondered at length how Jerdan had avoided the early influences of his youth that had so benefited his exalted friends. He too lit upon Jerdan's comment about learning how debt was a curse, but observed that Jerdan's words remained merely that, and were never trans-lated into actions. Hypocritically, he claimed that it was harder for him to write the truth than for Jerdan to peruse it, but insisted that "Literature is in no way responsible for the calamities of William Jerdan. How many of them are trace-able to violation of the domestic affections it is not for us to decide."

The *Literary Gazette* echoed the other reviews in choosing to quote Jerdan's paragraph of dire warning, but did not bother to cloak its response in guarded language. "What a tissue of falsehood and unpardonable misrepresentation is here! ... The social failings that rendered Mr Jerdan's abilities of no avail to him in literature would have been his stumbling block in every profession and in any trade. Has he ever taken the trouble to calculate the self-denial, the steady perseverance, the patient self-devotion ... " of Pollock, Truro and the others, he asked angrily. Other writers had not expressed Jerdan's "fallacious hopes" etc. "They are not the lot of Hallam, of Macaulay, of Dickens; they are not the lot of Southey ... " The virtuous and hard-working do not incur "the righteous doom of the spendthrift and the libertine". Harsh words indeed.

The critic pointed to Jerdan's handsome remuneration as editor of the *Sun* and as editor and part proprietor of the *Literary Gazette*

> it is a matter of notoriety that he drew for years a considerable income. If Mr Jerdan has been foolish enough, year after year, to spend more than he earned – to make no provision for his family when Providence put the means in his way – to exhibit no self-government and no moral strength, we are sorry for him and can pity his present blank and dreary lot. But let him not visit upon literature the calamities of his own creating or slander the profession of his adoption ...

This fulminating and vituperative attack on Jerdan as an individual, concluded by noting that there was no reason to have included Hood's poem in the book, and that some of Jerdan's anecdotes were interesting, others improbable. The *coup de grâce* was swiftly administered – that the whole book was done with "a view of an instant return – ever a cruel necessity in Mr Jerdan's life – the wholesome confessions of a literary man, who has travelled through the world in pain, trouble and sorrow, only because he did not choose to live prosperous, happy and respected".

In a note to Bennoch, Jerdan told his friend:

> The *Literary Gazette* has given me (not my book) a malevolent notice which is so far satisfactory as it proves what bitter enemies I had assailing me, and how unscrupulous their means. For the rest it is too contemptible.
>
> The *Spectator* about the soundest, most impartial and rather severe of our weekly Journals is very favourable ... [10]

Jerdan did not identify the writer of the *Literary Gazette* review, although he must have known who it was who harboured such a violent hatred for him.

The *Eclectic Review* waited until its September issue to review Volume I of the *Autobiography* and did so in tandem with a review of R. P. Gilles's *Memoirs of a Literary Veteran*, published by Bentley the previous year. Jerdan would probably have found this juxtaposition galling, that his long-time associate had chosen to publish a work similar to his own. Both the authors reviewed had been editors, both were Scotsmen, and both had dwelt upon their hardships and misgivings about the literary life, and Gilles had been thrown into prison. The *Eclectic's* account of Gilles, from his Memoirs, made Jerdan's shortcomings seem quite trivial. The reviewer, disagreeing with *Tait's* opinion about "not an atom of spleen", remarked that Jerdan's book "is much better written", but that it "is equally pervaded by that spirit of acrimonious raillery and that tone of melancholy" as Gilles's book. Jerdan's circumstances had been less favourable than Gilles's but "he attained a much higher position as a man of letters". Noting that, by his own account, he had not been ill-paid, Jerdan had looked back upon his life as made up of "uncertain rewards" and "broken hopes". The reviewer found these comments contradictory, especially in view of Jerdan's assertion that he "got his first lesson of that fatal truth, that debt is the greatest curse which can beset the course of a human being". He seemed to have been burdened with this curse for a great part of his life, remarked the critic, noting with little sympathy how Jerdan himself admitted that his start in life had been on equal terms with men who had attained the height of their professions. Had Jerdan confronted the question of their rise and his own less worldly attainments earlier, his life might have been different. He had given up his studies in the law whilst his friends had persevered, kept to their goals, and focussed on their careers. Jerdan blamed his condition on his dependence on "the fragile crutch of literature", rather than on his own shortcomings. Quoting the same bitter extract as the other reviews, the *Eclectic* thought this was "mistaken counsel". "It is a fallacious excuse for an ill-regulated life", it noted sternly.

Before the reviews appeared, Jerdan wrote, probably to *Blackwood's*, saying that the first Volume was to be sent for review in the *Magazine*, and that in the second volume would be "letters etc. from my old friend Blackwood".[11] He had sent a Review of American Lay Sermons and asked if it was to be used, or for the return of the manuscript. (No contribution from Jerdan has been indexed in the *Magazine*.) In the same note he said "As I have some correspondence of Delta, it would gratify me much to have his Biography, and as I am Newspapering a bit again, I will give you a Notice in return."[12]

The "Newspapering" was being undertaken concurrently with Jerdan's writing of the second volume of his autobiography, and was providing him with much-needed income. The *London Weekly Paper, Organ of the middle classes*, priced at 4 pence, was a large broadsheet paper advertised as "a record of political, domestic and foreign news, literature, arts, sciences etc. under the direction of William Jerdan Esq. late editor of the *Literary Gazette*". The proprietor, Frederick Tallis, had his office at Crane Court, Fleet Street. Jerdan wrote to Bennoch that the first issue was to be on 15 May, and asked his friend for a contribution: "I feel that a series of articles on the L.[London] corporate body and city affairs wd be more likely to bring it at once into notice in the Metropolis. If you agree and will do the business, a brief introduction concocted between us cd be desirable."[13] In June Jerdan reported that from the second issue circulation had increased weekly, "unparallelled in newspaper enterprise", and by the fifth issue the weekly increase had risen to nine hundred and seventy-five, a vindication of its aim to be independent of all political parties, its object being the welfare of the people. In November Tallis added his name to the masthead, the paper then being called *Tallis's London Weekly Paper.*

Jerdan would have welcomed the income from editing this paper, but it was not primarily about literature, his real forte. Whilst he wrote the next volume of his *Autobiography*, he was also interested in offering his writings to America. The well-known publisher from Boston, J. T. Fields, was also a friend of Francis Bennoch and Jerdan hoped to use this mutual acquaintance to his advantage. "Any news of Fields and 'pastures ever new'?" he asked Bennoch in April.[14] In May Fields wrote from Paris, in response to Bennoch's mention of Jerdan's *Autobiography,* commenting:

> You tell me Jerdan's book is out. I long to be at it. I know I shall devour every word with interest for I am convinced if any man in England knows how to make a readable book it is our friend Wm. Jerdan and wish I were the owner of a good sound fortune if for no other reason than the satisfaction it wd afford me to say to Jerdan and such as he "There, take that little sum and be jolly the rest of yr days with no further thoughts of £.s.d. – If we had the sale of his LG in America I shd propose to our firm to allow him just the same copyright as we give Am'n. authors. It wd make a great difference in the sake my being absent because I shd take extra pains to advertize the great men's(?) of the work and spread its fame about the country if I were at home. I supposed <u>Virtue</u> would not allow the early publication to any one in America because I know he has a house in New York where all his pub'ns are offered at American prices. However when I arrive in London if anything can be done for Jerdan's interests in America, doubt not it shall be done. I consider that he has done more for good literature and has befriended more young writers than any living man and I love (?) him accordingly.[15]

Such warmth of feeling and intention should have boded well for Jerdan's hopes of an American market for his writings. The effervescent writer Martin Tupper also waited with anticipation for Fields's arrival, telling Bennoch:

> Fields is reminded to bring me more than his usual Graces with him, to

consort with our Greenwood condition hereabouts: and we'll all eat gooseberry fool in character among the haycocks.

Jerdan is to be drest out on the occasion in straw hat ribbons and knee-nuffens, as an "Arcadian" pastor: Mrs Bennoch shall sing; you shall dance; Grace aforesaid shall be our shepherdess; and Fields shall have his congenial fill (tell him) of silly-bub and goosberry fool.[16]

Tupper remembered this festivity long afterwards: "Do I not pleasantly remember the jolly haymaking, when old Jerdan calling out 'More hay! More hay!' covered Grace Greenwood with a haycock overturned, and had greeted a sculptor guest appropriately and wittily enough with 'Here we are, Durham, all mustered!' the 'we' being besides others, Camilla Toulmin, George Godwin and Francis Bennoch."[17] The hay-covered Grace Greenwood recalled the same party, especially "Mr Jerdan, or 'old Jerdan' as he is familiarly called, a man of nearly 70 years, yet retaining the joyous spirit of 17, one of the finest wits and most remarkable personages of his time".[18]

Fields had arrived in London by the summer, but although he had expressed himself so encouragingly about prospects for the *Literary Gazette* in America, Jerdan was anxious, telling him:

> My dear Sir,
> Our meeting is so uncertain and the strain of your business engagements so great and the Bennochian return before you go so uncertain – that I am re- or in-duced to write.
>
> I should like much to know what you think probable about the Auto-biography in America; and if you wd buy any copies, or secure the embellishments – Canning's is the least likeness of him ever published.
>
> Again, would you have anything to say to my Paraphrase of old Proverbs – full of wise sayings and modern instances – with curious annotations and delightful illustrations by A. Crowquill – at least as far as can be judged by the specimens I have received.
>
> To turn a few dollars wd not hurt one's health or spoil one's appetite, and I have been sickly and out of spirits for nearly all this week, so want comforting, which please afford to, my dear Sir, Yours very cordially,[19]

While he waited for news of an American debut from Fields, Jerdan completed the second volume of his *Autobiography* by August 1852, three months after the first had made its appearance. This volume was dedicated to the memory of George Canning. In the 'Prefatory Chapter', Jerdan referred to the favourable reception of his first volume, "by the almost unanimous voice of those critics in whom the public reposes confidence . . . ". He had been mistaken, however, by some critics, and attempted to set them straight on their misunderstanding that he had disparaged the practice of literature and been ungrateful for his success. As *Chambers'* had noted, he said, he had aimed to present his life candidly, thereby pointing a moral at the expense of "adorning" his tale; he was not writing a novel, but "the genuine life", and "as for the vilifications of the Holy Willies of the earth, I am disposed to take, even for them, the blame that I may deserve in a repentant spirit and despise all the rest". The facts of the author's life, maintained Jerdan, "has very little to do with his text . . . It is an unwholesome principle, therefore, to attempt the rebuke of virtuous precepts, merely because they may be uttered by some one who may not have fulfilled the duties of the decalogue: it is a mode of judging that must be condemned." He returned to the charge of disparaging the profession of literature to refute it absolutely, maintaining that his statements were the very reverse. "Literature is neither appreciated, encouraged, nor honoured as it should be . . . " His first book had merely exposed his own experiences with its errors and blunders, he wrote, in the hope that others pursuing literature would avoid at least the same mistakes. His intention was to show the evils, enjoyments and disappointments that can befall the writer, "the injustice and wrongs he is doomed to meet with". Jerdan's naïvety is surely assumed; he went on to claim, in the name of warning others, but in fact reflecting on his own individual experiences,

> the abstraction of his mind from the needful details of accurate business, and its aptness to seek refuge from dull realities in the brighter idealities of imagination as the result; and his often blameable inattention, impunctuality and want of order, which leave him almost a helpless prey, to be preyed upon by the sordid, the grasping, the scheming and the rascally, who are not slow to take full advantage of their opportunities to plunder and defame their victims.[20]

He had plainly not taken to heart the *Literary Gazette* reviewer's remarks that such a fate had not befallen Dickens, Hallam, Southey and others, and that it was Jerdan's own failings that had caused his downfall. He disputed this analysis, however, pointing out that tens of thousands have experienced heartache and poverty, and not all were "careless, extravagant, reckless, vicious!"

The second volume commenced more or less where the first ceased, covering some stories about Canning, the row with Taylor over the *Sun*, Trotter's Bazaar and many reminiscences and anecdotes of old friends from the world of literature, as well as letters which he scattered throughout his four volumes. Jerdan wanted to include examples of his friends' and his own writings within his *Autobiography*, and his placements were not always relevant. He admitted, " . . . no matter what the taste of readers may be, I have a lot of poetry to deposit somewhere in the course of my Biography". One was a doggerel verse on the illness and death of a pet dog found to have died of a seventy-yard tapeworm, the suicide of his distraught mistress, and the accidental death of her maid on beholding such horrors. More poetically, Jerdan included the verse, *Lines written by the Sea Side* which had appeared in *The Poetical Album* in 1828, but here entitled it *The Waves*. His alter-ego 'Teutha' was quoted in a four stanza poem called *Moonlight* and to lighten things up, a small Impromptu, *The Painter's Defence*:

> A Bride's likeness was painted, where only *one hand*
> Was seen, to the critic's dismay;
> But the artist, when blamed, cried 'What would you demand?'
> *She has just given the other away*!

Based upon an old Scottish saying, "It wants a new stock, a new lock, and a new barrel, like the Highlandman's pistol", Jerdan used the opportunity to regale his readers with a long poem entitled *The Highlandman's Pistol; a Fable for the present time*. The Highlandman, Donald, treasured an old pistol inherited from his ancestors, rusty and old-fashioned but reliable and prized. Wicked counsellors persuaded Donald to despise it, to change it, Lock, Stock and Barrel. When he needed it to defend himself against attack it burst asunder, allowing the enemy to kill him. The story ended that his place was desolate, deserted by Heaven as he had refused its gifts. The poem itself ended with a 'Moral':

> In Britain's Isle, so matchless fair,
> Of Innovation's wiles beware.
> Your glorious Constitution rears
> Its fabric through a thousand years,
> Impregnable to every storm,
> Immortal, if insane Reform,
> Vision'd Perfection, and wild Change,
> Within are ne'er allowed to range.
> Then doubt Improvement's specious cry,
> And prize substantial blessings high;
> Warn'd by our tale, not told in vain,
> Believe not every spot a stain,
> Nor every ancient form misspent,
> Nor useless each rich ornament.
> *Experience* proves, at endless length,
> *These* may be glory, wisdom, strength;
> And *Fable* only strives to show,
> Aptly, that from rash counsels flow,
> Guilt, Madness, Ruin, Slavery, Woe!![21]

This would appear to have been written twenty years earlier, at the height of the Reform crisis, but Jerdan still considered it worthy of a place in his memoir.

Other poems of slight merit appeared throughout, but Jerdan never lost sight of his chief purpose. He was at pains to point out that men of fortune did not have "to make literature their staff", and indeed for several it had cost them money to be published. He picked this topic up again in an Appendix, having in this volume meant to demonstrate "beyond controversy from the multitude of the unsuccessful and unfortunate and the paucity in numbers of those who reached any moderate degree of opulence, the truth of the positions I have laid down in regard to literary pursuits. But the task has grown too large . . . " and would be pursued in future. Loath to leave his pet subject entirely, Jerdan listed in two columns ten painters and ten poets, to compare their achievements with their pecuniary remuneration, from which he concluded that "higher intellect being requisite in one case than in the other – not that the artist is too liberally encouraged, but that the author is ill requited and wronged".

The reviews for this second volume were less divided than for the first one. The *Athenaeum*'s review followed the hitherto derided methods of its old rival, the *Literary Gazette*, by saying very little and extracting at length:

> Our reasons for specifying the contents of this work instead of subjecting it to the usual amount of critical annotation are not likely to be misunderstood, and claim no minute statement or explanation. We will therefore pass through this second volume lightly, and let Mr Jerdan tell his own story with as little disturbance as may be. The first chapter is an essay on the sorrows and difficulties of literature as a profession – on which theme Mr Jerdan descants as often as digression is permissible . . . [22]

Tait's Edinburgh Magazine focussed on Jerdan's attempted vindication of his views on the literary profession, sympathized with his examples of those who achieved great ends but carefully avoided any judgment on the merits of the book as a whole.[23]

The *Westminster Review* expended an amazing twenty-five pages reviewing the first two volumes of the Autobiography. The author embarked upon a cruelly vindictive character assassination, causing Jerdan to comment in a footnote in Volume III (page 306), that he had read the article,

> and perceive it to be furnished by the same individual who has got his pay for the same matter in other quarters . . . the whole diatribe proceeds, and, with the inveterate inconsistency of conceding *all* my argument whilst abusing myself, on grounds which no human being has a right to assume against another, especially in the braggard style of this ubiquarian hangman reviewer. I must have been poor game to him, after Dickens! – but he is not a Tory in the *Westminster*![24]

This was a mild protest in response to the viciousness with which he was treated by the critic. The long article observed that a man who wrote his 'life' should have something to tell, and a reason to tell it; something unusual should have happened to him, to justify his writing, or there would be a "plague of autobiographies". Nothing of the kind had been found in Jerdan's volumes, he claimed, the most memorable event being his birth. Being a mere editor was nothing remarkable, and a man had to have produced his own writings to earn a position of respect. The status of the *Literary Gazette* was attacked, arguing against Jerdan's claim for its exalted position in periodical literature.

Turning to the *Autobiography* itself, the *Westminster Review* critic highlighted Jerdan's statement that his 'spoiling' as a child was detrimental to his adult life, commenting spitefully that "If we get no more in the way of a moral from the book than this, we may congratulate ourselves on getting so much." Jerdan's inclusion of much detail met with derision: "He finds himself writing his life, and having once placed himself in the position of the hero of a book, he falls into the belief that everything personal to the actor who monopolizes the foreground must possess a certain value and attraction . . . " Ironically, Jerdan had omitted most of his personal life from his book thus, too late, giving the lie to his critic's accusation. Jerdan was a literary failure, crowed the critic, chortling over the success of the highly placed men of Jerdan's circle, and laughing, as had other critics, at Jerdan's putting the blame on literature for his failure to be as successful as his friends. At this juncture the critic became exceptionally personal, asking rhetorically many questions along the lines of:

> Has he ever thought of comparing his life with theirs? – his wasteful habits with their persevering industry and self-denial? Does he believe that they achieved their distinction by dining out; by the indulgence of idle pleasures; by dallying with time and fortune; and living for today without a thought of tomorrow?

The remainder of this lengthy review was in similar vein, the tone sarcastic and biting. Pages were devoted to exposing the flaws in Jerdan's attributions to literature of failure and poverty; much that is written, the reviewer commented, is transitory, worthless, uninformed, fugitive. Jerdan was accused of seeing the profession of literature solely in terms of money. "He never asks the question, did such or such a writer <u>deserve</u> a great reward? – he only inquires, did he <u>get</u> it". Even Jerdan's many anecdotes were found to be wanting: "The names of his celebrities flit through his pages, and scarcely leave an impression on them. We learn nothing of their ways of life, their conversation, their specialities, . . . " he carped, somewhat unjustifiably, as Jerdan had indeed sketched in some personal characteristics, especially in the case of Canning.

The *Westminster Review* differed notably from all other reviews in the very small number of extracts it used, preferring to fill its pages with scalding criticism of Jerdan's work, self-confessed kindliness, personality, opinions and experiences. In a final barb the reviewer noted:"Few men connected with current literature have enjoyed better opportunities than Mr Jerdan of attaining a final position of credit and security; and if he have not succeeded, we must seek the causes in other sources of misfortune than his overflowing good nature, and the imputed ingratitude of the world." The deliberate unkindness of this entire review suggests that the critic had a very personal score to settle with Jerdan as, although many of his points are similar to those of other reviewers, none had attacked Jerdan in such a personal manner, or in such bitterly sarcastic language.

The *Spectator*, whose review of Volume 1 Jerdan had thought the best, completely changed their tune now, complaining of "excessive stuffing . . . tedious discussions . . . .reprints of fugitive pieces, whose attraction has for the most part long ceased, (if the bulk of them ever had any)".[25] This was cruel and harsh and not wholly justified. Jerdan's *Autobiography* can – and has been – mined for nuggets of information about any one of the myriad of people he mentioned, but his fragmentary style can be off-putting if one seeks a coherent narrative. More rewarding is to accept that his books are a series of recollections in no particular order, and often his connections are between one thought and another, an anecdote leading on to an account of a dinner leading to a poem or a memory of some contributor to the *Gazette*, or an incident in his own life; interesting in his terms and if expectations of readers are not met, this does not diminish the validity of Jerdan's own train of thought and associations of ideas.

Jerdan must have dreaded the *Literary Gazette's* reaction to his second volume. He had reason: it was just as vindictive as before.

> Another volume of inconsistent grumbling, unjustifiable invective and puerile complaint! . . . a miserable but unauthorized whining over the literary profession relieved by scarcely a page of biography or original composition that an indifferent reader will care to peruse. We entreat Mr Jerdan for his own sake, to desist from this unmanly and unnecessary wailing.[26]

He was not the man to give advice, it went on, as whatever he earned he always spent more. The critic attacked Jerdan's alleged profligacy: "When his income has not been sufficient to pay for the ordinary necessaries of a man of family, has he not wantonly and madly persisted in the indulgence of gross sensual luxuries." This was a very personal charge and one which, in the circumstances, Jerdan was powerless to refute. The *Gazette* critic repeated his earlier assertion that Jerdan's calamities were the fault of his own shortcomings, not of literature.

Listen to his sickening groans and you would really conclude that he had nothing to tell you but the story of a wretch starving in a garret, nibbling at a goose quill, unblessed with a friend, not recognized by a solitary acquaintance. Believe nothing of the kind! Take Mr Jerdan's account of himself from his own lips, and he is an object of interest and of envy at every turn of his life. In virtue of literature he has lived all his days upon the fat of the land, and been honoured by the friendship and regard of some of the greatest men of the time.

Sneeringly, the *Gazette* pointed to Jerdan's friendship with de Tabley and Canning, his familiarity with Caroline Lamb and his self-confessed good deeds in regard to various people mentioned in his *Autobiography*. All this, believed the reviewer, happened because of his literary position. But now, he has forfeited respect; "he has wearied his well-wishers and deliberately cast asunder his friendships . . . so Mr Jerdan has sunk, and in his misery unjustifiably and uselessly upbraids an honest calling for disasters for which he alone stands culpable in the eyes of the world." The *Gazette* was "curious to follow Mr Jerdan as he progresses in his story. If he dare write his 'confessions' – he has indeed an instructive tale to tell. But he must dig deep down, and not be content to skim – with eye averted – the mere surface of his long and singularly-spent life." This was a large gauntlet to throw in Jerdan's path and one that he could not accept without betraying his wife, Landon, and even his current 'wife', Mary Maxwell. His impotent rage can be imagined as he prepared for his third volume, where he finally steeled himself to the subject of Letitia Landon.

He told Bennoch:

My present work in Volume 3 is very painful and perplexing. I have come to the advent of L.E.L: and knowing all the scandals that have been circulated, it is most difficult to treat. Her perfect idolatry of her first tutor and guide in poetry was an enthusiasm which none but poetic souls can feel or comprehend: and yet her poetry is quite unintelligible without this key. It is enough to make me ill, and I cannot review her fate or think of her tragic end, without weeping so much that I cannot see my paper. Even now I must stop.[27]

Close as Jerdan was to Bennoch, and much as Bennoch aided him financially in desperate times, Jerdan was not being entirely honest with him about Landon, and his letter reads almost like a draft for what he wrote about Landon in this section of the *Autobiography*. His servant had gone away, he complained, and he had mixed up his medicines; the Doctor had told him to stay in bed. "I am a poor hand by myself, having been so cockered all my life by affectionate help . . . " he told his friend pathetically, trading on his usual excuse that his early "spoiling" had tainted his life, a theme he mentioned again in Volume III.

This third book carried on its fly-leaf the date of 1853, but the dedication was dated October 1852 and read, "To the memory of the deeply lamented L.E.L. to whose genius the Literary Gazette was, during many years, indebted for its greatest attractions, this volume is gratefully inscribed by W. Jerdan." The first chapter dealt, as before, with his critics. He complained that he had been treated unfairly by having his warnings concerning the uncertainties of a livelihood from literature misinterpreted as a personal bemoaning of his own circumstances. Quite the reverse, he stated:

> I have throughout represented my success as a repetition of the spoiling which marked my earlier years (see Vol. I), and acknowledged that I was lifted far above what my deserts in almost any other calling could have effected, without some lucky accident. I have shown that as the happy result even of my literary efforts, I lived all my life with the noble in station and intellect, which I could hardly have done under any other circumstances; and I have substantially reaped, in the sterling coin of the realm, a very handsome remuneration for my labours, such as they have been, in a successful periodical.

His "handsome remuneration" did not mean that he had saved any money, having been burdened with debt from his earlier years. In support of his warning thesis Jerdan revealed, "I have written or published ten or twelve separate volumes – not one a failure – and yet all I reaped from them would not have fed a grasshopper!" (His calculation includes multi-volume books such as Fisher's *National Portrait Gallery* and *The Paris Spectator* so is a little misleading, but this does not alter his meaning.)

The early chapters of Volume III reminisced over many of Jerdan's acquaintance in literature, including the publisher John Murray, the poet Hook, and the Irish poet Ismael Fitzadam whose verse Jerdan quoted and greatly admired. He covered his appointment at Editor of the *Literary Gazette*, which jogged his memory of many other writers, and mentioned in passing his great interest at that time in new treatments for the insane developed in Italy and brought to England, whereby patients were treated in beautiful surroundings with little restraint. He could not have imagined back then how this topic would touch him so closely in his later life. Jerdan went on to provide a detailed history of the Royal Society of Literature and finally, at page 168, he came to the core of this volume, two chapters on L.E.L.

He chose for his epigraph, "We love the bird we taught to sing", the same phrase of L.E.L.'s which he quoted to Lady Blessington on Landon's death, but which has not been identified in any of her extant writings. This was followed by "I cannot but remember such things were/ And were most dear to me." "The foregoing lines may suggest that I have arrived at the most difficult point in these memoirs", he continued in a vein of eulogy over Landon's genius and divinity, their closeness as teacher and pupil: "every line and every motion of a soul imbued with a quenchless thirst for literary distinction and poetic glory was submitted for my advice". He acknowledged that his return was Landon's inestimable assistance with his work on the *Literary Gazette* as well as her invaluable poetic contributions. Thinking back to this period of his work on the *Gazette* and its pre-eminent place amongst "the clashing of rivalry", Jerdan told his readers:

> It is not easy to apprehend the station and influence of the Literary Gazette in its palmy days. It was the court of appeal for all literature of the period; its voice was potential, and its character held high throughout the sphere it essayed to occupy, in letters, and sciences, and fine arts . . . [28]

Modestly, he continued, "it was only my good fortune as its editor, to have much of the credit it so fairly won, reflected upon me." Jerdan included the letters from Landon's mother with Letitia's early poetry, and reprinted her first published poems from the *Literary Gazette*. No-one, of course, knew as much about Landon as Jerdan did, but he wrote not a word or a hint of their long love affair, their three children or of his own true feelings for her, excepting his opaque reference to the "master-key" without which her critics "will make nothing of their reveries". Touchingly, however, he implored his reader to

> shut out the present from contemplation, and throw back his glance to the date of which I am writing – to recognize, if congenial, the character whose outline I have traced, and the circumstances which developed it: through the intervening gloom, the retrospect, even to the sympathising stranger, must be uninviting; to me it is as the Valley of the Shadow of Death, and attempted to be recalled through floods of unavailing tears flowing from aged eyes, it is impossible to declare whether the impenetrable darkness is more dismal or the revealing light more distressing.

One wonders what Mary Maxwell, mother of so many of Jerdan's children, made of his floods of tears at the memory of his past love, dead now these twelve years.

As if his first chapter on Landon might have shown too much emotion, the next one opened briskly, listing Landon's earnings from her various works, and her grandmother's legacy. He could not keep up this business-like tone, reverting at once to praising Landon's "ceaseless consideration for the feelings of others . . . a sweet disposition, so perfectly amiable . . . ". To demonstrate her character, Jerdan printed her letters to him from Paris in 1834, which have been mentioned earlier in this present work,[29] concluding his tribute to her memory by observing that these letters "re-create a vivid portrait of the lamented writer". In writing his *Autobiography* Jerdan could hardly have omitted Landon, even if solely for the substantial amount of her input to the *Literary Gazette*, and as he was trying to maintain at least a semblance of chronology her appearance was fitted in to the right time, the first few years of his editorship of the *Gazette*. There is however, (but perhaps with the benefit of hindsight), a highly emotional note to these two chapters, and certainly more space given to one individual, than appears anywhere else in the four volumes of Jerdan's memoir.

Jerdan then reverted to his usual pattern of associated reminiscences, conscious that they did not form a coherent narrative. He excused this by noting:

> Biography, especially if as various as mine, cannot be constructed with the consistency of an invented plot. My web is not woven of a fancy-pattern with the main design running from end to end, and the accessory sprigs and embroideries in apple-pie order; but more like that spun by the Moenian Arachne, where there is indeed a centre, but from which the threads diverge in every fashion, now apparently tied together in mathematical-looking angles and circles, now flowing freely in wider weft, now throwing out long filaments, whither, and for what purpose, it is not easy to tell, yet altogether displaying an irregular regularity which is pleasant to look upon, when once leisurely examined and properly understood!

This rather verbose description of himself at the centre of a spider's web does indeed describe not only the structure of his *Autobiography*, but also of his literary and personal life; had he made this idea clear at the outset, perhaps some of his sterner criticis would have been kinder in their reviews of the apparently random nature of his reminiscences and associations of thought.

The by now familiar Appendices included letters and poems by Barry Cornwall and William Read, and in the final appendix Jerdan appealed, "I hope there is no reader on earth who would be so cruel to an autobiographer – a person who acts the part of a great medicine for the cure of the bile – as to deny him the comfort of two or three pages of Appendix to fill up the sheet with a few trifling specimens of his other writings." The trifles were amusing, comprised of quips and puns, and a brief *Last Love Song*.

The *Spectator's* review of Volume III was short and neutral, commenting that there was "less of the wonted topic . . . the misfortunes of literary men and the disadvantages of literature as a profession, than there was in the second volume . . . but the volume wants the reality of the youth and early manhood of its author". The critic found that the two chapters on L.E.L. "tell very little and are somewhat mysterious to boot".

Tait's, which had been positive about the first two books, greeted the third warmly: "a treasury of readable matters culled with a liberal profusion from the hoarded stores of a long literary life". The reviewer noted Jerdan's "generous and kindly spirit" when introducing *Literary Gazette* contributors such as Pyne and especially Maginn, on whom *Tait's* extracted the descriptive passages. Regarding L.E.L., the critic looked "for further information at his hands, and shall probably have it in a future volume", and regretted that he had run out of space after mentioning only one-third of the "varied contents of this somewhat discursive but engrossing book".

The *Athenaeum* gave Volume III nearly three columns, much of which contained extracts from Jerdan's text. Ignoring Jerdan's own explanatory metaphor of the spider's web, the reviewer carped:[30]

The farther these confessions and experiences of a literary life proceed, the more discursive and reclamatory do they become. There is a perpetual reference either backward or forward. Something already written needs to be corrected or confirmed, – something not yet written is to be anticipated. Critics have yet to be answered, enemies defied, – forgotten papers to be brought in, with or without regard to time and theme. So that, altogether, instead of a regular narrative, with anecdotes, repartees and character introduced artistically to enliven and illustrate the individual story, the reader has in these volumes a literary *olla*,[31] which would probably have little less of sequence if its articles were first put into a box, well shaken, and printed as they might happen to come out again.

Taking up the chief bone of contention between Jerdan and the majority of his critics, the *Athenaeum* declared that the topic was referred to in almost every chapter. "We have taken no part so far in this discussion, – and, for reasons which our readers will appreciate, we still refrain from discussing with Mr Jerdan a topic so important and so delicate." The review entirely overlooked the chapters on L.E.L., and extracted several anecdotes in a lighter vein for the entertainment of their readers.

In the interval between sending off his manuscript for Volume III, and awaiting its reviews, Jerdan was still working on his latest paper, *Tallis's Weekly*. It was not doing well, and in January 1853 its proprietor was trying a new idea to encourage subscriptions by offering "a superb steel engraving" worth two guineas, entitled "Liberty and Captivity" to anyone who signed up for six months. Jerdan told Bennoch that he had not heard how the paper was succeeding, but "I think it ought to make its way and will: but my position has some drawbacks, from the erroneous notion that I am too Derbyish;[32] and a hankering to be Liberal whilst pretending to hold equal scales."[33] However, Jerdan's article on "The Magazines" in the issue of 6 November, sounded like sour grapes, as if he was missing his job on the *Literary Gazette*, and was using the opportunity to air some old grievances:

> The magazines seem to us on the whole unusually dull this year. Whether it be the weather, or the prospect of the duke's funeral [Wellington], or something else, we know not, but something certainly has happened to cast a rather lugubrious tone over them all. *Bentley's* indeed appeared so heavy . . . a certain sameness about [the articles] which would almost induce one to believe that they were all by the same writer . . . *Fraser*, which is also rather dull . . . the tone and style of *Blackwood* is the same, contains, if anything, less novelty than usual . . .

He was more complimentary about other periodicals such as *Tait's, Gentleman's Magazine* and the *New Monthly Magazine*, perhaps because they had not annihilated his *Autobiography*.

Jerdan was still considered by some to have influence. Lord Lennox assured him that he would receive the first bound copy of his *Memoirs of being aide de camp to Wellington*, asking for an early notice "to start me well".[34] In the 4 December issue of *Tallis's Weekly*, Jerdan unashamedly took advantage of his position as Editor to give himself some free publicity, quoting at some length "an amusing instance" from Volume III of his *Autobiography*, concerning the difficulties of sending a package to the Duke of Wellington.

Jerdan, with two of his daughters (unnamed), spent nearly two weeks over Christmas and the New Year 1853 with the Polar explorer Sir James Ross and his wife at their home in Buckinghamshire.[35] Even in his penurious state he was still invited to his friends' homes. His finances were to slightly improve when in March 1853 Jerdan's pension of one hundred pounds a year was finally granted by the intervention of Lord John Russell, a previous Prime Minister, to the current PM the Earl of Aberdeen. It was grudgingly announced in the *Literary Gazette*:

> We are happy to announce that a pension of £100 a year has been granted to Mr Jerdan, editor of this Journal from its commencement in 1817 to the close of 1850, in consideration of his literary labours. Although we have thought it right to repel the unwarrantable attacks made by Mr Jerdan on the profession of letters, and been thus driven to state the facts which have been the cause of his personal misfortunes, we are not the less sensible of his claim to literary sympathy. The award of a pension under such circumstances supplies a crowning proof of the consideration which literary position and connexion have procured for Mr Jerdan, although to this profession he attributes all his calamities.[36]

This was a churlish way to score more points off Jerdan's misfortune, under the guise of seeming to congratulate him on his pension award. Jerdan appreciated the pension and believed that there was nothing left in the fund to make him a more generous allowance. The lithographer and sculptor, R. J. Lane told Jerdan, "I am glad the Lord John thanked you (as he ought) – the term 'pension' is wrong it seems – as the grant is one hundred a year for two years, but then comes the intimation that no minister would be likely to discontinue it – this <u>entre nous</u> as it is a private letter."[37] A rather more munificent pension of £200 a year had been granted to Leigh Hunt in 1847, with the bonus of an accompanying letter from Lord John Russell saying "the severe treatment you formerly received in times of unjust persecution of liberal writers, enhances the satisfaction with which I make this announcement". Hunt had earned his larger pension by the long term he had spent in prison for publicising his liberal views, a sacrifice Jerdan had avoided by keeping away from politics for most of his working life.

After a hiatus of nearly a year, in November 1853 Jerdan published the fourth and final volume of his *Autobiography* and dedicated it to Sir Edward Lytton Bulwer Lytton. The frontispiece was adorned by a flattering engraving of Bulwer and another of the Lytton ancestral home, Knebworth in Hertfordshire. Jerdan opened with his usual theme of commenting upon his critics. He said that "exhibitions of spite and rancour have demonstrated a truth of which I have long been aware, namely, that gratitude was the shortest lived of human virtues; but the compensation on the other hand of liberal sentiments and generous sympathies have far outweighed the inflictions of literary coxcombic pertness, and sheer stupidity and unprovoked malevolence". He affected to "grin" at the double-sided portrait of himself given by his various reviewers. He quoted from letters he had received, mostly praising him, and noted that he had been encouraged to expand and to reduce, to include and to omit; taking full responsibility for his work, he remarked that "it will be my own fault at the end of my journey if I am discovered to be carrying my OWN ASS: and after all, it is better to ride an ass that carries, than a horse that throws, you".

This volume focussed on contributors to the *Literary Gazette*, reminiscences of his old friends, his purchase of a share in the *Literary Gazette* and of Grove House. He also documented, albeit very vaguely, the financial trouble which necessitated selling his grand home, and proudly listed the committee which oversaw his Testimonial. The Appendices in this volume included his story, "Baby", which had been published in the *Mirror* in 1831, and matters concerning the foundation of the Royal Geographical Society and the Literary Fund. He self-indulgently added what he called "a playful note" from Landon, sent probably around 1830, which he believed "will farther show from what a height I have fallen". As her letter asked him to procure a theatre box for a friend, something he habitually did, asked for his opinion on her latest review, and wished his sore throat better, this hardly indicated the "fall" to which he alluded. Perhaps this was Jerdan's way of pre-empting his critics from pointing too spitefully to his reduced condition.

Jerdan concluded his life story by observing that "Autobiography as it ought to be, was defined by a great man as 'a portrait of the mind of the writer', and in order to come somewhat within this canon, I have not hesitated to give such truthful lineaments as occurred to my pencil, though I was not artist enough to paint a complete picture ... " He had been accused of egotism, he said, but that was something inseparable from his task.

The *Spectator* dismissed the fourth volume, saying that all it contained were "not digressions, but only variations of the theme – Self and Gazette".[38] What else did they expect, one wonders, from the autobiography of a man who had spent thirty-four years on his influential periodical? The *Athenaeum* was unhappy with Jerdan's claims of ingratitude and with the sounding of "the trumpet of his own virtues".[39] His publication of private letters was called into question; the reviewer was "not sorry that this work had come to a close ... Mr Jerdan has evidently lost his temper, and with it his discretion". The critic foresaw an angry response to this book, "though this may not be the case in the *Athenaeum*" he recorded smugly, having decimated the work in a single paragraph.

The faithful *Tait's* waited a while before its review appeared, excusing itself by remarking that the volume "comes late to hand, like a tardy dessert after a dinner of three courses". It was worth waiting for, full of things piquant, odd, funny and touching. *Tait's* revived the old argument about publishers' demands for good reviews in the periodicals they owned, gently chiding Jerdan's kindly nature:

> There are some curious revelations in this volume of the soreness of publishers with regard to the works which they issue to the public. Surely no man in such a position ever dealt more leniently with authors than Mr Jerdan while at the head of the *Literary Gazette*; but it would appear that with certain publishers, nothing short of unqualified praise will please them ... we fear, that Mr Jerdan has really some offences to atone for. His generosity has sometimes outrun his judgment and from hints dropped here and there in this concluding volume, it is to be suspected that some who have been most favoured, have been the least grateful.[40]

Their review concluded by urging readers that Jerdan's *Autobiography* was "the fullest and most amusing history which he can possibly meet with of the literary world of the last half century".

The *Literary Gazette* refrained from reviewing Volumes III and IV, perhaps feeling that enough bitterness and gall had been expended on the first two books.

Taken all in all, Jerdan's *Autobiography* was more 'stream of association' than it is organized chronological information. Although his avowed intention was to warn young people off a career in literature, the four volumes are peppered with boasting of the high, mighty and powerful whom he met through his long career. It is fruitless to search for almost any hard fact in their pages, the absence of dates being just one of the frustrating omissions. As might be expected Jerdan made little reference to anything after the glory days of 1830, and only tenuous, teasing remarks on the catastrophes that he suffered after that date. Almost nothing about his family found a place in his memoir although considerable space was devoted to Landon. It is conceivable that he intended a fifth volume which may have treated these matters in more detail, but that his publisher Virtue decided there was no demand for one. (He was correct, as the *Autobiography* was advertised in the *Athenaeum* in November 1858 at the reduced price of 10s for all four volumes.)

On the other hand, if his volumes are accepted for what they are, the somewhat rambling reminiscences of an elderly man who had recently suffered the loss of his life-long employment and his own journal, one can appreciate his mental connections between one anecdote and the next, whether driven by personality, time, topic, or some other personal connection only Jerdan could make. No-one would wish to dwell on the downside of their life when writing their memoirs, at least a man such as Jerdan for whom success seemed to be measured not so much in money, but in the kindness and influence he could offer to striving authors, and in the names of the great and the good he could call his friends.

The curmudgeonly Samuel Carter Hall, who had known – but not liked – Jerdan, looked back thirty years later to pronounce:

> He left an autobiography; considering his vast opportunities it is deficient in interest, of little use for reference, and giving us but a shadowy idea of the many great men and women to whom it makes reference and whom he has personally known. Indeed, he had personally known nearly all who flourished during the second quarter of the century. I have myself vainly sought in his four volumes for the help he might have given – and ought to have given – the writers who should come after him.[41]

This was an unnecessarily spiteful comment on the work of a man then long dead, a man whose usual *joie de vivre* was a characteristic quite foreign to Hall. Jerdan himself had already given his response to such criticism; he acknowledged his shortcomings, but said that "fifty years of literary life, mixed up with 'all the world' defies system",[42] and system was not one of Jerdan's virtues.

Six weeks before Volume IV went to press, and despite the temptations of steel engravings and Jerdan's efforts, his association with *Tallis's London Weekly*

Paper ran into difficulties. Its early success at fourpence had quickly fallen off, and it needed to sell twenty thousand copies to be profitable.[43] Jerdan reported that they could not sell above half that amount; the price was raised to sixpence and circulation fell by half. In August they offered another engraving, this of Her Majesty on Horseback painted by Count d'Orsay; an advertisement for *Tallis's* noted that it was "of the full extent allowed by law, containing 3060 square inches of reading matter, is of Liberal Politics, sound Protestant Principles and the best Family Paper issued from the Metropolitan Press". None of this was enough to save it, and Jerdan's role as editor came to an end in November 1853 with issue no. 77. The paper itself was absorbed into the Empire New Series at that time ("Pharoahs who knew nothing of Joseph" Jerdan claimed), and ran for a further three years. The reincarnated paper did not employ Jerdan, as was evident from his anguished letter to Bennoch of November 1853. Fields, despite his avowed intentions, had not found any work for him, and there was another matter which Jerdan needed to discuss with Bennoch. He sounded desperate:

> I enclose a copy of the letter I have addressed to Messrs Cook Son & Co as you advised.
>
> I am sorry that <u>after</u> circumstances should impress you with the opinion that I committed a social injury in being carried away (it may be somewhat imprudently) by Mr Thomson's flattering and seductive inducements. The failure of the Boston Correspondence and of Tallis' Paper could not be foreseen at the time, and my plunge into difficulties was both sudden and unexpected. I have not now to learn however that Poverty is a moral taint.
>
> I cannot, if I would, take the benefit of the Insolvent Court. My antecedents in 1850 prevent it and if Messrs Cook persevere in their merciless course, I must, as I have stated be made an outlaw, or sent to a Gaol till Death relieved me of my sufferings.
>
> I think that with two years' arrested life I cd do much to improve my circumstance – do something for the Children – and leave a memory better preserved from censure or calumny and higher in the literature of my country. But alas I see no way to this repose and can only groan forth Oh that I could flee away to be at rest.
>
> I hope in my reference to you I have not exceeded the licence you prescribed. Much as I value yr friendship I would not press upon it even to a stretch of commercial convenance, to save me from ruin. As it is I am all but broken hearted
> Yrs most sincerely,
> WJ
> I am of necessity away from Home, and all destitute enough.[44]

The nature of Messrs Cook's action is unknown, but was plainly very serious. Jerdan confided to Bennoch that he was in a "dreadful state" and had tried to see Frank Cook, but he was out of England; he had written instead to a Mr Jones, and enclosed his response for Bennoch to see. Jerdan was not optimistic: "If he apprehends me, the destruction of all belonging to me and my incarceration for life and the certain results. For God's sake help me if you can to avert this terrible stroke. I am obliged to flee from home. Can scarcely write this scrawl."[45] He was understandably terrified of being imprisoned for debt, a fate suffered by so many other literary men before him. He wrote often to Bennoch, to whom he was forced to apply for funds to keep going.

Jerdan's letters asking friends for money often had a ring of melodrama, but these last two to Bennoch seem to have been wrung from his heart as he looked back over his life and realized, finally, that he was possibly nearing its end without having achieved security for his family or a place for himself in posterity. "Want, my dear Friend, and not Economy, is the order of the day with me, unless some replacement of the cash is effected," he remarked to Bennoch in another letter. The children had to play their part too. "Charles has been a week in his trial at the [Press?] office. The girls talk of going out to service or teach."[46] Charles would have been about 15 or 16, the girls 17 and 18. How different the lives of this family to that of Jerdan's legitimate children, steady in their careers or marriages.

In *Fraser's Magazine* of September 1853 Jerdan contributed a four verse poem called *Après Moi*, about children's happiness continuing, even though "The dead must rest – the dead shall rest". His frame of mind spoke for itself.

22

Widened Horizons

Following publication of his *Autobiography*, Jerdan was commissioned by Routledge to prepare "Remarks on his Writings and a Sketch of His Life" at the beginning of *The Works of the Rev. George Herbert*, published in 1853. He was paid ten pounds for this essay, and two thousand copies of the book were printed.[1] Routledge chose an old-style type face for this book, with the letter 's' looking like an 'f', understandable perhaps in the body of a work written two centuries earlier, but an anachronism as far as Jerdan's contribution was concerned. Jerdan's Introduction is particularly interesting as it is a rare example, outside of the *Literary Gazette*, of his opinion on literary and especially poetical work. His personal predilection was biased more towards poetry than prose, a bias which was likely to have been a key factor in the decline of the *Literary Gazette*. A study of three contemporary Introductions to Herbert's poetry concluded that Jerdan's best expressed the understanding of Herbert's work as a template of Christian ethics and "of the broader Victorian Evangelical movement".[2]

Herbert's verse, almost all in a collection entitled "The Temple" comprised one hundred and sixty poems and contains unusual imagery. The collection was of a religious nature which made the choice of Jerdan, who was not especially religious, a curious one. However, he was well known as a literary pundit and it was on this basis that he approached his task. Jerdan's Preface, reflecting his eternal passion for poetry, remarked:

> The mission of Poetry is refining, pure and holy. If it be not, it will not last, descend the stream of time, and be cherished from generation to generation through succeeding ages. It is only as the heroic partakes of this influence, in the form of noble sentiment, that it enjoys a similar immortality: whilst wit, humour and description are doomed, however admirable in their way, to a much more limited existence.

Jerdan acknowledged Herbert's earlier biographers included Sir Isaak Walton and, basing his study on these works, gave a brief outline of the main events of his subject's life. He then discussed why Herbert's "orb has beamed more brightly through the shade of so many years" when those of his contemporaries have faded. (Jerdan omitted to mention Milton, whose orb had not faded much at all.) Putting Herbert into his historical context Jerdan noted that the beginning of the seventeenth century was "unsettled in religious principle", with many clergy positively irreligious. This gave rise to an opposite extreme, of the religious fanatic. The Civil War polarised allegiances even more, and as a result of the turmoil religion was almost banished, in disgust at its "violences, hypocrisies and crimes". During the "Popish struggles" of James II, men changed their religion to suit their convenience. All this occupied nearly a century.

Into the midst of such chaos and confusion came Herbert, aspiring to walk in the footsteps of his "Master". Jerdan remarked that in Herbert's period the standard of poetry was not high, although he found some worthwhile work of lesser poets, naming four. Declaring he was not an apologist on either side, Jerdan said that many Restoration poets veered into licentiousness, but suggested that "polished vice is less obnoxious and injurious than coarse and vulgar profligacy in word or deed". Jerdan seldom let his literary judgment overpower his strong sense of morality even though his actions so often belied his creed. Herbert's popularity, he thought, lay in his ideals being the antidote to loose living, ensuring his "descent to our day with a halo of righteous glory about him". Herbert was passionate about music, his chief occupation besides "Piety and Poetry". His own influence had permeated through seven generations. He "diffused a vast amount of holiness throughout the British Empire and the Universe", said Jerdan, and attributed to Herbert "the wisdom of Solomon with the inspiration of David", saying that over his subject's prose and verse "is shed that divine Spirit which transports us to another sphere far beyond the cares and afflictions of our present sojourn".

Whilst passing quickly over Herbert's *The Country Parson*, observing merely that it would benefit the Church and its congregants to take its lessons to heart, Jerdan pointed out that this was a topic foreign to the purposes of his essay. From this point on in his Introduction, Jerdan was on surer ground: he finally started to discuss poetry. As was usual in the seventeenth century, a poet or playwright's work was often introduced by "commendatory verses" written by others. It was Jerdan's opinion that these were characterised by poverty of composition, "full of commonplace compliments and exaggerated laudation in unpoetic language". These defects, however, served to demonstrate Herbert's superiority.

Jerdan quoted from the first epigram of *The Church Porch*, "A verse may find him who a sermon flies [/ and turns delight into a sacrifice.]" He maintained this was the key and touchstone to all Herbert's works. "His whole nature is developed in its nine words!" he eulogised. "The love and service of God: the love and use of Poetry!" Only verse, asserted Jerdan, was exalted enough to light the sacred flame; prose appeared to Herbert to be the effort of a stammerer.

Jerdan's critical faculties were alert to the danger of critiquing work produced in a different age. Herbert's penchant for "sprinkling strange and quaint conceits over all" were usual in his day, and were understood then to be moral pointers. Jerdan quoted some of Herbert's verses in order to demonstrate what he meant by "conceits", showing how phrases that were acceptable and admired two centuries earlier would, in the present time, be considered profane.

Long years in the periodical and magazine business made Jerdan aware of production details of a first edition of Herbert's work, published in 1633, which another reviewer may have overlooked. He commented on the enhancement of some poems by "the fanciful devices in which they were typographically moulded into the shapes of angels' wings, hour-glasses, altar-pieces and other forms analogically connected with their matter". Jerdan saw these decorative elements as in some way dictating the shape of the verse, whilst he in no way detracted from the "substance" of the poetry. He gave several examples of the "sweet or pathetic ideas" which overflow Herbert's pages, more suited to decoration than were the "sacred exhortations and mysteries". Herbert's verses, so moral and impressive in their own era were, with the effluxion of time, "liable to be lost on our fastidious era, when partial education is more widely extended, and minute criticism more largely indulged".

Jerdan proceeded to discuss Herbert's opening poem of "The Temple", entitled *The Church Porch*, praising the way in which Herbert, in the name of the Church, admonished drunkenness, idleness, lying and other vices, but did so in a voice of "kindness, earnestness and love". This was why, Jerdan believed, his writing stood the test of time. He selected a quotation to illustrate his observation, on a subject with which he had a close familiarity:

> Be temperate
> Drink not the third glass, which thou canst not tame,
> When once it is within thee
> He that is drunken . . .
> He hath lost the reins,
> Is outlawed by himself.

Jerdan quoted twenty-four lines on another matter which spoke directly to his own life, some lines of which were:

> Be thrifty, but not covetous; therefore give
> Thy need, thine honour, and thy friend his due.
> . . . By no means run in debt . . .
> . . . if with thy watch, that too
> Be down, then wind up both. Since we shall be
> Most surely judged, make thy accounts agree.

These words must have struck a deep chord within the critic, who had never in his life made his accounts agree. He concluded by commending Herbert's poems to his readers as a blessing passed down the ages.

Reflecting this solemn and intellectual work on Herbert, and reminiscent of his work for the Camden and Percy Societies, Jerdan prepared a paper for the British Archaeological Association on "Documents relative to the Spanish armada and the defence of the Thames".[3] Somewhat startlingly, in his opening paragraph setting the armada in its historical context, Jerdan remarked that the Pope had blessed the Spanish expedition, "the result of which showed that the benediction of his holiness was so ineffectual as to be turned into a curse". Jerdan drew his readers' attention to the "curious coincidences with the present day", such as the "menaces of invasion". He discussed three documents, the first, of December 1585, showing "Queen Elizabeth and her ministers adopting measures for putting the navy in an effective state to meet the enemy." This dealt with wages paid to the militia, and allowances for victuals. Jerdan remarked on the smallness of the scale of such preparations, but noted that the queen had "the enthusiasm of her people to sustain her against all foreign aggression . . . ". The second document, a lengthy one, gave the Duke of Parma's twelve orders previous to sailing the armada from Lisbon in May 1588. Several of these orders were concerned with Catholic observances on board their ships, and instructions for the fair and equal treatment of all sailors. Jerdan noted that it was "interesting from the particular painstaking to reconcile, or at least postpone, all existing differences, and produce a unity of zeal and daring in the sacred cause of a religious crusade". The final document was a report dated 25 August 1588 concerning the defence of the kingdom against Spanish invasion. Some of the soliders at Tilbury had not received their full pay as their captains had spent it on entertainments, and other sections dealt with the pay of conscripted men. Jerdan commented that this document "is principally deserving of attention from the insight it affords into the interior of the military service of the age, and of the determined purpose to effect all requisite reforms and redress all real grievances". He acknowledged that these three documents were widely known, and that he could not add "any novel matter of importance" to them, but that his intention was to show his support for the British Archaeological Association, "in the prosperity of which I have taken so warm an interest since its first institution at Canterbury".

In the same year, 1853, Jerdan worked on an entirely different and contrasting piece: an Introduction for the American book, *Yankee Humour and Uncle Sam's Fun*, published by Ingram, Cooke & Co. His work was featured in *Eliza Cook's Journal*, and that article was subsequently copied in *The Eclectic Magazine* of June 1855.[4] The book was a London-published adaptation of *Dow's Patent Sermons*, humorous articles originally published in the *New York Sunday Mercury*. Jerdan's lengthy and erudite introduction pointed out that whilst many American writers had achieved considerable popularity overseas, very little was known about the "humorous exhibitions of the press". His purpose was to make readers better acquainted with American humour of the various regions of the country – the far west, south west and Yankee versions. Taking *Dow's Sermons* as his text-book, he said, he also took several other publications into account when researching his subject. He could not write the scholarly treatise such a subject deserved, but noted how little we know of the humour of antiquity:

> how the Hebrews joked, if they did joke, in their dialects without points; how the Egyptians punned, if they did pun, in hieroglyphics; or how the Chinese, Assyrians, Babylonians, Medes, or Persians jested when in a merry mood, and laughed at the good sayings of their Joe Millers and Sydney Smiths. Of Greece we have some Attic and dramatic remains, which enable us to judge of the fineness and asperity of Greek humour. From Rome, little of what we (i.e. England and modern tastes,) consider to be wit or humour, has descended to us. Biting satire, and epigrams, the spirit of which generally depends upon the brevity of the dictum, or turn of expression, barely afford us grounds for comparing and contrasting these two ancient aggregations of human intellect, and showing us how dissimilar they were in their playful moments and movements."

He remarked that no vestige of what made Druids, Celts or Britons laugh has remained; the Saxons left caricatures in their church carvings, and the national humour of Britain, for centuries, was ridicule or satire. Shakspeare (sic) commenced the present era, embracing every variety of humour "from the purest and loftiest range to the inferior sports of badinage, equivoque and pun". Jerdan expounded his discussion through the wit of Swift, after which he believed there had followed a half century of "remarkable mediocrity and dulness. "School of authorship" had led to quantities of imitators of Johnson, Sterne, Smollett, Scott and others, but "we have nothing like Don Quixote or Gil Blas to light up the retrospect".

Jerdan noted that English, Irish or Scottish humour were very dissimilar, just as Anglo-Saxon humour transported to America became nothing like its original. He gave examples of the "droll system of exaggeration" which was popular in the "idleness of the far West": "a man being so tall that he had to get up a ladder to shave himself; an oyster being so large as to take two men to swallow it whole", and similar examples. He quoted from popular stories published in America in 1846, commenting astutely that "In the exhibition of American humour, so much depends upon the language, that it is requisite to have some notion, not only of the newly-coined phraseology, but of the distinctive localization of the patois which belongs to various States and divisions and subdivisions of the Union." He quoted at some length from "A Stray

Yankee in Texas" which set out such distinctions, with many examples of words, phrases and pronunciations reflecting Spanish and French influences in various States.

Having covered in detail the genesis of humour in America, Jerdan finally approached his subject of Dow's Sermons, "so full of good sense, endorsed by burlesque and whim". Before starting on his putative subject however, he discussed the adventures of Captain Suggs who embodied the daring rascality of the go-ahead characters of the new world with a propensity for foul play to achieve his ends. Jerdan dismissed this type of story-telling as "rather a specimen of the characteristic than the humorous". Despite this caveat, Jerdan filled a further seven pages with Suggs's exploits, following this with a further long extract from "Georgia Scenes"; these sketches of the South, he thought, showed a "more jocular quality". After several more pages of quotations from a successful contemporary book published in Philadelphia, concerning Major Jones's Courtship, Jerdan filled more space by extracting from a similar book, *Travels from Georgia to Canada*, to demonstrate a style he said was "full of merriment, with some little spaces of sentiment".

After dealing with what he called "Facetiae Americanae", only on page twenty-seven did he finally come to Dow's Sermons, of which there were more than two hundred. They attracted notice for "their Yankee style, sly sub-acid banter and quaint originality both in design and execution". The writer, Jerdan thought, was "well versed in Scottish publications". The sermons displayed both jest and earnest, and Jerdan noted that "The American press compares the author with Boz . . . " A little over a page of extract is given, whereupon Jerdan said he did not need to introduce or remark at length upon the Sermons. His whole article was very much in the *Literary Gazette* tradition of lengthy extracts to fill his space, but the first part was his own disquisition on the origins of humour, and displayed his not inconsiderable knowledge of history and etymology. The critic of the *New Quarterly Review* did not appreciate the book, dismissing it as "A catchpenny for the railways, to which we are sorry to see Mr Jerdan's name prefixed. It consists of very bad facetiae collected from the back numbers of the *New York Mercury*."[5] It may not have been the quality to which Jerdan had normally aspired, but in his present penurious condition any work was better than none.

Although Jerdan had completed his *Autobiography* and moved on to other work, there were some repercussions from his memoir. Richard Bentley had been seriously offended by one paragraph in Volume IV of the *Autobiography*. On page 209, headed "Publisher's Profit", Jerdan had described how Bulwer paid Bentley £750 to recover a copyright and that Dickens too had paid the publisher to return his copyright in *Oliver Twist* for £2250, so that Bentley had profited by £3000. True to form, Jerdan omitted any dates, but these transactions had taken place in 1837, sixteen years earlier.

Jerdan heard from Bentley setting out his grievance, which apparently bewildered Jerdan, who responded on 7 January:

> If I have committed any mistake about you, Sir B Lytton [Bulwer], or Mr Dickens, I shall be happy to correct it, on your informing me what it is: as I cannot guess aught from a vague generality, I really do not know to what your letter alludes. I shall regret any possible mis-statement unpleasing to you.
>
> As for any abuse of 'confidence' I repudiate the charge, and think it comes with an ill grace from you. From your <u>first</u> publication to your last, I was your steady friend, as many a warm acknowledgement from you remains to show, if I am wrongfully accused. But I wish to close my days with the good feelings which have ever governed them, and hope there is nothing to prevent a reciprocal sense on your part.
>
> Many mutual kindnesses have passed between us, and on which side any obligation for services rendered may rest, I am willing to leave to the oblivion of yours. 'No more pipe, no more dance', is no novelty to, Dear Sir, yours truly, W. Jerdan.[6]

On 9 January Bentley protested vehemently, "There is a universal feeling amongst right-minded men that communication made in private intercourse should be regarded as sacred."[7] He accused Jerdan of misrepresentation and gross inaccuracy and demanded that the paragraph be "cancelled", although he failed to suggest how this might be achieved in a book already published. Indignantly, Jerdan told him:

> I need not enter into any argument on the general principle as to what ought to be deemed confidential communications every opinion varying on the extent to which it should be carried, and every individual case resting on its own circumstances.
>
> I do not feel that I have transgressed any gentleman's obligation, and have only to repeat that if you will point out any error into which I may have fallen, and of which I am unconscious, I will do my best to remedy it . . .[8]

Bentley declined his offer to make a public statement which could only "call attention to what ought <u>never</u> to have been published" and repeated his demand for cancellation of the paragraph.[9] Bentley was infuriated to hear again from Jerdan, still affecting to be mystified as to the reason for his ire:

> It seems to me that, for some reason of your own, which I cannot comprehend, you desire to fasten an unprovoked censure upon me; and I have

only to repeat that unless you will state distinctly and explicitly of what it is you do complain, I cannot deal with the subject.

You surely cannot expect me to acknowledge errors of which I am utterly unconscious, though I am still very truly your friend W. Jerdan.[10]

Beyond patience now, Bentley told him, "It is idle to waste any more words on the subject . . . Do you, or do you not intend to cancel the statement to which I so strongly object?" He gave Jerdan until the end of the week, after which "I shall conclude that you refuse and shall be compelled to seek reparation in some other way."[11]

On 15 January Jerdan, perhaps fearful of a law suit, tried once again to protest that he did not understand what had caused Bentley offence:

After so long a period of friendly intercourse I cannot be so discourteous as to allow you to interpret things from my silence. I repeat that what you persist in calling your "distinct and explicit explanation" is beyond my wit to comprehend. If I could discover any error I would do my best to remedy it.[12]

Taking the matter into his own hands, Bentley asked *The Critic* to publish his letter stating that Jerdan's account of the two transactions was grossly incorrect and indiscreet.[13] Naturally, Jerdan rose to defend himself in a letter to *The Critic* of 1 February, protesting that he would never wish to cause Bentley the slightest injury, that at the time he had acted as Bentley's arbiter and would not have sanctioned a "disreputable arbitration" which was then "perfectly satisfactory to all concerned". Forster wrote an unsolicited note of support to Bentley, with Dickens's approval, in which he recalled that at the time of the transaction unresolved matters between Dickens and Bentley had been taken into account when the price for the copyrights was fixed. Bentley asked if he might publish this letter and it duly appeared in *The Critic* of 15 February. The editorial comment preceding it hoped that this would "close the discussion so unfortunately commenced by Mr Jerdan" who had been guilty of a breach of confidence. However, he had not "designedly misrepresented" but had "an imperfect memory of the facts after so long an interval". This did indeed close the publicity *The Critic* gave to Bentley's dudgeon. The consequence of Jerdan's indiscretion was a low point in the often sticky relationship between himself and Bentley, whose name had not appeared in the list of Testimonial subscribers Jerdan included in Volume IV of his *Autobiography*.

Jerdan had also seriously upset Thomas Crofton Croker by printing three letters from Mrs Croker in this Volume. There was nothing in her letters to cause offence, but Jerdan had not asked permission to include them. Croker, whom Jerdan considered a close friend, exploded to Robert Balmanno:

Jerdan is beneath my notice . . . Profligacy – recklessness – debt – coupled
with the most brazen audacity – are melancholy things to see in a man
whose years must make him verge on the grave. Who has deserted his
wife – ruined his son–in–law – swindled the most noble of Charities –
and involved many of his best friends in difficulties.[14] (Balmanno noted:
"The Literary Fund" after the mention of charities, referring to the not-
proven charge of embezzlement in 1840.)

Croker had retired from his official post at the Admiralty in 1850, and just
three months after writing this angry letter about his friend of so many years,
he died aged 56, and was buried in the Brompton Cemetery, an ironic twist to
his assumption that it was the 72-year old Jerdan who was verging on the grave.
Jerdan did not include Croker in his *Leisure Hour* studies of "Men I Have
Known" in 1865 and 1866, although the Irishman had been a prolific writer
and collaborated with Jerdan on the Camden, Percy, Noviomagians and many
other societies. Plainly their rift was never healed, a situation which must have
caused Jerdan some grief. He had second thoughts on the matter and featured
Croker affectionately in a more minor series in the *Leisure Hour* in 1868, entitled 'Characteristic Letters'.

Two poems signed W.J. appeared in *Fraser's Magazine*. In March, *To a Pleasant
Companion* celebrated the birth of a child thirteen years earlier, recalling that

> The smiling sisters did ordain
> That thou someday with jest and whim
> Should rain thy merriment on him
> Whose life, when thou wert born, was pain.

Jerdan seems to have had his son William in mind, who was born in 1841.
Fraser's October 1854 issue printed *Thirty One to Fifteen*, a title with no
apparent relevance to the poem itself, which addresses "Charlie"; the poet's face
is wrinkled, he has resigned hope and urges, "Upward thou must climb Charlie!"
and ends,

> I shall not tread thy battle–field,
> Nor see the blazon on thy shield;
> Take thou the sword I cannot wield,
> And earn the prize I miss, Charlie!
> Earn the prize I miss.
> Be fairer, braver, more admired,
> So win a bride by all desired;
> Just tell her who thy soul inspired
> With dreams of love and bliss, Charlie!
> Dreams of love and bliss.

This "Charlie" would seem to be his son Charles Stuart Jerdan, born in 1838, who eventually sailed to Australia, but returned to settle in England. Jerdan sounded tired, as if he had struggled long enough, but still wanted to be fondly remembered.

In June Jerdan wrote a long and careful review covering two columns of the *Illustrated London News*. This was about Sir Roderick Murchison's *Siluria*, a geological history. On the eve of the review's publication Jerdan wrote to the author to tell him, "Though more removed out of the circle of your remembrance than in past times, I do not forget your friendly courtesies of old; and hope if you see the *Illustrated News* tomorrow, you will not dislike my effort to popularize, as far as the limits allowed, your *momentum ore perennus*."[15] He hinted that he would cherish a copy of the book signed by Murchison. Reviews in the *Illustrated London News* were unsigned, and it is possible that others by Jerdan were published; this one has come to light only because of Jerdan's letter; others may be revealed in due course if an office book is found for the *News*.

Following the failure of Tallis's paper, Jerdan was now engaged on a project outside of his usual activities. Although reminiscent of his *Bank to Barnes* spoof of 1829, this next project was not a spoof but the real thing. He told Grissell, High Sheriff of Surrey, in May,[16] that having just completed his *Main Line S E Rail Manual*,[17] "I have got to Boxhill on the Guildford and Reading Branch" presumably for his next production. He reminded Grissell of his offer to introduce him to the local chaplain, from whom he could glean information on items of interest in the area. Bennoch was to accompany him as 'Assistant'. The project of the Rail Manual was a commission from the South Eastern Railway to write a guide to all the landmarks and neighbourhoods along the train's route from London Bridge to Ashford in Kent; and thence from Ashford along the three different routes available to Margate, Dover and Hastings. Jerdan wrote a detailed and highly informative guide, commencing with a description of the geology on which London Bridge Station was founded, its historic antecedents, and the cost of the present structure, noting that it had been made of iron and masonry to protect it from the fires common in that area. Lines and branches of the South Eastern railway covered in his book were 280 miles long, and employed between two and three thousand people. Jerdan indulged himself in a vivid description of the crowds rushing through the station, observing the differences between passengers who arrive and those who depart:

> The whistle is heard, and the coming train, gradually lessening its speed, approaches its destination. In a few minutes its living freight are all crowded upon the platform, and trunks, boxes, bags, parcels, cases, bundles, and all the paraphernalia of travelling, are dragged from their repositories, and allotted to their owners for further transport by other means and in other vehicles . . .

The departing scene is of a different description and nowhere is the tide in the affairs of men more remarkably illustrated; nowhere does it ebb and flow with greater regularity.... Faster and faster gathers the crowd; hundreds of pedestrians and, from every description of conveyance, descending parties jostling together, eagerly press forward to secure their tickets and to select their carriages. While without the Station walls all is a mixture of chaos and Babylon – the natural consequence of universal individual independence – within all is symmetry and regularity. To each is his place allotted and to each his allotted time.

Details of many sights to be spotted along the route or very nearby were given, noticing especially Beulah Spa near Norwood and the Philanthropic Farm School near Redhill, for which Prince Albert had laid the foundation stone in 1849, and was for the housing of young offenders, so that they could learn agriculture:

Thousands of brands would be plucked from the fire and saved; the criminality of the country would be relieved from contagion and greatly reduced; our colonies would reap an important benefit, and every country in England would find such an economy of expenditure as would show not how doubly but tenfold blessed are the well-conducted works of mercy and charity.

Close to his own personal interests was the Asylum for Idiots being built nearby: "Long considered to be beyond the pale of efficacious succour, the idiot and the imbecile were left to their hapless fate; but since 1847 at Park House, Highgate, and Essex Hall Colchester, chiefly through the arduous exertions of Mr Alderman Wire and the skilful direction of Dr John Conolly, with the co-operation of other zealous philanthropists a special treatment of this affliction has been successfully applied, and many cures been the result. Thus encouraged, the cause is now undertaken on an extensive scale and liberally supported."

Jerdan's guide continued giving, as its subtitle set out, historical, antiquarian and picturesque facts about everything remarkable along the way; engineering details of Folkestone harbour were taken from a report focussing on the "eight splendid steam-vessels" owned by the South Eastern and Continental Steam Packet Company, an offshoot of the Railway Company which had commissioned him to write the Guide. Dover Harbour (which did not belong to the company) was dismissed as it did "not rank high as one of security or refuge". The hotels he recommended at Hastings, however, did belong to the Railway Company, so the guide was a kind of advertorial exercise, but he was extremely thorough in his information and did not hesitate to give his own opinions. St Leonards, for instance, designed by Decimus Burton only twenty-five years previously, "is a gem, a toy, a pretty fancy of a town, and from its charming situation, its sunny serenity of look, its attractive promenades and gardens and its fine pure air of healthful vitality, it looks more like the realization of some romance or some scene in a drama, than an every-day town, such as have sprung out of the congregated wants of a community! *Floreat,* St Leonards!" Jerdan the journalist was in his element, especially as this was a part of the country he knew well, having visited Hastings and its surroundings on many occasions. He skated over Ramsgate, "a petty London transferred to the most beautiful beach of this portion of the coast and adorned with all the means and appliance for the enjoyment of Cockney idleness", and warned travellers about Margate: "Alas! The glory of Margate, like the age of chivalry, is gone. Its grand Square is deserted, and what used to be considered in old warlike cities a dangerous indication, but which in Margate was a grateful sound, namely the footsteps of the stranger, is more unfrequently heard in its streets."

The *Manual* combined Jerdan's broad knowledge of history, archaeology, personalities and so on in an entertaining and informative book of a hundred and eight pages. From his comment to Grissell about the Guildford and Reading Branch he was expecting to produce another, similar book for that line, but no further mention of it occurs, nor has any copy been found. It would seem, from a later letter of Jerdan's, that the first book ran into trouble: "My Railbook is so far settled that it (the 1500 copies) are secured from the rogue who has sacked the advertizement money, to my infinite discomfort, and within 48 hours of delivery; I have however to pay the binding, out of torn pockets."[18] Jerdan was, as so often, most unfortunate and no doubt having to pay for the binding cost almost as much as he earned for the work itself. (In one of those ironic coincidences, the British Library's copy of Jerdan's *Manual* has lost its binding.)

Repeating a pattern that had dogged Jerdan frequently in his life, he was receiving letters from lawyers and writs for five and six thousand pounds. Bennoch had offered financial assistance, but asked Jerdan for a clear statement of his affairs. Jerdan responded irritably:

In answer to your comforting letter of the 6th I stated as explicitly as possible the circumstances which harassed me and by causing expences consumed my efforts and left me in a condition of arrear instead of progress . . . unless I can do something promptly I shall not be torn but scratched to death.[19]

In 1854 Jerdan and Mary added yet another son to their brood. Edward, known as Teddie, was likely to have been born in Maidstone, where, on 12 October, his mother was in a lunatic asylum in Barming Heath. Records of admissions to this asylum have not survived, so the precise dates of her incarceration and the reason for it are now lost. For Jerdan, her illness was a disaster:

there were so many youngsters still at home, although possibly Mary's mother was still living with them and could help, as would the older children. Mary had had a hard life, so many children in quick succession and no security in the later years. She probably suffered from depression, which saw many women sent into asylums. Jerdan did not desert her, and indeed the following year saw the birth of yet another son, Charles Stuart, curiously named the same as their earlier Charles who had gone to Australia and later returned to settle in Devon.

London was again rife with cholera, this outbreak centering around the Broad Street Pump; Bennoch took his family to Scotland for six weeks, and was "well off out of the way of cholera and its concomitant alarms", Jerdan told Fields.[20] In June Jerdan moved his family from Swanscombe to Old Charlton. Their home, St Ann's Cottage in Landsdowne Road, was only a mile or so from their earlier home in Blenheim Villas, next door to Bennoch. From their cottage they heard "waggon-loads of nightingales singing every night up to July".[21] From here Jerdan concentrated on his American ventures, corresponding with Fields in Boston, and on the Letters he had been sending to the Boston *Traveller* and the *Saturday Evening Gazette,* an opportunity arranged by the kindly Fields who thought highly of his abilities. The *Traveller* had been founded in 1825 as a twice-weekly bulletin for stagecoach listings, but twenty years later had become a daily paper. The *Saturday Evening Gazette* had been published by W.W. Clapp since 1851. When Fields, because of ill health, had to postpone a visit to England, Jerdan wrote to tell him:

> I was personally anxious to see you to learn if I had fulfilled the expec-
> tations created by your (I fear too favourable) presentations of my talent
> for Journalism Correspondence. I can only say that I spare no pains to
> acquire information as distinct from our newspapers which are usually
> inaccurate and to render my letters as various as possible. I shall be glad
> to hear how they are liked, and must confess when I meet with some of
> the New York papers and observed their London communications, I am
> rather inclined to think well of my own. I wish I cd obtain other chan-
> nels in the other cities of the Union.[22]

He told Fields in the same letter, "My project of an Edition of ancient Scottish poets of which Mr Ticknor . . . thought so well – my Proverbs with Crowquill's illustrations and other enterprizes of great faith and moment are all paralyzed by your non-appearance."[23]

A month later he had received no reply and wrote anxiously, "By this day's packet my letters to the *Traveller* from April to the last of August will have numbered eighteen, and when agreeable to remember the writer, I shall be well pleased with the honorarium." After chattily giving Fields news of his friends Bennoch and Tupper, Jerdan continued "I want more work to keep me young;

for let me tell you that it is better for an old horse to keep in harness, if not too heavy, than to have alternate pull and play – as the latter gets to preponderate and make the draught (never easy) distasteful."[24] To his evident relief he heard from Fields soon after, in response to which Jerdan thanked him for his letter and told him:

> I am taking great pains with my Boston Letters (as I hope you may see by the result of this day's post to both organs) and I purpose going to Liverpool on the 16th to the British Association for original observation. I am greatly obliged to you for your promise to look out for other channels. From the few New York papers I see, I confess I am proud of my own efforts. In plain truth I often read in my Boston Correspondence, news quite equivalent to the London News of the date of my reception of it. In fact, our Newspapers are darkling, jobbing and ill informed and good sifting as well as authentic sources are required for genuine intelligence.[25]

He felt time passing, and remembering the picnic in a hayfield a couple of years before, exclaimed to Fields, "Well, well, D.V. [Deo volente – God willing], we will do such things together next year – only I am getting older than the "Old Jerdan" of Grace Greenwood and no "More hay!"

Whilst Jerdan had been assiduously writing his 'Letters' to the Boston papers, payment for them had not arrived, as he had already hinted to Fields. In September, Clapp of the *Gazette* advised him that no more letters were required. In October he wrote to Clapp, "I have taken the liberty to draw on you also for seventy dollars, which approaches as near as I can calculate to very nearly the end of my letters at ten dollars each and posterior to the remittance of ten pounds for which I had to thank you some months ago."[26] This would amount to a total of twenty-four pounds for his *Gazette* 'Letters'. As far as he knew at this stage, he was still supplying the *Traveller* with material, but this was about to change as his American connection proved ultimately unsuccessful. His two most supportive friends corresponded about him; Fields wrote to Bennoch in December:

> I am sorry that the Boston papers do not wish to keep Mr Jerdan any longer in their pay. I tried every way to have him retained but it was of no avail. I also tried the other papers but without success. This grieves me, for dear old William is my admiration and I wish to show him how much I regard him. I do not think I have answered his last letter for I hate always to chronicle bad news.[27]

Fields had just married, and hoped to bring his bride to England in the

Spring. He had the warmest regard for Bennoch, who was so supportive of his less fortunate friends, including Jerdan: "Dear Bennoch, I often think of how your kind heart must throb with gladness at the thought of relief you have in so many ways bestowed among your less happy friends. Poor Haydon! and Jerdan! And Miss M[itford]! Ah, it was a bright day when FB saw the daylight."

Jerdan would certainly have agreed with Fields about that. Of all his many hundreds of acquaintance and friends over the years Jerdan's closest confidant was Francis Bennoch, some thirty years his junior, but a man he deeply respected both for his literary and business achievements, and also for his highly princi-pled, respectable way of life. Bennoch was popular with the Jerdan children, too: "As my boy Henry said one day, 'I wish Mr Bennoch was in danger in the river drowning (how kind?) and I could rush in and extricate him!' Not so ungrateful though not so convenient a wish!" Jerdan wrote to Bennoch.[28] Jerdan's heart was heavy at this time as Mary Maxwell's mental illness took its toll on the family. In that same letter to Bennoch, Jerdan confessed, "My poor invalid is a sad trial for us all and I get more and more terrified at the want of employment as we cannot make shifts so economically with her, as we managed to do before, and the boys from school is another heavy grief."

With so much on his mind, Jerdan was vastly relieved to receive an offer which he hastened to tell Bennoch:

> A ship owner . . . having offered to take one of my boys to try how he likes the sea, Henry has accepted the chance and will be received on board the Ralph Waller, 1500 tons bound from Liverpool to Australia and India. This has come very suddenly upon me, and there are only four or five days to provide everything before the ship sails.[29]

He was "clean drained" and needed Bennoch's help to negotiate a draft from Boston to outfit Henry for his new life. "[Henry] is the first of the lads to go and others must speedily follow . . . I hope Henry may be as fortunate as my last two exports – for Stuart is going on prosperously in Trinidad and his sister Ella so well married in Melbourne as to be able to send him £50 to clear off early settling scores. These are loads off [my] mind." Stuart, that is Fred Stuart, Landon's son now aged twenty-eight and Ella, Landon's eldest daughter aged thirty-two, were thus known, at least by name, to Bennoch, the only surviving indication that Jerdan had acknowledged them as his own children.

Fred Stuart had not followed his sister Ella to Australia but went instead to Trinidad. Only one letter from him survives in the family's possession; this was written to Ella from Port of Spain, calling her "My own dearly loved Nelly" and signed "Your affectionate loving brother". The long letter is undated, but thanked Ella for her Christmas gift, possibly the fifty pounds that Jerdan mentioned. From his letter it is plain that Fred was not "going on prosperously" as Jerdan had said but was in despair, "penniless and homeless" and recovering from a severe illness, "bad West Indian fever". Following in his (probable) father's footsteps, Fred told his sister that he had been asked to edit one of Trinidad's newspapers, and would accept as he was in need of cash. He noted that Ella's letter had come to him enclosed in a "short cold note" from Laura, their sister in London, "the first she has favoured me with since I left England – tho' the very last words she spoke to me the night before my departure was a most solemn promise to write regularly and freely . . . ". Why Laura should be "cold" to her brother is not known, unless she was afraid of his importuning her for funds.

Fred mentioned that his only correspondent from home had been "poor dear Uncle", whose constant theme was to wonder what had become of "dear Nelly . . . poor girl, hard has been her lot thro' life". It is just possible that the term "Uncle" was a euphemism for his father, but as Jerdan knew what had become of Ella, and that she had done well for herself, it is more likely that the term referred to Fred's real uncle, Landon's brother Whittington, indicating that he was party to the existence of the secret children. This raises the question of whether Landon had told him at the time of the children's births, or possibly had kept her secret until she married Maclean and left for Africa, needing someone she trusted to watch over them as they became adults. Whenever Whittington knew of his illegitimate nieces and nephew, it would have been especially difficult for him, as a clergyman from a family of churchmen, to accept. The language of Fred's letter suggests that he was well educated, "a mist of that precious salve for wounded vanity", "so many thousand miles of that envious briny ocean between us"; it seems therefore that Landon and maybe Jerdan, had taken care to place their children in homes where they would be well brought up. The only other known document surviving from Fred Stuart's life is a photograph sent to Ella, of a little girl about two years old, taken in a photographic studio in Port of Spain Trinidad. It is undated, and marked on the reverse "Emily Ella Stuart" (see illustration no. 7). Family lore is that Fred married the daughter of a Governor of Trinidad; he may indeed have done so, but no evidence to support this claim has yet come to light, and it could be another of those myths that Ella, through her granddaughter Ethel, handed down to their descendants to validate the family line.

Perhaps as a consequence of his stress over money, losing both his American columns, the cost of binding the *Rail Manual*, and Mary's mental troubles, Jerdan became ill. Writing to his constant friend Bennoch he confided:

> Few friends, my dear Bennoch, will be more concerned than yourself (for I have found you a good and true one) to learn that I have had a great warning, in a partial attack of paralysis. It has been confined to my right leg which was suddenly struck on Sunday noon on the shore at Hastings. I got immediate medical aid and was doctored in the Hotel room where you slept at our last visit! Yesterday I was able to come to town and say

(sic) Dr Copland who prescribed and the Pres. Coll. Phys. Dr Paris accidentally, who approved. Today I feel more power and the numbness going
off though the circulation is but imperfectly restored.

I must work on and do my best to 'die with harness on my back'. Long
weakness and helplessness would be a sad business. Do you know that I
have wondered how even my hearty and sanguine temperament could
resist the cares and anxieties with which I have been oppressed. But no
spirits can last for ever.[30]

Although Fields had been reluctant to inform Jerdan that the Boston papers
did not wish to continue with his Letters, Jerdan had already heard from
Worthington and Flanders, publishers of the *Traveller*, that "We are compelled to
discontinue our London Correspondence from this date. Will you do us the
favour to send your bill and draft for the amount due to you . . . "[31] He wrote
at once to his benefactor in Boston,

I have received a sad shock today by the countermand of the *Traveller*
correspondence on which I have been bestowing such great pains that I
absolutely flattered myself it was unique. I am sure no journal in America
obtained such authentic and early political information – and if you read
the paper I think you will observe much of interest in literary and other
matters. There is however no help for it and I shall feel the vacuum
severely. Mr Clapp Jnr has not redeemed his credit, which I am very sorry
for. I rely on the *Traveller's* remittance, 180 dollars by the earliest mail – as
"Times is hard". If you can throw anything else in my way, it will essentially serve me, I say no more.[32]

Others were feeling economic pressures too, even Bennoch who was
spending more time in Manchester, and had joined the Nightingale Fund
committee, to send nurses to the Crimea.[33] "Our hilarity is much checked,"
Jerdan told Fields. "Indeed, we are very grave." He had not received his payment
by mid-March, when he again begged Fields to intercede on his behalf, reiterating his disappointment at the cessation of his Letters and how hard he had
worked on them. Vital as the money was, it was not the only thing that worried
Jerdan. "I should be very glad of any other literary employment, as having little
to do is my bane – relaxing my mind and collapsing my purse."[34] He was forced
to follow up again on 30 March, as he had still not received payment.

A task much nearer to Jerdan's heart came along in 1855. Charles Rogers
was preparing a six-volume work, to be published in Edinburgh, on *The Modern
Scottish Minstrel, or The Songs of Scotland of the Past Half Century*. Jerdan was asked
to make a contribution in two respects. The first was to provide a biography of
his highly-esteemed friend Francis Bennoch, fifteen of whose songs or poems

were featured in the volume. Jerdan's account of Bennoch's life ran over several pages, concentrating largely on his poetic achievements, from youth to the present, giving examples especially of his songs to Margaret his wife. Jerdan spoke admiringly of Bennoch's ability to combine his literary talent with the daily life of business; he pointed to the assistance Bennoch gave "poor Haydon", who had "never applied in vain". Had Bennoch not been abroad at the time, Jerdan suggested, Haydon would not have committed suicide. His help to Mary Russell Mitford was also mentioned, and Bennoch's membership of the Society of Arts, Royal Society of Antiquaries, Royal Society of Literature and the Scottish Literary Institute were noted. Jerdan's warm regard for Bennoch is evident throughout this biography, which also noted that he was fortunate in his wife, "a woman whom a poet may love and a wise man consult; in whom the sociable gentleman finds an ever cheerful companion, and the husband a loving and devoted friend". How different, Jerdan could not have helped thinking, from his own "wife" shut away in the lunatic asylum in Maidstone.

Jerdan's other contributions to *The Modern Scottish Minstrel* were two songs or verses of his own; *What Makes This Hour?* is a short, sad dirge that his love had not kept her tryst, so that an hour seems like a day. The second, *The wee bird's song*, was annotated, 'Here first published'. The very title echoes that phrase that Jerdan used repeatedly about Landon, "We love the bird we taught to sing". The speaker in this poem is female, listening in her chamber to the bird's song:

> And I had long been pining,
> For my Willie far away –
> When I heard the wee bird singing.

Her lover is nearby and hears the song too, and they are joyfully reunited:

> The true bells had been ringing,
> And Willie was my own.
> And oft I tell him, jesting, playing,
> I knew what the wee bird was saying,
> That morn, when he, no longer straying,
> Flew back to me alone,
> And we love the wee bird singing.

Was "Willie" himself harking back to the days with Landon, when he and she were often straying, and fruitlessly wishing that life had turned out differently for them both?

Looking back was inevitable in these days of enforced idleness, and Jerdan used his time to send a second contribution to *Notes & Queries*, reminded by a republication of the 'Noctes' from *Blackwood's Magazine*. This was a letter he had received from Thomas Pringle between 1820–25, (a some time editor of *Friendship's Offering*), whom John Wilson had asked to be his literary agent in London, which he declined. He mentioned that Wilson's claim of Hogg being the 'main projector' for Blackwoods was incorrect as he himself had been the instigator. Jerdan made no comment on the content of the letter, leaving it to speak for itself. It was to be eleven years before he again appeared in *Notes & Queries*, but not under his own name.

Known for his concern about the welfare and remuneration of writers, Jerdan's charity extended further afield when, in July 1855, he originated the "Pensioners Employment Society", from which arose the still extant Corps of Commissionaires. S. C. Hall, no admirer of Jerdan because of his bibulous and other habits, disclosed the venture in his *Retrospect of a Long Life*. Jerdan's aim for this society was to find employment for wounded soldiers returning from the Crimea. Several people lent their names to the project, but did nothing further; Hall remarked that of the fifteen members, ten did not attend a single meeting, and that the brunt of the work fell upon himself and a W.E.D. Cumming. "It was no wonder that things went wrong", Hall wrote. "Mr Jerdan was called upon to retire from the position he held as 'Registrar and Honorary Secretary', a very few weeks after his appointment to it, and in the then working secretary no confidence was placed." However, a letter from Jerdan survives, dated 14 January 1856, on the blue notepaper of the "Army and Navy Pension Employment Society", at 22 Parliament Street.[35] The Society was still going strong in 1882 when Hall penned his *Retrospect*; it was then under the guidance of a Captain Walter, and offered employment to large numbers of needy soldiers. Hall did not elaborate on why Jerdan was ousted from his honorary position, but whatever the reason, Hall openly credited Jerdan with the idea and the energy to start the organisation to help the soldiers.

23

Poverty in Old Age

In 1856 a book was published in Philadelphia which referred to Jerdan's wife, the single clue which has led to her identification. The book was by Charles Lanman, entitled *Adventures in the Wilds of the United States and British American Provinces*. In New Brunswick, now Canada, Lanman had come across Robert Eggar, brother of Jerdan's wife Frances, six years her junior. Eggar "claimed a good name for his family", and told how he had come to New Brunswick in 1809 at the age of twenty-two. He was a government agent, transacting business in the fur trade. His claim to fame was his sister's marriage to William Jerdan. Lanman was clearly impressed with Eggar, dubbing him 'The Hermit of Aroostook' and recalling his meeting in a further book, *Haphazard Personalities*, published in Boston in 1886. The timing of this unexpected revelation of Frances's identity coincided almost exactly with news of her death.

Frances and her daughter Elizabeth had moved some years earlier to Bentley in Hampshire, but she became ill with digestive problems and then contracted a chronic gastroenteritis, from which she died at 6 Albert Cottages, Stoke Field, Guildford on 23 February 1856. She was seventy-six and her death certificate noted her as "wife of William Jerdan, Gentleman". Her death was mentioned in the *Gentleman's Magazine* and in the *Leader*. The notation of "wife" (taken together with Robert Eggar's claim to be Jerdan's brother-in-law, although no marriage certificate has been found), indicates that they were still legally married, or at least accepted as such, so that it would not have been possible for Jerdan to have married Mary Maxwell before this time, unless bigamously, for which there is no evidence. There is also no evidence that he married Mary subsequently, although on the majority of her children's birth certificates she is called "Jerdan". After her mother's death, Elizabeth Hall Dare Jerdan, now aged thirty-six, had to earn her own living and, like so many single middle-class women of the times, became a governess,

Her older brother, William Freeling, had worked with his father for many years, as an assistant on the *Literary Gazette*. His health had suffered from the constant strain of Jerdan's acute poverty and the demands of his father's large family, as well as his own cramped living conditions in Southwark. In 1856 he was listed as a Supplementary Clerk in the Post Office at St. Martins-le-Grand, in the office of the Secretary Rowland Hill. On 17 May 1856, aged 40, he took the unusual step of writing to Puttick & Simpson, leading auctioneers of music and art, enclosing a batch of autograph letters for safekeeping until the death of the authors and in the event of his own death.[1] Many "literary autographs" appeared in the auctioneers' catalogue of April 4 1860, including some addressed to Jerdan. This sale was after William Freeling's death, and the letters were very probably those he sent to them at this time.

These letters caused some problems for Jerdan, who had mentioned them to Bennoch, and the matter became generally known to some of their authors. "With regard to the autographs you may justify me and satisfy our fussy friends," Jerdan told Bennoch indignantly:

> There is not a letter of Wrights (tho' I have many which we wd not like published at the Cross) such as loans to him when pushed and very free opinions of mutual <u>friends</u> – of Tuppers, there are two or three mere notes with his signature – and indeed such is the character of all I have sent of any living writer and therefore there can be no offence.
>
> Mackay's "wrath" I might deem unseemly. Does he imagine I wd make public his letters of everlasting gratitude to me for procuring him aid from the L. Fund when he required it? Surely there are of those who censure me not a few who might well be afraid of my letting the world see what returns I have had for most essential services. But let that pass. Only it is dangerous to provoke, instead of striving to serve an Old Friend whose friendship has been of so much value, as mine has been to <u>These</u>.[2]

Jerdan had found letters of his own catalogued for sale; he insisted that he had no idea how they had been obtained and that he had known nothing about them. "I went on the day previous, looked over the lots, and retired every letter of a nature to be deemed private," he informed Bennoch. The whole affair had stung him to the quick: "Let any enemy of mine meet me face to face and allow fair play for explanation, and if they can convict me of an act unbecoming for a gentleman and man of honour, I will trouble not one friend any more." Destitute as he was, he would not stoop so low as to try and make money on letters from friends, or from any correspondence he had received over his long career – at least until their authors were dead.

Jerdan and Bennoch had paid a courtesy visit to Nathaniel Hawthorne, the American novelist, when he first came to England in 1853 as Consul, settling in Liverpool. At the time Hawthorne had wondered about Jerdan, "What there was in so uncouth an individual to get him so freely into polished society."[3] Hawthorne and Bennoch had stayed in touch, perhaps because of mutual liking or because of trading arrangements. (Bennoch, Twentyman and Rigg's wholesale silk company had been formed ten years earlier.) Hawthorne certainly had a soft spot for Bennoch, writing of him, although anonymously in *Our Old Home* as "the man to whom I owed most in England, the warm benignity of whose nature was never weary of doing me good".[4] On 22 March 1856 Hawthorne travelled to London, complaining of the usual dull and monotonous journey. It was Good Friday, so the streets "had on their Sunday aspect. If it were not for the human life and bustle of London, it would be a very stupid place, with a heavy and dreary monotony of unpicturesque streets."[5] Already in this grumpy mood, and made more weary by a walk in the drizzle, Hawthorne took himself out again after lunch to Wood Street in the City to visit Bennoch's place of business. Hawthorne enjoyed his friend's bluff, kindly manner and after discussing matters of mutual interest, enquired after Jerdan.

At this point in Hawthorne's journal, his record is strangely at odds with what is known about the relationship between Jerdan and Bennoch, coloured perhaps by his depressed and damp state at the time. Concerning Jerdan, Hawthorne noted:

Mr Bennoch spoke of him as a very disreputable old fellow, who had spent all his life in dissipation, and has not left it off even now in his old age. I do not see how such a man has attained vogue in society, as he certainly did; for he had no remarkable gifts, more than scores of other literary men, and his manners had, to my taste, no charm. Yet he had contrived to live amongst and upon whatever is exquisite in society, and in festivity, and had seduced (according to Bennoch's statement) innumerable women, and had an infinity of illegitimate children, besides an unconscionable number born in wedlock, of more than one wife. I asked Bennoch whether he supposed that there was any truth in the scandalous rumors in reference to Jerdan and L.E.L. He replied that he did not think that they were true to the utmost extent, although he conceived that there had been great freedom, and even licentiousness, of intercourse between her and Jerdan – great looseness of behaviour – only falling short of the one ultimate result. He said that Jerdan had assured him, on his honour, that L.E.L. had never yielded her virtue to him; and Bennoch thought he would not have denied it, had the case been otherwise. But, in short, the impression on my mind about Jerdan is, that he is a good-for-nothing old wretch, always disreputable, and now drunken and rowdyish on the edge of the grave. He is shameless even in begetting legitimate children; being now much above seventy, and his youngest child only about three years old.

Hawthorne himself had the reputation of a highly moralistic man; this account has a ring of Bennoch attempting to tell his visitor what he thought he wanted to hear, rather than disclosing the close nature of his friendship with, and boundless generosity to, Jerdan. Bennoch was on good terms with Jerdan's children by Mary Maxwell and, if recent family information is correct, Ella Stuart, Landon's daughter, came to stay with them at least once, so that Bennoch would have known that she was Jerdan's daughter, in contradiction of his assurances to Hawthorne.

Hawthorne's social rounds in London included many of Jerdan's own acquaintance, including Samuel Carter Hall whose effusiveness Hawthorne found overwhelming. Hall however, found Hawthorne "one of the most lovable of men", of "painful shyness in general society".[6] On 10 July Hawthorne sat through a long dinner party and then met Bennoch, travelled back by train and cab to Blackheath. Next day the Bennochs left for a continental journey and wishing to relax, Hawthorne happened to pick up Volume IV of Jerdan's *Autobiography*. He was dozing over it, "(wretched twaddle, though it records such constant and apparently intimate intercourse with distinguished people)", when Jerdan himself was announced. Remembering his earlier opinion of the "uncouth individual", Hawthorne's vivid but sympathetic portrait of Jerdan now reflected the parlous state his visitor was in at the time:

> He now looks rougher than ever; time-worn but not reverend; a thatch of grey hair on his head; an imperfect set of false teeth; a careless apparel, checked trowsers, and a stick; for he had walked a mile or two, from his own dwelling. I suspect (and long practice at the Consulate has made me keen-sighted) that Mr Jerdan contemplates some benefit from my purse; and, to the extent of a sovereign or so, I would not mind contributing to his comfort. He spoke of a secret purpose of Bennoch and himself to obtain me a degree or diploma in some Literary Institution – what one, I know not, and did not ask; but the honour cannot be a high one, if this poor old fellow can do aught towards it. I am afraid he is a very disreputable senior, but certainly not the less to be pitied on that account; and there was something very touching in his stiff and infirm movement, as he resumed his stick and took leave, waving me a courteous farewell, and turning upon me a smile grim with age, as he went down the steps. In that gesture and smile I fancied some trace of the polished man of society, such as he may have been once; though time and hard weather have roughened him.[7]

Hawthorne was writing in the middle of the Victorian period, and perhaps needed some grit in the oyster of his generally positive report on England for his American readers – a touch of the disreputable to spice his journal. During this same period Jerdan paid a call on Hawthorne at his home, recalled in great detail by Hawthorne's son Julian, half a century later, a portrait of Jerdan more vivid and evocative than any which his contemporaries have furnished:

One Sunday forenoon . . . we descried an old gentleman approaching up the winding street. As he drew nearer he presented rather a shabby, or at least, rusty appearance. His felt hat was not so black as it had been; his coat was creased and soiled; his boots needed a blacking. He swung a cane as he stumped along, and there was a sort of faded smartness in his bearing, and a knowingness in his grim old visage, indicating some incongruous familiarity with the manners of the great world. He came to a halt in front of the house, and, after quizzing it for a moment, went up the steps and beat a fashionable tattoo with the knocker.

Summoned in-doors soon afterwards, we found this questionable personage sitting in the drawing-room. His voice was husky, but modulated to the inflections of polite breeding; he used a good many small gestures, and grinned often, revealing the yellow remains of his ancient teeth; he laughed, too, with a hoarse sound in his throat. There was about him an air of determined cheerfulness and affability, though between the efforts the light died down in his wrinkled old eyes and the lines of his face sagged and deepened. He offered to kiss my sisters, but they drew back; he took my hand in his own large, dry one with its ragged nails and swollen joints. At length he inveigled my younger sister to his knee, where she sat gazing unflinchingly and solemnly into him with that persistence which characterizes little girls of four or five who are not quite sure of their ground. Her smooth, pink-and-white cheeks and unwinking eyes contrasted vividly with his seamed yellowness and blinking grin; for a long time he coquetted at her, and played peep-bo, without disturbing her gravity, making humorous side comments to the on-lookers meanwhile. There was a ragged and disorderly mop of gray hair on his head, which showed very dingy beside the clear auburn of the child's. One felt a repulsion from him, and yet, as he chatted and smirked and acted, there was a sort of fascination in him, too. Some original force and fire of nature still glowed and flickered in his old carcass; something human stirred dimly under the crust of self-consciousness and artificiality. Rose's adamantine seriousness finally relaxed in a faint smile, upon which he threw up his hands, emitted a hoarse cackle of triumph, and exclaimed, "There – there it is! I knew I'd get it; she loves me – she loves me!" He then permitted her to slip down from his knee and withdraw to her mother, and resumed the talk which our entrance had interrupted. It was chiefly about people of whom we youngsters knew nothing . . . he had the nobility and gentry at his finger-ends; he was privileged, petted, and sought after everywhere; if there were any august door we wished to enter, any high-placed personage we desired to approach, any difficult service we wanted rendered, he was the man to help us to our object. Who, then, was he? He has long been utterly forgotten; but he was well known, or notorious, during the first half of the last century; he was such a character as could flourish only in England. His name was William Jerdan; he was born in 1785, and was now, therefore, about seventy years old. He had started in life poor, with no family distinction, but with some more or less useful connections either on the father's or the mother's side. He had somehow got an English education, and he had pursued his career on the basis of his native wits, his indomitable effrontery and persistence, his faculty of familiarity, his indifference to rebuffs, his lack of shame, conscience, and morality. How he found the means to live nobody could tell, but he uniformly lived well and had enjoyed the good things of the world . . . Now, however, in his age, he was wellnigh at the end of his tether; what we should call his "pull" was losing its efficiency; he was lapsing to the condition where he would offer to introduce a man to the Prince of Wales or to Baron Rothschild, and then ask him for the loan of five pounds – or half a crown, as the case might be. He was a character for Thackeray. He haunted my father for a year or two more, and then vanished I know not where.[8]

At this point, Jerdan had absolutely no work at all, no income besides his pension and no expectations. His debts were necessarily mounting daily and he was unable to keep his promise to repay any of Bennoch's loans, or those of his partner Mr Riggs. In yet another heart-rending letter to his benefactor he begged Bennoch, "Cannot you hear of some place [for the older boys], however moderate and humble? As for my own exertions I wish I were a Copying Clerk rather than endure the strange chances of a job here and there . . . I am as much distressed as a human being can be by sheer misfortune."[9] As ever, Jerdan was in denial that his misfortunes were any of his own making, and his failure to save anything from the considerable sums he had earned in the past was somehow not his fault. He must have sorely tried Bennoch's patience, just as he had formerly caused Macready to withhold any more 'loans' that were in reality gifts.

Three weeks later Jerdan was again telling his friend, "My boys hang on hand and I can procure no regular pen-work, and the load on my back increases in weight as I grow the weaker to sustain it. But hence to useless complaining. The bed is made and I only wish it were deeper and quieter."[10] Having got his troubles off his chest he brightened up, enclosing a book written by a Glasgow merchant as a consequence of Jerdan's *Plan of Polity and Finance* in 1827; he asked Bennoch to glance at it, so that they could compare their opinions. To assist Bennoch Jerdan also enclosed the only copy he could find of the essays which he and John Trotter had published at the time of their financial Plan. (Three months later Bennoch had still not responded to this request, and Jerdan was being harassed by the Glasgow merchant.) As soon as Jerdan had something outside of his own troubles to think about, his old ebullient self was reasserted.

"What do you think of the Wallace Night move in Scotland?", he asked his compatriot. "Should London reflect the patriotic idea?"

The 'patriotic idea" was for a memorial to William Wallace, the Scottish patriot who had died in 1305. Jerdan had been asked for his opinion about fundraising and advised his correspondent (unnamed, but probably Charles Rogers, editor of *The Modern Scottish Minstrel*),

> I am all for a National, chiefly Scottish Dinner, at the London Tavern, with Lord Elgin, Lord Eglinton and other distinguished men at the head of it (vide my list for Burns in 1816); and I have no fear of raising a Fund of more than you want for the Monument and a surplus for some patriotic purpose to keep the maker annually, constantly, in the Country's memory. Command my best sources if they can be of use in promoting the design.[11]

With this letter he enclosed a collection of his "versifying published and unpublished" and noted that *The Wee Bird's Song* was his favourite. He especially requested that his papers be returned, "the sooner the better, as I was born in 1782 – and hardly expect to see 1882 as an Anniversary." Two months later he told Rogers that he had called at the office of his London Secretary and offered his help, mentioning the prominent part he had played in the Burns and Ettrick Shepherd festivals. Jerdan strongly supported the idea of a Dinner at the London Tavern (when did he not?), and thought "some hundreds of pounds" could be raised.[12] "The mere revival of the National feeling in the British Capital, every now and then, is an excellent object – nutriment to Scottish brotherhood, good feelings and charities." The old convivial Jerdan had not completely disappeared under the crushing weight of penury and "no pen-work", and he would have been flattered that his opinion and assistance were still thought, in some quarters, to be useful.

In *Notes & Queries* of September 1856 an H. G. Davis suggested that Jerdan could write "a most interesting paper" on his recollections of the area of Cromwell House where he used to live and where he had dug up "statues and other pieces of sculpture". He believed Cromwell had occupied Cromwell House and if not the Protector himself, then Chief Justice Hale. However, Jerdan did not publish any such history in *Notes & Queries*; he needed to spend his writing time to make money, interested as he would have been in such a project. It has been suggested[13] that he may have done a little work as a publisher's reader, evidenced by a letter reporting on the manuscript of a novel, "praising character and dialogue, objecting to a lack of variety from chapter to chapter", but his addressee is not named, so the evidence is slight.

In the autumn Jerdan was once again unwell, and confined to bed. The faithful Bennoch referred him to a Dr Thomson for a consultation.[14] By suggesting that Jerdan consult a particular doctor, Bennoch may have been indicating that he would meet the Doctor's fees. (This was not the Dr Thomson who had treated Landon, as he had died in 1849.)

Jerdan was in constant financial straits. On recovering from his illness he acknowledged Bennoch's advice that 'Gentlemen in difficulties' consult with friends, and asked him, "I have some pictures, curious and of value, if I could avail myself of such property to tide over the year. Can you advise or promote this object and essentially benefit . . . W. Jerdan."[15] Times were hard, when he was forced into selling his personal possessions. Yet again, he reflected Leigh Hunt's enforced selling of his precious books to keep his family fed, back in 1834; Hunt however was later able to re-purchase them, although after Hunt's death his son Thornton disposed of his father's library of two thousand books, mainly to J. T. Fields in Boston.

By November Jerdan was desperate enough to forget about being a "Gentleman in difficulties", and wrote from his heart to Messrs. Cook, whose writ made him fear imprisonment. Mustering all his skills of eloquence he pleaded to be released from his debt:

Gentlemen,

I am advised by friends who also know you well to make a final appeal to your humanity to stop a proceeding against my person which must either make me a fugitive or a prisoner for life. My viability to meet your claim has been rendered more and more afflicting by unfortunate circumstances and a vain struggle to regain the means I had when I contracted the debt and which were swept away through no fault of mine, from employments both in America and London.

Thus reduced I have had to subsist on very precarious and inadequate resources, to support in the humblest way a family of eleven children, unhappily deprived of a Mother's care by the heaviest calamity that can befal a living soul – the loss of reason, and consequent charge in a lunatic asylum.

I am blamed, Gentlemen, for contracting this debt as if at the time I had no reasonable prospect of paying it, but such is not the case, and it may also be remembered in my favour that I used the best of my literary efforts and connections with the American and Australian press to be of service to your great concerns.

But I urge no merits. I can only now throw myself, in old age, and sinking under other miseries, upon your merciful consideration. To destroy me utterly beyond a hope in this world, and with me (. . .) on helpless offspring, would surely be a punishment more cruel than any offence I have given you ought to provoke in Christian breasts, taught to pray to God to forgive them as they forgive others.

In inexpressible distress I therefore once more appeal to you. In a letter to Mr Jones I have a reference to Mr Bennoch as cognizant of my situation and I go no farther than to state that while he censures the manner of my having contracted this debt he affords me some relief by expressing his opinion that in so sad a case such a House as yours will not proceed to extremities against me.[16]

Three weeks later, in a dazed confusion, he asked Bennoch,

Did I understand you to say, yesterday, that Messrs Cook had withdrawn their proceedings? It was not merely Mr. Ald. W's presence which confused me, but just before you came up, I am sorry to say me head gave me a stagger and nearly a fall on the floor with the Paper in my hand. It arose, I think, from stooping over it, but these sensations are significant. Thanks for the good and merciful help – I cannot describe the benefit – only once more perhaps and then wait the falling due. Pray say about Messrs. C.[17]

Bennoch was to come to his aid yet again at Christmas, by giving young Henry, now aged 19, a trial for a position in his company. "I cannot say how thankful I am to you for the great service you have done to Henry and to us all. It is a fair and most welcome opening and I trust he will acquit himself so as to do credit to his friends. Mr F. thought him not strong, from his pale looks, but he is perfectly healthy and with regular meals and habits will soon show better. Of late we have been strangely un-provisioned, and suffered a good deal more than I shd like the world to know."[18] His other son, Charles, was to start work at Mr Penn's and Jerdan asked Bennoch to advance him some funds to set up both his boys appropriately.

For a short time Jerdan's letters carried the address of 16 Park Walk, West Brompton, but this was a temporary measure, and he was shortly to make a move to his final home.

After a desperate year in which he had virtually no work at all, Jerdan would have been relieved to find Dickens amenable to a contribution or two to *Household Words*. His first article, "The Gift of Tongues", earned him two guineas, in line with Dickens's normal payment of one guinea for a two-column page.[19] Unlike his many contributions to Bentley's *Miscellany*, Jerdan's articles for *Household Words* were not fiction. Being now quite free from regular editorial duties he had more time than he would have liked to write up these essays, and to a certain extent they are an outlet for the opinions and knowledge he had amassed.

The first such essay published in *Household Words* of 10 January 1857 is a heartfelt and reasoned argument for the practical necessity of teaching eastern languages in England. Jerdan noted that the recent war had brought western armies into contact with a Babel of tongues, including Persian, Croatian, Bulgarian and many others including, of course, Russian. He asks, "Who was so much at a loss for the gift of tongues as the Englishman? Who was so little as the Russians?" Using agents and interpreters to acquire supplies, he argued, left the English open to double-dealing; their inability to converse with prisoners lost opportunities to obtain useful information. Russian officers, on the other hand, always spoke French and English and often other languages such as Polish and Cossack tongues.

Jerdan noted that Sir Charles Trevelyan[20] commissioned assistance from Professor Max Müller, a 'philosophical linguist' which, although too late to be useful in the war, highlighted faults in the English educational system. This was said to demand very little thought and deliberation from pupils, and concentrated on training the mind by mathematics especially Euclid. This, Jerdan (and Müller) believed, "excludes all human interest from calculation, and every accident that could bring judgment and discretion into play". Mathematics had a definite place in education, but the study of living language is a better way of teaching boys to think. The "mere study" of words assists the development of reason.

From this theoretical position, Jerdan described Müller's attempts to illustrate the practical benefits of the proposal. He took common military terms, to "see how much thought is suggested by them". One example serves to explain this process: "Caballus, a cart-horse rather than a charger, gives us not only cavalry and a horseman, but a chevalier; and we must needs take the terrible cannon from canna, a cane or hollow tube. Musket (French, mousequet; Italian, moschetto) was the name of a sparrow-hawk, stood godfather to the German terzerol, a small pistol." Other terms given similar treatment included infantry, soldier, corporal and marshal. Müller's rationale was that each word has a story to tell, changing in form and meaning, becoming exalted or lowly according to the times. The huge diversity of languages in a small geographical region around the Black and Caspian Seas and the Danube, formed an obstacle for inhabitants wishing to resist Russian occupation as they had no common form of communication. Russia, in contrast, used the Cyrillic alphabet, "one of the greatest barriers between that empire and the intellectual world of Europe". Moreover, Russian officers were taught many languages, including Arabic, Tartaric and Tscherkessian (Circassian).

The essay made a plea for English statesmen to follow this example and establish language schools in tongues that related to England's great Asiatic and Indian interests. From Sanskrit to Chinese and Indian dialects, Englishmen who transact the business of empire should be able to speak these languages. St Petersburg boasted a chair for every branch of oriental literature, the French Academy's members represented every department of eastern philology; Vienna, Denmark

and Prussia encouraged oriental scholars and used them as consuls and interpreters. English universities, especially Oxford and Cambridge, should remove
difficulties for oriental scholars, award them honours and scholarships and
increase the number of oriental professorships. Other universities would follow
suit once they saw the benefit. As a parting thrust, to underline the paucity of
England's openness to oriental languages, Jerdan pointed out that in all of
England there was not a supply of oriental type to print Professor Müller's essay.
This had to be undertaken in Leipzig.[21]

The two guineas he received for this article did not begin to meet his
commitments and he still fretted about his boys. Henry's trial month with a
company recommended by Bennoch, was coming to an end; Charles was about
to start work in Mr Penn's factory, and Jerdan explained to Bennoch that he was
forced to beg for an advance (presumably on his pension) of seven pounds, as
the boys' needs had straitened his resources. He had still not been told officially
whether Cooks had withdrawn proceedings against him, and still suffered
"painful apprehensions" on that account. Now that the two older boys had some
employment Jerdan turned his attention to the rest of his family. "The young
ones are in dismal lodging and I am most anxious to flee away with them and
be at rest in some retired spot suited to our reduced circumstances. Charles and
Henry being off my hands may make the move possible", he told Bennoch.[22]
Jerdan's head had been troubling him and he felt himself confused at times, his
memory failing. Young Henry had seemingly satisfied his employers, and entered
upon a formal apprenticeship. Jerdan wrote happily to Bennoch:

> The first wish expressed by Henry after signing his indentures was to
> come across and thank you, with which I was much pleased as it showed
> a right disposition which I trust will continue with him, so that he may
> be a credit to your recommendation and 'conduct himself' (as on his trial)
> to his Master's 'entire satisfaction.'[23]

Jerdan was proud of his son's instincts, and knew that of all his children, Henry
was the one who most admired Bennoch, and a few years earlier was the one
who had dreamed of saving his benefactor from drowning.

Whilst he did his best to provide for these sons of his and Mary Maxwell's,
he received the worst news about his son with Frances, George Canning. On
26 February 1857 George died in Calcutta, aged only 39. His two-line obituary
in the *Gentleman's Magazine* said that "He was for several years connected with
the *Calcutta Englishman* newspaper", another of Jerdan's offspring who were
connected with the Press. It is unknown whether he married or left any issue.

In the dark days of the previous year Jerdan had been forced to pawn some
of his possessions, and they were now due to be redeemed or lost. "Some of
them were once left with Mrs. B." he reminded Bennoch, "and I think were

liked for her table. They are of much more value than what would redeem them . . . I should never need them again and from five to ten pounds would recover (I imagine) what could not be purchased for thrice the amount."[24] How humiliated Jerdan must have felt to be reduced to asking his highly-esteemed friend not just for the usual loan, but to buy his household goods. The days when he had hob-nobbed with Prime Ministers and Lords, and his influence sought by so many, were far behind him. Now Bennoch was the one involved in politics. On 30 March Jerdan rejoiced:

> Bravo, My Dear Bennoch!
> I congratulate you on your victory; and only wish those in want of public or private support, might find themselves aided by such a friend. As for your Protégé, I think it would have been a shame to London to throw him over, though the family-loving author of Don Carlos would not grant a pension to his kind and amiable Reviewer. Never mind! Forget and forgive. I presume – he will put himself at the head of Reform, and if the cunning Premier does not anticipate and outbid him, be again Prime Minister of England. In that event I rely on you to have my shabby Pension increased, agreeably to the merits of
> My Dear Bennoch, Yrs most sincerely, W Jerdan

The cause for celebration was Lord John Russell's overthrow of the government of Prime Minister Palmerston, which had been defeated on Richard Cobden's motion censuring the resort to force against China and condemning the Second Opium War. The Earl of Derby was appointed to his second brief conservative administration and Russell survived the attempt to oust him from his City seat. As Bennoch had had much influence in the City, it was this on which Jerdan congratulated him, but Bennoch's influence was on the wane: his business was in a bad way and notice of its bankruptcy had been printed in the *Times*. Alarmed, Nathaniel Hawthorne hurried to see him, finding Bennoch and his two partners shadows of their former selves. Bennoch confided that, unknown to him, his partners had speculated and lost the company's money. All hope Bennoch had of civic appointment had vanished and he was reduced to being dunned for his gas bill. Sorrowfully, Hawthorne noted that his friend "had to begin life again, as he began it twenty-five years ago, only under infinite disadvantages . . . Every other man, into whatever depths of poverty he may sink, has still something left . . . the merchant has nothing."[25]

Trying to keep his own income afloat, Jerdan made his second contribution to *Household Words*. The article entitled "Old Scraps of Science" published in the 11 April 1857 issue, concerned scientific advancements in the present age compared to those of two centuries earlier. Jerdan's topic had been suggested by a speech at the British Association Meeting in Cheltenham which praised recent achievements. Because Jerdan recognized the debt owed to discoveries of an earlier age, he moralized that they should "teach us to modify the ultra high valuations of our noble selves". Acknowledging the giants of the past as "oracles in the sciences", he recounted some of the findings in natural sciences by sixteenth and seventeenth century figures. Some of these discoveries sounded far-fetched, but had been ratified by later and more scientific experiments. Jerdan's detailed knowledge of revered figures such as Besler, Scaliger and Gesner from more than two centuries earlier was impressive, as was his grasp of aspects of their work that he described. He chose items which would be of interest to *Household Words* readers, more than to a scientific audience. Thus he mentioned a moss (usnea), the application of which stopped bleeding; whelk shells to remedy baldness, butterflies as a diuretic and burnt mussel shells as dentifrice. He discussed many other discoveries of the distant past which had been appreciated in the present, and pondered that in two centuries time, AD 2056, "our enlightened descendants may enjoy a laugh at the absurdities of our grand philosophy!"

An event which would have been of interest to Jerdan during 1857 was the opening of the South Kensington Museum, later to become the Victoria and Albert Museum. Nearby, the Royal Albert Hall was rising on the site of Lady Blessington's Gore House. Jerdan, however, was looking in another direction. He had at last found the quiet country place he yearned for, where his youngest children could enjoy clean air and a place to grow. He moved with them to Bushey Heath in Hertfordshire, to a small cottage; the local churchwarden's rate book valued this cottage in 1859 at £16.10.0, on which Jerdan paid first 2s 9d and later 1s 4½d of tax,[26] confirming the impression of a crowded dwelling too small for the numbers of children living there. He wrote to Frederick Pollock, his friend from boyhood, on the eve of his own 75th birthday, 15 April 1857, telling him, "I am safely lodged here, whither, thanks to your providence, I contrived to get down, finding that, with the utmost economy, the cost of moving consumed the last 'splendid shilling' . . . " He asked after Pollock's family and confessed, "My philo-progenitiveness is almost a mania. I cannot bear the sight or thought of children ill; and I am not sure that I do not connive at the vagaries even of ill children."[27] The village was on an omnibus route to London, so that when occasion demanded Jerdan could go into town. This he did on 1 June, asking Bennoch for yet more financial aid as "The moving and a new place have been severe on my limited means" and Henry needed "tailorage".[28] Bennoch was planning a trip to Russia, and Jerdan was keen to help:"I trust you will remember my offer of letters to our Consul. I would also advise you to think a little of Masonic introduction and taking your clothing etc. with you. I have been told that such things have been productive of much pleasure and advantage." Jerdan had been a Freemason in earlier years, but just as he had to resign from all other societies from inability to pay his dues, he would also have had to absent himself from Masonic gatherings, unless invited as a guest.

In the next surviving letter three weeks later, Jerdan sounded more like his old self, interested in literary matters which he had barely mentioned in many months. Bennoch had sent Marion Jerdan a gift, perhaps for her 21st birthday: "Mop is charmed with your gift of the portrait", Jerdan noted. "It is certainly very true and replete with character. I am surprized that with such a look of poetry and genius you can maintain your reputation and credit as a City Merchant. A tithe part sufficed to ruin me as a man of business. Ask Mr Rigg."[29] Their mutual friend, the poet Charles Swain, had just had a new book of poems published by Whittemore and Hall. "I hope they pay in proportion", Jerdan remarked, as they had boasted of the book's sterling qualities. "I am sure Mackay (if still chief Redacteur of the *Illustrious*) would cheerfully give his brother bard a lift, and at any rate that being forwarded by you to the proper Channel would secure attention. I will try the only Editor I know, the M[orning] Post, with a similar notice." Jerdan had again been suffering with his leg: "My lameness is getting much better – the inflammation and swelling nearly reduced, and simply gout twinges induced by the affection – no one can imagine what the poison was, or whence proceeding. It resembled locally what we read of in tropical climes."

Following his efforts on Swain's behalf, Jerdan made another foray into the world of literature, sending some work to the son of his old friend Blackwood for the *Maga*, about Scotland "in elder time". "I will not say more than that I have taken much pains with it and that if self-opinion does not deceive me, it is calculated to be popular and deemed worthy of *Maga* in the maturity, experience and vigour of 'Five Hundred'. I set out with the *Literary Gazette* in the same year, 1817 – what a contrast now!"[30] It appears that Blackwood decided not to use this piece.

Jerdan's old friend, the Danish writer of fairy stories, Hans Christian Andersen, returned to London after an absence of ten years. He stayed with Dickens for five weeks, during which time he saw various theatrical performances, met many new people and renewed acquaintance with old friends. He did not, however, see Jerdan, now living too far away from town in Bushey Heath. Jerdan wrote to him sadly:

Learning from the newspapers that you are again in London I cannot resist the wish to hear of your 'whereabouts', and to have the great pleasure of meeting you occasionally during your stay. I am, unfortunately, farther from Town than when we used to be much together on your former visit, and am besides at this moment confined to my cottage by indisposition; but I hope to be able to go out within a few days and make some arrangement for seeing you. I observe that you are with our mutual friend C. Dickens, to whom I had the gratification of making you personally acquainted . . . .I look to your Portrait now before me with the loved inscription "the excellent kind hearted Jerdan from his true friend H. C. Andersen" and trust not to be forgotten, though more out of the busy world, and having to lament the loss of several distinguished parties whose hospitalities we so cordially enjoyed in company together.[31]

No record survives as to whether Andersen ever replied to this letter. He outstayed his welcome with the Dickens family and when he finally departed for Paris Dickens wrote to Jerdan that "He had spoken of you with much regard, and I understand, or fancied, had seen you."[32] Andersen had been "utterly conglomerated", Dickens went on, "unintelligible", and getting into "wild entanglements". Dickens sounded as if he was trying to console Jerdan for Andersen's apparent neglect, but Jerdan must have been hurt that his erstwhile friend, for whom he had done so much both in the *Literary Gazette* and personally, had not made time to visit him. Andersen published an intimate account of his visit with Dickens and his family, without warning his host who was on the point of separating from his wife. A few weeks after Andersen's departure, Dickens fell in love with Nelly Ternan, thus rendering somewhat absurd Andersen's account of a cosy, happy family life. He never understood why he had offended Dickens, who failed to reply to any of his letters until the day of his death, thirteen years later.

Although Dickens was obviously greatly distracted by his domestic upheavals he had incorporated *Household Words* into his new journal, *All the Year Round*, overlapping them for five weeks in May 1859. In the issue of 26 September Jerdan contributed "Old Hawtrey". This filled four and a half columns, but no payment was listed in the Office Book. It has been noted that the Office Book payment record is not entirely complete, and "In a letter to Jerdan, Dickens recorded sending him Wills' cheque in payment for the item which the Office Book records no payment; the letter does not state the amount of the cheque."[33] "Old Hawtrey" described a rural walk near Windsor in June, and a meeting between the narrator and a countryman of eighty-four. The main part of the story comprised his memories of youth, seeing King George III out hunting with his dogs, "a hallooing and barking and howling (the gift of tongues I think they called it)" – a cheeky reference to Jerdan's earlier story in the magazine; he recounted how he met his wife when he was 21, and the "parcel of bairns" they had, "thinned off" by smallpox and even those who lived into adulthood had died before him. He was all alone. He remembered the jubilation over "Peace with Bonnyparty", and walking to "Lunnun" with friends, where they were robbed; the Jubilee of George's fifty years on the throne. Finally, as the sun went down, the old man said his prayers to himself, and "Amen" aloud, and retired to his cottage. The narrator, taking the same road after the harvest, decided to call on the old man, arriving just as his coffin was carried out, inscribed 'Thomas Hawtrey Aged 84 years.' Although Jerdan was only seventy-five not eighty-four, this little piece was clearly a trip down his own memory lane, and would have resonated with the older readers of Dickens's magazine.

Jerdan's last contribution to Dickens's paper was a 'Chip', i.e. a short piece entitled "A British Nuisance", for which he received one guinea. It was published in the issue of 23 January 1858, and told of the narrator's escape from his Kentish village to Paternoster Row in London, the centre of education and enlightenment. A short walk from here took the narrator to nearby Newgate Prison, and a small square where sheep and bullocks were being slaughtered, watched by groups of young men and small boys. Open slaughterhouses, Jerdan wrote, were "calculated to be very hurtful to the children who assemble and meet together to witness these detestable spectacles. They must corrupt the heart and the head and pave the way, by a training not to be withstood, to cruelty and crime." Animals should be killed mercifully, he proposed, out of public sight and preferably in the Moslem way of instant death. Animal welfare was a subject he had mentioned in his *Autobiography* as a cause which he had always espoused and this 'Chip' gave him an opportunity to make known his thoughts on the matter.

~24~

Biographies – Concerning Madness

Tucked away in his cottage on Bushey Heath with a tribe of young children, Jerdan was utterly cut off from his former life and from his friends. Most painfully, he missed his exchanges with Francis Bennoch. Henry had been unwell and had come home to recover, nursed by "Mop". Jerdan wrote to Bennoch in March,

I long exceedingly to see and converse with you.

I have been poor and poorly all the winter, and thrice to London in nearly four months. Without any thing to stir me after my busy life I am snuffing out, with little intercourse with society even by letters. The last two days, I have hobbled about the garden, looking at green things breaking through the clod, and picking up stones with the bairns off the borders.

I look back, and seem to have lost my identity. Perhaps I have. But I am not altered with regard to the friends I esteem and love. While this lowly life lasts, they, and they are wondrous few, will occupy their warmest place in my affections.[1]

One bright spot had occurred in their lives: " Matilda has been proposed to, by a worthy fellow, yet only a merchant's clerk, and that one of our perplexities brings you both so home to our minds was, O, that we could advise with Mrs Bennoch about marrying and marriage preparations." The lack of a wife at such a delicate time would have been a real problem for Jerdan.

Bennoch apparently did not respond to this letter as on 10 May 1858 Jerdan wrote to him again, regretting the "absence of all correspondence between us [which] makes a melancholy blank to me",[2] using as excuse for his letter a question about some contribution of Bennoch's to *Welcome Guest* publication. Always grateful for Bennoch's sound advice, Jerdan explained that he had, two months previously, proposed to Fields a new publication which he "wished to give, in the first instance anonymously, from America". Not having received a reply, he asked Bennoch what he should do: to wait, to write again, or let the matter drop.

Tilly's marriage, he told his friend, was set for 26 June, "a very important event in a family like mine, and in such circumstances. God send it well through! She is a fine girl and of economical disposition – of habits I will say nothing for necessity has formed in a cruel school." He did not discuss with Bennoch the fact that before she could marry, Matilda had to be christened. This event took place on 30 May, and on 26 June the twenty-one year old Tilly married Charles Condamine Bickley, aged twenty. Their witnesses were her father and her sister Marion. Charles's father Samuel was a merchant of Albion Grove Islington, with two younger children. Tilly was making a good match, considering that her father was in dire penury and her mother in a lunatic asylum.

In the same newsy letter Jerdan told Bennoch that he had been invited to the Surrey Archaeological Meeting, and intended to go. "I so rarely go anywhere that such things appear to be quite events." More interesting, he then divulged that he had been looking at records of the huge sums he had deposited at Drummonds Bank between 1825 and 1829:

> and to think how I am, raises a doubt of my identity. It is however but too true, and my chief consolation is like your own that I was <u>guilty</u> of as many kindnesses as I well could commit. If the gratitude you meet with is equal to what I have experienced 'O save me from my friends' may join in the voice of My Dear Bennoch. Yours most sincerely,

Inevitably, Jerdan was still completely unwilling to accept that his present condition had anything to do with his poor judgment in financial matters, his carelessness about keeping accounts, or his bad management of all his affairs. His poverty now was due solely to his "kindnesses", and not to his failings. He had enjoyed a considerable income in those early years, and this was likely to have continued for several years after that until the *Literary Gazette* started its rapid decline.

Jerdan was still producing as much as he could; one piece was "A Chapter on Dogs", which appeared in the July issue of *Chambers' Journal*. This, as other pieces in *Chambers'*, was unsigned, and has been identified only by a note in which Jerdan sent a copy to Bennoch, using his son Henry as a messenger.[3] His inspiration was the recent novel by Edward Bulwer Lytton entitled *What will he do with it? By Pisistratus Caxton*, which had as its hero a poodle called Sir Isaac. Acknowledging this work as his starting point, Jerdan discoursed on the subject of dogs in general. He referred to a pair which had been exhibited fifteen years previously in the Regent's Circus. They had been trained by a Frenchman, Adrien Leonard, who had produced an octavo book of over four hundred pages on the education of animals. Jerdan said this book contained "some new, and much curious matter". The subject was not unworthy of science, as Descartes was inclined to the belief that animals had souls, and many other eminent men had examined canine attributes. Jerdan carefully analyzed Leonard's discussion, comparing the training of dogs with that of children and weighing evidence for intelligence versus instinct. Lightening the tone at the end of his four page article, Jerdan chose to quote from Leonard's book what happens when a dog is spoilt and petted. "'With such an education,' observes our author severely, 'a dog cannot fail to be surly and mischievous, and occasion very unpleasant scenes; all which would be avoided if he were taught promptly to obey.' Perhaps we might for 'dog' read 'child'", concluded Jerdan who should have learnt this lesson from his vast experience as father of at least twenty-three children.

There was nothing in this article of Jerdan's originality but, as he had done many times before, he took a weighty book and made it accessible and digestible to a lay readership, with a light touch that avoided being patronising to those less well educated or well read than he was himself. He felt, however, that he was out of step with the times. He complained to Bennoch: "The popular rising Periodicists of the present day are so smart that old prosers, like me, seem dull and heavy; but I cannot say I admire all the sparkling froth which swims a-top. I do like a little depth, and do fancy that even clever men must read a little before they can write what is either truly entertaining or useful."[4] Perhaps he had not yet read the just-published books, Darwin's *On the Origin of Species*, or Mill's *Essay on Liberty*, which would have given him the 'depth' he desired.

In September 1858 the *Leisure Hour* published Jerdan's recollections of London in two instalments, entitled "About Sixty Years Ago".[5] Remarking that the adage about 'nothing new under the sun' was inaccurate, Jerdan anticipated many new changes would occur in the future, as they had in the past sixty years, even until the year 2000, "the commencement of a new millenary". He described how, when he came to the capital, "My London was comparatively a quiet and sober city . . . with a few small clumps of suburban cottage retreats within a mile or two." He had planned to describe the London of his youth, but found it easier to compare then and now by small homely details, such as the cries of the street vendors no longer heard, the difficulty of striking a light before the invention of matches, even the act of letter-writing, sealing and posting a letter in those days before envelopes and stamps. He mused on the filth of Butchers Row in his youth and the present fine new squares of Russell and Tavistock, walked to Charing Cross through what had become, when he was writing, Trafalgar Square, and remarked on the respectable shops of earlier times which did not, as now, sport "indistinct and dubious prices".

Jerdan noted that one of the most significant differences between now and sixty years previously was the advent of street lighting. In his youth shopkeepers had been forced to close by eight, it being too dark to see; the shopboys retired to bed, "their masters went to their evening relaxation or symposium". He found here the greatest difference: in earlier times tradesmen and shopkeepers of all kinds, "as well as persons engaged in professional pursuits – resided and slept in the houses in which their several occupations were carried on". This encouraged frequenting of nearby taverns, to talk over politics and news. This train of thought led him inevitably to recall the 'Charlies', night-watchmen with lanterns, he had reason to know from his more bibulous and riotous evenings out as a younger man. Now there were 'Bobbies', Peel's policemen, patrolling the streets which were lit with fifteen hundred miles of gas lights. The Thames, back at the turn of the century was truly silver, now he called it a "desperately polluted stream". The peace of 1814 had marked a great change in English society, said Jerdan, and noted the rapid growth in learning both for the elite and the masses. Chiswick and Regents Parks had not been created nor the Zoological Gardens. The closest one could get to a wild animal were those caged in at Exeter 'Change. Railways and omnibuses had replaced sedan chairs, but he felt that people had "less individuality of character" now. Jerdan had been in Parliament to hear the debate about allowing its proceedings to be reported in the newspapers, and the papers themselves were poor things compared to the modern variety. He closed his reminiscences of London by agreeing with Racine, "Everything changes, arts, habits, wit and wisdom's self. We are not as we were, and we shall not remain as we are."

These recollections must have met with approbation, as in December he wrote the first instalment of "A Walk from London to Edinburgh about Sixty Years Ago", with a footnote referring readers back to his London articles.[6] The nineteen-year-old Jerdan had shaken off the sights and sounds of London with only a change of shirt and stockings, "a little bit of coxcombry in dress and decoration to demonstrate, at first sight, that I did not walk from sheer poverty", a handsome purse with ten guineas, a gold watch and chain, and a sparkling ring. He walked forty or sometimes fifty miles a day, refusing an offer to ride in the carriage of an acquaintance. On the Great North Road he encountered vast herds of cattle destined for London cooking pots, losing weight after a four hundred mile, three week journey. What he remembered from such a long-ago adventure was that there was opportunity to talk to local people who knew everything about their area, unlike the days of railway travel rushing one between places, so that one knows "as little (or less) of the country and its inhabitants, as of the polar regions and the Esquimaux. New forms of transport are a wonderful improvement", he acknowledged, "but only that all is not gain." The remainder of his article recounted the highlights of his journey, via Holy Isle, Alnwick Castle and the banks of his beloved Tweed. He finally arrived in Edinburgh, "castle-crowned and palace-footed, splendid and filthy, philosophical and foolish, refined and rude, sober and drunken, religious and licentious".

The second article dealt with the city itself. There was a considerable English as well as Scottish military presence there and Jerdan recalled the social structure of the civilian population, notably as a city of ministers and of "lawyers, *par excellence*". He noted the preponderance of the unfortunate results of inbreeding, and how they were treated kindly as characters, but not reviled. He recollected Edinburgh nights with their "superabundance of wine and spirits ... Edinburgh was very considerably drunken", and from his distance of almost sixty years, wondered "that so much, both of physical and moral abomination, was ever endured". He believed that "the New Town was a necessity of the period: it was the creation of a civilizing crisis", and recounted some of the mad exploits of earlier days to amuse the *Leisure Hour* readers. Jerdan spoke of the 'caddies', Highland Celts who were found on street corners, ready to run errands, and told how he despatched one man to run with an urgent message forty miles over hilly countryside and return, a feat accomplished at a steady trot of seven-and-a-half miles per hour. He surveyed the intellectuals who had sprung from Edinburgh, highlighting the start of the *Edinburgh Review* in 1802, and acknowledged that these men "created a new political and literary era, not only for the north, but extending to the utmost limits of the British empire". *Blackwood's* and the *Quarterly* were mentioned, and Jerdan moved on to the famed wit of legal men and some quaint Scottish phrases of the day. He recalled the romance of Calton Hill, "then uninvaded by unfinished Parthenons and monumental memorials" and the miles of open country with only a few 'country seats', now covered by the modern populous city. He wrote about the Highland pipes at Leith race week, with their clan tartans, and the "vivid remembrance of the '45' and a feeling of sympathy and passionate admiration for Jacobite legend, song and music." Burns had only recently died, Wallace was still revered as a hero. Bringing what he called his "desultory retrospect" to a close, Jerdan quoted Montaigne: "Old men should retreat from life backwards" and hoped that his look at the past would prove instructive, "looking back with experience, that we may look forward with warning, wisdom and hope."

Such optimistic words seem particularly cruel when in February, life gave Jerdan another terrible blow. His son William Freeling died aged 41, of "pulmonary consumption", the fifth of his children by Frances to predecease him. His obituary in the *Gentleman's Magazine* revealed that he had tried several careers:[7]

By his birth connected with the literary world, he did not, however, devote himself to literature, and was only a casual contributor of lighter matter to the press. In office business he was very able and expert, and had realized a moderate competency, when the fearful railway crash (he being then secretary to the Great Northern of France) wrecked him in the gulph of extended ruin. He afterwards turned more assiduously to literary employment; became a principal shareholder in, and administrator of, the 'Literary Gazette', out of which he retired to make room for Messrs Benham and Reeve. For several years, and at the time of his premature death, he was a clerk in the General Post Office. Gifted with more than common talent, he was one of the kindest-hearted beings that ever existed, and his loss is not only sincerely lamented by his family and relatives, but by a numerous circle whom he had attached by his ever-obliging disposition and readiness to serve by any means that lay in his power.

Of all his children William Freeling had been the closest to Jerdan in terms of working with him and for him, even though this was plainly not his son's first choice of occupation. Once more life had drawn a sad parallel between Jerdan and Leigh Hunt, whose beloved son Vincent had also died of TB in 1852, at not yet thirty years old. As one son was dying, Jerdan tried to use his remaining influential friends to find positions for others, writing to Bulwer he asked, "Can you do nothing for my lads? My back is broken with an aimless burden. Has Columbia no opening for youth and activity?"[8]

By July Jerdan had heard from Fields that "publishing in the US is quite stagnant" and that therefore his proposed anonymous volume would not happen. He had wanted to write about "the miseries incident to the middle classes in our condition of civilization, interspersed with short, poetical sketches". It was half done already, but Jerdan was discouraged and thought that now it would never be completed. "I must be content to rust out," he ended his letter to Bulwer. "I am afraid I am not quite so happy, but I am sure I am always happy in the happiness of those I love."

He was not the only one of his old circle unhappy in 1858. Edward Bulwer Lytton incarcerated his wife Rosina into a lunatic asylum, after many years of mutually distressing and abusive treatment, even though they had long been separated. She had written to prominent people accusing her husband of mistresses and illegitimate children, and even suggested a sexual relationship between him and Disraeli. She had been a successful writer herself, publishing thirteen novels and other works. She quickly proved that she was sane and was released after three weeks. Although Jerdan now rarely socialized with Bulwer, who was now an eminent politician as well as a successful novelist, they were still on friendly terms. At the end of July 1858 he asked Bulwer to use his influence with Lord Stanley to promote Irwin to the Auditorship of the East India Board.[9] His daughter Agnes's husband was currently employed in the Audit Office and seeking a better position to support his growing family. Jerdan may have offered to approach Bulwer on his behalf not only in his daughter's interest, but also as an effort to compensate Irwin for the failed *Literary Gazette* partnership which had landed his son-in-law in Court. Jerdan reinforced his request with another note to Bulwer a few days later,[10] but heard nothing from him. In September he asked for a brief interview,[11] but in November had to acknowledge that Irwin's claim had been supplanted by another appointment. He hinted broadly that he would welcome an invitation to Knebworth the following summer, and noted that Irwin's cousin William Grove had been offered the Chief Trusteeship of Bombay.[12]

At a dinner in Park Lane Bulwer had introduced Jerdan to the Private Secretary to Lord Malmesbury, to whom Jerdan wrote a long letter apologizing for his "garrulous intrusion". At the dinner conversation had turned to ciphers and the purpose of Jerdan's letter was to mention the "secret cypher" which he had invented back in 1802, and which seemed to be still in use. Jerdan was not seeking any reward but was merely "curious about it, though far too late for any ground to augment the recognition of my literary deserts by even a government composed of such literary elements as the present – upon whose productions, including those of two Secretaries of State and a Chancellor of the Exchequer, I have had the honour and imprudence to sit in critical judgment". He enclosed an article referring to the time when, as he wistfully recalled, "I was much in the confidence of eminent official men and knew as much as some members of the Cabinet. I was engaged in higher pursuits then."[13]

On Monday 29 November 1858 the *Times* reported that Bulwer, in his capacity as HM Principal Secretary of State for the Colonies, had "at once instituted a most searching inquiry, sparing no exertion by day or night, until he succeeded in obtaining evidence which justified him in authorizing the present prosecution against the prisoner at the bar". The prosecution concerned Sir John Young's Ionian Despatches which the prisoner was accused of stealing from the Colonial Office and allowing to be printed in the *Daily News*. Bulwer was "fearful that some person in the public service had betrayed his trust by disclosing a private communication". Jerdan leapt to his defence against the *Times'* implied criticism. On two large sheets of blue paper he set out his arguments in Question and Answer form, and enclosed this to Bulwer's secretary, expressing his ire at Bulwer's treatment. "The attack upon Sir EBL in *The Times* – setting the sordid against the noble in spirit – has induced me to throw a few thoughts (loosely) together on the subject of that Journal, and, as far as I know, supineness of the government in relation to its unrelaxing hostility. I have known much of newsprint matters, and I am sure that in neglecting this continual outpouring of rancour Ministers avoid a duty (disagreeable and difficult no doubt) and leave a dangerous field open to the injury of the Country as well as of their government."[14]

Jerdan's mood was more cheerful the next day when he wrote jovially to an old friend, "Fuk show chuang tseven – oh! I forgot that, with all your knowledge of languages, French, Italian, German, Hebrew, Sansskrit, Pali, Russ, Cherokee, etc. etc. you do not understand Chinese and so began my letter thoughtlessly in an unintelligible tongue, but have therefore good reason and better, for not going on with it."[15] He mentioned receiving an invitation to attend the Burns Centenary the following month, which he had "declined on three sufficing accounts, viz. distance, expence and old age. It wd have been a temptation, 'Ere I was old!'" Jerdan had not lost his sense of humour, regaling his correspondent with his "last *Jeux*", and then giving her a "family abstract" of each of his children still at home, from Mop who "blows me up like a wife for spoiling the young uns", to Teddy, "a marvellous pretty pet". He seems never to have hidden his almost-worship of small children and enjoyment of their company.

A reminder of Jerdan's former life and activities was the fight between Dickens backed by Charles Dilke and John Forster, and Jerdan's erstwhile favourite charity, the Royal Literary Fund. In a sixteen-page pamphlet entitled "The Case of the Reformers in the Literary Fund", they accused the Fund of mismanagement and of spending too much on administration. Their other complaint was of a more technical nature and concerned the constitution of the Managing Committee. The Fund responded by issuing an eighteen-page refutation, pointing out that some of the reformers' allegations referred to incidents that had occurred thirty years earlier. Dickens's involvement was not new. His fight to reform the Royal Literary Fund had been waged for several years without much effect. In March 1856 Dickens in *Household Words*, and Dilke in the *Athenaeum* had bitterly attacked the extravagant administration of the Fund. Dickens repeatedly tried to reform the Fund, but his censure motion was defeated by seventy votes to fourteen. In March 1859 John Forster made an anonymous and generous offer, through Dickens, in a final attempt to reform the Royal Literary Fund: "a magnificent library . . . and the sum of ten thousand pounds for its maintenance and enlargement in perpetuity" on condition of an amended Charter. Still the Fund refused to reform and Forster's library was eventually left to the Victoria and Albert Museum. Jerdan watched these efforts from the sidelines, willing Dickens and his supporters to succeed, but no changes to the Fund occurred during Jerdan's lifetime, and the Fund for which he had worked so hard and to which he had made applications for so many destitute writers, went on in the same way until the turn of the century.

In the summer of 1859 Jerdan had been overjoyed to be once again with his treasured friend Bennoch, who had been experiencing some difficulties in his business. Jerdan's delight bubbled over in his letter:

> I cannot explain to you the <u>extent</u> of the pleasure I felt at our late meeting. The present enjoyment seemed to be not only a proof that the storm was over but a pledge that the prospect was bright. Old as I am I may live to see you as high, and more firm in the struggle of this weary world than ever before, and believe me not those nearest and dearest to you will rejoice more fervently than I.[16]

In a change of mood, Jerdan told Bennoch that he had been "inexpressibly shocked" by the suicide of William Cumming, an underwriter at Lloyds and a neighbour at Charlton, who had died aged 48, leaving a wife and children. Jerdan felt guilty as they had quarrelled, "(or rather he had quarrelled), but he was deceived by the most base and artful hypocrite that ever it was my lot to encounter, or even to fancy as a possibility in human nature. Quilp is the only prototype of the wretch that I can imagine – the villainy of his plotting is incredible." Jerdan was convinced that had they remained friends, Cumming would not have taken his life. Ending on a lighter note, Jerdan gave Bennoch some "Apothegms" (sic).

> For Bennoch. No more pipe, no more dance – Experienced. Begin to play again and dancing will be renewed; but you have learnt the worth of the Dancers.
> For Jerdan. When the candle is snuffing out, people forget the light it shed on their early meeting and how it shone on their continued company. They can now clearly see their own way. I refer to all the past as an <u>Inward</u> <u>Sight</u>!"
> So be it! You I trust will make a good use of the tunes you hereafter play and I, Dear Bennoch, gratefully and affectionately yours, will flicker out regardless of matters too late to mend.
> Love to the Wife.

In a faint echo of his heyday in the literary world, Jerdan introduced John Blackwood to an old friend, B. P. Ainslie, who had a manuscript he wanted published. "He neither cares for nor expects profit", Jerdan advised Blackwood.[17] Presumably neither did Jerdan, whose days as an agent were long over.

However he embarked on a new project in the autumn, one which was to carry him through the next few years. This was a series for the weekly magazine the *Leisure Hour*, entitled 'Men I Have Known', and published anonymously. Commencing on 20 October 1859 with Lord Chancellor Truro, a friend from his youth, six subsequent issues that year featured George Canning, the Ettrick Shepherd, Henry Hallam, the Earl of Ripon and Bishop Burgess. These articles covered between two to three pages of the *Leisure Hour*, and were written very much from Jerdan's personal knowledge of those he discussed. He leavened the plain biographical details with personal observations and opinions, and chose only subjects who were now dead. The editors must have received positive responses from readers as the series continued for some time.

Leigh Hunt, whose life experiences so often ran parallel to Jerdan's own, died in August 1859 having become increasingly frail. Not until ten years later did Samuel Carter Hall, an unlikely champion of one who was the star of the 'Cockney School', arrange for a monument to be erected on Hunt's tombstone. Dickens, Procter, Carlyle, Browning and others helped to provide the funds.

Durham sculpted a bust of Hunt, the whole being unveiled in October 1869, three months after Jerdan's own death.

As 1860 began, the New Year brought back many memories to Jerdan, and whilst thinking of the past, he wrote to Bennoch with good wishes for the future. He was seldom in town, he told his old friend, and

> I get dumpish sometimes from so little intercourse with the few for whom I entertain a sincere affection, and my new neighbourhood, though pleasant in many respects, does not compensate for the old relations. So
> I walk by myself,
> And say to myself
> By way of reverie –
> Look to thyself
> And take care of thyself
> For nobody cares for Thee!
>
> There is great quiet humour, as it appears to me, in this quaint old humdrum, and especially in one word
> Then I answered myself,
> And said to myself,
> By way of _Repartee_
> Look to thyself
> Or look not to thyself
> 'Tis the selfsame thing to me![18]

He had been "strongly invited" to go to the Masonic Lodge at Watford, but was "bare of 'clothing'", asking Bennoch if he could borrow his apron etc. The invitation was important to Jerdan: "My object is to <u>show</u> a leetle to two or three men hereabouts who have not <u>shown</u> as they should to an In-comer, whilst strangers have done much more." He went on to say that "Miss Marion Jerdan is a little over age on Tuesday 17th. She has been a great comfort to me. And she is of good family, do you know? A Hist. of my native county has just appeared wherein my ancestor (I believe) John Jerdone is mentioned as the proprietor of land, held of the Abbot of Kelso – a field or two only – but the same is in the possession of my nephew John Jerdan. It is remarkable that so small a holding should date from AD 1300." The comment about Marion's birthday may mean that she was to be 22, but she might have been older, as no birth record has been found for her, indicating that she was born before records began in 1837.

The _Leisure Hour_ provided Jerdan with an outlet for 'Men I Have Known' as well as for some other articles, and therefore with a vitally necessary income. In the issue of 23 February appeared one entitled "Pickles and Preserves", identified as Jerdan's by a letter in March to Crowquill, (Alfred Forrester), mentioning it. Without such confirmation it would be impossible to identify this as Jerdan's work, it being of an entirely new nature and content, although the subject of food adulteration was something the *Literary Gazette* had discussed in 1843; the topic had now come to the forefront of public awareness, following articles in *The Lancet*. This latest piece, like the one he wrote for Trotter's Soho Bazaar, read more as an extended advertisement for the products of Crosse & Blackwell, the company he discussed, coincidentally also of Soho Square. (Mr Blackwell had advised the House of Commons' Committee on the adulteration of food, in 1855, that his company no longer used colourants.)

Jerdan had visited their factory in July at the height of the season, and described in great detail every aspect of their various processes under separate headings of Pickles, Sauces, Preserves and Preserved Provisions. He described the different methods, and set out an impressive number of statistics for the quantities of jars produced. He was careful to record the source of the vegetables, meats and fish used in the various preparations, and discussed the size of the workforce required to carry out the work. Jerdan compared their work with that of the women in Hood's famous poem, *The Song of the Shirt*:

> Stitch, stitch, stitch,
> Seam, and gusset and band,
> Band and gusset and seam.

He was gratified, he wrote, to learn that "the average wages were two shillings, and that a clever picker could earn half a crown by her day's work." Crosse & Blackwell's calf's foot jelly he noted, had been "sent to the Crimea as presents, was found to be so beneficial to our sick soldiers that it is now being ordered for all the government hospitals". Jerdan was particularly impressed by the company's policy not to use artificial colourings, and he concluded that "it seems to me that this immense business was the triumph of the grand principle that honesty is the best policy". The firm treated its workers well, thought Jerdan, who was amazed that in their newest building in Dean Street a system of ventilators drew off the steam and hot air from the pickling process and brought in fresh air to "invigorate the exhausted workers". In this article Jerdan brought his long-dormant journalistic abilities to the fore, producing an article that was full of facts yet written in an interesting and entertaining style.

The subject continued to interest him, as he told Crowquill in March: "I have a fancy for doing a small volume on the Adultery of Food, first title, Death Dinnering."[19] He suggested that Crowquill might care to provide relevant illustrations, and set out his own ideas for the cover:

My notion is a table, the front so far open as to show that it was supported upon grotesque skeleton claws, and perhaps a thigh bone or two as cross pieces. Several Courses set like Sancho Panza at Baratgaria, a figure like the Doctor forbidding the touch of a splendid dish, a butler of the skeleton genus doing the wine duties – another servant deadly bringing in a tray . . . etc etc.

Crowquill appeared to like the project, as a few days later Jerdan told him that his "dish gets me into a scrape." Everyone wanted to keep his sketch, but Jerdan gleefully recounted how his visitors coveting Crowquill's work were shown "some of your old treasured fancies, held in lavender by sons and daughters of this wealthy house; and it is quite painful to notice what envy and malice are excited!"[20] Crowquill had enquired about paper sizes and publishers, but Jerdan had not thought his project through. "My idea was to produce a lot of copies and go with them in hand to Smith & Son, or other great Vendor, and sell them in the lump of one, two, three or more thousands." He asked Crowquill's advice as to price, thinking himself of a one shilling volume. In addition to the *Leisure Hour* article on Crosse & Blackwell, he referred the illustrator to his own papers in the *Literary Gazette* of 1843, "Accum's Death in the Pot". "The work will treat of the deleterious and fraudulent extent of deterioration – exemplified in a multitude of ways and instances", he explained. Despite Jerdan's enthusiasm and Crowquill's agreement, the book does not appear to have ever been published.

The *Leisure Hour* provided Jerdan with the opportunity to add four more characters to his 'Men I Have Known' series. In July he wrote on Sir Mark Isambard Brunel, in August on Sir James Mackintosh and Sir Joseph Jekyll, and then there was a gap until the November issue on Samuel Rogers.

Only two letters survive from 1861, one being from Bulwer, thanking Jerdan for a "little volume" he had sent, which must have been a manuscript as Bulwer, in praising it most warmly, told Jerdan, "it is a book that should be <u>published</u> and its merits will be appreciated in proportion to the intellect of the reader – the judgment of the Few will make it a permanent addition to the literature of the many."[21] The tone of Bulwer's comments, and his remark that "it has the chance of a classic in its great truthfulness and unconscious power", suggest that this was not Jerdan's planned book on food adulteration, but some other work of a more literary nature, possibly his biography of Thomson. The second surviving letter, dated on the penultimate day of the year, was from solicitors concerning a debt of Jerdan's to a Mr Collis.

'Men I Have Known' continued to appear in the *Leisure Hour*. February covered Captain Crozier, whilst Gifford of the *Quarterly* and Sir Walter Scott appeared in the Spring. Mountstuart Elphinstone and Richard Brinsley Sheridan shared an issue in June, and in July was the turn of Lord Chancellor Eldon. An August issue featured the odd pairing of William Huskisson and

Thomas Campbell, and Jerdan's last contribution in 1861 was in October, on Sir John Malcolm.

A Census was again held in 1861 and Jerdan's little cottage on Bushey Heath was recorded as home to him as Head of the household, aged 78; he listed himself as "Widower", a clear reference to Frances's death five years earlier, and a sure sign that he did not marry Mary Maxwell thereafter. His unmarried daughter Marion, aged 24, was listed as housekeeper, together with five sons and one other daughter, Agnes, ranging in age from 19 to five years, Edward being the youngest, born to Mary Maxwell in the Barming Heath lunatic asylum. A daughter, Emma, who appeared on the 1851 Census as a five-year old, was not mentioned on this one.

Although Jerdan had long ago resigned from the many societies of which he had been a member he had remained on the list of the Garrick Club, which he had helped to establish in 1831. In February 1862 he wrote to Lord William Lennox, regretting that he had to ask for his name to be withdrawn:

The infrequency of my visits to town, and the increase of the subscription determined me to forgo the pleasant tie (almost the last) with old and gratifying associations. I have thought that in forming the new rules an exception might have been made with regard to those who, like yourself and myself, went through the labour of the foundation. I, in my case, as you may remember, went to considerable expense towards furnishing the cellar, and other provisional arrangements. I should have been well content to catch a glimpse of my old friends now and then before the fall of the curtain, but having laid my small share of ashes in the original fire, I must now only hope that the Phoenix about to arise from the nest may flourish and grow great in the good system of love and literature, and patronage of the Drama. Your plate and crockery will still remind you of the inventor of your symbol, and suggest to the youthful and sanguine that 'All the World's a Stage'.[22]

Jerdan's isolation, loneliness and sadness is palpable. He did receive occasional visits from the poet Eliza Cook, who came in the summer months to visit friends in Heath Cottage on Bushey Heath.

In April, Jerdan sent a note to an unnamed person, saying apologetically, "I daresay it is hardly worth your remembrance that you asked for and I had the pleasure to send you some memoranda for the first edition of your Biographical Dictionary."[23] He mentioned some additional information on the sculptor Durham, and ended rather pathetically, "I am still _alive_ at Bushey Heath and if I can render you any little service you may call on [me]." The addressee was most likely to have been Edward Walford, whose _Biographical Dictionary_ was published in 1862. The entry on Durham was a new insertion into his existing Dictionary, and its style suggests that Jerdan was the author. The entry for Jerdan himself was a straight-forward sketch of his working life, which could have been taken directly from his *Autobiography*.

Jerdan's own biographical endeavour was picking up speed, as in the first half of the year the 'Men' he knew for the *Leisure Hour* were Sir John Franklin, Lisle Bowles and Charles Dibdin. He had a break over the summer, reappearing in October to present Richard Martin of Galway, and Coleridge. Three issues in December were devoted to Richard Porson, Sharon Turner, Barham and Douce.

In July Jerdan made a rare visit to London, to the Reading Room of the British Museum. He tried to find the works of Lt. Holman, the Blind Traveller, which he had reviewed long ago in the *Literary Gazette*. Failing to find what he sought, he wrote to ask the Museum whether it was his "blundering, not being a very customary visitor to the BM", or a lapse in their Catalogue. He could not resist remarking that "in the course of the day I had the pleasure of shaking hands with both Sir H. Ellis and M. Panizzi".[24] His love of "tuft-hunting", or name-dropping, was a lifetime trait. Henry Ellis had been the ineffective but titular head of the British Museum who had resigned aged seventy-nine, in 1856, while Sir Anthony Panizzi, keeper of printed books, had been Head in all but name, until finally appointed to the post on the resignation of Ellis.

The end of summer found Jerdan in pensive mood, dwelling on the past, and musing on the inherent problems of literature. He unloaded what he called his "periodical prosing" to Bulwer:[25]

> When the lamp is flickering out, there are shadowy intermittent periods during which the <u>reflections</u> of its early light and burning assume vivid hues from their nature imperceptible to the world. It is at such times that I am apt to recall the memory of friends who were near and dear to me – much in Communion – and of circumstances once so deeply inter-esting. Even not yet forgetting the past, and hoping against being quite forgot, accidental matters will stir up the lambent flame of former years and get one a-wishing for some intercourse to prove that I am the Ipse [*he himself*] I fancy to have been.

Moving on to mention a recent article in *Blackwood's* on literary pursuits, Jerdan continued:

> The mechanical and the intellectual cannot be co-ordinate. The simple act of putting pen to paper will ever affect the thought desired to be expressed. The emanation cannot be transferred to a material medium so pure and so entire as the conception and shaping in the mind. Thus no man of any genius could be satisfied with what he wrote. The nearer he approached the standard, he would be the better pleased; but he never

could reach it. Grateful readers might applaud the greatness of his achievement – the while he was lamenting the measure in which it fell short of his ideal. Their triumphale is to him almost an aggravation of his sense of failure.

His own sense of failure, added to his sense of isolation, intensified when on 12 September his long-time partner, Mary Maxwell, died of 'chronic mania' in the asylum at Barming Heath, Maidstone. She was forty-five years old. Unfortunately for posterity, she left no known letters or diaries to illuminate her life with Jerdan, unlike Leigh Hunt's Marianne, who had also succumbed to years of stress and poverty, but kept a journal partly as a defence against accusations levelled against her.[26] The diagnosis of "chronic mania" as cause of death might, in today's terms, have covered conditions which had nothing to do with lunacy but rather be depression, which would not be surprising given her thirteen children in less than twenty years, her aging sick 'husband', and several house moves whilst endeavouring to support Jerdan in his struggles to create some income for his large family. Other conditions for which women were sent to asylums were hysteria, anorexia and perceived sexual problems. A woman could be incarcerated for no longer permitting conjugal relations, but it would seem this is not the reason why Mary was put away, as she gave birth whilst in the asylum. Jerdan would have known that in the 1840s Thackeray's wife became depressed after the birth of her second child, and stayed in an asylum for the rest of her life. Mary Wollstonecraft's *Maria, or the Wrongs of Woman* published in 1798 involved a woman whose marriage broke down due to her husband's misbehaviour, and was imprisoned by him in a madhouse. Things had improved in the intervening years, and Jerdan had been interested in the treatment of madness since the early days of the *Literary Gazette*. He made reference to this topic throughout his editorship; one instance was in August 1828 when there was a review of *Commentaries on the Causes, forms, Symptoms and Treatment, Moral and Medical, of Insanity*.[27] This treatise traced insanity "in all items forms of mania, melancholia, demency, idiocy etc. etc. to the various moral and physical causes which produce that almost worst of human afflictions". Jerdan devoted over two pages to this book, an indication of his own interest in the subject at a time long before it became a factor in his own life.

Later, he drew attention to the second edition of *An Inquiry as to the Expediency of a County Asylum for Pauper Lunatics*, mentioning that this was a subject of general interest, and that the author had striven to campaign for "a suitable asylum in his native county for the proper care and treatment of a most helpless class of our afflicted fellow-creatures".[28] The reviewer referred to a paper published the previous year, revealing that more than one in a thousand "was actually mad", and that "the disease" was increasing. Parliamentary figures now confirmed that nearly fourteen thousand people in England and Wales were insane. There had been no attempt at a cure, merely incarceration, even in private madhouses, a practice which exacerbated mental problems. Now that the "magnitude of evil" was known, it was to be hoped that proper provision would be made for the afflicted. In response to the call for county asylums, the 1845 Lunatics Act compelled local authorities to provide asylum care. Bryan Waller Procter, a barrister better known as the poet Barry Cornwall who had been an early contributor to the *Literary Gazette*, had become one of the first two legal Metropolitan Commissioners in Lunacy from 1832 until his death in 1861. Jerdan would have been keen to hear his inside knowledge of the matter.

Jerdan's campaigning interest in the subject reappeared in the *Literary Gazette* in March 1840, in a review of *Aphorisms and management of the insane, with consideration on public and private lunatic asylums, pointing out the errors in the present system.*[29] The reviewer noted, "the disease is a frightful one and ages have passed over generations of men and women without its being sufficiently investigated or understood. In later days, some steps have been taken towards remedying this crying evil, but much, very much, yet remains to be done; and with such a guide before us, we trust it will not be long before that great desideration is partially if not wholly accomplished . . . " An issue of the *Literary Gazette* in 1844 gave the front pages to a review of *The General Report for 1843 of Bridewell and Bethlem.*[30] Most unusually, extracts formed only one-third of Jerdan's article which rejoiced that treatment of the insane had, over time, moved from the punitive to the gentle; science had at last realised that there was still "a spark among the ashes which, by care and skill, may be fanned into the natural and regulated illumination of soul, and the rational be reclaimed from the irrational, and the wretched restored to society, usefulness and peace". He told readers that "when our *Gazette* was young", "it was the first public journal in England to direct attention to the course of remedial and alleviating lunatic treatment adopted at Aversa in Italy . . . at Massachusetts, at York and at Perth". To write his article, Jerdan himself went to visit Bethlem and described in much detail the excellent conditions he found there. He then quoted some statistics from the Report, highlighting the benefits of providing useful employments for the insane. He made a case for England to have a "self-supporting asylum" on the lines of one in Paris, explaining how his would work.

An article on "Insanity from Chloroform" highlights the possibility of understanding what might have happened to Mary Maxwell.[31] It discussed three cases of insanity following the administration of chloroform during childbirth, reported at a meeting of the Westminster Medical Society. One woman became maniacal and was removed to an asylum where, after twelve months, she recovered her reason and was released. A second woman never recovered at all, whilst the third became excitable and behaved like a child, a condition which lasted five months. Chloroform could also cause instant death, a high price to pay for "stupefaction during labour". By the 1850s there was a huge increase in the number of women admitted to asylums and this was, perhaps, one of the reasons. The 1850s was also the time when Jerdan's general interest became more personal. He devoted the front pages of the *Literary Gazette* to several publications under the heading of "Treatment of Insanity". As he had in his article six years earlier, he referred to the *Gazette*'s early notice of progressive treatment in Italy and other places, where "lenient or soothing treatment" superseded whips, chains and dark dungeons. The achievements of Dr John Conolly of the Middlesex Lunatic Asylum at Hanwell were discussed and praised, and extracts from his 'Croonian Lectures' delivered to the Royal College of Physicians took up most of the remaining review. Brief mentions were made of other writings on "Lunatics."

Jerdan also strongly supported the efforts of Dr Haslam, noting affectionately that he had "a tinge of that eccentricity which seems frequently to have accrued from scientific devotedness to the medical treatment of insanity, and mingling much with insane patients". By the time Jerdan wrote this, he could add a footnote, saying that "the aberrations of the afflicted have not the same tendency to affect the minds of those who are charged with the most trying and interesting of all human trusts, the care of them, and the device of means to restore them to their sorrowing friends".[32]

~~25~~

Men I Have Known

Writing his usual new year letter to Francis Bennoch, Jerdan thanked him for the "Carte" with which Marion was "much gratified", and "admires the likeness and expression".[1] The 'Carte de Visite' was a small photograph mounted on a card the size of a normal visiting card, and had been introduced in France in 1854; it was a popular format in Britain throughout the second half of the nineteenth century. Not to be outdone, Jerdan reported that he had "sat to Mr Carrick according to orders, but the sun was not favourable and the artist feared there was not force enough to afford the Negatives". The Carrick mentioned was most likely to have been Thomas Heathfield Carrick, miniature painter turned photographer. Between 1841 and 1866 Carrick exhibited his miniatures at the Royal Academy, his sitters including some of Jerdan's associates and acquaintance, such as Lord John Russell, Eliza Cook, William Macready and William Farren of the Garrick Club. Towards the end of this period Carrick started a photographic studio in Regent's Circus, London which failed in 1868. Because of Jerdan's mention of negatives, he was clearly sitting for a photograph rather than a miniature. This photograph has not been found, and the only known photograph of Jerdan was by Charles Watkins, whose studio, with his brother John, was well known for its portraits of "artists and culturally influential people in the years between 1840 and 1875."[2] (See illustration no. 3.) This photograph shows Jerdan seated, holding a cane in his right hand, and looking squarely into the camera. His hair has thinned, and his raven locks have turned to white or grey, and he sports a drooping moustache. The strong similarity to the earlier sketches and engravings attest to the various artists' skill in depicting their subject.

The children of Jerdan's third family were close, as he told Bennoch: "Willie [William, born 1841], was down for two of our birthdays, (Marion's with Teddie's added)", and Jerdan was grateful to Bennoch for undertaking to write a letter of recommendation for William junior, and also to ask him to visit. "We know the value of a little countenance in the struggling time!" He had been to Town, and enjoyed his visit, and was cheered to find several letters on his return home. He had not been entirely forgotten. He felt his health considerably mended, to the point where "If the pressure was not so very – very – heavy, I do believe I might yet show a few flares of light before my sinking taper went out. But when 'Give us this Day' and 'Deliver us from evil' are the most anxious burthens of the Prayer, it is of small use to think of mental exertion or literary effort."

He did, however, make strenuous literary efforts in this period, the *Leisure Hour* carrying fifteen 'Men I Have Known' articles over twelve issues from February to November. These included Perry of the *Chronicle*, d'Israeli the Elder, Pinnock and Maunder, Dean Buckland, John Trotter and the Rev. T. Frognall Dibdin. The subject of his failed attempt to research him in the British Museum, James Holman the Blind Traveller, was published in June, followed by Robert Southey, the Earl of Aberdeen, Thomas Cubitt and William Bullock of the famous Egyptian Hall. The final contenders in this year were Wordsworth, Sir David Wilkie and Archdeacon Nares.

Jerdan sometimes sent a copy of these occasional pieces to his old friends and frequent hosts, Lord and Lady Willoughby de Eresby at Drummond Castle near Crieff in Scotland. He was happy when Lady Willoughby replied, and now and again sent him a basket of produce from the estate, no doubt well received in his crowded cottage full of ever-hungry children. His gratitude was pathetic, plainly demonstrating his fall from sought-after editor and jolly companion to impoverished and lonely old man. "I assure you in perfect truth", he told her, "it has become almost a passion – a basket (I have to give thanks for one three weeks ago) – a letter – any sign of my not being forgotten, is a jubilee, of which it is impossible for your Ladyship or my Lord to imagine the enjoyment."[3] He sent her the *Leisure Hour* with his sketch of the late Lord Aberdeen, and mentioned that he had read of Earl and Lady Sefton visiting Drummond Castle recently. This had prompted old memories, and he asked his patient correspondent,

> Can your Ladyship recollect a sudden storm on the Lake which drenched the fair Lady, in thin costume, whom I was trying to boat, to the skin. I remember your Ladyship's amusement when I brought my half-drowned charge home and presented her as Lady Muslin or Muslineux ... I trust that this, like other of my exploits at Drummond Castle, may not come to be misrepresented – but Albrecht [Lady Willoughby's son] told my friend Durham, the sculptor, that I went out shooting in my dress-shoes – which is certainly a libel, to be denied if ever I should meet my young friend of old.

His humour was laboured, and at last he confessed:

> I have passed a sad year, amid painful privations, reducing me so low as to render even partial recovery very precarious. As it is, I am now brought

face to face with the cold, wintry weather, most unprepared for the struggle and liking to hum Dibdin's ballad.[4] Whether to live or die, the Doctor did not know, and it is all I can now do, as patiently as possible await the issue, avert the dark thoughts, and encourage the cheerful . . . P.S. Oh, I might hope for another letter – angel visits.

In December he wrote to Lady Willoughby again, to thank her husband for his "vital succour", quoting a French writer:" 'Woe to him who depends wholly on his pen . . . ' I am afraid that disappointment and woe are only too certain to the man who has sacrificed a life to literature and depended upon the result. Always unapt for business it has made a sad wreck of my closing years, for the comparative blest comfort of which I again and again return my heartfelt acknowledgements."[5] Jerdan had not taken to heart the many criticisms of his *Autobiography* about his constant complaint that literature had caused his poverty when in fact it had been his own profligacy.

He enclosed for her Ladyship some of his "latest trifles in print", telling her with some disgust that the editor of the *Leisure Hour* had taken his story, "The Godless Ship", "and docked it in the *Sunday at Home* without my cognisance, where I do not like it so well and I like still less a small splice or two of lower-church phraseology, which is not in my style". The *Sunday at Home*, sister paper to the *Leisure Hour* started two years later, was designed to promote wholesome family reading. Jerdan's tale appeared in two instalments, on 7 and 14 November 1863. It was based on a true incident about a competent master mariner whose single fault was his ignorance of religion. No services were held aboard his ship, no thanks were given to God for nature's wonders or deliverance from storms. Jerdan told the story of a voyage to Australia in 1859 when the ship was embroiled in a terrible hurricane, badly damaging the vessel. The skill of the captain and crew repaired it, but neglected to offer prayers for their salvation. The narrative centred upon a death leading to such a brawl that the Captain had the instigator put in irons. Morale on the ship became low, and the vessel was "a hell upon the face of the tranquil waters". The captain refused to land, as he would then have had to commit his prisoner to gaol, and preferred him to suffer his punishment on the ship. Vengeance and rage was rife, leading inevitably to a climax, when the first instalment ended.

The second instalment took up the tale when "the avalanche of evil was at hand". Suspicious officers, discontented crew, and wretched, beaten boys ruled over by a tyrannical captain made for a desperate situation. Suddenly, the ship struck an iceberg creating a huge leak which only the strength and skill of the imprisoned sailor could repair. The captain was forced to release him from his chains; he dived into the icy waters and covered the hole with a sail, stemming the inrushing water. Afterwards however, he was responsible for another death. The crew mutinied and the murderer killed the captain. Jerdan vividly described the ensuing mayhem. All officers were murdered and thrown into the sea – no evidence could be left to indict the murderers. "Oh, what a reckoning for those who had never bent a knee in supplication to their God; who had never acknowledged his infinite mercy in a Redeemer . . . " were not Jerdan's words, but the Editor's, determined to reinforce the Christian message of his paper. The ship's owners, believing after many months that the vessel had been lost at sea, were paid out by the insurers, and were amazed one day, when two boys, the only survivors from its crew, appeared in their offices to tell their tale: how they had waited until all the men were insensibly drunk, and killed them, and how the two had somehow brought the ship to shore.

The dreadful fate of all these men was, in the *Sunday at Home*, put down to the captain running a "Godless ship"; the Christian message was spelled out more clearly than Jerdan would have originally written, an editorial intervention he was unhappy about but powerless to amend, not having been asked for his views or permission to alter his story. The two boys did not escape retribution for their own killing spree. They were awarded salvage money, with which one drank himself to death within three months, and the other embarked on an emigrant ship which never arrived at Sydney. Jerdan told Lady Willoughby that he had heard the tale from "the freighter of the vessel, my neighbour here, Mr Hodgson, Governor of the Bank".[6] The Editor had somewhat softened the details, Jerdan told her, "to avoid sensation writing, as in truth the crew were killed by the boys literally cleaving the sculls (sic) of their persecutors with hatchets when they were drunk".

This was a violent story without any morality, transformed by the Editor into a tale where Christian redemption would have saved everyone had they only been believers. Jerdan's own Christianity was an integral part of his upbringing but not, from his actions, central to his life; he would have been far more interested in the narrative and action of his story than its Christian message. He also sent his correspondent other extracts, these from the *Leisure Hour*, including "a brief sketch of Wilkie and the account of the painting of the Rent Day for the King of Bavaria." Jerdan sent a small packet to Drummond Castle before Christmas, "to repair some blundering I discovered in my last enclosure".[7] He also sent, marked as "For Lady Willoughby de Eresby", an old Jacobite song entitled *Culloden* by Nicholson. It began "The heath-cock craw'd o'er muir and dale", and the last two lines read "The sword has fallen frae aut his hands,/His bonnet blue lies stained and bloody!" Jerdan commented that "The change of chorus in the last verse seems to me most touching and the mere allusion to the sword and bonnet the soul of poetry."[8]

He never lost his innate love of literature. Acknowledging that he wanted a favour, he told Bulwer of his novel *The Caxtons*, "if ever there was a classic in any language will last as such in the English tongue. How great a success in so small a compass!"[9] The favour was once again on behalf of one of his sons, this time Henry, who was now twenty-six. Jerdan's sketch of his son's life to this point is poignant and telling:

> As the Great Patron of the Drama I have sent you a Bill in which I am deeply interested. Do you remember helping me to redeem my son from the harsh military servitude. That effort failed and the effort was dissipated; my poor lad remaining, as you may see, from the Bill, playing female characters, which bespeak no athlete form or constitution. He is indeed a gentle boy, affectionate and deserving. Once before he came home the only soul saved from a fine merchantman in which he sailed from Liverpool; and it was upon another visit to that Port in which he failed in his object that he enlisted rather than return to be a burden on his father. Well, you may truly say What is that to me, and I can only reply it is dear to me on the very out-boundary of life, and the help of friendship will be a delightful illumination of the flickering lamp. His companion [. . .] the <u>husband</u> in The Rifle[10] is being bought off, and if Henry can be restored to liberty, has offered to take care of his "Wife" till better can be accomplished. Thus has been my urgency but I am very powerless.

The following year Jerdan reported to Bennoch that 'Harry' was a Corporal in Canada, a life that may not have been appropriate for "a gentle boy". Later in life he did indeed become a professional actor.

In November, Jerdan's son Walter, now aged twenty, came for his Sunday visit to the family on Bushey Heath. Jerdan gave him some money to deliver to Bennoch, on the way to his office in Gresham House. The money was to repay Bennoch for helping him with the draper's bill. Jerdan also sent some papers for the archives of the Noviomagians, marvelling how time had flown since his convivial days in their society. Now, he told Bennoch, "I am pottering out and near the end of my journey. It may be that we have a few cheerful meetings yet, but such angel visits cannot be far between."[11] Jerdan's references to "angel visits" may have been his attempt to avert the evil eye but he had a few more years still left to him and a major book to produce. In December he wrote to an unnamed lady, "It is a well-known fact that I am not a millionaire. Yet, though set down for it, I never was a careless man. I was naturally and simply regardless of money, as I am still, and shall be till cemetery time . . . "[12] Jerdan seemed oblivious of the fact that his being "regardless of money" had caused hardships to his family, annoyance and embarrassment to his friends, and the loss of his own hard-won good reputation.

The *Leisure Hour*, having featured of many of the "Men" Jerdan had known in the previous year, soft-pedalled in 1864 with his series appearing in only three issues. Sir James Ross and the gastronome Dr Kitchiner were featured together in October, with John Britton the following week, while Sir Francis Chantrey the sculptor made an appearance in December.

The year began and ended with letters to Halliwell, the first enquiring for information about Shakspere's (sic) purchase of the Stratford property, and offering to call on an imminent visit to town. The old tone of friendship had disappeared, the greeting being "My dear Sir", but in his Christmas letter he was back to "Dear Halliwell". This letter was used as an excuse to wish his friend happy years ahead, and was ostensibly to draw Halliwell's attention to his "correcting Clare's Poems for a friend, and have met with a number of Northamptonshire archaisms . . . ".[13] He listed several, including "soodling: up and down strolling" and "chumbled: food storing by dormice". The novelty of such localized words might have charmed Jerdan now, although in earlier years he had criticised Clare's *The Village Minstrel* for words judged "radically low and insignificant . . . too decidedly provincial . . . ".[14] Always ready for any kind of word-play, especially puns, he explained to Halliwell, "Some time ago I amused myself by putting together a collection of slang and fashionable mis-used words to send to some magazine, and when I saw Mr Hotter's publication reviewed, I wrote him a note to say I had such matter to which he was welcome, without fee or reward, if he thought it might be of any use to him. He had not the civility to acknowledge my letter. If you have any intercourse with him, you may say that I tell the anecdote not to his credit." Jerdan had conveniently forgotten the times when he himself had delayed responding to similar letters. He was thirsty for any news, asking Halliwell for advice on the best Shakespeare editions, and whether Halliwell had made any new discoveries. "Aught to relieve my monot-onous life (after all my busy one) will always be prized . . . " A while later he was still thinking of Clare's Northamptonshire poems, illustrating his love of unusual words: Attempting a synonym for "dandering" he told Halliwell, was "Wandering helplessly, does not quite express it"; for "hirpling", "Crippling is not feeble enough" and so on.[15] He had recently been to London and dined with Vice Chancellor Stuart and slept in Brompton, but had not managed to call on Mrs Halliwell; his letter was "merely a passing thought to show that I am still alive and mindful of old friends".

He was not entirely forgotten, as a booklet published in March by the London Society called "London Papers and London Editors" devoted more than four of its sixteen pages to him. It referred to his *Autobiography*, written to "coin his own life into money" after literary interest in him failed. The writer called the volumes "Queer, rambling, gossiping, egotistical books the most of them are, in which a good story, or a curious bit of local history, or some half-forgotten incident of parliamentary warfare is found overlaid with heaps of rubbish . . . the reader [must] surrender himself to the illusion that of all the men there described, Jerdan was the foremost – of all the scenes he was the hero." The rest of the article paraphrased the *Autobiography* and featured the quasi-sonnets on Byron which Taylor and Jerdan had printed in the *Sun,* forty-seven years earlier.

Jerdan's main focus now was on his family, and in response to an enquiry from Bennoch as to their welfare, he set out what his "boys" were now doing. The "boys" he referred to were his sons with Mary Maxwell, the children of his first two families being now either deceased or grown up, some with families of their own. This letter reveals more details about his family than any other single document yet discovered, and one can feel Jerdan's relief that some of his brood were making their own way in the world:[16]

> You ask about the "Boys".
> 1. **Charles**, a first Engineer, Galatea. Has just earned high praise by his gallantry in descending six or eight times in Diving dress to ascertain the injury the fine vessel had received in a hurricane. I am told the service is likely to promote him,[17] as the repairs of the ship abroad or at home rests on this examination of the very machinery he helped to make at Penns!
> 2. **Harry**, your old vis-à-vis in Canada – a Corporal!
> 3. **Wm** at Penns. Has been home a fortnight covered like Lazarus with boils. Is better and hopes to go with his regiment to the Review on Monday.
> 4. **Walter** in the Telegraph office Gresham House – under £40 pr ann. He and Wm mess together at Greenwich.
> 5. **Gilbert** at home – poor gardener nothing to do etc. Ahoy
> 6. **George (Tiny)** has been a fortnight with Mr Bickley a stock and insurance broker Union Court, Wood Street. He is brother of C. Bickley Matilda's husband – a character – but seems willing to give Tiny an introductory training at nominal wages.

> The younger boys are thriving on the Heath and short Commons – the youngest a vast pet, and very interesting in countenance and manners.

> As for me, I am off and on. Now and then expecting the Crisis; then rallying, and holding on through coughs, colds and the long etceteras that pertain to fourscore. When I am in good case I really thrive wonderfully and it is only at straining epochs (too frequent) that I bid so fair to fall off my perch.

> Oh if I had the power to show you how I value yr friendship by lending you a lift, you would not be able to fancy me a mere Begging Letter Importer. I am sick of myself, yet always the same.

The "Penn's" mentioned as ex-employers of Charles and where William was currently employed, made ships' machinery; the boils suffered by William, and at an earlier time by Charles, could well have been caused by the lead used in such a manufacturing process. "Harry" was the Henry who, in his youth, had so admired Bennoch, and who was following in the family Army tradition in the footsteps of his uncle and older half-brother, having recently tried his luck upon the stage.

Jerdan's final group of 'Men' for his series in the *Leisure Hour* featured Lord de Tabley, founder of the first Gallery for British art, coupled in February with the famous artist Sir Thomas Lawrence, followed by another artist Sir David Roberts, in June. August was given to Jerdan's dear friend Sir Willoughby de Eresby, September to Forbes and the final contribution in this series in October was devoted to John Galt.

From the depths of his isolation and despair, his fear of being forgotten and abandoned in the previous two or three years, Jerdan seemed to have taken on a new lease of life in the summer of 1865. He accepted an invitation from Halliwell delivered by Wright – his two collaborators on the Camden and Percy Societies – to attend a dinner in town. His good mood continued although he had been ill again, telling Halliwell in September,

> Dic mitic who was the author of Chrononhotonthologus – about what period etc. I hope you are all well with Mrs Halliwell and daughter enjoying the country or returned like Chinese gigantics refreshed, to partake of the comforts of home. I have just weathered an attack of gout on the head, which is a very grave matter; but I may yet live to see you with a better vis-à-vis at table than, Dear Halliwell, Yours very sincerely,[18]

His better mood was because he had been hard at work again on his final book, *Men I Have Known*, based on his *Leisure Hour* articles.

Jerdan was very unwell[19] and his hand-writing was unusually shaky, when he asked Halliwell in December to vote for a Mr Acworth at a meeting of the Society of Antiquaries.[20] Having left the Society many years earlier, he had no direct influence, but would have been happy to think that his opinion could still make a difference.

He still managed to keep in touch with his daughters by Landon. A surviving letter to Ella in Australia reads:

> My dear Ella, I send you my Autograph at the age of Eighty-four and upwards – rather downwards. I think you have neglected me a good deal, but I rejoice, not the less, that you are well-doing in the world. Laura is a dear Creature and I love her beyond expression. I have been greatly pleased with the accounts of your children. Perhaps the new generation in the next few years may lead to many acceptable recognitions when I am in the grave. Till I go, believe me Ella to be most affectionately Your, W Jerdan.[21]

Jerdan's letter to Ella did not use the terms 'daughter' or 'father' perhaps from a sense of concern that such acknowledgement could somehow compromise him, his latest young family or Ella herself. His rather wistful hope that his paternity might eventually be recognized is a touching insight into the heart of a loving and gentle man whose faults were many, but never included neglect of any of his children. Jerdan took a great interest in them all, using whatever influence he had to assist them in gaining positions or advancement. Unfortunately, nothing has been found to support this interest in the case of Fred Stuart in Trinidad, but the absence of surviving evidence does not mean that it never existed. Laura Landon had been well placed with the Goodwins and needed no support from Jerdan, and Ella Stuart had married well and was secure. Ella and her half-brother Charles met in Melbourne during the visit of the *Galatea* on which 'Coz Charlie' was an engineering officer. It was a ceremonial trip captained by HRH The Duke of Edinburgh.[22] (See illustration no. 8.) There were several weeks between November 1867 and January 1868 whilst the ship was in Melbourne when the officers had considerable free time, and it was likely to have been during this period that the two children of the same father but different mothers forged a friendship which continued to future generations.

Suddenly, Jerdan was busy again. He told Gaspey, "I am plunged in press-correcting and know not of the hour to spare; and, my friend, I am not so alert as I was with brain, pen and limbs. I cannot walk far . . . I am seeing my volume of Eminent and Exemplary Men I Have Known through the press – and the task has been and is quite and more than quite enough for my old head. I expect little from the publication but hope it will be some small help."[23] His activity was a welcome distraction, as he had other news to tell his old friend: "My two boys sailed for Adelaide on Tuesday and I have just had a good (female) cry over their Farewell letters from Plymouth". The boys were George, known as 'Tiny', and Gilbert, who arrived on 16 April 1866 on the *Atalanta*. Their voyage of eighty-one days had been plagued by severe winds and then long calms; seven children died on the journey.[24] Worse than two sons going off to make their lives in Australia was the untimely death of his daughter Tilly at the age of 29. She left two daughters for her husband Charles Bickley to care for. He remarried at the beginning of September 1868, a Julia Archer, and died in 1877 aged thirty-eight.

Jerdan compiled his book from the *Leisure Hour* articles with no certainty of getting it published. He originally offered it to Richard Bentley, whom he had yet again somehow offended greatly, without knowing why.

> I was sorry to hear from Mr Macaulay that you did not think my Volume had sufficient interest for the risk of publication. Your letter, declining it, has somewhat touchingly recalled my memory to other times, when, for many years, you and I held on together in very friendly and pleasant inter-

course and I passed many happy social days in the enjoyment of your personal intercourse, not uncongenial with our little literary concerns.

I am aged now, and regret the more that any misunderstanding should have broken off this agreeable state of relation, but I never felt otherwise toward you but to wish you well with all my heart, and so it was not in my power to mend the rent.[25]

In April, *Men I Have Known* was published by George Routledge and Sons. The genre of biographical sketches mixed with memoirs was popular at the time and, with the vast acquaintance he had accumulated over the years, coupled with his experience of biography writing for *Fisher's National Portrait Gallery*, Jerdan was well placed to make his own contribution in a huge effort to swell his coffers. Routledge printed one thousand copies. Their costs of composition, engraving, machining and paper totalled just over £189. Jerdan's royalties were a few pence over £48.[26] Considering that much of the material had already been paid for by the *Leisure Hour*, this was a sum he would have been satisfied to receive. The book was a collection of all his pieces for the *Leisure Hour*, and Jerdan dedicated it to his "Dear Friend", Rt. Hon. The Lord Chief Baron Pollock, referring him to the entries on Truro and Hallam especially, as they mentioned Pollock. Emotionally, Jerdan's dedicatory letter continued, "But, above all, an intimate friendship rendered (to my feelings) almost sacred by the extent of its period from youth to age, inspires my earnest wish to dedicate the last of my literary efforts to One who has cheered my path and comforted my toil, throughout every concomitant vicissitude and anxiety. It is but a faint expression of the faithful attachment and affectionate regard . . . "

The subjects Jerdan chose had all, to some extent, been friends or acquaintances, and he had selected them from amongst writers, poets, artists, scientists, politicians and explorers; very few had appeared in his biographies in *Fisher's National Portrait Gallery* in the 1830s, but where there were duplications, Jerdan's treatment of them was completely different. His entry on Wilkie is an example, as in the *Portrait Gallery* Wilkie's status and artistic achievements were paramount, but in *Men I Have Known*, Jerdan wrote warmly of the artist as a man and a friend in a much more intimate style. He necessarily omitted an article on his Dedicatee, Frederick Pollock, as all other subjects in his book were dead. The book was arranged alphabetically, not in the order the articles had appeared in the *Leisure Hour*, and could thus not cause offence to anyone sensitive to hierarchy. Jerdan wrote a brief Preface, which was mainly an apology to those who might consider such a book to be egotistical, "but its very nature precluded the use of any other style, and its Author hopes he has neither transgressed the rules of propriety, nor laid himself open to the charge of weak vanity". All those harsh critics of his *Autobiography* had apparently left their mark on his self-confidence. On revising his *Leisure Hour* articles, he noted, "some congenial additional matter" had become available and been appended to the original papers. In some cases, such as the entry on Lord Truro, the Addendum was far longer than the original piece and quoted a letter from Pollock, surprised that Jerdan had not mentioned their three-sided friendship. To the piece on Lord Willoughby de Eresby, Jerdan had added an extra sketch, of Lady de Eresby for whom he had great affection and who had been kind to him whilst he struggled with poverty.

Jerdan's style throughout was, as the title indicated, that of personal experience of the history and character of his diverse subjects, positive and uncritical, but not sycophantic. His articles and Addenda formed a substantial octavo book of four hundred and ninety pages, and included a Postscript in which he vouched for the truthfulness of his sketches and begged "indulgence for its imperfections". He had looked back at a panorama of a long life and remarkable personages and others who had been forgotten. "For the rest," he continued, "it is a weary journey to look back upon; and at an age beyond fourscore, with flagging brain and wavering hand be reminded that my work must be very nearly done." Endeavouring to pre-empt criticism of some anecdotes thought to be "too trivial to contribute effectually to the elucidation of character", Jerdan invoked the dictum of Horace Walpole who observed that trifles may appear in a stronger light in retrospect. He apologized in advance that only the memory and experience of age can "reveal, verify and satisfactorily discuss", and that "there are many interesting things which must suffer when left to report and conjecture to determine". He pleaded unashamedly to any potential critic:

> I am still so beset with saucy doubts and fears about my own production, that I would fain bespeak the gentle handling which my shortcomings need ... My revelations ought to have been of a higher order; but there are things that cannot be told, and I can only offer my contribution, in its unassuming form, to the fund of general information. May it be accepted!

Such insecurity was sad in a man who, for over thirty years, had been an arbiter of literary taste; here was Jerdan at eighty-four, running scared of adverse criticism such as he had suffered with his *Autobiography*. It is remarkable that he had managed to produce such a substantial quantity of work over the previous few years, and then added extra material to bolster his book.

Whilst awaiting the reviews Jerdan remarked on his efforts to a friend, "I hope it may be liked. I deserve some praise as revealing some curious facts and exhibiting not a few characteristic traits of my time and Men though in the poor cloudy amber of querulous age."[27] He had not too long to wait. On 2 June the *Athenaeum* noticed his book, only mildly sarcastically:

For many reasons, including the recollection of past controversies (hard enough in their time), this book by Mr Jerdan can be here spoken of only in a tolerant, rather than critical spirit. It is a republication of scattered papers contributed to the *Leisure Hour*, with annotations and corrections. If literary historians to come fail to find in it those marking anecdotes which are welcome as 'illustrating character', they may recognize the placid and gentle spirit befitting one who (as we are here told) in its pages, closes accounts with a long and busy life. There is no reckoning with faults of taste and judgment under the circumstances.

In stark contrast the July issue of the *London Review*, under the heading 'Contemporary Celebrities', moaned:

How wearisome is that class of literature, if indeed it be literature at all, which thrives and flourishes on the rank soil of scandalous gossip, and is popular just in proportion as it gratifies an idle, if not an impertinent, curiosity! 'Men Whom I Have Known' – 'Men whom I Have Seen' – 'Places I Have Visited' – how well we know the contents before reading a page of the volume! Next we shall have 'Wives I Have Flirted With' – 'Cabmen who have cheated me' – and 'Women who object to smoking'. These, indeed would be an agreeable change after the inanities under which we have suffered so long. Would that somebody would give us an account of 'Men he has *not* seen', or of 'Places he has *not* visited'.

Having complained thus bitterly, the reviewer grudgingly observed, "By these remarks we would not imply that Mr Jerdan's book is among the worst of its class: there are many things in it which deserve recording, and, were it not so, we could willingly overlook its failings out of respect to the writer's great and lengthened services to literature." A few of Jerdan's factual errors were pointed out, followed by descriptions of his articles on several of his 'Men'. The review concluded fairly positively that although it could not name all of the 'Men', they "refer readers to the volume, where they will find Mr Jerdan's pen-and-ink sketches lively enough, if not always very new."

The *New Sporting Magazine* was much more enthusiastic and right on Jerdan's wavelength: "Mr Jerdan's style is delightful to every reader and there is no book in our literature on which we would so readily stake the fame of the old unpolluted English language – no book which shows so well how rich that language is in its own proper wealth and how little it has been improved by all that it has borrowed."[28] *Notes & Queries* gave the book a warm review posssibly prompted by the prospect of advertisements for it such as duly appeared on 23 June, promising that it "will be read by the public with the greatest pleasure and the greatest profit".

Just as Jerdan had created *Men I Have Known* from his *Leisure Hour* articles, now he attempted to create a further commission from his book. In September he wrote to John Blackwood, son of his old Edinburgh friend William, mentioning his book and in particular the article on John Galt. Galt's son was now Finance Minister of Canada, and "when he was over in England he and I had some intercommunion about his Father's life and works". [29] Blackwood owned the copyright and Jerdan asked him whether he thought "there is any fair prospect for a good biography and a new edition of the best of Galt's works?" Playing on his old associations Jerdan took the opportunity of enclosing a contribution asking for "a place in *Maga*" or if not, that it be sent to his nephew at the *Kelso Mail*. Not receiving a reply Jerdan approached Blackwood's London colleague, a Mr Langford, asking if his letter had been delivered. "I am sure no pooh-poohing can be meant. To repel a friendly correspondence which existed 49 years ago when Mr Blackwood and *Maga* and William Jerdan and the *Literary Gazette* started together. He never published a Work respecting which I was not immediately informed and frankly interested – not only, indeed, as an influential kinsman but a personal and family friend." [30] His appeal did not go unanswered, and Jerdan responded gratefully, explaining to Blackwood that he had been "retired and quiet" for more than ten years, and understood that others were "immersed in the engrossing business of life". His idea for the Galt biography had emanated from his book, he said, but "I fear it must remain an idea". Regarding the contribution he had enclosed with his earlier letter, he was "half-ashamed to say it was a rhyming attempt to depict 'The Working Man' as the coming dictatorial power of the Country and which, if accepted, might have procured me the pride of once more appearing on the page of Maga. Most likely you think that there can be no *Jeu d'esprit* in a brain over four score years, ramshackling, and I am, myself, pretty much of that opinion." Blackwood would be fifty in April, Jerdan noted, the same month in which he would be eighty-five.

Jerdan's brain was not "ramshackling" at all, but reinvigorated by his renewed activity. He took up his interest in the magazine *Notes & Queries* and in the second half of 1866 there appeared thirteen entries under his pen name, 'Bushey Heath'. These covered topics as diverse as a Relic of Charles I which he had seen as a young man, some explanations of Scottish and common sayings, and a note on the witty sayings of Lord Erskine. His fourth entry was about Blackwoods, a detailed enquiry about a preface found in one early edition but not another. This is signed 'T.B.' and does not read like a letter from Jerdan, but it is indexed under the name 'Bushey Heath'. Jerdan's fascination with words is evident in several of his contributions, as is his humour. As an example, in August he offered, "Is not <u>smittle</u> equivalent to, or a mere variation of <u>smitten</u> i.e. smitten by a disease which if contagious, becomes a <u>smittle</u> complaint?" He discussed the meaning of the farewell blessing "God speed", and "salamagundy", "a north country saladian concoction of which a salt herring (instead of the southern lobster) is the primary ingredient. It was a favourite dish years ago, and very relishing and toothsome". One can hear his lips smacking over his ill-fitting false teeth at the memory! The variety of Jerdan's *Notes & Queries* is astonishing; in the same issue he offered a schoolboy version of an old song and a disquisition on the pronounciation and etymology of the surname of the poet Cowper. In December he railed against the careless idiomatic use of English, noting that even in respectable publications one finds 'neither' followed by 'or' rather than 'nor', and other misuses. If he had no other occupation at this time one could understand these detailed and varied contributions, but he was busier than he had been for a long time, so it is evident that such miscellaneous matters were of importance to him, and that he was keen to have his opinion known in the world; but then, if so, why use a pen name?

In July 1866 Jerdan's long-time friend the novelist and politician Edward Bulwer was elevated to the peerage, becoming Lord Lytton Bulwer-Lytton. Writing to congratulate him, Jerdan said:

> My dear Bulwer, I will once, before I write 'my Lord', address you by the old familiar name, to say that in all that can contribute to your honour and happiness I continue to feel the deepest interest. When you were in your youth and I was about my prime, our intimacy began, and in all that has happened to you since – every step by step – it has been my joy and pride, and I may add my acceptable privilege, to go along with you, if possible with good offices and always with good wishes. No living soul can more sincerely congratulate you on your wholly earned elevation to be an English baron. Soft and long auspiciously worn may the coronet be.[31]

Their ways, once so intertwined, had gone in such very different directions, especially since Landon's marriage and untimely death, but it was Jerdan's instinct to be generous and not envious of his friend's ennoblement and success.

Jerdan was extremely sensitive about being forgotten in his old age. He had spent many decades in the centre of activities both cultural and political and it was not surprising that his resentment occasionally boiled over, albeit thinly disguised. Evidence for this is a letter he wrote to Halliwell in 1867, having watched his erstwhile close friend and colleague being extremely busy in the preceding period. In 1865 Halliwell was involved in thirteen publications, all of a scholarly nature, in which he edited documents related to his Shakespearian studies. In 1866 a further three appeared, and the catalyst for Jerdan's letter was yet another volume edited by Halliwell which had just been published in 1867, "Selected Extracts from the ancient registry of the causes tried in the Court of Record at Stratford-upon-Avon in the time of Shakespeare; including many entries respecting the poet's family." Most of these and subsequent publications were printed in only ten copies, a fact Jerdan chose to ignore. His April letter to Halliwell read, in part:

> Is it not a strange thing that as soon as <u>one</u> is out of the way, people forget <u>their</u> old friends and publish, and publish, and publish, without ever thinking that it might gratify the aforesaid to be complimented with a remembrance. Now, you see I am particularly sensitive on this subject . . . I seem to feel, as it were, rather neglected. There is a wise old Scottish proverb, "No more pipe, no more dance" and indeed I can suggest no earthly reason . . . why there should be any dancing to keep up the ball, after the music has ceased . . . I have been confined to bed and chair since March 20th with a severe and dangerous illness, but am again slowly and wonderfully recovering . . . [32]

His purpose was to make Halliwell feel guilty about neglecting to send him his publications, but for Halliwell, as with so many other of Jerdan's one-time friends, it seems to have been a case of out-of-sight, out-of mind.

Jerdan took a break from his entries in *Notes & Queries* during 1867, with a single exception in February where he commented on historical books dealing with George III. He reported that he had heard, from an informant of "eminent qualifications", that the King had been able to deal with his correspondence speedily and effectively, demonstrating a clear understanding of the Constitution, contrary to reports in the books under review. Jerdan's loyalty to the late King is touching if, in the light of better informed history, misguided. He signed his name to a column of "Varieties" in the *Leisure Hour* of 1 March 1867, which included topics as diverse as nightingales, the American book trade and discharged prisoners.

26

Characteristic Letters

Following his long series in the *Leisure Hour* Jerdan started a new series for the same magazine in February 1868 called 'Characteristic Letters', with the tag line "Communicated by the author of 'Men I Have Known'." His column appeared once a month and the first instalment opened with the challenging question: "Why should a man 'be *dead* a hundred years' – by which time nobody cares much about him – before it is reckoned quite timely to illustrate his character by publishing any of his correspondence? . . . a single letter, or a single expression in a letter, has often marked a striking trait in the character of the writer, which might furnish a key to the right interpretation of much of his outward life and action."[1] Jerdan claimed that he had selected from his mass of papers those which would not "hurt a feeling of the living or violate a sanctuary of the dead". With a ring of false modesty, he assured readers that he had to print a complete letter even though this could mean the inclusion of "passages complimentary to myself", in his former capacity as editor of the *Literary Gazette*. The chosen letters represented a wide range of correspondents, and Jerdan alternated the letters with brief personal memories, anecdotes or observations about each correspondent. His first subject was the scientist Michael Faraday, whose letter informing Jerdan that the Royal Institution had chosen him as its first Chair of Chemistry was reprinted here. Jerdan's second subject in this initial column was Hans Christian Andersen, whose warm letters of 1847–48 Jerdan was proud to include.

Despite being overlooked on the occasion of Andersen's last visit to England in 1857, Jerdan wrote to him in February 1868, enclosing a copy of the *Leisure Hour* featuring his article on Andersen's letters. His accompanying note was friendly and personal:

I dare say you will be surprized to see a letter from One you left so old a personage that you could hardly expect to hear from him after so long a period of time had elapsed. Yet here I am in the breathing world, still, though verging on my 86th birthday, and still remembering with true-hearted feelings every circumstance which united us in mutual regard and esteem during your visit to London – to London, wonderfully, and, to me, sadly changed since you were here.

But why am I induced to you now. I hope you will receive with this the monthly part of a periodical of vast circulation, *The Leisure Hour*, to which I have ventured to contribute a memorial of our friendly intercourse. I trust you will rather be pleased with it, than blame it as a liberty with private correspondence. Tell me?!

Do you recollect the sweet pretty mother whom you enchanted with a Poet's kiss? She has been eleven years in her grave, leaving a fine boy of that age – the one knowing nothing of her gift, and the other nothing of his loss. The little girl whom you also kissed, declares she remembers it perfectly well, and consequently reads your Tales at our nightly fireside with important emphasis, as if one of the initiated. These Tales I enjoy as much as ever, though I observe errors in translations which do not do justice to the exquisite touches of the original, nor the finest of spirit and nature which only a few congenial souls can truly appreciate. Still, there is enough left for great popularity, and I see editions everywhere advertized by the "Trade". One of these, Routledge, borrowed from me the portrait engraving of yourself which you gave me with an inscription of praise and cordial affection, which I valued beyond prize. And it is most unpardonable – my picture is mislaid or lost – "strict search" is to be made for it! Confound the Trade and all who belong to it. I am on tenter hooks, as the saying is, and the wall of my little room despoiled, vacant, deplorable.

Might I hope for the delight of a letter from you? If?

It would, my dear friend, make me exceedingly happy.[2]

The "sweet pretty mother", Mary Maxwell, had in fact died in 1862, only six years previously, although to Jerdan it may have seemed like eleven. Her last child, as far as is known, was born in 1855, but from Jerdan's comment there seems to have been a later birth from which she died. No evidence for this "fine boy" has come to light.

The March issue of *Leisure Hour* reprinted letters from Benjamin Haydon, painter of vast pictures, thanking Jerdan for his kindness and sending a drawing in appreciation, with another letter from the time in 1846 when the Egyptian Hall made hundreds of pounds by exhibiting the midget, General Tomb Thumb, whilst takings for Haydon's own exhibition did not cover the room rent. These, said Jerdan, were examples of his opening claim, illuminating the true character of a man in a few strokes of the pen. There was a correspondent however, Jerdan admitted, who could not be delineated were all of his letters to be collected. His reference was to the volatile Dr Maginn, and the letters he chose to print were those from way back in 1821 when he first met the young Irishman. One of these quoted, "showed a bit of the temper of my friend"; having seen a copy of the *Literary Gazette*, Maginn confronted Jerdan with, "Do you intend to list yourself in the business of libelling me, or copying those who do? I ask merely for information; because if such be your design, it is a game at which two can play, and I hate being under an obligation to any man which I do not intend to return." Sorting through Maginn's letters must have brought back many bitter, as well as enjoyable, memories to Jerdan, especially their rivalry for Landon's affections. Jerdan made no reference to Maginn's slide into drink, destitution and early death, commenting only, "His eccentricity was a constant source of pleasantry to friends and no heinous offence to enemies."

Some of Jerdan's 'Characteristic Letters' throughout the year struggle to fit into his claim of illuminating character and have more the feel of filling his column inches, although this was definitely not the case with his April contribution, stirred by the appearance in January's *Quarterly Review* of Lockhart's *Life of Sir Walter Scott*. Jerdan did not know who the *Quarterly*'s reviewer was, but thought that "he is one of the very few remaining who are conversant with the facts and competent to handle the subject". Saying how Scott, eleven years his senior, had lived in the same landscape, and attended the same school as he had, and how they had both collected ballads, Jerdan identified closely with Scott. He purported to be "amused" at their similarities and yet acknowledged their great difference in the pursuit of literature. Jerdan had displeased Scott once in reviewing a late novel, he recalled, and Scott evaded Jerdan's visit to him at Abbotsford, although friendly at a subsequent meeting. "I felt some satisfaction in having a sad posthumous revenge", wrote Jerdan, "by being one on the sub-committee of management for preserving Abbotsford in the family and by my zeal in adding a considerable amount to the subscription." He paired letters from Scott with some from James Ballantyne, and gave a brief note on John Ballantyne, from whom he had no letters to print.

On 1 May Jerdan chose the letter he had received from Wordsworth irritably rejecting his suggestion of recording an imminent tour of the continent for publication in the *Literary Gazette*. The poet scolded, "Periodical writing, in order to strike, must be ambitious, and this style is, I think, in the record of tours and travels, intolerable, or at any rate the worst that can be chosen." Reinforcing his theme of poets, Jerdan printed James Hogg's letter of December 1832 discussing *inter alia*, his desire to marry Mary Jerdan to his nephew, together with those of two more minor figures.

In preparing for this series, Jerdan, in a note of 24 May, requisitioned some material from his old friend Francis Bennoch, accepting his offer for letters from Mary Russell Mitford.[3] Sympathizing with his friend's current troubles, Jerdan told him how, although he could "bear my own sickness and troubles as well as may be," he could not so well endure those of a friend who had given him so much sympathy and assistance in times of want. He had heard from "all the

Australian boys . . . the Queenslanders have a hard and rough fight with that new world", he confided to Bennoch. A subsequent letter, three weeks later, returned one of the four letters of Mitford's, and asked Bennoch whether he had seen the column on Haydon, as he had been alluded to. "The Sculptor has cut me dead, though I am still alive," he complained, possibly referring to Durham. "Strange it is. I was his earnest friend in his early life – we have been friends through not a few intervening years, and he has been the friend of my decline. But I have not heard from him for months . . . I fear I have lived too long and tired out remembrance of auld lang syne in some instances!"[4] This neglect, or perceived neglect, of old friends hurt Jerdan deeply, especially in the many cases where he had been the means by which the writer or artist came into public recognition. But he was very old now, living far from Town and of no more practical use in promoting his friends. As he told Bennoch, "it is a way of the world, but I did not expect it in that quarter". When Jerdan returned Mitford's letters to Bennoch he explained that "The *Leisure Hour* does not afford much space or honorarium, but it is all very well towards the pot-boiling as far as it goes."[5] He was enjoying old copies of a magazine, the *Once a Week* (published between 1859–1865) which had been lent to him, and asked Bennoch to identify his contributions. Jerdan was feeling better and thought he may even visit London again. "But uncertainty rather predominate after 86, and when the bad bits happen, I can only reconcile myself to a quiet look up at Mr. Auctioneer Death's uplifted hammer and bide to see whether the lot is put off unsold, or it is to come down "Going – Gone!" and I shall be no more."

Before the hammer fell, however, Jerdan had more 'Characteristic Letters' to send to the *Leisure Hour*. In June he mentioned the Irish bard James Sheridan Knowles, and the novelist and poet Barbara Hofland, but the greater part of the issue of 1 June was reserved for his great friend of many years Crofton Croker, even though Croker had died before the rift between them could be mended. Celebrating Croker's writings about his homeland, Ireland, Jerdan noted sadly, "He was taken from us before Ireland had fallen upon the evil days of which we hear so much". What would Croker have thought now, he wondered; "Where are the Irish characteristics – the good humour, the sportiveness, the nonchalance, the open-heartedness, and the brave endurance of hardship or misfortune." Jerdan mused that he hoped the visit of the Prince and Princess of Wales would be the harbinger of better days for Ireland – he would have been appalled to know that it would take more than a hundred and thirty years before this could happen. He shared two of his friend's letters from 1828, explaining how Croker often "engrafted the pencil on to the pen", reproducing a drawing Croker had sent to accompany his account of suffering from gout, his left arm in a sling, a nightcap on his head, and hobbling on crutches. The letter was about *Literary Gazette* matters and then, responding to a note he had received from Jerdan, said, "I really sympathize hand and foot with our poor poetess. The possibility of one who possesses so much innate fire as L.E.L. catching cold, never entered my head." Even at the expense of reprinting such a trivial note, Jerdan could not resist a reference to Landon. He completed his section on Crofton Croker with an anecdote of the occasion when Mrs Croker and he, knowing friends were seeking a female servant, dressed Crofton Croker up as an applicant. Whilst waiting in the kitchen to be interviewed, he was regaled by the cook with confidential gossip about his prospective employers, painting such an awful picture that he took his leave hastily, before they saw him.

The July column was solely devoted to the Scottish poet Allan Cunningham, and August's to the "thorough socialist" Edward Forbes, whose comic verse on a British Association meeting at Dudley he printed, together with one on the *Anatomy of the Oyster* and other examples of Forbes's offerings. Jerdan coupled this with a smaller section on Edward Jesse who had recently died aged eighty-eight, formerly a Deputy Surveyor of Royal Parks and Palaces. Jerdan recounted the time when he told Jesse that a large and elusive trout had been caught at Windsor by a hook baited with apple blossom; believing him implicitly, Jesse included the story in a book he was currently seeing through the press, until persuaded that Jerdan had hoaxed him and so removed it.

Even though he now had enjoyable work again, Jerdan felt lonely and isolated. In July he wrote to his long-time friend Thomas Gaspey, wishing they

> were nearer for a gossip about the old times. You always refresh my mind, and stir up (as well as rectify) remembrances of the past. My memory, I regret to say gets confused and unsettled; so that a Flapper of Laputa would be very useful. The infirmity of deafness is also a sore drawback and to One who was, you know, a good deal courted for social circles, to be bravely tolerated in a very limited sphere is rather damaging to dear self-conceit.
>
> I cannot but fancy that either you or I might do something profitable in the periodical press; but the young puppies in possession of the kennel do not like the old dogs to intrude.
> Sic transit,
> Though ever the same Dear Gaspey, Yrs truly[6]

In the midst of assembling his letters for the *Leisure Hour* Jerdan's family suffered another unexpected bereavement. Writing again to Gaspey on black-bordered paper on 11 August, Jerdan told him, "I have been visited by one of the most dreadful calamities that could have befallen me, in the death of my son in law Irwin, who only at Lady Day entered into the possession of Macready's property at Elstree."[7] Irwin, aged fifty-eight, had been an Examiner in the Audit Office, and was the husband of Jerdan's oldest daughter, Frances-Agnes, whom he married in 1844. They had five children and seem to have been in comfortable circumstances. That Jerdan mourned Irwin's death in the terms he used, that it was a calamity for *him*, rather than for his daughter and grandchildren, would seem to indicate that Irwin made him an allowance or at least gave him money from time to time, the cessation of which would cause Jerdan much hardship. If Irwin had indeed helped Jerdan out in this way it was generous of him, as it had been his father-in-law's inability to pay *Literary Gazette* expenses which had landed Irwin, briefly a partner in the enterprise, in court. Frances-Agnes survived her husband by twenty-three years, dying in 1891 aged eighty-one.

Sad as he was at Irwin's early death, Jerdan still had to produce his column for the *Leisure Hour*. His September contribution concentrated on two famous literary Scotsmen, John Gibson Lockhart and the publisher John Murray. In introducing the section on Lockhart, Jerdan said that he was glad to have the chance to leave a brief tribute to him, as "few characters have ever been less understood or more misrepresented. But mine is a simple statement: neither an apology nor a defence . . . " Jerdan set Lockhart into the political context of his time, the high Tory against the opposition Whig press. Even so, Jerdan believed that "the style of criticism at the period referred to was less envenomed than it had previously been, and less dictatorially, and domineeringly offensive than it is generally at the present day". This was an odd statement from a man who had been personally subjected to venomous abuse in the period he was discussing. Lockhart and he had been on "the most confidential footing for twenty years", Jerdan claimed, and "a kinder hearted man did not exist". He printed Murray's letter of 1825 advising him that Lockhart was appointed editor of the *Quarterly Review*, a position he held for eighteen years. As son-in-law and biographer of Walter Scott, Lockhart had perforce been involved in the subscription committee to save Scott's home, Abbotsford, as had Jerdan. In addition to his other work Lockhart had written several works of fiction and Lives of Burns and Napoleon, as well as that of Scott. When he came to John Murray, Jerdan reported how Murray had turned down a proposal Jerdan made to him for a joint venture, claiming that he would make a "restless and fretful partner", and in another note a "restless and teasing partner". He remained on good terms with Jerdan, however, as the short note Jerdan printed, confirmed, "I am really yearning to see you . . . "

In October, Jerdan featured the novelist Mary Russell Mitford, commenting "How different the mental from the physical portrait! The first, a likeness of graceful form and simple beauty; the last, a picture of what Byron rudely called, 'a dumpy woman'." He smoothed this with praise of her writing, and mentioned that the Rev. Harness was her literary executor, and Francis Bennoch her friend. Between them they had planned to publish her correspondence and collected works; she had died thirteen years previously, and it was to be hoped that this intended plan would be executed. He included three of her letters to Bennoch, those which he had borrowed earlier in the year, and one of her verses. One letter was in response to Bennoch's request for a complete list of her works and a few notes on her life, as he knew she was ailing. Her letter was adamantly against writing any sort of autobiography but she did eventually comply with his wishes, and Bennoch was then able to write a brief but accurate biography of her in the *Fine Arts Journal*. Jerdan made Mary Mitford's experience of financial difficulties despite being a successful author an opportunity to reiterate the major theme of his *Autobiography*, by printing her letter asking for his intervention to obtain money due to her for editing the *Bijou Almanac* after Landon had given it up.

Jerdan's next subject, in November, was William Blackwood, publisher of *Maga* in Edinburgh, which started at the same time as Jerdan joined the *Literary Gazette*. His introduction contemplated the nature of publishers in general, arguing against a current view which saw them as patrons of literature; instead, he believed that "A publisher, educated and endued with the rare gifts of good and sound judgment, who superadds the management of a magazine or periodical to his ordinary business, is in a position peculiarly favourable to be of use to literary aspirants and to promote the best educational interests of the country". Blackwood, 'Old Ebony', he said, was just this type of publisher. Jerdan listed the famous writers whom Blackwood had nurtured in their youth; he abstained, he said, from noticing questions of acrimony, lampooning and so on, levelled against *Maga*: "much of it was the language common to all parties in those days of 'pot and kettle', when people were really more in earnest than they are now. We gladly acknowledge a better tone in the press, and that there are far fewer outbursts of foul words, misrepresentations, and violence. For this we must be thankful." Jerdan's analysis here of the difference between the acrimony common in days gone by and his present day, is in contrast to his analysis of the same subject in his piece on Lockhart, where he opined that the earlier press had been <u>less</u> "dictatorially and domineeringly offensive" than at the present day. Returning to the man, however, Jerdan noted that for Blackwood, his work was his hobby, "It was not mere trade". Jerdan illustrated this by selecting three brief business letters asking or thanking Jerdan for help in promoting a friend and a fourth, which Jerdan called "rather curious" concerning the *Edinburgh Review*. From the hundreds and hundreds of letters Jerdan must have received from Blackwood over a long association, he selected one from 1830 which mentioned L.E.L., evidently in response to Jerdan's request for a notice of her latest work. As with other such requests, Blackwood chided him, "I have laid it down as a rule never to urge any of my friends to notice a book unless it is their own free will to do so, and that they can make an article which will be worthy of *Maga* . . . All the same, you must have observed how kindly she is mentioned whenever there is incidental occasion for it." Jerdan concluded his column, observing that "the renown and profit of Scotland were far and wide extended by the impulse given to its press by William Blackwood". Jerdan, the expatriate Scot, sounded wistful, possibly envying his Edinburgh colleague for his pre-eminent position in his native city.

The 'Characteristic Letters' in December were from the writer and dear friend of Jerdan, the Irishman Samuel Lover. Like Bulwer, Jerdan wrote, Lover's work had been met by hostile criticism, marring his success and inhibiting him from reaping his just deserts. Jerdan quoted from a letter he had received from Lover, speaking of a "grief that smote my heart this morning, seeing the announcement of my dear friend Edward Forbes's death. I cannot tell you how bitterly I feel his loss . . . we can't make *old* friends – and at our age new ones are not good for much – *they don't fit.*". How Jerdan must have agreed whole-heartedly with this sentiment – he had outlived nearly all his old friends and many of his own family. Jerdan printed a letter dated January 1865, six months before Lover died, enclosing a "photo-proto-type of an owld sojer boy for Mop"[8] – he was god-father to Marion, Jerdan's first daughter with Mary Maxwell. Although then 68 years old, he had joined the London Irish Volunteers, telling Jerdan his reason, that "Ireland was behaving so badly at that time, and about that grand movement, that I thought it incumbent on every Irishman in England with a spark of gentlemanly feeling and loyalty in him, to enrol himself among the volunteers". Jerdan too set much store by "sparks of gentlemanly feeling and loyalty", clearly finding a fellow spirit in his Irish friend.

Around this time Gaspey had evidently asked Jerdan's advice about a piece he thought of submitting to the *Leisure Hour.* Jerdan told him that the magazine was running mostly Irish stories and suggested that Gaspey find another manu-script that might be better. He told his old friend that "my bairns take precious care of me now and all guard me against fatigue and risk of catching cold". It was "tortuous or inconvenient" to get to Bushey Heath he knew, and anyway had no bed to offer, but there was one nearby. He hoped that both he and Gaspey would live until the Spring when perhaps he could tempt his friend to a visit.[9] Jerdan's mention of the care the children took of him is a rare glimpse into his home life.

At the same time as he was producing his 'Characteristic Letters' Jerdan renewed his interest in *Notes & Queries*. In January he wrote about popular superstitions, citing "a worthy laundress neighbour, in some distress" because a cock had crowed on two or three nights at nine o'clock, "a sure sign of an early death in her family". It was indeed the hour she lost her last daughter. He also told how a robin "weeping" foretold death, and asked whether these supersti-tions were generally known. Another contribution was his version of a satirical song on the Four Ages of Mankind he once sang at a party, and in the same issue a brief note on the "salacious nature of shell-fish food". February saw him ener-getically defending the record of the Royal Society of Literature against attack on its failure, followed by another two snippets of folk lore. His two contribu-tions in May concerned the meaning of the word "Latten" and the border dialect word "skelp". In August he referred to Walter Scott's saying that "Old times are changed, old manners gone", and recorded detailed accounts of some games played in his boyhood on Tweedside, already unknown to the present generation of children. There is something quite touching about an old man, nearing death, taking the trouble to ensure that his childhood games were described so minutely for posterity, and his observation that the times had changed so much that now the idea of boys and girls playing together was unacceptable. Later he remembered more games, and offered them to *N & Q*'s readers in December. He particularly recalled how swimming and splashing in the Tweed was enjoyed by the majority of boys, and that "It was a common custom to take to the river a bit of bread, which was called the 'shuddering' or the 'shivering bite' and eaten immediately on coming out of the water, to reanimate the exhausted frame. Is this a fashion elsewhere to restore the system? Is it done in the cold–water cure?" he asked. Another time he asked readers if they knew the word "nying" used in a book of 1580, and whether anyone could tell him about "Old Taylor the artist".

Jerdan's sense of humour, mostly of the practical joke kind, was legendary. In the *New Sporting Magazine* of November 1868 a writer, F. Greville, related an anecdote about him in an article "Down and Up Again", a collection of tales and myths about recipes and cures found in the natural world, that he was imparting to a companion: "I recollect once meeting Mr William Jerdan, of the *Literary Gazette,* who assured me, without a muscle of his face displaying a smile, that he was on his way to the London Tavern to see the exhibition of a new power whereby a man got into a common market-basket, and taking the two handles with his hands lifted himself off the ground." A pointless kind of joke, but one can imagine it giving Jerdan a chuckle.

He tried hard to keep his spirits up; in a letter written to Bennoch in October,

I wither very slowly; but take matters in quiet; and can even (when I have breath enough in *play*) utter a jest. Being verbally pitied is a trial and the other day a caller consoling me with the assurance that I had in good time realized the fall into the sere and yellow leaf I comforted the Job-ber by acknowleding (sic) the fact that I must expect very speedily to hop the twig . . . my cup runs low![10]

The end of the year was more cheerful when his daughter Marion, "Mop", married Frederic Martin, the first of three marriages between Jerdan and Martin siblings. Marion was about 32 and Frederic also "of full age", possibly younger than his bride. He gave his occupation as 'Sailor', and his father Charles's as 'Civil Engineer'. Charles Bickley, husband of Marion's late sister Tilly and his new wife Julia, were witnesses to the marriage which took place not in Bushey where the bride had been living with her father and his young children, but at the Parish Church in Islington, close to Frederic Martin's home.

Jerdan's late burst of energy showed no signs of diminishing in his 87th year. With a wry sense of humour he marked Valentine's Day with an entry in *Notes & Queries*: "A long while ago I knew St Valentine and was indeed privy to some of his little affairs . . . " His next note was about an architect, Arthur Ashpitel, wishing "something more had been said" in a previous issue, and another answering a query about an author and composer whom he had known briefly "five or six-and-thirty years ago, as an emaciated shadowy creature, passing slowly away. If I could compare him to anything, it was to the last cadence of music sinking into the air . . . " A Scrap of Border Ballad, and an accurate reply to a query about the author of 'The Hermit in London' first featured in the *Literary Gazette* of 1818, appeared in March. Jerdan's last contribution to *Notes & Queries* was, fittingly, about da Vinci's painting of The Last Supper:

> *Ne sutor ultra crepidam* [do not offer opinions on things outside your competence] is my ardent motto, yet I fancy I sometimes notice things in productions of art which have escaped great critics. Thus, negatively, *veluti in speculum* [as in a mirror], in carefully examining the immortal Last Supper by Leonardo da Vinci, I discovered that, though there were twelve disciples, there were only eleven glasses. I would fain inquire if the artist meant a fling at Judas – a slight which might inflame his treachery? It is a curious question relating to so famous a work.[11]

'Characteristic Letters' were still in full flow. The new year 1869 opened with "Rajah Brooke", the late Sir James Brooke famous as the Rajah of Sarawak, and included two drawings by his subject. John Claudius Loudon was February's man; he had written monthly for the *Literary Gazette* on gardening and horticultural topics. Horrifyingly, Jerdan reported how ill Loudon had become and called in Dr. Thomson (who had also attended L.E.L.) Thomson told Jerdan that he had "repaired" Loudon. "He had treated him, he said, just as he would have treated an old decaying tree in his arboretum – lopped off a huge withered branch here, cut away several diseased members there, scraped off gangrenes and stopped injurious holes and cracks, all which the patient had borne with a firmness worthy of the aged tree itself!" In 1825 Thomson had amputated one arm at the shoulder and some fingers of Loudon's left hand – upsetting reading for the *Leisure Hour*. A note on Ackermann completed this issue, although Jerdan forbore to quote his friend's letters as, "like his German pronounciation of the English tongue, so droll, that they might convey quite an erroneous impression of his solid common sense and enterprising attention to business". In August *Notes & Queries* published some corrections to this section, but by then it was too late for Jerdan to care.

As Jerdan had noted of Loudon, that he had barely survived by his writing, so did he stress this point again in March when he spoke of Patrick Tytler, an "eminent historian". Jerdan had enlisted him to write a *History of Scotland* for the ill-fated 'Juvenile Library', and took this opportunity to list many of the other eminent writers he had similarly commissioned. He "could never divine", he said, "why the series had been "broke off i' the middle" but was plainly still upset about it, thirty-five years later.

He then made an opportunity to tell of his part in the romance of George Croly, when he was instrumental in introducing him to his future wife through her poetry. His role as Cupid culminated in him giving the bride away, "as a friend of her deceased father". Jerdan generously believed that Croly's writings were as worthy of posterity as Charles Lamb's *Essays of Elia*, but regretted that they had not remained as popular. The letters he printed included two in which Croly had scolded him roundly, one concerning a bad review in the *Literary Gazette* which Croly had not read himself but merely heard about; in the other, which Jerdan called "curious", Croly stated, "I wish, of course, to be always on the thickest terms with you, but yesterday you used careless language . . . you said also that I was 'holding a candle to these persons'. This was an ill-considered expression. Do you mean to say that whoever writes for a periodical work necessarily *holds a candle to its editor*, or that I, in contributing to the *Literary Gazette* hold a candle and act the menial to you?" Jerdan thought this letter was "replete with character", and his publishing it alongside more poetic letters of Croly, demonstrated that his eagerness to present all sides of his subjects over-rode any vanity on his own part, where his behaviour was called into question.

The section on Sir James Ross in May throws another light on the way Jerdan's expertise was asked for and freely given, with or without the label of 'literary agent'. Ross knew that Jerdan had negotiated the sale of his colleague Fisher's book to Longmans, and in 1843 was deciding on placing his own account of the expedition to the South Pole.

> I have an offer from Mr Murray of the same kind as that of Longmans & Co., – namely sharing the profits. I am so little conversant in these matters that I am not aware whether their offers or that of Mr Bentley are the most advantageous, and am desirous of availing myself of your very kindly offered assistance in coming to a decision in the matter. I have always heard of the difficulty of knowing the amount of profit, and been rather led to prefer money down.

Ross finally chose John Murray's higher bid. One of Ross's letter referred to "Jerdan Island", giving its dedicatee the chance to tell his readers how Captain Waddell (sic) had named a large island off Cape Horn after him, and that it was "illustrated by a chart (now in the British Museum Library)". Jerdan hero-worshipped Ross, concluding his column by noting, "It related to one whom, from his extraordinary labours in both hemispheres (planting his foot upon the

Arctic and penetrating within 160 miles of the Antarctic Pole), I esteemed 'the noblest Roman' of all that illustrious band of explorers with whom I held intimate acquaintance, from Captain Parry to nearly the latest."

Jerdan's June contribution to 'Characteristic Letters' was more interesting for the idea behind it than for the individuals portrayed. He grouped together the editors of daily newspapers, men of vast influence: "The great voice of the nation, or what is commonly called 'public opinion' is the real power in a free country like England . . . An editor is sagacious and skilful as he has judgment to know and tact to follow and to express the national will. Doing this well, editors of daily journals are among the real rulers of the people." Who are these unknown men, he asked. "They are men of rare and superior talent and ability, placed by circumstances in a position which affords them immense authority over not merely the multitude, but all classes of society." Such praise of editors cannot but raise the question as to whether Jerdan had seen his own long role in the *Literary Gazette* in the same light, as knowing how to "follow and to express the national will", although in his case it would be "the national taste". Was his early success at the *Literary Gazette* because he <u>followed</u> public taste rather than <u>formed</u> it, or perhaps it was a balance of the two. He chose Burns of *The Times* as the first editor to feature, recalling how he had annihilated Jerdan's hopes of becoming an MP with his "trenchant" leader, "denouncing the pretensions of literary men to become legislators". Jerdan charged Burns with treachery, but they soon restored good relations. Jerdan's other editors were John Black of the *Morning Chronicle* and William Mudford of the *Courier*; he wound up by noting that it was not only their "leaders" that created their influence but that "It is the promptitude, the judgment, the decision, which is demanded from them at every hour of their difficult lives, which constitute their real value and right to the power they possess. Each must not only be the central moving wheel, but he must direct the lesser motions; he must take care that none of the smaller wheels get out of order, he must regulate the entire action so that all tends to the end in view, and that there is perfect unison and consistency in every part of the wonderful and complex machine."

Appearing in July were letters from the popular historical novelist G.P.R. James, whom Jerdan had known since his youth. The *Literary Gazette* had favourably reviewed James's first work, *The Ruined City*, thirty-two pages published privately in 1828. He printed James's letter of thanks and astonishment that such a small work was noticed at all; Jerdan felt it necessary to add a footnote exonerating himself from any blame of egotism, as "To him, as to many aspirants during the third of a century, it so happened, from my position as editor of the *Literary Gazette* that I was of some service. There were many authors, artists, antiquaries, inventors and others, thus introduced to the public. Lending a hand up the first steps of the ladder is no great service, but the grateful remembrance of it is even now warmly expressed by the few survivors of that now distant and all but forgotten day." This really summed up Jerdan's thoughts on the whole matter of being an editor, to help people on their way, and to be thanked for his help was all he desired – although gifts were always welcome too. It was ingratitude he could not tolerate, a theme which had found its way into his *Autobiography* on several occasions.

Thinking back over his life, or perhaps on looking over his papers for 'Characteristic Letters', something must have jogged Jerdan's mind about Fox Talbot, one of the inventors of photography with whom he had corresponded on and off for thirty years, Fox Talbot's descriptive letters featured often in the pages of the *Literary Gazette* as well as the journal's biting response to the *Quarterly's* criticism of his *English Etymologies*. Even after Jerdan relinquished the *Literary Gazette* the paper printed an account, in November 1852, from Fox Talbot of "The Traveller's Camera". Jerdan's sad note to him dated 8 March 1869 read:

> It is so long since our agreeable correspondence ceased, and I remember from fighting the great Photographic battle by your side, that I am afraid to address this letter – as if we pilot a balloon to discover what wind blows.
>
> I am so deep in the sere and yellow leaf of age and jaundice that you could hardly believe I was still of this world. But I am, and if you are and hold the memory of former days, it will afford me a very great gratification to hear from you.[12]

In March 1869, four months before he died, Jerdan's article entitled "The Grand Force" was published in *Fraser's Magazine*. For an old ailing man it is a surprisingly vigorous attack on the power of advertising. He had reason to be suspicious of advertising in all its forms: he could not have avoided recalling the controversy over his so-called "puffing" of Colburn's books in the *Literary Gazette* some thirty years earlier and the problems that accusation caused him. In this contribution to *Fraser's,* he used the device of challenging a Professor at the Royal Institution lecturing on Mechanical Forces, on the grounds that he did not include the greatest force of all. He maintained it was a Force that can stir the world, "compelling mere words to alter, confuse, and confound the realities of things".

In support of this large claim, Jerdan's article gave examples of the power that advertising wielded, none in praise, but rather showing clearly the economic consequences of this fast-expanding phenomenon. "The Advertisement can import millions of chests of tea direct from China, and sell cheaper than sloe leaves and carpet sweepings!" "The Advertisement can cleanse the Augean stable of millions of boxes of bottles of quack medicine, and induce millions of fools to anoint their bodies with, or swallow their contents!" Advertisements for adulterated wine and beer were included in his tirade, as was promotion of the railways; these, he raged, created huge profits but admitted they had never been known to "kill even One of the well-assured multitude who trust their lives to consequences so satisfactorily accredited."[13] Jerdan became particularly exercised in referring to advertisements supporting foreign loans (i.e. Greek); promoting 'bubble' companies, and lending money to individuals without security which, as he knew to his cost, can "gull hundreds of thousands of idiots into disastrous loss or utter ruin". The press incurred his wrath too. Advertising supported countless good, bad and indifferent periodicals which in turn promulgate "sensationalism, spiritualism, ritualism, political associations, monster meetings, nonsense, trash, rubbish, imposture, and poison of every possible kind . . . ". His frustration boiled over, and he finally got to what was at the core of his complaint. Times had moved on and left him behind. The extent of advertising is "one of the most extraordinary proofs of the mighty change which has taken place in the manners, morals and doings of the civilised world". Jerdan focussed on the injustice he perceived: low rogues and thieves were transported, whilst nothing is done against rogues and thieves who are wealthy mercantilists.

Advertising, Jerdan was trying to prove, was responsible for most of society's ills. The dishonest used it to tempt the public, leaving "the honest, in self-defence . . . to have recourse to the Greatest of all Forces". His hopeless solution to these iniquities was Silence. A postscript to his article noted that since writing it "about four-fifths of a new Parliament has been elected by means of the grand force; which has thus demonstrated its power to shape the course and determine the destiny of the British Empire". The image of Canute trying to keep back the waves, or the boy with a finger in the dyke, is the image of Jerdan, hating the new world around him, unable to participate in it and railing angrily against progress.

Following Jerdan's diatribe about advertising in *Fraser's* issue of March 1869, in April he contributed a companion piece, "The Greatest Wonder". This time his target was the law. Despite all the advantages of being British, "the Greatest Wonder of the age appears to be the entire absence of common sense and simplicity in the legislation of our prosperous and gifted land!" The progress of civilization, he wrote, has become so complicated and the world so crowded, that the rule was now "Every man for himself", unlike olden days where wise men guided the people and only two religions, Deism and Pantheism reigned. Now, he complained, there are numberless creeds and sects, leading to endless quarrels. This is analogous with the law: previously there were rules and subjects (generally tyrants and slaves), with no "Peoples" of middle class to disturb the system. Jerdan went on to say that the same change and enlargement permeated all aspects of modern life. There had been a great mistake in the belief that for every ill, social or medical, there was a cure. This was not necessarily the case, but in the endless search for remedies, absurdities and worse occur.

Taking the law as his quarry and example, Jerdan posited what happens when a Lord Chief Justice cannot rule on a case; he calls in three other judges, and if agreement cannot be found the case goes to the House of Lords. Here the whole House rules on a case about which they know nothing and are therefore, quipped Jerdan, "impartial". Furthermore, law has little to do with justice – a judge may deem a litigant's claim just, but must follow a precedent which could indict him. This discrepancy frustrated Jerdan who asked irritably " . . . has it not occurred to our legislators to render law intelligible". Laws had been promulgated in vast numbers, in an attempt to "stop every hole, strengthen every flaw, fill up every crack . . . ", resulting in monster legislation with deleterious effects. He thought it was a gamble, a lottery.

Acknowledging that serious debates upon law reform had taken place, Jerdan nevertheless wanted to throw his "little arrow" to penetrate "where a spear could not be thrust", by proposing some ideas towards reform and improvement of common and criminal law, and their administration. Taking common law first he focussed on shop-keeping, where there were laws laying down punishments for cheating and fraud, but in practice these powers are seldom exercised. Jerdan asserted that this had resulted in a lax moral system where goods are habitually adulterated and nothing is what it should be. This, coupled with fraudulent weights and measures, had the worst effect upon the poor, where "we are utterly shocked by the universal prevalence of gross impositions, injurious alike to economy and health". In former times rules relating to weights and measures were enforced by a Court Leet, efficient once but now barely functioning. The Custom House and Excise office possessed powers, but loosely employed. Could there not, he suggested, be a National Minister of Justice over an unimpeachable Court Leet, to redress the evils of adulteration and fraudulent weights. In addition to the obvious moral improvement to society, Jerdan insisted this would relieve the country financially too. The cost of penal settlements, penitentiaries and poor rates would dramatically reduce and the whole community would be happier. As if realizing that this may be too heavy for *Fraser's* readers, he commented that his remedy may seem a jest, and that he tried to make the subject light, but that even so he thought that some good may arise from his idea.

His treatment of criminal law was even more robust than his discussion of common law. Its "farces, pantomimes, spectacles and tragedies . . . its effeteness and hazard-game are enough to condemn it to all rational minds . . . ". Jerdan expostulated about the financial cost involved in legal actions against all criminals who, when imprisoned, have to be kept at the expense of the public purse or, as he more picturesquely remarked, "The tax-payers pay dear for their wild beasts". He calculated the cost to be between £700 to £1000 per criminal. His solution, a "little game" which may go some way to reforming convicts and opening a door for them to rise in the world. He presented this idea for the consideration of the Foreign Minister, Lord Clarendon.

As the threat of transportation to the colonies had not significantly decreased the crime rate, Jerdan suggested entering into alliances with various African rulers, whereby England would provide say twenty convicts a year at no cost, the number varying according to the size of the nation. The rulers could then use the convicts as they wished, taking advantage of such talents as they had. The prisoners would thus have the opportunity to "mount in the African scale". Jerdan recognized that this might seem an attractive option for some leading to an increase in crime, so "cargoes of Thames pirates" could be sent to Timbuctoo or the Ashantee kingdoms, to take their chances under despots who enjoy "butchering thousands at a single festival". This plan would dispose of all undesirables from our shores and if successful, Jerdan satirically hoped for a Statue of Gold in his honour, for restoring a golden age to the British Empire.

This was Jerdan's final article published in his lifetime, appearing in April, the month he celebrated his eighty-eighth birthday, and was a neat conclusion to an exceptionally long life and literary career. The *Theatrical Journal* of June 1869 noticed this article, commenting that "Mr Jerdan is still vigorous, his intellects are unimpaired by time, and he is now engaged upon the MSS of his old friend Samuel Lover, whose unpublished works he is preparing for the press." Jerdan did not manage to complete this task.[14]

In May, Jerdan received a note from Charles Dickens:[15] "I grieve to find you describing yourself as 'sorely crippled', but I hope and trust that the departure of these horrible winds and the coming in of balmy weather will let in a shower of genial influences upon you. In the meantime I can declare this: that I never saw a handwriting as unchanged as yours, My dear fellow, the out of the way village made a triumphant appearance immediately." This note was endorsed by Jerdan "A botch! The whole sequel story's left out", an unexplained reference. Dickens's reference to an "out of the way village" may be to Jerdan's signature on his many offerings in *Notes & Queries*, where he signed himself 'Bushey Heath'.

Part VI

Remembrances

27

Death, Obituaries, Posthumous Publications

William Jerdan died on 11 July 1869. His death certificate identified the cause as 'Decay of Nature', in other words old age. His son John was with him. Francis Bennoch, the sculptor Joseph Durham and a local pillar of society Mr Noakes, attended his burial. The *Times* considered him worthy of an obituary on 13 July, on the basis that:

> Forty years ago[1] there were few names better known in London society and in the world of letters than that of William Jerdan … His genial spirit, ready wit and abundant anecdote made him a welcome guest in other than mere literary circles … the last two parts of the *Gentleman's Magazine* contain an article on the celebrated Beefsteak Club, which no other living man could have written from personal knowledge … His kindly help was always afforded to young aspirants in literature and art, and his memory will be cherished by many whom he helped to rise to positions of honour and independence."

A shorter notice of Jerdan's death was published in the *New York Times* of 17 July, which did not make any mention of his brief connection with the American press. The *Gentleman's Magazine* itself noted that Jerdan's last articles in its pages, on the Beef Steak Club, had now acquired "a special and melancholy interest". He had died, they reported,

> full of years and honours. For half a century he had been a successful worker in the field of literature and politics. There were few men of note during that time with whom he was not personally acquainted … In his eighty-eighth year it was singular to note with what zest he applied himself to the history of the 'Beef Steaks'. He seemed to live again in transcribing his notes of the famous Club. Nothing, he said, had given him so much pleasure for many years as the telling of this story, and it was a great

satisfaction to him that the record should appear in the *Gentleman's Magazine* . . . [2]

Jerdan had apparently written the notes for these two articles at an earlier time; the language is vigorous and robust, befitting his subject, "The Steaks", subtitled "Vulgarly the 'Beef', Classically the 'Sublime'". He introduced his subject by railing against "Progress! Aye that is the word now. It is in everybody's mouth; everybody boasts of it. It is the grand feature of the age." He was not against progress, but had a strong reservation:" . . . it does, now and then, obliterate what was good of old, and the Sublime Steaks afford a striking example."

Many years before he had been taken to the last meeting of "a Club which had defied time from the reign of Charles II". Jerdan described, with evident relish, the customs of the original old dining and drinking society, and the club which took over from it in 1735. Art and furniture belonging to The Steaks had recently been auctioned and throughout his articles Jerdan noted the prices fetched for many items. He wrote with great authority on the drinking habits of the club: "Port wine being the living element of the Steaks and the very essence of their existence"; it was odd to find Jerdan, renowned for his love of drink, insisting, "In uttering my diatribe against the prevalence of intoxication and consequent debauchery, during the last forty years of the past century, I desire to be understood as directing it only against the excess. Let us not be unjust. In the worst there is always something of good." The "good" was the fellowship and intimacy of the members. Jerdan told anecdotes of famous figures who had belonged to The Steaks, and described in detail the windowless room behind the Lyceum Theatre built especially for their meetings, with a huge gridiron on view in the adjacent kitchen on which the beefsteaks were cooked, and served with "choice salads (mostly of beetroot), porter and port".

This first instalment ran to over twelve pages, while the final article following in the next month was fourteen pages. Jerdan's own nature was a perfect fit to write about high class, witty, jolly gatherings of men whose sole aim was good company, good food and good drink. His pleasure in repeating stories, puns and sayings of The Steaks is plain, and the *Gentleman's Magazine* the ideal place for such an article to appear. Fittingly it was an essentially eighteenth-century club, whose history was related by an essentially eighteenth-century man at the very end of his long life. Somewhat surprisingly, Henry Irving quoted substantial passages from the articles on The Steaks in his discussion of clubs, in his book *Impressions of America* published in 1884; he noted that "the late William Jerdan was the first to attempt anything like a concise sketch of the club . . . ". Jerdan, that great admirer of the theatre, would have been delighted to be quoted by one of its greatest actors. In the same December issue of the *Gentleman's Magazine* which carried the final article on The Steaks, was an article linking Jerdan with another writer, H. H. Dixon. This noted that "they were both kindly, genial scholarly men worthy of our most respectful remembrance; and their names will be ranked high on the national muster roll of famous journalists".

The *Gentleman's Magazine* articles appeared several months after Jerdan's death, and stood as some kind of memorial to him. In a final echo of Jerdan's parallel life events to those of Leigh Hunt, the family were too poor to mark his resting-place.[3] It was five years before Jerdan's grave in the churchyard of St. James's, Bushey village, was marked by a tombstone erected by his friends. On one side it bore the inscription in Roman capitals: "William Jerdan, F.S.A.; born at Kelso, April 16, 1782, died at Bushey, July 11, 1869. Founder of the Literary Gazette and its Editor for 34 years". On the other side was inscribed: "Erected as a tribute to his memory by his Friends and Associates in the Society of Noviomagus, 1874." The event was duly recorded in *Notes & Queries* on 10 October 1874.

Nine days after her father's death, his daughter Agnes Maxwell was christened at the age of 23, and two days later married Charles Martin, brother of Frederic, her sister Marion's husband. The haste to marry so quickly after Jerdan's death was plain when their daughter, also Agnes, was born soon after but lived only a few months. The couple made their home in Willington, Derbyshire, where Charles was a Railway Clerk. By 1881 they had four children and he had become Chief Stationmaster.

As far as the *Leisure Hour* was concerned, Jerdan lived on. In August 1869 an article on the early history of the Royal Geographical Society appeared; it was unsigned but bore the hallmarks of Jerdan's intimate knowledge of the nascent Society. No mention was made of his death at the time, and the magazine continued to print his series of 'Characteristic Letters' right through until December. Uncharacteristically, Jerdan had obviously planned ahead and prepared several future issues. He covered Hudson Gurney, a wealthy fellow antiquarian in a brief entry; David Macbeth Moir, a doctor and frequent contributor to *Blackwood's* under the penname 'Delta', whose poem to his dead child Jerdan included; Harry Goodsir, surgeon and naturalist to the Franklin expedition appeared in October with only a few lines of comment, the article being mainly a long letter written from Baffin's Bay in 1845 describing the natural world he found there. The following month was devoted to George Mogridge, known to *Leisure Hour* readers as 'Old Humphrey'; his career, like so many others, had begun in the *Literary Gazette*, and in his memoirs appeared a recollection of meeting L.E.L. in Jerdan's study, where she engaged in lively conversation. Jerdan included a long, rather sycophantic letter from Mogridge written in 1830, begging him to 'notice' his book of poems, and full of praise for Jerdan's judgment. The final entry in the series appeared in December and concerned the Rt. Hon. Thomas Grenville whose assistance Jerdan had sought in 1830 when he was struggling to write dozens of biographies for *Fisher's National Portrait Gallery*, and in this instance, the entry for Lord Grenville himself. Grenville considered his life to have been of only "trivial interest" and agreed only to correct dates and facts in Jerdan's entry. He was the brother of the late Prime Minister but had preferred books to politics, leaving his vast and valuable collection to the British Museum. Jerdan claimed to have enjoyed Grenville's "almost intimate acquaintance", and that a breakfast and a morning's conversation with him "was a treat that any Prince in Europe might envy".

The final subject of this long-running series of 'Characteristic Letters' shared Grenville's entry, and returned Jerdan to his very early days in Cromwell Cottage, before his editorship of the *Literary Gazette* had started. There he met 'Isabella Kelly', penname of his neighbour Mrs Hedgeland, novelist since 1795. The last letter was from her son, by then Lord Chief Baron, correcting a few details in a reference to his mother's works. And so this strangely posthumous series came to an end, and it was not until the same issue, in December 1869, that the *Leisure Hour* finally acknowledged the death of their author, with a selection of his very own 'Characteristic Letters'.

In the same issue of the *Leisure Hour* as Jerdan's final 'Characteristic Letters' appeared the magazine made a tribute to him with a column under the same heading, the letters this time featuring Jerdan himself. The writer noted that on Jerdan's death obituaries linked him to the *Literary Gazette*, and "there were many to whom the name of both the paper and its editor were strange. They both belonged to a generation which had passed away." The *Leisure Hour* quoted the *Times* obituary in full, noting that unlike other such notices, it made no mention of the *Literary Gazette*. The first letter printed was an unfinished one to his daughter Frances-Agnes, wife of Thomas Irwin. It was dated 12 August 1866, written when Jerdan had himself been ill for a week and felt his end was imminent. He gave her a brief outline of his life, from his first poem on Wilberforce in 1804, life on the *Gladiator*, his early jobs as a journalist, and then listed all of his writings that he could remember. Most of this information was of course already in his *Autobiography*. He also mentioned writing "much" for the *Kelso Mail* and for the *London Review*. Very few copies of the *Kelso Mail* covering the period of Jerdan's lifetime survive, and those which do have no authors' names appended to articles. They do feature an occasional brief paragraph copied from the *Literary Gazette*, but these could not be the writings to which Jerdan referred. The *London Review* articles are similarly unattributed.

Three of Jerdan's letters to Chief Baron Frederick Pollock were printed, one dated when he moved to Bushey Heath, the second included a mention of receiving proofs of his first article for the *Leisure Hour*, on 'About Sixty Years Ago' and wishing Pollock were nearby to see them. He talked about his "inherent anti-historical spirit" of liking Charles II, admiring Richard III and so on, interrupting himself to tell Pollock that his "little fellow" had just asked him "to go and dig some potatoes for his dinner, and as I understand that better than your square roots, I shall bid you goodbye for the present . . . ". The image of the old man digging for his children's dinner is a touching one, remembering that same man in better days in the glittering surroundings of Lady Blessington's salon or George Canning's drawing room. On 11 November 1859 Jerdan had sent Pollock several of his *Leisure Hour* articles on 'Men I Have Known', asking if he would find time to proof subsequent ones. He was "much affected by the death of Lady de Tabley," he told his friend, especially as only three months earlier she had invited him to Tabley House but he had been unable to go. "She was one of the loveliest and most fascinating creatures I ever saw, and my regrets are deepened by the simple accident of having failed in this *tryst*, which can never more be offered in this world." Jerdan had had a genuine fondness for this woman, namesake and godmother to his deceased infant Georgiana, so this was a real sorrow not merely the sentimental ramblings of an old man.

The *Leisure Hour* noted that later letters from Jerdan to various correspondents made "frequent references to the *res angusta domi*, [hand to mouth existence]". The magazine tried to show different aspects of Jerdan's character in the letters they selected, in the spirit of the title of his series; his playful, one might almost say childish side was evidenced by a letter to the sculptor Joseph Durham in 1851 after a visit to his studio. Jerdan teased him about "an extraordinary work by a young sculptor", the tools he invented for his purpose, his artistry and skill. Puzzled, Durham asked for an explanation, to be told that it was a description of himself preparing the beefsteak for Jerdan's dinner.

His grand-daughter Maymé, likely to be his pet name for Mary, the eleven-year old daughter of Frances-Agnes and Thomas Irwin, was the recipient of a unique extant letter to a grandchild, which has survived only because in print in the *Leisure Hour*. The letter was dated August 1857. Jerdan was glad they were settled in their "pretty country lodging", he said, and that the boys were "soapy (so (h)appy)," and that she and Agnese (Felicity-Agnes her seven year old sister) were going to take music lessons. He had had new jam for breakfast and gave his grand-daughter instructions on collecting blackberries and making jam, and hoped she would invite him over to visit. "You must not think me an idle foolish old granny, for writing all this "nonstence" to you, and if you and the boys will write to me in return, I shall be soapy myself. I am impatient to see you all ruddy and stout, and your mother beginning to turn a fattish old lady – not too fat either – but the picture of a strong-minded woman, laughing at care, and as usual petting (My dear children) Your Affectionate grand-pa."

Another rare letter to one of his close family was also included in the *Leisure Hour* selection; these must have been lent to the magazine by his daughter to whom this one was sent, dated 7 February, with no year given:

My very dear Agnes, I was prepared for your sad letter,[4] but it makes me unspeakably miserable. The vision of the wasted life and the suffering form cannot be driven from my mind for any period of time. I try to write, and it may beguile a few minutes; I sink into my chair, and ponder; I cannot be long after. It is a mercy there are no children there.

I fancy I am something better, I was out ten minutes in the sunshine on Saturday, and thought I could walk ever so far. But I am best in my bedroom, where, thank Heaven! We can, as yet, keep a fire – for without warmth I am perished. But enough of self – I will go out whenever the weather admits.

How grieved and anxious I am about you! Remember how much depends, and take all the care you can of yourself. And poor (sister) Pussy – what trials she has of woes, yet she is safe herself, and will I trust live to enjoyment, when time has softened the regret for those who have gone before. The inversion of the order of nature is the worst to bear. Why do I linger on, and where are those who should have laid my head in the grave!

. I am unable to write more. May heaven strengthen and bless you. My poor love to all. Your affectionate father.

As the *Leisure Hour* pointed out:

These letters may not appear very 'characteristic' to those who knew Mr Jerdan in his early years, when he was the life of many a social circle. But we prefer giving letters which pertain to the later period of his life, when he had relations with this magazine. To the same period belongs the following:

FAILINGS ARE COMFORTS AT 80.
I have got very deaf. What a blessing! There is such a lot of silly talk I cannot hear – such scandals, etc.

My eyes are failing. How fortunate I do not see a tythe of the folly and wickedness that is going on around me! I am blind to faults which would provoke me to censure.

I have lost my teeth, and my voice is not very audible. Well, I find it is of no use babbling to folks who won't listen, so I save my breath for better purposes. I don't show my teeth where I can't bite. I venture on no tough meal.

My taste is not as discriminating as of yore, and the good is that I am more easily satisfied, don't keep finding fault, am contented and thankful. A nice palate is a plague I have got rid.

My joints are rather stiff. Well, if they were ever so supple, I do not want to go to see sights, hear concerts, make speeches, carouse at feasts.

I am not so strong as I was; but for what do I need to be stout. I am not going to wrestle or fight with anybody. My morals are greatly improved.

My brain is not so clear as in my younger days, and all the better, for I am neither so hot-headed, nor so opinionated. I forget a thousand injuries.

If these were Jerdan's own words and not copied from elsewhere, the fragment gives a clear sketch of the old man ever trying to be optimistic, finding some good things to say about the ravages of age. The day before he died he wrote a note to the little daughter of his medical attendant who would take no money for his services. Jerdan wrapped two guineas, a great sum for him, into the note, which told her, "Dear Lilian, A wee bird bids me send you a gold penny to buy a pretty dress for the Heath Road on sunny summer days." This charming story encapsulates so much of Jerdan's complex personality: the "wee bird" echoes his mis-quote of his beloved L.E.L., "we love the bird we taught to sing", his legendary kindness and generosity, and his evident love of and empathy with children, and his profligacy with money.

Apart from this tribute in 'Characteristic Letters,' and the *Times* notice of Jerdan's death, which was copied in other papers and periodicals, few people commented on his passing. Most of his closest circle had predeceased him, so it was left to a younger man to have the final word. Samuel Carter Hall's character was totally at odds with Jerdan's: he was teetotal, married to Anna Maria for a lifetime, childless, in employment throughout his career. In the *Art Journal* which he had edited for many years, Hall was generous in his farewell to a man of whom he had never approved:

It is but justice to say of Mr Jerdan that he ever 'did his spiriting gently', was always ready to help, and never willing to depress, the efforts of men striving for fame; and many are they who achieved greatness mainly as a consequence of the encouragement received at his hand, whom severity of rebuke might have depressed into oblivion. It is scarcely too much to say that during his fifty years of labour there was hardly a young author who did not gratefully thank him for good words.[5]

Jerdan treated artists well too, Hall observed: "his judgment was sound and his verdicts were seldom questioned . . . ". Hall suggested that present-day critics would do well to emulate Jerdan's example.

When Hall came to write his *Retrospect of a Long Life* in 1883 he was eighty-three years old. He still treated Jerdan as fairly as he could and his words are those most often quoted in any later description of Jerdan. He acknowledged that the *Literary Gazette* had been "a power in the Press. Its good or ill word went far to make or mar an author's reputation, and the sale of a book was often large or limited according to its fiat . . . he was far less given to censure than to praise."[6] Hall echoed Hawthorne's opinion of Jerdan as "time-worn but not reverend", but went on to say,

> yet in old age he retained much of his pristine vigour, and when he was past eighty could be, and often was, witty in words and eloquent in speech. Yet his life is not a life to emulate, and certainly not one for laudation. Many liked, without respecting him. No doubt he was of heedless habits, no doubt he cared little for the cost of self-gratification, and was far too lightly guided all his life long by high and upright principles.

This, at least, Jerdan would have agreed with, having said many times how his childhood 'spoiling' had had an adverse effect upon his life. Piously, Hall could not "turn a deaf ear to the prayer, that is half an apology" in the *Autobiography*, when Jerdan hoped that "some fond and faithful regret might embalm the memory of the sleeper . . .". But Hall also reminded his readers, lest they become too sentimental, that Jerdan had also written "I have drained the Circe cup to the dregs". "Alas!" grieved Hall, "the dregs were pernicious to heart, mind and soul." He noted, as mentioned elsewhere, that he found the *Autobiography* uninteresting and devoid of help to writers. He ended his piece on the editor with a most ambivalent paragraph:

> I wish I could say something to honour the memory of William Jerdan, for personally I owed him much; I had always his good word, and so had my wife; there is no one of her books that did not receive generous and cordial praise in the *Literary Gazette*. I grieve that now he is in his grave I can give so little for so much.

Eliza Cook wrote a short poem in memory of the man, who had guided and helped her, and with whom she had shared many a stroll on Bushey Heath:[7]

> *To the Late William Jerdan*
> If my poor Harp has ever poured
> A tone that Truth alone can give;
> Thou wert the one who helped that tone
> To win the echo that shall live.
>
> For thou didst bid me shun the theme
> Of morbid grief, or feigned delight;
> Thou bads't me *think* and *feel;* not dream
> And 'look into my heart and write'.

> And looking in that heart just now;
> 'Mid all the memories there concealed;
> I find thy name still dearly claim
> The thanks in these few lines revealed.

In December 1871, more than two years after Jerdan's death, the journal Once A Week published an article entitled 'Gossip from an Editor's Book'. It acknowledged that "Few people outside of literary circles have heard much of William Jerdan, or know that for half a century, in his various capacities of editor, contributor, and reviewer, he enjoyed a sort of critical supremacy of his own." The article noted that the *Autobiography*, and *Men I Have Known* "are a store-house of reminiscences of his contemporaries, told in a light and fluent style and replete with much interesting anecdote". The article then drew largely on *Men I Have Known*, especially the sections on Coleridge and Campbell, selecting the lightest and most amusing stories of the poets. The writer observed that Jerdan's admiration of Wordsworth "seems somewhat qualified", and repeated Jerdan's story of his visit to Wordsworth at Rydal Mount. Amusing incidents from Jerdan's accounts of several more minor characters were mentioned, the writer concluding with, "We dismiss Mr Jerdan in the belief that we have shown how pleasant a companion he is."

In the issue of *All the Year Round* of 18 December 1873, in an article entitled "Forty Years Ago", readers were told:

> Among the lesser lights – great lights in their day – whose names have scarcely come down to the newer folk of this generation, the first in *'Fraser's Gallery'* is a conspicuous example.
>
> William Jerdan, editor of the *Literary Gazette*, was once a power in the Republic of Letters. It was thought that he could make and unmake literary reputations, though he could do nothing of the kind, and he was flattered and feared accordingly by all the smaller fry of literature. He was not unhonoured by the greater fry; for he was hospitable, generous, cordial, and the best of company, and lent a helping hand to young and struggling genius whenever it came in his way.

In 1875 Richard Henry Stoddard edited a book called *Personal Reminiscences by Moore and Jerdan*. This was published as one of the Bric-a-Brac series by Scribner, Armstrong & Co. in New York. The section on Moore drew from the eight-volume *Journal, Memoirs and Correspondence* edited by Lord John Russell, and that on Jerdan from what Stoddard called the 'essence' of anecdotes in the more than fourteen hundred pages of the *Autobiography*. Stoddard clearly despised Jerdan, commencing his introduction with

William Jerdan was a man of note at one time, it is not easy to see why now. He was not a man of letters, though he wrote books, but a journalist ... the reader will judge what it is ... if it be not as sprightly as he could wish, he should remember that it was written by one who began to remember when most begin to forget ... The brilliant poet [Moore] and the laborious journalist will now speak for themselves.

One wonders why, when he thought so little of him, Stoddard chose Jerdan as one of two people to 'Reminisce' about. The fact that his book was published in New York indicates that Jerdan's name still had some meaning in America, maybe because of his articles in the Boston newspapers, although these had been published twenty years earlier.

Epilogue

Jerdan's name was kept alive in odd corners, not quite forgotten by the popular press although more often quoted in the venerable magazine *Notes & Queries*, devoted as it was to words and literature, and to which Jerdan had contributed frequently at the end of his life; his name continued to appear throughout the years. Quotations from the *Literary Gazette*, his *Autobiography*, and from *Men I Have Known*, and Fisher's *National Portrait Gallery*, were often used for answers to many queries posted on a wide variety of topics. Jerdan had become metamorphosed into a kind of oracle, whose word was taken as the ultimate, definitive pronouncement. Between 1875 and the end of the century at least thirty-seven different queries were related to him, by which time any contributor to *Notes & Queries* who had any personal acquaintance with him, had died. Jerdan's voice lived on, however, into the twentieth century, some twenty-four references to him appearing in the magazine until the 1980s.

Naturally enough, with the explosion in Regency and Victorian literary studies over the last hundred years, Jerdan's *Autobiography*, as well as the *Literary Gazette*, have proved fruitful, if frustrating, ground for researchers. In part, this was what he had in mind, especially concerning the *Literary Gazette*, wanting it to be a literary history for posterity when he said: "I am conscious that productions of this kind are rarely more than popular for a limited period; and then are to be found in libraries for future references, perhaps by authors who may be investigating portions of the literary history of past times."[1] Such scholarly journals as *The Year's Work in English Studies*, *The Nineteenth Century*, *Past and Present*, and *The Review of English Studies* have mined Jerdan's output exhaustively. This is only to be expected, for he created the first weekly literary periodical in the country, and wrote widely of his personal knowledge and experience of the great (and not-so great) men and women of half a century. More surprising perhaps, are the instances where Jerdan is cited in non-literary studies. A cursory trawl on a computer search engine shows his work being used in studies on art, crime, antiquarianism, photography, electricity, gas lighting and animals, to name but a few; he has been widely quoted in biographies, and the *Oxford Dictionary of National Biography* includes his name thirty-five times in connection with other entries.

There is a small mystery too, in his legacy: in September 1875 a Maxwell Jerdan wrote a novel entitled *Kate Elder*, published by Tinsley who reprinted a new six shilling edition in October, which was advertised throughout the following year. The combination of Maxwell and Jerdan must surely indicate the author as one of the offspring of Mary Maxwell and William Jerdan, but no further information on this author has yet come to light.

Jerdan perhaps made a posthumous appearance as a character in literature, although neither in life nor in death has he been previously noted to appear in Thackeray's *Pendennis*, which famously includes Maginn, L.E.L., Colburn and Bentley. Unless (and this is only a wild guess or wishful thinking,) Thackeray turned him into a bit part, a Mr Doolan, who was an Irishman who read the *Dawn*, a liberal newspaper – a possible inversion of a conservative Scotsman who edited the *Aurora*. Doolan worked as a reporter for the 'Tom and Jerry' newspaper, talked about men of letters with whom he was very familiar, particularly "about Tom Campbell and Tom Hood . . . as if he had been their most intimate friend". Pointedly, Thackeray had the coach travelling through Brompton as the conversation of which this was a fragment, was taking place. Halfway through the novel Doolan is killed off: "They buried honest Doolan the other day; never will he cringe or flatter, never pull long-bow or empty whisky-noggin any more." This may be a brief sketch of Jerdan or some other journalist, and it is possible that a figure as well-known and colourful as Jerdan appeared in other books of the period, but has so far been unidentified. His name did appear, though, in two stories published long after his death. The *Belgravia Annual* of Christmas 1883 carried a story by a James Payn entitled "Why he married her"; the heroine is 'Miss Letty Jerdan', conflating L.E.L. with her ex-lover, but the stockbroker husband is called Richard Taunton, a name with no Jerdan resonance. In July 1898 the *London Quarterly Review* noted a book, *A Woman Worth Winning*, by George M. Fenn, in which Sir Martin Jerdan is madly jealous of his wife's former lover and Lady Jerdan is a noblewoman. Her former lover is immured in a lunatic asylum because of the baronet's jealousy. Apart from the incidence of the Jerdan name there is the introduction of madness, a subject with which Jerdan had been only too familiar. So long after his death this may have been merely coincidence, so not too much should be read into this.

A more lasting legacy of Jerdan's is the continuation of his far-flung progeny, many proudly bearing the names of Jerdan or Stuart often as traditional family middle names regardless of gender. Some who consider themselves cousins are likely to have sprung from different mothers, whether Frances Jerdan, Letitia Landon or Mary Maxwell. They live in America, in Japan, Australia and Canada, and probably in many other countries too. The name of William Jerdan is memorialized in Isola Jerdan, that barren inhospitable island off Cape Horn, named for him by Captain Weddell, and also somewhere that could not be more different – a small pedestrian street in Fulham, West London, called Jerdan Place (see illustration on back cover). This name was approved by the Metropolitan Board of Works on 11 August 1876, changed from its previous incarnations as

Frederick Place and Market Place. The Minutes of this meeting show that no discussion took place as to the reason for the change; it was odd that Jerdan was chosen for a street in Fulham, an area where he had never lived. He was, however, known in his day as a frequent guest at Pryors Bank nearby; the honour of having a Place named for him came seven years after his death.

None of Jerdan's many offices or homes still exist; even his gravestone was removed within fifty years of its being erected over his resting-place, to make way for other interments.[2] The cottage where he died is no more, though other cottages of the same period can still be found on Bushey Heath. The armlets in the British Museum are the only relics which he touched, together with the three hundred-plus letters in his hand lodged in various archives. We have his *Autobiography*, the bound volumes of the *Literary Gazette*, and his stories, verses and biographies. The contribution Jerdan made to literature and to the history of periodicals, his encouragement to authors, artists and others, and his struggle against his own indulgent personality, deserve more than the cursory mentions of him offered by his contemporaries, and it is hoped that this work will go some way towards redressing the balance.

Appendix

Jerdan's Descendants

Immediate descendants of William and Frances Jerdan

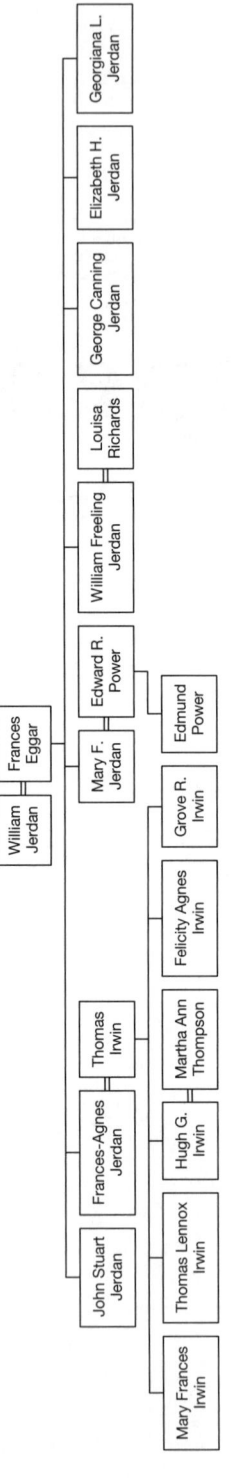

Descendants of Jerdan's Families[1]

The Children of William Jerdan and Frances (Eggar) Jerdan

Of their seven children, one died in infancy, one was unmarried, and one childless. It is probable that John, who died young in Jamaica had no children although he had recently married the daughter of the engraver John Vendramini. Whether George Canning Jerdan who lived in Calcutta, had married and had issue, is not known.

Of the remaining children of William and Frances's marriage, Mary Power's son Edmund, a coffee planter in Ceylon, was unmarried at the age of twenty-nine but his circumstances not known thereafter. There may also have been one other child of Mary's marriage who died early.

The most prolific of the legitimate Jerdan offspring was Frances Agnes, married to Thomas Irwin of the Audit Office. The family is traceable as far as the 1861 Census which enumerates that they had five children: Mary Frances in 1845, Thomas Lennox in December 1846, Hugh Grove Jerdan born in March 1848, Felicity Agnes in March 1850, all born in Brompton, and Grove R., born in Chelsea in 1852.[2] The father of the family died in 1868, but neither the 1871 Census nor those following have any record of either his wife Frances Agnes, nor his daughter Mary Frances, although it is known that Frances Agnes lived until September 1891, and should therefore be discoverable in three Censuses. A Mary Frances Irwin of Gainsborough, Lincolnshire, lived until the age of 52, dying in 1899, and a Mary F. Irwin died in 1922 aged 78, at East Preston, Sussex. Either or neither of these could have been Jerdan's granddaughter, but if so, in either case she had not married, so presumably had no issue.

Of Thomas Lennox Irwin there is no trace, but his brother Hugh Grove Irwin married on 23 February 1874 in Trinity Church, Paddington, to Martha Ann Thompson, giving his occupation as Warehouse man.[3] Hugh's mother was not named as a witness on the marriage certificate. A Hugh G. J. Irwin, with a birth date of "circa 1847", matching Jerdan's grandson, emigrated alone on the S.S. *Baltic*, arriving in New York on 25 February 1882. His occupation was given as 'Merchant'. If this is indeed Jerdan's grandson, his young wife may have died prematurely, or the marriage proved unsuccessful. No trace of Hugh Irwin's subsequent life or death has been found.

Felicity Agnes and Grove R. Irwin have not come to light in any record, embodying the difficulty of establishing any certain legitimate descendants from William and Frances Jerdan's marriage.

Immediate descendants of William Jerdan and Letitia E. Landon

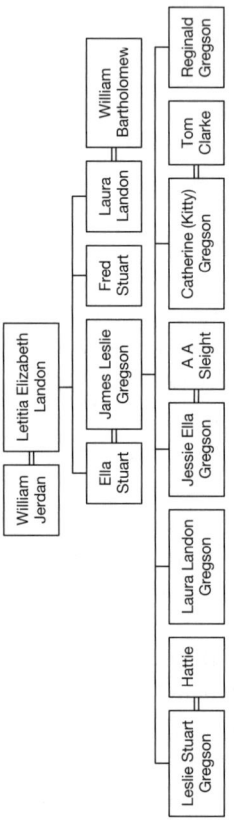

The Children of William Jerdan and Letitia Elizabeth Landon

Ella Stuart
Ella and Captain Leslie James Gregson had five children, all born in Australia:
Laura Landon Gregson remained unmarried and died in Shanghai in December 1924.
Kitty married Tom Clarke, lived in Shanghai, and died childless in 1950, in San Francisco.
Reginald, died 1919.
Leslie (d. 1916) had two children (Evelyn who became Mrs Hunt, and Colin who became an explorer).
Jessie (1854–1930) married under age, in 1874[4] to Alfred Augustus Sleight, (d. 1896) an undertaker whom Ella abhorred. The underage marriage might indicate that Jessie was pregnant, or known to have had relations with Alfred Augustus.

The Sleights produced a large family. Names of their children were : Kitty Bell (no issue), Queenie, Harold Stuart (illegitimate issue: one son, one daughter), Sony; Vernon and Ruby, both of whom were one year old when they died. There may have been two other children who died as infants, Augustus Leslie and Laura. Of the remaining Sleight children:

Lola Landon Sleight, echoing the Landon name Ella had given to her own daughter Laura, married Frederick Brockhoff, and had three sons: Harold, whose children were Bruce and Sue; Jack who was knighted as Sir Jack Stuart Brockhoff, and Alan. Alan's first marriage to Joyce Johnston produced Peter and John; Peter had three sons of his own, Peter, Steven and Ricky, and John had two children. Alan's second marriage to Neon resulted in three children, Michael, Sarah and Fiona.

Gordon Stuart Sleight (1880–1961) married Lydia Coleman. Their daughter Shirley Stuart (b. 1915) married Eric Frederic Gorman of London. They became the parents of Michael Stuart Frederic (b. 1944) and Christopher George Stuart (b. 1946) both born in Christchurch, New Zealand. Michael married Mizue Nakanishi of Kurashiki City, Japan. Christopher married Philippa Margaret Kempthorne and has two sons, Nicholas Eric (b. 1974) and Richard Stuart (b. 1977). Nicholas married Annabel Lucy Ensor of Canterbury New Zealand; their son George Frederic was born in 2009. Richard's partner is Victoria Barnett, and their daughter Charlotte Olivia Margaret was born in 2009.

Roy, the youngest son of Jessie Ella and Alfred Augustus Sleight, had four daughters, all of whom had children of their own. One daughter, Zara Kitty (1916–2005), married Richard Gamble (1916–1992), and had two sons Anthony and Simon. Anthony Amherst Gamble (1936) married Penelope Hopkins. Their daughter Letitia married William Alexander McClean – thereby becoming, extraordinarily, the namesake of her ancestor Letitia Maclean, née Landon. Letitia's two children were Xander Timothy and Olive Kitty. The second daughter of Anthony and Penelope Gamble was Jessica Elizabeth. Zara and Richard Gamble's second son, Simon, had three sons: Duncan, Roger and Phillip.

Yvonne, another of Roy Sleight's daughters, married Theo Troedel, and had four sons: Dennis, Andrew, William (Bill) and James, born between 1937–1946. In turn, Dennis married Heather Sutherland and their daughter Anouche was born in 1979. Andrew married Margaret Rowell and had Sally (1970) and Lucy (1972); following the death of Margaret he subsequently married Pru Downie whose two children, Martine and Brooke, assumed the family name of Troedel. Sally married Jonathan Bare and had four children, Nicholas, Stephanie, Madeline and Zara. Lucy married Craig Shaw and had Arthur and Frances. William (Bill) married Prue Hamilton, and had Alastair (1972), James (1974) and Penelope(1977). Alastair married Miranda Scarff and had Rupert and Oliver; James married Kirsten Madden and had Noah; Penelope married Thomas Paton and their children were William and Angus. The fourth son of Yvonne Sleight and Theo Troedel, James, married Priscilla Watson and had Amy (1973), Harald (1977) who married Nerissa Broban and had Indigo, Freya Letitia (1979) who married James Wong, and Roland (1982).

Lola Janet, Roy Sleight's third daughter, married Bill McNeice, and had two sons, Shane (two children) and Connor (two children).

Roy Sleight's fourth daughter Valda married Joseph Dixon. Their children were Skye, Jonathon, Stephen and Fabian.

Ethel, who married George Fred Barnes. Ethel knew her grandmother Ella well as they lived nearby for nearly thirty years (from 1875–1910). Ethel was thirty-four years of age when Ella died. All the family stories have emanated from this connection. Ethel Barnes's daughter Margaret, "Peg", married Henri Malval and remained childless. She became the keeper of the family archives on Ethel's death at 105, and on her own death aged 95 in 2008, in the U.S.A, these archives were sent to Michael Gorman now living in Japan, who has generously shared his family's information concerning Ella Stuart and her descendants.

Ella (Stuart) Gregson died in 1910 at the age of 87,[5] and was buried above her husband. Their sons Leslie who died in 1916, and Reginald, who died in 1919, were buried in the same grave as their parents.

According to notes left by Ethel Barnes concerning her grandmother Ella Stuart Gregson, and conversations between family archivist Michael Gorman and Ethel Barnes, and also with Peg Malval, Ethel's daughter, Ella was reputedly a strict mother with no patience for frivolity and ruled her family with an iron hand. She appears to have been protective towards her consumptive brother Fred, " but had no time for her sister Laura, disliked Jerdan intensely – and was very bitter always about her Mother"[6] (L.E.L.). Ella struck up a close friendship with

"Coz" Charlie Jerdan – who was in fact her half-brother. They met when he went to Australia on the steamship *Galatea* as an Engineer.[7] When he returned to England and settled in Devon, the ties between their families were maintained for three generations. Ethel Barnes, Ella's granddaughter, was friendly with Alice Jerdan, "Coz" Charlie's daughter, born within five months of each other. Ethel and her daughter Peg stayed with Alice on a visit to Devon in the 1930s, and noted that Alice was terrified at the idea of raking up old stories about L.E.L., the shadow of illegitimacy reaching down a century later.[8]

Laura Landon

Since at least 1851 Laura lived with her foster parents, Theophilus and Mary Goodwin at Alford Cottage, Rosebery Place, Islington.[9] (They had listed a Laura under their own name, as a ten-year old in the 1841 Census; this could have been Laura Landon or Laura White, another child they fostered as their own.) The 1851 Census lists her as "Laura Landon, niece". In the 1861 Census Goodwin had described himself as a Master Silk Manufacturer employing 320 people.[10] Ten years later he said his occupation was "Mercantile Cl.", possibly meaning Clerk. The heyday of the silk industry was over when, in 1860, the Anglo-French treaty removed protection from French imports of silk. The Goodwins, with Laura Landon, had moved by 1871 to 65 Graham Road Hackney, a large terraced house on a broad straight street.[11] In 1879 Mary Goodwin died, aged 69.[12]

On 2 March 1880 at St. Paul's, Canonbury, Laura, claiming to be forty-seven years old, when in fact she was fifty-one, married William Charles Bartholomew, age fifty-four, a widower, whose occupation was Outfitter.[13] On her marriage certificate the name of her father is given clearly as 'William Landon, deceased, Gentleman", a neat elision of the first and last names of her father and mother, and one that would raise no questions, as 'Jerdan' certainly would have done. Theophilus Goodwin witnessed the marriage.

The newly married couple continued to live with Theophilus Goodwin; perhaps marriage was a necessarily respectable step to enable Laura to continue to take care of Goodwin after his wife's death.[14] In January 1891 Goodwin himself died, aged eighty-four.[15] He left many charitable bequests and legacies, including £1000 to his god-son, the son of his other foster-daughter, Laura White. He left Laura Landon, now Bartholomew, a life annuity of £100, and a half share with the other Laura, of his furniture, linen, china, wines and liquors, excepting some presentation silver salvers which went to family members. Laura also received a one-seventh share of any residue after the bequests had been fulfilled. Goodwin had been a wealthy man, leaving an estate of almost £18,000.[16]

Laura and her husband remained in the same house with a boarder and a servant. On 23 December 1891, William Bartholomew died of chronic bronchitis at the age of sixty-five, and Laura, married for only eleven years, was left a widow.[17] She moved to Streatham where, in the 1901 Census, she was listed as a Boarding House Keeper aged fifty-nine — she was actually seventy-two — with four lodgers and a servant.[18] She died on 25 January 1913, aged eighty-four (although her death certificate states eighty-six).[19] She had died of broncho-pneumonia and heart failure. She left an estate of £207, and several bequests of her personal effects to the family of her foster-sister Laura White, now Robinson. The residue of her estate was for her friend, Edith Maud Smith.[20]

Laura Landon Bartholomew was buried with her husband in Abney Cemetery, Stoke Newington, North London.[21] Their grave is marked by three square stones of graduated size; the top stone shows evidence of having had some monument placed on it, perhaps a cross as was common for monuments of this type, but that has now disappeared.

Fred Stuart

All that is known of Fred is that he went to Trinidad and was in dire financial straits.[22] Family lore says that he married the Governor's daughter.[23] One photograph taken in a Port of Spain, Trinidad, studio is of a little girl, and marked on the reverse, "Emily Ella Stuart". Fred has defied every attempt to discover more about his life, neither has it so far been possible to trace what happened to his daughter Emily.

Immediate descendants of William Jerdan and Mary Maxwell

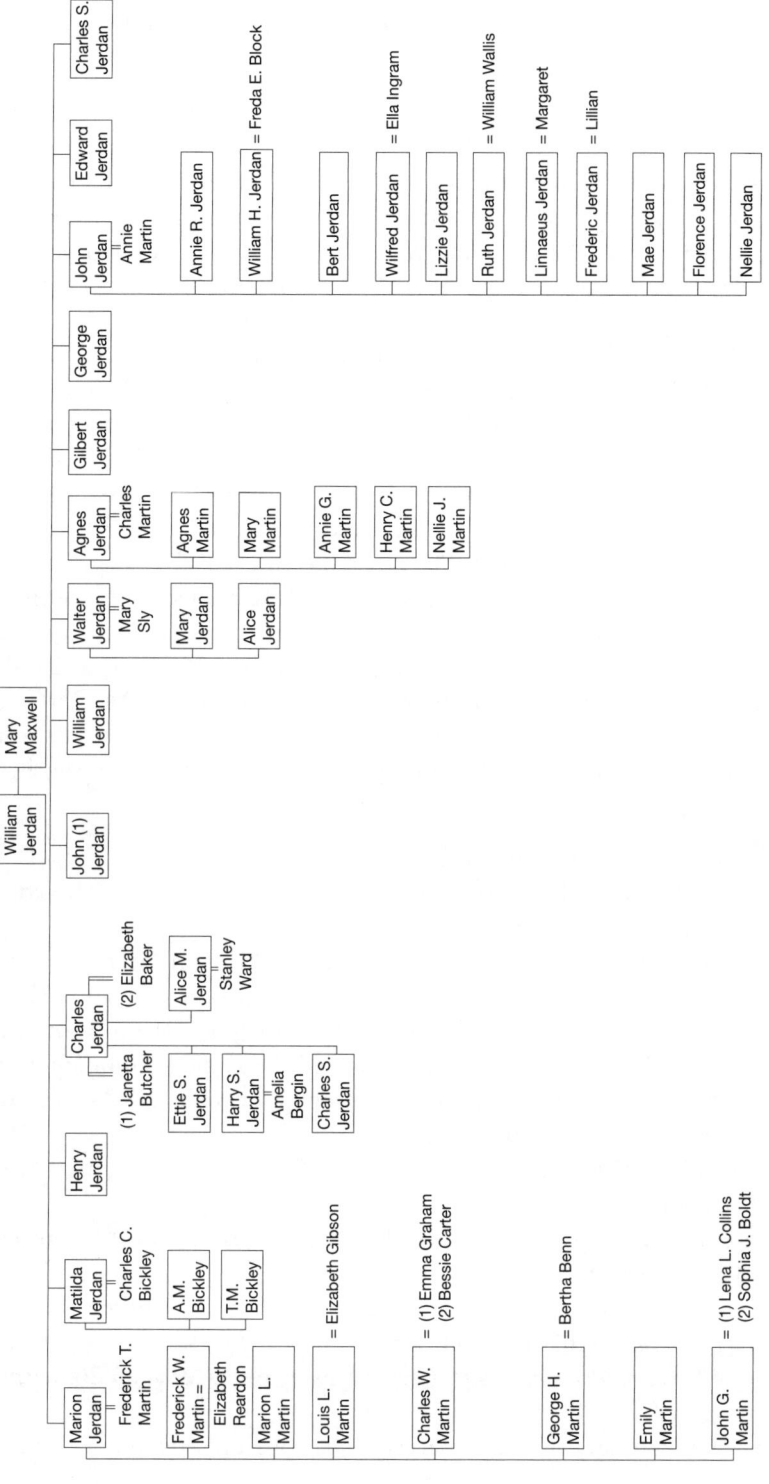

The Children of William Jerdan and Mary Maxwell

Mary Maxwell was about 18 or 19 when she and the 53-year old William Jerdan started their family of thirteen children.

Marion (Jerdan) Martin was born before 1837 when births had to be registered; she was probably born in 1835–6, and appeared on the Census of 1841 as 'Marion Stewart'. Whilst living with her aging father and her young siblings in Bushey Heath, on 23 December 1868, seven months before Jerdan's death, Marion married a sailor, Frederick Thomas Martin, several years younger than herself.[24] They had Frederick William born June 1870, Marion Lousia born March 1872 who died aged one month, Louis in June 1873 and Charles Walter in April 1875. Three months after the latter's birth, the young family emigrated on the S.S. *Greece* to New York, docking on 29 July 1875. Frederick Martin's occupation was listed as 'Railway Inspector'. On Christmas Day 1877 George Henry was added to the family, followed by Emily A. on 13 October 1879 and John Gilbert on 20 March 1881. By 1891 the family had moved to Toronto, Canada, possibly drawn by the proximity of Marion's brother John, married to Annie Martin, Frederick's sister. By the time of the 1891 Census, Frederick's occupation was given as Policeman,[25] and at the 1901 Census Emily and John were still living at home with their parents in E. Toronto.[26] Marion Jerdan Martin died at the age of 85 on 18 August 1921 at 296 Sackville Street, Toronto, having suffered three years of 'senile debility' (raising thoughts of her mother's 'chronic mania' – perhaps there was an inherited trait.).[27]

Of Marion's six surviving children:
Emily has proved impossible to trace, although 'Emiline A. Martin' witnessed the marriage of her brother:
John Gilbert Martin to Lena Lepper Collins on 25 February 1909. The newly-weds went to live in Nipissing, Ontario. Another marriage of a John Gilbert Martin, aged 39, is recorded on 14 July 1919 in Ontario, to Sophia Jane Boldt. This may mean that his wife Lena died young, or they divorced, or the record could refer to a different John Gilbert Martin. No record of John's death has been found.
Frederick William married Elizabeth Reardon in December 1893 in York, Ontario.
George Henry married Bertha Belinda Benn in November 1904 in Wentworth Ontario.
Charles Walter married twice, once when he was 24, to the 18 year old Emma Armstrong Graham, in Hamilton Ontario. His second marriage, at the age of 42, as a widower, was to Bessie d'Esterre Carter aged 26, witnessed by his brother John Gilbert.
No issue from any of these marriages has been discovered. Thus it is probable

that of Marion Jerdan and Frederick Martin's marriage, only their son Louis Linnaeus provided them with grandchildren.

Louis married Elizabeth (Lizzy) Gibson in Ontario in September1892 when he was almost twenty years old and working as an electrician. Their family comprised Frederick Charles, born in May 1893, Louis Arthur in March 1900, Marion Margaret in November 1902, Lloyd Gotherold in December 1903, and George Henry in July 1906.

Of these five great-grandchildren of William Jerdan, no marriages or census records have been found for three of them.

Frederick enlisted in the Canadian Over-seas Expeditionary Force in September 1915,[28] giving his trade as 'Light and Power Cashier'.
The only other person who left a trace was Lloyd Gotherold Martin, who crossed the border from Canada into the United States on 3 April 1924, naming his father 'Lewis' as a contact. He crossed again at the Detroit border a year later, this time reverting to 'Louis', giving the same Toronto address for his father as appeared on his brother Frederick's Attestation Paper for the Expeditionary Force. At the time of this immigration into the U.S. Lloyd described himself as molding for an aluminum company. At the age of 24 he married 18 year old Evelyn Agnes Axford from Wisconsin, who had an Irish father and a Danish mother. They married in Detroit on 10 October 1927. Their son Lloyd L. arrived on 31 October 1928. Lloyd Gotherold Martin died in St Paul, Minnesota in November 1988, aged 60. Lloyd L. enlisted in the U.S. Army in November 1945, joining the Air Corps enlistment for the Hawaiian Department. He had three years of high school education and, like his father, was a sheet metal worker. He died in November 1988 in Minnesota. These descendants of William Jerdan were far removed from his world of politicians, artists and writers. The line of descendants from Marion Jerdan appears to have ended with Lloyd L. Martin for whom no issue has been found.

Matilda Maxwell (Jerdan) Bickley, William Jerdan and Mary Maxwell's second daughter died aged 29, in 1866. She left two daughters whose names are known only by their initials appearing on the 1861 Census:[29] they were A.M.S., born in Islington in 1859 and T.M. born in Peckham in 1860. Matilda's husband Charles Bickley remarried in 1868, but the family does not appear on the 1871 Census, although they were still young enough to be living with their father and his new wife. He died, aged 38, in June 1877. Matilda's children have not been traceable.

Henry Jerdan, usually called 'Harry' by his father, is known to have been a Corporal in Canada in 1864, although more suited to the life of an actor. He somehow got to Australia where another Harry, son of his brother Charles, had also emigrated. He married Julia Harwood and finally became a professional actor, according to his death certificate of 9 June 1922 at the age of 80.[30] The Informant was his nephew and namesake, Harry Stuart Jerdan, who gave his uncle's birthplace as Bushey and his mother's name as Marion Stuart, two small errors which must have been related to him by his uncle. Henry or 'Harry' and Julia Harwood had no children.

Charles Jerdan's birth certificate of 1838[31] does not add "Stuart" to his name, although the Charles born to the same parents in 1855 in the Barming Asylum *is* named Charles Stuart.[32] The descendants of the first Charles are now scattered in England and in Australia. Charles had joined the Royal Navy and in July 1861 was Assistant Engineer Second Class; three years later he was appointed First Class Assistant Engineer whilst on the S.S. *Galatea*, a wooden screw frigate, whose maiden voyage was five years earlier. At the time of his promotion, Charles married at the age of 23, in February 1862, to Janetta Henrietta Butcher, aged 16.[33] Her father was a wine merchant in Plymouth. Janetta and Charles's daughter Ettie Stuart Jerdan was born early in 1865 and their son Harry Stuart Jerdan on 6 October 1866. The 1871 Census shows mother and children living with Janetta's parents.[34]

Charles sailed on the S.S. *Galatea* which left Plymouth on 24 January 1867 captained by H.R.H. Alfred Ernest Albert, Duke of Edinburgh, Queen Victoria's fourth child. They embarked on a world tour which took them to Gibraltar, the Cape of Good Hope and then across the Indian Ocean to Australia, arriving at Glenelg near Adelaide, on 31 October 1867. In December of that year Charles was promoted to Engineer. Prince Albert toured Australia for five months, the first Royal visit ever made to that continent, marred by an assassination attempt in Sydney, by a Fenian who was hanged soon afterwards. The *Galatea* was used for coastal visits, but the Prince was taken by a special royal train from Victoria to inland provincial towns. It is probable that it was during this royal visit that Charles Jerdan met up with his half-sister Ella Stuart Gregson, daughter of Jerdan and L.E.L. They became close, Ella referring to him as "Coz Charlie", distancing herself from a more direct blood relationship. The friendship thus started was to last beyond their own lifetimes to the next generations of their families.

The *Galatea* returned to England in June 1868 after an absence of seventeen months. Charles and Janetta's third child, a son named after his father, was born in 1869 but lived only a few months. Janetta herself died aged 26 in 1872.[35] From the beginning of 1873 until December 1876 Charles served three voyages on the *Indus*, and also served on the *Pembroke*, *Nymphe* and *Pearl*.

In December 1876 he was pensioned, and his service record adds a comment "with a note as to his Bankruptcy".[36]

In 1878 Charles remarried, to Elizabeth Ann Baker, five years his senior. The following year their daughter Alice Marion Stuart Jerdan was born.[37] Their household included Ettie, child of Charles's first marriage, but by the 1881 Census there is no mention of his son Harry Stuart, aged 15.[38] Charles died in 1887 aged 47 but his widow lived on until 1911, aged 78.

Alice Marion Stuart Jerdan, daughter of Charles's second marriage, married Stanley May Ward in 1906 and they continued to live in Devon.[39] They were visited by Ethel Barnes (L.E.L.'s granddaughter) and her own daughter Peg on a trip from Australia to England in 1930. Ethel Barnes noted that they had talked about a recent book by Michael Sadleir which contained erroneous information about L.E.L. Alice allegedly was most anxious that the matter not be discussed lest their illegitimacy come to light.[40] In fact, as her ancestor was Mary Maxwell she herself was not a descendant of L.E.L. although Ethel and Peg were, but they did of course share a common ancestor in William Jerdan.

Harry Stuart, who had vanished from the 1881 Census, is next found in Sydney, Australia, in 1885 when, at the age of 19, he married Amelia Priscilla Bergin, 19, from Parramatta, New South Wales.[41] By 1892 Harry Stuart Jerdan had become an optician in Sydney, also offering a mail order service for 'Magic Lanterns' for country customers; between 1904–7 he was in partnership and the company was called Osborne and Jerdan Opticians, but by 1913 it reverted to Jerdan's Limited.[42] Harry Stuart and Amelia had five children, Harry Stuart born on 1 January 1886 in Redfern, N.S.W., then Walter Reginald Charles Stuart, followed by Ruby born in 1890, Ernest in 1895 and Audrey Millicent Stuart Jerdan in 1901.[43]

Of these children, Harry Stuart married twice, and died in Darlington N.S.W. in November 1948.[44] His son Peter Stuart Jerdan was born in 1935, of his second marriage to Lina Boesch. Peter's career was as a military and commercial and pilot, something that his great-great-grandfather William Jerdan, who had watched Lunardi's balloon flight with amazement, would have found incomprehensible. Peter Jerdan has two sons who carry the name of Stuart, two daughters and ten grandchildren.

Walter Reginald Charles Stuart Jerdan married Doris M. Bradley in 1913, and lived in Mosman N.S.W. until at least 1931. His sister Audrey was either living or staying with them at the time of the Electoral Registration in 1930.[45] Walter died in 1948.[46]

Ruby died in 1913 at the age of only 23, and was unmarried.[47]

Ernest and Audrey, the two youngest siblings, were known to Ethel Barnes, granddaughter of L.E.L., the next generation continuing the friendship of Ella Stuart and "Coz Charlie". Ernest became a brilliant barrister and lecturer at Sydney University. He married Rachael Mandelbaum in 1920 in Sydney, but this ended in divorce.[48] Ernest travelled on the S.S. *Demosthenes* to London, arriving in April 1924.[49] He stayed first at the Devonshire Club in St. James Street, before moving to Harley Street where he lived with Dr. Norman Haire. He spent the summer of 1929 in Germany visiting Bayreuth and Leipzig, flying on to Berlin where he met many famous psycho-analysts. He travelled on through the Tyrol and into Italy which he thought was like a great barracks full of Fascist militia. A few months later he went to the house of some friends in Hove, Sussex, knowing that they were away and put his head in the gas oven. His inquest delivered a verdict of suicide while of unsound mind, even though he had left money to compensate for the inconvenience and a note warning his friends to keep their children out of the kitchen. His doctor friend was reported as saying that Ernest had been under treatment for mental trouble, and had been very clever but overstrung.[50] With hindsight, it may have been genetically significant that his ancestor, Mary Maxwell, was "a lunatic", dying in an asylum, her "chronic mania" perhaps handed down to yet another member of her family.

Ernest's sister Audrey married Ferris A. Glennie in 1934.[51]

John Jerdan 1

The John Jerdan born to William Jerdan and Mary Maxwell in December 1839[52] has vanished from the record. Another son born in March 1850 was also called John, which may indicate that the first John had died.

William Jerdan; Walter Jerdan

All that is known is what their father told Bennoch in 1863: that William worked at Penn's machinery factory, and Walter at the Telegraph Office. No further information on William has been discovered. Walter Jerdan went to Australia like his older brothers Henry and Charles, and his younger brothers George and Gilbert. He married Mary Jane Sly[53] and they had two daughters, Alice and Mary. Walter lived in Queensland from about 1873 until his death on 8 August 1890 at the age of 41, when his occupation was described as Clerk in the Municipal Division Board.[54] As occurred for his brother Henry, the Informant was his nephew Harry Stuart Jerdan, who knew that the name of his uncle's father was William [Stuart] (sic) Jerdan, journalist, but did not know the name of his mother.

Agnes Maxwell Jerdan

A few days after Jerdan's death his daughter Agnes had herself christened, and two days afterwards she married Charles Martin, the third Jerdan sibling to marry a Martin sibling.[55] Their daughter Agnes was born very shortly after the marriage, but survived only a few months. They lived in Willington,

Derbyshire, where, in 1871 Charles Martin was a railway ticket collector. By 1881 their family included Mary aged 11, Annie aged 8, Harry aged 5 and Nellie, aged 2. Charles Martin had risen to become Chief Stationmaster in Willington.[56]

Gilbert Jerdan; George 'Tiny' Jerdan

These two sons of William Jerdan and Mary Maxwell had sailed to Australia in 1866.[57] The only Australian records found are of a single man, George Gilbert Jerdan who, in 1925, was a sub-accountant in Queensland. In 1930 he was an accountant at the Kalamia Estate, and by 1936 had become business manager at the Imperial Hotel in Kennedy, Queensland.[58] It is probable that this man was a son of either George or Gilbert.

John Jerdan 2

The John Jerdan born in 1850[59] married Annie Martin, sister to Frederick and Charles who were each married to Jerdan sisters. John and Annie married in 1872, when she was still 'under-age', probably about 16.[60] In 1877 they emigrated to N. Dumfries Township, Waterloo, Ontario in Canada. Later they moved to Toronto where John was a clerk. (See illustration no. 8.) Their first child Annie Rosa Stuart was born on 22 August 1878; William Henry Stuart arrived on 23 January 1881, and Wilfred Walter Stuart on 7 March 1886. The repeated use of the Stuart name, harking back to the mother of their ancestor William Jerdan, reappears in many descendants on various continents. There may have been another son, Bert, for whom no birth registration is listed, although a relative heard that he disliked America and emigrated to South Africa, where he founded a diamond mine.[61]

Annie Martin Jerdan died on 5 November 1923 in Philadelphia, aged 64. John Jerdan died on 19 March 1925, also in Philadelphia. His interment record shows his age as 71, but in fact he was 74.

No further record of Annie Rosa's life has been found, and from later information it is probable that she died young.

The brothers William Henry and Wilfred Walter moved to Philadelphia. By 1910 William Henry was married to Freda, née Block, whose parents were from Germany. They had three children, William Henry Stuart Jr. born on 17 June 1915, Gladys Anna Stuart in September 1916 and Vera Emma Stuart in May 1920. The first William Henry's World War I Draft Registration card shows him at age 37, as a spot welder for the Budd Wheel Corporation. By the 1930 Census he was a 'Puter Out' in a leather mill, but when his World War II Draft Registration card was issued at the age of sixty-one, he was noted as unemployed. He died in Philadelphia in August 1944 at the age of 63. The official record after the 1930 Census is silent on William Henry Stuart's children, but his living descendants have provided much information to fill this gap. His daughter Gladys did not marry, and died in Philadelphia in February 2010. Vera married A. Malcontento in 1973, and died in Philadelphia in February 2007.

William H. S. Jr., the namesake and son of William Henry Stuart Jerdan, married Eleanor Isabelle McCullough in June 1939; they had five sons and a daughter. William Henry Stuart Jerdan Jr. became a presiding Bishop of the Reformed Episcopal Church of North America, and died in March 2001 at the age of eighty-five, in Summerville, S. Carolina.

Their sons were:

William Stuart Jerdan, born November 1944, married Diane Hagen. Their children are Stephanie Lynn, Daniel Stuart, Benjamin William, Jonathan Hagen. Of these, Daniel married Dulcia Frisinger and they have Ailish Kaylee, Colin Stuart and Ian Russell. Benjamin married Sarah Haberkamp and their children are Nathan William Stuart and David Allen Stuart.

Bruce Alan Jerdan, born 20 August 1947. No issue.

Barry Dean Jerdan, born 10 May 1949, married Nancy Susan Roppelt. Their children are Barbara Lois and Andrew Carl.

Brian Scott Jerdan, born 18 September 1952, married Kathleen Hill. Their children are Olivia (married Bjorgvin Fredriksson; their daughter is Isabelle Joy Bjorgvinsdotter), Brian Isaac Stuart (married Jerrica Clark; their daughter is Teagan Marie), Philip, Elizabeth Bahar, Ozgur Paul, and Onur Peter.

Robert Mark Jerdan, born 28 July 1956 married (1) Cynthia Beales, and their sons are Matthew Stuart and Stephen Maxwell. This middle name of Maxwell echoes the name of his great-great-great-grandmother, Mary Maxwell. However, this was genealogy previously unknown to the family and it is coincidental that Stephen Maxwell Jerdan derives his name from a completely different ancestor on his mother's side, thus unknowingly linking both sides of his family tree in the one name. Robert married (2) Ronda Schuman.

Bonnie Eleanor, born 20 February 1958, married Frank Sayles Jr. Their son is Nicholas. Bonnie Sayles has been the untiring source of much information about the younger Jerdans.

Many of these children are continuing the tradition of holding William Jerdan's mother's name of Stuart.

John and Annie Jerdan's next son, Wilfred Walter Stuart, married Ella Ingram (1892–1975) and, like his brother, was enlisted in World War I. Wilfred's World War II Draft Registration card at age fifty-six, reveals him as working for the railroad. He died in June 1982 in Bensalem, Bucks County, Pennsylvania, at the age of ninety-four. Wilfred and Ella's twin sons Linnaeus and Walter were born on 29 November 1913, followed by another set of twins, Ada May and William. This William's son, also William, is practising as a Doctor in Pennsylvania. Linnaeus appears to have married Marion

Lebrun, lived all his life in Pennsylvania, and had two sons, one of whom was named Edward. Ada May married and had three children.

Lizzie Jerdan, born in 1888, married and had two daughters, one of whom was named Nancy who married and had three children. When Lizzie was 22, at the time of the 1910 Census, all three were living with her parents John and Annie in Philadelphia, together with her sister Ruth and two brothers, Linnaeus and Fred.

Ruth married William Wallis, and their son Roy was born in 1919, but died at the age of fourteen. Their second son William Roy was born in 1929 and died in 2008. Ruth died at the age of 85. A daughter, Gail, was adopted and still lives in Pennsylvania; she has kindly provided some of the information about the older generation of this branch of the family.

Linnaeus Arthur Stuart, seventh child of John and Annie Jerdan, married Margaret and had two sons, Joseph who died in about 2005, and John Linnaeus known as Jack who, in 2009, was living in Las Vegas. He was told that the name Linnaeus had been given to him in memory of the captain of the ship in which his grandparents had sailed from England.

The next son, Frederick Edward Stuart, was born in 1895, and married Lillian; their daughter, also Lillian, was born in 1920, and their two sons were named Frederick and Edward.

Of the last three daughters of John and Annie Jerdan, Mae apparently had a son and a daughter Annie; Florence married a military man, but died of consumption; Nellie married and had several children. Many of John and Annie's family moved to Atlantic City, New Jersey.

Edward 'Teddie' Jerdan; Charles Stuart Jerdan

These two youngest sons of William Jerdan were living with him until not long before he died, by which time they were aged about 14 and 15. No trace of their lives has been discovered, and it is possible that they emigrated to North America or to Australia where they had brothers and a sister who may have given them a home. An Edward Stuart Jerdan is recorded on Electoral Rolls in Western Australia between 1906–1925; this Edward could be William Jerdan's youngest son, or a grandson of one of the earlier emigrants. As with so many details of William Jerdan's life, this is yet a further unsolved mystery.

❧ Notes ❧

A Note on Money

1 Paul Lewis, <u>VICTORIA@listserv.indiana.edu</u>, 15 December 2008.
2 Jeffrey G. Williamson, "The Structure of Pay in Britain, 1710–1911", *Research in Economic History*, 7 (1982), pp. 1–54.

Part I The Early Years, 1782–1817

Chapter 1   From the River Tweed to the River Thames

1 *The Statistical Account of Scotland Drawn up from the Commmunications of the Ministers of Different Parishes*: Sir John Sinclair Bart: Vol. Tenth: William Creech: Edinburgh, 1794. The entry for Kelso by Dr Christopher Douglas, Physician in Kelso.
2 William Jerdan, *Autobiography* I, p. 10.
3 Many years later he remarked that one of his daughters was noticed to bear a strong resemblance to a particular portrait by Traill of Mary Queen of Scots. However it has been pointed out (by Dr Julie Watt, Edinburgh) that all Stewart and royal portraits in Holyrood Palace were painted at the same time by the same artist, and closely resembled each other, no Stewarts or royals being present at their production. It is therefore unlikely that any similarities between Jerdan's daughter and the Queen's portrait would indicate royal ancestry. However, Jerdan must have been delighted with such public recognition, and not made any attempt to discourage the notion of such a connection.
4 *Auto.* I, p. 8.
5 *Auto.* I, p. 9.
6 Notes and Queries, 4ᵗʰ series, ii, 12 August 1868, p. 97; 12 December 1868, p. 554.
7 These officers, under the authority of the Baillie, imposed a tax on the inhabitants of the town, the amount dependent upon their judgment of individual means.
8 Goose Gibbie, a half-witted boy in Sir Walter Scott's tale *Old Mortality*, published 1819.
9 Lunardi's ballooning career in Great Britain ended in tragedy in Newcastle in 1786, when a young man became entangled in the ropes as the unmanned balloon came loose; he fell to his death from five hundred feet.
10 The village of Ednam still exists, unlike many of Scotland's eighteenth-century villages.
11 *Auto.* I, p. 211.
12 Ibid.
13 *Auto.* I, p. 10.

14 *Auto*. I, p. 12.

15 *Auto*. I, p. 14.

16 *Auto*. I, p. 16.

17 *The Statistical Account of Scotland*, op. cit.

18 Whilst staying with the Scotts at Rosebank in 1783, Walter Scott attended Kelso High School for a few months, where he met James Ballantyne. They met again at Edinburgh University, after which Ballantyne returned to Kelso to practice law. This was apparently unsuccessful as he responded enthusiastically to the proposals made by John Jerdan and others in 1797 to establish a Tory newspaper, the *Kelso Mail*, in opposition to the radical *Kelso Chronicle*. The *Mail* was to be the newspaper of a more reactionary view. There were initially three holders of copyright in the *Mail*: John Jerdan, Walter Scott and James Ballantyne. The Jerdan family retained the copyright for eighty-four years. James Ballantyne continued to edit the *Kelso Mail* until 1809, then handed it on to his brother Alexander. In 1824 William Jerdan's brother George borrowed £1500 with which he bought the *Kelso Mail* and the property accommodating its printing office at 12 Bridge Street. George Jerdan was a practising lawyer and a fervent Tory who, like his father, saw the *Mail* as a vital weapon to combat the rampant radicalism of its competitor, the *Kelso Chronicle*. Ten years after taking over the *Mail* George Jerdan proposed the addition of a weekly journal to encourage conservative support and to "counteract the revolutionary tendency of the present weekly paper", the same ideal which had prompted his father to found the *Mail* back in 1797. His attempt was unsuccessful, and in 1840 George Jerdan wanted to dispose of his interest in the *Mail,* but there was no sale, and when George died in 1849, the paper was leased to Alexander Elliot until 1861 when George's son, another William, took over as proprietor. He was still running the newspaper in 1866, at which time it was the second oldest extant provincial newspaper in Scotland. (Ironically, at a later date it merged with the hated *Kelso Chronicle*, an arrangement that would have appalled both John and George Jerdan.)

19 *Auto*. I, 20.

20 *Auto*. I, 21.

21 *Auto*. I, 23.

22 The Fifth Meeting of the British Association was held in Dublin in 1835.

23 *Auto*. I, 30.

24 *Auto*. I, 39.

25 *Auto*. I, 47.

26 *Auto*. I, 40.

27 He wrote about this journey at some length in the *Leisure Hour*, September 1858, p. 564, mentioning that he had been aged 19.

28 *Auto*. II, 316.

29 Jerdan's name was registered as a Member on 21 January 1808, covering initiates between 1802–1807. Grand Lodge of Scotland.

30 In 1809 Scott was half owner (John and James Ballantyne owned the other half) of John Ballantyne & Co. Scott thus profited in three ways: publishing, printing and copyright, from his own works. The company fell into crippling debt, and was forced to ask Archibald Constable to take over its remaining assets. Constable & Co.

collapsed into bankruptcy in 1825 as a result of the crash of Hurst, Robinson & Co., their agents. Scott's debts from these two disasters were not finally paid off until 1847.

31 *Auto.* I, p. 72.

32 *Auto.* I, p. 99.

33 *Auto.* I, p. 75.

34 *Auto.* I, p. 78.

35 *Auto.* I, p. 80. No copies exist in the British Library of the *Portsea, Portsmouth and Gosport Journal*, which was the probable publisher of this work. The *Hampshire Telegraph*, the only other Portsmouth paper of that time, carries no poems on Wilberforce until 1807, when an indifferent poem signed with the initials J.H. appeared. It therefore seems likely that Jerdan's first published work is lost to posterity.

36 An article in the *Sun* in 1805 has been attributed to Jerdan, probably incorrectly, on the grounds that the author's penname of Viator was that used by Jerdan when he worked for the *Sun* several years later. The article, later turned into a pamphlet entitled "Observations on Indecent Sea-Bathing as Practised at Different Watering-Places on the Coast of this Kingdom" has a tone of indignant morality unlikely to be that of the 23-year old William Jerdan. Viator was frequently used as a penname by a variety of writers.

Chapter 2   Embarking on Journalism

1 *Auto.* I, p. 119.

2 *Auto.* I, p. 100.

3 *The Oxford Dictionary of National Biography* cites a marriage entry in the parish records of Temple, Edinburgh, 5 September 1806. However, this entry does not refer to the William Jerdan of this biography, but to a different William Jerdan (possibly a cousin) who married Margaret Olridge.

4 Every English County Record Office and many Scottish Offices have been requested to search for a record of the marriage, but none has been found.

5 *Auto.* I, p. 83.

6 The first issue and a few subsequent issues are held by the Newspaper Library of the British Library.

7 *Auto.* I, p. 89.

8 G. Pyle, *The Literary Gazette under William Jerdan*, unpublished PhD dissertation, 1975, p. 15, quoting from "Passages of a Working Life During Half a Century", C. Knight.

9 Ibid.

10 S. C. Hall, *Retrospect of a Long Life*, p. 113.

11 *Auto.* I, p. 84.

12 *Auto.* I, p. 85.

13 Bishops Transcripts, St. Mary Abbot, Kensington DL/T.47/14.

14 *Auto.* I, p. 91.

15 A. Andrews, *History of British Journalism*, 1859.

16 *Auto.* I, p. 110.

17   Ibid.
18   There is a book by this name in the British Library, published in 1811, by Oliver Outline, Major-General. Jerdan's name is not mentioned.
19   A possible reference to the chapter, 'The Life of Mahomet' in Gibbon's *Decline and Fall of the Roman Empire*, an abridged edition of which was published in 1807, in which he says that "the jurisdiction of the magistrate was mute and impotent".
20   Instances of Jerdan's use of his pseudonym are noted *seriatim*.
21   A copy is in the British Library, dated 25 October 1809.
22   Frederick, Duke of York, was the second and favourite son of King George III, and Commander-in-Chief of the Army. He was disgraced in 1809 when it was revealed that his mistress, Mary Ann Clarke, had acted as a broker for military commissions and promotions. A committee was set up to investigate the matter, which was taken up in the House by a Colonel Wardle, demanding that the Commander in Chief be removed from office. Canning asked the House to treat the Duke fairly, without prejudice, but also without favour, showing the House how even an innocent letter he himself had written could be wilfully misinterpreted by anyone wishing to casti-gate him. He pointed out that only the testimony of Mrs Clarke herself, a known prostitute, linked the Duke of York with the practices of which he was accused, and that only she had "proved the privity of the Duke of York", i.e. had claimed that they shared a secret knowledge. Canning's powerful argument showed how the Duke's partnership with Mrs Clarke had ceased in 1806, but that she continued her malpractice of commissions for cash with a Colonel Sandon, having nothing more to do with the Duke. Despite Canning's best endeavours, the Duke of York was charged, but Mrs Clarke and Colonel Sandon escaped the consequences.
23   *Auto*. I, p. 111.
24   *Auto*. I, p. 114 . An invasion by 40,000 British troops of the Isle of Walcheren in the Scheldt, with the aim of capturing Antwerp and destroying the French fleet. It was a disastrous failure.
25   *Auto*. I, p. 126.
26   James Morgan, Engineer of the Regent's Canal, drafted plans in 1811 which became the basis of the Regent's Canal Bill which passed Parliament after a stormy passage in July 1812.
27   *Auto*. I, p. 128.
28   *Examiner*, 29 December 1811.
29   www.number-10.gov.uk.
30   *Auto*. I, p. 134.
31   *Auto*. I, p. 136.
32   *Auto*. I, p. 138.
33   In 1804 Bellingham had left his native Liverpool and travelled to Russia, engaged in his business of trading, where he was imprisoned for some connection which he strenuously denied, with the loss of a ship for which the Lloyds underwriters refused to pay insurance. He appealed to Lord Gower, then British Ambassador to Russia, who did request his release from the military governor of Archangel. This request was refused on the grounds that Bellingham was imprisoned for a legal cause, and he was kept incarcerated for six years, being moved from dungeon to dungeon, fed

on bread and water, and sometimes marched through the streets with hardened criminals, once under the very windows of the British Minister. He was eventually released from prison.

34 So thoroughly did Jerdan claim his place in history, that when a question was raised in *Notes & Queries* in April 1855 as to whether it was Jerdan or Hume who had seized Bellingham, the respondent quoted Jerdan's words and concluded "I should have thought the fact that it was Mr Jerdan who seized Bellingham to have been as well known as that Wellington was at Waterloo."

35 *Auto.* II, p. 309.

36 'A voice and nothing more'.

37 *Auto.* II, p. 313.

38 *The Satirist*, 1 August 1812 and *Auto.* II, p. 314.

39 *Catalogue of Personal and Political Satires preserved in the Department of Prints and Drawings in the British Museum.* Ref. No. 11894. W. H. Ekoorb (Brooke).

40 *The Satirist*, p. 394. Advertisement for Ladies' Riding Habits.

41 Alvin Sullivan, *British Literary Magazines 1789–1836.* The Romantic Age, p. 386.

42 *The Satirist*, 1 September 1813.

43 A. Sullivan, op. cit., p. 386.

44 *Auto.* II, p. 315.

45 A. Sullivan, op. cit., p. 386.

Chapter 3 Editor of the *Sun*

1 *Auto.* I, p. 159.

2 Jerdan and Perry were cited as exceptions to the prevailing view that until the 1820s journalism "was regarded as neither a dignified nor a reputable profession". A. Aspinall, *The Social Status of Journalists at the beginning of the 19th Century.* RES 21 (1945), 216–32, quoted in G. Pyle, op. cit., p. 19. However, this view is at odds with Collins, *Profession of Letters*, p. 203 who says that from the beginning of the century "journalism stands out henceforth as the great avenue to success in the profession of letters".

3 *Auto.* I, p. 161.

4 Proby had never left London, never been on a horse or boat, walked with a cane his own height, later exchanged for an umbrella which he was never without. He could memorise and report on entire debates in the Lords, without making a note, and wrote novels on the social manners of the times. He was addicted to confectionery, for which debts Jerdan and Taylor bailed him, and was known to be so punctual there was no need for his observers to carry a watch. He ended his life in a Lambeth workhouse, from which he visited his friends clad in its grey garments, and in which he exulted at being permitted to teach the workhouse children their ABC. Jerdan shared in a subscription of a few pounds a year to bring Proby some modest comforts.

5 Founded in 1805, the British Institution opened in Pall Mall, London, in January 1806. Its aim was to promote the Fine Arts in the United Kingdom. Two exhibitions were held each year, one of old, the other of new pictures.

6 *Auto.* I, p. 176.

7 Bishops Transcripts, St. Mary Abbott, Kensington. DL/T/47/23.

8 The Corn Laws were protectionist, encouraging export and limiting import of corn when prices fell below a fixed point; these Laws later became the focus of fierce contention between landowners and the working classes.

9 Letter from Walter Scott to W. Jerdan, 2 November 1814. Historical Society of Pennsylvania, Dreer Collection.

10 Entries from 22 April to 10 September 1814 are numbered to 32, but No. 26 is missing; No. 25 appeared on 26 August and No. 27 the following day. The latter refers to a topic in his 'last letter' i.e. No. 26, which appears not to have been printed, or was incorrectly numbered.

11 *Sun*, 29 May 1814.

12 *Auto*. I, p. 177.

13 *Sun*, 28 April 1814.

14 *Sun*, 29 April 1814.

15 Jerdan did not mention, until his *Autobiography* many years later, that to avoid currency losses, he sent his excess gold home with a friend, Turner, who was never heard of again, and was presumed to have been murdered for the gold.

16 *Sun*, 2 May 1814.

17 *Sun*, 3 May 1814.

18 *Sun*, 14 May 1814.

19 *Sun*, 16 May 1814.

20 *Sun*, 20 May, 1814.

21 N. Davies, *Europe*, p. 752.

22 *Sun*, 20 May 1814.

23 *Sun*, 27 May 1814.

24 A phrase from Hamlet Act V sc. 1, meaning literally that it irritates a chilblain.

25 *Sun*, 20 May 1814.

26 *Sun*, 16 May 1814.

27 Ibid.

28 *Auto*. I, p. 187.

29 *Auto*. I, p. 193.

30 *Sun*, 29 May 1814.

31 *Sun*, 16 August 1814.

32 *Sun*, 18 August 1814.

33 Loutherberg's popular Eidophusikon, a model theatre with movable scenes lit by variable lighting, had been enormously popular in London some years earlier; at this time he was better known for his ambitious and brilliantly executed scenery for Garrick's Drury Lane Theatre.

34 *Sun*, 6 August 1814.

35 *Auto*. I, p. 195.

36 *Sun*, 29 May 1814.

37 *Sun*, 13 August 1814.

38 *Sun*, 6 September 1814.

39 *Sun*, 16 June 1814.

40 *Sun*, 5 July 1814.

41 *Sun*, 6 September 1814.
42 *Sun*, 7 September 1814.
43 *Sun*, 10 September 1814.

Chapter 4 Turbulent Times

1 The name of Mrs Charlemont was also spelled Charlmont or Clermont in contemporary documents. Jerdan recounts the story about Byron's challenge to a duel in his *Autobiography*, but Byron's *Sketch from Private Life*, was not published until 1815, a year after his journey with Kinnaird. Their discussion must therefore have occurred on another occasion and become confused in Jerdan's memory so many years later.

2 *Auto*. II, p. 26.

3 *Sun*, 4 August 1814.

4 *Auto*. II, p. 29.

5 Jerdan's boyhood friend, David Pollock, was involved in promoting the new invention of gas and for thirty years was governor of the Chartered Gas Light and Coke Company. Pollock rushed to London to watch the lighting of the bridge and pagoda with this new invention. Mortifyingly, the bridge caught fire, and everything was plunged into darkness. Pollock was the butt of his friends' jokes for quite a while afterwards.

6 *Auto*. I, p. 204

7 *Auto*. IV, p. 171 (I am the daughter of a hero; the wife of a zero).

8 George Canning was born in 1770 into an Anglo-Irish family. He became an MP in 1793. Three years later he was appointed parliamentary under-secretary for Foreign Affairs, under Lord Grenville. He briefly edited the pro-government, anti-republican, anti-reform journal, the *Anti-Jacobin*, for which he also wrote. At the age of thirty he married an heiress, paid off his debts, and acquired property. When Pitt's government fell, Canning resigned his various offices, and refused to serve under the next Prime Minister, Addington. He was not a minister in the Grenville parliament either. In 1808 he became Foreign Secretary in the government of Portland, who was his brother-in-law. He negotiated treaties with Portugal and Spain, and planned the seizure of the Dutch fleet, thus thwarting Napoleon's scheme of invasion. He believed that Lord Castlereagh was mishandling the War Office, in particular the disastrous Walcheren expedition, and refused to work with him, threatening to resign from the Foreign Office unless Castlereagh was removed. Castlereagh got wind of this and challenged Canning to a duel, in the course of which Canning received a wound to his thigh. On Portland's death, Canning offered himself to the King as the next Prime Minister, but was rejected. He then resigned as Foreign Secretary, refusing to serve under the ill-fated Spencer Perceval who was briefly Prime Minister until his assassination. Soon after this event, Canning carried a motion in the House of Commons in favour of Catholic Emancipation, to which Perceval had been staunchly opposed. Canning turned down Prime Minister Lord Liverpool's offer of his old job as Foreign Secretary, because he did not wish to work under Castlereagh, now Leader of the House of Commons. He was elected MP for Liverpool in 1812, a seat he held for eleven years.

9   *Auto.* II, p. 10.
10 *Auto.* II, p. 15.
11 Charlotte had been happily married to Prince Leopold of Saxe-Coburg. She was the only eligible heir to George III in her generation, so her death was a national disaster. Her baby son also died.
12 Huskisson later became President of the Board of Trade, and Colonial Secretary; he was an active proponent of free trade. He famously received fatal injuries at the opening of the Liverpool & Manchester Railway in 1830, when he was knocked down by Stevenson's *Rocket*.
13 *Auto.* II, p. 22.
14 *Auto.* I, p. 203.
15 *Auto.* II, p. 73.
16 *Auto.* II, p. 71.
17 *Auto.* II, p. 73.
18 *Auto.* II, p. 46.
19 *New Monthly Magazine* of November 1857 quoted M. Clarigny, late Editor of "The Constitutional", writing of this time, that Jerdan "was a man of talent and good sense, but deficient in taste and but an average writer. He had sound views in politics." Taylor was "Gay, sharp, sparkling . . . he was a lion of supper parties . . . [but] no serious idea could lodge in the head of this intelligent man . . . He once saluted Scotland as "Hail, sister island!"; his daily contact with celebrated men left no trace on his mind."
20 *Auto.* II, p. 76.
21 Pyne's *History of the Royal Residences* was published in three volumes in 1819, and provides an invaluable insight into the decorative schemes of the palaces, and the placement of art within the rooms.
22 *Auto.* II, p. 117.
23 W. Jerdan, *Men I Have Known*, p. 458.
24 Bishops Transcripts, St. Mary Abbott, Kensington. DL/T/47/23.
25 In 1830 the humorist Thomas Hood named his daughter Frances Freeling in honour of her godfather.
26 Letter from W. Jerdan to Walter Scott, 7 October 1815. National Library of Scotland, 3886/195.
27 *Auto.* II, p. 91.
28 *Auto.* II, p. 103.
29 *Auto.* II, p. 109.
30 Trotter's and other Bazaars are discussed in "The 'Vanity Fair' of 19th century England: Commerce, women and the East in the Ladies' Bazaar", G. R. Dyer, *Nineteenth Century Literature*, Vol. 46, No. 2, September 1991.
31 *New Monthly Magazine*, February 1816, p. 26.
32 "A Visit to the Bazaar" by 'A Lady', published in 1818 by Harris, is a promotional detailed account of the Bazaar and its offerings. This was possibly based on Jerdan's original work. The Bazaar was in existence until 1855.
33 The writer whose life had many parallels to Jerdan's own, Leigh Hunt, had the same difficulty: "To this day I cannot do a multiplication sum, or any other."

Quoted in A. Holden, *The Wit in the Dungeon: A Life of Leigh Hunt*, p. 226.

34 Mulock was still writing 40 years later in support of Louis Napoleon; he wrote three letters to the *Literary Gazette* under the name 'Satan', which stirred attention at the time, and he also gave a course on English Literature in Geneva and London.

35 *Auto*. II, p. 148.

36 *The Diary of Joseph Farington*, Vol. 14, 1817

37 James Grant, *The Newspaper Press*, assessed that this sum shows that the *Sun* was a good property; at that time *The Courier* was divided into 24 shares, *The Times* into 16.

38 Jerdan did not bear a grudge, and in a typically generous gesture in the *Literary Gazette* of 5 August 1826 announced a subscription to publish a volume of Taylor's poems. It referred briefly to "the misconduct of some person . . . has rendered the present measure . . . essential to his comforts. We trust the public, especially the town, will not be deaf to the invitation."

Part II The *Literary Gazette* – The First Decade, 1817–1827

Chapter 5 The *Literary Gazette* – An Ideal Occupation

1 *Auto*. IV, p. 382.

2 *Auto*. II, p. 165.

3 *Auto*. II, p. 167.

4 B. Colbert, *Bibliography of Travel Writing, 1780–1840*.

5 The book is catalogued in the British Library as written by Eaton Stannard Barrett, a lawyer who became a playwright and satirist. However, in his *Autobiography* Jerdan confessed to being the author.

6 Gary Dyer, *British Satire and the Politics of Style 1789–1832*, p. 104.

7 *Auto*. II, p. 177.

8 *Auto*. II, p. 176.

9 A. Holden, *The Wit in the Dungeon: A Life of Leigh Hunt*, p. 126.

10 Waterloo Directory, entry for *New Monthly Magazine*. www.victorianperiodicals.com.

11 French writer, whose work on education was influential on Mary Wollstonecraft.

12 *Auto*. II p. 174.

13 S. C. Hall, *The Book of Memories*, p. 285.

14 G. Pyle, *The Literary Gazette under William Jerdan*, p. 8.

15 Ibid., p. 40.

16 *Auto*. II, p. 179.

17 R. Duncan, *William Jerdan and the Literary Gazette*, iii, pp. 7, 16, 38–40.

18 G. Pyle, op. cit., p. 129.

19 *Literary Gazette*, 23 August 1823, p. 538.

20 Auto. II, p. 178.

21 *The Longman Companion to Victorian Fiction*, ed. J. Sutherland, from *Dictionary of National Biography*.

22 *Auto*, III, p. 11.

23 *Auto*, II, p. 187.

24 *Auto.* II, p. 192.
25 Proceedings of the Old Bailey, ref. T18170917-252.
26 One pound was twenty shillings.
27 *Auto.* II, p. 196.
28 R. Duncan, op. cit., p. 179.
29 *Literary Gazette*, 26 July 1817.
30 *Auto.* II, p. 213.
31 William St Clair, *The Reading Nation in the Romantic Period*, p. 316.
32 *Auto.* II, p. 234.
33 Stamp tax was payable on newspapers and periodicals, and was required if these were sent by post; unstamped copies were illegal until after the "wars" on this tax in the 1830s, resulting in the law being repealed in 1836.
34 *Auto.* III, p. 11.
35 A. A. Watts, *Alaric Watts*, p. 189.
36 *Auto.* III, p. 232.
37 *Auto.* III, p. 277.
38 *Auto.* II, p. 235.
39 *Auto.* II, p. 215.
40 *Auto.* II, p. 238.
41 G. Pyle, op. cit., p. 127.
42 Letter W. Jerdan to P. G. Patmore, 15 April 1818, Bodleian Library, University of Oxford, MS. Eng. Let. e.86 f7.
43 Letter W. Jerdan to W. Blackwood, 10 May 1819, National Library of Scotland, 4004/163-4.
44 Barry Cornwall (Bryan Procter), *The Literary Recollections of Barry Cornwall*, ed. R. W. Armour.
45 *Literary Gazette*, 22 May 1819, p. 321.
46 *Literary Gazette*, 31 October 1818, p. 698.
47 English Poetry 1579–1830: Spenser and the Tradition. http://wiz2.cath.vt.edu.
48 This incidence of negotiating Hippesley's copyright and of assisting Murray is one of the earliest noted when Jerdan acted as agent for an author, a role he played frequently in subsequent years, and is discussed later.
49 W. Jerdan, *Men I Have Known*, p. 308.
50 Dated from a letter sent to him at that address.
51 *Survey of London*, Vol. 41.
52 Bishops Transcripts, St. Mary Abbott, Kensington. DL/T/47/23.
53 Janet Adam Smith, *The Royal Literary Fund*: a short history.
54 Nigel Cross, *The Royal Literary Fund 1790–1918*, World Microfilms.
55 Ibid., p. 14.
56 Ibid., p. 14.
57 *Auto.* IV, p. 34.
58 *Auto.* II, p. 237.
59 *Auto.* II, p. 242.
60 *Auto.* II, p. 243.
61 *Literary Gazette*, 3 April 1819, p. 220.

62 *Auto.* II, p. 257.
63 In Autumn 1818 Turner visited Edinburgh in connection with Sir Walter Scott's 'The Provincial Antiquities of Scotland'. His visit to Tabley House may well have been a stop-over on his return to London.
64 W. Jerdan, *Men I Have Known*, p. 476.
65 R. D. Altick, *The Shows of London*, p. 240.
66 W. Jerdan, *Men I Have Known*.
67 *Auto.* II, p. 301.
68 W. Jerdan, *Men I Have Known*, p. 481.
69 *Auto.* II, p. 88.
70 *Auto.* II, p. 288.
71 *Auto.* II, p. 290.
72 Letter John Miller to W. Jerdan, 11 November 1820, National Library of Scotland, 948/26.
73 G. Pyle, p. 68.
74 *Auto.* III, p. 324.
75 Letter Cosmo Orme to W. Jerdan, 2 March y.n.d. Bodleian Library, University of Oxford, MS.Eng. lett d. 114, f121.
76 Freeling had corresponded with Walter Scott, certain that he was the author of the Waverley novels. (All Scott's novels were published anonymously until after Scott's bankruptcy in 1826.) Freeling claimed that Scott made reference to him in the Preface to 'Ivanhoe', which he took as confirmation that his guess was correct.
77 *Auto.* III, p. 64.
78 Noted in Indenture dated 27 November 1829. University of Reading, Longman Archives II, 129/8.
79 Edinburgh Register of Births, Marriages and Deaths, 1820.
80 *Auto.* III, p. 128.

Chapter 6   Love and Literature

1 www.british-history.ac.uk
2 Kensington Land Tax Record Book No. 4925 for 1819.
3 C. Lawford, *The early life and London worlds of Letitia Elizabeth Landon, a poet performing in an age of sentiment and display*, p. 337.
4 *Auto.* III, p. 175.
5 Ibid.
6 Ibid.
7 S. C Hall, *Book of Memories*, p. 269.
8 W. Jerdan,. "Memoir of L.E.L." in *Romance and Reality*, Bentley, 1848, p. xi.
9 Letter from Catherine Landon to W. Jerdan, Bodleian Library, University of Oxford, n.d. MS. Eng. lett. d. 114 f9.
10 *Auto.* III, p. 177.
11 *Auto.* III, p. 178.
12 F. J. Sypher, *Letitia Elizabeth Landon: A Biography*, 2009, p. 364, n.13, suggests a possible additional poem, *Sonnet*, published in the *Literary Gazette* on 18 November 1820.

13 Named after his friend Robert Westley Hall (he added Dare to his name in 1823) who wrote a series of letters in Dec.1819 and Jan. 1820 under the name of "An Essex Freeholder" in the *Essex Herald*, which were republished as pamphlets.

14 Bishops Transcripts, St. Mary Abbott, Kensington. DL/T/47/26

15 C. Lawford, *Thesis,* p. 185.

16 *Auto.* III, p. 170.

17 *Auto.* III, p. 181.

18 C. Lawford, *Thesis,* p. 198.

19 John Landon's brother Whittington, was Provost of Worcester College.

20 L. Blanchard, *Life & Literary Remains of LEL*, p. 55.

21 *Auto.* III p. 169.

22 K. Thomson, (Grace and Philip Wharton) *Queens of Society*, Vol. I, p. 277.

23 L. Blanchard, *Life*, p. 74.

24 S. C. Hall, *A Book of Memories*, op. cit., p. 274.

25 R. Duncan, *Thesis.*

26 W. Jerdan, *Men I Have Known*, p. 475.

27 R. Duncan, *Thesis*, p. 216.

28 *Literary Gazette*, 22 May 1819, p. 321.

29 Quoted in R. Duncan. *Thesis*, p. 222: D. Hewlett, *Adonais: A Life of John Keats.*

30 *Literary Gazette*, 19 May 1821, p. 305.

31 Ibid., p. 307.

32 *Literary Gazette*, 1 April 1820, p. 206.

33 *Literary Gazette*, 17 July 1824, p. 451.

34 *Auto.* III, p. 135.

35 *Auto.* III, p. 138.

36 *Auto.* III, p. 139.

37 It is ironic that in 1827 Scott accepted a medal from the RSL.

38 *Auto.* III, p. 149.

39 *Auto.* III, p. 153.

40 *The Times*, 10 July 1821.

41 Letter signed R.C. to W. Jerdan, 5 January 1821, National Library of Scotland 791 217-9.

42 Letter Bryan Procter to W. Jerdan, 27 November 1820, MsL C8213je3, University of Iowa Libraries, Iowa City, Iowa.

43 Letter Bryan Procter to W. Jerdan, n.d., MsL C8213je, University of Iowa Libraries, Iowa City, Iowa.

44 Letter Bryan Procter to W. Jerdan, December 1820, MsL C8213je3, University of Iowa Libraries, Iowa City, Iowa.

45 *Literary Gazette*, 25 March 1820, p. 207.

46 *Literary Gazette*, 24 May 1823, p. 332.

47 Letter T. C. Hofland to W. Jerdan, 28 January 1821, MsL H7125j, University of Iowa Librearies, Iowa City, Iowa.

48 Letter W. Porden to W. Jerdan, 31 December 1821, Bodleian Library, University of Oxford, MS. Eng. Lett. d. 114, f147.

49 *Auto.* IV, p. 10.

50 A.A. Watts, *Alaric Watts*, Vol. 1 p. 224.
51 Letter Alaric Watts to W. Jerdan, n.d., MsL W348AC, University of Iowa Libraries, Iowa City, Iowa.
52 A.A. Watts, Vol. 1.
53 Ibid., p. 114.
54 Ibid., p. 115.
55 *Auto*. IV, p. 7.
56 *Literary Gazette*, 31 July 1824.
57 *Auto*. III, p. 83.
58 R. S Mackenzie, *Miscellaneous Writings of W. Maginn, Vol. V Fraserian Papers*.
59 Ibid, p. 5.
60 *Auto*. III, p. 85.
61 R. Duncan, p. 45.
62 Quoted in G. Pyle, p. 90.
63 *Auto*. III, p. 82.
64 C. Lawford, *Thesis*, p. 222.
65 Ibid., p. 235.
66 *Literary Gazette*, Dec. 1821, No. 257, p. 814.

Chapter 7   Out in Front – Problem Poetics

1 *Auto*. III, p. 236, and I, pp. 16, 226.
2 *Auto*. IV, p. 44.
3 C. Lawford, " 'Thou shalt bid thy fair hands rove': L.E.L.'s Wooing of Sex, Pain, Death and the Editor" and "Diary".
4 J. Rappoport, Buyer Beware: The Gift Poetics of LEL.
5 L. Blanchard, *Life and Literary Remains of LEL*, I, 30–31.
6 Edward Bulwer Lytton, *New Monthly Magazine*, Dec. 1831, Review of 'Romance & Reality'.
7 Quoted in C. Lawford, *Thesis*, p. 262.
8 W. Jerdan, *Men I Have Known*, p. 408.
9 *Literary Gazette*, 17 March 1821, p. 161.
10 A. Holden, *The Wit in the Dungeon: A Life of Leigh Hunt*, p. 176.
11 *Literary Gazette*, 19 January 1822, p. 41.
12 *Literary Gazette*, 2 November 1822, p. 694.
13 *Auto*. II, p. 3.
14 G. Pyle, *Thesis*, p. 134.
15 *Auto*, III, p. 210.
16 Quoted in G. Pyle, p. 140.
17 *Auto*. III, p. 211.
18 In 1827 Westmacott purchased *The Age* following its proprietor's bankruptcy, and ran it until 1834, continuing his trademark accusations.
19 *Literary Gazette*, 16 March 1822.
20 *Literary Gazette*, February 1823, p. 29.
21 C. Lawford, *Thesis*, p. 270.
22 Quoted in C. Lawford, *Thesis*, p. 277.

23 *Auto.* III, p. 172.
24 *Literary Gazette*, 26 June 1824, p. 411.
25 *Literary Gazette*, 10 May 1823.
26 *Literary Gazette*, 20 March 1824, p. 188.
27 *Literary Gazette*, 4 September 1824, p. 573.
28 *Literary* Gazette, 4 September 1830, p. 579.
29 R. Altick, *The Shows of London,* p. 339.
30 *Literary Gazette*, 31 December 1825, p. 843.
31 R. Altick, p. 273.
32 *Auto.* II, p. 88.
33 W. Jerdan, *Men I Have Known*, p. 74.
34 *Auto.* III, p. 173.
35 Glennis Byron, Entry on Landon, *Oxford Dictionary of National Biography*.
36 G. Pyle, p. 126.
37 In 1821 Thomas Campbell was paid £500 a year for editing Colburn's *New Monthly Magazine*, although the sub-editor did most of the work. Oxford DNB, Colburn, by P. Garside
38 *Literary Gazette*, August 10 1822, No. 290.
39 *Auto.* IV, p. 16.
40 C. Lawford, *Thesis*, pp. 294–296.
41 *Auto.* III, p. 168.
42 C. Lawford, *Thesis*, p. 298.
43 Ibid.
44 Ibid., p. 307.
45 Letter W. Jerdan to W. Blackwood, 15 March 1823, National Library of Scotland, 4010/205-6.
46 Letter B. Procter to W. Jerdan, 26 March 1823, MsL C8213je2, University of Iowa Libraries, Iowa City, Iowa.
47 G. Pyle, op. cit., p. 89 quoting M. Oliphant, *Annals of a Publishing House: Wm Blackwood and his Sons*.
48 *Auto.* IV, p. 241.
49 This is Jerdan's figure. The Oxford DNB puts the sum at over £200,000, presumably at today's rates.
50 *Auto.* IV, p. 243.
51 A. Holden, p. 28.
52 *Auto.* IV, p. 242.
53 Quoted in C. Lawford, *Thesis*, pp. 320–1.
54 F. J. Sypher, *Letters by L.E.L.*, August 1824.
55 C. Lawford, *Thesis*, p. 334.
56 *Auto.* III, p. 221.
57 *Auto.* III, p. 112.
58 Ibid.
59 *Auto.* III, p. 111.
60 Longmans' Archives. Ledger 1819–1843.
61 Amy Cruse, *The Englishman and His Books in the early Nineteenth Century*, p. 191:

"*Blackwood's* claimed in 1820 that its circulation was 'somewhere below 17,000', the *Edinburgh* upward of 7000 and the *Quarterly* about 14,000. The *Gentleman's Magazine* was about 4000. His figures cannot be taken as very reliable." Ms Cruse does not mention the *Literary Gazette* anywhere in her survey, despite its undoubted influence on the reading public.

62 Information from Michael Gorman, from a diary note by Ethel Barnes.

Chapter 8   Social Climbing

1 Baptismal record, St James, Paddington, County of Middlesex. Baptisms 1813–26. 4 April 1824, Microfilm X029/001. London Metropolitan Archives.

2 *Auto*. III, p. 162.

3 *Auto*. III, p. 163.

4 Letter A. A. Watts to W. Jerdan, n.d. Bodleian Library, University of Oxford, MS. Eng. Lett. d. 114, f288.

5 A. A. Watts, *Alaric Watts*, Vol. 1. p. 108.

6 Letters Owen Rees to Dr Campbell, 24 and 27 December 1824, University of Reading, Special Collections, Longman Archives, I, 101, 485A and 483B.

7 Quoted in S. C. Hall, *Book of Memories*, p. 269.

8 Letter W. Jerdan to Hurst, Robinson & Co., November 1823, University of Edinburgh, La II 171.

9 C. Lawford, *Diary*.

10 Quoted in G. T. Dibert-Himes, *Introductory Essay to the Work of Letitia Elizabeth Landon*, from 'Introduction', The Comprehensive Index and Bibliography to the Collected Works of Letitia Elizabeth Landon.

11 Letter from W. Jerdan to W. Blackwood, 13 July 1824, National Library of Scotland, 4012/208-9.

12 *Blackwood's Magazine* 16 August 1824, pp. 237–8.

13 S. C. Hall, *Retrospect of a Long Life*, Vol. I, p. 119.

14 Letter W. Maginn to W. Jerdan, 20 October 1823, Huntington Library, San Marino, California, Al 243.

15 R. Altick, *The Shows of London*, p. 269.

16 *Literary Gazette*, 23 February 1822, p. 123.

17 *Literary Gazette*, 17 April 1824.

18 *Literary Gazette*, 19 June 1824, p. 398.

19 R. Altick, *The Shows of London,* p. 316.

20 *Literary Gazette*, Nov. 24, 1843 quoted in Croker, *A Walk from London to Fulham*.

21 D. Griffin, *Life of Gerald Griffin by his Brother*.

22 Bishops Transcripts, St. Mary Abbott, Kensington. DL/T/47/26.

23 Society of Antiquarians, London, Minute Book Vol. XXXV. Jerdan misremembered the date, giving in his *Autobiography* 1826.

24 John Dix (afterwards Ross), *Pen and Ink Sketches of Poets, Preachers and Politicians*, p. 27.

25 S. C. Hall, *Book of Memories*, p. 17.

26 S. C. Hall, *Retrospect of a Long Life*, p. 25.

27 *Auto*. IV, p. 34.

28 *Auto*. III, p. 281.
29 *Quarterly Musical Magazine and Review*, Oct. 1827, p. 487.
30 *Age*, 1February 1829.
31 Letter J. Ballantyne to W. Jerdan, 5 July 1825, The Pierpont Morgan Library, New York, MA Unassigned.
32 *Auto*. IV, p. 34.
33 Archives of the Royal Literary Fund, British Library, M1077/16.
34 Letter W. Jerdan to J. Robinson, 30 July 1825, Boston Public Library. Quoted in G. Pyle, *Thesis*, p. 112.
35 G. T. Dibert-Himes, *Introductory Essay*.
36 Quoted in F. J. Sypher, *Biography*, p. 70.
37 F. J. Sypher, *Biography*, 2009, p. 58.
38 This may be the Pickersgill portrait referred to, although it is inscribed "Æt 25", which does not equate with Landon's age at this date. Sypher, *Biography 2009*, p. 313 also queries the veracity of this caption.
39 W. Jerdan, "Memoir" in *Romance and Reality*. p. xvii.
40 L. Blanchard, *Life and Literary Remains of L.E.L.*, p. 52.
41 *Auto*. III, p. 169.
42 K. Thomson, *Queens of Society*, p. 280.
43 W. Howitt, *Homes and Haunts of the Most Eminent British Poets*, p. 438.
44 Margaret Howitt, ed. Mary Howitt, *An Autobiography*. London: Isbister, 1891.
45 S. C. Hall, *Memories*, p. 270.
46 M. Sadleir, *Bulwer and his Wife: A Panorama 1803–1836*, p. 86.
47 For a detailed account, see "Turbans, Tea and Talk of Books: the Literary Parties of Elizabeth Spence and Elizabeth Benger". C. Lawford, Corvey Women Writers on the Web (CW3) Journal Issue No. 1, 2004.
48 Letter A. A. Watts to W. Jerdan, University of Oxford, Bodleian Library, 114–290.
49 *Literary Gazette*, 22 Oct. 1825, advertisement.
50 The house was demolished in 1844, (or 1846 according to T. Croker) and stood on the site now occupied by Ovington Gardens.
51 *Auto*. III, p. 303.
52 *Survey of London* Vol. XI Southern Kensington: Brompton.
53 T. Crofton Croker, *A Walk from London to Fulham*, p. 56.
54 W. Pitt, Lord Lennox, *Celebrities I have Known*, Vol. 2, p. 35 .
55 W. B. Scott, Ed., *The Poetical Works of L.E.L.* George Routledge & Sons, 1873 – with thanks to Dr Julie Watt for this extract.

Chapter 9   Financial 'Panic' – Personal Attacks

1 Information mainly from W. R. Bisschop, *The Rise of the London Money Market 1640–1826*.
2 *Auto*. III, p. 291.
3 R. A. Gettman, *A Victorian Publisher, a Study of the Bentley Papers*, p. 18.
4 *Auto*. IV, p. 18.
5 An Indenture dated 27 November 1829 refers to these arrangements. Two documents of February 1827 related to Twinings, to whom Jerdan owed £1368 plus

interest (presumably including the £1000 they 'gave' him on his moving into Grove House); a further document of 24 May 1827 related to the £1600 borrowed from a Joseph Heath, Grocer, of Rochdale, passed on to a Banker, John Roby. Jerdan was to pay £224.2.6 a year for his lifetime, even more than the 'ruinous' sum he recorded later. University of Reading, Special Collections, Longmans Archive, 129/8.

6 *Auto*. II, p. 228.

7 Letter W. Jerdan to E. Dubois, 4 April n.y. British Library, 20081 f252.

8 The *Wasp* was published by W. Jeffreys between 30 September and 16 December 1826, in twelve issues.

9 I am indebted for these quotations from *The Wasp* to C. Lawford's *Diary*, London Review of Books, 21 Sept. 2000.

10 C. Lawford, *"Thou shalt bid thy fair hands rove": L.E.L.'s Wooing of sex, pain, death and the Editor*, Romanticism on the Net No. 29–30, www.erudit.org 2003.

11 The *Ass; or Weekly Beast of Burden* appeared from 1 April until 15 July 1826.

12 *Auto*. III, p. 212.

13 L. Blanchard,. *Life and Literary Remains of LEL*, p. 54.

14 F. J. Sypher, *Letters by L.E.L.*, letter dated "early 1826".

15 *Auto*. III, p. 216.

16 *Auto*. IV, p. 64.

17 A double layer of peritoneum attached to the back wall of the abdominal cavity which supports most of the small intestine.

18 *Auto*. IV, p. 65.

19 The parallels between Jerdan's and Hunt's lives will be noted as they occur chronologically.

20 N. Roe, *The First Life of Leigh Hunt: Fiery Heart*, p. 164.

21 *Auto*. I, p. 16.

22 N. Roe, p. 26.

23 Letter S. Maunder to W. Jerdan, 6 September 1826, Bodleian Library, University of Oxford, MS. Eng. Lett. d. 114, f85.

24 *Monthly Magazine*, Nov. 1826, p. 476.

25 *Literary Gazette*, 30 September and 14 October 1826.

26 Jerdan included his story in the *Auto*. IV, Appendix D, p. 396.

27 Letter R. Dagley to W. Jerdan, 3 October 1826, Bodleian Library, University of Oxford, MS. Autogr. C.9 f33.

28 Letter W. Jerdan to W. Blackwood, 2 December 1826, National Library of Scotland, 4017/168-9.

29 J. Weddell, *A Voyage Towards the South Pole . . . in 1822–24*.

30 *Auto*. IV, 394.

31 Isla Jerdan, next to Isle Hermite, Cape Horn.

32 *Auto*. IV, p. 394.

33 *Auto*. IV p. 395.

34 R. Altick, *The Shows of London*, p. 309.

35 See Chapter 1, p. 11.

36 J. McGann and D. Riess, *Letitia Elizabeth Landon: Selected Writings* "The poem is a Fragment from 'Ethel Churchill', pub. 1837, but possibly written at this earlier date

and appears elsewhere as [A Late Breakfast] in Blanchard, L. *Life and Literary Remains of L.E.L.* Vol. 2, Colburn 1841", p. 291.

37   *Auto*. IV, p. 161.

38   *Literary Gazette*, 30 December 1826.

39   Bentley Archive, British Library, Add.MS.46,674 – quoted in W. St. Clair, *The Reading Nation in the Romantic Period*, Appendix. 8.

40   *Auto*. IV, p. 130.

41   *Auto*. IV, p. 63.

42   *Auto*. IV, p. 64.

43   *Edinburgh Magazine*. March 1826, p. 845. "There is preparing for publication a quarto volume, British Ichthyology, with fine engravings of the principal Fish of Great Britain from drawings taken from nature, by Sir John Leicester and some of the first artists – with a Preface and Occasional Remarks by W. Jerdan." Jerdan gave details of the proposed book in *Auto*. IV, p. 144.

44   W. Jerdan, *Men I Have Known*, p. 161.

45   J. Lough J. and E. Merson, *John Graham Lough 1798–1876, A Northumbrian Sculptor*, p. 11.

46   Quoted in *John Graham Lough*, p. 30.

47   *Literary Gazette*, 1841, p. 224.

48   Letter W. Jerdan to R. Cadell, 2 June 1827, National Library of Scotland, 21002/31-2.

49   Letter W. Jerdan to R. Cadell, 25 October 1827, National Library of Scotland, 21002/43-4.

50   Letter W. Jerdan to J. Hogg, 30 April 1827, National Library of Scotland, 2245/98-9.

51   Letter W. Jerdan to W. Blackwood, 30 April 1827, National Library of Scotland, 4019/230-3.

52   Archives Royal Literary Fund, British Library, M1077/18.

53   *Auto*. I, p. 146.

54   F. J. Sypher, *Letters by LEL*. Sypher dates this 'perhaps 1832' from a mention of Medwin's translation of Agamemnon by Aeschylus. However, Medwin translated another Aeschylus, Prometheus Bound, in 1827. Jerdan's accident and Landon's affectionate concern, with her offer to take care of the *Literary Gazette* point to the earlier date as being more likely.

55   Ibid. Sypher dates this 1833.

56   W. Jerdan, *Men I Have Known*, p. 264.

57   *Literary Gazette*, 27 April 1827.

58   E. Stapleton, ed. *Some Official Correspondence of George Canning*, pp. 361–2.

59   *Auto*. IV, p. 150.

60   Asa Briggs, *The Age of Improvement*, p. 226, quoting 'The Formation of Canning's Ministry', Camden Society, 1937

61   Ibid., p. 226.

62   *Auto*. IV, p. 153.

63   *Auto*. IV, p. 156.

64   E. J. Stapleton, *Some Correspondence of George Canning*, p. 368.

65 S. C. Hall, *Retrospect of a Long Life*, Vol. I, p. 162.
66 Letter J. G. Lockhart to W. Jerdan, 24 April 1827, John Rylands University Library, The University of Manchester, English MS Vol. 2, p. 160.
67 M. Sadleir, *Bulwer and his Wife*, p. 86.
68 F. J. Sypher, *Biography*, p. 94.
69 W. St. Clair, *Reading Nation in the Romantic Period*, Appendix 9.
70 Letter W. Jerdan to W. Blackwood, 9 February 1827, National Library of Scotland, 4019/228-9.
71 Letter W. Jerdan to n.k. 31 March n.y. National Library of Scotland, 4720/112-4.
72 S. C. Hall, *Retrospect of a Long Life*, Vol. II, p. 191.
73 *Auto*. IV, p. 312.
74 R. Duncan, *Thesis*, p. 245.
75 *Auto*. IV, p. 311.
76 A. A Watts,. *Alaric Watts*, Vol. 2, p. 34.
77 *Age*, 16 December 1827.
78 Thunderbolts that strike blindly and in vain.

Part III The Editor's Life, 1828–1840

Chapter 10 *Athenaeum* Competition and Challenging Projects

1 *Auto*. IV, p. 68.
2 *Auto*, IV, p. 71.
3 Ibid.
4 The *Literary Gazette*, 11 Sept. 1830 reviewed this: "We opened this work more with the wish than the expectation that we should find it such as would warrant a great alteration in our general opinion of the writings of Lady Morgan. But in truth she has not improved by 20 years of authorship; her faults only become the more fatiguing by repetititon . . . flighty ebullitions . . . It is almost pitiable to look upon a mature person exhibiting such fantastic tricks; and even in a miss of seventeen the long continuation of the hoyden would be apt to create ennui if not disgust."
5 Quoted in G. Pyle, p. 185, from M. Oliphant.
6 *Literary Gazette*, 16 June 1827, p. 374.
7 *Literary Gazette*, 17 Nov. 1827, p. 742.
8 *Literary Gazette*, 22 Jan. 1827, p. 37.
9 Letter W. Jerdan to Allan Cunningham, 4 November 1827, Huntington Library. San Marino, California.
10 L. A. Marchand, *The Athenaeum – a Mirror of Victorian Culture*, p. 104.
11 *Auto*. IV, p. 360.
12 L. Marchand, p. 22n
13 *Blackwood's Magazine*, April 1829, p. 543.
14 L. Marchand, p. 24.
15 *Auto*. IV, p. 360.
16 A. S. Collins, *Profession of Letters*, p. 215. This substantially agrees with Jerdan's own figures at the end of Chapter 7.
17 L. Marchand, p. 44.

18 Letter C. H. Townshend to W. Jerdan, 3 March 1828, Courtesy of the Wisbech and Fenland Museum.

19 Quoted in A. Holden, *The Wit in the Dungeon*, op. cit., p. 218.

20 F. J. Sypher, *Biography*, 2004, p. 178, letter dated Late Feb/Early March 1827.

21 *Auto*. IV, p. 193.

22 Letter G.P.R. James to W. Jerdan, 16 May 1828, The Pierpont Morgan Library, New York, MA Unassigned.

23 Archives of the Royal Literary Fund, British Library, M1077/19.

24 Letter J. Lilley to W. Jerdan, undated. Edinburgh University Library, Special Collections Department. LaII 426/289.

25 Letter W. Jerdan to J. Lilley, undated. Huntington Library, San Marino, California.

26 *Auto*. IV, p. 229.

27 Bentley Papers, British Library, Add. 46674.

28 Letter W. Jerdan to F. Bennoch, 10 May 1858, MsLJ55bAc, University of Iowa Libraries, Iowa City, Iowa.

29 S. C. Hall, *Retrospect of a Long Life,* op. cit., 2, p. 504.

30 *Auto*. IV, p. 32.

31 *Auto*. IV, p. 33.

32 Letter W. Jerdan to H. Colburn, 12 February 1829, University of Reading, Special Collections, Longman Archives, I 102/100c.

33 Letter J. C. Fisher to W. Jerdan, 17 October 1829, Bodleian Library, University of Oxford, MS. Eng. Lett. d. 113, f185.

34 *Auto*. IV, 303.

35 Ibid.

36 *Auto*. I, p. 8.

37 *Auto*. IV, p. 308.

38 *Auto*. IV, p. 303.

39 In October 1862 *Notes & Queries*, 3rs s. II, p. 329, a question from 'H.C. Index' asked about the authorship of "this clever little book bearing this alliterative title." James Knowles replied (15 Nov., p. 396) that it was Jerdan of the *Literary Gazette*. "The idea, I apprehend, was taken from the *Voyage de Paris a St Cloud, par Mer, et de la Retour per Terre*, published long before at Paris, in which the captain of the *pacquebot* is made to astonish his *badaud* passengers by an assurance that, although he had for twenty years encountered the perils of the *trajet,* he had never once been drowned – jamais!"

40 *Literary Gazette*, 3 and 10 October 1829.

41 J. Wilson, quoted in C. Lawford, *Thesis*, op. cit., p. 351.

42 Codex MS 872, University of Chicago.

43 *Auto*. IV, p. 235.

44 R. Altick, *The Shows of London*, p. 146.

45 *Literary Gazette*, 22 August 1829.

46 *Literary Gazette*, 28 November 1829 p. 780. Edward Bulwer wrote a long poem based on this exhibit, entitled *The Siamese Twins.*

47 *Literary Gazette,* 5 July 1828.

48 *Literary Gazette*, 7 September 1833, p. 573.

49 Letter E. Bulwer to W. Jerdan, 7 August 1829, Bodleian Library, University of Oxford, MS. Eng. Lett. d. 114, f581.

50 R. Duncan, *Thesis,* p. 63.

51 Letter G. Hogarth to W. Jerdan, 28 October 1829, The Pierpont Morgan Library, New York. Purchased by Pierpont Morgan before 1913. MA 104 79.

52 Christening Record, 17 March 1850, St Michael's Queenhithe, City of London. LDS Film No. 0374509.

53 C. Lawford, *Diary.*

54 N. Page, et al. Eds., *Charles Dickens: Family History,* Vol. 5, p. 104. http://books. google.com.

55 Letter W. Jerdan to R. Bentley, 4 December 1829, Harry Ransom Humanities Research Center, The University of Texas at Austin.

56 Letter W. Jerdan to R. Bentley, n.d. 1830, Harry Ransom Humanities Research Center, The University of Texas at Austin.

57 Letter W. Jerdan to R. Bentley, n.d. 1830, Harry Ransom Humanities Research Center, The University of Texas at Austin.

58 Ransom, H. *William Jerdan, Editor and Literary Agent*, Harry Ransom Humanities Research Center, The University of Texas at Austin, 1948.

59 Letter W. Jerdan to W. Blackwood, 3 May 1829, National Library of Scotland, 4025/1-2.

60 Letter W. Jerdan to (probably) John Blackwood, 14 June n.y., National Library of Scotland.

Chapter 11   'Wing-spreading' Editor

1 *Auto.* IV, p. 273.

2 Letter W. Jerdan to Lord Burghersh, 26 October 1829, Bodleian Library, University of Oxford, MS. Eng. c. 4862.

3 *Auto.* IV, p. 175.

4 *Auto.* IV, p. 274.

5 Letter W. Scripps to W. Jerdan, n.d. Bodleian Library, University of Oxford, MS. Eng. lett. d. 114, f205.

6 *Age*, 24 January 1830.

7 Letter T. Carlyle to J P Eckermann 20 March 1830. Carlyle Letters Online (CLO). 2007. http://carlyleletters.org. Viewed September 2007.

8 *Foreign Literary Gazette*, March 1830.

9 *Athenaeum*, 17 July 1830, pp. 435–6.

10 Rogers was included in Jerdan's *Men I Have Known* in 1866, and is treated with a biting criticism almost unique in Jerdan's considerable biographical writings.

11 R. Duncan, *Thesis,* p. 65.

12 Chorley, p. 107 Quoted in R. Duncan, *Thesis,* p. 100.

13 *Athenaeum*, 7 August 1830, p. 491.

14 There appears to be no concensus as to the identity of "T.A." One source, E.V. Lucas, *The Life of Charles Lamb*, suggests that Lamb might have written the final epigram, but another doubts this as one of the epigrams is addressed to Lamb himself.

15 *The Works of Charles and Mary Lamb*, Vol. 6 Letters. www.ebooksread.com.
16 In the *Age*, 5 September 1830, from *Tatler*.
17 Letter W. Jerdan to W. Blackwood, 8 February 1830, National Library of Scotland, 4027/236-7.
18 W. Jerdan, *Men I Have Known*, 1866, p. 480.
19 University of Reading, Special Collections, Longmans Archive, II 129/8.
20 *Auto*. IV, p. 246.
21 *Auto*. IV, Appendix H. p. 405 (later identified as Thomas Watts: Records of the RGS, H. Mill, London 1930)
22 *Auto*. IV, p. 267.
23 Records of the Royal Geographical Society, p. 18.
24 Letter W. Jerdan to C. Barrow, Royal Geographical Society, RGS/CB1/28.
25 *Auto*. IV, p. 272.
26 L. Marchand, p. 106n.
27 Ibid., p. 98.
28 *Athenaeum*, Oct. 29 1831, p. 705 quoted in L. Marchand, p. 109.
29 Matthew Rosa, *The Silver Fork School* quoted in L. Marchand, p. 109.
30 L. Marchand, p. 111.
31 E. Bulwer, England and the English, 1833 (with thanks to C. Lawford for this quote).
32 L. Marchand, p. 109.
33 Quoted in Rosa, M. p. 198.
34 A. S. Collins, *The Profession of Letters*.
35 L. Marchand, p. 112.
36 M. Rosa, p. 204.
37 *Auto*. IV, p. 22.
38 *Auto*. IV, p. 23.
39 R. Duncan, *Thesis*, p. 74.
40 *Auto*. IV, p. 82.
41 *Auto*. IV, p. 24.
42 *Auto*. III, p. 102.
43 Bentley Papers, Harry Ransom Humanities Research Center, The University of Texas at Austin.
44 G. Pyle, *Thesis*, p. 189.
45 Bentley Papers, Harry Ransom Humanities Research Center, The University of Texas at Austin.
46 R. Gettman, op. cit., p. 40.
47 Letter W. Jerdan to R. Bentley, 29 April 1830, Bentley Papers, Harry Ransom Humanities Research Center, The University of Texas at Austin.
48 This is overwritten as £200 in heavy ink.
49 British Library. Add.MSS. 46611 f.137.
50 Letter W. Jerdan to R. Bentley, 1 May 1830, Bentley Papers, Harry Ransom Humanities Research Center, The University of Texas at Austin.
51 Letter W. Jerdan to R. Bentley, 29 June 1830, Bentley Papers, Harry Ransom Humanities Research Center, The University of Texas at Austin.
52 Quoted in R. Gettman, p. 40.

53 S. C. Hall, *Retrospect of a Long Life*, Vol. I, p. 312.
54 Later introduced by Jerdan to C. Loudon, writer on landscape gardening, whom she married.
55 Jane Webb to W. Jerdan, n.d., Bodleian Library, University of Oxford, MS. Eng. lett. d. 114, f300.
56 *Examiner*, 8 October 1830.
57 *Athenaeum*, 23 October 1830.
58 Letter W. Jerdan to R. Bentley, 2 October 1830, Bentley Papers, Harry Ransom Humanities Research Center, The University of Texas at Austin.
59 Letter W. Jerdan to R. Bentley, 3 October n.y. Bentley Papers, Harry Ransom Humanities Research Center, The University of Texas at Austin.
60 Letter W. Jerdan to R. Bentley, n.d. Bentley Papers, Harry Ransom Humanities Research Center, The University of Texas at Austin.
61 Letter W. Jerdan to R. Bentley, n.d. 1830, Bentley Papers, Harry Ransom Humanities Research Center, The University of Texas at Austin.
62 Letter W. Jerdan to R. Bentley, n.d. Bentley Papers, Harry Ransom Humanities Research Center, The University of Texas at Austin.
63 Letter W. Jerdan to R. Bentley, 16 October 1830, Bentley Papers, Harry Ransom Humanities Research Center, The University of Texas at Austin.
64 W. Jerdan, Notes. Bentley Papers, Harry Ransom Humanities Research Center, The University of Texas at Austin.
65 Quoted in R. Gettman, p. 39.
66 *Athenaeum*, 25 June 1831.
67 *The Times,* 15 June 1831.
68 R. Gettman, p. 42.
69 R. Gettman, p. 43.
70 *Auto*. IV, p. 376.
71 *Athenaeum*, July 17 1830 p. 440 (quoted in Marchand, p. 125).
72 *Athenaeum,* August 7, 1830 p. 491.
73 The four issues of September 1830 carried over 53 columns devoted to Colburn & Bentley publications, 10 to Longmans, 17 to Murray, 12 to Saunders and Otley and 14 to two other publishers.
74 *Athenaeum*, May 28 1831, p. 343, quoted in Marchand, p. 163.
75 *Athenaeum*, 4 September 1830, p. 566.
76 L. Marchand, p. 131.
77 *Athenaeum*, August 18 1830 p. 540 (quoted in Marchand p. 131).
78 F. G. Kitton, *Dickensiana*, 1886, p. 47.
79 Letter W. Jerdan to Colburn & Bentley, 27 August 1831, Harry Ransom Humanities Research Center, The University of Texas at Austin.
80 Letter W. Jerdan to R. Bentley, annotated 1832, Harry Ransom Humanities Research Center, The University of Texas at Austin.
81 L. Marchand, p. 153.
82 W. St. Clair, *The Reading Nation in the Romantic Period*.
83 J. H. Buckley, *The Victorian Temper*, p. 29.
84 P. Leary, *Fraser's Magazine and the Literary Life, 1830–1847*. Victorian Periodicals Review.

85 R. Duncan, *Thesis*, p. 41.

86 M. Thrall, *Rebellious Fraser's*, p. 185.

87 *Fraser's*, April 1830, pp. 318–20.

88 P. Leary, op. cit.

89 M. Thrall, *Rebellious Fraser's*.

90 S. C. Hall, *Retrospect of a Long Life*, Vol. II, p. 215.

91 A. A. Watts, *Alaric Watts*, Vol. 2, p. 88.

92 J. L. Fisher, *Victorian Periodicals Review*, Vol. 39, No. 2, 2006, pp. 97–135.

93 W. Bates, (ed.) Preface, *The Maclise Portrait Gallery of Illustrious Literary Characters*,

94 Reported in the *Literary Chronicle*, 31 January 1824, making the joke at the expense of 'Longuemann's Cunnynge Advertizer'.

95 Letter D. Maclise to W. Jerdan, 20 March 1830, University of Cambridge, Fitzwilliam Museum, MS149-1949.

96 Letter W. Jerdan to R. Bentley, February 1830, Harry Ransom Humanities Research Center, The University of Texas at Austin.

97 Letter W. Jerdan to R. Bentley, n.d. Harry Ransom Humanities Research Center, The University of Texas at Austin.

98 Letter W. Jerdan to E. Bulwer. Dated "Grove House Dec 23 Thursday". The only Thursday 23 December whilst Jerdan lived at Grove House was in 1830. Hertford Record Office. D/EK C/11/23.

99 *Gentleman's Magazine*, June 1830 p. 458.

100 *Auto*. III, p. 122.

101 Archives, Royal Literary Fund, British Library, M1077.

102 *Auto*. IV, p. 195.

103 *Auto*. IV, p. 196

104 Letter E. Bulwer to W. Jerdan, n.d. Huntington Library, San Marino, California, HM 7902.

105 Letter E. Bulwer to W. Jerdan, 15 July 1830, Bodleian Library, University of Oxford, MS. Eng. lett. d. 114, f56.

Chapter 12   The *Literary Gazette* Teeters

1 *Auto*. IV, p. 355.

2 F. J. Sypher, *Letters by LEL*, op. cit., Letter to W. Jerdan, 1831.

3 *Survey of London*, Vol. 41.

4 *Auto*. IV, p. 251.

5 Holy Trinity Church, Select Vestry Minutes Book, Feb. 1830–April 1851, London Metropolitan Archives.

6 Letter John and Ellen Carne to W. Jerdan, 18 July 1831, Bodleian Library, University of Oxford, MS. Eng. lett. d. 113, f98.

7 Letter Owen Rees to W. Jerdan, 1 August 1831, University of Reading, Special Collections, Longmans Archive, I, 102, 171C.

8 Letter Owen Rees to W. Jerdan, 2 August 1831, University of Reading, Special Collections, Longmans Archive, I, 102, 171D.

9 S. C. Hall, *Retrospect of a Long Life*, Vol. 2., p. 506.

10 Information supplied by M. Riddell, Librarian and Archivist, Garrick Club.

11 *Auto.* IV, p. 287.
12 Letter W. Jerdan to E. Bulwer, 22 December n.y. Norfolk Record Office, BUL 1.3.561X5.
13 John Timbs, *Club Life of London*, Vol. I, p. 257.
14 *Auto.* IV, p. 292.
15 *Edinburgh Literary Journal*, Dec. 1831, p. 366, poem by Henry Glasford Bell.
16 Letter W. Jerdan to R. Bentley, n.d., Harry Ransom Humanities Research Center, The University of Texas at Austin.
17 W. St. Clair, *The Reading Nation in the Romantic Period*, Apx. 9 quotes Bentley Archives Add MS 46,674 that only 1000 were printed and sold out.
18 Letter W. Jerdan to R. Bentley, n.d., Harry Ransom Humanities Research Center, The University of Texas at Austin. Cynthia Lawford dates this as November or December 1831.
19 Letter W. Jerdan to R. Bentley, 22 November n.y., Harry Ransom Humanities Research Center, The University of Texas at Austin.
20 A. Lee, *Laurels and Rosemary*.
21 Bulwer's management of the *Magazine* was disorganised and circulation fell; he resigned in September 1833. to concentrate on writing novels.
22 M. Sadleir, *Bulwer and his Wife*, op. cit., p. 258.
23 *Athenaeum*, 10 December 1831, pp. 793–5.
24 *Fraser's Magazine*, Vol. 6, August 1832, p. 112.
25 Letter W. Jerdan to n.k., 23 April, n.y., Special Collections Department, Temple University Libraries, Philadelphia, PA, USA.
26 *All the Year Round*, June 1887.
27 Without haste, but without dawdling.
28 *Athenaeum*, 22 October 1831, p. 695.
29 L. Marchand, *The Athenaeum*, op. cit., p. 45.
30 *Auto.* III, p. 210.
31 *Auto.* III, p. 211.
32 G. Pyle, *Thesis*, p. 133.
33 Society of Antiquaries, *Archaeologia*, Vol. xviii, p. 72.
34 *Gentleman's Magazine*, Letter 12 March 1831, p. 211 and Minor Correspondence July 1831.
35 *Fraser's Magazine*, February 1831.
36 "To manumit" is to free from slavery. The Slave Trade Act of 1807 outlawed the slave trade in the British Empire, but it was not until 1833 that the Slave Abolition Act was passed. This was therefore a topic of contemporary interest at the time of the outing.
37 A reference to Mungo Park (1771–1806) a Borderer, like Jerdan, who was a famous but unsuccessful African explorer.
38 A. A. Watts, *Alaric Watts*, Vol. 2, p. 83.
39 Letter W. Jerdan to n.k. 25 May 1832, The Pierpont Morgan Library, New York. Bequest, Gordon N. Ray; 1987, MA4500.
40 Letter W. Jerdan to Duke of Portland, 31 January 1832, British Library, ADD 40879.

41 Perhaps he harboured the same misgivings as *The Times* of 24 Nov, 1832, which said that the nation, having paid off Scott's debts, should not purchase Abbotsford; it should be for the family to take care of his house.

42 Letter W. Jerdan to Lord Goderich, 5 February 1832, British Library, ADD 40879.

43 Letter W. Jerdan to Lord Goderich, 20 April 1832, Britsh Library, ADD 40879.

44 *Auto*. IV, p. 295.

45 K. Miller, *Electric Shepherd. A Likeness of James Hogg*, p. 316.

46 *Auto*. IV, p. 297.

47 "Liston Bulwer's Song" in *Fraser's*, February 1832, had previously been published in *John Bull*, 17 December 1820 and February 1821, according to Sadleir, *Bulwer and his Wife*, p. 264.

48 Letter J. Hogg to W. Jerdan, 27 December 1832, National Library of Scotland, 20437/42-3.

49 W. Jerdan, *Men I Have Known*, p. 253.

50 *Auto*. IV, p. 298.

51 H. T. Stephenson, *The Ettrick Shepherd: A Biography*, Indiana University studies, 2004, p. 43.

52 W. Jerdan, *Men I Have Known*, p. 252.

53 S. C. Hall, *Book of Memories*, p. 275.

54 K. Miller, *Electric Shepherd*, p. 314.

55 *Literary Gazette*, 17 July 1824.

56 *Literary Gazette*, 25 Dec. 1824.

57 *Auto*. IV, p. 300.

58 W. Jerdan, *Men I Have Known*, p. 250.

59 *Auto*. IV, p. 300.

60 Jerdan and L.E.L.'s descendant, Michael Gorman, reads much into this sketch, interpreting the lyre as liar; the position of L.E.L.'s head indicating that the burning fire would be around her loins, the cat (pussy) having obvious sexual connotations as well as the 'cat being out of the bag' as stand-in for a baby, the cup (Circean) on the mantelpiece with a spoon suggesting it is not fresh, the three objects alongside, possibly buns (bairns) referring to the three children, Jerdan's position being a reverse of the famous Maclise portrait, possibly alluding to LEL's rumoured affair with Maclise, L.E.L. is wearing a loose chemise similar to night attire and other indications that this cartoon was a smear against which they could not dare to take legal action.

61 Michael Gorman suggests Hook as the author based on S. C. Hall's *Book of Memories*, mentioning Hook's artistic habits. Hook was well known for hoaxes and satire and Gorman's suggestion might well be accurate. Despite considerable searching, no other possible author has been revealed.

62 Letter to Croker, 10 Oct. 1831, in *Sharpe's Magazine*, February 1862, p. 64.

63 F. J. Sypher, 'The Occultation of Letitia Elizabeth Landon'. www.cosmos-club.org. 1999.

64 R. S. Mackenzie, *Miscellaneous Writings of the late Dr. Maginn*, Vol. V, Memoir of W. Maginn, p. lxxxvi.

65 F. J. Sypher, *Letters by L.E.L.* Letter dated circa 1834, p. 100.

66 J. H. Buckley, *The Victorian Temper*, p. 27.

67 Most of the information about Lady Blessington is from Sadleir, M. *Blessington D'Orsay, a Masquerade.*

68 S. C. Hall, *Book of Memories*, p. 270.

69 K. Thomson, *Queens of Society*, p. 291.

70 *Auto.* III, p. 185.

71 E. Disraeli, ed., *Lord Beaconsfield's Letters*, p. 71.

72 A. Cruse, *The Englishman and His Books*, p. 143.

73 Quoted in *New Monthly Magazine*, October 1832, p. 461. Blaikie died on 3 September 1832.

74 *Age*, 3 August 1832.

75 *Literary Gazette*, March 1832, p. 202.

76 Letter W. Jerdan to n.k. 8 October 1832, National Archives of Scotland, GD157/2029/6.

Chapter 13   Financial Ruin

1 W. Toynbee, ed., *Diaries of William Charles Macready 1833–1851.*

2 *Literary Gazette*, May 1833, p. 300.

3 R. S. Mackenzie, *Miscellaneous Writings of W. Maginn*, Vol. 5, Memoir of W. Maginn, p. lxxxv.

4 M. Sadleir, *Bulwer and his Wife*, p. 423.

5 S. C. Hall, *Book of Memories*, p. 278.

6 Ibid., p. 277.

7 L. Blanchard, *Life and Literary Remains of L.E.L.*, p. 129.

8 M. Sadleir, *Bulwer and his Wife,* op. cit., p. 426.

9 K. Thomson, *Queens of Society*, p. 298.

10 Quoted in C. Lawford, *Thesis*, p. 325.

11 Letter W. Jerdan to R. Bentley, 21 April 1833, Harry Ransom Humanities Research Center, The University of Texas at Austin.

12 Quoted in entry 'Edward George Earle Lytton Bulwer Lytton' *Oxford Dictionary of National Biography.*

13 Letter John and Ellen Carne to W. Jerdan, 12 April 1833, Bodleian Library, University of Oxford, MSD. Eng. lett. d. 113, f100.

14 Letter O. Rees to W. Jerdan, 18 November 1833, University of Reading, Special Collections, Longman Archives, I, 102 198G.

15 Letter O. Rees to W. Jerdan, 23 November 1833, University of Reading, Special Collections, Longman Archives, I, 102 198H.

16 Letter W. Jerdan to R. Bentley, 21 June 1833, Harry Ransom Humanities Research Center, The University of Texas at Austin.

17 Letter W. Jerdan to R. Bentley, 16 October 1833, Harry Ransom Humanities Research Center, The University of Texas at Austin.

18 *Auto.* II, p. 193.

19 *Literary Gazette*, 23 February 1833, p. 122.

20 *Literary Gazette*, 2 March 1833, p. 140.

21 Ibid., p. 137.

22 *Literary Gazette*, 23 February 1833.

23 *Literary Gazette*, 14 September 1833, p. 586.
24 J. Conlin, *The Nation's Mantelpiece: A History of the National Gallery*, p. 366.
25 Ibid.
26 N. Cross, *The Royal Literary Fund 1790–1918*, p. 15.
27 *Literary Gazette*, 14 September 1833, p. 580.
28 *Auto*. IV, p. 34.
29 A letter from W. Jerdan to Colburn and Bentley requests them to send him £75 for Mr James's MSS payable to the Literary Fund. This was for James's "String of Pearls"; this may have been a different occasion which would account for the discrepancy in the sum named. Harry Ransom Humanities Research Center, The University of Texas at Austin.
30 Vizetelly, H., *Glances Back Through 70 Years*, Vol. I, p. 85.
31 F. J. Sypher, *Letters by L.E.L*, Letter June 10, 1834, p. 101.
32 *Auto*. III, p. 187.
33 *Auto*. III, p. 191.
34 *Literary Gazette,* 8 November 1834.
35 *Auto*. III, p. 203.
36 *Auto*. III, p. 206.
37 C. Lawford, *Diary*.
38 M. Sadleir, *Bulwer and his Wife*, p. 423.
39 Letter W. Landon to W. Jerdan, 14 July 1834, University of Oxford, Bodleian Library, 114-11.
40 *Literary Gazette*, December 1834, p. 849.
41 F. J. Sypher, *Letters by L.E.L.*, Letter 23 December 1834.
42 H. F. Chorley, *Autobiography: Memoirs and Letters*, 1873, reprinted in *Chorley, Planché and Young*, Stoddard, R. H. ed. Kessinger Publishing, p. 81.
43 Besant, B. *Fifty Years Ago*.
44 R. Duncan, *Thesis*, op. cit., p. 160. This opinion is at variance with Jerdan himself who pointed out in "The Publishing Trade" articles that he had omitted reviewing "fashionable novels" to a great extent.
45 *Fraser's Magazine, No.* 9 (Jan.–June), 1834, p. 724.
46 *The Times*, 14 July 1834.
47 *Auto*. IV, p. 358.
48 *Auto*. IV, p. 361.
49 Letter W. Jerdan to R. Bentley, n.d., Harry Ransom Humanities Research Center, The University of Texas at Austin.
50 W. Toynbee, ed. *Diary of William Macready*.
51 Quoted in A. Holden, *The Wit in the Dungeon*, p. 240.
52 Jerdan's old friend and rival William Blackwood died in 1834 and was succeeded by his son.
53 A. Holden, *The Wit in the Dungeon*, p. 241.
54 Ibid., p. 245.

Chapter 14   Notoriety and a New Family

1 *Gentleman's Magazine*, March 1839, p. 325.

2 Letter W. Jerdan to R. Bentley, 30 March 1835, Harry Ransom Humanities Research Center, The University of Texas at Austin.

3 Letter W. Jerdan to R. Bentley, 2 June n.y., Harry Ransom Humanities Research Center, The University of Texas at Austin.

4 Letter W. Jerdan to Messrs. Blackwood, 29 December 1835, National Library of Scotland, 4040/302-3. William Blackwood died in 1834. The *Maga* was run by his sons Alexander and Robert, until John Blackwood took over in 1845.

5 Letter D. Maclise to W. Jerdan, n.d., Edinburgh University Library, Special Collections Department, La.II 648/149.

6 Letter L. E. Landon to W. Jerdan, n.d., Letitia Elizabeth Landon papers, John Alexander Symington Collection, Special Collections and University Archives, Rutgers University Libraries.

7 Letter W. Jerdan to T. Croker, 8 December n.y., Letitia Elizabeth Landon papers, John Alexander Symington Collection, Special Collections and University Archives, Rutgers University Libraries.

8 Letter W. Jerdan to Messrs. Blackwood, 29 December 1835, National Library of Scotland, 4040/302-3.

9 H. Vizetelly, *Glances Back*, Vol. I, p. 126.

10 F. J. Sypher, *Biography*, 2009, p. 172, provides a detailed discussion of contemporary sources, especially Berkeley, to support the idea of blackmail.

11 The Royal Bank of Scotland Group Archives DR/427/263. Messrs Drummond customer account ledger 1845, pp. 383 and 394. I am indebted to Dr Julie Watt for painstaking transcription of Jerdan's accounts.

12 Letter T. Carlyle to J. Carlyle 27 Nov. 1835. The Carlyle Letters online (CLO). 2007 http//:carlyleletters.org. Viewed September 2007.

13 L. Marchand, ed., *Letters of Thomas Hood from the Dilke Papers in the British Museum*,, p. 49.

14 Letter W. Jerdan to R. Bentley, 18 January 1835, Harry Ransom Humanities Research Center, The University of Texas at Austin.

15 *Journal of the Dutch Burgher Union of Ceylon*, Jan. 1934, No. 3 – with thanks to Michael Gorman. This magazine includes a photograph of Power.

16 Letter W. Jerdan to Sir W. Horton, 23 May 1836, Derbyshire County Council, Derbyshire Record Office, D3155/C7015.

17 This refers to Sir George Back, 1796–1878, *Back's Journey to the Arctic Sea* 1836.

18 Letter W. Jerdan to Sir W. Horton, n.d. 1836, Derbyshire County Council, Derbyshire Record Office, D3155/WH2824.

19 Spelt McClise in the Literary Fund Minutes, but more usually Maclise.

20 *Times*, 25 May 1836.

21 Letter J. Britton to W. Jerdan, 25 March 1836, Bodleian Library, University of Oxford, MS. Eng. lett. d. 113, f64.

22 *Soane Organisation Newsletter* No. 14, Spring 2007.

23 *Times*, 13 May 1836 – rejecting that he was 'one of a Radical faction', and 25 May, a long account of Taylor's view of the affair for the benefit of the public, and to relieve himself of responsibility.

24 W. Toynbee, ed., *Diary of Charles Macready*, 10 May, 1836.

25   Archives of the Royal Literary Fund. British Library, M1077/125.
26   *Auto.* IV, p. 402. 'Ochone', a Gaelic expression of sorrow or regret. This appeared in *The Ingoldsby Legends.*
27   by Helen Dorey, see *Soane Newsletter.*
28   Letter W. Thackeray to W. Jerdan, 22 April 1836. The Henry W. and Albert A. Berg Collection of English and American Literature, The New York Public Library, Astor, Lenox and Tilden Foundations. 223652B.
29   Letter W. Jerdan to R. Bentley, 7 July n.y. Harry Ransom Humanities Research Center, The University of Texas at Austin.
30   Letter G.P.R. James to W. Jerdan, 12 November 1836, Bodleian Library, University of Oxford, MS. Eng. lett. d. 113, f261.
31   *Literary Gazette*, 14 May 1836.
32   Quoted in L. Marchand, *Athenaeum*, p. 73 who notes that the *Athenaeum* had given a glowing encomium to Mitford's latest work, but her estimate of income was probably wrong, as Dilke was putting profits back into the business.
33   R. H. Stoddard, ed., *Personal Reminiscences by Chorley, Planché, Young*, Scribner, New York, 1874 reprinted Kessinger Publishing, p. 81
34   *Letters of Charles Dickens.* Intro to Pickwick Papers, Penguin edition.
35   W. Toynbee, W. ed. *Diary of William Charles Macready* op. cit.
36   H. Vizetelly, *Glances Back,* p. 126.
37   Quoted in C. Lawford, *Thesis*, p. 332.
38   *Sharpe's Magazine*, April 1862, p. 189. Letter 1 November 1836.
39   "Governor" was the contemporary term often used for Maclean . After the British government withdrew from Cape Coast, British administration continued under a committee of merchants who had a government allowance for maintenance of Cape Coast and other ports. Maclean was the first President of the Council of government, appointed in 1830.
40   L. Blanchard, *Life and Literary Remains of L.E..L.*, p. 136.
41   K. Thomson, *Queens of Society*, op. cit., p. 300.

Chapter 15   Conflict and Loss

1   H. Vizetelly, *Glances back through 70 years*, I, 202–3. The joke has also been attributed to others. A bad omen, "Miss Sell Any" was another popular joke.
2   Letter W. Jerdan to R. Bentley, n.d. Harry Ransom Humanities Research Center, The University of Texas at Austin.
3   Accompt with R Bentley. British Library, 46651 f.143.
4   *Oxford Dictionary of National Biography*, Entry on John Richardson by Paul Schlicke.
5   F. J. Sypher, *Biography*, 2004, p. 169.
6   *Sharpes Magazine*, April 1862, p. 190. Correspondence between L.E.L. and Croker.
7   Letter W. Jerdan to T. Croker, March 1837, Letitia Elizabeth Landon papers, John Alexander Symington Collection, Special Collections and University Archives, Rutgers University Libraries.
8   *Sharpe's Magazine*, Miss Landon's Correspondence, April 1862.
9   *Auto.* IV, p. 42.
10   A. Holden, *The Wit in the Dungeon*, p. 248.

11 *Letters and Private Papers of William Makepeace Thackeray*, p. 313.

12 *Letters of Charles Dickens*, 1837.

13 *Auto*. IV, p. 365.

14 Letter W. Jerdan to R. Bentley, 10 June n.y., Harry Ranson Humanities Center, The University of Texas at Austin.

15 From F. G. Kitton, *The Life of Dickens*, where the connection to Jerdan's story was not made, and the letter was incorrectly inferred as Literary Gazette business.

16 Mr Burn had resigned from the Literary Fund in January 1836, but was asked to remain, which he agreed to do, under the direction of the Treasurer. He was therefore known personally to Jerdan.

17 Letter W. Jerdan to J. Burn, 20 July 1837, Bodleian Library, University of Oxford, MS Montagu d.14 ff. 26,27.

18 J. Watt, *Poisoned Lives*, Chapter 12.

19 L. Blanchard, *Life and Literary Remains of L.E.L.*, p. 142.

20 Quoted in M. Rosa, *The Silver Fork School*, p. 170.

21 Letter W. Jerdan to R. Bentley, 16 December 1837, Harry Ransom Humanities Research Center, The University of Texas at Austin.

22 Letter W. Jerdan to R. Bentley, 10 January 1838, Harry Ransom Humanities Research Center, The University of Texas at Austin.

23 Letter W. Jerdan to R. Bentley, 19 February, n.y. Harry Ransom Humanities Research Center, The University of Texas at Austin.

24 Letter T. Croker to W. Jerdan, 23 May 1838, Bodleian Library, University of Oxford, MS. Eng. lett. d. 113, f144.

25 Letter W. Jerdan to J. Nichols, 11 June 1834, Bodleian Library, University of Oxford, MS. Eng. b. 2074 f68.

26 Letter W. Jerdan to J. Bruce, 14 June 1834, John Bruce Collection, James Marshall and Marie-Louise Osborn Collection, Beinecke Rare Book and Manuscript Library, Yale University.

27 Society of Antiquaries, *Archaelogia*, Vol. 28, p. 435.

28 Letter H. Ellis to W. Jerdan, 10 June 1836, British Library, ADD70842 f.56. They are held in the British Museum's Department of Prehistory and Europe, reg. Nos. 1838,7-14.3 a + b.

29 "Tom Noddy" was a colloquial term meaning a fool; it was used by Leech in his cartoons for *Punch* 1842–64.

30 Letter W. Jerdan to R. Bentley, 1838, Harry Ransom Humanities Research Center, The University of Texas at Austin.

31 Lambeth, Surrey, Registration Vol. 4, p. 250.

32 Lambeth, Surrey, Registration Vol. 4, p. 218.

33 Letter C. Swain to W. Jerdan, 3 March 1838, Manchester Archives and Local Studies, Msf091524 (38).

34 *Age*, 6 April 1838.

35 S. C. Hall, *Book of Memories*, p. 276.

36 K. Thomson, *Queens of Society*, p. 304.

37 S. C. Hall, *Book of Memories*, p. 279. F. J Sypher, *Biography*, 2009, p. 213, suggests that Maclean's words were ironic, to counter Hall's implied hostility to him.

38 S. C. Hall, *Retrospect of a Long Life*, Vol. II, p. 159.

39 F. J. Sypher, *Biography, 2009*, discusses many possibilities of the cause of Landon's death.

40 J. Watt, *Poisoned Lives*, Chapter 10.

41 D. E. Enfield, *L.E.L.: A Mystery of the Thirties*, p. 96.

42 M. Thrall, *Rebellious Fraser's*, p. 226.

43 M. Sadleir, *Bulwer and His Wife*.

44 R. Duncan, *Thesis*, p. 92 fn.

45 M. Gorman, *The Murder of L.E.L.*

46 *Auto*. IV, p. 378.

47 Letter W. Jerdan to Lady Blessington, British Library, MSS 43688 f64 (also includes a lock of LEL's hair).

48 Letter W. Jerdan to Mrs Hall, 5 January 1839. The Pierpont Morgan Library, New York. Bequest, Gordon N. Ray; 1987. MA 4500.

49 S. Mackenzie, *Miscellaneous Writings of W. Maginn*, Vol. V, Memoir of W. Maginn, p. lxxxvi.

50 M. Sadleir, *Blessington D'Orsay: A Masquerade*, p. 280.

51 Letter K. Thomson to W. Jerdan, n.d., Bodleian Library, University of Oxford, MS. Eng. lett. d. 114, f258.

52 The full verse seems to be a pastiche of Barton by Jerdan; a search has been carried out to discover if he was quoting Barton himself, but no evidence has been found.

Chapter 16   Encouraging Authors – Creating Fiction

1 On 17 December 1839 Dickens referred to Bentley as "the Brigand of Burlington Street" in a letter to T. Beard, (ref: L. Nayder, https://listserv.indiana. edu/archives/ victoria.html).

2 Archives of the Royal Literary Fund. British Library, M1077.

3 Letter W. Jerdan to T. Croker, 11 March, n.y., Royal Borough of Kensington & Chelsea, Family & Children's Service.

4 Letter T. Uwins to W. Jerdan, 4 March 1839, Ashcombe Collection, II 78.2, Fitzwilliam Museum, MS 215-1949, University of Cambridge.

5 *Gentleman's Magazine*, November 1839. *Notes & Queries* Vol. II 2nd S. March 9, 1861 p. 192 discussed Gray's works and mentioned his dedication to Jerdan.

6 In *Auto*. IV, p. 352, Jerdan refers to being the croupier of the 'Anonomi' Club, meeting monthly at the Freemasons' Tavern. He names Simon Gray as a member, "an odd character, clerk in the War Office, and author of several pamphlets on 'Finance'".

7 Letter W. Jerdan to R. Bentley, 25 May 1839, Harry Ransom Humanities Research Center, The University of Texas at Austin.

8 Letter W. Jerdan to R. Bentley, n.d. 1839, Harry Ransom Humanities Research Center, The University of Texas at Austin.

9 William Henry Fox-Talbot, inventor of photography.

10 Charles Babbage, 1791–1871, originator of the idea for a programmable computer with his Analytical Machine, and inventor of a Difference Engine for production of logarithm tables.

11 Charles Wheatstone invented a speaking machine in 1837, based on an 18th century design.

12 W. Jerdan, *Men I Have Known*, p. 50.

13 *The Correspondence of William Henry Fox Talbot*. http://foxtalbot.dmu.ac.uk.

14 W. Jerdan, *Men I Have Known*, p. 363.

15 W. Toynbee, ed., *Diaries of William Macready*, 5 Oct. 1839.

16 *Auto*. IV, p. 365.

17 Letter W. Jerdan to Sir T. N. Talfourd, 5 August n.y., MsL J55Ac, University of Iowa Libraries, Iowa City, Iowa.

18 Letter W. Jerdan to T. Croker, 1839, Autograph Letters, Houghton Library, Harvard University.

19 The Academia has failed to respond to requests for any surviving correspondence to support this honorary membership.

20 Quoting from the Prospectus – even though the arithmetic does not add up.

21 As example Letter W. Jerdan to J. Bruce, 7 December n.y., John Bruce Collection, Beinecke Rare Book and Manuscript Library, Yale University.

22 *Auto*. IV, p. 349.

23 Letter W. Jerdan to R. Bentley, 16 December n.y., Harry Ransom Humanities Research Center, The University of Texas at Austin.

24 Letter W. Jerdan to R. Bentley, 19 December n.y., Harry Ransom Humanities Research Center, The University of Texas at Austin.

25 T. C. Croker, *A Walk from London to Fulham*, p. 316.

26 R. A. Gettman, *A Victorian Publisher*, p. 23.

27 *Letters of Charles Dickens*.

28 Letter W. Jerdan to R. Bentley, 19 June 1840, The Henry W. and Albert A. Berg Collection of English and American Literature, The New York Public Library, Astor, Lenox and Tilden Foundations, 369758B.

29 Letter R. Bentley to W. Jerdan, 21 June 1840, The Henry W. and Albert A. Berg Collection of English and American Literature, The New York Public Library, Astor, Lenox and Tilden Foundations, 36963B.

30 Letter W. Jerdan to R. Bentley, 1840, The Henry W. and Albert A. Berg Collection of English and American Literature, The New York Public Library, Astor, Lenox and Tilden Foundations, 36975B.

31 www.dickenslive.com.

32 Letter W. Jerdan to R. Bentley, n.d., Harry Ransom Humanities Research Center, The University of Texas at Austin.

33 The year was noted as a turning point by analysing the number of applicants and times of applications between 1800 and 1840, and then from 1840–1880, indicating that Victorian writers were better remunerated than their Georgian counterparts. N. Cross, *The Royal Literary Fund*, p. 15.

34 Archives of the Royal Literary Fund, Committee Minutes, November 1840, British Library, M1077.

35 Archives of Royal Literary Fund, British Library, M1077.

36 Letter W. Jerdan to J. Britton, 8 June 1840, British Library, Manuscript Department, 38794/170.

37   Quoted in G. Pyle, *Thesis*, p. 202. P. F. Morgan, ed., *Letters of Thomas Hood*.
38   *Auto*. IV, p. 36.
39   Archives of Royal Literary Fund, British Library.

Part IV Times of Change, 1841–1851

Chapter 17   Sole Possession – Serious Pursuits

1   Letter W. Jerdan to J. Barrow, 1 February 1841, Royal Geographical Society, RGS/CB3/428.
2   Society of Antiquaries, *Archaelogia*, Vol. 29, p. 407.
3   Lambeth, Surrey, Registration Vol. IV, p. 233.
4   Quoted in G. Pyle, *Thesis*, p. 208. *An Almanack of the British Stamped Press Including all Stamped Newspapers, Literary or Scientific journals, and Commercial Lists for 1841*.
5   Letter H. Colburn to W. Jerdan, 11 May 1841, Bodleian Library, University of Oxford, MS. Eng. lett. d. 113, f124.
6   *Auto*. IV, p. 361.
7   Letter W. Jerdan to T. Wright, Courtesy of University of St. Andrews Library, Special Collections, MS PR4825 J.25.
8   *Literary Gazette*, 7 August 1841, p. 497.
9   C. Dickens, ed., *Pic Nic Papers*, Vol. 1 p. 256.
10 *Literary Gazette*, 20 March 1841, p. 177.
11 R. Duncan, *Thesis*, p. 185.
12 *Literary Gazette*, 25 September 1841, p. 620.
13 Letter G. P. R. James to W. Jerdan, 19 April 1842, Bodleian Library, University of Oxford, MS. Eng. Lett. d. 113, f 263.
14 The Copyright Act of 1842 repealed earlier Acts, extended intellectual property rights for the author's lifetime and seven years after his death; if this was less than 42 years from first publication, copyright was for 42 years regardless of date of death. For posthumous publication, the owner of the MSS was protected by the same 42 years.
15 Letter W. Jerdan to R. Bentley, 13 February, annotated 1842, Harry Ransom Humanities Research Center, The University of Texas at Austin.
16 *Auto*. IV, p. 365.
17 W. Thackeray, "On a Joke I once heard from the late Thomas Hood", *Roundabout Papers*.
18 W. Toynbee, ed. *Diaries of William Macready*, 8 May 1842.
19 Letter W. Jerdan to J. O. Halliwell, Edinburgh University Library, Special Collections Department, LOA 21/78.
20 Letter W. Jerdan to J. O. Halliwell, Edinburgh University Library, Special Collections Department, LOA 21/1.
21 *Literary Gazette*, 4 September 1847.
22 Letter J. H. Rodwell to W. Jerdan, 12 November 1842, Edinburgh University Library, Special Collections Department, LA II 647/331.
23 *Literary Gazette*, Feb. Nos. 1360 p. 92, 1362 p. 1233, August Nos. 1385 p. 515, No. 1388 p. 545.

24 Letter William Jerdan to M. Napier, 1 August 1843, British Library, MSS. 34624/41.

25 Letter M. Napier to W. Jerdan, 16 October n.y., Bodleian Library, University of Oxford, MS. Eng. lett. d. 114, f102.

26 Letter W. M. Thackeray to W. Jerdan, 12 February 1843, Huntington Library, San Marino, California, HM 15307.

27 *Letters of Charles Dickens*, 9 October 1843.

28 Letter R. Bentley to W. Jerdan, 3 March 1847, Bodleian Library, University of Oxford, MS. Eng. lett. d. 113, f40.

29 Letter R. Bentley to W. Jerdan, 5 April 1845, Bodleian Library, University of Oxford, MS. Eng. lett. d. 113, f42.

30 R. Gettman, *A Victorian Publisher*, p. 23.

31 Marylebone Registration Vol. I, p. 223.

32 Letter W. Jerdan to R. Bentley, 20 May 1843, Harry Ransom Humanities Research Center, The University of Texas at Austin .

33 The rules of the King's/Queen's Bench and Fleet were certain limits without the actual walls of the prisons, where the prisoner, on proper security previously given to the marshal of the king's bench, or warden of the fleet, may reside; those limits are considered, for all legal and practical purposes, as merely a further extension of the prison walls. The rules or permission to reside without the prison, may be obtained by any person not committed criminally; http://legal-dictionary. thefree-dictionary.com/ Rules. The detainee was allowed to carry on his business as usual, allowing him to earn money to meet his debts.

34 Charles Fourier (1772–1837) devised a system of phalanxes, both built and societal, whereby concerned co-operation would lead to improved productivity and social success.

35 Letter Duke of Rutland to W. Jerdan, 7 May 1843, Bodleian Library, University of Oxford, MS. Eng. lett. d. 114, f78.

36 J. Hamilton, *London Lights*, p. 279.

37 Letter M. Wyatt to W. Jerdan, n.d., Bodleian Library, University of Oxford, MS. Eng. lett. d. 114, f338.

38 *Literary Gazette*, 13 September 1845, p. 612.

39 Letter to Charles Mackay, 7 March 1844. *Letters of Charles Dickens*, Vol. IV, 1844–46.

40 Sir R. Murchison to W. Jerdan, 22 May 1844, Bodleian Library, University of Oxford, MS. Eng. lett. d. 114, f97.

41 Alton, Hampshire, Registration Vol. 7 p. 25.

42 *Auto*. IV, p. 292.

43 *Auto*. IV, p. 293.

44 Letter W. Jerdan to W. Whewell, 23 June 1845, Trinity College Cambridge Library, Add. MS.a.21630(1).

45 H. Vizetelly, *Glances back*, Vol. I, p. 33.

46 Letter W. Whewell to W. Jerdan, 23 June 1845, Trinity College Cambridge Library, A.MS.a.21632.

47 *Auto*. IV, p. 294.

48 Letter Sir M.A. Shee to W. Jerdan, 8 April, probably 1844, MS 206-1949. Fitzwilliam Museum, University of Cambridge.
49 Letter C. R. Weld to W. Jerdan, 18 December 1843, Bodleian Library, University of Oxford, MS. Eng. lett. d. 114, f303.
50 *Auto.* IV, p. 367.
51 Letter Ellen Carne to W. Jerdan, 26 April 1844, Bodleian Library, University of Oxford, MS. Eng. lett. d. 113, f104.
52 *Literary Gazette*, 4 May 1844, p. 290.
53 *Literary Gazette*, 7 Dec. 1844, p. 778.
54 Preface Vol. XVII Scottish Traditional Version of Ancient Ballads, pub. Percy Society, 1845.
55 Letter W. Jerdan to _____ Watts, 26 October 184, Aberdeen University, Library and Historic Collections, 2303/2/182.
56 Letter W. Jerdan to P. Buchan, 19 April 1847, Aberdeen University, Library and Historic Collections, 2303/2/198.
57 *Literary Gazette*, 31 August 1844.

Chapter 18 Struggle for Financial Survival

1 Letter W. F. Ainsworth to W. Jerdan, 23 February 1845, Bodleian Library, University of Oxford, MS. Eng. lett. d. 113, f17.
2 In article about Count D'Orsay's portraits in *Ainsworth's Magazine*, (ed. W Harrison Ainsworth) January 1845, p. 226. Later in the year this latter Ainsworth paid Colburn £2,500 for the *New Monthly Magazine*.
3 Letter W. Jerdan to R. Bentley, n.d., Harry Ransom Humanities Research Center, The University of Texas at Austin.
4 M. Sadleir, *Blessington D'Orsay*, p. 219.
5 *Literary Gazette*, 27 June 1846, p. 374.
6 The Royal Bank of Scotland Group Archives, DR/427/273. Messrs Drummond customer account ledger 1845, pp. 38 and 45.
7 *Auto.* IV, p. 32.
8 *Blackwood's Edinburgh Magazine*, October 1861, p. 473.
9 Letter Q. Harris to W. Jerdan, 24 April 1845, National Library of Scotland, 9814/108-9.
10 *Literary Gazette*, 10 May 1845.
11 Letter Gibbs to W. Jerdan, 13 November 1844, Bodleian Library, University of Oxford, MS. Eng. lett. d. 113, ff215, 216.
12 Irwin paid £52.10 to Jerdan's account in December 1845, possibly for his share of the partnership.
13 Information from *Oxford Dictionary of National Biography*, J. Mordaunt Crook.
14 Letter J. Britton to W. Jerdan, 22 May 1845, Bodleian Library, University of Oxford, MS. Eng.lett. d. 113, f66.
15 Letter J. Wood to W. Jerdan, 15 March 1844, Bodleian Library, University of Oxford, MS. Eng. lett. d. 114, f319b.
16 W. Toynbee, ed. *Diaries of William Charles Macready*, 7 September 1845.
17 *Literary Gazette*, 27 September 1845.

18 *Literary Gazette*, 6 September 1845.
19 The original house still fulfils its purpose, and from 1965 twenty-four modern bungalows were added. Now run by the Book Trade Benevolent Society, the house was renamed Dickinson House in 1979.
20 *Gentleman's Magazine*, October 1845, p. 411.
21 *Literary Gazette*, 14 March 1846.
22 G. Pyle, *Thesis*, p. 216.
23 *Auto*. IV, p. 187.
24 J. H. Buckley, *The Victorian Temper*, p. 119.
25 G. Pyle, *Thesis*, p. 71.
26 Charles Mitchell, *The Newspaper Press Directory*, 1846.
27 Letter W. Nicoll to W. Jerdan, 7 January 1846, Bodleian Library, University of Oxford, MS. Eng. lett. d. 114, f106.
28 Letter R. Bentley to W. Jerdan, 14 January 1846, Bodleian Library, University of Oxford, MS. Eng. lett. d. 113, f44.
29 Letter W. Jerdan to J. O. Halliwell, 22 March 1846, Edinburgh University Library, Special Collections Department, LOA 25/89.
30 Letter C. R. Smith to W. Jerdan, 27 October 1846, Bodleian Library, University of Oxford, MS Eng. lett. d. 114, f214.
31 Letter W. Jerdan to J. O. Halliwell, 28 March 1846, Edinburgh University Library, Special Collections Department, LOA 27/22.
32 Marylebone Registration Vol. I, p. 193.
33 *Tait's Edinburgh Magazine*, March 1846, pp. 137–145.
34 Letter J. Burton to W. Jerdan, n.d., National Library of Scotland, 9393/85-8.
35 Letter W. Jerdan to R. Bentley, 4 April n.y., Harry Ransom Humanities Research Center, The University of Texas at Austin.
36 In 1849 Bentley published *The Life and Remains of Theodore Edward Hook* by R. Barham.
37 Gore House, (on the site where the Royal Albert Hall now stands) was then in the country. The house was built at the beginning of the century, and between 1808–21 had been the home of William Wilberforce, just before he moved to Grove House, which Jerdan took over from him.
38 M. Boyle, ed. *Boyle's Fashionable Court & Country Guide and Town Visiting Directory*, 1847, p. 558.
39 Agnes's birth year from 1861 Census, born Chelsea.
40 Letter W. Jerdan to R. Bentley, 3 November n.y., Harry Ransom Humanities Research Center, The University of Texas at Austin.
41 Letter R. Bentley to W. Jerdan, 1846, British Library, MSS 46651/143.
42 Letter W. Jerdan to R. Bentley, 7 December 1846, Harry Ransom Humanities Research Center, The University of Texas at Austin.
43 Letter R. Bentley to W. Jerdan, 8 December, probably 1846, Bodleian Library, University of Oxford, MS. Eng. lett. d. 113, f46.
44 Letter W. Jerdan to R. Bentley, n.d., Harry Ransom Humanities Research Center, The University of Texas at Austin.

45 Ransom, H., *William Jerdan, Editor and Literary Agent*, 1948, Harry Ransom Humanities Research Center, The University of Texas at Austin.

46 R. Duncan, *Notes & Queries*, September 1968, p. 346.

47 The two theses submitted some years ago on the subject of Jerdan and the *Literary Gazette*, highlight one of the hazards of interpreting and transcribing manuscript letters. Both writers happened to select the same letter from Bentley to support their thesis that Jerdan acted as a literary agent. One transcribed it incorrectly, thus changing its meaning entirely, and then pronounced on the outcome. Jerdan had found a cleric to write a volume on an agreed topic and wrote to tell Bentley. Ransom correctly transcribed:

"But he is a poor scholar also, and says, 'I must have thirty or forty pounds to start with, and pay my expenses in a strange place, far away from my family.' If you approve, send the cheque and I will see that he fulfills his engagement." (Jerdan's letter did not actually use the quotation marks Ransom ascribes, but his sense is clear.) Duncan, however changed the letter to read: " . . . he is a poor scholar. Also I say I must have thirty or forty pounds to start with, [to] pay my expenses in a strange place, away from my family", omitting the final sentence. He went on to say that "It is doubtful that Bentley would have given Jerdan money for such a plan". However, the money requested was clearly for the "poor scholar" and Jerdan was trying to help Bentley get a promised book ready, not to make money for himself.

48 See Ch. 5, p. 85.

49 *Auto.* III, p. 111.

50 *Auto.* III, p. 47.

51 Pyle, G. *Thesis*, p. 115.

52 Letter C. Orme to W. Jerdan, 1 June 1826, University of Reading, Special Collections, Longmans Archive, I, 102 20A.

53 Letter R. Bentley to W. Jerdan, 8 March 1838, British Library, Bentley Papers, ADD 46640, f.193.

54 *Leisure Hour*, letter dated 2 April 1838, in 'Characteristic Letters', August 1869.

55 Letter W. Jerdan to R. Bentley, n.d., Harry Ransom Humanities Research Center, The University of Texas at Austin.

56 Letter A. Bray to W. Jerdan, 26 July 1845, Bodleian Library, University of Oxford, MS. Eng. lett. d. 113, f58.

57 *Auto.* IV, p. 321.

58 Letter W. Jerdan to R. Bentley, 10 August n.y., Harry Ransom Humanities Research Center, The University of Texas at Austin.

59 J. Hepburn, *The Author's Empty Purse and the Rise of the Literary Agent*, p. 26.

60 Ibid., p. 26.

61 Ibid., p. 30.

Chapter 19   Leading to Bankruptcy

1   Bodleian Library, University of Oxford, MS. Eng. lett. d. 114, f95, 113, f37, 113, f135, 114, f194, 113, f122.

2　Letter W. Jerdan to R. Bentley, 16 February n.y., Harry Ransom Humanities Research Center, The University of Texas at Austin.

3　Letter W. Jerdan to R. Bentley, 29 November n.y., Harry Ransom Humanities Research Center, The University of Texas at Austin.

4　*Auto.* III, p. 172.

5　According to 1861 Census, born Chelsea.

6　Letter W. Jerdan to R. Bentley, 23 April n.y., Harry Ransom Humanities Research Center, The University of Texas at Austin.

7　Examination of the Bentley Papers in the British Library has not revealed the author of this Biographical Sketch.

8　Letter W. Jerdan to J. O. Halliwell, 12 May 1847, Edinburgh University Library, Special Collections Department, LOA 55.47.

9　Letter W. Jerdan to R. Bentley, 7 August 1847, Harry Ransom Humanities Research Center, The University of Texas at Austin.

10　Letter W. Jerdan to R. Bentley, 23 January n.y., Harry Ransom Humanities Research Center, The University of Texas at Austin.

11　Letter W. Jerdan to R. Bentley, 22 June n.y., Harry Ransom Humanities Research Center, The University of Texas at Austin.

12　The Hans Christian Andersen Center, University of Southern Denmark.

13　E. Bredsdorff, *Hans Christian Andersen, An Introduction to his Life and Works*, page 184.

14　*Letters of Charles Dickens*, 30 March 1847.

15　The Hans Christian Andersen Center, University of Southern Denmark.

16　Quoted in E. Bredsdorff, *Hans Christian Andersen*.

17　The Hans Christian Andersen Center, University of Southern Denmark.

18　Ibid.

19　J. Andersen, J., *Hans Christian Andersen*, p. 402.

20　Letter C. Dickens to W. Jerdan, 14 July 1847. The Hans Christian Andersen Center, University of Southern Denmark.

21　*Leisure Hour*, 1 February 1868, p. 144.

22　E. Bredsdorff, *Hans Christian Andersen*, p. 189.

23　Ibid., p. 197. Andersen's friend in Copenhagen, Edvard Collin, sent a copy of Jerdan's article to the *Berlingske Tidende* so that it could be quoted, but the Editor said it would be doing Andersen a disservice and make him a laughing-stock in Denmark if he quoted from an article in which he was seriously compared to Jenny Lind.

24　The Hans Christian Andersen Center, University of Southern Denmark.

25　Ibid.

26　Ibid.

27　Ibid.

28　Quoted in E. Bredsdorff, *Hans Christian Andersen*, p. 190.

29　Quoted in J. Andersen, J. *Hans Christian Andersen*, p. 404.

30　Letter W. Jerdan to n.k., 27 September 1847, Huntington Library, San Marino, California, Al 228.

31　Lanman, C., *Adventures of an Angler in Canada, Nova Scotia and the United States.*

Chapter XXI, 'The Hermit of Aroostook' is a detailed account of Lanman's meeting with Robert Eggar (spelling varies).

32 *Literary Gazette*, 25 Dec. 1847, p. 889.
33 The Correspondence of William Fox Talbot. http://foxtalbot.dmu.ac.uk. Doc. No. 2258.
34 Ibid. Doc. 6063.
35 Letter J. Prior to W. Jerdan, 17 May 1848, Bodleian Library, University of Oxford, MS. Eng. lett. d 114, f154.
36 *Literary Gazette*, 20 May 1848.
37 *Literary Gazette*, 27 January 1849.
38 *Literary Gazette*, 8 Dec. 1832, p. 773.
39 *Literary Gazette*, 19 Nov. 1842, p. 788.
40 *Literary Gazette*, 12 August 1848, p. 530.
41 R. Duncan, *Thesis*, p. 242.
42 Letter W. F. Jerdan to J. O. Halliwell, 11 July 1848, Edinburgh University Library, Special Collections Department. LOA 38/45.
43 W. Toynbee W., *Diaries of William Charles Macready*, 26 August 1848.
44 The Hans Christian Andersen Center, University of Southern Denmark, and *Leisure Hour*, 1 February 1868, p. 144.
45 The Hans Christian Andersen Center, University of Southern Denmark.
46 W. Toynbee, *Diaries*, 1 April 1848. Macready, D'Orsay, Forster, Thackeray and others. "A day interesting in its occasion but strangely assorted. Still, dear Dickens was happy ..."
47 The Hans Christian Andersen Center, University of Southern Denmark.
48 J. Andersen, *Hans Christian Andersen*, p. 408.
49 Quoted in E. Bredsdorff, *Hans Christian Andersen*, p. 221.
50 R. Fraser, *A People's History of Britain*.
51 Certificate from Royal Society of Literature to A. Layard.
52 Letter E. Cook to W. Jerdan, 10 February 1849, MsL C771je, University of Iowa Libraries, Iowa City, Iowa.
53 E. Bulwer to W. Jerdan, 15 January 1849, Bodleian Library, University of Oxford, MS. Eng. lett. d. 114, f52.
54 *Auto*. IV, p. 208.
55 Letter W. Jerdan to J. O. Halliwell, 14 February 1848, Edinburgh University Library, Special Collections Department, LOA 8/28.
56 Letter W. Jerdan to J. O. Halliwell, 16 June 1849, Edinburgh University Library, Special Collections Department, LOA 8/65.
57 Letter W. Jerdan to J. O. Halliwell, 24 June 1849, Edinburgh University Library, Special Collections Department, LOA 18/42.
58 Letter W. Jerdan to J. O. Halliwell, 6 July 1849, Edinburgh University Library, Special Collections Department, LOA 37/45.
59 Letter W. Jerdan to J. O. Halliwell, 25 August 1849, Edinburgh University Library, Special Collections Department, LOA 8/1.
60 *Auto*. IV, p. 320.
61 J. Britton, *Autobiography*, p. 134, 1849.

62 Ibid., p. 137.
63 National Archives, B/6/77.
64 *Literary Gazette*, Nov. 1849, p. 849.
65 According to 1861 Census, born Kilburn.
66 Edmund remained in Ceylon (although he visited London in 1858) and became a coffee planter, and was still unmarried at the age of 29. Mary's widower, Edward Power, remarried in 1863 to a woman half his age, eventually moving to Wales where he died aged 75 in 1886.
67 Registration of Deaths, St. Pancras, Vol. I, p. 286.
68 Letter G. Innes to W. Jerdan, 1 January 1850, Bodleian Library, University of Oxford, MS. Eng. lett. d. 113, f266.

Chapter 20   Losing the *Literary Gazette*

1 Birth Registrations, St. George, Southwark, Vol. 4, p. 484.
2 No death registration has been found to corroborate this supposition.
3 Christening Record, 17 March 1850, St Michael's Queenhithe. LDS Film No. 0374509.
4 *Auto.* IV, p. 362.
5 Letter W. Jerdan to J.O. Halliwell, 19 April 1850, Edinburgh University Library, Special Collections Department, LOA 54/77.
6 A. Lohrli, *Household Words 1850–59*, p. 3.
7 *Auto.* IV, p. 362.
8 Letter W. Jerdan to (?) J. O. Halliwell. Autograph Letters, Houghton Library, Harvard University.
9 Lovell Augustus Reeve and James Macaulay succeeded Jerdan as Editor either immediately, or within a year. The *Gazette* was to have a further eight editors, and merge with *The Parthenon* before it finally expired in 1863.
10 Letter Rev. W. Robertson to W. Jerdan, n.d., Edinburgh University Library, Special Collections Department, Gen. 1983/65.
11 *Auto.* IV, p. 368.
12 Letter W. F. Ainsworth to W. Jerdan, 26 December 1850, MsL A2969j, University of Iowa Libraries, Iowa City, Iowa.
13 A. Holden, *The Wit in the Dungeon*, p. 285.
14 B. Ford, ed. *Victorian Britain*.
15 W. Toynbee, ed., *Diaries*, 25 Feb. 1851.
16 *Times*, 18 February 1851.
17 N. Cross, *The Royal Literary Fund*, p. 18.
18 Ibid., p. 1.
19 *Auto.* IV, p. 37.
20 *Athenaeum*, 5 April 1851, p. 384.
21 Letter W. Jerdan to A. Forrester (pseud. Crowquill), 30 March n.y., Huntington Library, San Marino, California.
22 *Letters of Charles Dickens*, 8 February 1851.
23 Quoted G. Pyle, *Thesis*, p. 231 from Princeton University, Croker Collection, April 10, 1851.

24 Ibid., p. 230.
25 *Notes & Queries*, 16 and 30 August 1851.
26 *Auto*. IV, p. 375.
27 Letter W. Jerdan to not known, 22 June n.y., Bodleian Library, University of Oxford, MS. Autogr. b.10.
28 The IGI record gives the mother as "Marian Maxwell", but inaccurate transcription of names often arises and even in official documents Mary Ann was variously spelled as Maria, Mary Ann, Marianne or Marion.
29 Letter W. Jerdan to F. Bennoch, n.d., MsL J55bAc, University of Iowa Libraries, Iowa City, Iowa.
30 Hawthorne, Julian. *Hawthorne and his Circle*, p. 88.
31 Hawthorne, N., *The English Notebooks*, p. 291.
32 Letter W. Jerdan to Mrs. Bennoch, 1 November 1851, MsL J55bAc, University of Iowa Libraries, Iowa City, Iowa.
33 Letter W. Jerdan to Mrs. Bennoch, 4 November 1856 (probably), MsL J55bAc, University of Iowa Libraries, Iowa City, Iowa.
34 Letter W. Jerdan to F. Bennoch, n.d., Huntington Library, San Marino, California, Fl 2840-1.
35 Letter W. Jerdan to F. Bennoch, December n.y., MsL J55bAc, University of Iowa Libraries, Iowa City, Iowa.
36 Hookey Walker: reference to a bailiff, from a popular music-hall song.
37 Letter W. Jerdan to J. Durham, Courtesy of Senate House Library, University of London, AL 438.
38 Letter W. Jerdan to F. Bennoch, n.d., MsL J55bAc, University of Iowa Libraries, Iowa City, Iowa.
39 Letter W. Jerdan to F. Bennoch, December 1851, MsL J55bAc, University of Iowa Libraries, Iowa City, Iowa.

Part V   Life after the *Gazette*, 1851–1869

Chapter 21   Publication of *Autobiography*

1 Note by Margaret Malval, courtesy of Michael Gorman, great-great-great-grandson of Jerdan and L.E.L. Michael was raised in New Zealand and now lives in Japan. He is the generous source of all the family stories and notes concerning their descendants.
2 Private correspondence from Michael Gorman.
3 Ibid.
4 C. Lawford, *Diary*.
5 *Critic*, December 1851, p. 578.
6 N. Roe, *The First Life of Leigh Hunt*, p. 84.
7 Letter W. Jerdan to F. Bennoch, 13 April n.y., MsL J55bAc, University of Iowa Libraries, Iowa City, Iowa.
8 *Tait's Edinburgh Magazine*, June 1852, p. 380.
9 *New Quarterly Review*, July 1852, p. 270.
10 Letter W. Jerdan to F. Bennoch, n.d., Huntington Library, San Marino, California, Fl 2839.

11 Letter W. Jerdan to n.k. (likely to be Blackwood), 1 May 1852, National Library of Scotland, 4098/205.

12 'Delta' was the pseudonym of David Macbeth Moir, a physician and writer with close ties to Blackwoods, who had died on 6 July 1851 following an accident.

13 Letter W. Jerdan to F. Bennoch, 13 April n.y., MsL J55bAc, University of Iowa Libraries, Iowa City, Iowa.

14 Ibid.

15 Letter J. T. Fields to F. Bennoch, 11 May 1852, Huntington Library, San Marino, California, BE3.

16 Letter M. Tupper to F. Bennoch, 19 June 1852, Huntington Library, San Marino, California, BE233. Grace Greenwood was the pseudonym of Sara Jane Clarke Lippincott (1823–1904), American poet and essayist.

17 M. F. Tupper, *My Life as an Author*. Project Gutenberg, etext 17558.

18 G. Greenwood, *Haps and Mishaps of a Tour in Europe*, p. 41.

19 Letter W. Jerdan to J. T. Fields, 28 August 1852, Autograph Letters, Houghton Library, Harvard University.

20 *Auto*. II, p. 6.

21 *Auto*. II, p. 360.

22 *Athenaeum*, 14 August 1852, p. 863.

23 *Tait's*, September 1852, p. 569.

24 *Westminster Review*, 1852.

25 *Spectator*, 14 August 1852, p. 785.

26 *Literary Gazette*, 21 August 1852, p. 635.

27 Letter W. Jerdan to F. Bennoch, 1853, MsL J55bAc, University of Iowa Libraries, Iowa City, Iowa.

28 *Auto*. III, p. 173.

29 See Chapter 13.

30 *Athenaeum*, 13 November 1852, p. 1233.

31 *olla*: a large earthenware storage vessel.

32 The Earl of Derby, Tory Prime Minister, February to December 1852.

33 Letter W. Jerdan to F. Bennoch, 1853, MsL J55bAc, University of Iowa Libraries, Iowa City, Iowa.

34 Letter Lord Lennox to W. Jerdan, 24 January 1853, Bodleian Library, University of Oxford, MS. Eng. lett. d. 114, f28.

35 Letter W. Jerdan to Mrs Darby, 12 January 1853. The Pierpont Morgan Library, New York. Gift; Mr and Mrs Robert Cremin; 1982. MA 3553.

36 *Literary Gazette*, No. 1886, March 1853, p. 253.

37 Letter R. Lane to W. Jerdan, 12 February n.y., Bodleian Library, University of Oxford, MS. Eng. lett. d. 114, f15.

38 *Spectator*, 17 December 1853, p. 5 Supplement.

39 *Athenaeum*, 31 December 1853, p. 1592.

40 *Tait's Edinburgh Magazine*, February 1854.

41 S. C. Hall, *Retrospect of a Long Life*, p. 400.

42 R. H. Stoddard, ed. *Personal Reminiscences by Moore and Jerdan*, p. 175.

43 *Auto*. IV, p. 363.

44 Letter W. Jerdan to F. Bennoch, 1 November 1851 (probably), MsL J55bAc, University of Iowa Libraries, Iowa City, Iowa.

45 Letter W. Jerdan to F. Bennoch, 1857, MsL J55bAc, University of Iowa Libraries, Iowa City, Iowa.

46 Letter W. Jerdan to F. Bennoch, MsL J55bAc, University of Iowa Libraries, Iowa City, Iowa.

Chapter 22   Widened Horizons

1 Routledge Archives, RKP2, RKP6, Special Collections Library, University College London.

2 C. Armbrust, Nineteenth Century Presentations of George Herbert – Publishing History as Critical Embodiment. The *Huntington Library Quarterly*, Spring 1990, p. 142.

3 Published in the *Journal of the British Archaeological Association*, Vol. 9, 1854, pp. 330–6.

4 *The Eclectic Magazine* dated *Yankee Humor* as 1833, instead of 1853.

5 *New Quarterly Review*, January 1854.

6 Letter W. Jerdan to R. Bentley, 7 January 1854, Harry Ransom Humanities Research Center, The University of Texas at Austin.

7 Letter R. Bentley to W. Jerdan, 9 January 1854, British Library, Bentley Papers, Add 46641 f695.

8 Letter W. Jerdan to R. Bentley, 19 January 1854, Harry Ransom Humanities Research Center, The University of Texas at Austin.

9 Letter R. Bentley to W. Jerdan, 11 January 1854, British Library, Bentley Papers, Add 46641 f696.

10 Letter W. Jerdan to R. Bentley, 12 January 1854, Harry Ransom Humanities Research Center, The University of Texas at Austin.

11 Letter R. Bentley to W. Jerdan, 13 January 1854, British Library, Bentley Papers, Add 46641 f701.

12 Letter W. Jerdan to R. Bentley, 15 January 1854, Harry Ransom Humanities Research Center, The University of Texas at Austin.

13 *The Critic*, 16 January 1854.

14 Quoted in G. Pyle, *Thesis*, p. 202, from Princeton Univ. Croker Collection, Croker to Balmanno, Jan 6, 1854.

15 Letter W. Jerdan to Sir R. Murchison, 30 June 1854, British Library, Manuscripts Department, 46126/482.

16 Letter W. Jerdan to T. Grissell, 6 May n.y., Bodleian Library, University of Oxford, MA. Eng. Lett. e86 f9.

17 *Manual for Travellers upon the South Eastern Railway No. 1.*

18 Letter W. Jerdan to F. Bennoch, 13 September 1856 (probably), MsL J55bAc, University of Iowa Libraries, Iowa City, Iowa.

19 Letter W. Jerdan to F. Bennoch, February 11, n.y., MsL J55bAc, University of Iowa Libraries, Iowa City, Iowa.

20 Letter W. Jerdan to J. T. Fields, 25 August 1854, Huntington Library, San Marino, California, Fl 2832–38.

21 Letter W. Jerdan to J. T. Fields, 21 July 1854, Huntington Library, San Marino, California, Fl 2832–38.

22 Ibid.

23 Ticknor was Fields's partner in their publishing business; Crowquill was a pseudonym for Alfred Forrester.

24 Letter W. Jerdan to J. T. Fields, 25 August 1854, Huntington Library, San Marino, California, Fl 2832–38.

25 Letter W. Jerdan to J. T. Fields, 8 September 1854, Huntington Library, San Marino, California, Fl 2838.

26 Letter W. Jerdan to Mr Clapp, 27 October 1854, Huntington Library, San Marino, California. Contemporary evidence (Life of J. M. Whistler, Ch.V, 1854, Lippincott, Philadelphia) equates $350 to £70, therefore $5 is equivalent to £1.

27 Letter J. T. Fields to F. Bennoch, 18 December 1854, Huntington Library, San Marino, California, BE11.

28 Letter W. Jerdan to F. Bennoch, n.d., MsL J55bAc, University of Iowa Libraries, Iowa City, Iowa.

29 Letter W. Jerdan to F. Bennoch, 16 December 1856 (probably), MsL J55bAc, University of Iowa Libraries, Iowa City, Iowa.

30 Letter W. Jerdan to F. Bennoch, 13 September 1856 (probably), MsL J55bAc, University of Iowa Libraries, Iowa City, Iowa.

31 Letter W. Jerdan to J. T. Fields, 30 March 1855, Huntington Library, San Marino, California, Fl 2832–38.

32 Letter W. Jerdan to J. T. Fields, 2 February 1855, Huntington Library, San Marino, California, Fl 2837.

33 S. C. Hall, *Retrospect of a Long Life*, Vol. I, p. 449.

34 Letter W. Jerdan to J. T. Fields, 16 March 1855, Huntington Library, San Marino, California, Fl 2832–38.

35 Letter W. Jerdan to unknown, London Metropolitan Archives, Q/WIL/236.

Chapter 23   Poverty in Old Age

1 Letter W. F. Jerdan to Messrs. Puttick & Simpson, 17 May 1856, Bodleian Library, University of Oxford, MS. Eng. lett. d. 113, f270.

2 Letter W. Jerdan to F. Bennoch, 4 May 1856 (probably), MsL J55bAc, University of Iowa Libraries, Iowa City, Iowa.

3 N. Hawthorne, *The English Notebooks*, p. 379.

4 Ibid., p. 642 n. 296.

5 Ibid., p. 281.

6 S. C. Hall, *Retrospect of a Long Life*, Vol. II, p. 202.

7 N. Hawthorne, *The English Notebooks*, p. 378.

8 Julian Hawthorne, *Hawthorne and His Circle*. Briefer recollections of this same visit were recorded by Julian Hawthorne's sister Sophia, *Memories of Hawthorne*.

9 Letter W. Jerdan to F. Bennoch, 1 June 1856, MsL J55bAc, University of Iowa Libraries, Iowa City, Iowa.

10 Letter W. Jerdan to F. Bennoch, 21 June 1856 (probably), MsL J55bAc, University of Iowa Libraries, Iowa City, Iowa.

11 Letter W. Jerdan to not known, 4 July 1856, National Library of Scotland, 14303/262-3.

12 Letter W. Jerdan to C. Rogers, 15 September 1856, National Library of Scotland, 14303/276-7. The foundation stone of the Wallace Monument was finally laid in June 1861, overlooking the battlefield of Stirling.

13 G. Pyle, *Thesis*, p. 241.

14 Letter W. Jerdan to F. Bennoch, 4 October 1856, MsL J55bAc, University of Iowa Libraries, Iowa City, Iowa.

15 Letter W. Jerdan to F. Bennoch, 16 October 1856 (probably), MsL J55bAc, University of Iowa Libraries, Iowa City, Iowa.

16 Letter W. Jerdan to Messrs. Cook, 1 November 1856, MsL J55bAc, University of Iowa Libraries, Iowa City, Iowa.

17 Letter W. Jerdan to F. Bennoch, 20 November 1856, MsL J55bAc, University of Iowa Libraries, Iowa City, Iowa.

18 Letter W. Jerdan to F. Bennoch, 30 December 1856, MsL J55bAc, University of Iowa Libraries, Iowa City, Iowa.

19 A. Lohrli, *Household Words 1850–59*, p. 21.

20 A colonial administrator with a facility for languages, posted to India 1826–40. In 1854, together with Sir Stafford Northcote, he published "The Organisation of the Permanent Civil Service", of which institution he is known as the "father."

21 In 2010 the situation had not improved; in Iraq British soldiers cannot converse with Iraqi soldiers or civilians.

22 Letter W. Jerdan to F. Bennoch, 27 January 1857, MsL J55bAc, University of Iowa Libraries, Iowa City, Iowa.

23 Letter W. Jerdan to F. Bennoch, 10 February 1857, MsL J55bAc, University of Iowa Libraries, Iowa City, Iowa.

24 Ibid.

25 N. Hawthorne, *The English Notebooks*, p. 606. Bennoch somehow retrenched and Hawthorne's son, Julian, in *Hawthorne and his Circle* noted that he repaid all his creditors with interest and became once more active and happy. Quoted in *The English Notebooks*, p. 654 n. 472.

26 Information from Grant Longman, quoted in G. Pyle, *Thesis*, p. 259.

27 *Leisure Hour*, December 1 1869, p. 812.

28 Letter W. Jerdan to F. Bennoch, 1 June 1857, MsL J55bAc, University of Iowa Libraries, Iowa City, Iowa.

29 Letter W. Jerdan to F. Bennoch, 17 June n.y., MsL J55bAc, University of Iowa Libraries, Iowa City, Iowa.

30 Letter W. Jerdan to J. Blackwood, 28 June 1857, National Library of Scotland, 4124/238-9.

31 Letter 25 June 1857, Jerdan to Andersen, Hans Christian Andersen Center, University of Southern Denmark.

32 *Letters of Charles Dickens*, 21 July 1857.

33 A. Lohrli, *Household Words*, p. 36.

Chapter 24   Biographies – Concerning Madness

1   Letter W. Jerdan to F. Bennoch, 18 March 1858, MsL J55bAc, University of Iowa Libraries, Iowa City, Iowa.

2   Letter W. Jerdan to F. Bennoch, 10 May 1858, MsL J55bAc, University of Iowa Libraries, Iowa City, Iowa.

3   Letter W. Jerdan to F. Bennoch, 30 March 1857, MsL J55bAc, University of Iowa Libraries, Iowa City, Iowa.

4   Ibid.

5   *Leisure Hour*, September 1858, pp. 564, 588.

6   *Leisure Hour,* December 1858, p. 803; January 1859, p. 21; January 1859, p. 43.

7   *Gentleman's Magazine*, March 1859, p. 326,

8   Letter W. Jerdan to E. Bulwer, 1 January 1859, Hertfordshire Archives and Local Studies, D/EK 025/231.

9   Letter W. Jerdan to E. Bulwer, 31 July 1858, Hertfordshire Archives and Local Studies, D/EK 025/231.

10 Letter W. Jerdan to E. Bulwer, 4 August 1858, Hertfordshire Archives and Local Studies, D/EK 025/231.

11 Letter W. Jerdan to E. Bulwer, 21 September 1858, Hertfordshire Archives and Local Studies, D/EK 025/231.

12 Letter W. Jerdan to E. Bulwer, 1 November 1858, Hertfordshire Archives and Local Studies, D/EK 025/231.

13 Letter W. Jerden to Secretary to Lord Malmesbury, 28 November 1858, Hertfordshire Archives and Local Studies, D/EK 025/231.

14 Letter W. Jerdan to E. Bulwer, 4 December 1858, Hertfordshire Archives and Local Studies, D/EK 025/231.

15 Letter W. Jerdan to Mrs Darby, 5 December 1858. The Pierpont Morgan Library, New York. Gift; Mr and Mrs Robert Cremin; 1982. MA 3553.

16 Letter W. Jerdan to F. Bennoch, 14 July 1859, MsL J55bAc, University of Iowa Libraries, Iowa City, Iowa.

17 Letter W. Jerdan to J. Blackwood, 15 December 1859, National Library of Scotland, 4140/11.

18 Letter W. Jerdan to F. Bennoch, 12 January 1860, MsL J55bAc, University of Iowa Libraries, Iowa City, Iowa.

19 Letter W. Jerdan to A. Forrester (pseud. Crowquill), 6 March 1860, Huntington Library, San Marino, California, 130.

20 Letter W. Jerdan to A. Forrester (pseud. Crowquill), 12 March 1860, Huntington Library, San Marino, California.

21 Letter E. Bulwer to W. Jerdan, 3 May 1861, Bodleian Library, University of Oxford, M.S.Eng. Let. 48 f.24.

22 Lennox, Lord William Pitt, *Celebrities I Have Known*, Vol. 2, p. 42. The 'Phoenix' probably referred to a new home for the Garrick then being built, to which the Club moved in 1864.

23 Letter W. Jerdan to n.k., 9 April 1862, MsL J55bAc, University of Iowa Libraries, Iowa City, Iowa.

24 Letter W. Jerdan to J. Winter, 11 July 1862, British Library, Manuscripts Department, 70850/29.

25 Letter W. Jerdan to E. Bulwer, 1 September 1862, Hertfordshire Archives and Local Studies, D/EK/C/11/26.

26 A. Holden, *The Wit in the Dungeon*, p. 242.

27 *Literary Gazette*, No. 604, p. 516.

28 *Literary Gazette*, July 1830, p. 445.

29 *Literary Gazette,* March 1840, No. 1207, p. 147.

30 *Literary Gazette,* 20 April 1844, No. 1422.

31 *Literary Gazette*, Nov. 1849, p. 861.

32 *Auto*. III, p. 279.

Chapter 25   *Men I Have Known*

1 Letter W. Jerdan to F. Bennoch, 24 January 1863, MsL J55bAc, University of Iowa Libraries, Iowa City, Iowa.

2 Wikipedia on John Watkins. Photograph of Jerdan in Rob Dickens Collection, Watts Gallery.

3 Letter W. Jerdan to Lady Willoughby de Eresby, 25 September 1863, National Archives of Scotland, GD160/316/34.

4 Charles Dibdin (1740–1814) wrote 'Tom Bowling', a song mourning a dead sailor.

5 Letter W. Jerdan to Lady Willoughby de Eresby, 1 December 1863, National Archives of Scotland, GD160/316/35.

6 Kirkman Daniel Hodgson (1824–1879) lived across the road from Jerdan, in a mansion called Laurel Lodge, (later known as Sparrows Herne Hall) from 1845–1869. He was MP for Bridport and in 1863, Governor of the Bank of England.

7 Letter W. Jerdan to Lady Willoughby de Eresby, 5 December 1863, National Archives of Scotland, GD160/316/37.

8 Letter W. Jerdan to Lady Willoughby de Eresby, n.d., National Archives of Scotland, GD160/324/38.

9 Letter W. Jerdan to E. Bulwer, 6 October 1863, Hertfordshire Archives and Local Studies, D/EK C/11/25.

10 This play was probably "The Rifle and How to Use it", by I.V. Bridgeman, a Farce in One Act. First performed at the Theatre Royal, Haymarket, September 1859. Victorian Plays Project, victorian.worc.ac.uk.

11 Letter W. Jerdan to F. Bennoch, 1 November 1863, MsL J55bAc University of Iowa Libraries, Iowa City, Iowa.

12 *Leisure Hour*, December 1869 p. 813.

13 Letter W. Jerdan to J. O. Halliwell, 19 December 1864, Edinburgh University Library, Special Collections Department, LOA 6/24.

14 *Literary Gazette*, 6 October 1821. With thanks to Cynthia Lawford for bringing this to my attention.

15 Letter W. Jerdan to J. O. Halliwell, 8 February 1866, Edinburgh University Library, Special Collections Department, LOA 105/19.

16 Letter W. Jerdan to F.Bennoch, 15 March 1864, MsL J55bAc, University of Iowa Libraries, Iowa City, Iowa.

17 Charles Jerdan of the *Galatea* was promoted to First Class Assistant Engineer. *The Scotsman*, 29 August 1864.

18 Letter W. Jerdan to J. O. Halliwell, 23 September 1865, Edinburgh University Library, Special Collections Department, LOA 107/47.

19 He suffered from chronic bronchitis, "provoking cough and phlegm with considerable effort and exhaustion". Letter W. Jerdan to E. Bulwer, 14 March 1863, Hertfordshire Archives and Local Studies, D/EK C/11/24.

20 Letter W. Jerdan to J. O. Halliwell, Edinburgh University Library, Special Collections Department, LOA 104/13.

21 C. Lawford, *Diary*, op. cit.

22 J. Milner, *The Cruise of the Galatea*.

23 Letter W. Jerdan to T. Gaspey, 24 January 1866, Huntington Library, San Marino, California.

24 Immigrant Ships Transcribers Guild, *Arrival of the Atalanta with 394 Government Immigrants.*

25 Letter W. Jerdan to R. Bentley, 6 November 1865, Harry Ransom Humanities Research Center, The University of Texas at Austin.

26 Routledge Archives, Publication Book, Special Collections Library, University College London.

27 Letter W. Jerdan to Pigott, 1 May 1866, Huntington Library, San Marino, California.

28 *New Sporting Magazine*, July 1866.

29 Letter W. Jerdan to J. Blackwood, 5 September 1866, National Library of Scotland, 4201/15-16.

30 Letter W. Jerdan to _____. Langford, 18 September 1866, National Library of Scotland, 42201/17-18.

31 Letter W. Jerdan to E. Bulwer, July 8 1866, Hertfordshire Archives and Local Studies, D/EK C/10/106.

32 Letter W. Jerdan to J. O. Halliwell, 28 April 1867, Edinburgh University Library, Special Collections, LOA 82/12.

Chapter 26 *Characteristic Letters*

1 *Leisure Hour*, 1 February 1868.

2 Hans Christian Andersen Center, University of Southern Denmark.

3 Letter W. Jerdan to F. Bennoch, 24 May 1868, MsL J55bA, University of Iowa Libraries, Iowa City, Iowa.

4 Letter W. Jerdan to F. Bennoch, 13 June 1868, MsL J55bA, University of Iowa Libraries, Iowa City, Iowa.

5 Letter W. Jerdan to F. Bennoch, 17 June 1858 (probably), MsL J55bA, University of Iowa Libraries, Iowa City, Iowa.

6 Letter W. Jerdan to T. Gaspey, 28 July 1868, Autograph Letters, Houghton Library, Harvard University.

7 Letter W. Jerdan to T. Gaspey, 11 August n.y., MsL J55Ac, University of Iowa Libraries, Iowa City, Iowa.

8 Lover wrote and composed a song The Bowld Sojer Boy, c. 1845.

9 Letter W. Jerdan to T. Gaspey, n.d., City of London, London Metropolitan Archives, Q/WIL/237.

10 Quoted in G. Pyle, *Thesis*, p. 245.

11 *Notes & Queries* s.III, 27 March 1869, p. 287

12 Correspondence of William Fox Talbot. Doc. 9504.

13 This was not true. The first person to die was in September 1830. See Chapter 5, n.12. Further deaths had occurred on railways since then.

14 In 1874 a *"Life of Samuel Lover . . . with selections from his unpublished papers and correspondence"* was written by William Bayle Bernard. In 1880 A. J. Symington included a sketch of Lover, with a selection from his writings and correspondence in his book, *"Men of Light and Leading"*, London, 1880. They may well have used some of Jerdan's papers for these books.

15 *Letters of Charles Dickens*, op. cit., 14 May 1869.

Part VI   Remembrances

Chapter 27   Death, Obituaries, Posthumous Publication

1 Once again, Jerdan and Leigh Hunt's lives reflected each other: Hunt's obituary in a local newspaper of 1859 remarked "Some people will be surprised to hear not only that Leigh Hunt is dead, but that he only died on Sunday last . . . he was one of a generation long since passed away". But he was outlived by Jerdan for another decade.

2 *Gentleman's Magazine*, August 1869, p. 378.

3 Nine years after Hunt's death a subscription was raised for a memorial. The impecunious Jerdan gave one guinea, the same sum as Lord Lytton and S. C. Hall, an amazingly generous gesture to the man who had attacked him early in his career. Hunt's monument in Kensal Green was unveiled in October 1869.

4 Likely to refer to the death of his son William Freeling, who died on 6 February 1859, from consumption, and was childless.

5 *The Art Journal*, September 1 1869, p. 272.

6 S. C. Hall, *Retrospect of a Long Life*, pp. 164–6.

7 In *The Poetical Works of Eliza Cook*, Frederick Warne & Co., London, 1870.

Chapter 28   Epilogue

1 Auto. I, p. 4.

2 Listed as the grave of Wm Jerban (sic) FSA, his gravestone was marked to "Remove" in an undated clearances book lodged at Hertfordshire Archives and Local Studies, D/P26/6/93.

Appendix: Jerdan's Descendants

1 Much of the information following has been sourced from www.ancestry.com and findmypast.co.uk, as well as from Jerdan's descendants. Where individual births have not been found, approximate dates have been inferred from Census records.

2 1861 Census, Hendon Middlesex, RG 09/ 786.

3 Marriage Registration, Jan.–March 1874, Kensington, Vol. 1a, 273.

4 Bishop of Melbourne, Parish of St Peter's Melbourne, 15 April 1874. A note appended to the marriage certificate states that she married with written permis-

sion of her father. Thanks to Michael Gorman for this information.

5 Ella (Stuart) Gregson died 10 July 1910, Melbourne Supreme Court Registrar of Probate Jurisdiction, certificate 24 August 1910.

6 Handwritten note of Ethel Barnes, in possession of Michael Gorman.

7 Handwritten note of Ethel Barnes: "The Duke of Edinburgh arrived aboard the RN frigate HMS Galatea in 1867. On board was (gap) Jerdan a half brother of Grandma Gregson – and Charles Beresford who was a cadet – who later was Lord Charles Beresford – an Admiral – when in Melbourne he was escort to Mother – Jessie Gregson – we had the buttons he gave Mother off his coat – in one of her precious boxes." Thanks to Michael Gorman for this note.

8 Handwritten note of Ethel Barnes: "When in London I met the novelist Michael Sadleir – who mentioned L.E.L. in a couple of his books – I told him I was a great-granddaughter of L.E.L. – he was most anxious to know if I had any letters – Clemence Dane was also going to write a play about L.E.L. and when I mentioned that I would like to tell her the truth about L.E.L. Alice Jerdan whom I was staying with in Devon nearly passed out and made me promise not to rake up the old scandals – Kitty Clark was very upset also when I mentioned it – so did not do anything more about it – although many things in Sadleir's books are quite wrong." Thanks to Michael Gorman for this note.

9 1851 Census, H.O. 107/1504.

10 1861 Census, RG 9/155.

11 1871 Census, RG 10/322.

12 Greater London, Middlesex, Hackney, Registration Vol. 1b, July–September 1879.

13 Islington Registration Vol. 1b, 237.

14 1881 Census, RG 11/298.

15 Hackney Registration Vol. 1b, 376.

16 Theophilus Goodwin's Will, Principal Probate Registry, London.

17 Death Registration, Hackney Vol. 1b, 368.

18 1901 Census, RG 13/472.

19 Death Registration, 25 January 1913, Wandsworth, Vol. 1d, 752.

20 Laura Bartholomew's Will, Principal Probate Registry, London.

21 Abney Park Cemetery Trust, Section D06, Burial 120965.

22 See Chapter 22.

23 Ethel Barnes's written notes, in possession of Michael Gorman.

24 Marriage Registration, Islington, Vol. 1b, 487.

25 1891 Census of Canada, Province of Ontario, District 119 East Toronto.

26 1901 Census of Canada, Province of Ontario, District 119 Toronto East.

27 Death Registration, County of York, Toronto.

28 Attestation Paper, Library and Archives Canada, RG150 Accession 1992–93/166, Box 5978-36.

29 1861 Census, RG 9/130.

30 New South Wales Death Certificate, Registration No. 1922/007355.

31 Birth Registration, September 1838, Lambeth, Vol. 4, 250.

32 Birth Registration, March 1855, Maidstone, Vol. 2a, 409.

33 Marriage Registration, Plymouth, Vol. 5b, 428.

34 1871 Census, Plymouth, RG 10/2118.

35 Death Registration, Plymouth, Dec. 1872, Vol. 5b, 185.

36 Records of the Admiralty, Naval Forces, Royal Marines, Coastguard and Related Bodies, Admirality Officer's Service Records Series III, Engineering Officers, The National Archives, Ref: ADM 196/24.

37 Birth Registration, April–June 1879, Plymouth, Vol. 5b, 254.

38 1881 Census, Plymouth, RG 11/2190.

39 Marriage Registration, April–June 1906, Tavistock, Cornwall, Vol. 5b, 823.

40 Private correspondence from Michael Gorman, based on notes from Ethel Barnes.

41 New South Wales Registry of Births, Deaths and Marriages, Registration no. 2092/1885.

42 Information from Peter Jerdan, Australia.

43 New South Wales Registry of Births, Deaths and Marriages, Registration Nos. 10749/1886, 9128/1888, 25388/1890, 29848/1895, 14271/1901.

44 New South Wales Registry of Births, Deaths and Marriages, Registration No. 25144/1948.

45 Australian Electoral Rolls 1910–1936.

46 New South Wales Registry of Births, Deaths and Marriages, Registration No. 2770/1948.

47 New South Wales Registry of Births, Deaths and Marriages, Registration No. 10675/1913.

48 New South Wales Government, Department of Commerce, No. 258/1928.

49 www.ancestry.co.uk UK Incoming Passenger Lists, 1878–1960.

50 Newspaper cuttings, *Graphic* of 12 January 1930 and others, courtesy of Michael Gorman.

51 New South Wales Registry of Births, Deaths and Marriages, Registration No. 7818/1934.

52 Birth Registration, Oct–Dec 1839, Lambeth, Vol. IV, 218.

53 New South Wales Registry of Births, Deaths and Marriages, Registration No. 3066/1888.

54 New South Wales Registry of Births, Deaths and Marriages, Registration No. 10147/1890.

55 Marriage Registration, St Paul's. Deptford Kent, 22 July 1869, No. 408.

56 1881 Census, RG 11/2755.

57 On S.S. *Atalanta*. www.immigrantships.nt/1800/atalanta 660416.html.

58 Australian Electoral Rolls, 1901–1936.

59 Birth Registration, 6 March 1850, St. George, Southwark, Vol. 4, 484.

60 Marriage Registration, July–Sept. 1872, Hackney, Vol. 1b, 681

61 Information from Gail Wallis.

Bibliography

Primary Sources

Armour, R. W. ed., *The Literary Recollections of Barry Cornwall*. Boston: 1936.

Besant, W. *Fifty Years Ago*. London: Chatto & Windus, 1888.

Blanchard, Laman. *The Life and Literary Remains of L.E.L.* London: Henry Colburn, 1841.

Boyle, M. *Boyle's Fashionable Court & Country Guide and Town Visiting Directory*, J. Mitchell, 1847.

British Archaeological Association. *Journal*. Vol. 9, 1894.

Britton, John. *Autobiography*. 1849

Carlyle, T. *Letters of Thomas Carlyle*. http://carlyleletters.dukejournals.org.

Croker, T.C. *A Walk from London to Fulham*. (Partly re-written Beatrice Horne.) London: Kegan Paul, Trench, Trubner & Co. 1860, 2nd ed. 1896.

Dickens, C., ed. *Pic Nic Papers*. London: Henry Colburn, 1841.

Dickens, C. *A Charles Dickens Journal*. www.dickenslive.com.

Dickens, C. *Letters of Charles Dickens*.

Dix (later Ross) J. *Pen and Ink Sketches of Poets, Preachers and Politicians*. London: Bogue, 1845.

Fox Talbot, William. *The Correspondence of William Henry Fox Talbot*. De Montfort University Leicester and University of Glasgow, Project Director: Larry J. Schaaf. http://foxtalbot.dmu.ac.uk.

Garlick, K. and A. Macintyre, eds. *Diary of Joseph Farington*. New Haven & London: Yale University Press, 1978.

Greenwood, Grace. *Haps and Mishaps of a Tour in Europe*. 1852.

Griffin, D. *Life of Gerald Griffin*. London: 1843.

Hall, S. C. *Retrospect of a Long Life*, 2 vols. London: Richard Bentley & Son, 1883.

Hall, S. C. *The Book of Memories of Great Men and Women of the Age, from personal acquaintance*. 2nd ed. London: Virtue & Co. 1877.

Hawthorne, Julian. *Hawthorne and his Circle*. 1903. Project Gutenberg etext 6982.

Hawthorne, Nathaniel. *The English Notebooks*. London: Modern Language Association, 1941.

Hawthorne, Rose, ed. *Memories of Hawthorne*. New York: 1897.

Howitt, William. *Homes and Haunts of the Most Eminent British Poets*. London & New York: Routledge Warne & Routledge, 1847.

Howitt, Margaret, ed. Mary Howitt, *An Autobiography*. London: Isbister, 1891.

Jerdan, William. *Autobiography*. London: Arthur Hall, Virtue & Co., 1852–53.

Jerdan, William. *Manual for Travellers upon the South Eastern Railway, No. 1. Main Line to *the coast and continent: with historical, antiquarian and picturesque notices of the adjacent parts.* London: Mead & Powell, 1854.

Jerdan, William. *Men I Have Known.* London: Routledge & Co., 1866.

Jerdan, William, *The Rutland Papers,* Camden Society, 1842.

Jerdan, William, *The Perth Papers,* Camden Society, 1845.

Lamb, C. and M. *The Works of Charles and Mary Lamb.* Vol. 6, Letters. www.ebooksread.com.

Landon, L. E. *Romance and Reality.* London: Richard Bentley, 1848.

Lanman, Charles. *Haphazard Personalities.* Boston: Lee & Shepherd, 1886.

Lanman, Charles. *Adventures of an Angler in Canada, Nova Scotia and the United States.* London: Richard Bentley and http://books.google.com, 1848.

Lennox, Lord William Pitt. *Celebrities I Have Known.* London: 1876.

Sharpe's Magazine.

Stapleton, E. *Some Correspondence of George Canning.* London: Longman & Co., 1887.

Stoddard, R. H., ed. *Personal Reminiscences by Chorley, Planché and Young.* New York: Scribner, 1874. Reprinted Kessinger Publishing.

Stoddard, R. H., ed. *Personal Reminiscences by Moore and Jerdan.* New York: Scribner, Armstrong & Co. 1875. Reprinted Kessinger Publishing.

Thackeray, W. M. *Roundabout Papers.* Project Gutenberg etext 2608.

Thackeray, W. M. *The Letters and Private Papers of William Makepeace Thackeray,* Harvard University Press, 1945.

The Statistical Account of Scotland Drawn up from the Commmunications of the Ministers of Different Parishes: Sir John Sinclair Bart:Vol. Tenth, Edinburgh: William Creech, 1794.

Thomson, Katherine and J. C. (Grace and Philip Wharton). *Queens of Society.* Philadelphia: Porter & Coates, first pub. 1860.

Thomson, Katherine. *Recollections of Literary Characters and Celebrated Places,* 2 vols. New York: Scribner, 1874. Reprinted Kessinger Publishing.

Timbs, J. *Club Life of London.* London: Richard Bentley, 1866.

Toynbee, W., ed. *The Diaries of William Charles Macready 1833–1851,* 2 vols. London: Chapman & Hall, 1912.

Tupper, Martin. *My Life as an Author.* Sampson Low, Marston, Searle & Rivington, 1886. Project Gutenberg extext 17558.

Vizetelly, Henry. *Glances back through seventy years.* Kegan Paul, 1893.

Watts, A. A. *Alaric Watts.* London: Richard Bentley, 1884.

Weddell, J. *A Voyage Towards the South Pole . . . in 1822–24.* London: 1825.

Westmacott, C. M. *Cockney Critics.* J. Duncombe, 1823.

Secondary Sources

Altick, Richard A. *The Shows of London.* Mass. & London: Belknap Press, 1978.

Andersen, Jens. *Hans Christian Andersen.* New York & London: Overlook Duckworth, 2005.

Andrews, A. *History of British Journalism.* London: Bentley, 1859.

Armbrust, C. *Nineteenth Century Presentations of George Herbert – Publishing history as Critical Embodiment.* Huntington Library Quarterly, Spring 1990.

Bates, William. *The Maclise Portrait Gallery of Illustrious Literary Characters.* London: Chatto & Windus, 1898.

Bibliography

Bisschop, W. R. *The Rise of the London Money Market 1640–1826.* Batoche Books, 2001.

Bredsdorff, Elias. *Hans Christian Andersen, An Introduction to his Life and Works.* 1987.

Briggs, Asa. *The Age of Improvement.* London: Longmans, 1959.

Buckley, J. H. *The Victorian Temper.* Cambridge University Press, 1951, 2nd ed. 1969.

Colbert, Benjamin. *Biography of Travel Writing 1780–1840: The European Tour 1814–1818 excluding Britain and Ireland).* Cardiff Corvey: Reading the Romantic Text 13 (Winter 2004). Online: Internet, date accessed December 2008. http://www.cf.ac.uk/encap/corvey/articles/cc13_n01.html.

Collins, A. S. *The Profession of Letters – a Study of the Relations of Author to Patron, Publisher and the Public 1780–1832.* London: George Routledge & Sons, 1928.

Conlin, Jonathan. *The Nation's Mantelpiece: A History of the National Gallery.* London: Pallas Athene (Publishers) Ltd., 2006.

Cross, Nigel. *The Royal Literary Fund 1790–1918.* London: World Microfilms, 1984.

Cruse, Amy. *The Englishman and his Books in the Early Nineteenth Century.* London: George Harrap & Co., 1930.

Davies, Norman. *Europe: A History.* London: Pimlico, 1997.

Dibert-Himes, Glenn T. *Introductory Essay to the Comprehensive Index and Bibliography to the Collected Works of Letitia Elizabeth Landon.* Dissertation. Ann Arbor, Michigan. UMI 1997. www.people.iup.edu/ghimes/gdessay.htm.

Disraeli, R. ed., *Lord Beaconsfield's Letters 1830–1852.* London: John Murray, 1887.

Duncan, Robert. *William Jerdan and the Literary Gazette.* Unpublished Ph.D. dissertation, University of Cincinnati, 1955.

Dyer, Gary. The 'Vanity Fair' of Nineteenth Century England: Commerce, Women and the East in the Ladies' Bazaar. *Nineteenth Century Literature,* Vol. 46 (2), September 1991.

Dyer, Gary. *British Satire and the Politics of Style.* Cambridge: Cambridge UP, 1997.

Enfield, D. E. *L.E.L. A Mystery of the Thirties.* London: Hogarth Press, 1928.

Fisher, J. L., "In the Present Famine of Anything Substantial": Fraser's "Portraits" and the Construction of Literary Celebrity; or, "Personality, Personality Is the Appetite of the Age". *Victorian Periodicals Review,* Vol. 39 (2), pp. 97–135. University of Toronto Press, 2006.

Ford, Boris, ed. *Victorian Britain* (Cambridge Cultural History, Vol. 7). Cambridge: Cambridge University Press, 1989.

Fraser, Rebecca. *A People's History of Britain.* Chatto & Windus, 2003.

Gettmann, Royal A. *A Victorian publisher, A Study of the Bentley Papers.* Cambridge: University Press, 1960.

Gorman, Michael. *L.E.L. The Life and Murder of Letitia E. Landon.* London: Olympia Publishers, 2008.

Grant, James. *The Newspaper Press.* London: Tinsley Bros., 1871.

Hamilton, James. *London Lights.* London: John Murray, 2007.

Hepburn, James. *The Author's Empty Purse and the Rise of the Literary Agent.* London: Oxford University Press, 1968.

Holden, Anthony. *The Wit in the Dungeon: A Life of Leigh Hunt.* Little, Brown, 2005.

Jeffrey, Lloyd N. *Thomas Hood.* New York: Twayne Publishers Inc., 1972.

Kitton, F.G. *Dickensiana.* London: G. Redway, 1886.

Lawford, Cynthia. *"Thou shalt bid thy fair hands rove": L.E.L.'s Wooing of Sex, Pain, Death, and the Editor.* Romanticism on the Net, Issues 29–30, February–May 2003, accessed July 2007. http://id.erudit.org/iderudit/007718ar.

Lawford, Cynthia. *Diary.* London: London Review of Books, Vol. 22 (18), 21 September 2000.

Lawford, Cynthia. *Turbans, Tea and Talk of Books: The Literary Parties of Elizabeth Spence and Elizabeth Benger.* CW3 Journal. Corvey Women Writers Issue No. 1, 2004.

Lawford, Cynthia. *The early life and London worlds of Letitia Elizabeth Landon, a poet performing in an age of sentiment and display.* Unpublished Ph.D. dissertation, New York: City University, 2001.

Leary, P. *'Fraser's Magazine' and the Literary Life, 1830–1847. Victorian Periodicals Review,* Vol. 27 (2), University of Toronto Press, Summer 1994.

Lee, Amice. *Laurels and Rosemary, The Life of William and Mary Howitt.* Oxford: Oxford University Press, 1955.

Leighton, A. and M. Reynolds, eds. *Victorian Women Poets – An Anthology.* Oxford: Blackwells, 1995.

Lohrli, Anne. *Household Words – A Weekly Journal 1850–1859.* Canada: University of Toronto Press, 1973.

Lough John, and E. Merson. *John Graham Lough 1798–1876, A Northumbrian Sculptor.* Woodbridge, Suffolk: Boydell, 1987.

Mackenzie, R. S. *Miscellaneous Writings of the late Dr. Maginn.* Reprinted Redfield N.Y. 1855–57. Google Books.

Marchand, L., ed. *Letters of Thomas Hood from the Dilke Papers in the British Museum.* Rutgers University Press, 1945.

Marchand, L. *The Athenaeum – A Mirror of Victorian Culture.* University of North Carolina Press, 1941.

McGann, J. and D. Reiss. *Letitia Elizabeth Landon: Selected Writings.* Broadview Literary Texts, 1997.

Miller, Karl. *Electric Shepherd, A Likeness of James Hogg.* London: Faber & Faber, 2003.

Milner, John. *The Cruise of the Galatea.* London: 1869.

Mitchell, Charles. *The Newspaper Press Directory,* 1846.

Oxford Dictionary of National Biography, Oxford: 2004.

Page, N. et al. eds., *Charles Dickens: Family History, Vol. 5.* http://books.google.com.

Pyle, Gerald. *The Literary Gazette under William Jerdan.* Unpublished Ph.D. dissertation, Duke University, 1976.

Radcliffe, D. H. *English Poetry 1579–1830: Spenser and the Tradition.* Virginia Tech. http://wiz2.cath.vt.edu.

Ransom, Harry. *William Jerdan, Editor and Literary Agent.* University of Texas, 1948.

Rappoport, J. Buyer Beware: The Gift Poetics of L.E.L. *Nineteenth Century Literature,* Vol. 58 (4), March 2004.

Roe, Nicholas. *The First Life of Leigh Hunt: Fiery Heart.* London: Pimlico, 2005.

Rosa, M. W. *The Silver-Fork School.* New York: Kennikat Press, 1964.

Royal Geographical Society, London. *Records of the Royal Geographical Society.*

Sadleir, Michael. *Bulwer and his Wife: A Panorama 1803–1836.* London: Constable & Co. 1931.

Sadleir, Michael. *Blessington D'Orsay: a Masquerade*. London: Constable, 1933.

St. Clair, William. *The Reading Nation in the Romantic Period*. Cambridge: Cambridge UP, 2004.

Scott, W. B. ed., *The Poetical Works of L.E.L.* London: George Routledge & Sons, 1873.

Smith, Janet Adam. *The Royal Literary Fund, A Short History 1790–1990*. London: The Royal Literary Fund.

Stephenson, H. T. *The Ettrick Shepherd: A Biography*. Indiana University Studies, 1922.

Sullivan, Alvin. *British Literary Magazines 1789–1836: The Romantic Age*, London: Greenwood Press, 1983.

Sutherland, John, ed. *The Longman Companion to Victorian Fiction*. London: London Group UK Ltd., 1988.

Sypher, F. J. *Letitia Elizabeth Landon, A Biography*. Ann Arbor, Michigan: Scholars' Facsimiles & Reprints, 2004, 2nd ed. 2009.

Sypher, F. J., ed. *The Letters of Letitia Elizabeth Landon*. Delmar, New York: Scholars' Facsimiles & Reprints, 2001.

Sypher, F. J. *The Occultation of Letitia Elizabeth Landon*. www.cosmos-club.org, 1999.

Thrall, Miriam. *Rebellious Fraser's: Nol Yorke's Magazine in the days of Maginn, Carlyle and Thackeray*. New York: Columbia University Press, 1934.

Victorian Plays Project. www.victorian.worc.ac.uk.

Waterloo Directory, www.victorianperiodicals.com

Watt, Julie. *Poisoned Lives: Regency Poet Letitia Elizabeth Landon (L.E.L.) and British Gold Coast Administrator, George Maclean*. Brighton, Portland, Toronto: Sussex Academic Press, 2010.

Wellesley Index to Victorian Periodicals 1824–1900. W. E. Houghton, ed. et al. Toronto University Press; Routledge and Kegan Paul, 1966–1990.

❧ Index ❧

W.J. is William Jerdan   Lit. Gaz. is *Literary Gazette*

Index

Index

Index

Index

Nelson, Lord Horatio, 3, 134

New Monthly Magazine, 73, 82, 112, 159, 207, 211, 226, 232, 233, 246, 248, 249, 258, 264, 285, 286, 292, 297, 313, 315, 329, 338, 392, 425, 468

New Quarterly Review, 452, 479

New Sporting Magazine, 537, 549

Nichol, William, 399

Nichols, John Bowyer, 322. 340, 352, 367, 379

'Noctes Ambrosianae', 73, 147, 206, 217, 491

Normanby, Marquis of, 91, 162, 297, 388, 447, 448

North, Christopher, *see* Wilson, John

North Staffordshire Potteries Gazette, 85

Northampton, Marquis of, 186

Notes & Queries, 499, 537, 569; *and see* Jerdan, William, professional activities

Noviomagus, Society of, *see* Jerdan, William, charitable activities

Nugent, Michael, 22, 70

Ollier, Charles, 221, 244

Orme, Cosmo, 57, 94, 141, 224, 236

D'Orsay, Count Alfred, 360; *and see* Blessington, Countess of

Palmerston, Lord, 214, 414, 504

Parry, Captain W. Edward, 141, 172, 173

Patmore, P.G., 212, 280

Peacock, Thomas Love, 78, 261, 367

Peel, Robert, 188–89, 332, 348, 394

Perceval, Spencer, 25–27, 174, 213, 450

Percy Society, 380, 390, 432

Perry, James, *see Morning Chronicle*

Picken, Andrew, 260, 279

Pickersgill, Henry W., 104, 157, 410

Pinnock, William, 31, 74, 93–94, 174, 527

Pirie, John (Lord Mayor of London), 9

Pitt, William (later Lord Lennox), 162, 468, 521

Planché, James Robinson, 243,

Pledge of Friendship, 283

Poetical Album, 209, 459

Poetical March of Humbug, 282

Pollock brothers, 8–9, 596n5

Pollock, Frederick (Lord Chief Baron), 8, 60, 109, 162, 360, 436, 439, 449, 454, 505, 535, 562–63

Porden, William, 112

Portland, Duke of, 25, 277, 310

Power, Edmund, 430, 575, 630n66

Power, Edward Rawdon, 317, 326, 373, 430, 630n66

Prior, James, 420

Proby, Mr., 594n4

Procter, Bryan Waller ("Barry Cornwall"), 81, 83, 111, 133, 181, 266, 309, 427, 434, 440, 466, 517, 524

Prout, Father, *see* Mahoney, Francis Sylvester

Pyne, William, 56, 76, 92, 122, 209, 248

Quarterly Review, 72, 85, 115, 208, 248, 313, 318, 419, 513, 520, 543, 553

Ransom, Harry, 405

Read, William, 466

Red Lions, 394

Rees, Owen, 94, 144, 259

Reeve and Benham, 435, 513

Reynolds, Frederic Mansell, 218, 276

Richardson, D. L., 211

Roberts, Emma, 157, 160, 166

Rogers, Charles, 490, 499

Rogers, Samuel, 150, 226, 520

Rolleston, S., 10

Rolls, Mrs., 81

Roney, C. P., 322

Ross, Sir James, 468, 530, 551

Ross, Thomasina, 75, 82

Royal Academy, 295–96, 388, 427

Royal Geographical Society, 230–32, 373, 387, 469, 561

Royal Inst. of British Architects, 395

Royal Ladies Magazine, 274, 276

Royal Society of Literature, 107–9, 133, 143, 170, 185, 192, 230, 253, 360, 381, 382, 400, 419, 425, 438, 439–40, 464, 491, 548

Russell, Lord John, 249, 253, 332, 436, 468, 469, 504, 526, 567

Rutherford, Dr., 7

Rutland, Duke of, 109, 360, 379, 386

Satirist, 23, 27–31

Satirist or Censor of the Times, 274

Saunders & Otley, 259, 312, 337

Scorpion, 170

Scott, Sir Walter, early visits to Kelso, 5; assoc.

Index